HIDDEN HAWAII
The Adventurer's Guide

"Great." *Library Journal*

"A bible." *Honolulu Advertiser*

"Thorough." *Publishers Weekly*

"Don't leave home without it." *Los Angeles Herald Examiner*

"Will make a fine traveling companion." Stephen Birnbaum,
Nationally-syndicated columnist

"Riegert deserves high marks for solid and basic research."
Oakland Tribune

"Offers the best of all worlds to the Hawaii visitor."
Dallas Morning News

"History, low cost lodging, eating, intriguing nightspots, shell hunting, much more." *Mademoiselle*

"Exotic destinations are described in intimate and encyclopedic detail. . . . A view no travel agent can offer. Riegert's adventures are crammed with fascinating insider's advice." *Los Angeles Times*

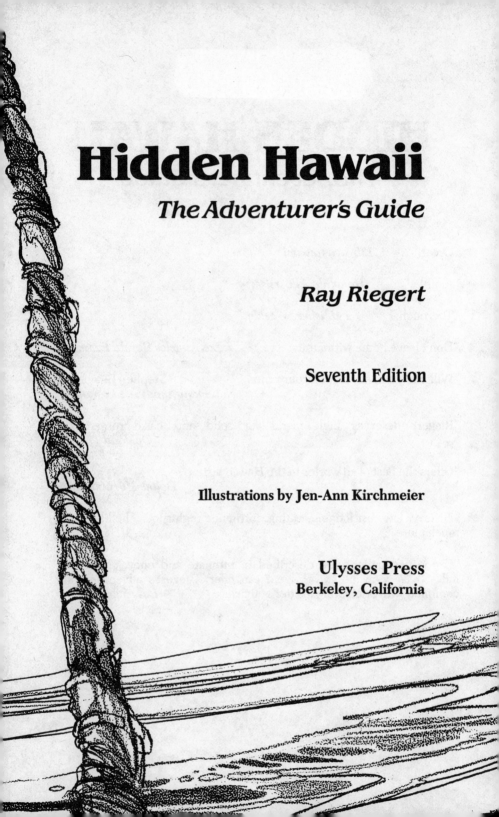

Hidden Hawaii

The Adventurer's Guide

Ray Riegert

Seventh Edition

Illustrations by Jen-Ann Kirchmeier

Ulysses Press
Berkeley, California

Published by: Ulysses Press
    3286 Adeline Street Suite 1
    Berkeley, CA 94703
    510/601-8301

Library of Congress Cataloging in Publication Data

Riegert, Ray, 1947–
  Hidden Hawaii.
  Seventh edition
  Bibliography
  Includes index.

Library of Congress Catalog Card Number 92-81058
ISBN 0-915233-65-7

Printed in the U.S.A. by the George Banta Company

20 19 18

Production Director: Leslie Henriques
Managing Editor: Claire Chun
Editorial Director: Roger Rapoport
Editor: Joanna Pearlman
Cover Design: Leslie Henriques and Bonnie Smetts
Research Assistance: Laurie Greenleaf, Cynthia Price and Lee Michaeux
Cover Photography: Front cover photo by Doug Peebles; back cover photos by Dave Houser (top) and Leslie Henriques (bottom)
Map Design: Wendy Logsdon and Phil Gardner
Index: Sayre Van Young
Computer Consultant: Robert Lettieri

Distributed in the United States by Publishers Group West, in Canada by Raincoast Books, and in Great Britain and Europe by World Leisure Marketing

To Jim Chanin,
for years of friendship

Acknowledgments

Since this book is now entering its seventh edition, there are several generations of people to thank. The person to whom I owe the deepest gratitude has been working on the project since the very beginning. I met my wife Leslie when I first arrived in the islands to write *Hidden Hawaii*. Since then she has contributed to the book as an editor, writer, researcher, and innovator. Her energy and spirit have been an inspiration throughout.

The current edition results from the efforts of several people. Claire Chun skillfully shepherded the book through many stages. Roger Rapoport contributed his expertise on numerous editorial matters; Joanna Pearlman did a great job editing the manuscript; Sayre Van Young once again lent her skills as indexer; my wife, Leslie, and Bonnie Smetts devoted their talents to the cover design; Phil Gardner contributed his expertise on the pasteup table and worked with Wendy Logsdon, our cartographer extraordinaire, on the map designs. Doug Peebles, Dave Houser and Leslie Henriques provided outstanding cover photos. Laurie Greenleaf, Cynthia Price, and Lee Micheaux aided and abetted with research and other matters large and small. My son Keith and daughter Alice also merit a warm note of thanks for their encouraging smiles and infectious energy.

I want to convey a special thanks to those people in the publishing industry who rarely receive credit for the vital work they do. Foremost are the distributors. Charlie Winton, Randy Fleming, Mark Ouimet, and all the other folks at Publishers Group West have contributed invaluable assistance and advice in nearly every phase of publishing and marketing. Bill Julius at Banta Company have also been particularly helpful over the years.

People to whom I am indebted for prior work on *Hidden Hawaii* include Carlene Schnabel, the project coordinator for the earlier editions; Jen-Ann Kirchmeier, who contributed her boundless enthusiasm as well as a collection of marvelous drawings; Marlyn Amann and Alison McDonald, who worked on the first edition; and Ed Silberstang, who offered expert assistance with the manuscript. I want to express my gratitude to Ronn Ronck, Doug Brown, Gail Brown and all my friends in Hawaii for assistance above and beyond the call of friendship. To the people of Kauai, I send a special *aloha*, and a thousand wishes for a swift recovery.

To everyone, I want to extend a *mahalo nui loa*—thank you a thousand times for your *kokua*.

Preface

Hawaii. What images does the word bring to mind? Crystal blue waters against a white sand beach. Palm trees swaying in a soft ocean breeze. Volcanic mountains rising in the hazy distance. Bronzed beach boys and luscious Polynesian women. Serenity. Luxury. Paradise.

To many it conjures still another dream—the perfect vacation. There is no more beautiful hideaway than this spectacular chain of tropical islands. For over a century Hawaii has been the meeting place of East and West, a select spot among savvy travelers. These adventurers are attracted not by Hawaii's famed tourist resorts—which are usually crowded and expensive— but by the opportunity to travel naturally and at low cost to an exotic locale.

As you'll find in the following pages, it is possible to tour economically through Hawaii's major sightseeing centers. It's even easier to explore the archipelago's more secluded realms. Few people realize that most of Hawaii's land is either rural or wilderness, and there's no price tag on the countryside. You can flee the multitudes and skip the expense by heading into the islands' endless backcountry. And if you venture far enough, you'll learn the secret that lies at the heart of this book: the less money you spend, the more likely you are to discover paradise.

Quite simply, that's the double-barreled purpose of *Hidden Hawaii*—to save you dollars while leading you to paradise. Whatever you're after, you should be able to find right here. When you want to relax amid the comforts of civilization, this book will show you good restaurants, comfortable hotels, quaint shops, and intriguing nightspots.

When you're ready to depart the beaten track, *Hidden Hawaii* will guide you to untouched beaches, remote campsites, underwater grottoes, and legendary fishing holes. It will take you to the Pacific's greatest surfing beaches, on hiking trails across live volcanoes, into flower-choked jungles, through desert canyons, and up to the top of the world's most massive mountain.

Hidden Hawaii is a handbook for living both in town and in the wild. The first chapter, covering Hawaii's history and language, will familiarize you with the rich tropical culture. Chapter Two describes how to get to the islands, what to bring, and what to expect when you arrive. The third chapter prepares you for outdoor life—swimming, hiking, camping, skindiving, and living off the land.

The last six chapters describe individual islands. Each island is divided geographically. Here you'll find specific information on sightseeing, hotels, restaurants, shops, night spots, and beaches.

This book is not intended for those tourists in plastic *leis* who plop down on a Waikiki beach, toast for two weeks, then claim they've seen Hawaii when all they've really seen is some bizarre kind of Pacific Disneyland. No, *Hidden Hawaii* is for adventurers: people who view a vacation not as an escape from everyday routine, but rather as an extension of the most exciting aspects of their daily lives. People who travel to faraway places to learn more about their own homes. Folks like you and me who want to sit back and relax, but also seek to experience and explore.

Ray Riegert
Honolulu, 1979

Notes From the Publisher

Throughout the text, hidden beaches, locales, special features, remote regions, and little-known spots are marked with a star (★).

✻ ✻ ✻

An alert, adventurous reader is as important as a travel writer in keeping a guidebook up-to-date and accurate. So if you happen upon a great restaurant, discover a hidden locale, or (heaven forbid) find an error in the text, I'd appreciate hearing from you. Just write to:

Ulysses Press
3286 Adeline Street   Suite 1
Berkeley, CA 94703

✻ ✻ ✻

It is our desire as publishers to create guidebooks that are responsible as well as informative. The danger of exploring hidden locales is that they will no longer be secluded.

We hope that our guidebooks treat the people, country, and land we visit with respect. We ask that our readers do the same.

No alien land in all the world has any deep, strong charm for me but that one, no other land could so longingly and so beseechingly haunt me, sleeping and waking, through half a lifetime, as that one has done. Other things leave me, but it abides; other things change, but it remains the some.... In my nostrils still lives the breath of flowers that perished twenty years ago.

Mark Twain, 1889

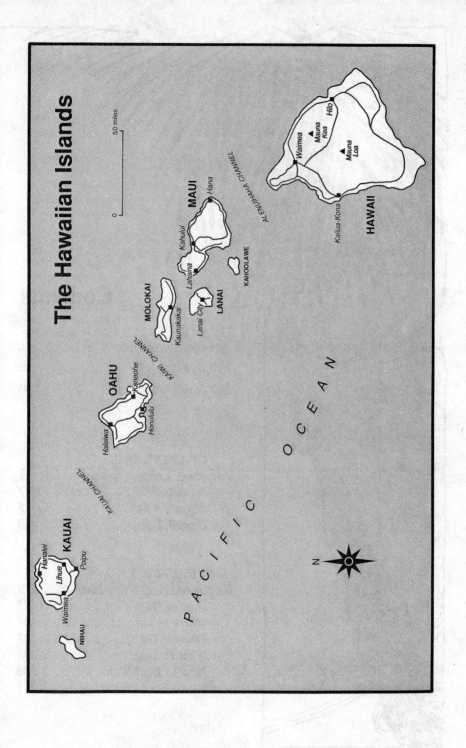

The Hawaiian Islands

50 miles

0

NIIHAU

KAUAI
Hanalei
Waimea
Lihue
Poipu

KAUAI CHANNEL

OAHU
Haleiwa
Kaneohe
Honolulu

KAIWI CHANNEL

MOLOKAI
Kaunakakai

Lanai City
LANAI

Lahaina
Kahului
MAUI
Hana

KAHOOLAWE

ALENUIHAHA CHANNEL

Waimea
Mauna Kea
Hilo
Mauna Loa
Kailua-Kona
HAWAII

P A C I F I C   O C E A N

N

Contents

Acknowledgments . . . . . . *vii*

Preface . . . . *ix*

Introduction . . . . *xxiv*

CHAPTER ONE
Paradise Lost 1
   Hawaii, B.C. *1*
   Hawaii, A.D. *5*
   Hawaii Today *18*

CHAPTER TWO
Rediscovering Paradise *25*
   How to Go *25*
   Where to Go *27*
   When to Go *28*
   What to Take *33*
   How to Deal With *36*

CHAPTER THREE
Paradise for Free **43**
   Camping and Hiking *44*
   Fishing and Gathering . . . *45*
   Picking Fruit *50*
   Relating to Drugs *51*

CHAPTER FOUR
Oahu **55**
   Waikiki *58*
   Downtown Honolulu *75*
   Greater Honolulu *88*
   Southeast Oahu *98*
   Windward Coast *104*
   North Shore *115*
   Central Oahu *123*
   Leeward Coast *124*
   Sporting Life *130*
   Transportation *137*
   Addresses *140*

CHAPTER FIVE

Hawaii **143**

    Hilo *146*

    Hamakua Coast *155*

    Waimea *160*

    Kohala Coast *163*

    Kailua-Kona Area *174*

    Kona/Kau District *185*

    Hawaii Volcanoes National Park *195*

    Saddle Road *201*

    Puna District *202*

    Sporting Life *206*

    Transportation *215*

    Addresses *218*

CHAPTER SIX

Maui **221**

    Kahului-Wailuku Area *224*

    Central Maui and the Road to Lahaina *232*

    Lahaina *233*

    Kaanapali-Kapalua *248*

    Northwest Maui *256*

    Kihei-Wailea Area *259*

    Hana Highway *269*

    Upcountry *280*

    Haleakala National Park *284*

    Sporting Life *288*

    Transportation *299*

    Addresses *302*

CHAPTER SEVEN

Lanai **305**

    Lanai City *308*

    Northeast—Shipwreck Beach and Naha *312*

    The Munro Trail *314*

    Southeast—Manele Bay *314*

    Southwest—Kaumalapau Harbor and Kaunolu . . . *317*

    Northwest—Polihua Beach *318*

    Sporting Life *319*

    Transportation *320*

    Addresses *321*

CHAPTER EIGHT

Molokai **323**
    Kaunakakai to East End *326*
    Kaunakakai to West End *333*
    Kalaupapa *342*
    Sporting Life *343*
    Transportation *345*
    Addresses *346*

CHAPTER NINE

Kauai **349**
    Lihue Area *353*
    Poipu Area *364*
    Waimea Area *373*
    Wailua-Kapaa Area *385*
    North Shore *396*
    Sporting Life *409*
    Transportation *417*
    Addresses *418*
Recommended Reading *421*
Index *423*
Also Available *438*
About the Authors and Illustrator *440*

SPECIAL FEATURES

Hawaiian Glossary *22*
The New Travel *34*
Fish Identification *46*
Relating to the Ocean *48*
Fruit Tree Identification *52*
How to Beat the Heat with a Sweet Treat *113*
Skindiving the Gold Coast *170*
Ski Hawaii *211*
Shell Hunting *246*
In the Belly of the Volcano *286*
Whale Watching *293*
Molokai's Outback *335*
Hidden Beaches and Cane Roads *363*
Hiking Kalalau *415*

MAPS

Hawaiian Islands . . . . *xvii*
Oahu 57
Waikiki 61
Downtown Honolulu 77
Honolulu 89
Southeast Oahu 99
Windward Coast 107
North Shore 117
Leeward Coast and Central Oahu 125
Hawaii 145
Hilo 149
Hamakua Coast 157
Kohala Coast 165
Kailua-Kona 175
Kona Coast 187
Hawaii Volcanoes National Park 197
Puna District 203
Maui 223
Kahului-Wailuku 225
Lahaina 235
Kaanapali-Kapalua 249
Northwest Maui 257
Kihei-Wailea 261
Hana Area 271
Upcountry 281
Haleakala National Park 287
Lanai 307
Molokai 325
Kauai 351
Lihue 355
Poipu 365
Waimea Area 375
Waimea Canyon 383
Windward Coast 387
North Shore 397

Introduction

Reading *Hidden Hawaii* brought back memories of my long and frustratingly unconsummated love affair with the islands. Throughout my childhood I listened spellbound as my father and uncles swapped tales of sun-washed beaches far across the Pacific. Like millions of other sailors and GIs, they had toured distant lands courtesy of that great travel agent, Uncle Sam. Between battles they recuperated under swaying coco palms, swilling warm beer and bartering with the natives. Stale Lucky Strikes were traded for hand-forged bolo knives and intricately carved hardwood spears. And though their travels took them far beyond "Pearl," to me the atolls, jungles, and magical reefs of which they spoke all spelled Hawaii.

"Hawaii Granted Statehood," the headline ran. I folded the damp newspaper, hurled it toward my customer's front porch, and pedaled angrily along my paper route. *They* had done it, by a simple stroke of an administrative pen. My dream of retiring to the islands at age fifteen gave a violent lurch. Hawaii suddenly shifted from the distant edge of the unknown Orient to just another state. The Iowa of the Pacific. Offshore California. No more need for a passport or an interpreter. No gorging on exotic mahimahi and *poi*—the fabled Sandwich Islands would now feed me on McBurgers and cola.

I survived the disillusionment of statehood and though, two years later, I squandered my meager savings (earmarked for passage to the islands) on a battered motorbike, the dream did not fade entirely. Friends-of-friends returned from two-week Hawaiian idylls, faces and arms tanned to an improbable richness. Wilted *leis* would be casually draped over lampshades and mantlepieces, a not-so-subtle reminder of their brief fling in the sun. I could only wait.

Later, the islands subverted my college career. In the storm clouds gathering above the campus, I saw the foam of a turquoise wave curling around a slender surfer. Rain-washed ivy dissolved into frangipani and bougainvillea. The neo-Gothic monstrosity of the campus library became a battered volcanic grotto, rumbling with echoes of ocean rollers. My instructors, unable to see beyond the tips of their umbrellas, rewarded my visions of paradise with neat lines of zeroes.

Flunking out of college, however, almost brought me my dream. I found myself low man on the totem pole on a disabled fishing boat, drifting helplessly across the gulf of Alaska. There seemed little promise of sunburns and coco palms in those cold, relentless waves. And then the captain took a close look at the charts.

"Well, boys, if this keeps up, we'll just have to head for Hawaii," he muttered. It had already been two endless weeks. Given the force of wind and current, we would hail the islands' sparkling shores within a month.

But it was just another lost chance, thwarted by an annoyingly efficient Norwegian chief engineer who dreamed of cod and boiled salmon heads rather than pineapple and passion fruit. The ancient engine coughed to life and took us north, back into the Big Grey.

Like many early explorers before me, I now took the only reasonable alternative left in my unsuccessful quest for the islands: I gave up. I went south instead, to a land where coconuts and tequila create a dream of their own. I traded my vision of a Polynesian outrigger for a ticket on the Greyhound, drawn to the irresistible warmth of a Mexican sun. Hawaii receded over the horizon.

A few years later, returning north through California, land of surprises, the dream suddenly reappeared. My partner Lorena and I were invited to a birthday *luau* honoring King Kamehameha, father of the islands. In the shade of a redwood forest we feasted on rich, greasy barbecued pork, delicate raw fish, tropical fruits, palm hearts, and that exotic beverage, Budweiser-on-tap. Frustrated Hawaiians weaving another year's dream from Maui smoke, we lay back on soft aromatic pine needles, lulled into fantasies of graceful sea canoes, the melancholy summons of conch shell trumpets, the rhythmic sweep of the paddles ... carrying us off to the islands.

We could resist no longer; we determined to make the big break with the mainland. Having already written a travel book on Mexico, I now had the ultimate justification. We would go to Hawaii and return with knowledge and advice to pass on to others—while also earning a royalty that would guarantee a long rest on a hidden beach. Lorena was enthusiastic; between the native herbs and tropical sunsets, she could pass many many days. The final lure was thrown to us by our publisher: the promise of an advance to finance the journey. "But only when you've finished your camping book on Mexico," he warned.

●   ●   ●

"Hey, Carl, remember the book you were going to do on Hawaii?" I held the phone in a white-knuckled grip. Publishers are notorious for their twisted humor. Surely "remember" and "were going to do" were just sad attempts to cheer me toward my deadline.

"Yeah," I answered, "I have my Hawaiian shirt on right now. The one you bought me at Goodwill. *Remember?*"

There was a short, cynical laugh.

"Well, Ray Riegert just wrote it for you. Looks like it's time to play spin-the-globe again."

I slammed the phone down. Moments later I was trudging through the dusty Mexican streets, snarling at burros and stray dogs. At least my new recipe for *mai tais* wouldn't be wasted!

● ● ●

Good travel writers must constantly walk a tightrope between telling too much and not telling enough. The lazy tourist demands to be led by the nose to a comfortable yet inexpensive hotel and from there to a tasteful, quaint cafe. Nothing can be left to the demons of surprise and chance. Restless natives laboring over tom-toms in the middle of the night must be courtesy of the local tourist bureau, a civic contribution to amuse the traveler, rather than an inconvenient rebellion.

And with the distance between the islands and the continental U.S. reduced to nothing more than a quick lunch and a few drinks on a passenger jet, the pressures of tourism have become enormous. Hawaii's very lure is in danger of becoming its downfall.

This has created a situation in which a responsible and imaginative writer can perform a service both to adventurers and to the places they travel to see. A sensitive and aware guidebook like *Hidden Hawaii* helps educate and, in so doing, creates sensitive and aware travelers. The vast majority of guidebooks are not actually guides but consumer directories: where to spend your money with a minimum of distraction. That type of book actually steers us away from the heart of a place and an understanding of its peoples, on to nothing more than a superficial tour of the "sights." Ray Riegert shows us a Hawaii blessed with an incredible richness of cultures, history, topography, and climates.

Hidden Hawaii not only points out attractive and inexpensive alternatives in meals, lodging, entertainment, and shopping, but also takes us beyond Hawaii's often overdeveloped facade: where to watch whales; how to find the best parks, trails, and campsites; how to live on the beach, foraging, fishing, and diving; where to go shell collecting, volcano gazing ... a variety of information as broad as the interests of travelers who want a lot out of a trip without going bankrupt. *Hidden Hawaii* demonstrates a very encouraging trend: I like guidebooks that are starting points for my own explorations, not addictive crutches. A little help can, and should, go a long way. Travel is a creative activity, one that should enhance the traveler as well as the places and people visited.

This is a book with an underlying attitude of respect and an awareness that it is more often one's attitude, rather than physical presence, that can be destructive. The hiker's motto, "Walk softly on the earth," is just as valid to the traveler strolling the streets of Lahaina as it is to the explorer on the trails of Kauai or the hidden beaches of Molokai.

It's up to *us* to keep hidden Hawaii unspoiled and enjoyable for everyone.

Carl Franz
San Miguel de Allende, 1979

CHAPTER ONE

Paradise Lost
Hawaii's History and Culture

Hawaii, B.C. (Before Cook)

GEOLOGIC TIME

More than 25 million years ago a fissure opened along the Pacific floor. Beneath tons of sea water molten lava poured from the rift. This liquid basalt, oozing from a hot spot in the earth's center, created a crater along the ocean bottom. As the tectonic plate that comprises the ocean floor drifted over the earth's hot spot, numerous other craters appeared. Slowly, in the seemingly endless procession of geologic time, a chain of volcanic islands, stretching almost 2000 miles, emerged from the sea.

On the continents it was also a period of terrible upheaval. The Himalayas, Alps, and Andes were rising, but these great chains would reach their peaks long before the Pacific mountains even touched sea level. Not until a few million years ago did these underwater volcanoes break the surface and become islands. By then, present-day plants and animals inhabited the earth, and apes were rapidly evolving into a new species.

For a couple of million more years, the mountains continued to grow. The forces of erosion cut into them, creating knife-edged cliffs and deep valleys. Then plants began germinating: mosses and ferns, springing from windblown spores, were probably first, followed by seed plants carried by migrating birds and on ocean currents. The steep-walled valleys provided natural greenhouses in which unique species evolved, while transoceanic winds swept insects and other life from the continents.

Some islands never survived this birth process: the ocean simply washed them away. The first islands that did endure, at the northwestern end of the Hawaiian chain, proved to be the smallest. Today these islands, with the exception of Midway, are barren uninhabited atolls. The volcanoes that rose last, far to the southeast, became the mountainous archipelago generally known as the Hawaiian Islands.

1

POLYNESIAN ARRIVAL

The island of Hawaii, the Big Island, was the last land mass created in this dramatic upheaval but the first to be inhabited by humans. Perhaps as early as the third century, Polynesians sailing from the Marquesas Islands, and then later from Tahiti, landed near Hawaii's southern tip. In Europe, mariners were rarely venturing outside the Mediterranean Sea, and it would be centuries before Columbus happened upon the New World. Yet in the Pacific, entire families were crossing 2500 miles of untracked ocean in hand-carved canoes with sails woven from coconut fibers. The boats were awesome structures, catamaran-like vessels with a cabin built on the platform between the wooden hulls. Some were a hundred feet long and could do twenty knots, making the trip to Hawaii in a month.

The Polynesians had originally come from the coast of Asia about 3000 years before. They had migrated through Indonesia, then pressed inexorably eastward, leapfrogging across archipelagoes until they finally reached the last chain, the most remote—Hawaii.

These Pacific migrants were undoubtedly the greatest sailors of their day, and stand among the finest in history. When close to land they could smell it, taste it in the seawater, see it in a lagoon's turquoise reflection on the clouds above an island. They knew 150 stars. From the color of the water they determined ocean depths and current directions. They had no charts, no compasses, no sextants; sailing directions were simply recorded in legends and chants. Yet Polynesians discovered the Pacific, from Indonesia to Easter Island, from New Zealand to Hawaii. They made the Vikings and Phoenicians look like landlubbers.

HAWAIIAN CULTURE

Hawaii, according to Polynesian legend, was discovered by Hawaii-loa, an adventurous sailor who often disappeared on long fishing trips. On one voyage, urged along by his navigator, Hawaii-loa sailed toward the planet Jupiter. He crossed the "many-colored ocean," passed over the "deep-colored sea," and eventually came upon "flaming Hawaii," a mountainous island chain that spewed smoke and lava.

History is less romantic. The Polynesians who found Hawaii were probably driven from their home islands by war or some similar calamity. They traveled in groups, not as lone rangers, and shared their canoes with dogs, pigs, and chickens, with which they planned to stock new lands. Agricultural plants such as coconuts, yams, taro, sugarcane, bananas, and breadfruit were also stowed on board.

Most important, they transported their culture, an intricate system of beliefs and practices developed in the South Seas. After undergoing the stresses and demands of pioneer life, this traditional lifestyle was transformed into a new and uniquely Hawaiian culture.

It was based on a caste system that placed the *alii* or chiefs at the top and the slaves, *kauwas*, on the bottom. Between these two groups were the priests, *kahunas*, and the common people or *makaainanas*. The chiefs, much like feudal lords, controlled all the land and collected taxes from the commoners who farmed it. Each island was divided like a pie into wedge-shaped plots, *ahupuaas*, which extended from the ocean to the mountain peaks. In that way, every chief's domain contained fishing spots, village sites, arable valleys, and everything else necessary for the survival of his subjects.

Life centered around the *kapu*, a complex group of regulations that dictated what was sacred or profane. For example, women were not permitted to eat pork or bananas; commoners had to prostrate themselves in the presence of a chief. These strictures were vital to Hawaiian religion; *kapu* breakers were directly violating the will of the gods and could be executed for their actions. And there were a lot of gods to watch out for, many quite vindictive. The four central gods were *Kane*, the creator; *Lono*, the god of agriculture; *Ku*, the war god; and *Kanaloa*, lord of the underworld. They had been born from the sky father and earth mother, and had in turn created many lesser gods and demigods who controlled various aspects of nature.

It was, in the uncompromising terminology of the West, a stone-age civilization. Though the Hawaiians lacked metal tools, the wheel, and a writing system, they managed to include within their short inventory of cultural goods everything necessary to sustain a large population on a chain of small islands. They fashioned fish nets from coconut fibers, made hooks out of bone, shell, and ivory, and raised fish in rock-bound ponds. The men used irrigation in their farming. The women made clothing by pounding mulberry bark into a soft cloth called *tapa*, dyeing elaborate patterns into the fabric. They built peak-roofed thatch huts from native *pili* grass and *lauhala* leaves. The men fought wars with spears, slings, clubs, and daggers! The women used mortars and pestles to pound the roots of the taro plant into *poi*, the islanders' staple food.

The West labeled these early Hawaiians "noble savages." Actually, they often lacked nobility. The Hawaiians were cannibals who sometimes practiced human sacrifice and often used human bait to fish for sharks. They constantly warred among themselves and would mercilessly pursue a retreating army, murdering as many of the vanquished soldiers as possible.

But they weren't savages either. The Hawaiians developed a rich oral tradition of genealogical chants and created beautiful lilting songs to accompany their hula dancing. Their musicians mastered several instruments including the *ukeke* (a single-stringed device resembling a bow), an *ohe* or nose flute, conch shells, rattles, and drums made from gourds, coconut shells, or logs. Their craftsmen produced the world's finest featherwork, weaving thousands of tiny feathers into golden cloaks and ceremonial helmets. The

Hawaiians helped develop the sport of surfing. They also swam, boxed, bowled, and devised an intriguing game called *konane*, a cross between checkers and the Japanese game of *go*. They built hiking trails from coral and lava, and created an elemental art form in the images—petroglyphs—that they carved into rocks along the trails.

They also achieved something far more outstanding than their varied arts and crafts, something which the West, with its awesome knowledge and advanced technology, has never duplicated. The Hawaiians created a balance with nature. They practiced conservation, establishing closed seasons on certain fish species and carefully guarding their plant and animal resources. They led a simple life, without the complexities the outside world would eventually thrust upon them. It was a good life: food was plentiful, people were healthy, and the population increased. For a thousand years, the Hawaiians lived in delicate harmony with the elements. It wasn't until the West entered the realm, transforming everything, that the fragile balance was destroyed. But that is another story entirely.

Hawaii, A.D. (After Discovery)

CAPTAIN COOK

They were high islands, rising in the northeast as the sun broke across the Pacific. First one, then a second, and finally, as the tall-masted ships drifted west, a third island loomed before them. Landfall! The British crew was ecstatic. It meant fresh water, tropical fruits, solid ground on which to set their boots, and a chance to carouse with the native women. For their captain, James Cook, it was another in an amazing career of discoveries. The man whom many call history's greatest explorer was about to land in one of the last spots on earth to be discovered by the West.

He would name the place for his patron, the British earl who became famous by pressing a meal between two crusts of bread. The Sandwich Islands. Later they would be called Owhyhee, and eventually, as the Western tongue glided around the uncharted edges of a foreign language, Hawaii.

It was January 1778. The English army was battling a ragtag band of revolutionaries for control of the American colonies, and the British Empire was still basking in a sun that never set. The Pacific had been opened to Western powers over two centuries before, when a Portuguese sailor named Magellan crossed it. Since then, the British, French, Dutch, and Spanish had tracked through in search of future colonies.

They happened upon Samoa, Fiji, Tahiti, and the other islands that spread across this third of the globe, but somehow they had never sighted Hawaii. Even when Cook finally spied it, he little realized how important a find he had made. Hawaii, quite literally, was a jewel in the ocean, rich in fragrant sandalwood, ripe for agricultural exploitation, and crowded with sea life. But it was the archipelago's isolation that would prove to be its greatest resource. Strategically situated between Asia and North America, it was the only place for thousands of miles to which whalers, merchants, and bluejackets could repair for provisions and rest.

Cook was 49 years old when he shattered Hawaii's quiescence. The Englishman hadn't expected to find islands north of Tahiti. Quite frankly, he wasn't even trying. It was his third Pacific voyage and Cook was hunting bigger game, the fabled Northwest Passage that would link this ocean with the Atlantic.

But these mountainous islands were still an interesting find. He could see by the canoes venturing out to meet his ships that the lands were inhabited; when he finally put ashore on Kauai, Cook discovered a Polynesian society. He saw irrigated fields, domestic animals, and high-towered temples. The women were bare-breasted, the men wore loincloths. As his crew bartered for pigs, fowls, and bananas, he learned that the natives knew about metal and coveted iron like gold.

If iron was gold to these "Indians," then Cook was a god. He soon realized that his arrival had somehow been miraculously timed, coinciding with the *Makahiki* festival, a wild party celebrating the roving deity Lono whose return the Hawaiians had awaited for years. Cook was a strange white man sailing monstrous ships—obviously he was Lono. The Hawaiians gave him gifts, fell in his path, and rose only at his insistence.

But even among religious crowds, fame is often fickle. After leaving Hawaii, Cook sailed north to the Arctic Sea, where he failed to discover the Northwest Passage. He returned the next year to Kealakekua Bay on the Big Island, arriving at the tail end of another exhausting *Makahiki* festival. By then the Hawaiians had tired of his constant demands for provisions and were suffering from a new disease that was obviously carried by Lono's archangelic crew—syphilis. This Lono was proving something of a freeloader.

Tensions ran high. The Hawaiians stole a boat. Cook retaliated with gunfire. A scuffle broke out on the beach and in a sudden violent outburst, which surprised the islanders as much as the interlopers, the Hawaiians discovered that their god could bleed. The world's finest mariner lay face down in foot-deep water, stabbed and bludgeoned to death.

Cook's end marked the beginning of an era. He had put the Pacific on the map, his map, probing its expanses and defining its fringes. In Hawaii he ended a thousand years of solitude. The archipelago's geographic isolation, which has always played a crucial role in Hawaii's development, had finally failed to protect it, and a second theme had come into play—the islands' vulnerability. Together with the region's "backwardness," these conditions would now mold Hawaii's history. All in turn would be shaped by another factor, one which James Cook had added to Hawaii's historic equation: the West.

KAMEHAMEHA AND KAAHUMANU

The next man whose star would rise above Hawaii was present at Cook's death. Some say he struck the Englishman, others that he took a lock of the great leader's hair and used its residual power, its *mana*, to become king of all Hawaii.

Kamehameha was a tall, muscular, unattractive man with a furrowed face, a lesser chief on the powerful island of Hawaii. When he began his career of conquest a few years after Cook's death, he was a mere upstart, an ambitious, arrogant young chief. But he fought with a general's skill and a warrior's cunning, often plunging into the midst of a melee. He had an astute sense of technology, an intuition that these new Western metals and firearms could make him a king.

In Kamehameha's early years, the Hawaiian islands were composed of many fiefdoms. Several kings or great chiefs, continually warring among themselves, ruled individual islands. At times, a few kings would carve up one island or a lone king might seize several. Never had one monarch controlled all the islands.

But fresh players had entered the field: Westerners with ample firepower and awesome ships. During the decade following Cook, only a handful had arrived, mostly Englishmen and Americans, and they had not yet won the influence they soon would wield. However, even a few foreigners were enough to upset the balance of power. They sold weapons and hardware to the great chiefs, making several of them more powerful than any of the others had ever been. War was imminent.

Kamehameha stood in the center of the hurricane. Like any leader suddenly caught up in the terrible momentum of history, he never quite realized where he was going or how fast he was moving. And he cared little that he was being carried in part by Westerners who would eventually want something for the ride. Kamehameha was no fool. If political expedience meant Western intrusion, then so be it. He had enemies among chiefs on the other islands; he needed the guns.

When two white men came into his camp in 1790, he had the military advisers to complement a fast expanding arsenal. Within months he cannonaded Maui. In 1792, Kamehameha seized the Big Island by inviting his main rival to a peaceful parley, then slaying the hapless chief. By 1795, he had consolidated his control of Maui, grasped Molokai and Lanai, and begun reaching greedily toward Oahu. He struck rapidly, landing near Waikiki and sweeping inland, forcing his enemies to their deaths over the precipitous cliffs of the Nuuanu Pali.

The warrior had become a conqueror, controlling all the islands except Kauai, which he finally gained in 1810 by peaceful negotiation. Kamehameha proved to be as able a bureaucrat as he had been a general. He became a benevolent despot who, with the aid of an ever-increasing number of Western advisers, expanded Hawaii's commerce, brought peace to the islands, and moved his people inexorably toward the modern age.

He came to be called Kamehameha the Great, and history first cast him as the George Washington of Hawaii, a wise and resolute leader who gathered a wartorn archipelago into a kingdom. Kamehameha I. But with the revisionist history of the 1960s and 1970s, as Third World people questioned both the Western version of events and the virtues of progress, Kamehameha began to resemble Benedict Arnold. He was seen as an opportunist, a megalomaniac who permitted the Western powers their initial foothold in Hawaii. He used their technology and then, in the manner of great men who depend on stronger allies, was eventually used by them.

As long a shadow as Kamehameha cast across the islands, the event that most dramatically transformed Hawaiian society occurred after his death in 1819. The kingdom had passed to Kamehameha's son Liholiho, but Kamehameha's favorite wife, Kaahumanu, usurped the power. Liholiho was a prodigal son, dissolute, lacking self-certainty, a drunk. Kaahumanu was a woman for all seasons, a canny politician who combined brilliance with boldness, the feminist of her day. She had infuriated Kamehameha by eating forbidden foods and sleeping with other chiefs, even when he placed a taboo on her body and executed her lovers. She drank liquor, ran away, proved completely uncontrollable, and won Kamehameha's love.

It was only natural that when he died, she would take his *mana*, or so she reckoned. Kaahumanu gravitated toward power with the drive of someone whom fate has unwisely denied. She carved her own destiny, announcing that Kamehameha's wish had been to give her a governmental voice. There would be a new post and she would fill it, becoming in a sense Hawaii's first prime minister.

And if the power, then the motion. Kaahumanu immediately marched against Hawaii's belief system, trying to topple the old idols. For years she had bristled under a polytheistic religion regulated by taboos, or *kapus*, which severely restricted women's rights. Now Kaahumanu urged the new king, Liholiho, to break a very strict *kapu* by sharing a meal with women.

Since the act might help consolidate Liholiho's position, it had a certain appeal to the king. Anyway, the *kapus* were weakening: these white men, coming now in ever greater numbers, defied them with impunity. Liholiho vacillated, went on a two-day drunk before gaining courage, then finally sat down to eat. It was a last supper, shattering an ancient creed and opening the way for a radically new divinity. As Kaahumanu had willed, the old order collapsed, taking away a vital part of island life and leaving the Hawaiians more exposed than ever to foreign influence.

Already Western practices were gaining hold. Commerce from Honolulu, Lahaina, and other ports was booming. There was a fortune to be made dealing sandalwood to China-bound merchants, and the chiefs were forcing the common people to strip Hawaii's forests. The grueling labor might make the chiefs rich, but it gained the commoners little more than a barren landscape. Western diseases struck virulently. The Polynesians in Hawaii, who numbered 300,000 in Cook's time, were extremely susceptible. By 1866, their population had dwindled to less than 60,000. It was a difficult time for the Hawaiian people.

MISSIONARIES AND MERCHANTS

Hawaii was not long without religion. The same year that Kaahumanu shattered tradition, a group of New England missionaries boarded the brig *Thaddeus* for a voyage around Cape Horn. It was a young company—many were in their twenties or thirties—and included a doctor, a printer, and several teachers. They were all strict Calvinists, fearful that the second coming was at hand and possessed of a mission. They were bound for a strange land called Hawaii, 18,000 miles away.

Hawaii, of course, was a lost paradise, a hellhole of sin and savagery where men slept with several wives and women neglected to wear dresses. To the missionaries, it mattered little that the Hawaiians had lived this way for centuries. The churchmen would save these heathens from hell's everlasting fire whether they liked it or not.

The delegation arrived in Kailua on the Big Island in 1820 and then spread out, establishing important missions in Honolulu and Lahaina. Soon they were building schools and churches, conducting services in Hawaiian, and converting the natives to Christianity.

The missionaries rapidly became an integral part of Hawaii, despite the fact that they were a walking contradiction to everything Hawaiian. They were a contentious, self-righteous, fanatical people whose arrogance toward the Hawaiians blinded them to the beauty and wisdom of island lifestyles. Where the natives lived in thatch homes open to the soothing trade winds, the missionaries built airless clapboard houses with New England-style fireplaces. While the Polynesians swam and surfed frequently, the new arrivals, living near the world's finest beaches, stank from not bathing. In a region where the thermometer rarely drops much below seventy degrees, they wore long-sleeved woolens, ankle-length dresses, and claw-hammer coats. At dinner they preferred salt pork to fresh beef, dried meat to fresh fish. They considered coconuts an abomination and were loath to eat bananas.

And yet the missionaries were a brave people, selfless and God-fearing. Their dangerous voyage from the Atlantic had brought them into a very alien land. Many would die from disease and overwork; most would never see their homeland again. Bigoted though they were, the Calvinists committed their lives to the Hawaiian people. They developed the Hawaiian alphabet, rendered Hawaiian into a written language, and, of course, translated the Bible. Theirs was the first printing press west of the Rockies. They introduced Western medicine throughout the islands and created such an effective school system that, by the mid-19th century, 80 percent of the Hawaiian population was literate. Unlike almost all the other white people who came to Hawaii, they not only took from the islanders, they also gave.

But to a missionary, *giving* means ripping away everything repugnant to God and substituting it with Christianity. They would have to destroy Hawaiian culture in order to save it. Though instructed by their church elders not to meddle in island politics, the missionaries soon realized that heavenly wars had to be fought on earthly battlefields. Politics it would be. After all, wasn't government just another expression of God's bounty?

They allied with Kaahumanu and found it increasingly difficult to separate church from state. Kaahumanu converted to Christianity, while the missionaries became government advisers and helped pass laws protecting the sanctity of the Sabbath. Disgusting practices such as hula dancing were prohibited.

Politics can be a dangerous world for a man of the cloth. The missionaries were soon pitted against other foreigners who were quite willing to let the clerics sing hymns, but were damned opposed to permitting them a voice in government. Hawaii in the 1820s had become a favorite way station for the whaling fleet. As the sandalwood forests were decimated, the island merchants began looking for other industries. By the 1840s, when over 500 ships a year anchored in Hawaiian ports, whaling had become the islands' economic lifeblood. More American ships visited Hawaii than any other port in the world.

Like the missionaries, the whalers were Yankees, shipping out from bustling New England ports. But they were a hell of a different cut of Yankee. These were rough, crude, boisterous men who loved rum and music, and thought a lot more of fornicating with island women than saving them. After the churchmen forced the passage of laws prohibiting prostitution, the sailors rioted along the waterfront and fired cannons at the mission homes. When the smoke cleared, the whalers still had their women.

Religion simply could not compete with commerce, and other Westerners were continuously stimulating more business in the islands. By the 1840s, as Hawaii adopted a parliamentary form of government, American and British fortune hunters were replacing missionaries as government advisers. It was a time when anyone, regardless of ability or morality, could travel to the islands and become a political powerhouse literally overnight. A consumptive American, fleeing the mainland for reasons of health, became chief justice of the Hawaiian Supreme Court while still in his twenties. Another lawyer, shadowed from the East Coast by a checkered past, became attorney general two weeks after arriving.

The situation was no different internationally. Hawaii was subject to the whims and terrors of gunboat diplomacy. The archipelago was solitary and exposed, and Western powers were beginning to eye it covetously. In 1843, a maverick British naval officer actually annexed Hawaii to the Crown, but the London government later countermanded his actions. Then, in the early 1850s, the threat of American annexation arose. Restless Californians, fresh from the gold fields and hungry for revolution, plotted unsuccessfully in Honolulu. Even the French periodically sent gunboats in to protect their small Catholic minority.

Finally, the three powers officially stated that they wanted to maintain Hawaii's national integrity. But independence seemed increasingly unlikely. European countries had already begun claiming other Pacific islands, and with the influx of Yankee missionaries and whalers, Hawaii was being steadily drawn into the American orbit.

THE SUGAR PLANTERS

There is an old Hawaiian saying that describes the 19th century: The missionaries came to do good, and they did very well. Actually the early evangelists, few of whom profited from their work, lived out only half the maxim. Their sons would give the saying its full meaning.

This second generation, quite willing to sacrifice glory for gain, fit neatly into the commercial society that had rendered their fathers irrelevant. They were shrewd, farsighted young Christians who had grown up in Hawaii and knew both the islands' pitfalls and potentials. They realized that the missionaries had never quite found Hawaii's pulse, and they watched uneasily as whaling became the lifeblood of the islands. Certainly it brought wealth, but whaling was too tenuous—there was always a threat that it might dry up entirely. A one-industry economy would never do; the mission boys wanted more. Agriculture was the obvious answer, and eventually they determined to bind their providence to a plant that grew wild in the islands—sugarcane.

The first sugar plantation was started on Kauai in 1835, but not until the 1870s did the new industry blossom. By then, the Civil War had wreaked havoc with the whaling fleet, and a devastating winter in the Arctic whaling grounds practically destroyed it. The mission boys, who prophesied the storm, weathered it quite comfortably. They had already begun fomenting an agricultural revolution.

Agriculture, of course, means land, and in the 19th century practically all Hawaii's acreage was held by the king and the chiefs. So in 1850, the mission sons, together with other white entrepreneurs, pushed through the Great Mahele, one of the slickest real estate laws in history. Rationalizing that it would grant chiefs the liberty to sell land to Hawaiian commoners and white men, the mission sons established a Western system of private property.

The Hawaiians, who had shared their chiefs' lands communally for centuries, had absolutely no concept of deeds and leases. What resulted was the old $24-worth-of-beads story. The benevolent Westerners wound up with the land, while the lucky Hawaiians got practically nothing. Large tracts were purchased for cases of whiskey; others went for the cost of a hollow promise. The entire island of Niihau, which is still owned by the same family, sold for $10,000. It was a bloodless coup, staged more than 40 years before the revolution that would topple Hawaii's monarchy. In a sense it made the 1893 uprising anticlimactic. By then Hawaii's future would already be determined: white interlopers would own four times as much land as Hawaiian commoners.

Following the Great Mahele, the mission boys, along with other businessmen, were ready to become sugar planters. The *mana* once again was passing into new hands. Obviously, there was money to be made in cane, a lot of it, and now that they had land, all they needed was labor. The Hawaiians would never do. Cook might have recognized them as industrious, hardworking people, but the sugar planters considered them shiftless. Disease was killing them off anyway, and the Hawaiians who survived seemed to lose the will to live. Many made appointments with death, stating that in a week they would die; seven days later they were dead.

Foreign labor was the only answer. In 1850, the Masters and Servants Act was passed, establishing an immigration board to import plantation workers. Cheap Asian labor would be brought over. It was a crucial decision, one that would ramify forever through Hawaiian history and change the very substance of island society. Between 1850 and 1930, 180,000 Japanese, 125,000 Filipinos, 50,000 Chinese, and 20,000 Portuguese immigrated. They transformed Hawaii from a chain of Polynesian islands into one of the world's most varied and dynamic locales, a meeting place of East and West.

The Chinese were the first to come, arriving in 1852 and soon outnumbering the white population. Initially, with their long pigtails and uncommon habits, the Chinese were a joke around the islands. They were poor people from southern China whose lives were directed by clan loyalty. They built schools and worked hard so that one day they could return to their native villages in glory. They were ambitious, industrious, and—ultimately—successful.

Too successful, according to the sugar planters, who found it almost impossible to keep the coolies down on the farm. The Chinese came to Hawaii under labor contracts, which forced them to work for five years. After their indentureship, rather than reenlisting as the sugar bosses had planned, the Chinese moved to the city and became merchants. Worse yet, they married Hawaiian women and were assimilated into the society.

These coolies, the planters decided, were too uppity, too ready to fill social roles that were really the business of white men. So in the 1880s, they began importing Portuguese. But the Portuguese thought they already *were* white men, while any self-respecting American or Englishman of the time knew they weren't.

The Portuguese spelled trouble, and in 1886 the sugar planters turned to Japan, with its restricted land mass and burgeoning population. The new immigrants were peasants from Japan's southern islands, raised in an authoritarian, hierarchical culture in which the father was a family dictator and the family was strictly defined by its social status. Like the Chinese, they built schools to protect their heritage and dreamed of returning home someday; but unlike their Asian neighbors, they only married other Japanese. They sent home for "picture brides," worshipped their ancestors and Emperor, and paid ultimate loyalty to Japan, not Hawaii.

The Japanese, it soon became evident, were too proud to work long hours for low pay. Plantation conditions were atrocious; workers were housed in hovels and frequently beaten. The Japanese simply did not adapt. Worst of all, they not only bitched, they organized, striking in 1909.

So in 1910, the sugar planters turned to the Philippines for labor. For two decades the Filipinos arrived, seeking their fortunes and leaving their wives behind. They worked not only with sugarcane but also with pineapples, which were becoming a big business in the 20th century. They were a boisterous, fun-loving people, hated by the immigrants who preceded them and used by the whites who hired them. The Filipinos were given the most menial jobs, the worst working conditions, and the shoddiest housing. In time, another side of their character began to show—a despondency, a hopeless sense of their own plight, their inability to raise passage money back home. They became the niggers of Hawaii.

REVOLUTIONARIES AND ROYALISTS

Sugar, by the late 19th century, was king. It had become the center of island economy, the principal fact of life for most islanders. Like the earlier whaling industry, it was drawing Hawaii ever closer to the American sphere. The sugar planters were selling the bulk of their crops in California; having already signed several tariff treaties to protect their American market, they were eager to further strengthen mainland ties. Besides, many sugar planters were second-, third-, and fourth-generation descendants of the New England missionaries; they had a natural affinity for the United States.

There was, however, one group that shared neither their love for sugar nor their ties to America. To the Hawaiian people, David Kalakaua was king, and America was the nemesis that had long threatened their independence. The whites might own the land, but the Hawaiians, through their monarch, still held substantial political power. During Kalakaua's rule in the 1870s and 1880s, anticolonialism was rampant.

The sugar planters were growing impatient. Kalakaua was proving very antagonistic; his nationalist drumbeating was becoming louder in their ears. How could the sugar merchants convince the United States to annex Hawaii when all these silly Hawaiian royalists were running around pretending to be the Pacific's answer to the British Isles? They had tolerated this long enough. The Hawaiians were obviously unfit to rule, and the planters soon joined with other businessmen to form a secret revolutionary organization. Backed by a force of well-armed followers, they pushed through the "Bayonet Constitution" of 1887, a self-serving document that weakened the king and strengthened the white landowners. If Hawaii was to remain a monarchy, it would have a Magna Carta.

But Hawaii would not be a monarchy long. Once revolution is in the air, it's often difficult to clear the smoke. By 1893, Kalakaua was dead and his sister, Liliuokalani, had succeeded to the throne. She was an audacious leader, proud of her heritage, quick to defend it, and prone to let immediate passions carry her onto dangerous ground. At a time when she should have hung fire, she charged, proclaiming publicly that she would abrogate the new constitution and reestablish a strong monarchy. The revolutionaries had the excuse they needed. They struck in January, seized government buildings and, with four boatloads of American marines and the support of the American minister, secured Honolulu. Liliuokalani surrendered.

It was a highly illegal coup; legitimate government had been stolen from the Hawaiian people. But given an island chain as isolated and vulnerable as Hawaii, the revolutionaries reasoned, how much did it really matter? It would be weeks before word reached Washington of what a few Americans had done without official sanction, then several more months before a new American president, Grover Cleveland, denounced the renegade action. By then the revolutionaries would already be forming a republic. They would choose as their first president Sanford Dole, a mission boy whose name eventually became synonymous with pineapples.

Not even revolution could rock Hawaii into the modern age. For years, an unstable monarchy had reigned; now an oligarchy composed of the revolution's leaders would rule. Officially, Hawaii was a democracy; in truth, the Chinese and Japanese were hindered from voting, and the Hawaiians were encouraged not to bother. Hawaii, reckoned its new leaders, was simply not ready for democracy. Even when the islands were finally annexed by the United States in 1898 and granted territorial status, they remained a colony.

More than ever before, the sugar planters, alias revolutionaries, held sway. By the early 20th century, they had linked their plantations into a cartel, the Big Five. It was a tidy monopoly composed of five companies that owned not only the sugar and pineapple industries, but the docks, shipping companies, and many of the stores, as well. Most of these holdings, happily, were the property of a few interlocking, intermarrying mission families— the Doles, Thurstons, Alexanders, Baldwins, Castles, Cookes, and others— who had found heaven right here on earth. They golfed together and dined together, sent their daughters to Wellesley and their sons to Yale. All were proud of their roots, and as blindly paternalistic as their forefathers. It was their destiny to control Hawaii, and they made very certain, by refusing to sell land or provide services, that mainland firms did not gain a foothold in their domain.

What was good for the Big Five was good for Hawaii. Competition was obviously not good for Hawaii. Although the Chinese and Japanese were establishing successful businesses in Honolulu and some Chinese were even growing rich, they posed no immediate threat to the Big Five. And the Hawaiians had never been good at capitalism. By the early 20th century, they had become one of the world's most urbanized groups. But rather than competing with white businessmen in Honolulu, unemployed Hawaiians were forced to live in hovels and packing crates, cooking their *poi* on stoves fashioned from empty oil cans.

Political competition was also unhealthy. Hawaii was ruled by the Big Five, so naturally it should be run by the Republican Party. After all, the mission families were Republicans. Back on the mainland, the Democrats had always been cool to the sugar planters, and it was a Republican president, William McKinley, who eventually annexed Hawaii. The Republicans, quite simply, were good for business.

The Big Five set out very deliberately to overwhelm any political opposition. When the Hawaiians created a home-rule party around the turn of the century, the Big Five shrewdly co-opted it by running a beloved descendant of Hawaii's royal family as the Republican candidate. On the plantations they pitted one ethnic group against another to prevent the Asian workers from organizing. Then, when labor unions finally formed, the Big Five attacked them savagely. In 1924, police killed 16 strikers on Kauai. Fourteen years later, in an incident known as the "Hilo massacre," the police wounded 50 pickets.

The Big Five crushed the Democratic Party by intimidation. Polling booths were rigged. It was dangerous to vote Democratic—workers could lose their jobs, and if they were plantation workers, that meant losing their houses, as well. Conducting Democratic meetings on the plantations was about as easy as holding a hula dance in an old missionary church. The Democrats went underground.

Those were halcyon days for both the Big Five and the Republican Party. In 1900, only five percent of Hawaii's population was white. The rest was comprised of races that rarely benefitted from Republican policies. But for the next several decades, even during the Depression, the Big Five kept the Republicans in power.

While the New Deal swept the mainland, Hawaii clung to its colonial heritage. The islands were still a generation behind the rest of the United States—the Big Five enjoyed it that way. There was nothing like the status quo when you were already in power. Other factors that had long shaped Hawaii's history also played into the hands of the Big Five. The islands' vulnerability, which had always favored the rule of a small elite, permitted the Big Five to establish an awesome cartel. Hawaii's isolation, its distance from the mainland, helped protect their monopoly.

THE JAPANESE AND THE MODERN WORLD

All that ended on December 7, 1941. The Japanese bombers that attacked Pearl Harbor sent shock waves through Hawaii that are still rumbling today. World War II changed all the rules of the game, upsetting the conditions that had determined island history for centuries.

Ironically, no group in Hawaii would feel the shift more thoroughly than the Japanese. When the Emperor declared war on the United States, 160,000 Japanese-Americans were living in Hawaii, fully one-third of the islands' population. On the mainland, Japanese-Americans were rounded up and herded into relocation camps. But in Hawaii that was impossible; there were simply too many, and they comprised too large a part of the labor force.

Many were second-generation Japanese, *nisei*, who had been educated in American schools and assimilated into Western society. Unlike their immigrant parents, the *issei*, they felt few ties to Japan. Their loyalties lay with America, and when war broke out they determined to prove it. They joined the U.S. armed forces and formed a regiment, the 442nd, which became the most frequently decorated outfit of the war. The Japanese were heroes, and when the war ended many heroes came home to the United States and ran for political office. Men like Dwight Eisenhower, Daniel Inouye, John Kennedy, and Spark Matsunaga began winning elections.

By the time the 442nd returned to the home front, Hawaii was changing dramatically. The Democrats were coming to power. Leftist labor unions won crucial strikes in 1941 and 1946. Jack Burns, an ex-cop who dressed in tattered clothes and drove around Honolulu in a beat-up car, was creating a new Democratic coalition.

Burns, who would eventually become governor, recognized the potential power of Hawaii's ethnic groups. Money was flowing into the islands—first military expenditures and then tourist dollars, and non-whites were rapidly becoming a new middle class. The Filipinos still constituted a large part of the plantation force, and the Hawaiians remained disenchanted, but the Japanese and Chinese were moving up fast. Together they comprised a majority of Hawaii's voters.

Burns organized them, creating a multiracial movement and thrusting the Japanese forward as candidates. By 1954, the Democrats controlled the legislature, with the Japanese filling one out of every two seats in the capital. Then, when Hawaii attained statehood five years later, the voters elected the first Japanese ever to serve in Congress. Today one of the state's U.S. senators and a congressman are Japanese. On every level of government, from municipal to federal, the Japanese predominate. They have arrived. The *mana*, that legendary power coveted by the Hawaiian chiefs and then lost to the sugar barons, has passed once again—to a people who came as immigrant farm-workers and stayed to become the leaders of the 50th state.

The Japanese and the Democrats were on the move, but in the period from World War II until the present day, everything was in motion. Hawaii was in upheaval. Jet travel and a population boom shattered the islands' solitude. While in 1939 about 500 people flew to Hawaii, now more than five million land every year. The military population escalated as Oahu became a key base not only during World War II but throughout the Cold War and the Vietnam War, as well. Hawaii's overall population exploded from about a half-million just after World War II to over one million at the present time.

No longer did the islands lag behind the mainland; they rapidly acquired the dubious quality of modernity. Hawaii became America's 50th state in 1959, Honolulu grew into a bustling highrise city, and condominiums mushroomed along Maui's beaches. Outside investors swallowed up two of the Big Five corporations, and several partners in the old monopoly began conducting most of their business outside Hawaii. Everything became too big and moved too fast for Hawaii to be entirely vulnerable to a small interest group. Now, like the rest of the world, it would be prey to multi-national corporations. By the 1980s, it would also be of significant interest to investors from Japan. In a few short years they succeeded in buying up a majority of the state's luxury resorts, including every major beachfront hotel in Waikiki, sending real estate prices into an upward spiral that did not level off until the early 1990s. Hawaii had arrived; it was fully a part of the modern world. An island chain that had slept for centuries had been rudely awakened by the forces of change.

Hawaii Today

THE LAND

Hawaii is an archipelago that stretches more than 1500 miles across the North Pacific Ocean. Composed of 132 islands, it has eight major islands, clustered at the southeastern end of the chain. Together these larger islands are about the size of Connecticut and Rhode Island combined. Only seven are inhabited: the eighth, Kahoolawe, serves as a bombing range for the U.S. Navy. Another island, Niihau, is privately owned and off-limits to the public. So in planning your trip, you'll have six islands to choose from.

They're located 2500 miles southwest of Los Angeles, on the same 20th latitude as Hong Kong and Mexico City. It's two hours earlier in Hawaii than in Los Angeles, four hours before Chicago, and five hours earlier than New York. Since Hawaii does not practice daylight-saving, this time difference becomes one hour greater during the summer months.

Each island, in a sense, is a small continent. Volcanic mountains rise in the interior, while the coastline is fringed with coral reefs and white-sand beaches. The northeastern face of each island, buffeted by trade winds, is the wet side. The contrast between this side and the island's southwestern sector is sometimes startling. Kauai, for instance, contains the wettest spot on earth, but its southwestern flank resembles Arizona. Dense rainforests in the northeast are teeming with exotic tropical plants, while across the island you're liable to see cactus growing in a barren landscape!

THE PEOPLE

Because of its unique history and isolated geography, Hawaii is truly a cultural melting pot. It's one of the few states in the union in which white people are a minority group. Whites, or *haoles* as they're called in the islands, comprise only about 33 percent of Hawaii's 1.1 million population. Japanese constitute 22 percent, Hawaiians and part-Hawaiians account for 21 percent, Filipinos 15 percent, Chinese about six percent, and other racial groups three percent.

It's a very young, vital society. More than half the community is under thirty-five and over one-quarter of the people were born of racially mixed parents. Three out of every four residents live on the island of Oahu, and almost half of those live in the city of Honolulu.

One trait characterizing many of these people is Hawaii's famous spirit of *aloha*, a genuine friendliness, an openness to strangers, a willingness to give freely. Undoubtedly, it is one of the finest qualities any people has ever demonstrated. *Aloha* originated with the Polynesians and played an important role in ancient Hawaiian civilization. When Western colonialists arrived, however, they viewed it not as a Hawaiian form of graciousness, but rather as the naivete of a primitive culture. They turned *aloha* into a tool for exploiting the Hawaiians, taking practically everything they owned.

Today, unfortunately, the descendants of the colonialists are being repaid in kind. The *aloha* spirit is still present in the islands, but another social force has arisen—racial hatred. There is growing resentment toward white people and other mainlanders in Hawaii.

Sometimes this hatred spills into ripoffs and violence. Therefore, mainland visitors must be very careful, particularly when traveling in heavily touristed areas. Try not to leave items in your car; if you absolutely must, lock them in the trunk. Don't leave valuable gear unattended in a campsite. And try not to antagonize the islands' young people.

It's exciting to meet folks, and I highly recommend that you mix with local residents, but do it with forethought and consideration. A lot of locals are eager to make new acquaintances; others can be extremely hostile. So choose the situation. If a local group looks bent on trouble, mind your own business. They don't need you, and you don't need them. For most encounters, I'd follow this general rule—be friendly, but be careful.

THE ECONOMY

For years, sugar was king in Hawaii, the most lucrative part of the island economy. Today, tourism is number one. More than four million Americans, and almost seven million travelers worldwide, including a rapidly increasing contingent of Japanese tourists, visit the Aloha State every year. It's now a 9.4 billion-dollar business that expanded exponentially during the 1970s and 1980s.

With 117,141 personnel and dependents stationed in Hawaii, the U.S. military is another large industry. Concentrated on Oahu, where they control one-quarter of the land, the armed forces pour more than three billion dollars into the local economy every year.

Marijuana is now Hawaii's foremost cash crop (the Department of Business, Economic Development, and Tourism estimates that the market totals over seven billion dollars). *Pakalolo* flourishes on Maui, Hawaii, and Kauai. Nurtured under ideal growing conditions, Hawaiian dope is especially potent and commands high prices all across the continental United States. It's a very controversial product, one which has created an underground economy.

Of course, no Chamber of Commerce report will list the demon weed as Hawaii's prime crop. Officially, sugar is still tops. While the $329 million sugar industry is small potatoes compared to tourism and the military, Hawaii remains one of America's largest sugar-producing states. But sugar, like everything else in the islands, is threatened by urban development. A ton of water is required to produce a pound of sugar. Since the construction industry is now a 2.2 billion-dollar business, new housing developments are competing more and more with sugarcane for the precious liquid.

Pineapple is another crop that's ailing. Stiff competition from the Philippines, where labor is cheap and easily exploitable, has reduced Hawaii's pineapple plantations to a few relatively small operations.

Hawaii is one of the only places in the United States that grows coffee. The islands do a booming business in macadamia nuts, orchids, anthuriums, guava nectar, and passion fruit juice. Together, these industries have created a strong economy in the 50th state. The per capita income is greater than the national average, and the standard of living is generally higher.

Important note: Hawaii has a higher cost of living than almost any other state in the union. As in the rest of the country, inflation is no stranger here; price increases are common. Therefore, don't be surprised if the prices quoted in this book are sometimes lower than those you'll actually be paying.

THE CUISINE

Nowhere is the influence of Hawaii's melting pot population stronger than in the kitchen. While in the islands, you'll probably eat not only with a fork, but with chopsticks and fingers, as well. You'll sample a wonderfully varied cuisine. In addition to standard American fare, hundreds of restaurants serve Hawaiian, Japanese, Chinese, Korean, Portuguese, and Filipino dishes. There are also fresh fruits aplenty—pineapples, papayas, mangoes, bananas, and tangerines—plus native fish such as *mahimahi*, marlin, and snapper.

The prime Hawaiian dish is *poi*, made from crushed taro root and served as a pasty purple liquid. It's pretty bland fare, but it does make a good side dish with roast pork or tripe stew. You should also try *lau lau*, a combination of fish, pork, and taro leaves wrapped in a *ti* leaf and steamed. And don't neglect to taste baked *ulu* (breadfruit) and *opihi* (limpets). A good way to try all these dishes at one sitting is to attend a *luau*. I've always found the tourist *luaus* too commercial, but you might watch the newspapers for one of the special *luaus* sponsored by civic organizations.

Japanese dishes include sukiyaki, teriyaki, and tempura, plus an island favorite—*sashimi*, or raw fish. Similarly, Chinese menus usually feature the dishes you've sampled at home as well as some less common treats. Among these are *saimin*, a noodle soup filled with meat and vegetables, and crack seed, a delicacy made from dried fruits.

You can count on the Koreans for *kim chi*, a spicy salad of pickled cabbage, and *kun koki*, barbecued meat prepared with soy and sesame oil. The Portuguese serve up some delicious sweets including *malasadas* (donuts minus the holes) and *pao doce*, or sweet bread. For Filipino fare, I recommend *adobo*, a pork or chicken dish spiced with garlic and vinegar, and *pochero*, a meat entrée cooked with bananas and several vegetables.

As the Hawaiians say, *"Hele mai ai."* Come and eat!

THE LANGUAGE

The language common to all Hawaii is English, but because of its diverse cultural heritage, the archipelago also supports several other tongues. Foremost among these are Hawaiian and pidgin.

Hawaiian, closely related to other Polynesian languages, is one of the most fluid and melodious languages in the world. It's composed of only twelve letters: five vowels—*a, e, i, o, u,* and seven consonants—*h, k, l, m, n, p, w.*

At first glance, the language appears formidable: how the hell do you pronounce *humuhumunukunukuapuaa*? But actually it's quite simple. After you've mastered a few rules of pronunciation, you can take on any word in the language.

The first thing to remember is that every syllable ends with a vowel, and the next to last syllable receives the accent.

The next rule to keep in mind is that all the letters in Hawaiian are pronounced. Consonants are pronounced the same as in English (except for the *w*, which is pronounced as a *v* when it introduces the last syllable of a word—as in *ewa* or *awa*. Vowels are pronounced the same as in Latin or Spanish: *a* as in *among, e* as in *they, i* as in *machine, o* as in *no,* and *u* as in *too.* Hawaiian has four vowel combinations or diphthongs: *au*, pronounced *ow, ae* and *ai,* which sound like *eye,* and *ei,* pronounced *ay.*

By now, you're probably wondering what I could possibly have meant when I said Hawaiian was simple. I think the glossary that follows will simplify everything while helping you pronounce common words and place names. Just go through the list, starting with words like *aloha* and *luau* that you already know. After you've practiced pronouncing familiar words, the rules will become second nature; you'll practically be a *kamaaina.*

Just when you start to speak with a swagger, cocky about having learned a new language, some young Hawaiian will start talking at you in a tongue that breaks all the rules you've so carefully mastered. That's pidgin. It started in the 19th century as a lingua franca among Hawaii's many races. Pidgin speakers mix English and Hawaiian with several other tongues to produce a spicy creole. It's a fascinating language with its own vocabulary, a unique syntax, and a rising inflection that's hard to mimic.

Pidgin is definitely the hip way to talk in Hawaii. A lot of young Hawaiians use it among themselves as a private language. At times they may start talking pidgin to you, acting as though they don't speak English; then if they decide you're okay, they'll break into English. When that happens, you be one *da kine brah.*

So *brah*, I take *da kine* pidgin words, put 'em together with Hawaiian, make one big list. Savvy?

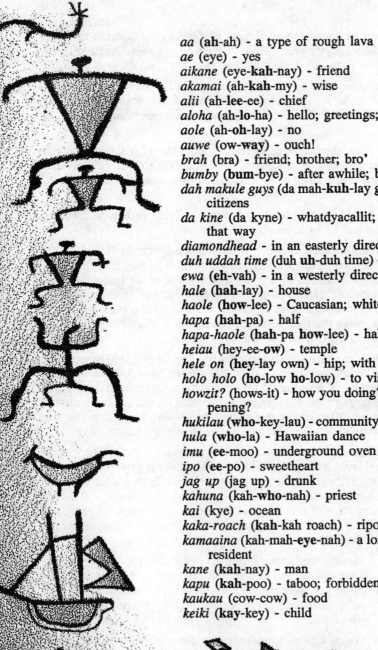

aa (**ah**-ah) - a type of rough lava
ae (eye) - yes
aikane (eye-**kah**-nay) - friend
akamai (ah-**kah**-my) - wise
alii (ah-**lee**-ee) - chief
aloha (ah-**lo**-ha) - hello; greetings; love
aole (ah-**oh**-lay) - no
auwe (ow-**way**) - ouch!
brah (bra) - friend; brother; bro'
bumby (**bum**-bye) - after awhile; by and by
dah makule guys (da mah-**kuh**-lay guys) - senior citizens
da kine (da kyne) - whatdyacallit; thingamajig; that way
diamondhead - in an easterly direction
duh uddah time (duh **uh**-duh time) - once before
ewa (**eh**-vah) - in a westerly direction
hale (**hah**-lay) - house
haole (**how**-lee) - Caucasian; white person
hapa (**hah**-pa) - half
hapa-haole (**hah**-pa **how**-lee) - half-Caucasian
heiau (hey-ee-**ow**) - temple
hele on (**hey**-lay own) - hip; with it
holo holo (**ho**-low **ho**-low) - to visit
howzit? (**hows**-it) - how you doing? what's happening?
hukilau (**who**-key-lau) - community fishing party
hula (**who**-la) - Hawaiian dance
imu (**ee**-moo) - underground oven
ipo (**ee**-po) - sweetheart
jag up (jag up) - drunk
kahuna (kah-**who**-nah) - priest
kai (kye) - ocean
kaka-roach (**kah**-kah roach) - ripoff; theft
kamaaina (kah-mah-**eye**-nah) - a longtime island resident
kane (**kah**-nay) - man
kapu (**kah**-poo) - taboo; forbidden
kaukau (cow-cow) - food
keiki (**kay**-key) - child

kiawe (key-**ah**-vay) - mesquite tree

kokua (ko-**coo**-ah) - help

kona winds (**ko**-nah winds) - winds that blow against the trades

lanai (lah-**nye**) - porch; also island name

lauhala (lau-**hah**-lah) or *hala* (**hah**-lah) - a tree whose leaves are used in weaving

lei (lay) - flower garland

lolo (low-low) - stupid

lomilomi (**low**-me-**low**-me) - massage; also raw salmon

luau (**loo**-ow) - feast

mahalo (mah-**hah**-low) - thank you

mahalo nui loa (mah-**hah**-low **new**-ee **low**-ah) - thank you very much

mahu (**mah**-who) - gay; homosexual

makai (mah-**kye**) - toward the sea

malihini (mah-lee-**hee**-nee) - newcomer; stranger

mauka (**mau**-kah) - toward the mountains

nani (**nah**-nee) - beautiful

ohana (oh-**hah**-nah) - family

okole (oh-**ko**-lay) - rear; ass

okolemaluna (oh-ko-lay-mah-**loo**-nah) - a toast: bottoms up!

ono (**oh**-no) - tastes good

pahoehoe (pah-**hoy**-hoy) - ropy lava

pakalolo (pah-kah-**low**-low) - marijuana

pakiki head (pah-**key**-key head) - stubborn

pali (**pah**-lee) - cliff

paniolo (pah-nee-**oh**-low) - cowboy

pau (pow) - finished; done

pilikia (pee-lee-**key**-ah) - trouble

puka (**poo**-kah) - hole

pupus (**poo**-poos) - hors d'oeuvres

shaka (**shah**-kah) - great; perfect

swell head - angry

tapa (**tap**-ah) - tree bark which is used as a fabric

wahine (wah-**hee**-nay) - woman

wikiwiki (**wee**-key-**wee**-key) - quickly; in a hurry

you get stink ear - you don't listen well

CHAPTER TWO

Rediscovering Paradise
How to Travel in Hawaii

How to Go

GETTING TO THE ISLANDS

During the 19th century, sleek clipper ships sailed from the West Coast to Hawaii in about 11 days. Today, you'll be traveling by a less romantic but far swifter conveyance—the jet plane. Rather than days at sea, it will be about five hours in the air from California, nine hours from Chicago, or around 11 hours if you're coming from New York.

There's really nothing easier, or more exciting, than catching a plane to Hawaii. No fewer than seven major airlines—**Northwest, United, Hawaiian, Continental, American, TWA,** and **Delta**—fly regular schedules to Honolulu. American and Delta also offer direct flights to Maui, and United flies directly to Maui as well as the Big Island. This nonstop service is particularly convenient for travelers who are interested in visiting the outer islands while bypassing Honolulu.

Whichever carrier you choose, ask for the economy or excursion fare, and try to fly during the week; weekend flights are generally higher in price. To qualify for lower price fares, it is sometimes necessary to book your flight two weeks in advance and to stay in the islands at least one week. Generally, however, the restrictions are minimal. Children under two years of age can fly for free, but they will not have a seat of their own. Each passenger is permitted two large pieces of luggage plus a carry-on bag. Shipping a bike or surfboard will cost extra.

In planning a Hawaiian sojourn, one potential moneysaver is the package tour, which combines air transportation with a hotel room and other amenities. Generally, it is a style of travel that I avoid. However, if you can find a package that provides air transportation, a hotel or condominium accommodation, and a rental car, all at one low price—it might be worth considering. Just try to avoid the packages that preplan your entire visit, dragging you around on air-conditioned tour buses. Look for the package that provides only the bare necessities, namely transportation and lodging, while allowing you the greatest freedom.

However you decide to go, be sure to consult a travel agent. They are professionals in the field, possessing the latest information on rates and facilities, and their service to you is usually free.

GETTING BETWEEN ISLANDS

Since cruise ships are the only commercial boats serving all six Hawaiian islands, most of the transportation is by plane. **Aloha Airlines** and **Hawaiian Air**, the state's major carriers, provide frequent inter-island jet service. If you're looking for smooth, rapid, comfortable service, this is certainly it. You'll be buckled into your seat, offered a low-cost cocktail, and whisked to your destination within about twenty minutes.

Without doubt, the best service aboard any inter-island carrier is on Aloha Airlines. They have an excellent reputation for flying on time. For several years running, the U.S. Department of Transportation has named them the top airline in the country for having the fewest passenger complaints. I give them my top recommendation.

Now that you know how to fly quickly and comfortably, let me tell you about the most exciting way to get between islands. Several small airlines—such as **Aloha Island Air** and **Air Molokai**—fly twin-engine propeller planes. These small airplanes travel at low altitudes and moderate speeds over the islands. Next to chartering a helicopter, they are the finest way to see Hawaii from the air.

The service is very personalized; often the pilot will point out landmarks along the route, and sometimes he'll fly out of his way to show you points of particular interest. I often fly this way when I'm in the islands and highly recommend these small planes to anyone with a sense of adventure.

Let me describe a typical flight I took between Honolulu and Kona. So that I'd get a better view, the captain suggested that I sit up front in the co-pilot's seat. After taking off in a wide arc around Honolulu, we passed close enough to Diamond Head to gaze down into the crater, then headed across the Kaiwi Channel to Molokai. Since we had to pick up passengers at Molokai's lonely airstrip, the pilot gave us a tour of the island. We paralleled the island's rugged north face, where sharp cliffs laced with waterfalls drop thousands of feet to the sea. Then we swept in toward Maui for a view of Haleakala Crater, and continued past the Big Island's snowtipped volcanoes before touching down in Kona. All for the price of an airline ticket!

Rates for these twin-engine propeller planes are very competitive when compared with the inter-island jets. Coupled with the fact that your ticket on the smaller carriers is worth a guided tour as well as a trip between islands, you really can't do better than booking your flights on these sturdy little planes.

Hawaii's grand oceanliner tradition is carried on today by **American Hawaii Cruises** (550 Kearny Street, San Francisco, CA 94108; 800-765-7000). Sailing the *S.S. Independence* and the *S.S. Constitution*, they cruise the inter-island waters, docking at Maui, the Big Island, and near Aloha Tower in Honolulu (stops in Kauai have been temporarily suspended because of Hurricane Iniki, the 1992 storm that devastated the island). The cruises are week-long affairs that evoke memories of the old steamship era.

One of the few ferry services in Hawaii is provided by **Sea Link of Hawaii** (533-6899). Their 118-foot *Maui Princess* provides road trips daily between Maui and Molokai.

Where to Go

Deciding to take a vacation in Hawaii is easy; the hard part comes when you have to choose which islands to visit. All six are remarkably beautiful places, each with unique features to offer the traveler. Eventually, you should try to tour them all, but on a single trip you'll probably choose only one, two, or three.

To help you decide which to see, I'll briefly describe the key features of each. For more detailed information, you can turn to the introductory notes in each of the island chapters.

My personal favorites are the Big Island and Kauai, and I often recommend to friends unfamiliar with Hawaii that they visit these two islands. That way they manage to travel to both ends of the chain, experiencing the youngest and most rugged, and the oldest and most lush, of all the islands. The two offer a startling contrast, one that quickly shatters any illusion that all the islands are alike. (Since Kauai is currently recovering from Hurricane Iniki, I am presently recommending that travelers visit the Big Island and one of the other islands.)

Oahu, Hawaii's most populous island, is dominated by the capital city of Honolulu. Featuring the Waikiki tourist center, this is the most heavily touristed island. It's too crowded for many visitors. But Oahu *is* a prime place to mix city living with country exploring. It's also rich in history, culture, and beautiful beaches.

The island of Hawaii, or the **Big Island**, is true to its nickname. Located at the southeastern end of the Hawaiian chain, and dominated by two 13,000-foot volcanoes, this giant measures more than twice the size of all the other islands combined. It's a great place to mountain climb and explore live volcanoes, to swim along the sun-splashed Kona Coast, or to tour orchid farms in the verdant city of Hilo.

Maui, the second largest island, is rapidly becoming Hawaii's favorite destination for young visitors. Haleakala alone, the extraordinary crater that dominates the island, makes the "Valley Isle" worth touring. The island also sports many of Hawaii's prettiest beaches and provides an offshore breeding ground for rare humpback whales.

Directly to the west, lying in Maui's wind-shadow, sits the smallest and most secluded island. **Lanai** is an explorer's paradise, with a network of jeep trails leading to hidden beaches and scenic mountain ridges. There are only 2,000 people and about twenty miles of paved road here. If you're seeking an idyllic retreat, this is the place.

Molokai, slightly larger but nearly as remote, provides another extraordinary hideaway. With white-sand beaches, a mountainous interior, and a large population of Hawaiians, the "Friendly Isle" retains a unique sense of old Hawaii. Here you can visit a leper colony on the windswept Kalaupapa Peninsula, a pilgrimage that could prove to be the most awesome of all your experiences in Hawaii.

Before it was struck by Hurricane Iniki in September 1992, **Kauai** was Hawaii's prettiest, most luxuriant island. Located at the northwestern end of the chain, it is filled with jewel-like beaches and uninhabited valleys. Along the north shore are misty cliffs that fall precipitously to the sea; from the island's center rises a mountain that receives more rainfall than any place on earth; and along Kauai's southern flank there's a startling desert region reminiscent of the Southwest. With its wildly varied climates and terrain, this island is like a small continent. With rebuilding and replanting operations currently in place, it hopefully will soon return to its former beauty.

When to Go

SEASONS

There are two types of seasons in Hawaii, one keyed to tourists and the other to the climate. The peak tourist seasons run from mid-December until Easter, then again from mid-June through Labor Day. Particularly around the Christmas holidays and in August, the visitor centers are crowded. Prices increase, hotel rooms and rental cars become harder to reserve, and everything moves a bit more rapidly.

If you plan to explore Hawaii during these seasons, make reservations several months in advance; actually, it's a good idea to make advance reservations whenever you visit. Without doubt, the off-season is the best time to hit the islands. Not only are hotels more readily available, but campsites and hiking trails are also less crowded.

Climatologically, the ancient Hawaiians distinguished between two seasons—*kau*, or summer, and *hooilo*, or winter. Summer extends from May to October, when the sun is overhead and the temperatures are slightly higher. Winter brings more variable winds and cooler weather.

The important rule to remember about Hawaii's beautiful weather is that it changes very little from season to season but varies dramatically from place to place. The average yearly temperature is about 75°, and during the coldest weather in January and the warmest in August, the thermometer rarely moves more than 5° or 6° in either direction. Similarly, sea water temperatures range comfortably between 74° and 80° year-round.

A key aspect to this luxurious semitropical environment is the trade wind that blows with welcome regularity from the northeast, providing a natural form of airconditioning. When the trades stop blowing, they are sometimes replaced by *kona* winds carrying rain and humid weather from the southwest. These are most frequent in winter, when the islands receive their heaviest rainfall.

While summer showers are less frequent and shorter in duration, winter storms are sometimes quite nasty. I've seen it pour for five consecutive days, until hiking trails disappeared and city streets were awash. If you visit in winter, particularly from December to March, you're risking the chance of rain.

A wonderful factor to remember through this wet weather is that if it's raining where you are, you can often simply go someplace else. And I don't mean another part of the world, or even a different island. Since the rains generally batter the northeastern sections of each island, you can usually head over to the south or west coast for warm, sunny weather. Or if you seek cooler climes, head up to the mountains; for every thousand feet in elevation, the temperature drops about 3°. If you climb high enough on Maui or the Big Island, you might even encounter snow!

Sometimes nasty weather engulfs the entire chain, but there's usually a sunny refuge somewhere. I once spent a strenuous period along the Kona Coast working on a suntan. Across the island near Hilo, flood warnings were up. Twenty-five inches of rain dropped in 24 hours; five feet of water fell in seven days. Toward the end of the week, when my major problem was whether the tan would peel, officials in Hilo declared a state of emergency.

CALENDAR OF EVENTS

Something else to consider in planning a visit to Hawaii is the amazing lineup of annual cultural events. For a thumbnail idea of what's happening when, check the calendar below. You might just find that special occasion to climax an already dynamic vacation.

JANUARY

Mid-January or February: The month-long **Narcissus Festival** begins with the Chinese New Year. During the weeks of festivities, there are open houses, street parties, and parades in Honolulu's Chinatown. The **Pipeline Body-surfing Classic** takes place on Oahu's North Shore. Maui celebrates with music and dance at **No Mele O Maui.**

FEBRUARY

February: Architecture students from the University of Hawaii challenge local professionals in the annual **Sandcastle Building Contest** at Kailua Beach Park, Oahu.

Mid-February: If weather conditions permit, the **Mauna Kea Ski Meet** is held on the 13,000-foot slopes of the Big Island volcano.

Late February through March: The Japanese community celebrates its **Cherry Blossom Festival** in Honolulu with tea ceremonies, *Kabuki* theater presentations, martial arts demonstrations, and crafts exhibits.

MARCH

During March: Island musicians perform at Waikiki's Kapiolani Park in the **Hawaiian Song Festival and Song Composing Contest.** On Kauai, athletes compete in the **Prince Kuhio Ironman/Ironwoman Canoe Race.**

March 26: Major festivities on Kauai and Oahu mark the **Prince Kuhio Festival,** commemorating the birthdate of Prince Jonah Kuhio Kalaniana-ole, Hawaii's first delegate to the U.S. Congress.

APRIL

Early April: The week-long **Merrie Monarch Festival** on the Big Island pays tribute to David Kalakaua, Hawaii's last king. Festivities include musical performances, pageants, and a parade.

Early April: Buddhist temples on all the islands mark **Buddha Day,** the luminary's birthday, with special services. Included among the events are pageants, dances, and flower festivals.

MAY

May 1: **Lei Day** is celebrated on all the islands by people wearing flower leis colorful Hawaiian garb. In Oahu's Kapiolani Park, there are pageants and concerts.

Late May: The **50th State Fair** features agricultural exhibits, food stalls, dances, music, and displays of island arts and crafts.

JUNE

During June: In Honolulu, the music, dance, and customs of more than 40 Pacific Rim areas are showcased at the annual **Festival of the Pacific**. This two-week event features performers from American Samoa, New Zealand, Guam, and Hawaii. Canoeists vie on Oahu in the 100-mile **Around-the-Island Canoe Race**. Also on Oahu, the **Hawaiian Bodysurfing Championships** are held at Point Panic on the weekend with the best surf. *Halaus* from around the world participate in Oahu's **Annual King Kamehameha Hula Competition**.

During June: On Maui, the **Kapalua Music Festival** features chamber music by internationally acclaimed artists.

June 11: **Kamehameha Day**, honoring Hawaii's first king, is celebrated on all six islands with parades, chants, hula dances, foot races, and exhibits.

JULY

During July and August: On Oahu and the other islands, Buddhists perform colorful **Bon Dances** every weekend to honor the dead.

Fourth of July: In addition to fireworks, Hawaii celebrates Independence Day with the **Makawao Rodeo** on Maui, and with the **Hilo Orchid Society Flower Show** on the Big Island.

Late July: Hundreds of ukelele players gather at Kapiolani Park in Waikiki for the **Annual Ukelele Festival**.

AUGUST

During August, on consecutive Sundays: Local artists perform at the **Hula Festival** in Waikiki's Kapiolani Park.

During August: The dramatic **Hawaii State Surfing Championships** and the **Wahine Bodyboard Championships** are held on Oahu. In Honolulu, dancers six to twelve years old gather to compete in the **Queen Liliuokalani Keiki Hula Festival**.

August 21: Local residents celebrate **Admission Day**, the date in 1959 when Hawaii became the 50th state.

SEPTEMBER

Early September: The **Queen Liliuokalani Canoe Regatta** is staged on the Big Island.

Mid-September: The **Hawaii County Fair** in Hilo on the Big Island features an orchid show, steer show, *lei* contest, agricultural displays, plus exhibits of Hawaiian arts and crafts.

Late September and during October: The highlight of Hawaii's cultural season is the **Aloha Week** festival, a series of week-long celebrations featuring parades, street parties, and pageants. Each week, a different island stages the festival, and the entire sequence ends with a **Molokai-to-Oahu Canoe Race.**

OCTOBER

During October: The **Honolulu Orchid Society Show** in Honolulu presents thousands of orchids and other tropical plants.

Early October: The **Maui County Fair** features agricultural exhibits and arts-and-crafts displays; the **Iron Man Triathlon** on the Big Island tests the stamina of the world's best-conditioned athletes.

NOVEMBER

Mid-November: The Big Island's **Kona Coffee Festival** celebrates the coffee harvest with a parade, international food bazaar, and musical entertainment.

Mid-November: Paniolos on the Big Island turn out for the **Bull and Horse Show.**

DECEMBER

Early December: Buddha's enlightenment is commemorated on all the islands with **Bodhi Day** ceremonies and religious services.

Mid-December: Runners by the thousands turn out for the **Honolulu Marathon.**

During December: The **Festival of Trees** at Honolulu's Blaisdell Center marks the Christmas season.

During December: Surfers and landlubbers alike gather for the **Hawaiian Pro Surfing Championships** on Oahu.

December through Early January: The world's greatest surfers compete on Oahu's north shore in a series of contests including the **Pipeline Masters, Men's World Cup,** and the **Women's World Cup.** With 20-foot waves and prize money topping $50,000, these are spectacular events.

What to Take

When I get ready to pack for a trip, I sit down and make a list of everything I'll need. It's a very slow, exact procedure: I look in closets, drawers, and shelves, and run through in my mind the activities in which I'll participate, determining which items are required for each. After all the planning is complete and when I have the entire inventory collected in one long list, I sit for a minute or two, basking in my wisdom and forethought.

Then I tear the hell out of the list, cut out the ridiculous items I'll never use, halve the number of spares among the necessary items, and reduce the entire contents of my suitcase to the bare essentials.

Before I developed this packing technique, I once traveled overland from London to New Delhi carrying two suitcases and a knapsack. I lugged those damned bundles onto trains, buses, jitneys, taxis, and rickshaws. When I reached Turkey, I started shipping things home, but by then I was buying so many market goods that it was all I could do to keep even.

I ended up carrying so much crap that one day, when I was sardined in a crowd pushing its way onto an Indian train, someone managed to pick my pocket. When I felt the wallet slipping out, not only was I unable to chase the culprit—I was so weighted down with baggage that I couldn't even turn around to see who was robbing me!

I'll never travel that way again, and neither should you. Particularly when visiting Hawaii, where the weather is mild, you should pack very light. The airlines permit two suitcases and a carry-on bag; try to take one suitcase and maybe an accessory bag that can double as a beach bag. Dress styles are very informal in the islands, and laundromats are frequent, so you don't need a broad range of clothing items, and you'll require very few extras among the essential items.

Remember, you're packing for a semitropical climate. Take along a sweater or light jacket for the mountains, and a poncho to protect against rain. But otherwise, all that travelers in Hawaii require are shorts, bathing suits, lightweight slacks, short-sleeved shirts and blouses, and summer dresses or *muumuus*. Rarely do visitors require sport jackets or formal dresses. Wash-and-wear fabrics are the most convenient.

For footwear, I suggest soft, comfortable shoes. Low-cut hiking boots or tennis shoes are preferable for hiking; for beachgoing, there's nothing as good as sandals.

There are several other items to squeeze in the corners of your suitcase—suntan lotion, sunglasses, a towel, and, of course, your copy of *Hidden Hawaii*. You might also consider packing a mask, fins, and snorkel, and possibly a camera.

(Text continued on page 36.)

The New Travel

Travel today is becoming a personal art form. A destination no longer serves as just a place to relax: it's also a point of encounter, where experience runs feverish and reality unravels. To many, this new wave in travel customs is labeled "adventure travel" and involves trekking glaciers or sweeping along in a hang glider; to others, it connotes nothing more daring than a restful spell in a secluded resort. Actually, it's a state of mind, a willingness not only to accept but seek out the uncommon and unique.

Few places in the world are more conducive to this imaginative new travel than Hawaii. Several organizations in the islands cater specifically to people who want to add local customs and unusual adventures to their vacation itineraries.

The Nature Conservancy of Hawaii (1116 Smith Street, #201, Honolulu, HI 96817; 537-4508), a nonprofit conservation organization, conducts week-long natural history tours of Oahu, Maui, and Molokai. Led by expert guides, small groups explore untrammeled beaches, rainforests, and an ancient bog. The tours provide a singular insight into the plant and animal life of the islands.

Pacific Quest (59-496 Pupukea Road, Haleiwa, HI 96712; 638-8338) features a 13-day camping and hiking adventure to Kauai, Maui, and the Big Island including whale-watching and snorkeling.

More in the Outward Bound tradition, **Wilderness Hawaii** (P.O. Box 61692, Honolulu, HI 96839; 737-4697) outfits four-day and 14-day expeditions in Hawaii Volcanoes National Park on the Big Island. The 14-day experience challenges your self-reliance and wilderness skills. Beginning at the 3000-foot elevation, you explore the 13,677-foot summit of Mauna Loa and are left alone in the outback for three days. The four-day trip is slightly less strenuous and includes a seven-mile back-packing hike to the coast.

Paradise Safaris (Box A-D, Kailua-Kona, HI 96745; 322-2366) offers a sunset stargazing trip. Small groups board a four-wheel-drive wagon to the summit of Mauna Kea to enjoy a sunset view and learn about the mountaintop observatory's telescope. There's a hands-on stargazing experience at mid-mountain before returning.

Hike Maui (P.O. Box 330969, Kahului, HI 96733; 879-5270) leads day hiking trips all around the Valley Isle. Ranging from five to twelve hours in duration, these treks can be custom designed to your interests.

If you prefer a day trip that is not overly strenuous, sign on with **Action Hawaii** (P.O. Box 75548, Honolulu, HI 96836; 944-6754), which sponsors an Oahu adventure that includes a guided hike to Diamond Head, boogie boarding, snorkeling, and a unique island tour.

To truly kick back, just **Go Native Hawaii** (P.O. Box 11418, Hilo, HI 96721; 935-4178). This bed-and-breakfast clearinghouse lists over 250 private homes that welcome guests. Located on the four major islands, these informal accommodations (priced in the budget range and higher) provide a chance to vacation in an island home.

When you're ready to take up the challenge of this new style of freewheeling travel, check with these outfits. Or plan your own trip. To traditional tourists, Hawaii means souvenir shops and fast-food restaurants. But for those with spirit and imagination, it's a land of untracked beaches and ancient volcanoes waiting to be explored.

If you plan on camping, you'll need most of the equipment required for mainland overnighting. In Hawaii, you can get along quite comfortably with a lightweight tent and sleeping bag. You'll also need a knapsack, canteen, camp stove and fuel, mess kit, first-aid kit (with insect repellent, water purification tablets, and Chapstick), toilet kit, a pocket knife, hat, waterproof matches, flashlight, and ground cloth.

How to Deal With . . .

CAR RENTALS

Renting a car is as easy in Hawaii as anywhere. Every island supports at least several rental agencies, which compete fiercely with one another in price and quality of service. So before renting, shop around: check the listings in this book, and also look for the special temporary offers that many rental companies sometimes feature.

There are several facts to remember when renting a car. First of all, a major credit card is very helpful; if you lack one, you'll often have to leave a cash deposit on the car. Also, some agencies don't rent at all to people under 25. Regardless of your age, many companies charge several dollars a day extra for insurance. The insurance is optional and expensive, but if you don't take it you're liable for the first several thousand dollars in accident damage. So before leaving home, check to see how much coverage your personal insurance policy provides for rental cars and, if necessary, have a clause added that will include rental car protection.

Rates fluctuate with the season; slack tourist seasons are great times for good deals. Also, three-day, weekly, and monthly rates are almost always cheaper than daily rentals; cars with standard shifts are generally less than automatics; and compacts are more economical than the larger four-door models.

Other than on the island of Lanai, I don't recommend renting a jeep. They're more expensive and less comfortable than automobiles, and won't get you to very many more interesting spots. Except in extremely wet weather when roads are muddy, all the places mentioned in this book, including the hidden (★) locales, can be reached by car.

CONDOMINIUM LIVING

Many people visiting Hawaii, especially those traveling with families, find that condominiums are often cheaper than hotels. While some hotel rooms come with kitchenettes, few provide all the amenities of condominiums. A condo, in essence, is an apartment away from home. Designed as studio, one-, two-, or three-bedroom apartments, they come equipped with full kitchen facilities and complete kitchenware collections. Many also feature washer-dryers, dishwashers, air-conditioning, color televisions, telephones, lanais, and community swimming pools.

Utilizing the kitchen will save considerably on your food bill; by sharing the accommodations among several people, you'll also cut your lodging bill. While the best way to see Hawaii is obviously by hiking and camping, when you're ready to come in from the wilds, consider reserving a place that provides more than a bed and night table.

HOTELS

Accommodations in Hawaii range from funky cottages to highrise condominiums. You'll find inexpensive family-run hotels, middle-class tourist facilities, and world-class resorts.

Whichever you choose, there are a few guidelines to help save money. Try to visit during the off-season, avoiding the high-rate periods during the summer and from Christmas to Easter. Rooms with mountain views are less expensive than ocean view accommodations. Generally, the farther a hotel is from the beach, the less it costs. Another way to economize is by reserving a room with a kitchen. In any case, try to reserve far in advance.

Throughout this book, hotels are described according to price category. *Budget* hotels have rooms starting from $50 or less per night for two people. *Moderate* facilities begin somewhere between $50 and $90. *Deluxe* hotels offer rates starting from $90 to $130. *Ultra-deluxe* establishments rent accommodations at prices above $130.

RESTAURANTS

A few guidelines will help you chart a course through Hawaii's countless dining places. Within a particular chapter, the restaurants are categorized geographically, with each restaurant entry describing the establishment as budget, moderate, deluxe, or ultra-deluxe in price. Dinner entrées at *budget* restaurants usually cost $8 or less. The ambience is informal café style and the crowd is often a local one. *Moderately* priced restaurants range between $8 and $16 at dinner and offer pleasant surroundings, a more varied menu, and a slower pace. *Deluxe* establishments tab their entrées above $16, featuring sophisticated cuisines, plush decor, and more personalized service. *Ultra-deluxe* restaurants generally price above $24.

Breakfast and lunch menus vary less in price from restaurant to restaurant. Even deluxe-priced kitchens usually offer light breakfasts and lunch sandwiches, which place them within a few dollars of their budget-minded competitors. These early meals can be a good time to test expensive restaurants.

MAIL

If you're staying in a particular establishment during your visit, you can usually have personal mail sent there. Otherwise, **American Express** will hold mail for no charge at its Honolulu office for 30 days, and will provide forwarding for cardholders. If you decide to use their facilities, have mail addressed to American Express, Client Mail, 2424 Kalakaua Avenue, Honolulu, Oahu, HI 96815 (922-4718). If you don't use this service, your only other recourse is to have mail sent to a particular post office in care of general delivery.

VISITOR INFORMATION

The **Hawaii Visitors Bureau,** a privately funded agency, is a valuable resource from which to obtain free information on Hawaii. With offices nationwide and branches on each of the four largest islands, the Bureau can help plan your trip and then offer advice once you reach Hawaii.

Details concerning the island offices appear in the "Addresses" section at the end of the Oahu, Hawaii, Maui, and Kauai chapters. On the mainland, you can contact the Hawaii Visitors Bureau at the following offices: on the West Coast—at 3440 Wilshire Boulevard, #502, Los Angeles, CA 90010 (213-385-5301), or at 50 California Street, Suite 450, San Francisco, CA 94111 (415-392-8173); in the Midwest—at 180 North Michigan Avenue, #2210, Chicago, IL 60601 (312-236-0632); and on the East Coast—at 441 Lexington Avenue, #1003, New York, NY 10017 (212-986-9203).

Another excellent resource is the **Hawaii State Library Service**. With a network of libraries on all the islands, this government agency provides facilities for residents and non-residents alike. The libraries are good places to find light beach-reading material as well as books on Hawaii. Visitors can check out books by simply applying for a library card with a valid identification card.

BEING DISABLED

The **Commission on Persons with Disabilities** publishes a survey of the city, county, state, and federal parks in Hawaii that are accessible to disabled people. For information, contact the Commission at 5 Waterfront Plaza, Suite 210, 500 Ala Moana Boulevard, Honolulu, HI 96813 (586-8121). You can pick up their "Aloha Guides to Accessibility," which covers Oahu, Maui, Kauai, and the Big Island, and gives information on various hotels, shopping centers, and restaurants that are accessible.

The **Society for the Advancement of Travel for the Handicapped** (347 5th Avenue, #610, New York, NY, 10016; 212-447-7284) offers information for disabled travelers. **Travelin' Talk** (P.O. Box 3534, Clarksville, TN 37043; 615-552-6670), a network of people and organizations, also provides assistance.

Be sure to check in advance when making room reservations. Some hotels feature facilities for those in wheelchairs.

BEING AN OLDER TRAVELER

Hawaii is a hospitable place for senior citizens to visit. Countless museums, historic sights, and even restaurants and hotels offer senior discounts that can cut a substantial chunk off vacation costs. The national park system's Golden Age Passport, which must be applied for in person, allows free admission for anyone 62 and older to the numerous national parks and monuments in the islands.

The **American Association of Retired Persons** (AARP) (3200 East Carson Street, Lakewood, CA 90712; 310-496-2277) offers membership to anyone over 50. AARP's benefits include travel discounts with a number of firms; escorted tours and cruises are available through AARP Travel Experience/American Express (400 Pinnacle Way, Suite 450, Norcross, GA 30071; 800-927-0111).

Elderhostel (75 Federal Street, Boston, MA 02110; 617-426-7788) offers reasonably priced, all-inclusive educational programs in a variety of locations throughout the year.

The federal government offers an informative brochure, *Travel Tips for Senior Citizens* (Superintendent of Documents, Government Printing Office, Washington, DC 20402; 202-783-3238) for a nominal fee.

Be extra careful about health matters. Consider carrying a medical record with you—including your medical history and current medical status as well as your doctor's name, phone number, and address. Make sure your insurance covers you while you are away from home.

BEING A WOMAN TRAVELING ALONE

It is sad commentary on life in the United States, but women traveling alone must take precautions. It's entirely unwise to hitchhike and probably best to avoid inexpensive accommodations on the outskirts of town; the money saved does not outweigh the risk. Bed and breakfasts, youth hostels, college dorms and YWCAs are generally your safest bet for lodging.

If you are hassled or threatened in some way, never be afraid to scream for assistance. It's a good idea to carry change for a phone call and to know the number to call in case of emergency.

BEING A FOREIGN TRAVELER

PASSPORTS AND VISAS   Most foreign visitors are required to obtain a passport and tourist visa to enter the United States. Contact your nearest United States Embassy or Consulate well in advance to obtain a visa and to check on any other entry requirements.

CUSTOMS REQUIREMENTS   Foreign travelers are allowed to bring in the following: $400 worth of duty-free gifts, and any amount of currency (amounts over U.S. $10,000 require a form). Carry any prescription drugs in clearly marked containers; you may have to provide a written prescription or doctor's statement to clear customs.

DRIVING   If you plan to rent a car, an international driver's license should be obtained prior to arrival. Some rental car companies require both a foreign license and an international driver's license along with a major credit card, and require that the lessee be at least 25 years of age.

CURRENCY   American money is based on the dollar. Bills in the United States generally come in six denominations: $1, $5, $10, $20, $50, and $100. Every dollar is divided into 100 cents. Coins are the penny (1 cent), nickel (5 cents), dime (10 cents), and quarter (25 cents). You may not use foreign currency to purchase goods and services in the United States. Consider buying traveler's checks in dollar amounts. You may also use credit cards affiliated with an American company such as Interbank, Barclay Card, VISA and American Express.

WEIGHTS AND MEASUREMENTS   The United States uses the English system of weights and measures. American units and their metric equivalents are as follows: 1 inch = 2.5 centimeters; 1 foot = 0.3 meter; 1 yard = 0.9 meter; 1 mile = 1.6 kilometers; 1 ounce = 28 grams; 1 pound = 0.45 kilogram; 1 quart (liquid) = 0.9 liter.

TRAVELING WITH CHILDREN

Hawaii is an ideal vacation spot for family holidays. The pace is slow, the atmosphere casual. A few guidelines will help ensure that your trip to the islands brings out the joys rather than the strains of parenting, allowing everyone to get into the *aloha* spirit.

Use a travel agent to help with arrangements; they can reserve spacious bulkhead seats on airlines and determine which flights are least crowded. They can also seek out the best deals on inexpensive condominiums, saving you money on both room and board.

Planning the trip with your kids stimulates their imagination. Books about travel, airplane rides, beaches, whales, volcanoes, and Hawaiiana help prepare even a two-year-old for an adventure. This preparation makes the "getting there" part of the trip more exciting for children of all ages.

And "getting there" means a long-distance flight. Plan to bring everything you need on board the plane—diapers, food, toys, books, and extra clothing for kids and parents alike. I've found it helpful to carry a few new toys and books as treats to distract my son and daughter when they get bored. I also pack a few snacks.

Allow extra time to get places. Book reservations in advance and make sure that the hotel or condominium has the extra crib, cot, or bed you require.

It's smart to ask for a room at the end of the hall to cut down on noise. And when reserving a rental car, inquire to see if they provide car seats and if there is an added charge. Hawaii has a strictly enforced car seat law.

Besides the car seat you may have to bring along, also pack shorts and T-shirts, a sweater, sun hat, sun dresses, and waterproof sandals. A stroller with sunshade for little ones helps on sightseeing sojourns; a shovel and pail are essential for sandcastle building. Most importantly, remember to bring a good sunblock. The quickest way to ruin a family vacation is with a bad sunburn. Also plan to bring indoor activities such as books and games for evenings and rainy days.

Most towns have stores that carry diapers, food, and other essentials. However, prices are much higher in Hawaii. To economize, some people take along an extra suitcase filled with diapers and wipes, baby food, peanut butter and jelly, etc., etc. If you're staying in Waikiki, ABC stores carry a limited selection of disposables and baby food. Shopping outside Waikiki in local supermarkets will save you a considerable sum: **Star Market** (2470 South King Street; 973-1666) is open from 6 a.m. to 1 a.m.

A first-aid kit is always a good idea. Also check with your pediatrician for special medicines and dosages for colds and diarrhea. If your child does become sick or injured in the Honolulu area, contact **Kapiolani Medical Center** (973-8511). On the Windward Coast of Oahu, call **Castle Medical Center** (263-5500); on the North Shore, **Kahuku Hospital** (293-9221); and on the leeward side, **Wahiawa General Hospital** (621-8411). On the Big Island's east side, there's **Hilo Hospital** (969-4111); in Kona, **Kona Hospital** (322-9311); Maui, **Maui Memorial Hospital** (242-2343); Lanai, **Lanai Community Hospital** (565-6411); Molokai, **Molokai General Hospital** (553-5331); and Kauai, **Wilcox Memorial Hospital and Health Center** (245-1100). There's also a **Poison Control Center** in Honolulu, which can be reached from the outer islands at 1-800-362-3585 or from Oahu at 941-4411.

Hotels often provide access to babysitters. On Oahu, a bonded babysitting agency is available: **Aloha Babysitting Service** (732-2029). In the Kaanapali area of Maui, you can try **Babysitting Services of Maui** (661-0558).

Some resorts and hotels have daily programs for kids during the summer and holiday seasons. Hula lessons, *lei* making, storytelling, sandcastle building, and various sports activities keep *keikis* (kids) over six happy while also giving Mom and Dad a break. As an added bonus, these resorts offer family plans, providing discounts for extra rooms or permitting children to share a room with their parents at no extra charge. Check with your travel agent.

When choosing the island to visit, consider how many diversions it will take to keep your children happy. Oahu offers numerous options, from the Honolulu Zoo to theme parks to museums, while the outer islands have fewer attractions. It might be helpful to read the introductory passages to each of the island chapters before planning your vacation.

CHAPTER THREE

Paradise for Free
Natural Living in Hawaii

With its luxurious parks, mountain retreats, and deserted beaches, Hawaii is a paradise for campers and backpackers. Because of the varied terrain and the islands' microenvironments, it's possible to experience all kinds of outdoor adventures. One day you'll hike through a steaming rainforest filled with tropical flowers; the next night you'll camp atop a volcanic crater in a stark, windblown area that resembles the moon's surface; then you'll descend to a curving white-sand beach populated only by shorebirds and tropical fish.

Paradise means more than physical beauty, however. It also involves an easy life and a bountiful food supply. The easy living is up to you; just slow down from the frantic pace of mainland life and you'll discover that island existence can be relaxing. As for wild food—you'll find it hanging from trees, swimming in the ocean, and clinging to coral reefs. With the proper techniques and a respect for conservation needs, it's yours to take.

In this chapter, I'll detail some of the outdoor skills necessary to camp, hike, and live naturally in Hawaii. This is certainly not a comprehensive study of how to survive on a Pacific island; I'm just passing along a few facts I've learned while exploring Hawaii. I don't advise that you plan to live entirely off the land. Hawaii's environment is too fragile to support you full-time. Anyway, living that way is a hell of a lot of work! I'll just give a few hints on how to supplement your provisions with a newly caught fish or a fresh fruit salad. That way, not only will you save on food bills, you'll also get a much fuller taste of the islands.

Obviously, none of these techniques were developed by me personally. In fact, most of them date back centuries to the early days, when Polynesian explorers applied the survival skills they had learned in Tahiti and the Marquesas to the newly discovered islands of Hawaii. So as you set out to fish along a coral reef, hunt for shellfish in tidepools, or gather seaweed at low tide, give a prayerful thanks to the generations of savvy islanders who have come before you.

Camping and Hiking

Camping in Hawaii usually means pitching a tent, reserving a cabin, or renting a camper. Throughout the islands there are secluded spots and hidden beaches, plus numerous county, state, and federal parks. All these campsites, together with hiking trails, are described in the individual island chapters; it's a good idea to consult those detailed listings when planning your trip. You might also want to obtain hiking maps; they are available from **Hawaii Geographic Maps & Books** (P.O. Box 1698, Honolulu, HI 96806; 538-3952). The camping equipment you'll require is listed in the preceding chapter.

Before you set out, there are a few very important matters that I want to explain more fully. First, bring a campstove: firewood is scarce in most areas and soaking wet in others. It's advisable to wear long pants when hiking in order to protect your legs from rock outcroppings, insects and spiny plants. Also, if you're going to explore the Mauna Kea, Mauna Loa, or Haleakala volcanoes, be sure to bring cold-weather gear; temperatures are often significantly lower than at sea level and these peaks occasionally receive snow.

Most trails you'll be hiking are composed of volcanic rock. Since this is a very crumbly substance, be extremely cautious when climbing rock faces. In fact, you should avoid steep climbs if possible. Stay on the trails: Hawaii's dense undergrowth makes it very easy to get lost. If you get lost at night, stay where you are. Because of the low latitude, night descends rapidly here; there's practically no twilight. Once darkness falls, it can be very dangerous to move around. You should also be careful to purify all drinking water. And be extremely cautious near streambeds as flash-flooding sometimes occurs, particularly on the windward coasts. This is particularly true during the winter months, when heavy storms from the northeast lash the islands.

Another problem that you're actually more likely to encounter are those nasty varmints that buzz your ear just as you're falling asleep—mosquitoes. Hawaii contains neither snakes nor poison ivy, but it has plenty of these dive-bombing pests. Like me, you probably consider that it's always open season on the little bastards.

With most of the archipelago's other species, however, you'll have to be a careful conservationist. You'll be sharing the wilderness with pigs, goats, tropical birds, deer, and mongooses, as well as a spectacular array of exotic and indigenous plants. They exist in one of the world's most delicate ecological balances. There are more endangered species in Hawaii than in all the rest of the United States. So keep in mind the maxim that the Hawaiians try to follow. *Ua mau ke ea o ka aina i ka pono:* The life of the land is preserved in righteousness.

Fishing and Gathering

While you're exploring the islands, the sea will be your prime food source. Fishing in Hawaii is good all year round, and the offshore waters are crowded with many varieties of edible fish. For deep-sea fishing you'll have to charter a boat, and freshwater angling requires a license; so I'll concentrate on surf-casting. It costs nothing to fish this way.

In the individual island chapters, you'll find information on the best spots to fish for different species; in the "Addresses" section of those chapters, you'll usually see a fishing supply store listed. For information on seasons, licenses, and official regulations, check with the Aquatic Resources Division of the State Department of Land and Natural Resources. This agency has offices on most of the major islands.

The easiest, most economical way to fish is with a hand-held line. Just get a 50- to 100-foot line, and attach a hook and a ten-ounce sinker. Wind the line loosely around a smooth block of wood, then remove the wood from the center. If your coil is free from snags, you'll be able to throw-cast it easily. You can either hold the line in your hand, feeling for a strike, or tie it to the frail end of a bamboo pole.

Beaches and rocky points are generally good places to surf-cast; the best times are during the incoming and outgoing tides. Popular baits include octopus, eel, lobster, crab, frozen shrimp, and sea worms. You can also fish with lures. The ancient Hawaiians used pearl shells to attract the fish, and hooks, some made from human bones, to snare them. Your friends will probably be quite content to see you angling with store-bought artificial lures.

TORCHFISHING AND SPEARFISHING

The old Hawaiians also fished at night by torchlight. They fashioned torches by inserting nuts from the *kukui* tree into the hollow end of a bamboo pole, then lighting the flammable nuts. When fish swam like moths to the flame, the Hawaiians speared, clubbed, or netted them.

Today, it's easier to use a lantern and spear. (In fact, it's all *too* easy and tempting to take advantage of this willing prey: Take only edible fish and only what you will eat.) It's also handy to bring a facemask or a glass-bottomed box to aid in seeing underwater. The best time for torchfishing is a dark night when the sea is calm and the tide low.

During daylight hours, the best place to spearfish is along coral reefs and in areas where the bottom is a mixture of sand and rock. You can use a speargun or make your own spear with heavy rubber bands and a piece of metal. Then, equipped also with mask, fins, and snorkel, you can explore underwater grottoes and spectacular coral formations while seeking your evening meal.

CRABBING

For the hungry adventurer, there are two important crab species in Hawaii—Kona crabs and Samoan crabs. The Kona variety are found in relatively deep water, and can usually be caught only from a boat. Samoan crabs inhabit sandy and muddy areas in bays and near river mouths. All you need to catch them is a net fastened to a round wire hoop and secured by a string. The net is lowered to the bottom; then, after a crab has gone for the bait, the entire contraption is raised to the surface.

SQUIDDING

Between June and December, squidding is another popular sport. Actually, the term is a misnomer: squid inhabit deep water and are not usually hunted. What you'll really be after are octopuses. There are two varieties in Hawaii, both of which are commonly found in water three or four feet

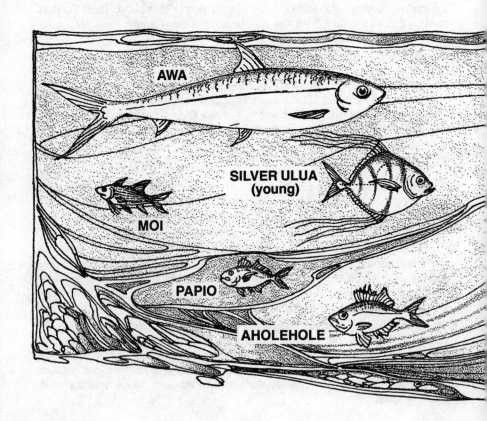

deep: the *hee*, a greyish-brown animal that changes color like a chameleon, and the *puloa*, a red-colored mollusk with white stripes on its head.

Both are nocturnal and live in holes along coral reefs. At night by torchlight you can spot them sitting exposed on the bottom. During the day, they crawl inside the holes, covering the entrances with shells and loose coral.

The Hawaiians used to pick the octopus up, letting it cling to their chest and shoulders. When they were ready to bag their prize, they'd dispatch the creature by biting it between the eyes. You'll probably feel more comfortable spearing the beast.

SHELLFISH GATHERING

Other excellent food sources are the shellfish that inhabit coastal waters. Oysters and clams, which use their muscular feet to burrow into sand and soft mud, can be collected along the bottom of Hawaii's bays. Lobsters,

(Text continued on page 50.)

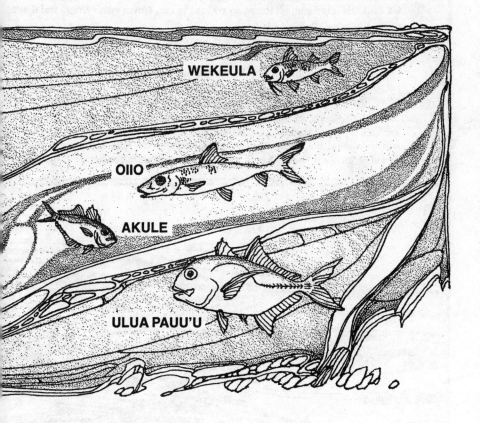

WEKEULA

OIIO

AKULE

ULUA PAUU'U

Relating to the Ocean

For swimming, surfing, and skin diving, there's no place quite like Hawaii. With endless miles of white-sand beach, the islands attract aquatic enthusiasts from all over the world. They come to enjoy Hawaii's colorful coral reefs and matchless surf conditions.

Many water lovers, however, never realize how awesome the sea can be. Particularly in Hawaii, where waves can reach 30-foot heights and currents flow unobstructed for thousands of miles, the ocean is sometimes as treacherous as it is spectacular. Dozens of people drown every year in Hawaii, many others are dragged from the crushing surf with broken backs, and countless numbers sustain minor cuts and bruises.

These accidents can be entirely avoided if you approach the ocean with a respect for its power as well as an appreciation of its beauty. All you have to do is heed a few simple guidelines. First, never turn your back on the sea. Waves come in sets: one group may be small and quite harmless, but the next set could be large enough to sweep you out to sea. Never swim alone, and don't swim immediately after eating.

Don't try to surf, or even bodysurf, until you're familiar with the sports' techniques and precautionary measures. Be extremely careful when the surf is high.

If you get caught in a rip current, don't swim *against* it: swim *across* it, parallel to the shore. These currents, running from the shore out to sea, can often be spotted by their ragged-looking surface water and foamy edges.

Around coral reefs, wear something to protect your feet against coral cuts. Particularly good are the inexpensive Japanese *tabis*, or reef slippers. If you do sustain a coral cut, clean it with hydrogen peroxide, then apply an antiseptic or antibiotic substance. This is also a good procedure for octopus bites.

When stung by a Portuguese man-of-war or a jellyfish, mix unseasoned meat tenderizer with alcohol, leave it on the sting for ten or twenty minutes, then rinse it off with alcohol. The old Hawaiian remedies, which are reputedly quite effective, involve applying urine or green papaya.

If you step on the sharp, painful spines of a sea urchin, soak the affected area in very hot water for 15 to 90 minutes. Another remedy calls for applying urine or undiluted vinegar. If any of these preliminary treatments do not work, consult a doctor.

Oh, one last thing. The chances of encountering a shark are about as likely as sighting a UFO. But should you meet one of these ominous creatures, stay calm. He'll be no happier to see you than you are to confront him. Simply swim quietly to shore. By the time you make it back to terra firma, you'll have one hell of a story to tell.

though illegal to spear, can be taken with short poles to which cable leaders and baited hooks are attached. You can also gather limpets, though I don't recommend it. These tiny black shellfish, locally known as *opihi*, cling tenaciously to rocks in areas of very rough surf. The Hawaiians gather them by leaping into the water after one set of waves breaks, then jumping out before the next set arrives. Being a coward myself, I simply order them in Hawaiian restaurants.

SEAWEED GATHERING

Few people think of seaweed as food, but it's very popular today among the Japanese, and it once served as an integral part of the Hawaiian diet. It's extremely nutritious, easy to gather, and very plentiful.

Rocky shores are the best places to find the edible species of seaweed. Some of them float in to shore and can be picked up; other species cling stubbornly to rocks and must be freed with a knife; still others grow in sand or mud. Low tide is the best time to collect seaweed: more plants are exposed, and some can be taken without even getting wet.

Picking Fruit

There's a lot more to Hawaii's tropical wonderland than gorgeous flowers and overgrown rainforests. The islands are also teeming with edible plants. Roots, fruits, vegetables, herbs, and spices grow like weeds from the shoreline to the mountains. By learning to identify key species, you can add numerous dishes to your table.

Here's a brief list of some of the islands' more common fruits. They can be picked by hand, poked with a stick, or plucked with a fruit-picker. This last device is easily made by threading a wire loop through a small sack, then fastening it to the end of a bamboo pole.

Banana: The Polynesians use banana trees not only for food but also for clothing, roofing, medicines, dyes, and even alcohol. The fruit, which grows upside down on broad-leaved trees, can be harvested as soon as the first banana in the bunch turns yellow.

Coconut: The coconut tree is probably the most important plant in the entire Pacific. Every part of the towering palm is used. You'll probably be concerned only with the hard brown nut, which yields delicious milk as well as a tasty meat.

Climbing a coconut palm is a task for the daring or foolhardy; personally, I wait for the nuts to fall and then pick them up off the ground.

If the coconut is still green, the meat is a succulent jelly-like substance. Otherwise, it's a hard but delicious white rind.

Papaya: These delicious fruits, which are picked as they begin to turn yellow, grow on unbranched trees. Summer is the peak harvesting season.

Guava: Roundish yellow fruits that grow on a small shrub or tree, these are extremely abundant in the wild. They ripen between June and October.

Mango: Known as the king of fruits, the mango grows on tall shade trees. The oblong fruit ripens in the spring and summer.

Breadfruit: These large round fruits grow on trees that reach up to 60 feet in height. Breadfruit must be boiled, baked, or fried.

Mountain apple: This sweet fruit grows in damp, shaded valleys at an elevation of about 1800 feet. The flowers resemble fluffy crimson balls; the fruit, which ripens from July to December, is also a rich red color.

Passion fruit: This delicious yellow fruit, oval in shape, grows to a length of about two or three inches. It's produced on a vine and ripens in summer or fall.

Avocado: Covered with a tough green or purple skin, this pear-shaped fruit sometimes weighs as much as three pounds. It grows on ten- to forty-foot-high trees, and ripens from June through November.

Relating to Drugs

For decades, Hawaii has been known for its sparkling beaches and lofty volcanoes. Agriculturally, the islands have grown famous by producing sugarcane and pineapples. But during the last several decades, the 50th state has become renowned for another crop, one which some deem a sacrament and others consider a sin.

In the islands it's commonly referred to as *pakalolo*. Mainlanders know it more familiarly by the locales in which it grows—Maui Wowie, Kona Gold, Puna Butter, and Kauai Buds. Because of Hawaii's lush tropical environment, marijuana grows year-round and has become the state's number-one cash crop. Plants easily reach ten- or twelve-foot heights; colas as thick as bottle brushes drip with resin.

Now that marijuana is big business, ripoffs have become a harrowing problem in Hawaii. Growers often guard their crops with guns and booby traps. Because of this armed protection, it can be very dangerous to wander through someone's dope patch. It might be on public land far from the nearest road, but in terms of the explorer's personal safety, a marijuana plantation should be treated as the most private property imaginable. In the words of the islanders, it is strictly *kapu*.

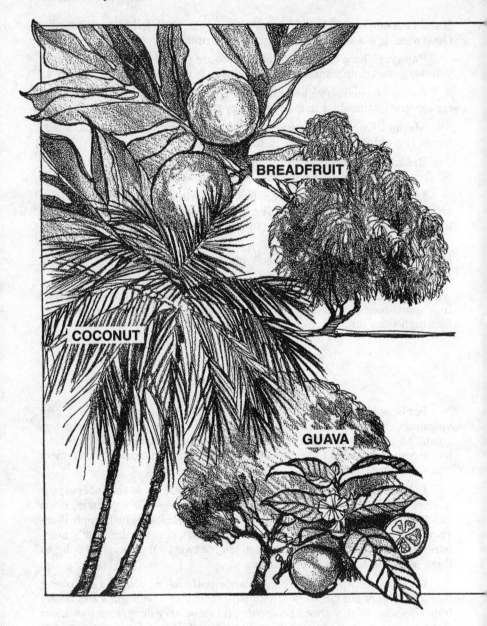

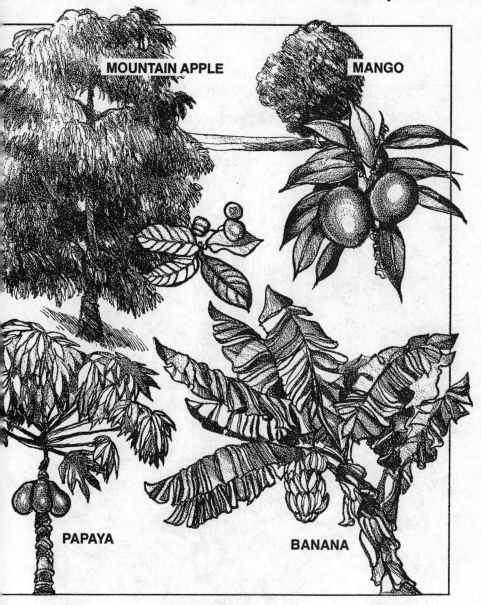

MOUNTAIN APPLE

MANGO

PAPAYA

BANANA

CHAPTER FOUR

Oahu

Honolulu, Somerset Maugham once remarked, is the meetingplace of East and West. Today, with its highrise cityscape and crowded commercial center, Hawaii's capital is more the place where Hong Kong meets Los Angeles. It's the hub of Hawaii, a city that dominates the political, cultural, and economic life of the islands.

And it's the focus of Oahu as well. Honolulu has given Oahu more than its nickname, The Capital Island. The city has drawn three-fourths of Hawaii's population to this third-largest island, making Oahu both a military stronghold and a popular tourist spot.

With military installations at Pearl Harbor and outposts seemingly everywhere, the armed forces control about one-quarter of the island. Most bases are off-limits to civilians; and tourists congregate in Honolulu's famed resort area—Waikiki. Both defense and tourism are big business on Oahu, and it's an ironic fact of island life that the staid, uniformly dressed military peacefully coexist here with crowds of sun-loving, scantily clad visitors.

The tourists are attracted by one of the world's most famous beaches, an endless white-sand ribbon that has drawn sun worshippers and water lovers since the days of Hawaiian royalty. In ancient times Waikiki was a swamp; now it's a spectacular region of world-class resorts.

Indeed, Waikiki is at the center of Pacific tourism, just as Honolulu is the capital of the Pacific. Nowhere else in the world will you find a population more varied or an ambience more vital. There are times when Waikiki's Parisian-size boulevards seem ready to explode from the sheer force of the crowds. People in bikinis and wild-colored *aloha* shirts stroll the streets, while others flash past on mopeds.

Since the 1980s this sun-splashed destination has also become a focal point for millions of wealthy tourists from Japan. Today the development craze that created modern-day Waikiki is continuing on to the southwest corner of the island. Here a major resort named Ko Olina is being built near Ewa Beach and plans are afoot to create Kapolei, a "second city" of as many as 200,000 people.

So hurry. Visitors can still discover that just beyond Honolulu's bustling thoroughfares stretches a beautiful island, featuring countless beaches and two incredible mountain ranges. Since most of the tourists (and a vast majority of the island's 836,000 population) congregate in the southern regions around Honolulu, the north is rural. You can experience the color and velocity of the city, then head for the slow and enchanting country.

As you begin to explore for yourself, you'll find Oahu also has something else to offer: history. *Oahu* means "gathering place" in Hawaiian, and for centuries it has been an important commercial area and cultural center. First populated by Marquesans around 500 A.D., the island was later settled by seafaring immigrants from Tahiti. Waikiki, with its white-sand beaches and luxurious coconut groves, became a favored spot among early monarchs.

Warring chiefs long battled for control of the island. According to legend, Kamehameha I seized power in 1795 by sweeping an opposing army over the cliffs of Nuuanu Pali north of Honolulu. Several years earlier the British had "discovered" Honolulu Harbor, a natural anchorage destined to be one of the Pacific's key seaports. Over the years the harbor proved ideal first for whalers and sandalwood traders and eventually for freighters and ocean liners.

In 1850 the city, which had grown up around the shipping port and become the focus of Hawaii, became the archipelago's capital as well. Here in 1893 a band of white businessmen illegally overthrew the native monarchy. Almost a half-century later, in an ill-advised but brilliantly executed military maneuver, the Japanese drew the United States into World War II with a devastating air strike against the huge naval base at Pearl Harbor.

There are some fascinating historical monuments to tour throughout Honolulu, but I recommend you also venture outside the city to Oahu's less congested regions. Major highways lead from the capital along the east and west coasts of this 608-square-mile island, and several roads bisect the central plateau en route to the North Shore. Except for a five-mile strip in Oahu's northwest corner, you can drive completely around the island.

Closest to Honolulu is the east coast, where a spectacular seascape is paralleled by the Koolaus, a jagged and awesomely steep mountain range. This is Oahu's rainswept Windward Coast. Here, traveling up the coast past the bedroom-communities of Kailua and Kaneohe, you'll discover beautiful and relatively untouched white-sand beaches. On the North Shore are some of the world's most famous surfing spots—Waimea Bay, Sunset, the Banzai Pipeline—where winter waves 20 and 30 feet high roll in with crushing force.

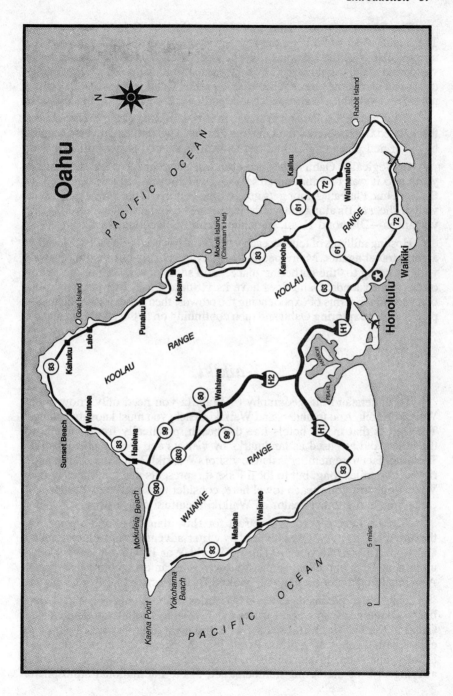

The Waianae Range, rising to 4040 feet, shadows Oahu's western coast. The sands are as white here, the beaches as uncrowded, but I've always felt uncomfortable on the Leeward Coast. Racial hostility is sometimes aimed at visitors on Oahu, as evidenced by theft, vandalism, and beatings. It is particularly bad along this shore. Wherever you go on Oahu you have to be careful not to leave valuables unattended, but be particularly watchful around Waianae.

Between the Koolau and Waianae ranges, remnants of the two volcanoes that created Oahu, spreads the Leilehua Plateau. This fertile region is occupied by sugar and pineapple plantations as well as several large military bases.

Geologically, Oahu is the second-oldest island in the chain; two million years ago it was two individual islands, which eventually were joined by the Leilehua Plateau. Among its geographic features is the *pali*, an awesome wall of sheer cliffs along the windward coastline, and three famous tuff-cone volcanoes—Diamond Head, Punchbowl, and Koko Head.

Hosting millions of tourists each year, Oahu has become a favorite location among travel agents. Many people can't even conceive of visiting Hawaii without going to "the gathering place," and some never venture out to any of the other islands. Oahu does have its virtues. But if, like me, you think of a vacation in terms of experiencing the crowds, then leaving them behind—plan on fully exploring Oahu and then continuing on to the neighbor islands.

Waikiki

To understand the geography of Waikiki you need only know about Waikiki Beach. And to understand Waikiki Beach, you must know two things. The first is that major hotels line the beach, practically from one end to the other, and are used as landmarks by visitors and local residents alike. The other fact to remember is that to visitors Waikiki Beach is a single sandy ribbon two miles long, but to local folks it represents many beaches in one. When you park your beach towel here, consider that every few strides will carry you into another realm of Waikiki's culture and history.

Waikiki once served as a retreat for Hawaiian kings and queens. By the turn of the century it was favored by writer-adventurers like Jack London and Robert Louis Stevenson. During World War II, GIs on leave soaked up its sun. Then in the jet age that followed it became a highrise resort area. As a result, different sections of Waikiki Beach answer to different names.

This fabled peninsula extends two miles from the Ala Wai Yacht Harbor to Diamond Head and measures a half-mile in width from the Ala Wai Canal to the Pacific. Kalakaua Avenue, the main drag, is packed elbow to elbow with throngs of visitors. Paralleling the ocean, this broad boulevard is noisy, annoying, cosmopolitan, and fascinating. Today visitors from Japan, arriving in ever-increasing numbers, add to the international atmosphere.

But the main appeal is still the district's white-sand corridor. Dotting the beach are picnic areas, restrooms, showers, concession stands, and beach equipment rentals. Most of the beach is protected by coral reefs and sea walls, so the swimming is excellent, the snorkeling fair. This is also a prime area for surfing. Two- to four-foot waves, good for beginners and still challenging to experienced surfers, are common here.

The western flank of Waikiki Beach sits near the **Ilikai Hotel** (1777 Ala Moana Boulevard). Here you will find a pretty lagoon that is fringed by palm trees.

The curving strand nearby, fronting Hilton Hawaiian Village (2005 Kalia Road), is called **Kahanamoku Beach**. Named for Hawaii's great surfer, Duke Kahanamoku, it features numerous facilities. Beach stands here rent everything from towels, chairs, and air mattresses to snorkel sets, surfboards, and Hobie-cat sailboats.

Also here is Port Hilton, the pier from which the resort complex launches catamaran cruises. One of these boats will take you to what may be the only hidden attraction around Waikiki, the **Atlantis Submarine** (536-2694), a 46-passenger sub located just off the coast that carries visitors to the bottom for a close-up look at coral reefs and tropical fish.

Fort De Russy Beach, owned by the military but open to the public, features the area's widest swath of white sand. It is also beautifully backdropped by a grove of palm trees. There are restrooms, picnic tables, and barbecues, plus tennis, squash, and volleyball courts.

The nearby **Fort De Russy Army Museum** (Kalia Road; 438-2821) has every weapon from Hawaiian shark teeth blades to modern-day instruments of destruction. You can also trace the United States' unending series of military campaigns from the uniforms (ours and theirs) on exhibit here.

Past Fort De Russy Beach stretches a palisade of highrise hotels. Lining the beachfront, they provide numerous facilities for thirsty sunbathers or adventuresome athletes. Continue on and you will pass the Sheraton strip, a lengthy stretch of Waikiki Beach fronted entirely by Sheraton hotels. This section marks Waikiki's center of action. The first hotel is the **Sheraton Waikiki** (2255 Kalakaua Avenue). A highrise structure built with two curving wings, it resembles a giant bird roosting on the beach.

The hotels here are so famous that the nearby strand is named **Royal-Moana Beach**. Stretching between the Royal Hawaiian and Moana hotels, it has been a sun-soaked gathering place for decades. That's because these two grande dames are Waikiki's oldest hotels. The **Royal Hawaiian** (2259 Kalakaua Avenue; 923-7311) is Hawaii's "Pink Palace," a Spanish Moorish-style caravansary painted shocking pink. Built in 1927, it is a labyrinth of gardens, colonnades, and balconies; the old place is certainly Waikiki's most interesting edifice. The woodframe **Sheraton Moana Surfrider Hotel** (2365 Kalakaua Avenue; 922-3111), built in 1901, was Waikiki's first resort. Its vaulted ceilings, tree-shaded courtyard, and spacious accommodations reflect the days when Hawaii was a retreat for the rich. This beach is also the site of one of Waikiki's most renowned surfing spots, Canoe's Surf.

Here and elsewhere along Waikiki Beach, concessions offer rides on **outrigger canoes**. They are long, sleek fiberglass crafts resembling ancient Polynesian canoes. Each seats four to six passengers, plus a captain. For several dollars you can join the crew on a low-key wave-riding excursion that will have you paddling as hard and fast as you can to catch waves and ride them far into the shore.

Just beyond the Moana Hotel is **Kuhio Beach Park** (2453 Kalakaua Avenue), which runs along Kalakaua Avenue from Kaiulani to Kapahulu avenues. In addition to a broad sandy beach, there are numerous facilities here—picnic areas, beach equipment rentals, showers, restrooms, and lifeguards on duty. The shady pavilions in this public park also attract local folks who come to play cards and chess. Needless to say, this convenient beach is often quite crowded. Diners like it because of its proximity to many Waikiki budget restaurants; parents favor the beach for its protective sea wall, which provides a secure area in which children can swim; and people-watchers find it an ideal place to check out the crowds of tourists and local residents.

The strand just beyond is called **Queen's Surf**. Here also are picnic areas, shady pavilions, restroom facilities, and showers. Something of a Bohemian quarter, this pretty plot draws gays, local artists, and a wide array of intriguing characters. On the weekends, conga drummers may be pounding out rhythms along the beach while other people gather to soak in the scene.

Kapiolani Park next door extends across 140 acres on both sides of Kalakaua Avenue. Hawaii's oldest park, this tree-studded playland dates back more than 100 years. Perhaps more than anything else, it has come to serve as a jogger's paradise. From dawn 'til dark, runners of all ages, colors, sizes, and shapes beat a path around its perimeter. But Kapiolani offers something to just about anyone. There are tennis courts, a driving range, an archery area, and much more. To fully explore the park, you must visit each of its features in turn.

First is the **Waikiki Aquarium** (2777 Kalakaua Avenue; 923-9741), the place where you can finally discover what a *humuhumunukunukuapuaa*, that impossibly named fish, really looks like. (Don't be surprised if the name proves to be longer than the fish.) Within the aquarium's glass walls, you'll see more than 300 different fish originating from Hawaiian and South Pacific waters. Ranging from rainbow-hued tropical fish to menacing grey sharks, they constitute a broad range of underwater species. Then there are seals and other intriguing creatures.

The **Kapiolani Rose Garden** is planted across the park at the corner of Monsarrat and Paki avenues. With its colorful flowerbeds and shady pavilion, this is a pretty place to stroll and picnic.

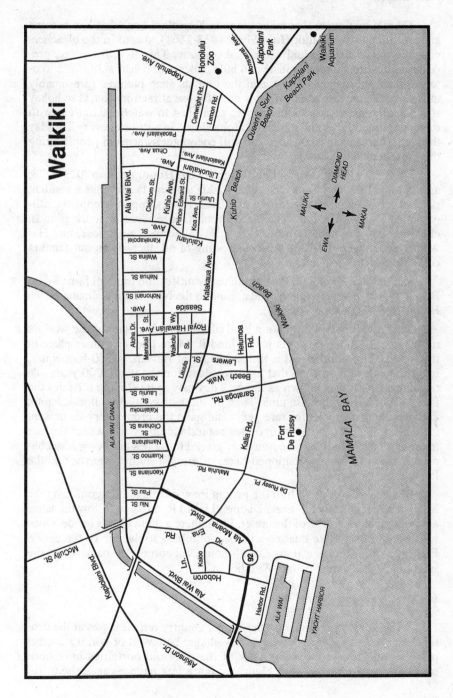

There's one event that takes place in Kapiolani Park that has become an institution—the **Kodak Hula Show** (833-1661), staged in the bleachers near the Waikiki Shell and Monsarrat Avenue. This free, hour-long presentation features ukulele music and hula dancers in ti-leaf skirts. The ukuleles plunk, the dancers sway, and the tourists snap pictures (presumably using Kodak cameras and film). It is one of those attractions that is so hokey it is actually interesting. Some people come just to watch the tourists with their sunburned faces and matching aloha shirts. In any case, every Tuesday through Thursday at 10:00 a.m. you will encounter swarms of people lining the bleachers.

The park's most outstanding feature is the **Honolulu Zoo** (923-7723; admission). Like city zoos everywhere, this tropical facility has a resident population of elephants, giraffes, ostriches, zebras, hippos, leopards, alligators, and so on. But it also includes animals more common to the islands, creatures like the nene (a rare goose), Hawaiian pig, mongoose, and Hawaiian wild sheep. Perhaps most interesting of all, there is an outstanding collection of tropical birds.

Just beyond Kapiolani Park stretches beautiful and tranquil **Sans Souci Beach**, which extends from the Natatorium to the New Otani Kaimana Beach Hotel (2863 Kalakaua Avenue).

Sans Souci is certainly not a hard place to find, as one of the world's most famous landmarks rises just behind it. More than any other place in the islands, **Diamond Head** is the trademark of Hawaii. A 760-foot crater, it is the work of a volcano that has been dead for about 150,000 years. To the Hawaiians it was known as *Leahi*. They saw in its sloping hillsides the face of an *ahi*, or yellowfin tuna. Then, in the 19th century, sailors mistook its volcanic glass rocks for rare gems and gave the promontory its present name. Formed 350,000 years ago, this natural landmark was a sacred place to the ancient Hawaiians. A *heiau* once graced its slopes and King Kamehameha is said to have worshipped here, offering a human sacrifice to the Polynesian war god.

It is possible to drive into the gaping maw of this old dragon. Just take Kalakaua Avenue until it meets Diamond Head Road, then follow the latter around to the inland site of the crater. From there a tunnel leads inside. Once within, there is a three-quarter-mile trail climbing to the rim of the crater. From here you can gaze along Oahu's southeast corner and back across the splendid little quarter called Waikiki.

WAIKIKI HOTELS

While it may no longer be the simple country retreat it was at the century's turn, Waikiki does have one advantage: believe it or not, it's a great place to find low-rent hotels. A lot of the cozy old hostelries have been torn down and replaced with highrises, but a few have escaped the urban assault. Some of those skyscrapers, too, are cheaper than you might think. So let's take a look at some of the better bargains Waikiki has to offer.

The **Malihini Hotel** (217 Saratoga Road; 923-9644) will give you a feel for Honolulu's earlier, lowrise era. An attractive complex that spreads out instead of up, this 30-unit hotel is just a short stroll from the beach. Though pretty on the outside, its sparse furnishings, scant decoration, and cinderblock walls give a vacant feel to the place. But the studios are spacious and come equipped with kitchenettes. The one-bedroom apartments will sleep up to five people. Budget.

Rising higher from the ground, while still keeping costs low, is the **Royal Grove Hotel** (151 Uluniu Avenue; 923-7691), a six-story, 87-unit establishment. If you can get past the garish pink exterior here, you'll find the rooms more tastefully designed. All are comfortably furnished, and some are decorated in simple but appealing styles. There are televisions, telephones, and carpeting in many of the higher-priced rooms upstairs, plus an almond-shaped pool and spacious lobby downstairs. Rents vary according to which wing of this sprawling building your bags are parked in. Some rooms even have kitchenettes and air conditioning, so it's hard to go wrong here. Budget.

If you'd like to stay directly across the street from the beach, check into the **Waikiki Circle Hotel** (2464 Kalakaua Avenue; 923-1571). This 14-story hotel-in-the-round has air-conditioned rooms at reasonable rates. Many have an ocean view, which is the main advantage here. Budget.

An inexpensive place for men in Waikiki is the **YMCA Central Branch** (401 Atkinson Drive; 941-3344). It's handily situated across the street from Ala Moana Center and a block from the beach. And you're welcome to use the gym, pool, saunas, television room, and coffee shop. You can also expect the usual Y ambience—long sterile hallways leading to an endless series of identical, cramped, uncarpeted rooms. But low prices help make up for the lack of amenities. Budget.

Interclub Waikiki (2413 Kuhio Avenue; 924-2636) is a sparkling clean hostel featuring dormitory and private rooms alike. Numbering 140 beds, it features a television lounge complete with checkerboard, dart board, and plenty of plump furniture. There is a laundry but no kitchen facilities. Budget.

It smells slightly musty, the furniture is old, and the walls are cinderblock, but at least the price is right at the **Waikiki Prince Hotel** (2431 Prince Edward Street; 922-1544). Many of the rooms are equipped with kitchenettes. Budget.

Budget travelers should also consider the **Hale Aloha Hostel** (2417 Prince Edward Street; 926-8313). This helpful facility features dormitory-style accommodations and private studio units available for couples. The latter are plain cinder block rooms with televisions and private baths; some have mini-refrigerators and hot plates. Open to both men and women, the hostel provides bedding, requires a daily chore, and creates a family-style atmosphere conducive to meeting other travelers.

There are three places in the moderate-price category that I particularly recommend. All are small, intimate, and close to the beach. First is the **Hale Pua Nui** (228 Beachwalk Avenue; 923-9693), a congenial home away from home. There are 22 studio apartments here, each spacious, well-furnished, and cross-ventilated. The rooms are quaintly decorated, carpeted, and equipped with kitchenettes. The personalized service you receive from the management makes the Hale Pua Nui an ideal vacation spot.

The second is **Kai Aloha Apartment Hotel** (235 Saratoga Road; 923-6723) just around the corner. Here intimacy is combined with modern convenience; each room has air conditioning, an all-electric kitchen, radio, telephone, cable television, and carpeting. Studio apartments have lovely rattan furniture and are attractively decorated with old drawings and paintings. The one-bedroom apartments will comfortably sleep four people. Daily maid service. Moderate.

A lowrise hotel tucked away in the shadow of vaulting condominiums, **The Breakers** (★) (250 Beach Walk; 923-3181) is truly a find. Dating to the 1950s, this Waikiki original consists of 64 rooms surrounding a pool and landscaped patio. *Shoji* doors add to the ambience while kitchenettes in every room and a location one block from the beach round out the features. Moderate.

If you're willing to sacrifice intimacy, you may find that the **Coral Seas Hotel** (250 Lewers Street; 923-3881) is the best deal in Waikiki. This seven-story hostelry, located just a hundred yards from the beach, has rooms at moderate prices. They are appealing accommodations with air conditioning, telephones, wall-to-wall carpeting, and small lanais. In some units you can add a mini-kitchenette to the list of extras. If you want, just for the hell of it, to directly experience the Waikiki tourist scene, this is the place. The Coral Seas Hotel is at the heart of the action, and has a pool.

Also in the center of Waikiki is the nearby **Edgewater Hotel** (2168 Kalia Road; 922-6424). Located a stone's skip from the beach, this 180-unit colossus offers excellent accommodations at low prices. Each room comes with telephone, carpeting, television, cable movies, and a shared lanai. The decor is bland but the furniture comfy. Downstairs is an open-air lobby with adjoining restaurant and pool. Moderate; rooms with kitchenettes are deluxe in price.

The **Honolulu Prince Hotel** (415 Nahua Street; 922-1616) was once a college dormitory. Today it's a ten-story hotel with a comfortable lobby. The standard rooms are small and blandly decorated; some are equipped with full kitchens. Located near the beach, this hotel also has one- and two-bedroom apartments available. Moderate.

Waikiki White Sands Resort (431 Nohonani Street; 923-7336) is more expensive but also more fashionable. This is a modern, attractive complex of three low-slung buildings surrounding a garden and swimming pool. The rooms come with all-electric kitchenette, telephone, color television, and air conditioning. Quite posh for the price: moderate.

Dominating the mid-range hotel scene in Waikiki are the Outrigger hotels. It seems like everywhere you turn in this tourist enclave another one looms above: There are almost two dozen. While prices range across the entire spectrum, one facility that offers a special value is the **Outrigger Coral Seas** (250 Lewers Street; 923-3881). Located on a busy street a block from the beach, it offers rooms with or without kitchenettes at moderate cost. You can expect street noise, and the lobby caters more to vendors than guests, but there is a pool next door at, you guessed it, another Outrigger. (For reservations and information on this entire chain of touristy but convenient hotels, call 926-0679.)

The Coconut Plaza (450 Lewers Street; 923-8828), a ten-story highrise, has moderately priced accommodations with kitchenettes. Decorated in Mexican tile and furnished with wicker, the guest rooms are attractively appointed. The lobby adds elements of elegance in the form of waterfalls, an open-air lounge, and pool. Breakfast included. Moderate.

The **Ewa Hotel** (2555 Cartwright Road; 922-1677) has 90 rooms starting in the moderate price range. Tucked away on a back street one block form the beach, this pastel-and-rattan establishment has a spiffy 1980s' aura about it. Close to Kapiolani Park and offering kitchenettes in many rooms, it is particularly convenient for families.

About the same size is the **Waikiki Hana Hotel** (2424 Koa Avenue; 926-8841), a 73-room place that offers a restaurant and small lobby. Quiet (for Waikiki), friendly, and comfortable, its rooms are brightly decorated and trimly appointed. Moderate.

One of the islands' few gay establishments, **Hotel Honolulu** (376 Kaiolu Street; 926-2766) rests on a quiet side street just off Kuhio Avenue. It's a three-story deco post-modern structure that has been beautifully landscaped and finely decorated. Guest rooms are bright, carpeted wall-to-wall, and equipped with tile bathrooms, stall showers, and kitchen facilities. Each is decorated along a different theme: Japanese, English, Chinese, Hollywood, Safari, and so on. There's also a rooftop garden sundeck to round off this well-run facility. Moderate.

If the **Waikiki Surf Hotel** (2200 Kuhio Avenue; 923-7671) has no space in its central facility, they can probably fit you into one of their two other buildings. All are located in central Waikiki. The rooms are adequately, if unimaginatively, decorated and come with television, air conditioning, telephone, and lanai. Moderate.

Hawaii Dynasty Hotel (1830 Ala Moana Boulevard; 955-1111), another good bargain, is easy walking distance from both Ala Moana Center and the beach. For the price, accommodations at this 17-story caravansary are relatively plush. Each room has air conditioning, television, telephone, decorations, carpeting, a shower-tub combination, and comfortable furnishings. The room I saw was quite spacious and contained a king-size bed. Moderate.

Also consider the **Waikiki Grand Hotel** (134 Kapahulu Avenue; 923-1511), across the street from lush Kapiolani Park. The standard rooms are comfortable, pleasant places to park your bags. Downstairs there's a wind-swept lobby. Moderate.

If you'd prefer to go native and stay in a private home, contact one of the bed and breakfast referral numbers. These include **Bed and Breakfast Honolulu** (595-7533), **Pacific Hawaii Bed and Breakfast** (262-6026), or **Bed and Breakfast Hawaii** (536-8421). They offer accommodations on all islands, priced in the moderate range.

Tabbed at the low end of the deluxe range and offering good value is the **Queen Kapiolani Hotel** (150 Kapahulu Avenue; 922-1941), a 313-room facility that rises 19 stories above nearby Kapiolani Park. There's a spacious lobby, three floors of public rooms, several shops, and a swimming pool here. The guest rooms are plainly decorated and modest in size. Located one block from the beach.

There are also two attractive facilities on the edge of Waikiki that are removed from the crowds. The **New Otani Kaimana Beach Hotel** (2863 Kalakaua Avenue; 923-1555) rests beside beautiful Sans Souci Beach in the shadow of Diamond Head. Its two restaurants and oceanside bar lend the feel of a big hotel, but the friendly staff and standard rooms create a family atmosphere. Deluxe.

Another hotel, equally secluded, has been nicely refurbished. Located even closer to the fabled crater, the **Diamond Head Beach Hotel** (2947 Kalakaua Avenue; 922-1928) is an ultra-contemporary establishment. The rooms are done in soft pastel tones and adorned with quilted beds and potted plants. Located on the ocean, this 13-story facility is one of the most chic resting places around. Continental breakfast is served to the guests and some rooms come with a kitchen. Deluxe.

There are two hotels right on the beach at Waikiki that capture the sense of old Hawaii. Waikiki was little more than a thatch-hut village when its first deluxe hotel went up in 1901. Today the **Sheraton Moana Surfrider Hotel** (2365 Kalakaua Avenue; 922-3111) retains the aura of those early days in its colonial architecture and Victorian decor. Insist on a room in the main building with its traditional appointments and turn-of-the-century ambience. Downstairs you'll find restaurants, bars, a lobby filled with wicker furniture, and an ancient banyan tree beneath which Robert Louis Stevenson once wrote. Ultra-deluxe.

Just down the beach resides the grande dame of Hawaiian hotels. Built in 1927 and affectionately known as "The Pink Palace," the **Royal Hawaiian** (2259 Kalakaua Avenue; 923-7311) is an elegant, Spanish Moorish-style building complete with colonnaded walkways and manicured grounds. This castle away from home is decorated in French provincial fashion and features a fabulous lobby bedecked with chandeliers. Worth visiting even if you never check in. Ultra-deluxe.

WAIKIKI CONDOMINIUMS

The **Royal Kuhio** (2240 Kuhio Avenue; 923-2502), a good bet for families, is a 389-unit highrise two blocks from Waikiki Beach. One-bedroom units feature fully equipped kitchens, balconies with ocean or mountain views, and special recreational programs for children. Prices start at $95.

Kaulana Kai Resort at Waikiki (2425 Kuhio Avenue; 922-7777) has 90 comfortable units with kitchenettes and private lanais. The suites, which include a full living room, are a good value for families. Studios run $85 to $95 and suites begin at $130.

At the **Aston Waikiki Beach Tower** (2470 Kalakaua Avenue; 926-6400) all 85 suites and penthouses feature contemporary furniture, wetbars, kitchens, and beautiful lanais. The kids will enjoy the game room, pool and paddle tennis court. One-bedroom units begin at $230 to $280. Suites for up to six guests start at $360 to $425. This is Waikiki's finest condominium.

Aston Waikiki Shore (2161 Kalia Road; 926-4733) offers 80 studios and one- and two-bedroom units. These condos feature complete kitchens, washer/dryers, and great views. Studios run $115 to $150. One bedroom units are $150 to $195. Two-bedroom units accommodating up to six cost $185 to $345.

Waikiki Lanais (2452 Tusitala Street; 923-0994) is located on a quiet street near the Ala Wai Canal and has 160 one- and two-bedroom units, each with a good-sized living room and kitchen. One-bedroom accommodations start at $90. Two-bedroom condos, sleeping up to six guests, begin at $125.

The **Pacific Monarch** (142 Uluniu Avenue; 923-9805) has studio apartments from $95 to $105 and one-bedroom units for $130 to $140 for up to four. These carpeted accommodations offer full kitchens and lanais. Two blocks from the beach.

At **Waikiki Banyan** (201 Ohua Avenue; 922-0555) one-bedroom units are $130 to $180 for one to four people. These highrise ocean and mountain view units have full kitchens, rattan furniture, and lanais. One block from the beach.

Several services rent condominiums on Oahu. They include **Condo Rentals of Waikiki** (413 Seaside Avenue; 923-0555), **Condofree Resorts** (2155 Kalakaua Avenue; 926-5900), and **Hawaiiana Resorts** (523-7785).

WAIKIKI RESTAURANTS

This tourist mecca is crowded with restaurants. Since the competition is so stiff, the cafés here are cheaper than anywhere else on the islands. There are numerous American restaurants serving moderately good food at modest prices, so diners looking for standard fare will have no problem. But as you're probably seeking something more exotic, I'll list some interesting Oriental, Hawaiian, health food, and other offbeat restaurants.

To find a budget-priced meal on Kalakaua Avenue, the oceanfront strip, you'll have to seek out **Woolworth's Restaurant** (2224 Kalakaua Avenue; 923-1713), an all-American lunch counter with meat-and-potato entrées, noodle dishes, sandwiches, and hamburgers.

Or try the bottom floor of the **Waikiki Shopping Plaza** (2270 Kalakaua Avenue). Here about a dozen ethnic and American restaurants offer take-out food as well as full course sitdown dinners. Budget.

For just a tad more you can dine overlooking the water at **Waikiki Circle Restaurant** (2464 Kalakaua Avenue; 923-1571). There's a varied dinner menu that includes teriyaki steak, shrimp tempura, and mahimahi as well as such standard fare as chops, chicken, and steak. Budget to moderate.

Near the center of the action on busy Lewers Street, about 50 macadam-paved yards from the beach, is **J.R.s** (226 Lewers Street; 924-8444). This glorified take-out stand has balcony seating overlooking the street. Downstairs you place your order for incredibly cheap breakfast specials, sandwiches, and plate lunches. Budget.

Up on the third floor of the Royal Hawaiian Shopping Center you'll happen upon **Spaghetti! Spaghetti!** (2201 Kalakaua Avenue, Suite A-213; 922-7724). At lunch or dinner there's an all-you-can-eat spaghetti buffet and salad bar. The spread includes several different types of pastas as well as an array of sauces. A great place to pack away those carbohydrates. Budget.

Even if the religious literature at **Country Life Vegetarian Buffet** (421 Nahua Street; 922-5010) doesn't satisfy your soul, the all-natural cuisine will certainly cleanse your body. Lunch and dinner are sold by the pound here, and with a menu that changes daily, they may be tipping the scales with vegetarian pizza, meatless tacos, or lasagna. The decor is simple café style. Budget.

By way of popular eateries, **Dee Dee's Café** (444 Hobron Lane; 951-0006) is one of those coffee shops that bakes its own pies and draws a primarily local crowd. Breakfast, lunch, and dinner are standard American affairs. There's fried chicken, grilled pork chops, and ground sirloin. Since this *is* Hawaii they add fried noodles and a few Japanese dishes. Budget.

Over on Kuhio Avenue, just a block in from the beach strip, there's a cluster of good, inexpensive restaurants. Foremost is **Hamburger Mary's Organic Grill** (2109 Kuhio Avenue; 922-6722), a sidewalk café fringed with potted plants. The adjoining bar is gay, but Mary's organic-panic sandwiches attract gays and straights alike. You can pull up a producer's chair, kick back in the sunshine, and order a plain Hamburger Mary, a salsa-smothered Hamburger Maria, or any of several vegetarian sandwiches. All are tagged at competitive rates and served on whole-grain bread. There's also a concoct-your-own omelette: just add avocado, shrimp, sprouts, pineapple, cheese, or several other goodies. Moderate.

Club 58 (2139-A Kuhio Avenue; 922-6588), a gay bar by night, serves lunch, dinner, and Sunday brunch to a mixed crowd earlier on. An open-air patio restaurant, it offers New York steak, veal marsala, chicken piccata, and a couple seafood dishes at moderate prices.

Perry's Smorgasbord, with its two locations—at the Outrigger Coral Seas Hotel (250 Lewers Street; 923-3881) and at 2380 Kuhio Avenue (926-0184)—has an inexpensive buffet at dinner, lunch, and breakfast. With an extensive salad bar, plus a host of meat and fish dishes, this all-you-can-eat emporium is hard to beat. I'd suggest the Outrigger branch; it's right on the waterfront. Moderate.

A great place for breakfast, the **Waikiki Broiler** (200 Lewers Street; 923-8836) has inexpensive specials every morning. Dining is outdoors under thatched umbrellas or in a small dining room. It's on a busy corner so the atmosphere is not exactly idyllic, but it's hard to match the prices—at dinner you can enjoy steak, shrimp, scallop, and chicken entrées at prices that are just a tad above the budget category.

The Rigger (2335 Kalakaua Avenue; 922-5544) sits along Waikiki's main drag and serves up family-style meals at reasonable rates. Breakfast specials are particularly cheap here. At lunch and dinner the selections are American all the way—from the fried shrimp platter and New York steak to the teriyaki chicken and seafood combination plate. You can sit at the counter or slip into a naugahyde booth. Moderate.

The young crowd gathering at the **Shore Bird Beach Broiler** (Reef Hotel, 2169 Kalia Road; 922-2887) is attracted by the disco. But this beachfront dining room is also a great place to enjoy a moderate-priced dinner and an ocean view. This is a cook-your-own-food facility that offers steak kabob, fresh fish, teriyaki chicken, and barbecued ribs. One of the best bargains on Waikiki Beach, the Shore Bird is inevitably crowded, so try to dine early.

For oceanfront dining at a moderate price, **The Beachside Café** (Sheraton Moana Surfrider Hotel, 2353 Kalakaua Avenue; 922-3111) is true to its name. With indoor and patio dining, it's a standard-fare American restaurant lacking in imagination but filled with beautiful views. Open for breakfast, lunch, and dinner, the café serves steak, seafood, hamburgers, and egg dishes. Ask for a table outside.

Honolulu's wackiest restaurant has to be **Bobby McGee's Conglomeration** (2885 Kalakaua Avenue; 922-1282). First there's the interior, a high-gauche design with gilded mirrors, woodstoves, and a salad bar served in an old bathtub. Then there are the waiters and waitresses, each dressed in a different costume and simulating caballeros, magicians, dancehall girls, referees, etc. The menu is more predictable, consisting of steak, seafood, fowl, and combinations thereof. A culinary adventure.

Caffe Guccini (2139 Kuhio Avenue; 922-5287), with indoor and al fresco dining, features spaghetti carbonara lasagna, veal scallopine, and other Italian favorites. This informal espresso bar does not serve breakfast or lunch, but it's a great place for bistro-style dining. Moderate.

Next door at **Hernando's Hideaway** (2139 Kuhio Avenue; 922-7758) you can munch on nachos and taquitos at the bar or settle on the patio and order from a full Mexican menu. There are enchiladas, tostadas, and burritos plus steak picado and a spicy Yucatán-style sirloin. Moderate.

Apart from the bustle of Waikiki but still right on the beach is the **Hau Tree Lanai** (2863 Kalakaua Avenue; 923-1555). Here beneath the interwoven branches of twin *hau* trees you can enjoy patio dining with a view that extends across Waikiki to the distant mountains. I particularly favor the place for breakfast (the French toast is delicious), but they also have a lunch and dinner menu that ranges from steamed vegetables to curried chicken to fresh island fish. In the evening the place is illuminated by torches, and soft breezes wisp off the water, adding to the enchantment. Deluxe.

The food is pretty standard fare at the Sheraton Waikiki's **Ocean Terrace** (2255 Kalakaua Avenue; 922-4422) but the view deserves five stars. Set poolside next to the beach in one of the state's largest hotels, this open-air dining room provides a welcome means to dine on the water. Popular for breakfast, lunch, and dinner, the Ocean Terrace's evening menu includes filet mignon, lobster, teriyaki steak, and mahimahi. Deluxe.

If you decide to go to **Nick's Fishmarket** (2070 Kalakaua Avenue; 955-6333), plan on eating seafood. You have never seen such a list of fresh fish dishes. Not that much of it will seem familiar, but there is ono, onaga, opakapaka, and ulua. Or if you prefer to dine on something you recognize, how about shrimp scampi, soft-shell crab, abalone, lobster, or scallops? Very chic; highly recommended. Deluxe.

Dishes like sautéed opakapaka garnished with watercress and ginger, medallions of veal with sautéed apples, and saddle of lamb baked in puff pastry make **Bali-By-The-Sea** (Hilton Hawaiian Village, 2005 Kalia Road; 949-4321) a special favorite. Plush seating, nautical lamps, marble sculptures, and soft ocean breezes add to the charm of this elegant restaurant. Ultra-deluxe. Dress code.

A great choice for romantic dining, **The Secret** (2552 Kalakaua Avenue; 922-6611) features continental entrées like blackened ahi salad, curry of tiger prawns, and French lamb chops with ohelo berry sauce. This gracious establishment in the Hawaiian Regent Hotel is centered around a carp pond. High-backed rattan chairs and private booths help the dining room live up to its name. Deluxe to ultra-deluxe.

For high dining I also like **Michel's** (Colony Surf Hotel, 2895 Kalakaua Avenue; 923-6552), a white-tablecloth French restaurant replete with chandeliers, statuettes, and oil paintings. The lovely ocean view highlights an haute cuisine atmosphere. The à la carte menu features a host of gourmet delights. Michel's serves a few beef dishes and a wealth of seafood selections, including lobster, a surf platter with shrimp, lobster, and crab, and a similar dish, baked avocado with crabmeat, prepared in Michel's unique style. Then of course there are tournedos, veal *médaillons*, filet mignon, châteaubriand, and on. For the ultimate in elegance try Michel's, but remember your dinner jackets, please. Ultra-deluxe.

It's not surprising that Waikiki's most fashionable hotel, the Halekulani, contains one of the district's finest restaurants. Situated on an open-air balcony overlooking the ocean, **La Mer** (2199 Kalia Road; 923-2311) has a reputation for elegant dining in intimate surroundings. The menu combines Continental and island cuisine to create such dishes as opakapaka sautéed with shiitake mushrooms, broasted duckling with wild rice, and lamb Provençal. Add the filigree woodwork and sumptuous surroundings and La Mer is one of the island's most attractive waterfront dining rooms. Dinner only; ultra-deluxe.

WAIKIKI MARKETS

The best grocery store in Waikiki is also the biggest. Prices at **The Food Pantry** (2370 Kuhio Avenue; 923-9831) are inflated, but not as much as elsewhere in this tourist enclave.

ABC Discount Stores, a chain of sundry shops with branches all around Waikiki, are convenient, but have a very limited stock and even higher prices.

If you are willing and able to shop outside Waikiki, you'll generally fare much better price-wise. Try the **Foodland** supermarket in the Ala Moana Center (1450 Ala Moana Boulevard; 949-5044) just outside Waikiki. Cheaper than Waikiki groceries, it's still more expensive than Greater Honolulu stores.

Vim and Vigor has a standard stock of natural food items in its store in Ala Moana Center (1450 Ala Moana Boulevard; 955-3600).

WAIKIKI SHOPPING

This tourist mecca is a great place to look but not to buy. Browsing the busy shops is like studying a catalog of Hawaiian handicrafts. It's all here. You'll find everything but bargains. With a few noteworthy exceptions, the prices include the unofficial tourist surcharges that merchants worldwide levy against visitors. Windowshop Waikiki, but plan on spending your shopping dollars elsewhere.

One Waikiki shopping area I do recommend is **Duke's Lane**. This alleyway, running from Kalakaua Avenue to Kuhio Avenue near the International Market Place, may be the best place in all Hawaii to buy coral and jade jewelry. Either side of the lane is flanked by mobile stands selling rings, necklaces, earrings, stick pins, bracelets, and more. It's a prime place to barter for tiger's eyes, opals, and mother-of-pearl pieces.

The main shopping scene is in the malls. **Waikiki Shopping Plaza** (2270 Kalakaua Avenue) has six floors of stores and restaurants. Here are jewelers, sundries, and boutiques, plus specialty shops like **Waldenbooks** (922-4154), with an excellent line of magazines as well as paperbacks and bestsellers.

The nearby **Royal Hawaiian Shopping Center** spans Kalakaua Avenue from Lewers Street all the way to the Royal Hawaiian Hotel. Along this four-tiered marathon course, you can purchase coral, cameras, or ice cream. There are boutiques, sporting-goods stores, surf shops, jewelry stores, art galleries, craft shops, and practically everything else conceivable—all at the very center of Waikiki.

Then there's **King's Village** (on Kaiulani Avenue between Kalakaua and Kuhio avenues), a mock Victorian town which represents how Britain might have looked had the 19th-century English invented polyethylene. The motif may be trying to appear antiquated, but the prices are unfortunately quite contemporary.

International Market Place (2330 Kalakaua Avenue) is my favorite browsing place. With tiny shops and vending stands spotted around the sprawling grounds, it's a relief from the claustrophobic shopping complexes. There's an old banyan spreading across the market, plus thatched treehouses, a carp pond, brick sidewalks, and woodfront stores. You won't find many bargains, but the sightseeing is priceless.

The **Waikiki Trade Center**, located at Kuhio and Seaside avenues, is another strikingly attractive mall. With an air of Milanese splendor about it, this glass-and-steel complex is a maze of mirrors. In addition to the stained-glass windows and twinkling lights, there are several worthwhile shops. The **Waldenbooks** (924-8330) outlet here is an excellent resource for books on Hawaii as well as general trade titles.

Some of Hawaii's smartest shops are located in **Hemmeter Center** at the Hyatt Regency Hotel (2424 Kalakaua Avenue). This triple-tiered arcade is *the* place to look when you are seeking the very best. Glamour and style are passwords around here. There are fine-art shops, designer apparel stores, gem shops, and much more.

Hilton Hawaiian Village (2005 Kalia Road) contains the **Rainbow Bazaar**, an array of shops spread around the grounds of Hawaii's largest resort complex. This plaza contains a number of stores specializing in island fashions, plus gift shops and import emporia. The shopping center has been designed in Oriental style, with curving tile roofs and brilliantly painted roof beams. You can stroll along an Asian arcade, past lofty banyan trees and flowering gardens, to stores filled with rare art and Far Eastern antiquities.

Actually it's the other 20 percent that predominates at **80% Straight Inc.** (2131 Kuhio Avenue; 923-9996). This gay men's shop has cards, clothes, videos, and gift items. Located on the 2100 block of Kuhio Avenue, it's in the heart of Waikiki's gay district.

WAIKIKI NIGHTLIFE

Hawaii has a strong musical tradition, kept alive by a number of excellent groups performing their own compositions as well as old Polynesian songs. I'm not talking about the "Blue Hawaii"–"Tiny Bubbles"–"Beyond the Reef" medleys that draw tourists in droves, but *real* Hawaiian music as performed by the Brothers Cazimero, Keola and Kapono Beamer, Marlene Sai, Melveen Leed, and others.

If you spend any time in Honolulu, don't neglect to check out such authentic sounds. One or more of these musicians will probably be playing at a local club. Consult the daily newspapers, or, if you want to hear these groups before paying to see them, listen to KCCN at 1420 on the radio dial. This all-Hawaiian station is the home of island soul.

The Brothers Cazimero are featured regularly at the posh **Monarch Room** (★) (the Royal Hawaiian Hotel, 2259 Kalakaua Avenue; 923-7311). There's a stiff cover but the show is well worth the price. Reservations are highly recommended.

Over at **Nick's Fishmarket** (2070 Kalakaua Avenue; 955-6333) the hot sounds of a contemporary band draw flocks of local folks and visitors alike nightly.

On weekends Jimmy Borges, a leading Hawaiian jazz singer, stars at the **Paradise Lounge** (2005 Kalia Road; 949-4321). Contemporary music also keeps the dancefloor busy weeknights at this Hilton Hawaiian Village nightspot. Choose between table or lounge seating in the carpeted club decorated with Hawaiian landscapes painted by local artists.

The **Esprit Nightclub** (Sheraton Waikiki Hotel, 2255 Kalakaua Avenue; 922-4422) is a congenial spot. Situated right on Waikiki Beach, this cozy club features two live shows and spectacular ocean views every night of the week. Cover charge for the early show only.

Waikiki is definitely rock-and-roll central. Every big hotel seems to have converted a dusty ballroom or sluggish restaurant into a throbbing strobe-lit dance hall. Out-of-town folks and locals alike pack these electric night spots. **Spat's** (2424 Kalakaua Avenue; 923-1234), the Hyatt Regency Waikiki's contribution to the dance scene, is one of the poshest. With stuffed chairs, oil paintings, and stained glass, it looks more the part of a fashionable restaurant. And until the deejay cranks up his Victrola nightly at eight o'clock, that's exactly what it is. But after the witching hour, anything goes. Cover; dress slacks and closed-toe shoes required.

Kentos, nestled in a corner of the Hyatt Regency (2424 Kalakaua Avenue; 923-7400), is an oldies nightclub featuring sounds from the '50s and '60s. Memorabilia from those halcyon days crowd the walls and swingers crowd the dancefloor. Cover.

For a quiet drink in an intimate atmosphere, I also recommend **The Library** (2552 Kalakaua Avenue; 922-6611). This relaxing bar is located in the Hawaiian Regent Hotel. It's a choice spot to sit back and recollect at the end of an enervating day. Good drinks, good service—who could ask for more?

The Point After (Hawaiian Regent Hotel, 2552 Kalakaua Avenue; 922-6611) is a hot young club. As you might guess from the name, the design motif is football, with more flashing lights than an exploding scoreboard. There is a cover charge.

After The Point After you can ride 30 stories in a tubular glass elevator to **Annabelle's,** a luxurious club located atop the Ilikai Hotel (1777 Ala Moana Boulevard; 949-3811). Starting early in the evening with big band sounds, the place segues into pop music and rocks 'til 4 a.m. Cover.

The **Maharaja Restaurant** (Waikiki Trade Center, 2255 Kuhio Avenue; 922-3030), an establishment as formal and upscale as its name implies, offers dancing to Top-40 deejay music. Cover and dress code.

The Jazz Cellar (205 Lewers Street; 923-9952) specializes in loud rock, serious drinking, and lively crowds rather than jazz. It's a top spot for a hot night. Cover charge.

At **Malia's Cantina** (311 Lewers Street; 922-7808) there is live local entertainment. You're liable to encounter The Peter Moon Band, Willy K, or Bruddah Waltah performing in this cozy cabaret. Cover.

For progressive music check out **The Pink Cadillac** (478 Ena Road; 942-5282), where the deejay sound is alternative rock and the color scheme is pink and black. Cover.

Or, for a live version, cruise into **Wave Waikiki** (1877 Kalakaua Avenue; 941-0424) and catch the progressive rock bands that perform nightly.

Cilly's (1909 Ala Wai Boulevard; 942-2952) is a Top-40 dance club geared to the 18-to-25-year-old crowd. This basement venue has tropical decor, stained-glass mirrors, and colorful pictures of Hawaii's early surfing days.

With room for 300 of your closest friends, **Moose McGillycuddy's Pub and Café** (310 Lewers Street; 923-0751) is the place to dance to live bands. Known for its weird pictures, this establishment is easily spotted. Just look for the only building on Lewers Street sporting a stuffed moose head.

At the antique-filled **Bobby McGee's Conglomeration** (2885 Kalakaua Avenue; 922-1282) you can dance to Top-40 tunes played by a deejay. This night club/bar is decorated with a variety of mementoes including old license plates and historic photos.

GAY SCENE The gay scene centers around several clubs on Waikiki's Kuhio Avenue. **Hamburger Mary's** (2109 Kuhio Avenue; 922-6722) is the most dynamic. There's dancing to recorded music as well as drinking and carousing. It's simply a U-shaped bar with a side patio, but the place draws huge crowds. Together with **Hula's Bar and Lei Stand** (923-0669) next door, it forms an unbeatable duo. Hula's, a disco complete with strobe-lit dancefloor, rocks nightly until 2 a.m.

The manager at **Club 58** (2139-A Kuhio Avenue; 922-6588) characterizes it as "the quiet bar on the street." Located in the center of the Waikiki gay district and drawing both gay men and women, it features taped music and a pool table. It's set on a patio.

Also predominantly gay is **Garbo's** (2260 Kuhio Avenue; 922-1405), where dancing to 1980s-era music is combined with regularly scheduled drag shows and karaoke contests.

Just upstairs from Garbo's, **Fusion Waikiki** (2260 Kuhio Avenue; 924-2422) is another gay after-hours club that stays open until 4 a.m. Looser and more underground, this third-floor hot spot features dancing to progressive deejay music. There are male strip shows four nights a week. Cover for shows.

Downtown Honolulu

For a historical and cultural tour of Hawaii's state capital, simply head toward Downtown Honolulu. A financial center for the entire Pacific Rim, Honolulu's importance to both North America and Asia is manifest in the highrise cityscape. The historical significance of this port city is evident from the 19th-century buildings that lead to the financial district in the heart of the city. A fitting place to begin your tour is among the oldest homes in the islands. The buildings at the **Mission Houses Museum** (553 South King Street; 531-0481; admission) seem to be borrowed from a New England landscape, and in a sense they were. The Frame House, a trim white wooden structure, was prefabricated on the East Coast and shipped around the Horn to Hawaii. That was back in 1821, when this Yankee-style building was used to house missionary families.

Like the nearby Chamberlain Depository and other structures here, the Frame House represents one of the missionaries' earliest centers in Hawaii. It was in 1819 that Congregationalists arrived in the islands; they immediately set out to build and proselytize. In 1831, they constructed the Cham-

berlain Depository from coral and used it as a storehouse. The neighborhood's Coral House, built of the same durable material ten years later, was
used by the first press ever to print in the Hawaiian language. The Mission
Houses complex tells much about the missionaries, who converted Hawaiian into a written language, then proceeded to rewrite the entire history of
the islands. The museum is run by members of the Hawaiian Mission Children's Society.

Opposite, at South King and Punchbowl streets, is the **Kawaihao Church**.
This imposing edifice required 14,000 coral blocks for its construction.
Completed in 1842, it has been called the Westminster Abbey of Hawaii,
because coronations and funerals for Hawaiian kings and queens were once
conducted here. Services are still performed in Hawaiian and English every
Sunday at 10:30 a.m.; attending them is not only a way to view the church
interior, but also provides a unique cultural perspective on contemporary
Hawaiian life. Also note that the tomb of King Lunalilo rises in front of
the church, and behind the church lies the cemetery where early missionaries
and converted Hawaiians were buried.

Across South King Street, that brick structure with the stately white
pillars is the **Mission Memorial Building**, constructed in 1916 to honor
those same early church leaders. The nearby Renaissance-style building with
the tile roof is **Honolulu Hale**, the City Hall. You might want to venture
into the central courtyard, an open-air plaza surrounded by stone columns.

As you continue along South King Street in a westerly direction toward
the center of Honolulu, **Iolani Palace** (522-0832) will appear on your right.
Built for King Kalakaua in 1882, this stunning Renaissance-style mansion
served as a royal residence until Queen Liliuokalani was overthrown in 1893.
Later the ill-starred monarch was imprisoned here; eventually, after Hawaii
became a territory of the United States, the palace was used as the capitol
building.

Today it represents the only royal palace in the United States. The king
who helped design the place, David Kalakaua, was a world traveler with
a taste for the good life. Known as the Merry Monarch, he planned for his
coronation the greatest party Hawaii had ever seen. He liked to spend money
with abandon and managed to amass in his lifetime a remarkable collection
of material goods, not the least of which was this beautiful mansion. He
filled the palace with precious furniture, outfitted his guards in sparkling
uniforms, and entertained on a scale befitting a king. Guided tours lead you
along the *koa* staircases and past the magnificent chandeliers and Corinthian
columns that lend a touch of European grandeur to this splendid building.

Also on the palace grounds are the **Iolani Barracks**, where the Royal
Household Guards were stationed, and the **Bandstand** upon which the "Champagne King" was coronated. You can tour the palace grounds for free, but
there is an admission charge for the building. Reservations are advised.

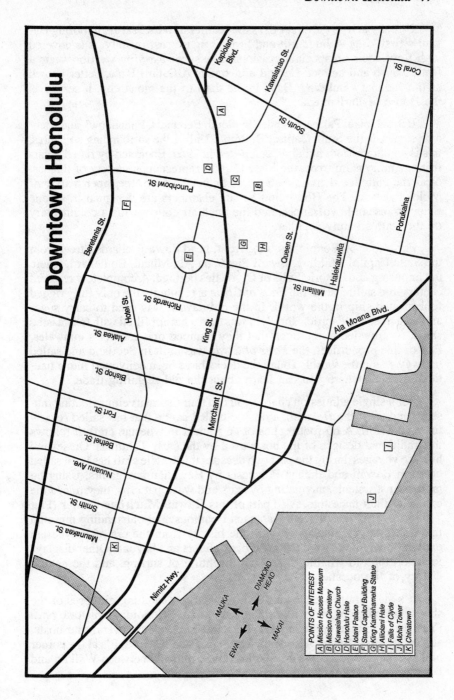

Downtown Honolulu

POINTS OF INTEREST

A	Mission Houses Museum
B	Mission Cemetery
C	Kawaiahao Church
D	Honolulu Hale
E	Iolani Palace
F	State Capitol Building
G	King Kamehameha Statue
H	Aliiolani Hale
I	Falls of Clyde
J	Aloha Tower
K	Chinatown

Kapiolani Blvd.
Kawaiahao St.
Coral St.
South St.
Punchbowl St.
Pohukaina
Beretania St.
Queen St.
Halekauwila
Hotel St.
Richards St.
Mililani St.
Ala Moana Blvd.
Alakea St.
King St.
Bishop St.
Merchant St.
Fort St.
Bethel St.
Nuuanu Ave.
Smith St.
Maunakea St.
Nimitz Hwy.

MAUKA
DIAMOND HEAD
EWA
MAKAI

Directly across the street rises the **Kamehameha Statue,** honoring Hawaii's first king. A huge gilt-and-bronze figure cast in Italy, it is covered with flower leis on special occasions. The spear-carrying warrior wears a feather cape and helmet. Behind him stands **Aliiolani Hale,** better known as the Judiciary Building. Back in the days of the monarchy, it served as the House of Parliament.

Behind Iolani Palace, bounded by South Beretania, Punchbowl, and Richards streets, is the **State Capitol Building.** Unlike the surrounding structures, this is an ultramodern building, completed in 1969. Encircled by flared pillars that resemble palm trees, the State Capitol represents a variety of themes. Near the entrance there is a statue of Father Damien, the leper martyr of Molokai Island. The House and Senate chambers are designed in a cone shape to resemble volcanoes, and the open-air courtyard is a commentary on the state's balmy weather.

For a tour of Honolulu's waterfront, head down Richards Street from the State Capitol Building toward Pier 7 on Ala Moana Boulevard, where the imposing and historic **Falls of Clyde** lies berthed. A completely restored century-old sailing ship, the *Falls of Clyde* is reputedly the only fully rigged four-masted ship in the world. In the old days it was used to carry sugar and oil across the Pacific. Honolulu was then a harbor filled with tall-masted ships, so crowded at the dock that they bumped one another's gunwales. Part of this proud fleet, the *Falls of Clyde* was built in Scotland and sailed halfway round the world. Today the decks have been converted into a nautical museum where you can learn about the old seafaring trade.

For a single admission charge you can tour this marvelous floating museum and view the *Hokulea,* a double-hulled canoe that has sailed several times to Tahiti. A 60-foot replica of an ancient Polynesian craft, it follows the traditional designs of the boats used by the early Tahitians. On several historic voyages during the past two decades this fragile craft has been sailed between Hawaii and French Polynesia by Hawaiian navigators. Using no modern instruments, navigating by stars and wave patterns, they traced the course of their ancestors. Also part of this **Hawaii Maritime Center** (Pier 7, 536-6373) is the adjacent Kalakaua Boathouse, an outstanding museum that traces the archipelago's maritime history from the era of Polynesian exploration to the days of the great ocean liners and beyond. Other displays focus on the old whaling trade, the invention of surfing, and the natural history of the ocean.

It's also fun to wander the nearby wharves, catching glimpses of the shops and pleasure boats that still tie up around Honolulu's historic port. (You can also take in the city's fishing fleet, as well as several tour boats, at **Kewalo Boat Basin.** Also known as Fisherman's Wharf, it's at the corner of Ala Moana Boulevard and Ward Avenue, midway between Waikiki and Downtown Honolulu.)

From the Hawaii Maritime Center, follow the roadway along the water to **Aloha Tower** at Pier 9. You'll see it nearby, rising like a spire along the water's edge. Earlier in the century, when many visitors arrived in luxurious ocean liners, this slender structure was Hawaii's answer to the Statue of Liberty. It greeted guests when they arrived and bade them farewell upon departure. Now dwarfed by the skyscrapers of Downtown Honolulu, proud Aloha Tower still commands an unusual view of the harbor and ocean. Any day between 8 a.m. and 9 p.m. you can ride an elevator to the tenth floor observation deck for a crow's nest view. For ship arrival and departure information, call 537-9260.

Today **American Hawaii Cruises** carries on the ocean-liner tradition in part. They operate the *SS Independence* and the *SS Constitution*, which ply the waters between the islands regularly, docking at Kauai, Maui, and the Big Island, and in Honolulu near Aloha Tower. For information on their week-long cruises around the Hawaiian islands, call 800-227-3666.

Back at ground zero, head *mauka* (toward the mountains) across the highway and up **Fort Street Mall**. This seven-block stretch of Downtown Honolulu has been refurbished and converted into an attractive pedestrian thoroughfare. There are restaurants galore here. The mall is also a good place to spend a little time shopping. Miles from the Waikiki tourist beat, the stores here cater to local people, so you'll be able to discover objects unobtainable in kitschier quarters.

Fort Street Mall leads to **Merchant Street**, center of the old downtown section of Honolulu. The 19th- and early-20th-century buildings in this neighborhood re-create the days before Hawaii became the 50th state, when the islands were almost totally controlled by "The Big Five," an interlocking group of powerful corporations. Today the brick-rococo district remains much the same on the outside. But the interiors of the buildings have changed markedly. They now house boutiques and gourmet restaurants downstairs and multi-national corporations on the upper floors.

After proceeding away from the waterfront all the way to the end of Merchant Street, take a right on Nuuanu Avenue, then a left on Hotel Street. As you walk along this thoroughfare, which seems to change its identity every block or two, you will pass from Honolulu's conservative financial district into one of its most intriguing ethnic neighborhoods, **Chinatown (★)**.

The Chinese first arrived in Hawaii in 1852, imported as plantation workers. They quickly moved to urban areas, however, became merchants, and proved very successful. Many settled right here in this weather-beaten district, which has long been a center of controversy and an integral part of Honolulu's history. When bubonic plague savaged the Chinese community in 1900, the Caucasian-led government tried to contain the pestilence by burning down afflicted homes. The bumbling white fathers managed to raze most of Chinatown, destroying businesses as well as houses.

Today Hotel Street, the spine of Chinatown, is undergoing a major renovation. Numerous buildings have already been restored and newly refurbished shops now stand cheek-by-jowl with quaint, time-worn stores. Even here, however, you can still encounter the other side of Chinatown, the seedy, late-night face of the neighborhood. Strung like a neon ganglion along the thoroughfare are porno movie places, flophouses, barrooms, and pool halls. This was once a booming red-light district, the haunt of sailors and ragged characters.

The ultimate emblem of Chinatown's revitalization is **Maunakea Marketplace** (Hotel and Maunakea streets). This Amerasian shopping mall, with a statue of Confucius overlooking a brick courtyard, houses an Oriental antique shop, a Chinese art store, and the Chinatown Visitor Center (537-2586). The most interesting feature is the produce market, a series of traditional hanging-ducks-and-live-fish stalls inside an air-conditioned building.

Some of Chinatown's woodframe buildings still suggest the old days and traditions. Wander down side streets like Maunakea Street and you will encounter import stores, Chinese groceries, and noodle factories. You might also pop into one of the medicinal herb shops, which feature strange potions and healing powders. There are chop suey joints, acupuncturists, and outdoor markets galore, all lending a priceless flavor of the Orient.

The best way to visit this neighborhood is on one of the Chinatown Walking Tours sponsored by the **Chinese Chamber of Commerce** (533-3181). Chinatown today is an eclectic community, containing not only Chinese, but Filipinos, Hawaiians, and recent arrivals from Vietnam and Laos. To fully understand Hawaii's melting-pot population, it is important that you visit this vibrant district. The walking tour will carry you past temples and other spots all around the neighborhood before stopping for a Cantonese-style lunch.

Continuing north along Hotel Street across Nuuanu Stream, turn right on College Walk and follow it a short distance upstream. You'll pass the **Izumo Taishakyo Mission**, a Shinto Shrine. In the course of a few short blocks you have passed from Hong Kong into Tokyo.

Proceed farther and you will arrive at **Foster Botanical Garden** (50 North Vineyard Boulevard; 531-1939). This 20-acre plot is planted with orchids, palms, coffee trees, poisonous plants, and numerous other exotic specimens. There are about 4,000 species in all, dotted around a garden that was first planted over 125 years ago. You can meditate under a bo tree or wander through a "prehistoric glen," a riot of ancient ferns and unusual palms. Or you can stroll through and marvel at the universe of color crowded into this small urban garden.

On the way back to Chinatown, walk along the other side of Nuuanu Stream and stop at the **Cultural Plaza**. This Asian-style shopping mall is bounded by Kukui, Maunakea, and Beretania streets, and by the stream. Here you'll find porcelain, Chinese jewelry, spices, and perhaps even acupuncture supplies.

Another important cultural point in the downtown district is the **Honolulu Academy of Arts** (900 South Beretania Street; 538-3693). This outstanding museum often displays author James Michener's collection of woodblocks from Japan. There are also classic works by European and American masters, as well as important art by local painters and sculptors. Several elegantly landscaped courtyards add to the beauty here.

Farther afield lies **Dole Cannery Square** (650 Iwilei Road; 548-6600; admission), site of Hawaii's largest pineapple cannery. Known for its 195-foot-high pineapple tower, the factory is one of Honolulu's most recognizable landmarks. Touring this 56-acre operation you'll see Hawaii's golden fruit peeled, cored, and canned.

The adjacent **Hawaii Children's Museum** (650 Iwilei Road; 522-0040; admission) has an ingenious collection of exhibits devoted to culture, science, and technology. Kids can explore a giant tooth complete with cavity, create five-foot bubbles in a bubble-making room, wander through a tropical bamboo jungle, and view a baby dinosaur fashioned with moveable parts.

DOWNTOWN HONOLULU HOTELS

Centrally located between Waikiki and Downtown Honolulu is the **Nakamura Hotel** (1140 South King Street; 537-1951). It's a pleasant place, but the only reason I can conceive for staying here is the locale. The hotel itself is adequate; the rooms are neatly furnished, carpeted, and equipped with private telephones for guests (though phone service is cut off at night). I'd ask for accommodations on the *mauka* side, since the other side fronts noisy King Street. Budget.

The **Pagoda Hotel** (1525 Rycroft Street; 941-6611) is sufficiently removed from the crowds but still within striking distance of the beach. Spacious studio and one-bedroom units put the accent on rattan furniture. The carpeted rooms feature views of the hotel garden or distant mountains. Two-bedroom units in the adjoining Pagoda Terrace offer kitchens. Moderate to deluxe.

On the outskirts of Chinatown is the **Town Inn** (250 North Beretania Street; 536-2377). This is an excellent spot to capture the local color of Honolulu's Chinese section, though the hotel itself is rather nondescript. The rooms are clean, carpeted, and sparsely furnished—some even have air conditioning—and all are practically devoid of decoration. Budget.

DOWNTOWN HONOLULU RESTAURANTS

Rather than list the city's restaurants according to price, I'll group them by area. As you get away from Waikiki you'll be dining with a more local crowd and tasting foods more representative of island cuisine, so I would certainly advise checking out some of Honolulu's eating places.

Right next to Waikiki, in Ala Moana Center (1450 Ala Moana Boulevard), there are numerous ethnic take-out restaurants that share a large dining pavilion called Makai Market. Best of all is **Patti's Chinese Kitchen** (946-5002), a crowded and noisy gathering place. At Patti's you can choose two or more main dishes plus a side order of fried rice, chop suey, or *chow fun*. The courses include almond duck, lemon-sauce chicken, tofu, beef tomato, sweet-and-sour pork, barbecued ribs, pig's feet, and shrimp with vegetables. It's quite simply the best place near Waikiki for a low-cost meal. Budget.

There's also the **Poi Bowl** (949-8444), a take-out stand serving Hawaiian dishes, and **Lyn's Delicatessen** (941-3388), featuring a full line of deli sandwiches as well as chicken baskets and plate lunches. Budget.

Or you can ride the escalator to the upper level of Ala Moana Center. Here **Shirokiya** (973-9111), a massive Asian department store, features an informal Japanese restaurant and deli. Moderate.

Hawaiian regional cuisine accented by island fruits is featured at the **Prince Court** (100 Holomoana Street; 956-1111). The Hawaii Prince Hotel's harborside restaurant, this dining room is known for dishes like sea scallops, kahuku shrimp, lobster, and mahi salad niçoise. A big wine list is another plus at this Polynesian-style dining room appointed with beautiful floral bouquets. Deluxe.

Ward Centre, located at 1200 Ala Moana Boulevard, midway between Waikiki and Downtown Honolulu, is a focus for gourmet dining. A warren of wood-paneled restaurants, it features several outstanding eateries. Particularly recommended is **Il Fresco** (523-5191), a California-style dining room decorated in brass and tile and featuring a wood-burning oven. In addition to pasta dishes and calzone, this moderate-priced nook offers grilled fresh fish, chicken entrées, and outrageous desserts.

Also consider **Compadres** (523-1307), upstairs in the same complex. This attractive Mexican restaurant, with oak bar and patio dining area, prepares a host of dishes from south of the border as well as sandwiches, steaks, and seafood. Priced moderately, it specializes in tropical ambience, good food, and fishbowl-size margaritas.

Located in the ultra-contemporary Restaurant Row shopping mall, **Sunset Grill** (500 Ala Moana Boulevard, #1A; 521-4409) is a minimalist's delight. Track lights, exposed pipes, raw wood, and poured concrete establish a kind of early-21st-century motif. The only area devoted to excess is the kitchen, which serves up a lavish array of mesquite-grilled dishes. Deluxe.

The menu at **Rex's Black Orchid** (500 Ala Moana Boulevard; 521-3111), in the same complex, features Italian specialties with a Hawaiian touch such as Maui onion and tomato salad with caper and pimento vinaigrette, Hawaiian lobster tail, angel hair pomodoro, and black-and-blue ahi seared rare. The Italian contemporary dining room offers booth and table seating and there's live jazz and contemporary music in the adjacent lounge. Paintings by Luigi Fumigalli grace the walls. Moderate to deluxe.

Fresh ono, ulua, spearfish, ahi, and marlin highlight the vast seafood menu at **John Dominus** (43 Ahui Street; 808-523-0955). A sprawling establishment midway between Waikiki and Downtown Honolulu, it features huge pools filled with hundreds of live lobsters. The wood-paneled dining room overlooks the water and the chefs know as much about preparing seafood as the original Polynesians. Steak and veal are also on the menu. Moderate to deluxe.

For sushi, sukiyaki, tempura, and other Japanese specialties, try the **Pagoda Floating Restaurant** (1525 Rycroft Street; 941-6611). This restaurant-in-the-round sits above a pond populated with gaily colored koi fish. Several cascades and a fountain feed the pond. The surrounding grounds have been carefully landscaped. This two-level dining room, which offers a lunch buffet, also serves steaks, scampi, and other Western dishes. Moderate to deluxe.

Honolulu has numerous seafood restaurants. Some of them, fittingly enough, are located right on the water. But for an authentic seafront feel, it's nice to be where the fishing boats actually come in. **Fisherman's Wharf** (1009 Ala Moana Boulevard; 538-3808) provides just such an atmosphere. Boasting "two decks of superb dining," this sprawling facility is festooned with nautical gear. The "Captain's Bridge" topside has a shoalful of seafood selections ranging from broiled salmon to Alaska king crab, priced in the deluxe range.

There are several other dining spots situated along interior streets away from the water that I particularly like. These are also located between Waikiki and Downtown Honolulu. For Italian-style seafood, **Philip Paolo's** (2312 South Beretania Street; 946-1163) is highly recommended by local residents. Set in a trim woodframe house, it features shrimp scampi, frutti di mare (seafood combination), and a host of pasta dishes. By moderate-priced restaurant standards, the interior is very fashionably done. Dinner only, lunch on Fridays.

In the same part of town sits one of Honolulu's best budget-priced Chinese restaurants. The decor at **King Tsin Restaurant** (1110 McCully Street; 946-3273) is rather bland, but the Mandarin cuisine adds plenty of spice. You can order Szechuan dishes like shredded pork or a Mongolian beef dish. These are plenty hot; you might also want to try the milder seafood, pork, vegetable, fowl, and beef dishes. Budget.

Auntie Pasto's (1099 South Beretania Street; 523-8855) is a popular, budget-priced Italian restaurant with oilcloth on the tables and a map of the mother country tacked to the wall. Pasta is served with any of a dozen different sauces—meat sauce, clams and broccoli, creamy pesto, carbonara, and seafood. There are salads aplenty plus an assortment of entrées that includes veal marsala, chicken cacciatore, and calamari steak.

For Southeast Asian cuisine, try the **Thai Chef** (1246 South King Street; 526-3772). At this modest café you can savor kang som (hot-and-sour fish soup), fried pork with garlic and pepper, or a tasty garlic prawn dish. Budget.

In Downtown Honolulu, near the city's financial center, there's a modest restaurant that I particularly like. **People's Café** (1310 Pali Highway; 536-5789) has been serving Hawaiian food for over 40 years. The place is owned by a Japanese family, which helps explain the teriyaki dishes on the menu. But primarily the food is Polynesian: This is a splendid spot to order *poi, lomi* salmon, *kalua* pig, and other island favorites. *Ono, ono!* Budget to moderate.

For Chinese food, try **Yong Sing Restaurant** (1055 Alakea Street; 531-1367). This high-ceilinged establishment, catering to local businesspeople, has some delicious dishes. I thought the oyster sauce chicken particularly tasty. With its daily lunch specials, Yong Sing is a perfect stopoff when you're shopping or sightseeing downtown. Budget to moderate.

But for the true flavor of China, head over to Chinatown, just a few blocks from the financial district. Amid the tumbledown buildings and jumble of shops, there's one restaurant you must not miss—**Wo Fat** (★) (115 North Hotel Street; 533-6393). Operating since 1882, this is the area's oldest eating place, an institution in itself. If you don't eat here, at least tour the place. This cavernous establishment contains three floors and a knockout decor. The second story, where I'd recommend dining, is painted from pillar to ceiling with dragons and ornate Oriental designs. Add Chinese lanterns, brush paintings, and a mural, and you have an extravagant display of Chinese art. The cuisine, too, is varied: You'll have to go to Hong Kong for a wider choice of delicious Cantonese dishes. There are hundreds of pork, beef, duck, seafood, vegetables, and chicken dishes, plus old standbys like won ton, chop suey, and chow mein. All are generally priced in the budget-to-moderate range.

There's **A Little Bit of Saigon** (1160 Maunakea Street; 528-3663) right in the heart of Chinatown. Decorated with batiks by local artists, this moderate-priced Vietnamese restaurant has gained a solid reputation among Honolulu regulars. The menu covers every culinary desire from noodle soups to "seven courses of beef."

And there's a little bit of every other ethnic cuisine at the food stalls in **Maunakea Marketplace** (Hotel and Maunakea streets). Here you'll find vendors dispensing steaming plates of Thai, Chinese, Japanese, Hawaiian, Filipino, Korean, Vietnamese, and Italian food at budget prices. Italian? Small tables are provided.

DOWNTOWN HONOLULU MARKETS

Midway between Waikiki and Downtown Honolulu there's a **Times Supermarket** (1290 South Beretania Street; 524-5711) and a **Safeway** store (1121 South Beretania Street; 538-7315). There's another **Safeway** in Downtown Honolulu (1360 Pali Highway; 538-3953).

Also look for **The Carrot Patch** (700 Bishop Street; 531-4037) with its health and diet products.

You might want to browse around the mom 'n' pop grocery stores spotted throughout Chinatown. They're marvelous places to pick up Chinese foodstuffs and to capture the local color.

Don't miss the **Open Market** (along North King Street between River and Kekaulike streets) in Chinatown. It's a great place to shop for fresh foods. There are numerous stands selling fish, produce, poultry, meat, baked goods, and island fruits, all at low-overhead prices.

DOWNTOWN HONOLULU SHOPPING

Ala Moana Center (1450 Ala Moana Boulevard), on the outskirts of Waikiki, is the state's largest shopping center. This multi-tiered complex has practically everything. Where most self-respecting malls have two department stores, Ala Moana has four: **Sears** (947-0211), **Penney's** (946-8068), Hawaii's own **Liberty House** (941-2345), and a Japanese emporium called **Shirokiya** (941-9111). There's also a **Woolworth's** (941-3005) and **Long's Drug Store** (946-7707), both good places to buy inexpensive Hawaiian curios. For imported goods you might try **India Imports International** (955-3213); and for contemporary fashion there is **Benetton** (943-0629). You'll also find an assortment of stores selling liquor, antiques, tennis and golf supplies, stationery, leather goods, cameras, shoes, art, tobacco, etc., etc., etc.

And, in a paragraph by itself, there's the **Honolulu Book Shop** (941-2274). Together with its sister store downtown at 1001 Bishop Street, this is Hawaii's finest bookstore. Both branches contain excellent selections of Hawaiian books, bestsellers, paperbacks, calendars, magazines, and out-of-town newspapers.

One of Honolulu's sleeker shopping malls is **Ward Centre** (1200 Ala Moana Boulevard), an ultramodern facility. Streamlined and stylized, it's an elite enclave filled with designer shops and spiffy restaurants. In addition to boutiques and children's shops, there's a bookstore and a gourmet grocery, **R. Field Wine Co.** (521-4043). Adorned with blond-wood facades, brick walkways, and brass-rail restaurants, the shopping complex provides a touch of Beverly Hills.

Ala Moana may be the biggest, but **Ward Warehouse**, located on Ala Moana Boulevard between Waikiki and Downtown Honolulu, is another very interesting shopping center.

If you're seeking Oriental items, then Chinatown is the place. Spotted throughout this refurbished neighborhood are small shops selling statuettes, pottery, woodcrafts, and other curios. It's also worthwhile wandering through the **Cultural Plaza** (521-4934), on the corner of Beretania and Maunakea streets. This mall is filled with Oriental jewelers, bookstores, and knick-knack shops.

At the edge of Chinatown along Nuuanu Avenue are several galleries and shops worthy of a visit. The **Pegge Hopper Gallery** (1164 Nuuanu Avenue, 524-1160) is here, displaying the odalisques and other female portraits for which she is renowned. Next door at the **Waterfall Gallery** (1160-A Nuuanu Avenue; 521-6863) you'll find everything from Balinese flying frogs to photos by the award-winning owner, William Waterfall.

DOWNTOWN HONOLULU NIGHTLIFE

The first thing you'll see upon entering the Prince Kuhio Hotel is **Cupid's Lobby Bar** (2500 Kuhio Avenue; 922-0811). The lounge area features tropical palms, tapestries, rock walls and a small mirrored bar. Order drinks and *pupus* while enjoying light piano music and vocalists. An outdoor garden is adjacent.

At **Rumours** (410 Atkinson Drive; 955-4811) theme nights are the spice of life. Ballroom dancing, beach life, and karaoke are all featured, along with dancing to Top-40 music provided by live bands and deejays. Located in the Ala Moana Hotel, this two-level club is decorated with artwork and neon fixtures.

A harbor view and Hawaiian/contemporary music played by an acoustic guitarist make **Horatio's** (1050 Ala Moana Boulevard; 521-5002) a good choice for a relaxing evening. This lounge is part of a popular Honolulu restaurant.

Located east of Waikiki, the **Hard Rock Café** (1837 Kapiolani Boulevard; 955-7383) is always a kick. Decorated with tons of rock-and-roll memorabilia, this restaurant/bar is a popular nightspot for those who like loud music and a big crowd.

Near Downtown Honolulu, the ultra-contemporary Restaurant Row (500 Ala Moana Boulevard) offers several nightspots. At **Studebaker's Hawaii** (526-9888) a deejay spins '50s and '60s platters. Cover. Live Top-40 bands rock the lounge at **Rex's Black Orchid** (521-3111) nightly. There's a cover on weekends.

For something more refined and classical, consider **Chamber Music Hawaii** (261-4290), which presents 20 to 25 concerts annually at several different locations around the city.

The **Honolulu Symphony** (942-2200); with a season that runs from September to April, provides a delightful schedule of programs. During summer months it sponsors an outdoor series at the Waikiki Shell in Kapiolani Park.

At the **Hawaii Opera Theater** (Neal Blaisdell Concert Hall, Ward Avenue and King Street; 521-6537) you can see works like Saint-Saens' *Samson and Delilah*, Puccini's *Madame Butterfly*, and *Die Fledermaus* by Strauss. This regional company features stars from the international opera scene.

A number of youth- and family-oriented productions are offered at the **Honolulu Theater for Youth** (2846 Ualena Street; 839-9885) at a variety of venues throughout Oahu. The company also tours the neighbor islands twice a year.

At the other end of the cultural spectrum (and at the other end of town), the Honolulu red-light scene centers around Hotel Street in Chinatown. This partially refurbished, partially run-down strip is lined with hostess bars and adult book stores. Prostitutes, straight and gay, are on the street regularly.

DOWNTOWN HONOLULU BEACHES AND PARKS

Ala Moana Regional Park (★)—Located directly across from Ala Moana Center, this 76-acre park is a favorite with Hawaii residents. On weekends every type of outdoor enthusiast imaginable turns out to swim, fish, jog, fly model airplanes, sail model boats, and so on. There's a curving length of beach, a grassy park area, recreation facilities galore, and a helluva lot of local color.

Facilities: Picnic area, restrooms, showers, concession stands, tennis courts, recreation building, bowling green, and lifeguards. Markets and restaurants are nearby. *Swimming:* Good. *Snorkeling:* Fair. *Surfing:* There are three separate breaks here: "Concessions," "Tennis Courts," and "Baby Haleiwa" all have summer waves. *Fishing:* The most common catches are papio, bonefish, goatfish, and moano.

Getting there: Located on Ala Moana Boulevard at the west end of Waikiki, across from Ala Moana Center.

Sand Island State Park—This 140-acre park wraps around the south and east shores of Sand Island, with sections fronting both Honolulu Harbor and the open sea. Despite the name, there's no sandy beach here, and jet traffic from nearby Honolulu International might disturb your snoozing. But there is a great view of Honolulu.

Facilities: Restrooms and picnic area. Markets and restaurants are nearby. *Swimming:* Poor. *Snorkeling:* Poor. *Surfing:* Summer breaks. *Fishing:* Bonefish, goatfish, papio, and moano are the prime catches.

Camping: State permit required for tent camping in the grassy area facing the ocean.

Getting there: From Waikiki, take Ala Moana Boulevard and Nimitz Highway several miles west to Sand Island Access Road.

Greater Honolulu

Framed by the Waianae Range in the west and the Koolau Range to the east, Honolulu is a non-stop drama presented within a natural amphitheater. Honolulu Harbor sets the stage to the south; at the center lie Waikiki and Downtown Honolulu. Wrapped around these tourist and business centers is a rainbow-shaped congeries of sights and places that for lack of a better name constitutes "Greater Honolulu."

It extends from navy-grey Pearl Harbor to the turquoise waters of the prestigious Kahala district and holds in its ambit some of the city's prettiest territory. These points of interest are dotted all across the city, and to see them you must ride buses or taxis or rent a car. But all are well worth the extra effort. Many are visited more by local residents than tourists and offer a singular perspective on island life and culture. Others contain an interesting mix of local folk and out-of-towners. In any case, be sure to visit a few of these outlying spots.

NUUANU AVENUE   The first district is actually within walking distance of Downtown Honolulu, but it's a relatively long walk, so transportation is generally advised. Nuuanu Avenue begins downtown and travels uphill in a northeasterly direction past several interesting points. First stop is **Soto Mission of Hawaii** (1708 Nuuanu Avenue), home of a meditative Zen sect. Modeled after a temple in India where the Buddha gave his first sermon, this building is marked by dramatic towers, and beautiful Japanese bonsai plants decorate the landscape. Here and at nearby **Honolulu Myohoji Temple** (2003 Nuuanu Avenue) the city seems like a distant memory. The latter building, placidly situated along a small stream, is capped by a peace tower.

Uphill from this Buddhist shrine lies **Honolulu Memorial Park** (22 Craigside Place). There is an ancestral monument here, bordered on three sides by a pond of flashing carp, and a striking three-tiered pagoda. This entire area is a center of simple yet beautiful Asian places of worship. For instance, **Tenrikyo Mission** (2236 Nuuanu Avenue) is a woodframe temple that was moved here all the way from Japan. One intriguing fact about this fragile structure is that large sections were built without nails.

The Hawaiian people also have an important center here. The **Royal Mausoleum** (2261 Nuuanu Avenue) is situated across the street from the Tenrikyo Mission. This was once the final resting place for two of Hawaii's royal families, the Kamehameha and Kalakaua clans. Together they ruled 19th-century Hawaii. Today the area is landscaped with palms, ginger, plumeria, and other beautiful plants and flowers.

PUNCHBOWL AND TANTALUS   It is a few miles from Downtown Honolulu to **Punchbowl**, the circular center of an extinct volcano. You'll

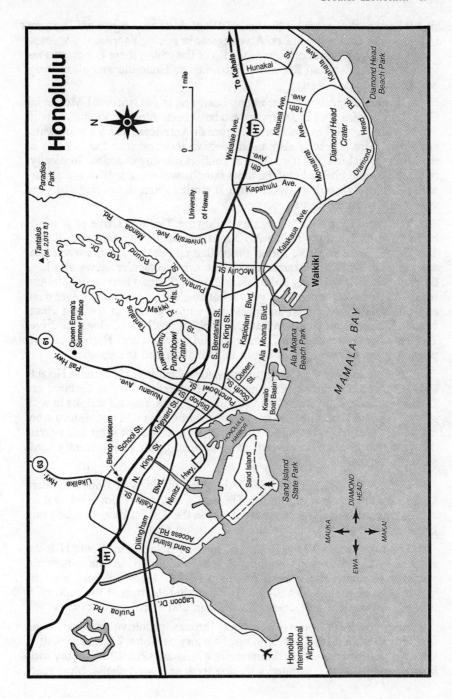

find it northeast of town, at the end of Ward Avenue and just off Prospect Drive, which circles the crater. A youngster in geologic terms, the volcano is a mere 150,000 years old. From the lip of the crater, there is a marvelous vista sweeping down to Diamond Head, across Honolulu and all the way out to the Waianae Range.

The most important feature here, however, is the **National Memorial Cemetery**, where over 25,000 war dead have been interred. Victims of both World Wars, as well as the Korean, Spanish-American, and Vietnam wars, are buried here. There is also an impressive monument to the "Courts of the Missing," which lists the names of soldiers missing in action. Ironically, of all the people buried here, the most famous was not a soldier but a journalist—Ernie Pyle, whose World War II stories about the average GI were venerated by an entire nation.

You can explore the heights by following Tantalus Drive as it winds up the side of **Tantalus** (★), a 2013-foot mountain. Together with Round Top Drive, Tantalus Drive forms a loop that circles through the residential areas hidden within this rainforest. There are spectacular views all along the route, as well as hiking trails that lead from the road into verdant hilltop regions. Here you'll encounter guava, banana, eucalyptus, and ginger trees as well as wildflowers and an occasional wild pig. One of the best views of all is found at **Puu Ualakaa Park**, a lovely retreat located along the drive. The vista here extends from Diamond Head west to Pearl Harbor, encompassing in its course a giant swath of Honolulu and the Pacific.

En route stop by the **Contemporary Arts Center** (2411 Makiki Heights Drive; 526-1322; admission). Among the hundreds of artists featured are David Hockney, John Ahern, and Rigoberto Torres. Hawaii weighs in with several sons and daughters of its own, including Jean Charlot, Satoru Abe, and Madge Tennet. Boasting five galleries, an inspired gift shop, and a gourmet café, the museum is nevertheless upstaged by its magnificently landscaped grounds.

CROSS-ISLAND EXPRESS   Along the outskirts of Honolulu, there are several more points of interest. The best way to tour them is while traveling along the two highways that cut across the Koolau Range, connecting Honolulu directly with the island's Windward Coast.

The Likelike Highway, Route 63, can be reached from Route H-1, the superhighway that serves Honolulu. Before heading up into the mountains, you will encounter the **Bishop Museum** (847-3511; admission) near the intersection of Routes 63 and H-1. Built around the turn of the century, it houses an excellent collection of Hawaiian and Pacific artifacts.

Here you'll find outrigger canoes, thrones, primitive artworks, royal feather capes, and fascinating natural-history exhibits. There are plaited mats woven from pandanus, drums made with shark skin, 19th-century surfboards, and helmets decorated with dog teeth and pearl shells. Most spectacular of all are the cloaks worn by Hawaiian kings and fashioned from tens of thousands of tiny feathers. The 19th-century whaling trade is represented with menacing harpoons and yellowing photographs of the oil-laden ships. There are displays capturing the Japanese, Chinese, and Filipino heritage in Hawaii and a hall devoted to other cultures of the Pacific.

The museum also offers a planetarium, a Hall of Discovery with children's activities, and classes in quilting, hula dancing, lei-making, and weaving. The Bishop is truly one of the finest museums of its kind in the world.

The other, more scenic road across the mountains is the Pali Highway, Route 61. As it ascends, it passes **Queen Emma's Summer Palace** (595-3167). Constructed in 1843, the palace was originally used by King Kamehameha IV and his wife, Queen Emma. Today the gracious white-pillared house is a museum. Here you can view the Queen's personal artifacts, as well as various other period pieces.

You can also walk the tree-shaded grounds of **Nuuanu Pali Drive** and follow until it rejoins the highway. This residential boulevard, with its natural canopy and park-like atmosphere, is one of Honolulu's many idyllic hideaways.

Farther along Pali Highway, there is a turnoff to **Nuuanu Pali Lookout**. It is a point that must not be missed, and is without doubt Oahu's finest view. Gaze down the sheer, rugged face of the Koolau cliffs as they drop 3000 feet to a softly rolling coastal shelf. Your view will extend from Makapuu Point to the distant reaches of Kaneohe Bay, and from the lip of the cliff far out to sea. It was from these heights, according to legend, that a vanquished army was forced to plunge when Kamehameha I captured Oahu in 1795.

PEARL HARBOR   Many people consider a trip to Pearl Harbor a pilgrimage. It was here on a sleepy Sunday morning, December 7, 1941, that the Japanese launched a sneak attack on the United States naval fleet anchored in the port, immediately plunging the nation into World War II. As Japanese planes bombed the harbor, over 3000 Americans lost their lives. Eighteen ships sank that day in the country's greatest military disaster.

The battleship *USS Arizona* was hit so savagely by aerial bombs and torpedoes that it plunged to the bottom, entombing over 1100 sailors within its hulk; today they remain in that watery grave. A special **Arizona Memorial** (422-0561) was built to honor them; it's a museum constructed directly above the ship, right in the middle of Pearl Harbor. In addition to the museum displays, the memorial includes a shrine with the name of each sailor who died aboard the ship carved in marble. Gazing at this too, too long list of names, and peering over the side at the shadowy hull of the ship, it's hard not to be overcome by the tragic history of the place. Daily from 7:30 a.m. to 5:00 p.m., the United States Navy sponsors free boat tours out to this fascinating memorial. Before boarding, be sure to remember, no bathing suits, bare feet, or children under 45 inches are permitted. Pearl Harbor, several miles northwest of Downtown Honolulu, can be reached by car or bus.

Anchored nearby the Arizona is the USS **Bowfin/Pacific Submarine Museum** (423-1341; admission). This World War II-era sub is a window into life beneath the waves. It provides an excellent opportunity to tour the claustrophobic quarters in which almost 100 men spent months at a time. The accompanying museum, filled with aquatic artifacts, will help provide an even fuller perspective.

MANOA VALLEY   Residents of a different sort are found in the city's beautiful Manoa Valley, a couple of miles northeast of Waikiki. Among the elegant homes decorating the region are some owned by the New England families that settled in Hawaii during the 19th century.

The **University of Hawaii** has its main campus here; over 20,000 students and 2,000 faculty members attend classes and teach on these grounds. Of particular interest on campus is the **East-West Center** (1777 East-West Road; 944-7111), a gathering place for foreign students. Designed by noted architect I. M. Pei, the center is devoted to the study of Asian and American cultures. The center also contains a number of priceless Asian artworks, well worth viewing.

From here you can head deeper into Manoa Valley along Oahu Avenue and Manoa Road. You'll pass the **Waoli Tea Room** (3016 Oahu Avenue; 988-2131), a cozy dining room tucked into a garden setting. Here also is the **Little Grass Shack** that was once occupied by Robert Louis Stevenson (or so the story goes) and a small chapel replete with stained glass windows.

Also set within Manoa Valley's fragrant realm is **Paradise Park** (3707 Manoa Road; 988-6686; admission). This tropical theme park was once the haunt of King Kamehameha and his courtiers. They relaxed and played in the forests that eventually became part of the park's 15 acres. Today the facility is a lovely complex featuring flower gardens, waterfalls, lagoons, ponds, and winding pathways. The plant life here is as rich and thick as that found in a tropical rainforest. Among the park's many highlights is a walk-through aviary. As you wander through the grounds, you can witness a theatrical presentation starring macaws and cockatoos, take in an exhibit of robotic dinosaurs, and tour an intriguing historical gallery.

Adjacent to the park is **Lyon Arboretum** (3860 Manoa Road; 988-3177), a magnificent 124-acre garden with greenhouses, a herbarium, and over 8000 plant species.

KAHALA   On the far side of Diamond Head, along a string of narrow beaches, lie many of Honolulu's most admired addresses. To reach this residential promised land follow Diamond Head Road.

Diamond Head Beach Park, a twisting ribbon of white sand, nestles directly below the famous crater. Whenever the wind and waves are good, you will see windsurfers and surfers galore sweeping in toward the shoreline. The coral reef here makes for good skindiving, too. It's a pretty beach, backdropped by the Kuilei cliffs and watched over by the **Diamond Head Lighthouse**.

From Diamond Head, continue east along Diamond Head Road and Kahala Avenue. These will lead through the Kahala District, home to the island's elite. Bordered by the ocean and the exclusive Waialae Country Club is a golden string of spectacular oceanfront homes with carefully manicured lawns.

GREATER HONOLULU HOTELS

The **Nuuanu YMCA** (1441 Pali Highway; 536-3556) has budget-priced accommodations for men. Complete athletic facilities are available.

Hawaii's foremost bed-and-breakfast inn rests in a magnificent old mansion near the University of Hawaii campus. Set in the lush Manoa Valley, the **Manoa Valley Inn** (★) (2001 Vancouver Drive; 947-6019) is a 1915 brown-shingle house featuring seven guest rooms and an adjacent cottage. Decorated with patterned wallpaper and old-style artworks, the rooms are furnished in plump antique armchairs. Guests enjoy a sun room and parlor, as well as the mansion's spacious porch and lawn. For luxury and privacy, this historic jewel is one of the island's finest spots. Deluxe to ultra-deluxe.

Also in Manoa Valley, the **Fernhurst YWCA** (1566 Wilder Avenue; 941-2231) is an appealing three-story lowrise that provides a residence for women. Guest rooms are single or double occupancy with connecting baths. Among the facilities are hot plates and refrigerators, laundry, dining room, swimming pool, and lounge. The budget-to-moderate rates include breakfast and dinner.

The **Atherton YMCA** (1810 University Avenue; 946-0253) is a co-ed facility with budget-priced accommodations for men and women. Located across the street from the University of Hawaii campus, it is open year-round to students and during summer months to the general public.

The **Honolulu International Youth Hostel** (2323-A Sea View Avenue; 946-0591) is a dormitory-style crash pad with separate living quarters for men and women. Shared kitchen facilities are available. Budget.

One of Hawaii's finest hotels is the **Kahala Hilton Hotel** (5000 Kahala Avenue; 734-2211). Located five miles outside Waikiki, this luxurious resort is ideally situated, far enough from Waikiki to escape the throngs but sufficiently close to enjoy Waikiki's restaurants and night spots. With a lovely white-sand beach, an oceanfront pool, and a waterfall tumbling through its beautiful grounds, the Kahala Hilton is an impressive retreat. The hotel acreage is landscaped with a variety of palm trees, plus bougainvillea and countless other flowering plants. The private guest rooms are equally outstanding. Ultra-deluxe.

GREATER HONOLULU RESTAURANTS

Liliha Seafood Restaurant (1408 Liliha Street; 536-2663), a neighborhood café out past Downtown Honolulu, comes highly recommended by local people. This could very well be the only Hawaiian dining spot that offers sweet-and-sour sea bass, squid with sour mustard cabbage, and fried squid with *ong choy*. In addition to two dozen seafood dishes, they have a host of chicken, pork, vegetable, and noodle selections, all at budget prices.

One of the ethnic restaurants most popular with local folks is **Keo's Thai Cuisine** (625 Kapahulu Avenue; 737-8240). Fulfilling to all the senses, this intimate place is decorated with fresh flowers and tropical plants. The cuisine includes such Southeast Asian dishes as the "evil jungle prince," a sliced beef, pork, and chicken entrée in hot sauce. You can choose from dozens of fish, shellfish, fowl, and meat dishes. The food is moderate to deluxe in price, very, very spicy, and highly recommended. Dinner only.

For Japanese dining, my favorite moderate-priced restaurant is **Irifune** (563 Kapahulu Avenue; 737-1141), a charming place with a warm and friendly ambience. There are tasty sukiyaki, curry, teriyaki, and tempura dishes here, plus several other Asian delectables.

For local-style plate lunches, cruise in to **Rainbow Drive-In** (3308 Kanaina and Kapahulu avenues; 737-0177). Popular with *kamaainas* and tourists alike, the menu includes hamburger steak, beef curry, chili, and fried chicken served with two scoops of rice and macaroni salad. Budget.

Ono Hawaiian Foods (★) (726 Kapahulu Avenue; 737-2275) is a must for all true Hawaii lovers. It's a hole-in-da-wall eatery on a busy street. But if you're lucky enough to get one of the few tables, you can feast on *laulau*, *kalua* pig, *pipikaula, poi,* and *haupia.* The walls are papered with signed photographs of local notables and the place is packed with locals, notable and otherwise. Budget.

To combine fine dining with a unique Polynesian experience, book a lunch or dinner reservation at **The Willows** (901 Hausten Street; 946-4808). The flowering trees and thatch-topped roofs are reminiscent of ancient Hawaii. There's a koi pond adding to the atmosphere, and a menu that features excellent Hawaiian and seafood dishes. Dedicated to "the very best that nature and Hawaii provide," the restaurant serves delicately prepared fish, sautéed scallops, scampi, and a traditional Hawaiian dinner (with island favorites like *laulau, poi,* and *lomi* salmon). Sunday brunch features strolling Hawaiian musicians. Deluxe in quality and price.

Near the University of Hawaii campus, there are pizzas, hero sandwiches, spaghetti, and a salad bar at **Mama Mia** (in Puck's Alley, 1015 University Avenue; 947-5233). Open for lunch and dinner, it's a great place to snack or stop for a cold beer. Moderate.

Or you can check out **Anna Banana's** (2440 South Beretania Street; 946-5190), a combination bar and Mexican restaurant that draws a swinging crowd. Located a half-mile from campus, this dim eatery serves burritos, enchiladas, and other south-o'-the-border favorites. Decorated in slapdash fashion with propellers, antlers, boxing gloves, and trophies, Anna's is the local center for slumming. Budget to moderate.

Waialae Avenue, a neighborhood strip several miles outside Waikiki, has developed into a gourmet ghetto. **Azteca Mexican Restaurant** (3569 Waialae Avenue; 735-2492) is a vinyl-booth-and-plastic-panel eatery that serves a delicious array of Mexican food at budget-to-moderate prices.

For spicy and delicious Asian dishes, it is hard to find a more appealing place than **Hale Vietnam** (1140 12th Avenue; 734-7581). A family restaurant that draws a local crowd, it features traditional Vietnamese soup and a host of excellent entrées. Moderate.

Out at the Kahala Mall (4211 Waialae Avenue), **La Salsa** (732-4042) is just one in a strip of small cafés. But the salsa at La Salsa is as spicy as life itself and could make it one of the biggest little restaurants around. What you put that hot sauce on—fajitas, quesadillas, burritos, enchiladas, tacos—is equally delicious. To keep your eyes as well as those taste buds occupied, the walls are painted in tropical colors and decorated with three-dimensional murals. Budget.

A spiral staircase leads down to one of Oahu's finest dining rooms, the **Maile Restaurant** (Kahala Hilton, 5000 Kahala Avenue; 734-2211). The continental menu offers entrées like roast duckling, chicken Wellington, roast veal tenderloin, and beef tournedos with Maine lobster. The atmosphere is graceful and subdued with an interior fountain, orchids, chandeliers and lace tablecloths. Ultra-deluxe.

GREATER HONOLULU MARKETS

A good place to shop near the University of Hawaii's Manoa campus is at **Star Market** (2470 South King Street; 973-1666).

The best place in Honolulu to buy health foods is at **Down To Earth Natural Foods** (2525 South King Street; 947-7678). **Kokua Co-op** (2357 South Beretania Street; 941-1922), a local-run market nearby, is another excellent choice.

GREATER HONOLULU SHOPPING

Scattered around town are several shops that I recommend you check out. At **Lanakila Crafts** (1809 Bachelot Street; 531-0555) most of the goods are made by the disabled, and the craftsmanship is superb. There are shell necklaces, woven handbags, monkeypod bowls, and homemade dolls. You'll probably see these items in other stores around the islands, with much higher price tags than here at the "factory."

The **Foundry Arts Center** (899 Waimanu; 538-7288) consists of a network of artisans producing ceramics, metal sculptures, jewelry, silk screens, and topiary. It's a very informal affair: You can tour the workshops and sometimes bargain with craftspeople for their wares.

Out at the Bishop Museum (Routes H-1 and 63) be sure to stop by **Shop Pacifica** (848-4158), which offers a fine selection of Hawaiiana. There are books on island history and geography, an assortment of instruments that include nose flutes and gourds, plus cards, souvenirs, and wooden bowls.

For secondhand items you might try the flea market at the **Kam Drive-In Theatre** (98-850 Moanalua Road; 483-5933). It's a great place to barter for bargains, meet local folks, and find items you'll never see in stores. It's open on Wednesday, Saturday, Sunday, and some holidays.

Honolulu's most upscale shopping center is **Kahala Mall** (4211 Waialae Avenue), where you'll find designer shops galore. This attractive complex also hosts an array of moderately priced stores.

GREATER HONOLULU NIGHTLIFE

Outside Honolulu there are a couple of prime spots to hear Hawaiian music. **Jubilee** (1007 Dillingham Boulevard; 845-1568), past Downtown Honolulu, has live bands every night.

Over by the University of Hawaii's Manoa campus, there's **Anna Banana's** (2440 South Beretania Street; 946-5190). A popular hangout for years, this wildly decorated spot has live entertainment several nights a week. There's likely to be a local band cranking it up and a local crowd headed for the dancefloor. Cover.

GREATER HONOLULU BEACHES AND PARKS

Keaiwa Heiau State Recreation Area—Amazing as it sounds, this is a wooded retreat within easy driving distance of Honolulu. Situated in the Koolau foothills overlooking Pearl Harbor, it contains the remains of a *heiau*, a temple once used by Hawaiian healers. There's an arboretum of medicinal plants, a forest extending to the far reaches of the mountains, and a network of hiking trails.

Facilities: Picnic area and restrooms. Markets and restaurants several miles away.

Camping: Tents only. State permit required.

Getting there: Located in Aiea Heights. To get there from Honolulu, take Route 90 west to Aiea, then follow Aiea Heights Drive to the park.

Diamond Head Beach Park (★)—A heaven to windsurfers, this twisting ribbon of white sand sits directly below the crater. It's close enough to Waikiki for convenient access but far enough to shake most of the crowds. The Kuilei cliffs, covered with scrub growth, loom behind the beach.

Facilities: Shower. It's about two miles to markets and restaurants in Waikiki. *Swimming:* Mediocre. *Snorkeling:* Good. Coral reef extends offshore throughout this area. *Surfing:* Year-round juice at "Lighthouse" breaks. Outstanding windsurfing. *Fishing:* Your chances are good to reel in ulua, papio, or *mamao*.

Getting there: Located just beyond Waikiki along Diamond Head Road at the foot of Diamond Head; watch for parked cars.

Kuilei Cliffs Beach Park and **Kaalawai Beach**—Extending east from Diamond Head Beach Park, these sandy corridors are also flanked by sharp sea cliffs. Together they extend from Diamond Head Lighthouse to Black Point. The aquatic attractions are the same as at Diamond Head Beach Park and both beaches can be reached from it (or from cliff trails leading down from Diamond Head Road). A protecting reef makes for good swimming at Kaalawai Beach (which can also be reached via a public accessway off Kulumanu Place).

Waialae Beach Park—Smack in the middle of Honolulu's prestigious Kahala district, where a million dollars buys a modest house, sits this tidy beach. Its white sand neatly groomed, its spacious lawn shaded by palms, Waialae is a true find. There are bathhouse facilities, beachside picnic tables, and a footbridge arching across the stream that divides the property. To the west of the park lies **Kahala Beach**, a long, thin swath of sand that extends all the way to Black Point.

Facilities: Restrooms, showers; groceries several miles away in Waikiki or along Waialae Avenue. *Swimming:* Good. *Snorkeling:* Good at nearby Kahala Hilton. *Surfing:* Poor. *Fishing:* Good.

Getting there: The park is located on the 4900 block of Kahala Avenue in Kahala.

Southeast Oahu

Out past Honolulu, beyond the lights of Waikiki and the gilded neigh-borhoods of Kahala, the pace slackens, the vistas open, and Oahu begins to look more like a tropical island. As the sunny south shore gives way to the windward side of the island, you'll encounter volcanic craters, famous bodysurfing beaches, and a dramatic blowhole. A major road, Route 72—the Kalanianaole Highway—leads from Honolulu along this southeastern coast.

This thoroughfare streams through Hawaii Kai and other residential areas, then ascends the slopes of an extinct volcano, 642-foot **Koko Head**. Here Madame Pele is reputed to have dug a hole for the last time in search of fiery volcanic matter. **Koko Crater**, the second hump on the horizon, rises to over 1200 feet. This fire-pit, according to Hawaiian legend, is the vagina of Pele's sister. It seems that Pele, goddess of volcanoes, was being pursued by a handsome demigod. Her sister, trying to distract the hot suitor from Pele, spread her legs across the landscape.

From the top of Koko Head, a well-marked sideroad and trail lead down to **Hanauma Bay**, one of the prettiest beaches in all Hawaii. This breath-taking place is a marine preserve filled with multicolored coral and teeming with underwater life. The word *hanauma* means "the curved bay," and you will clearly see that this inlet was once a circular volcano, one wall of which was breached by the sea. Little wonder that Hollywood chose this spot as the prime location for Elvis Presley's movie, *Blue Hawaii*. Elvis' grass shack was right here, and the strand was also a setting in *From Here to Eternity*.

The swimming and snorkeling are unmatched anywhere and the maze-work of coral formations along the bottom adds to the snorkeling adventure. Or you can stroll along the rock ledges that fringe the bay and explore **Toilet Bowl**, a tidepool that "flushes" as the waves wash through it. The best time to come is early morning before other swimmers stir up the waters. Hanau-ma Bay is an extremely popular picnic spot among local folks, so it is also advisable to visit on a weekday rather than face bucking the crowds on Sat-urday and Sunday.

Hanauma Bay is located about 12 miles east of Waikiki. From here the highway corkscrews along the coast. Among the remarkable scenes you'll enjoy en route are views of Lanai and Molokai, two of Oahu's sister islands. On a clear, clear day you can also see Maui, an island that requires no in-troduction.

At an overlook you will encounter **Halona Blowhole**, a lava tube through which geysers of seawater blast. During high tide and when the sea is tur-bulent, these gushers reach dramatic heights. *Halona* means "peering place," and that is exactly what everyone seems to do here. You can't miss the spot,

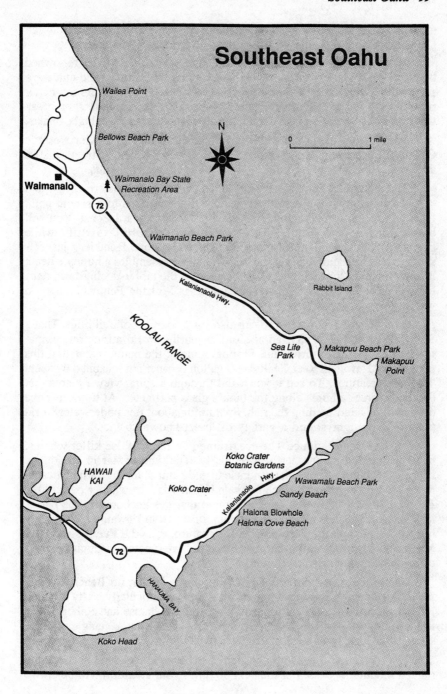

Southeast Oahu

Wailea Point

Bellows Beach Park

N

0   1 mile

Waimanalo

Waimanalo Bay State
Recreation Area

72

Waimanalo Beach Park

Kalanianaole Hwy.

Rabbit Island

KOOLAU RANGE

Sea Life
Park

Makapuu Beach Park

Makapuu
Point

Koko Crater
Botanic Gardens

Kalanianaole Hwy.

Wawamalu Beach Park

HAWAII
KAI

Koko Crater

Sandy Beach

Halona Blowhole
Halona Cove Beach

72

HANAUMA BAY

Koko Head

since the roadside parking lot is inevitably crowded with tourists. Between December and April this vista is also a prime whale-watching spot.

Just beyond spreads **Sandy Beach,** one of Hawaii's most renowned bodysurfing spots. It's a long, wide beach piled with fluffy sand and complete with picnic areas and showers. Inexperienced bodysurfers are better off enjoying the excellent sunbathing here, since the dramatic shorebreak that makes the beach so popular among bodysurfers can overwhelm beginners.

Across from the beach a side road leads up to **Koko Crater Botanic Gardens** (next to the Koko Crater Stables at 408 Kealahou Street), a 200-acre collection of cacti, plumeria, and other flowering plants.

Past this pretty spot, Route 72 rounds Oahu's southeastern corner and sets a course along the eastern shoreline. It also climbs to a scenic point from which you can take your first view of the Windward Coast. You will be standing on **Makapuu Point.** Above you rise sharp lava cliffs, while below are rolling sand dunes and open ocean. The slope-faced islet just offshore is **Rabbit Island.** It's ironic that this place resembles a bunny's head; it wasn't named for that, but rather because of the rabbit-raising farm once located on its shores. The distant headland is Mokapu Peninsula, toward which you are bound.

From this perfect perch you can also spy a complex of buildings. That's **Sea Life Park** (923-1531; admission), a marine-world attraction comparable to those in California and Florida. Among the many features at this park is the "Hawaiian Reef," a 300,000-gallon oceanarium inhabited by about 4000 sea creatures. To see it you wind through a spiral viewing area that descends three fathoms along the tank's glass perimeter. At times a scuba diver will be hand-feeding the fish. Swimming about this underwater world are sharks, stingrays, and a variety of lesser-known species.

At the Ocean Science Theatre, trained dolphins, false killer whales, penguins, and sea lions perform regularly. The whales star in an aquatic pageant, while the other entertainers leap and gambol through sophisticated routings. You can feed the sea animals if you wish, or wander over to the *Essex,* a 70-foot replica of a whaling ship that lies anchored in the park's lagoon. Since whalers played such an important part in Hawaii's 19th-century history, this is a particularly interesting feature, as is the **Pacific Whaling Museum,** where Hawaii's harpoon heyday is re-created through displays of artifacts and scrimshaw artistry.

Across the road from Sea Life Park spreads **Makapuu Beach,** another fabled but daunting bodysurfing spot that is set in a particularly pretty location. Nearby black lava cliffs are topped by a white lighthouse and Rabbit Island is anchored just offshore. The beach itself is a short, wide rectangle of white sand. It's an ideal place to picnic, but when the surf is up, beware of the waves.

The road continues along the shoreline between soft sand beaches and rugged mountain peaks. For the next 30 miles your attention will be drawn back continually to those rocky crags. They are part of the **Koolau Range,** a wall of precipitous mountains that vault up from Oahu's placid interior. Their spires, minarets, and fluted towers are softened here and there by lush, green valleys, but never enough to detract from the sheer beauty and magnitude of the heights. Light and shade play games along their moss-covered surfaces, while rainbows hang suspended between the peaks. If wind and weather permit, you will see hang gliders dusting the cliffs as they sail from the mountains down to the distant beach.

The road continues through **Waimanalo,** an old sugar plantation that today has been turned to fruit and flower cultivation. Outside town you will see **Olomana Peak.** Favored by rock climbers, it is a double-barreled peak that seems to belong in the Swiss Alps.

SOUTHEAST OAHU RESTAURANTS

Spotted along Oahu's southeastern shore are a number of moderately priced restaurants (and a couple of expensive but worthy ones) that may prove handy if you're beachcombing or camping. Most are located on or near Route 72 (Kalanianaole Highway). For the sake of convenience, I'll list the restaurants as they will appear when you travel east and north.

You're bound to feel Eurocentric at the **Swiss Inn** (Niu Valley Shopping Center, 5730 Kalanianaole Highway; 377-5447) where the menu includes wienerschnitztel, veal with a cream mushroom sauce, and cheese fondue. There's also a beef fondue with 24-hour advance notice. On the dessert menu you'll find Swiss chocolate mousse, peach melba, and fresh fruit tarts. The wood-paneled Old World look features pictures of villages that make you yearn for the Matterhorn. Deluxe.

Tucked away in unassuming fashion in a business park is one of the area's top dining spots. You'll have to travel all the way to Hawaii Kai, several miles east of Waikiki, to find **Roy's Restaurant** (6600 Kalanianaole Highway; 396-7697). It's small, intimate, and ultracontemporary, from the magazine clips framed on the walls to the cylindrical fish tank near the door. One of the most innovative of Hawaii's "Nouvelle Pacific" cuisine dining rooms, it specializes in fresh local ingredients. The main complaints you hear about this wildly popular restaurant are that it's too crowded and *too* noisy. Ultra-deluxe.

In Waimanalo, **Waimanalo Bar-B-Q** (41-857 Kalanianaole Highway) has breakfasts, plate lunches, and sandwiches at greasy-spoon prices. No gourmet's delight, this tiny eatery is well placed for people enjoying Waimanalo's beaches.

A few doors down is one of Hawaii's great Mexican restaurants. **Bueno Nalo** (41-865 Kalanianaole Highway, Waimanalo; 259-7186) may be short on looks, but is definitely long on taste. Good food at budget prices.

SOUTHEAST OAHU MARKETS

A convenient place to shop in Oahu's southeast corner is at the Koko Marina Shopping Center's **Foodland** (7192 Kalanianaole Highway; 395-3131) in Hawaii Kai. Open 24 hours a day.

Proceeding north along the coast, there's **Mel's Market** (41-1029 Kalanianaole Highway; 259-7550), a small store in Waimanalo.

SOUTHEAST OAHU BEACHES AND PARKS

Hanauma Bay Beach Park—One of Oahu's prettiest and most popular beaches, this curving swath of white sand extends for almost a half-mile. The bottom of the bay is a maze of coral reef, and the entire area has been designated a marine preserve. As a result, the skindiving is unmatched and the fish are tame enough to eat from your hand. You can also hike along rock ledges fringing the bay and explore some mind-boggling tidepools. Crowded though it is, this is one strand that should not be bypassed. Get here early—the beach closes at 7 p.m. every day.

Facilities: Picnic area, restrooms, showers, snack bar, snorkeling equipment rentals, and lifeguards. One mile to restaurants and markets at Koko Marina Shopping Center. *Swimming:* Very good. *Snorkeling:* Superb. But beware of "Witches Brew," a turbulent area on the bay's right side, and the "Molokai Express," a wicked current sweeping across the mouth of the bay. No fish spearing. *Surfing:* None. *Fishing:* Strictly prohibited.

Getting there: Located about nine miles east of Waikiki. Take Route 72 to Koko Head, then turn onto the side road near the top of the promontory. This leads to a parking lot; leave your vehicle and walk the several hundred yards down the path to the beach.

Halona Cove Beach—This is the closest you'll find to a hidden beach near Honolulu. It's a patch of white sand wedged between Halona Point and the Halona Blowhole lookout. Located directly below Kalanianaole Highway (Route 72), this is not exactly a wilderness area. But you can still escape the crowds massed on the nearby beaches.

Facilities: None. It's two miles to the markets and restaurants in Koko Marina Shopping Center. *Swimming:* Good when the sea is gentle, but extremely dangerous if it's rough. *Snorkeling:* Good. *Surfing:* None. *Fishing:* Prime catches are ulua, papio, and mamao.

Getting there: Stop at the Halona Blowhole parking lot on Route 72, about ten miles east of Waikiki. Follow the path from the right side of the lot down to the beach.

Sandy Beach—This long, wide beach is a favorite among Oahu's youth. The shorebreak makes it one of the finest, and most dangerous, bodysurfing beaches in the islands. It's a pleasant place to sunbathe, but if you go swimming, plan to negotiate a pounding shoreline. Should you want to avoid the crowds, head over to **Wamamalu Beach Park** next door to the east.

Facilities: Picnic area, restrooms, showers. Three miles to the restaurants and markets in Koko Marina Shopping Center. *Swimming:* Mediocre. *Snorkeling:* Poor. *Surfing:* Good, and very popular. Beware of rip currents. *Fishing:* Among the principal catches are ulua, papio, and mamao.

Getting there: Head out on Route 72 (Kalanianaole Highway) about 12 miles east of Waikiki.

Makapuu Beach Park—It's set in a very pretty spot with lava cliffs in the background and Rabbit Island just offshore. This is a short, wide rectangle of white sand favored by Hawaii's bodysurfers. With no protecting reef and a precipitous shoreline, Makapuu is inundated by awesome swells that send wave riders crashing onto shore. Necks and backs are broken with frightening regularity here, so if the waves are large and you're inexperienced—play the spectator. If you take the plunge, prepare for a battering!

Facilities: Restrooms, lifeguard. There's a restaurant across the road in Sea Life Park. *Swimming:* Though okay in summer, at other times the ocean is too rough. This is Hawaii's most famous bodysurfing beach. *Snorkeling:* Usually poor. *Surfing:* Not permitted. *Fishing:* Looks good for ulua, papio, and mamao.

Camping: County permit required.

Getting there: Located on Route 72 (Kalanianaole Highway) about 13 miles east of Waikiki.

Waimanalo Beach Park—Located at the southeast end of Waimanalo's three-and-a-half-mile-long beach, this is a spacious 38-acre park. It's studded with ironwood trees and equipped with numerous recreation facilities. Waimanalo Beach Park and **Waimanalo Bay State Recreation Area**, a mile farther north, are both excellent spots for picnicking, swimming, and sunbathing. The latter is farther removed from the highway in a grove of ironwood trees known to local residents as "Sherwood Forest."

Facilities: Picnic area, restrooms, showers, playground, basketball court, baseball field at Waimanalo Beach Park. Restaurants and markets nearby. Swimming: Good; well-protected. State park has good bodysurfing. *Snorkeling:* Good. *Surfing:* Poor. *Fishing:* Good at Waimanalo Bay for papio, bonefish, milkfish, and goatfish.

Camping: County permit required at both parks for tent and trailer camping.

Getting there: Waimanalo Beach Park is located at 41-471 Kalanianaole Highway (Route 72) about 15 miles east of Waikiki. Waimanalo Bay State Recreation Area is on Oloiloi Street a mile farther north.

Bellows Beach Park—This is one of Oahu's prettiest parks. There's a broad white-sand beach bordered by ironwood trees, with a marvelous view of the Koolau mountains. Sounds great, huh? The catch is that Bellows Park is situated on a military base and is open to visitors only from Friday noon until 8 a.m. Monday.

Facilities: Picnic area, showers, restroom, lifeguard. Restaurants and markets are about a mile away in Waimanalo. *Swimming:* Very good. *Snorkeling:* Good. *Surfing:* Good for beginners. *Fishing:* The most abundant species at Bellows is papio, followed by bonefish, milkfish, and goatfish.

Camping: County permit required.

Getting there: Turn off Kalanianaole Highway (Route 72) toward Bellows Air Force Station. The park is located near Waimanalo, about 17 miles east of Waikiki.

Windward Coast

Named for the trade winds that blow with soothing predictability from the northeast, this sand-rimmed shoreline lies on the far side of the *pali* from Honolulu. Between these fluted emerald cliffs and the turquoise ocean are the bedroom communities of Kailua and Kaneohe and the agricultural regions of the Waiahole and Waikane valleys. As suburbs give way to small farms, this florid region provides a relaxing transition between the busy boulevards of Honolulu and the wild surf of the North Shore.

From the southeastern corner of the island, the Kalanianaole Highway flows into Kailua, where it intersects with Route 61, or Kailua Road. If you go right for a quarter of a mile along this road you will encounter **Ulupo Heiau** (it's behind the YMCA). According to Hawaiian legend, this temple (which stands 30 feet high and measures 150 feet in length) was built by *Menehunes*, who passed the building stones across a six-mile-long bucket brigade in a one-night construction project. The *Menehunes*, in case you haven't been introduced, were tiny Hobbit-like creatures who inhabited Hawaii even before the Polynesians arrived. They were reputed to be superhumanly strong and would work all night to build dams, temples, and other structures. Several mysterious man-made objects in the islands that archaeologists have trouble placing chronologically are claimed by mythmakers to be *Menehune* creations.

Heading back to the main highway, you will find that Route 72 immediately merges into Route 61, which then continues for two miles to Route 83, the Kahekili Highway. Above this thoroughfare, spreading across 400 acres at the foot of the pali is **Hoomaluhia Park** (★) (off Route 83 at the end of Luluku Road, Kaneohe; 235-6636), a botanic garden and nature conservancy. With sheer cliffs rising on one side and a panoramic ocean view opening in the distance, it is a special place indeed. There is a 32-acre lake as well as a visitor center and hiking trails. The fruits, flowers, and trees include hundreds of species native to Hawaii.

The Kahekili Highway will also carry you to the graceful **Haiku Gardens,** located just outside Kailua at 46-336 Haiku Road. Formerly a private estate, the gardens rest in a lovely spot with a lofty rockface backdrop. Within this preserve are acres of exotic plant life, including an enchanting lily pond as well as numerous species of flowers. Hawaii specializes in beautiful gardens; the frequent rains and lush terrain make for luxuriant growing conditions. This happens to be one of the prettiest gardens of all.

Farther along you'll encounter the "Valley of the Temples," a verdant chasm folded between the mountains and the sea. Part of the valley has been consecrated as a cemetery honoring the Japanese. Highlighting the region is the **Byodo-In Temple** (47-200 Kahekili Highway, Kaneohe; 239-8811; admission). Rimmed by 2000-foot cliffs, this Buddhist shrine is a replica of a 900-year-old temple in Kyoto, Japan. It was constructed back in 1968 in memory of the first Japanese immigrants to settle in Hawaii. The simple architecture is enhanced by a bronze bell weighing seven tons that visitors are permitted to ring. A statue of Buddha dominates the site. Walk along the placid reflecting pool with its swans, ducks, and multihued carp and you will be drawn a million miles away from the bustle of Honolulu.

An alternate route through Kailua and Kaneohe will carry you near the water, though the only really pretty views of Kaneohe Bay come near the end. Simply follow North Kalaheo Avenue through Kailua, then pick up Kaneohe Bay Drive, and turn right on Route 836, which curves for miles before linking with Route 83. At Heeia Kea Boat Harbor you can take an hour-long glass bottom boat ride aboard the **Coral Queen** (235-2888).

Kaneohe Bay is renowned for its coral formations and schools of tropical fish that are as brilliantly colored as the coral. This expansive body of water possesses the only barrier reef in Hawaii. Along its shores are ancient Hawaiian fish ponds, rock-bound enclosures constructed by the early Polynesians to raise fresh seafood. Though they once lined the shores of Oahu, today only five remain; four rest along this Windward Coast. As a matter of fact, the largest of all is located at **Heeia State Park** (along Route 836 a few hundred yards before it merges with Route 83). It's an impressive engineering feat that measures 500 feet in length and once contained an 88-acre fish farm. The stone walls in places are 12-feet thick.

High above Kaneohe, gazing down upon the bay, is **Senator Fong's Plantation and Gardens** (47-285 Pulama Road, Kaneohe; 239-6775; admission). Here you can take a narrated tram tour of 725 acres of gardens and orchards. This luxurious preserve was donated by one of Hawaii's most famous U.S. senators, so be prepared to venture from Eisenhower Valley to Kennedy Valley (sugarcane) to the Johnson Plateau (fruit orchards) to Nixon Valley (gardens) to the Ford Plateau (pine trees)!

Route 83 soon becomes known as the Kamehameha Highway as it courses past *taro* patches and lazy fishing boats, then enters **Waiahole Valley** and **Waikane Valley**, the last places on the island where Hawaiian farmers grow crops in the traditional way.

That cone-shaped island offshore is **Chinaman's Hat**. It was named for its resemblance to a coolie cap, though the Hawaiians had another name for it long before the Chinese arrived in the islands. They called it Mokolii Island, or "little dragon," and claimed it represented the tail of a beast that resided under the water. Watch for frigate birds and delicate Hawaiian stilts flying overhead.

Just down the road, the **Old Sugar Mill**, Oahu's first, lies in ruin along the side of the road. Built during the 1860s, it fell into disuse soon after completion and has since served only as a local curiosity.

Three miles later you will arrive at a rock profile that resembles a **Crouching Lion**. To the ancient Hawaiians, who had never experienced the king of the jungle, the stone face was, in fact, that of Kauhi, a demigod from the island of Tahiti.

Next is coral-studded **Kahana Bay**. Then the road, still crowding the coastline, traverses the tiny towns of Punaluu and Hauula. The old **Hauula Door of Faith Church**, a small chapel of clapboard design, is surrounded by palms. Not far from here is another aging woodframe sanctuary, **Hauula Congregational Christian Church**, built of wood and coral back in 1862.

The nearby town of Laie is populated by Mormons. The Hawaii campus of **Brigham Young University** is located here, as well as the **Mormon Temple**. The Mormons settled here back in 1864; today there are about 25,000 in Hawaii. The courtyards and grounds of the temple are open to the public, but only Mormons are permitted to enter the temple sanctuary.

The Mormons also own Oahu's most popular tourist attraction, the **Polynesian Cultural Center** (293-3000; admission). Set right on Kamehameha Highway in Laie, it represents one of the foremost theme parks in the entire Pacific, a 42-acre attempt to re-create ancient Polynesia.

As you wander about the grounds you'll encounter ersatz villages portraying life in the Marquesas, Tahiti, Fiji, Tonga, New Zealand, and old Hawaii. Step over to the Tahitian hamlet and you will experience the rocking *tamure* dance. Or wander onto the islands of Samoa where the local inhabitants demonstrate how to climb coconut trees. In Tonga a native will be beating *tapa* cloth from mulberry bark, while the Fijians are pounding rhythms with poles of bamboo. These mock villages are linked by waterways and can be visited in canoes. The boats will carry you past craftsmen preparing *poi* by mashing *taro* roots and others husking coconuts.

The most popular shows are the "Pageant of the Long Canoes," in which the boats head up a lagoon amid a flurry of singing and dancing, and "This is Polynesia." The latter is an evening show similar to Waikiki's Polynesian

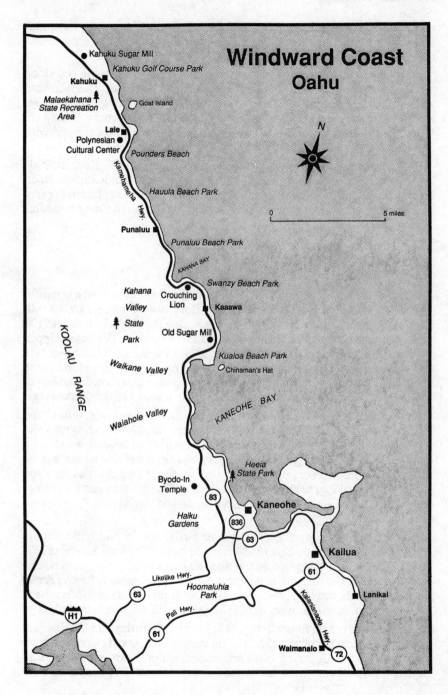

Windward Coast
Oahu

Kahuku Sugar Mill

Kahuku Golf Course Park

Kahuku

Malaekahana State Recreation Area

Goat Island

Laie
Polynesian
Cultural Center

Pounders Beach

Hauula Beach Park

Kamehameha Hwy.

Punaluu

Punaluu Beach Park

KAHANA BAY

Swanzy Beach Park

Kahana
Valley

Crouching
Lion

Kaaawa

State

Park

Old Sugar Mill

Waikane Valley

Kualoa Beach Park

Chinaman's Hat

Waiahole Valley

KOOLAU RANGE

KANEOHE BAY

Heeia State Park

Byodo-In
Temple

83

Kaneohe

Haiku Gardens

836

63

Kailua

Likelike Hwy.

61

Hoomaluhia Park

63

Lanikai

Pall Hwy.

Kalanianaole Hwy.

H1

61

Waimanalo

72

0   5 miles

revues, though generally considered more elaborate. Most of the entertainers and other employees at this Hawaiian-style Disneyland are Mormon students attending the local university.

Be sure to take in the town's natural wonder, **Laie Point**, situated along Anemoku Street, a side road just off Kamehameha Highway. This headland provides extraordinary ocean views sweeping for miles along the shoreline. Since the breezes and surf are wilder here than elsewhere on the Windward Coast, you'll often encounter waves lashing at the two offshore islets with amazing force.

Then the main road goes past the **Kahuku Sugar Mill** (Kahuku; 293-2444), a turn-of-the-century plant that is open for self-guided tours. In an effort to refurbish the old mill, gears and crushers have been painted tropical hues and the entire complex has been turned into an entertaining museum-cum-shopping mall.

WINDWARD COAST HOTELS

Out in the suburban town of Kailua, where trim houses front a beautiful white-sand beach, you'll discover **Kailua Beachside Cottages** (204 South Kalaheo Avenue; 262-4128). Overlooking Kailua Beach Park and about 100 yards from the beach sits a cluster of woodframe cottages. Each is equipped with a full kitchen and cable television. Don't expect the Hilton—only a few cottages have telephones and some of the furniture is nicked, but these duplex units are clean and cozy. They sit in a yard shaded with *hala* and breadfruit trees and provide an excellent bargain at the low end of the deluxe range.

You can't get much closer to the water than **Schrader's Windward Marine Resort** (★) (47-039 Lihikai Drive, Kaneohe; 239-5711). With about 50 units for rent, this unusual resting place consists of several woodframe buildings right on the edge of Kaneohe Bay. There are picnic tables, a pool, and a spa on the two-acre property, as well as a tour boat that can take you snorkeling, kayaking, or sightseeing on the bay. The guest rooms are cottage style with kitchen facilities; many have lanais and bay views. Prices begin in the moderate range.

When you're ready for a week-long meditation in an idyllic setting, consider **The Plantation Spa** (5150 Kamehameha Highway, Kaaawa; 237-8685). Check your hang-ups at the door and enjoy the pool, jacuzzi, and garden grounds, not to mention the backdrop of lush rainforest. Spread across seven acres, this retreat has a guesthouse with private rooms. Most stays are a week in duration; ultra-deluxe in price with all meals included.

If you don't mind funky living, check out the **Countryside Cabins** (53-224 Kamehameha Highway; 237-8169) in Punaluu. These old clapboard structures, complete with fading paint and linoleum floors, are set in beautiful garden surroundings across the street from the ocean. Depending on your taste, you'll find the one-room cottages either claustrophobic or quaint. But no one will find fault with the budget prices on these units and the two-bedroom cottages, or with Margaret Naai, the charming Asian woman who runs this unique establishment.

Just down the road, but a world away, you'll find **Pat's Hotel At Puna-luu** (53-567 Kamehameha Highway; 293-8111), a 136-unit highrise condo on the Punaluu beach. The one-bedroom "lodge" units come complete with lanai, kitchen, washer-dryer, and shower-tub combinations. Brick walls and carpeting create a pleasant atmosphere. Even cozier, however, are the four-plex cottages next to the beach, which house up to four people. "Lodge" accommodations are less expensive. All rooms have an ocean view; the condo also contains a pool, sauna, and exercise room. Moderate to deluxe.

Laniloa Lodge (55-109 Laniloa Street, Laie; 293-9282) is a low-slung motel with two floors of rooms surrounding a swimming pool. This is a standard Coke-machine-in-the-courtyard facility located next to the Poly-nesian Cultural Center. Moderate.

WINDWARD COAST RESTAURANTS

Kailua is a bedroom community with little to offer the adventurer. But since you might find yourself nearby at lunchtime or when returning from the beach, I'll briefly describe a few restaurants. You can try **Times Coffee Shop** (43-3 Oneawa Street, Kailua; 262-7122) for fried rice, hamburger steaks, or sandwiches. Budget.

Saeng's Thai Cuisine (315 Hahani Street, Kailua; 263-9727) is a freshly decorated ethnic restaurant with a hardwood bar and potted plants all around. Located in a strip mall, it nevertheless conveys a sense of elegance. The menu focuses on vegetarian, seafood, and curry dishes. Budget.

It's dinner only at **L'auberge Swiss** (117 Hekili Street, Kailua; 263-4663), a popular local restaurant that serves up fondue, bratwurst, beef stroganoff, wienerschnitzel, and chicken piccata in a red-checkered oilcloth atmo-sphere. Moderate to deluxe.

What sets **The Chart House at Haiku Gardens** (46-336 Haiku Road, Kailua; 247-6671) apart is its idyllic setting. A terraced dining area over-looks sharp cliffs and peaceful flower beds, making this a choice stop for dinner (lunch is served on Friday). Even though the atmosphere here varies from the average Chart House, the menu remains the same: steak, seafood, and prime rib at deluxe prices.

In Kaneohe you might like **Koa Omelette House** (46-126 Kahuhipa Street; 235-5772). Budget in price, it's a tastefully appointed restaurant with a breakfast bill of fare that includes pancakes and crepes suzette and a lunch menu with salads, sandwiches, teriyaki chicken, and seafood.

Or, if you want to take a snack to the beach, check out **Fuji Delicatessen and Restaurant** (45-270 William Henry Road; 235-3690) with its inexpensive sandwiches and Japanese plates.

The **Crouching Lion Inn** (51-666 Kamehameha Highway, Kaaawa; 237-8511), set in a vintage 1927 wood-shingle house, serves sandwiches and hamburgers, mahimahi, and teriyaki steak for lunch. At dinner there's a moderately priced surf-and-turf menu. Enjoying a beautiful ocean view, this attractive complex is popular with tour buses, so try to arrive at an off-hour.

"Paniolo" is Hawaiian for cowboy and the decor at the **Paniolo Café** (53-146 Kamehameha Highway, Punaluu; 237-8521) is a literal translation. Wagon wheels and longhorns set the scene at this steak-and-seafood roadhouse. There's beef brisket (that "melts in your mouth"), beef ribs ("da kine!!"), and country smoked sausage; among the seafood selections—mahimahi, scallops, and black tiger shrimp. Moderate.

There's one restaurant on the Windward Coast that fits the bill when location and price are both important. That's **Banana Beach Bar and Grill** (53-567 Kamehameha Highway; 293-8502). Wicker chairs, *lauhala* wall-hangings, and a windswept patio create an inviting atmosphere; the view at this beachfront establishment adds to the tropical ambience. At dinner there's a surf-and-turf menu, priced from moderate to deluxe, that includes grilled lamb, steak, barbecued ribs, Tahitian shrimp, crab, and the catch of the day. Lunch is served à la carte and features *kalua* pig, stir-fried vegetables, and other Hawaiian specialties.

You won't find shellfish any fresher than at **Royal Hawaiian Shrimp and Prawns** (293-8531), a roadside stand on Kamehameha Highway a few miles northwest of Kahuku. That's because they raise them in those shrimp beds next to the stand, then serve them up steaming and delicious. Budget to moderate.

WINDWARD COAST MARKETS

In Kailua and Kaneohe, you'll encounter large supermarkets. **Times Supermarket** (in Kailua Shopping Center on Kailua Road; 262-2366) and **Foodland** (Windward City Shopping Center at Kamehameha Highway and Kaneohe Bay Drive in Kaneohe; 247-3357) are the most convenient.

For health food, you might try the **Vim and Vigor** store (301-B Hahani Street; 261-4036) in Kailua.

These are good places to stock up, since the next large supermarket is **Lindy's Food** (Hauula Kai Center on Kamehameha Highway; 293-9722) in Hauula.

Between these major shopping complexes there are smaller facilities like the **7-11** (51-484 Kamehameha Highway, Kaaawa; 237-8810).

All along the Kamehameha Highway in Waiahole and Waikane valleys, there are small stands selling **fresh fruit**. The produce is grown right in this lush area and is sold pretty cheaply along the roadside.

You can get fresh fish at **Masa and Joyce Fish Market** (239-6966) in the Temple Valley Shopping Center on the Kahekili Highway (Route 83), just north of Kaneohe.

WINDWARD COAST SHOPPING

Kailua Shopping Center (571 Kailua Road, Kailua; 947-2618) offers a wide range of services at 40 stores. **Kaneohe Shopping Center** (94050 Farrington Highway, Kaneohe; 537-4519) also serves the region with 26 stores. These malls represent the prime shopping opportunities on this side of the island and provide a full assortment of shops.

Up in Punaluu, the **Punaluu Art Gallery** (★) (53-352 Kamehameha Highway; 237-8221) features batik work, calabash bowls, pottery, oil paintings, photography, blown glass, hand-carved candles, and unusual pieces like landscapes made from banana leaves, all by local artists.

WINDWARD COAST NIGHTLIFE

At **Fast Eddie's** (52 Oneawa Street, Kailua; 261-8561) you can dance to disco music in the lounge or listen to recorded music and watch games in the sports bar. There's also karaoke for anyone with the nerve to sing along.

Paniolo Café (53-146 Kamehameha Highway, Punaluu; 237-8521), a get-down, western-style saloon, draws hordes of Windward Coast regulars on Friday, Saturday, and Sunday night. That's when live bands are highlighted; the rest of the week it's jukebox city.

WINDWARD COAST BEACHES AND PARKS

Kualoa Beach Park—You could search the entire Pacific for a setting as lovely as this one. Just 500 yards offshore lies the islet of Mokolii, better known as Chinaman's Hat. Behind the beach the *pali* creates a startling background of fluted cliffs and tropical forest. The beach is a long and narrow strip of sand paralleled by a wide swath of grass parkland. Little wonder this is one of the Windward Coast's most popular picnic areas.

Facilities: Picnic areas, restrooms, and showers. *Swimming:* Good. *Snorkeling:* Good. *Fishing:* Try for papio, bonefish, milkfish, and goatfish.

Camping: Tent camping permitted. County permit required.

Getting there: Located along Kamehameha Highway (Route 83) about ten miles north of Kaneohe.

Swanzy Beach Park, Punaluu Beach Park, and Hauula Beach Park—
These three county facilities lie along Kamehameha Highway (Route 83)
within seven miles of each other. Camping is allowed at all except Punaluu,
but none compare aesthetically with other beaches to the north and south.
Swanzy is located on the highway but lacks a sandy beach; Punaluu, though
possessing a pretty palm-fringed beach, is cramped; and Hauula, a spacious
park with beach, is visited periodically by tour buses. So put these parks
near the bottom of your list, and bring them up only if the other beaches
are too crowded.

Facilities: All three have picnic areas and restrooms; all are within
a few miles of markets and restaurants. *Swimming:* Generally good. *Snorkeling:* Best diving is at Swanzy. *Surfing:* Swanzy has surfing for experts
only at nearby "Crouching Lion" breaks. Hauula's winter breaks are for beginners. *Fishing:* Along this coast the most abundant fish is papio, followed
by bonefish, milkfish, and goatfish.

Camping: Tent and trailer camping allowed at Hauula Beach Park as
well as at Swanzy Beach Park on weekends. County permit required.

Getting there: These parks are all located along Kamehameha Highway (Route 83). Swanzy lies about 12 miles north of Kaneohe, Punaluu is about
four miles north of Swanzy, and Hauula is about three miles beyond that.

Kahana Valley State Park—This 5228-acre paradise, set on a white-
sand beach, offers something for every adventurer. You can pick fruit in
a lush forest, picnic in a coconut grove, and sightsee the ancient Huilua
Fishpond. A 4.9-mile trail leads past old Hawaiian farms deep into the florid
Kahana Valley.

Facilities: Picnic areas, restrooms. Markets and restaurants nearby.
Swimming: Generally good. *Snorkeling:* Poor. *Surfing:* Mediocre. *Fishing:* Good spot for papio, bonefish, milkfish, and goatfish.

Camping: Across the street at Kahana Beach Park. A county permit
is required.

Getting there: Located along Kamehameha Highway (Route 83)
about 14 miles north of Kaneohe.

Kakela Beach—Here's one of the prettiest beaches on the Windward
Coast. With trees and a lawn that extend toward the white-sand beach, it's
a highly recommended spot for day-tripping.

Facilities: Picnic area, restrooms. Restaurants and markets nearby.
Swimming: Good. *Snorkeling:* Mediocre. *Surfing:* Winter breaks up to six
feet, with right and left slide. Bodysurfing is also good. *Fishing:* The most
frequent catch? Papio, then bonefish, goatfish, and milkfish.

Getting there: Located at 55-051 Kamehameha Highway (Route
83) in Laie about 20 miles north of Kaneohe.

How to Beat the Heat with a Sweet Treat

Since the early days of Hawaiian royalty, people have complained about Honolulu's shirt-sticking weather. Come summer, temperatures rise and the trade winds stop blowing. Visitors seeking a golden tan discover they're baking without browning. And residents begin to think that their city, renowned as a cultural melting pot, is actually a pressure cooker.

With the ocean all around, relief is never far away. But a lot of folks, when not heading for the beaches, have found another way to cool off. Shave ice. Known as ice frappes among the Japanese originators and snow cones back on the mainland, these frozen treats are Hawaii's answer to the Good Humor man.

They're made with ice that's been shaved from a block into thin slivers, packed into a cone-shaped cup, and covered with sweet syrup. Health-minded people eat the ice plain, and some folks ask for a scoop of ice cream or sweet black beans (*azuki* beans) underneath the shavings. Most people just order it with their favorite syrup flavors—grape, root beer, cola, cherry, orange, lemon-lime, vanilla, fruit punch, banana, strawberry, or whatever.

Whichever you choose, you'll find it only costs about a buck at the many stands sprinkled around town. Near Waikiki, you might try **Island Snow Hawaii** (2201 Kalakaua Avenue), which has a second location on the Windward coast (130 Kailua Road in Kailua). Watch for stands up on the North Shore, too. No doubt you'll see a long line outside Oahu's most famous shave ice store, **Matsumoto's** (66-087 Kamehameha Highway in Haleiwa).

As a matter of fact, anyplace where the sun blazes overhead you're liable to find someone trying to beat the heat by slurping up a "snow cone" before it melts into mush.

Pounders Beach—Named for the crushing shorebreak that makes it a popular bodysurfing beach, this quarter-mile-long strand features a corridor of white sand and a sandy bottom.

Facilities: None. Restaurants and markets nearby. *Swimming:* Good near old landing at the western end of the beach. *Fishing:* Good for ono, moi, and papio.

Getting there: Located along Kamehameha Highway just north of Kakela Beach.

Hukilau Beach—This privately owned facility fronts a beautiful whitesand beach that winds for more than a mile. Part of the beach is lined with homes, but much of it is undeveloped. Several small islands lie anchored offshore, and the park contains a lovely stand of ironwood trees. All in all this enchanting beach is one of the finest on this side of the island.

Facilities: There are no facilities here, but you'll find both markets and restaurants located nearby. *Swimming:* Good; bodysurfing is also recommended. *Snorkeling:* Fair. *Surfing:* Small waves with left and right slides. *Fishing:* Principal catch is papio; milkfish, bonefish, and goatfish are also frequently caught.

Getting there: Located on Kamehameha Highway (Route 83) in Laie about 22 miles north of Kaneohe.

Malaekahana State Recreation Area and **Goat Island** (★)—This is a rare combination. The Malaekahana facility is one of the island's prettiest parks. It's a tropical wonderland filled with palm, *hala*, and ironwood trees, and graced with a curving, white-sand beach. And then there's Goat Island, just offshore. Simply put, if you visit Oahu and don't explore Goat Island, you'll be missing an extraordinary experience. I hope you'll make an extra effort to get here. It's a small, low-lying island covered with scrub growth and scattered ironwood trees. On the windward side is a coral beach; to leeward lies a crescent-shaped white-sand beach that seems drawn from a South Seas dream. Goat Island (which no longer contains goats) is now a state bird refuge, so you might see wedge-tailed shearwaters nesting. You can camp, picnic, swim, do anything here, as long as you don't disturb the birds. Goat Island will return the favor—there'll be nothing here to disturb you either.

Facilities: Showers, bathrooms, barbecue pits, and electricity in cabins. *Swimming:* Good; the leeward beach is shallow and well-protected. *Snorkeling:* Good. *Surfing:* Long paddle out to winter breaks with left slide. *Fishing:* You may well reel in papio, the most abundant fish along here; goatfish, milkfish, and bonefish are also caught.

Camping: Tent camping. State permit required. There are also very rustic cabins available here. These beachfront units rent from $25 a night (one-bedroom cabin) to $100 a night (six-room cabin). Tent sites are $4 nightly.

Bring your own bedding and cooking gear and be prepared for funky accommodations. For information, call 293-1736.

Getting there: Located on Kamehameha Highway (Route 83) in Laie about 23 miles north of Kaneohe.

Kahuku Golf Course Park—Other than Goat Island, this is about the closest you'll come to a hidden beach on the Windward Coast. Granted, there's a golf course paralleling the strand, but sand dunes hide you from the duffers. The beach is long, wide, and sandy white.

Facilities: Restrooms at the golf course; a restaurant and market are nearby. *Swimming:* Fair, but exercise caution. *Snorkeling:* Poor. *Surfing:* "Seventh Hole" breaks have winter surf up to eight feet. Right and left slide. *Fishing:* Most likely you'll catch some papio, but bonefish, goatfish, and milkfish may turn up, too.

Camping: Unofficial camping perhaps.

Getting there: In Kahuku, about 25 miles north of Kaneohe, turn off Kamehameha Highway (Route 83) toward the ocean. Then walk across the golf course to the beach.

North Shore

Wide, wide beaches heaped with white, white sand roll for miles along the North Shore. Some of them have become famous throughout the world. Not, however, for their size or their sand, but rather because of their waves. If you have ever owned a surfboard, or even a Beach Boys album, you know Waimea Bay and Sunset Beach. The names are synonymous with surfing. They number among the most challenging and dangerous surf spots anywhere. During the winter 15- to 20-foot waves are as common as blond hair and beach buggies. The infamous "Banzai Pipeline," where surfers risk limb and longevity as thunderous waves pass over a shallow reef, is here as well.

Curving in a bowl shape from Kahuku Point in the east to Kaena Point in the west, the coast is backdropped by both Oahu mountain ranges. Most dramatic are the Waianaes, dominated by 4025-foot Mt. Kaala, the island's highest peak.

While the aquatic oriented zero in on the international surfing competitions that occur annually, many other residents work the small farms and ranches that checkerboard the tableland between the mountains and sea. All of them look to Haleiwa, a refurbished plantation town, as their primary gathering place.

Stretching for two miles and averaging 200 feet in width, **Sunset Beach** (Kamehameha Highway) is one of Hawaii's largest strands. When the surf is up you can watch world-class athletes shoot the curl. When it's not, Sunset becomes a great place to swim. The best place to go is **Ehukai Beach Park**, just off Kamehameha Highway about seven miles northeast of Haleiwa. Just 100 yards to the west sits the **Banzai Pipeline** (Ke Nui Road), where a shallow coral shelf creates tubular waves so powerful and perfect they resemble pipes. First surfed in 1957, it lays claim to cracked skulls, lacerated legs, and some of the sport's greatest feats.

On a plateau between Sunset Beach and Waimea Bay is **Puu o Makuha Heiau**, Oahu's oldest temple. A split-level structure built of stone, it once was used for human sacrifices. Today you will encounter nothing more menacing than a spectacular view and perhaps a gentle breeze from the ocean. To get there from Kamehameha Highway, turn left near the Sunset Beach Fire Station on to Pupukea Road, then follow the Hawaii Visitors Bureau signs.

At **Waimea Falls Park** (638-8611; admission), on Kamehameha Highway five miles northeast of Haleiwa, you can wander through a tropical preserve stretching across 1800 acres. Once a Hawaiian village, it is an amazingly luxurious area crisscrossed with hiking trails and filled with archaeological ruins. A tram carries visitors to the waterfalls, where you can swim or picnic. The arboretum in the park features tropical and subtropical trees from around the world. There are also beautiful botanical gardens, including a particularly fascinating one featuring local Hawaiian species. Then there are the birds, caged and wild, that populate the complex; since this nature park serves as a bird sanctuary, it attracts a magnificent assortment.

Across the street looms **Waimea Bay**, another fabled place that sports the largest surfable waves in the world. When surf's up in winter, the monster waves that roll in are so big they make the ground tremble when they break. Salt spray reaches as far as the highway. Thirty-foot waves are not uncommon. Fifty-foot giants have been recorded; though unsurfable, these are not tidal waves, just swells rising along the incredible North Shore. In summer Waimea is a pretty blue bay with a white-sand beach. The water is placid and the area perfect for picnicking and sunbathing. So when you visit Waimea, remember: swim in summer, sunbathe in winter.

Next, the Kamehameha Highway crosses a double-rainbow-shaped bridge en route to **Haleiwa**, an old plantation town with a new facelift. Fortunately, the designers who performed the surgery on this village had an eye for antiquity. They planned it so the modern shopping centers and other facilities blend comfortably into the rural landscape. The community that has grown up around the new town reflects a rare combination of past and future. The old Japanese, Filipinos, and Hawaiians have been joined by blond-mopped surfers and laidback counterculturalists. As a result, this clapboard town with wooden sidewalks has established itself as the "in" spot on the North Shore. Its stylish nonchalance has also proved popular among canny travelers.

From here, head west and pick up Farrington Highway (Route 930). This country road parallels miles of unpopulated beachfront, and arrives

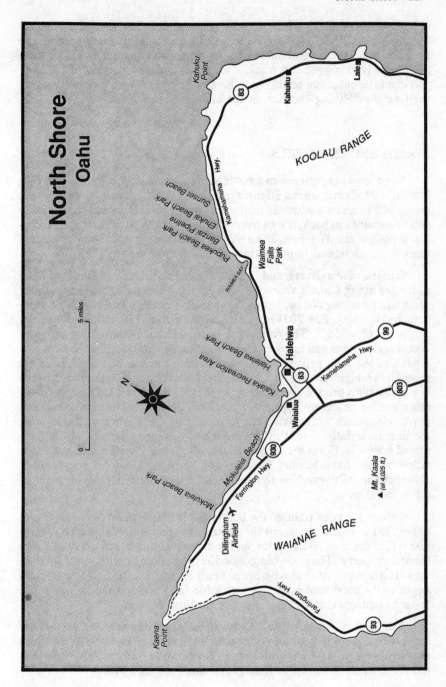

at Dillingham Airfield, where you can take a **glider ride** along the Waianae Mountains (call 677-3404 for information). Beyond this landing strip, the road continues for several miles between ocean and mountains before turning into a very rugged dirt track. Along this unpaved portion of roadway you can hike out about ten miles to **Kaena Point** on Oahu's northwest corner (see the "Hiking" section at the end of this chapter).

NORTH SHORE HOTELS

For a resort experience in a rustic setting, consider the **Turtle Bay Hilton** (57-091 Kamehameha Highway; 293-8811). This rural retreat sprawls across 808 acres on a dramatic peninsula. With a broad beach at the doorstep and mountains out back, it's an overwhelming spot. Add to that riding paths, a golf course, tennis courts, and a pair of swimming pools. Every room features a sea view and is priced in the ultra-deluxe range.

Surfers, scuba divers, and budget-minded travelers will find two ideal addresses along Oahu's vaunted North Shore. Managed by the same folks, and within walking distance of each other are **Vacation Inn** (59-788 Kamehameha Highway; 638-7838) and **Plantation Village** (59-754 Kamehameha Highway; 638-8663). The first consists of a central building that provides hostel-style rooms and features a television lounge and kitchen. There's also a back house with private rooms that share a kitchen and bath. Like the hostel it is budget-priced. Across the street, and directly on the beach, there is a house with private apartments that include their own kitchen and bathroom and are moderate in price. Plantation Village consists of nine restored plantation houses with private kitchens and baths. Set on a landscaped acre, the accommodations rent in the moderate-to-deluxe range, but budget-priced hostel facilities are also available. Both the Vacation Inn and Plantation Village have laundry facilities and barbecue areas for guests. They also sponsor daily activities and provide excellent opportunities for meeting other travelers.

Offering houses right on the beach, **Ke Iki Hale** (59-579 Ke Iki Road; 638-8229) is located between the Banzai Pipeline and Waimea Bay. Here you'll find duplexes, four-plexes, and cottages on an acre-and-a-half of palm-shaded property. They are basic woodframe buildings with plain furnishings. The complex includes barbecue facilities and a volleyball court. Prices begin in the moderate range for streetside facilities and the deluxe range for a beachfront duplex; the cottages are ultra-deluxe.

Turtle Bay Condos (56-565 Kamehameha Highway; 293-2800) has one-, two- and three-bedroom units with kitchen facilities and private lanais that overlook an 18-hole golf course. Studios run $85 to $105; one-bedrooms units sleeping up to four guests are $130 to $145.

NORTH SHORE RESTAURANTS

The Turtle Bay Hilton (57-091 Kamehameha Highway; 293-8811) features three good restaurants. At the **Palm Terrace**, overlooking the hotel's lovely grounds, you'll encounter moderate-priced dining in an attractive environment. The restaurant, serving three meals, offers everything from hamburgers to *saimin* and teriyaki to linguine. Or, for a splurge meal, try **The Cove**. This gourmet establishment, priced deluxe, serves lobster, lamb chops, filet mignon, a seafood gumbo dish, and a host of other delights. The newest addition, Asahi, also priced deluxe, features fine Japanese cuisine (dinner only). Reservations are required at The Cove and Asahi.

When you're around Sunset Beach, **D'Amico's** (59-026 Kamehameha Highway; 638-9611) is quite convenient. It's a roadside restaurant serving pizzas, sandwiches, and other surfer fare.

Otherwise, the best place to chow down is in Haleiwa, the main town on the North Shore. For a fashionable spot overlooking the ocean, try **Jameson's By The Sea** (62-540 Kamehameha Highway; 637-4336). This split-level establishment features a patio downstairs and a formal dining room upstairs. For lunch there are sandwiches, chowders, and fresh fish dishes; at dinner they specialize in seafood. Deluxe in price.

Haleiwa Beach Grill (66-079 Kamehameha Highway; 637-6777), a small café in the center of Haleiwa, is as colorful as coral. Matter of fact, the tropic-hued walls are adorned with carvings of fish from the nearby reefs. Read the menu that's posted on a surfboard and you'll discover fried chicken, grilled sandwiches, burritos, and "islander plates." There are kalbi ribs, shoyu pork, and a mixed grill dish that includes mahimahi. No extra charge for the rock music. Budget.

Steamer's (Haleiwa Shopping Plaza, Kamehameha Highway, Haleiwa; 637-5071) must be one of the world's only condominium restaurants—a two-in-one complex. By day it is Steamer's, a mirror-and-brass-rail dining room with an adjacent patio. Then every evening the terrace becomes **Mario's Italian Caffe**, serving a selection of "pastabilities" that includes fettucine with mahimahi, chicken linguine, and rigatoni bolognese, all at budget prices. In its Steamer's mode the place is a surf-and-turf restaurant with fresh fish (prepared Cajun style, Thai style, or grilled) and assorted beef dishes at moderate prices.

At **Café Haleiwa** (66-460 Kamehameha Highway, Haleiwa; 637-5516) surfers swear by the huevos rancheros, pancakes, and "the Barrel"—a blend of eggs, potatoes, green salsa and cheese wrapped in a tortilla. Located in a century-old building featuring local artwork, surfboards, and surfing memorabilia, this local favorite also serves an excellent quesadilla and grape/cashew salad. Budget.

Surfers also pour into **Kua Aina Sandwich** (66-214 Kamehameha Highway, Haleiwa; 637-6067), where they order hamburgers, fries, and mahimahi sandwiches at the counter, then kick back at one of the roadside tables. Great for light meals, the place is a scene and a half. Budget.

Celestial Natural Foods (66-445 Kamehameha Highway, Haleiwa; 637-6729) has a juice bar and vegetarian restaurant serving sandwiches, soups, and salads.

And **Banzai Bowl** (66-200 Kamehameha Highway, Haleiwa; 637-9122), a small Japanese restaurant, has a selection of Korean plates as well as Japanese dishes, omelettes, and hamburgers. No dinner served. Budget.

Years ago Haleiwa was home to Da Cuppa Kope, a great café and gathering place. Today it has been supplanted by an even better coffeehouse, the **Coffee Gallery** (North Shore Marketplace, 66-250 Kamehameha Highway; 637-5571). In addition to the best cappuccino on the island, this homespun restaurant, decorated with coffee sacks, serves pastries, waffles, bagels, and a variety of sandwiches. Every evening they also offer a special vegetarian dinner. Budget.

NORTH SHORE MARKETS

Haleiwa Supermarket (66-197 Kamehameha Highway, Haleiwa; 637-5004), one of the few large markets on the entire North Shore, is the best place to shop. Out by Sunset Beach you'll find a **Foodland Super Market** (59-720 Kamehameha Highway; 638-8081). There's also **Sunset Beach Store** (59-026 Kamehameha Highway; 638-8207), which has a small stock but is also conveniently located near Sunset Beach.

Celestial Natural Foods (66-445 Kamehameha Highway, Haleiwa; 637-6729) has an ample supply of health foods and fresh produce.

NORTH SHORE SHOPPING

Trendy shoppers head for the burgeoning town of Haleiwa. During the past several years boutiques and galleries have mushroomed throughout this once somnolent town. Now there's a modern shopping center and an array of shops. Since Haleiwa is a center for surfers, it's a good place to buy sportswear and aquatic equipment.

Iwa Gallery (66-119 Kamehameha Highway, Haleiwa; 637-4865) features a stained-glass studio as well as a unique collection of artwork by a number of local artists.

One local painter decorated the walls of **Sunset Hawaii Kid's Store** (Haleiwa Shopping Plaza, Kamehameha Highway, Haleiwa; 637-0474), which makes it worth stopping by even if you don't have kids.

For an excellent selection of women's clothing and accessories, **Pomegranates In The Sun** (637-9260) occupies the same shopping mall.

Tropical Dreams Emporium (66-037 Kamehameha Highway, Haleiwa; 637-7710) offers women's wear and jewelry.

NORTH SHORE NIGHTLIFE

Entertainment is a rare commodity on the North Shore, but you will find contemporary Hawaiian music at the **Bay View** at the Turtle Bay Hilton (57-091 Kamehameha Highway; 293-8811); on Friday and Saturday they feature disco music and charge a cover.

There's disco music every Thursday, Saturday, and Sunday, and a live band each Friday at **Steamer's** (Haleiwa Shopping Plaza, Kamehameha Highway, Haleiwa; 637-5071).

NORTH SHORE BEACHES AND PARKS

Sunset Beach—While Sunset Beach is actually only a single surfing spot, the name has become synonymous with a two-mile-long corridor that includes Banzai Beach and the adjacent Pipeline. I think the best way to do Sunset is by starting from **Ehukai Beach Park**. From here you can go left to the "Banzai Pipeline," where crushing waves build along a shallow coral reef to create tube-like formations. To the right lies "Sunset," with equally spectacular surfing waves.

Facilities: Ehukai Beach Park has picnic areas, restrooms, and showers. Nearby there are also markets and restaurants.   *Swimming:* Fair in summer; extremely dangerous in winter. From September to April, high waves and strong currents prevail. Be careful!   *Snorkeling:* Poor; but some of the island's best snorkeling is at **Pupukea Beach Park**, a marine reserve on Kamehameha Highway six miles northeast of Haleiwa. This 80-acre park, fringed by rocky shoreline, divides into several section. Foremost is "Shark's Cove," located on the north side of the fire station, which contains spectacular tidepools and dive sites.   *Surfing:* This is the place!   *Fishing:* Papio, menpachi, and ulua are common.

Getting there: Ehukai Beach Park is off Kamehameha Highway (Route 83) about seven miles northeast of Haleiwa.

Waimea Bay Beach Park—If Sunset is *one* of the most famous surfing spots in the world, Waimea is *the* most famous. The biggest surfable waves in the world roll into this pretty blue bay. There's a wide white-sand beach and a pleasant park with a tree-studded lawn. It's a marvelous place for picnicking and sunbathing. During the winter crowds often line the beach watching top-notch surfers challenge the curl; in summer the sea is flat and safe for swimming.

Facilities: Picnic area, restrooms, showers, lifeguard. Restaurant and market about a mile away near Sunset Beach.   *Swimming:* Good in summer; extremely dangerous in winter. Good bodysurfing in shorebreak.   *Snorkel-*

ing: Good when the bay is calm. *Surfing:* See above. *Fishing:*Papio, menpachi, and ulua are common.

Getting there: On Kamehameha Highway (Route 83) about five miles northeast of Haleiwa.

Haleiwa Beach Park—This is an excellent refuge from the North Shore's pounding surf. Set in Waialua Bay, the beach is safe for swimming almost all year.

Facilities: Picnic area, restrooms, showers, snack bar, ballfield, basketball court, volleyball courts, and playground. *Swimming:* Good. *Snorkeling:* Fair. *Surfing:* None here but "Haleiwa" breaks are located across Waialua Bay at Alii Beach Park. *Fishing:* The primary catches are papio, menpachi, and ulua.

Getting there: On Kamehameha Highway (Route 83) in Haleiwa.

Kaiaka Recreation Area—The setting at this park is beautiful. There is a secluded area with a tree-shaded lawn and a short strip of sandy beach. A rocky shoreline borders most of this peninsular park, so I'd recommend it more for picnics than water sports.

Facilities: Picnic area, restrooms. Restaurants and markets are nearby in Haleiwa. *Swimming:* Mediocre; rocky bottom. *Snorkeling:* Good. *Surfing:* Poor. *Fishing:* Good area for papio, menpachi, and ulua.

Camping: Permitted.

Getting there: Located on Haleiwa Road just outside Haleiwa.

Mokuleia Beach Park and **Mokuleia Beach** (★)—The 12-acre park contains a sandy beach and large unshaded lawn. An exposed coral reef detracts from the swimming, but on either side of the park lie beaches with sandy ocean bottoms. You'll have to contend with noise from nearby Dillingham Airfield, but the park is an excellent starting point for exploring the unpopulated sections of Mokuleia Beach.

To the west of the park, this beach stretches several miles along a secluded coast. You can hike down the beach or reach its hidden realms by driving farther west along Farrington Highway (Route 930), then turning off onto any of the numerous dirt side roads.

Facilities: Picnic area, restrooms, and showers at the park. Markets and restaurants are several miles away in Haleiwa. *Swimming:* Good, but exercise caution, especially during winter months. *Snorkeling:* Good. *Surfing:* Winter breaks up to ten feet near Dillingham Airfield. Right and left slide. *Fishing:* Common catches include papio, menpachi, and ulua.

Camping: Tent and trailer camping are allowed in the park, with a county permit. Unofficial camping along the undeveloped beachfront is quite common.

Getting there: The beach park is on Farrington Highway (Route 930) about seven miles west of Haleiwa.

Central Oahu

The 1000-foot-high Leilehua Plateau, a bountiful agricultural region planted with sugar and pineapple, extends from the North Shore to the southern reaches of Oahu. Situated in the middle of the island between the Waianae and Koolau ranges, this tableland has become a vital military headquarters. Wheeler Air Force Base, Schofield Barracks, and several other installations occupy large plots of land here.

Wahiawa, a small, grimy city, is the region's commercial hub. Somehow, between the agriculture and the armed forces, I've never found much in this part of Oahu. I usually pass quickly through this area on my way north or south. But there are a few places you might find worth touring.

From Haleiwa south to Wahiawa you can take Route 803, Kaukoahuna Road, a pretty thoroughfare with excellent views of the Waianaes, or follow Route 99, the Kamehameha Highway, which passes through verdant pineapple fields. The **Dole Pineapple Pavilion** (64-1550 Kamehameha Highway; 621-8408), often crowded with tourists, sells (who would have guessed) pineapple products. And the **Pineapple Variety Garden** (Kamehameha Highway and Kamananui Road) displays many different types of the fruit in a garden museum.

The highway also passes near **Kukaniloho** (follow the dirt road across from Whitmore Avenue just north of Wahiawa), a cluster of sacred stones marking the place where Hawaiian royalty gave birth to the accompaniment of chants, drums, and offerings. Studded with eucalyptus trees, this spot has held an important place in Hawaiian mythology and religion for centuries.

For a scenic and historic detour from Route 99, pull up to the sentry station at Schofield Barracks and ask directions to **Kolekole Pass**. On that "day of infamy," December 7, 1941, Japanese bombers buzzed through this notch in the Waianae Range.

You'll be directed through Schofield up into the Waianaes. When you reach Kolekole Pass, there's another sentry gate. Ask the guard to let you continue a short distance farther to the observation point. From here the Waianaes fall away precipitously to a plain that rolls gently to the sea. There's an astonishing view of Oahu's west coast. If you're denied permission to pass the sentry point, then take the footpath that begins just before the gate, leading up the hill. From near the cross at the top, you'll have a partial view of both the Waianaes' western face and the central plateau region.

Wahiawa Botanical Gardens (1396 California Avenue, Wahiawa; 621-7321), spreading across 27 acres, offers a handsome retreat studded with tropical vegetation. There are plants from Africa and Australia, Asian camphor trees, and gum trees from New Guinea.

From Wahiawa, Route H2 provides the fastest means back to Honolulu; the most interesting course is along Route 750, Kunia Road, which skirts the Waianaes, passing sugarcane fields and stands of pine.

Along the way you can take in the **Hawaiian Plantation Village** (94-695 Waipahu Street; 676-6727; admission), a re-created village that spreads across three acres of Waipahu Cultural Park in Waipahu. Comprised of over two dozen buildings, it includes a Japanese Shinto shrine, company store, and a Chinese Society building. Hawaii's many ethnic groups are represented in the houses, which span several architectural periods of the 19th and 20th centuries. Together they provide visitors with a window into traditional life on a sugar plantation.

Leeward Coast

Out along the west coast of Oahu, less than 30 miles from the sands of Waikiki, Hawaiian culture is making a last stand. Here on the tableland that separates the Waianae Range from the ocean, the old ways still prevail. Unlike the cool rainforests of the Windward Coast or the rain-spattered area around Honolulu, this is a region of stark beauty, resembling the American Southwest, with rocky crags and cactus-studded hills.

Hawaiian and Samoan farmers populate the place. Since much of the rest of Oahu has been developed, the Leeward Coast has become the keeper of the old ways. Residents here jealously guard the customs and traditions that they see slipping away in the rest of Hawaii.

Few tourists pass this way and few tourist amenities line the roadway. The scenery consists of farmyards with chicken-wire pens, dusty houses, and sunblasted churches. Sideroads off the main highway often turn to dirt and climb past truck farms and old homesteads. For entertainment there are family luaus, cockfights, and slack-key guitarists.

Travelers who do venture out here have sometimes been hassled by local residents seeking to keep the *malihinis* in Honolulu. But if you are considerate and careful, you should do just fine. This is one of those places that really should be seen, and seen soon, for it too is falling to the forces of change. Ko Olina Resort, the massive complex currently being developed outside Ewa, is only the beginning of the inevitable encroachment along this side of the island.

From Honolulu you can visit the region by traveling west on Route H-1 or Route 90. If you want to tour a prime sugar-growing area, take Route 90 past Pearl Harbor, then turn left on Fort Weaver Road (Route 760). This

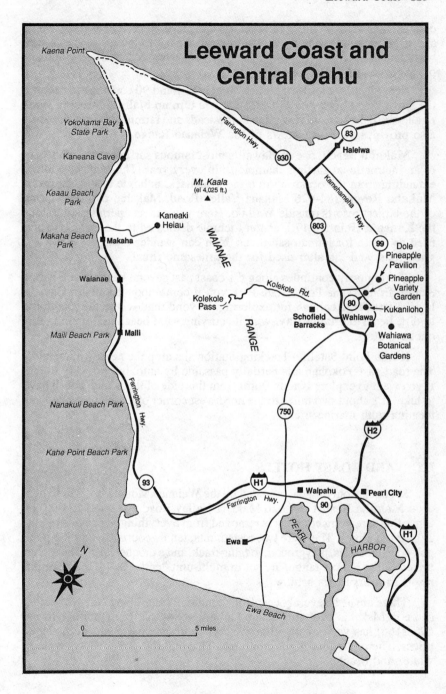

Leeward Coast and Central Oahu

Kaena Point

Yokohama Bay
State Park

Kaneana Cave

Keaau Beach
Park

Kaneaki
Heiau

Makaha Beach
Park

Makaha

Waianae

Maili Beach Park

Maili

Nanakuli Beach Park

Kahe Point Beach Park

Farrington Hwy.

Mt. Kaala
(el 4,025 ft.)

WAIANAE

RANGE

Kolekole Rd.

Kolekole
Pass

Schofield
Barracks

Farrington Hwy.

Halelwa

Kamehameha Hwy.

Dole
Pineapple
Pavilion

Pineapple
Variety
Garden

Kukaniloho

Wahiawa

Wahiawa
Botanical
Gardens

H2

93

H1

Farrington   Hwy.

Waipahu

Pearl City

Ewa

PEARL

HARBOR

H1

Ewa Beach

N

0   5 miles

country lane leads to the plantation town of **Ewa**. With its busy sugar mill and trim houses, Ewa is an enchanting throwback to the days when sugar was king. This town is a slow, simple place, perfect for wandering and exploring.

Near Oahu's southwest corner, Routes H-1 and 90 converge to become the Farrington Highway (Route 93). If you turn up Mailiilii Street in **Waianae**, you'll pass placid Hawaiian homesteads and farmlands. This side road also provides sweeping views of the Waianae Range.

Makaha Beach, one of Hawaii's most famous surfing spots, is the site of an international surfing championship every year. The Makaha Valley, extending from the ocean up into the Waianaes, is home to the **Sheraton Makaha Resort** (84-626 Makaha Valley Road, Makaha; 695-9511), one of the largest resorts outside Waikiki. Here you can ask permission to tour the **Kaneaki Heiau**, a 17th-century temple dedicated to the god Lono and used as a site for human sacrifices. You can wander past prayer towers, grass huts, and the altar used for the gruesome ritual.

The highway continues along the coast past several beaches and parks. Across from Kaena Point State Park you'll come upon **Kaneana Cave**, a lava cavern large enough for exploring. Beyond that, where the road turns to dirt, lies **Yokohama Bay**, with its curving sand beach and inviting turquoise waters.

Kaena Point Satellite Tracking Station sits atop the nearby mountains. The road past Yokohama is partially passable by auto, but it's very rough. If you want to explore **Kaena Point** from this side of the island, you'll have to hike. It's about two miles to the northwest corner of Oahu, past tidepools teeming with marine life.

LEEWARD COAST HOTELS

Set back from the sea, bounded by the Waianae Mountains, is the **Sheraton Makaha Resort** (84-626 Makaha Valley Road, Makaha; 695-9511). Since this sprawling complex is removed from everything, it provides a host of guest facilities. There are two restaurants, tennis courts, swimming pool, golf course, stables, playground, jogging track, and a croquet lawn. The rooms, priced in the deluxe range, are set in multi-unit "cottages." It's a beautiful resort in a luxurious setting.

There are also several oceanfront condominiums along Oahu's western shore in Makaha: **Makaha Beach Cabanas** (84-965 Farrington Highway; 696-2166) has very small, attractive one-bedroom apartments at moderate prices. There is a four-night minimum. This highrise condo fronts a pretty white-sand beach.

Makaha Surfside (85-175 Farrington Highway; 696-6325) offers one-bedroom units at ultra-deluxe prices. This sprawling facility fronts a rocky beach and has two swimming pools, a sauna, and a jogging path. Four-day minimum.

Makaha Valley Towers (end of Kili Drive, Makaha; 695-9055) is a highrise set along the slopes of Makaha Valley. The minimum stay is one week with rates for a studio unit starting at $350 for seven days.

LEEWARD COAST RESTAURANTS

This sparsely populated strip of shoreline has several dining spots. All are located on Farrington Highway, the main road, and most are in the town of Waianae. Within a short distance of one another are **Cathay Inn Chop Suey** (86-088 Farrington Highway; 696-9477), a good choice for Chinese cuisine, and **Hannara Restaurant** (85-888 Farrington Highway; 696-6137) for Korean and Hawaiian food. Budget to moderate.

Nearby **E. J.'s Pizza** (85-773 Farrington Highway; 696-9676) operates from a tiny roadside stand, but the owners boast that they'll "make you a pizza you can't refuse." They might just be right; not only is the food delicious, it's cheap too. In addition to pizzas, E. J.'s also serves Mexican snacks and sandwiches at budget prices.

Salvatore's By the Sea (87-064 Farrington Highway, Waianae; 696-6121) sports an ocean view and a mixed local/tourist clientele. Serving breakfast, lunch, and dinner, this moderate-priced eatery offers up pasta, steak, and seafood dishes. For decoration there are television sets (television sets?) and potted plants.

Out at the luxurious Sheraton Makaha Resort (84-626 Makaha Valley Road, Makaha; 695-9511) there are two restaurants. The **Pikake Café**, overlooking the pool and golf course, serves lunch and dinner at moderate prices. In the evening guests also adjourn to the **Kaala Dining Room**, a vaulted-ceiling structure surrounded by plate glass. The cuisine at this deluxe-priced gathering place includes lobster, prime rib, teriyaki chicken, scallops, rack of lamb, and filet mignon.

LEEWARD COAST MARKETS

Big Way Supermarket (Waianae Mall Shopping Center, 86-120 Farrington Highway; 696-4271), located in Waianae, is the prime spot in this area for shopping.

LEEWARD COAST NIGHTLIFE

The **Lobby Lounge** at the Sheraton Makaha Resort (84-626 Makaha Valley Road, Makaha; 695-9511) features a Hawaiian soloist Wednesday and Thursday evenings and karaoke singing on Friday and Saturday.

LEEWARD COAST BEACHES AND PARKS

Hawaiian Electric Beach Park—This once privately owned park, across the highway from a monstrous power plant, is now run by the county. There's a rolling lawn with palm and *kiawe* trees, plus a white-sand beach and coral reef. The drawbacks are the lack of facilities and the park's proximity to the electric company.

Facilities: There's a picnic area. *Swimming:* Good. *Snorkeling:* Good. *Surfing:* Small breaks year-round with right slide. *Fishing:* Common catches include papio, ulua, moano, and menpachi.

Camping: Not allowed here; but tent and trailer camping are okay at nearby **Kahe Point Beach Park**, with a county permit.

Getting there: The park is located on Farrington Highway (Route 93) about seven miles south of Waianae.

Nanakuli Beach Park—This park is so large that a housing tract divides it into two parts. The main section features a white-sand beach, *kiawe*-studded camping area, and a recreation complex. It's simply a park with everything, unfortunately including weekend crowds.

Facilities: Picnic areas, restrooms, showers, ballfield, basketball court, and playground; information, 668-1137. *Swimming:* Good. *Snorkeling:* Good. *Surfing:* Winter breaks; right and left slide. *Fishing:* Frequently seen are papio, ulua, moano, and menpachi.

Camping: Tent and trailer camping are allowed, but a county permit is required.

Getting there: On Farrington Highway (Route 93) about five miles south of Waianae.

Maili Beach Park—A long winding stretch of white sand is the high point of this otherwise unimpressive facility. The park contains shade trees and a spotty lawn.

Facilities: Restrooms and showers. Market and restaurant are nearby. *Swimming:* Good. *Snorkeling:* Fair. *Surfing:* Winter breaks; right slide. *Fishing:* Principal game fish are papio, ulua, menpachi, and moano.

Camping: Not permitted here, but tent camping, with a county permit, is allowed in the summer at nearby **Lualualei Beach Park**.

Getting there: Located on Farrington Highway (Route 93) in Maili a few miles south of Waianae.

Makaha Beach Park—Some of the finest surfing in the world takes place right offshore here. This is the site of international competitions, drawing championship surfers from all across the Pacific. For more relaxed sports, there's a white-sand beach to sunbathe on and some good places to skindive. The precipitous Waianae Mountains loom behind the park.

Facilities: Picnic tables, restrooms, showers. A market and restaurant are nearby. *Swimming and Snorkeling:* Both are good when the sea is calm; otherwise, exercise extreme caution. *Surfing:* Terrific. *Fishing:* Primary game fish caught here are papio, ulua, moano, and menpachi.

Getting there: Located on Farrington Highway (Route 93) in Makaha, two miles north of Waianae.

Keauu Beach Park—Except for the absence of a sandy beach, this is the prettiest park on the west coast. It's a long, narrow grassy plot spotted with trees and backdropped by the Waianaes. Sunsets are spectacular here, and on a clear day you can see all the way to Kauai. There's a sandy beach just west of the park. Unfortunately, a coral reef rises right to the water's edge, hindering water sports other than snorkeling.

Facilities: Picnic area, restrooms, showers. Markets and restaurants are several miles away in Waianae. *Swimming:* Good, but entry into the water is difficult. Bodysurfing is also good. *Snorkeling:* Very good. *Surfing:* Good summer breaks; left slide. *Fishing:* Principal catches are papio, ulua, moano, and menpachi.

Camping: Tent and trailer. County permit required.

Getting there: Located on Farrington Highway (Route 93) about five miles north of Waianae.

Yokohama Bay State Park (★)—This curving stretch of white sand is the last beach along Oahu's northwest coast. With the Waianae Range in the background and coral reefs offshore, it's a particularly lovely spot. Though officially a state park, the area is largely undeveloped. You can walk from Yokohama past miles of tidepools to Oahu's northwest corner at Kaena Point. Yokohama Bay is a prime region for beach lovers and explorers both.

Facilities: Restrooms, showers. *Swimming:* Good when the sea is calm, but exercise extreme caution if the surf is up. *Snorkeling:* Excellent if the sea is calm. *Surfing:* Summer breaks up to 15 feet over a shallow reef; left slide. *Fishing:* Principal game fish caught in this area are papio, ulua, moano, and menpachi.

Getting there: Yokohama Bay State Park is located at the end of the paved section of Farrington Highway (Route 93), about nine miles north of the town of Waianae.

The Sporting Life

CAMPING

Along with its traffic and crowds, Oahu has numerous parks. Unfortunately, these disparate elements overlap, and you may sometimes find you've escaped from Honolulu's urban jungle and landed in a swamp of weekend beachgoers. So it's best to plan outdoor adventures far in advance and to schedule them for weekdays if possible.

Camping at **county parks** requires a permit. Tent camping is permitted every night except Wednesday and Thursday; there are no trailer hook-ups. Permits can be obtained from the Department of Parks and Recreation, Honolulu Municipal Building, 650 South King Street, Honolulu, HI 96813 (587-0300) or at any of the "satellite city halls" around the island.

State park permits are free. They allow camping for five days and work on a first-come, first-served basis. They are issued by the Division of State Parks, 1151 Punchbowl Street, Room 310, Honolulu, HI 96813 (548-7455). You can also write in advance for permits.

Remember when planning your trip, rainfall is heaviest on the Windward Coast, a little lighter on the North Shore, and lightest of all on the Leeward Coast.

For camping equipment, check with **Omar The Tent Man**. Located at 650 Kakoi Street (836-8785) in Honolulu, Omar rents and sells supplies. The following Honolulu sporting goods stores also sell gear: **The Bike Shop** (1149 South King Street; 531-7071) and **Honsport** (Ala Moana Center, 1450 Ala Moana Boulevard; 949-5591).

SKINDIVING

One of the great myths about Hawaii is that you need to go far off the beaten track to discover its secret treasures. The fact is that within half an hour of Waikiki are excellent snorkeling and diving opportunities. Only an hour away are excellent reefs easily reached by dive boats. From popular Hanauma Bay, just a short ride from the heart of Honolulu, to Kahe Point on the Leeward Coast, there are snorkeling and diving opportunities for beginners and certified pros alike. Because conditions vary, I strongly recommended seeking instruction and advice from local diving experts before setting out.

The **Haleiwa Surf Center** (Haleiwa-Alii Beach Park, Haleiwa; 637-5051) teaches such sports as snorkeling, surfing, swimming, lifesaving, windsurfing, and sailing. This county agency is also an excellent source of information on island water sports and facilities.

In addition, many shops rent and sell skindiving equipment and offer underwater tours. **South Seas Aquatics** (870 Kapahulu Avenue #109, Honolulu; 735-0437) features dives off a custom 38-foot dive boat. **Aqua Blue** (1050 Ala Moana Boulevard; 521-9459) conducts introductory diving lessons and rents equipment and underwater cameras. **Aloha Dive Shop** (Koko Marina Shopping Center, 7192 Kalanianaole Highway, Hawaii Kai; 395-5922) runs courses for certified divers and students at Maunalua Bay in the southeast corner of the island. Beginning lessons are taught at Hanauma Bay. **Hawaii Sea Adventures** (98-728 Moanalua Road, Pearl City; 487-7515; and 46 Hoolai Street, Kailua; 263-2311) features lessons as well as half- and full-day trips and charters. At **Aaron's Dive Shop** (602 Kailua Road, Kailua; 261-1211) you can choose between beach and boat dives, as well as special night trips. Up in the North Shore town of Haleiwa, check out **Surf 'n Sea** (62-595 Kamehameha Highway; 637-9887). During the spring and summer they offer beach dives on the North Shore and Windward Coast. There are also year-round dive trips to the shipwreck *Mahi* located off the Leeward Coast.

SURFING AND WINDSURFING

Surfing, a sport pioneered centuries ago by Hawaiian royalty, is synonymous with Oahu. Stars bring their boards from all over the world to join international competitions that take advantage of ideal surf and wind conditions. From the 30-foot winter rollers on the North Shore to beginner lessons off Waikiki, this is beach boy and girl territory. Windsurfing is equally popular in areas like Kailua Bay and along the North Shore.

If you'd like to surf Waikiki, you can rent a board from **Prime Time Rentals** (949-8952) on Fort De Russy Beach, **Waikiki Beach Services** (in front of the Outrigger Reef Hotel; 924-4940), or the **Aloha Beach Service** (in front of the Sheraton Moana Surfrider Hotel; 922-3111).

Kailua Sailboard Company (130 Kailua Road; 262-2555) will teach you the tricks of the trade or help you brush up on your technique. Rentals are also available here. In the same area **Naish Hawaii** (155A Hamakua Drive; 261-6067) offers lessons and rentals. This company manufactures its own boards and also operates a shop filled with the latest in sailboarding apparel and accessories.

A resource for both the participatory and spectator aspects of surfing and windsurfing is the **Haleiwa Surf Center** (Haleiwa-Alii Beach Park, Haleiwa; 637-5051) on the North Shore. Surf lessons normally run September through early May and windsurfing is taught from May through early September. In the same area surfing lessons and rentals are also available from **Surf and Sea** (62-595 Kamehameha Highway, Haleiwa; 637-9887).

A number of stores located in different parts of the island also rent boards and sails: **Local Motion** (1714 Kapiolani Boulevard, Honolulu; 955-7873), **Downing Hawaii** (3021 Waialae Avenue, Honolulu; 737-9696), and **Windsurfing Hawaii** (155-A Hamakua Drive, Kailua; 261-3539).

FISHING

From deep sea-fishing to trolling for freshwater bass, Oahu offers challenges to suit any angler. You can try game fishing out in the Pacific, head down to the beach for surf casting, or try one of the island's popular lakes.

A good way to catch marlin, mahimahi, yellowfin, and ono is to head out 20 to 30 miles off the Leeward Coast. There are also prime fishing grounds off the south coast of Oahu. Most of the island's fishing fleet dock at Kewalo Basin (Fisherman's Wharf) on Ala Moana Drive between Waikiki and Downtown Honolulu.

Among the outfits you'll find **Coreene-C Sport Fishing Charters** (Kewalo Basin, Honolulu; 536-7472), which fishes the Leeward Coast and the waters off Molokai. Departing on similar trips from Kewalo Basin is **Island Charters** (536-1555). Also consider **Ilima V Charter Fishing** (521-2087) and **Golden Eagle Marine Charter Services** (531-4966), which also tie up in Kewalo Basin.

For freshwater angling head up into the Koolau Mountains to fish the **Nuuanu Reservoir**. Another possibility is the **Wahiawa Public Fishing Area**. Both of these reservoirs are good places to catch Chinese catfish.

SAILING

One of the best ways to enjoy Oahu is aboard a sailboat. From brief cruises off Honolulu to a day-long charter along the North Shore, this is the perfect antidote to the tourist crowds. It's also surprisingly affordable.

Honolulu Sailing Company (47-335 Lulani Street; 239-3900) and the beach stands in front of Hilton Hawaiian Village in Waikiki sponsor cruises, whale watching trips, and interisland sailing. **Kono Charters Ltd.** (Kewalo Basin, Honolulu; 521-5660) offers sunset cruises and half-day and full-day trips featuring swimming and snorkeling opportunities aboard the 67-foot sailing cutter *Tchaika*. **Above Heaven's Gate** (41-010 Wailea Street, #2, Waimanalo; Keehi Lagoon, Honolulu; 259-5429) operates charter group cruises to the Diamond Head reef area aboard a 56-foot teakwood pirate ship. You can also take a guided Hobie cat tour off the Windward Coast to undiscovered islands most tourists miss. Along the way you'll enjoy Waimanalo, Lanikai, and Kailua Bay. You can also learn how to sail this swift 16-foot craft.

If you're eager to charter your own yacht, contact **The Yacht Connection** (1060 Young Street, Suite 210, Honolulu; 523-1383). The company charters all sizes of vessels ranging from fishing boats to luxury yachts.

KAYAKING

A sport well suited for Oahu, kayaking is an ideal way to explore the island's protected bays, islands, and inland rivers. **Kailua Sailboard Company** (130 Kailua Road, Kailua; 262-2555) and **Two Good Kayak Hawaii**

(171-B Hamakua Drive, Kailua; 262-5656) offer kayaking trips that explore the beautiful islands of Kailua Bay.

To rent or purchase kayaks and equipment, consider **Go Bananas** (732 Kapahulu Avenue; 737-9514) just outside Waikiki and **'Cuda Kayaks** (789 Kailua Road, Kailua; 261-8424) on the Windward Coast.

HORSEBACK RIDING

Located on the Windward Coast across from Chinaman's Hat, **Kualoa Ranch** (49-560 Kamehameha Highway, Kaaawa; 237-8515) leads one- and two-hour rides in Kaaawa Valley. A longer, four-and-a-half-hour trip includes a visit to a hidden beach near an ancient Hawaiian fish pond. Don't forget your swimsuit.

Two large resorts, the **Turtle Bay Hilton** (293-8811) on the North Shore and **Sheraton Makaha Resort** (695-9511) on the Leeward Coast, have riding programs for guests and the general public.

GOLF

For a round of golf in Honolulu, try the **Ala Wai Golf Course** (404 Kapahulu Avenue; 296-4653), Hawaii's first municipal course, or the **Hawaii Kai Championship Golf Course** (8902 Kalanianaole Highway; 395-2358), a popular spot with both tourists and *kamaainas*.

Over on the Windward Coast, the lush **Olomana Golf Links** (41-1801 Kalanianaole Highway, Waimanalo; 259-7926) has an 18-hole course. For a cheap round of golf ($5!) visit the **Bay View Golf Center** (45-285 Kaneohe Bay Drive, Kaneohe; 247-0451). Located below the Nuuanu Pali Lookout, the **Pali Golf Course** (45-050 Kamehameha Highway, Kaneohe; 261-9784) affords sweeping views of the rugged Koolaus and the windward coastline. If you want to play an inexpensive, casual game, try the nine-hole **Kahuku Golf Course** (Kahuku; 293-5842).

On the North Shore, two 18-hole courses are open to the public at the **Turtle Bay Hilton** (Kahuku; 293-8811). The newer of the two courses was designed by golf professional Arnold Palmer.

Set amid fields of sugarcane and pineapple along the Leilehua Plateau in the center of Oahu, the **Hawaii Country Club** (98-1211 Kunia Road, Wahiawa; 622-1744) is a bit run-down, but offers some challenging holes. The **Mililani Golf Club** (95-176 Kuahelani Avenue, Mililani; 623-2254), though not particularly demanding, provides lovely views of the Koolau and Waianae ranges. The flat **Ted Makalena Golf Course** (93-059 Waipio Point Access Road, Waipahu; 296-7888) is not well maintained, but is still popular with locals.

Out toward the Leeward Coast, a series of lakes, brooks, and waterfalls meanders through the 18 holes at **Ko Olina Golf Course** (3733 Alii Drive, west of Makakilo; 676-5309). Bounded by the Waianae Range, the beautiful

Sheraton Makaha West Golf Course (84-626 Makaha Valley Road, Makaha; 695-9544) is among Oahu's foremost courses.

TENNIS

Many Oahu resorts offer complete tennis facilities. But don't despair if your hotel lacks nets. There are dozens of public tennis courts around the island.

In the Waikiki area, try **Kapiolani Park** (Kalakaua Avenue), **Diamond Head Tennis Center** (Paki Avenue), and **Ala Moana Regional Park** (Ala Moana Boulevard). Greater Honolulu courts include those at **Keehi Lagoon** (off the Nimitz Highway, Honolulu) and **Manoa Valley District Park** (2721 Kaaipu Avenue, Manoa).

For your tennis needs on the Windward Coast, try **Kailua District Park** (21 South Kainalu Drive, Kailua) or **Kaneohe District Park** (45-660 Keaahala Road, Kaneohe). **Sunset Beach Neighborhood Park** (59-360 Kamehameha Highway, Haleiwa), with two lighted courts, is an option on the North Shore. Lighted courts are also available at **Waianae District Park** (85-471 Farrington Highway, Waianae) on the Leeward Coast.

Call the County Department of Parks and Recreation (523-4182) for more information on public courts, or the Hawaii Visitors Bureau (923-1811) for private courts.

BICYCLING

Oahu is blessed with excellent roads, well-paved and usually flat, and cursed with heavy traffic. About three-quarters of Hawaii's population lives here, and it sometimes seems like every person owns a car.

Honolulu can be a cycler's nightmare, but outside the city the traffic is somewhat lighter. And Oahu drivers, accustomed to tourists driving mopeds, are relatively conscious of bicyclists.

Keep in mind that the Windward Coast is the wet side, the North Shore is slightly drier, and the south and west coasts are the driest of all. And remember, rip-offs are a frequent fact of life on Oahu. Leaving your bike unlocked is asking for a long walk back.

If you'd like a little two-wheeled company, check out the **Hawaii Bicycling League** (Box 4403, Honolulu, HI 96812; 735-5756), which regularly sponsors bike rides.

RENTALS In Waikiki **Aloha Funway Rentals** (1984 Kalakaua Avenue; 942-9696) and **Blue Sky Rentals** (1920 Ala Moana Boulevard; 947-0101) both rent bicycles.

REPAIRS The following shops do repair work, plus sell bikes and accessories: **Eki Cyclery** (1603 Dillingham Boulevard, Honolulu; 847-2005), **The Bike Shop** (1149 South King Street, Honolulu; 531-7071), **Hawaiian**

Island Creations (354 Hahani Street, Kailua; 261-9213), and **Waipahu Bicycle** (94-320 Waipahu Depot Street, Waipahu; 671-4091).

HIKING

There are numerous hiking trails within easy driving distance of Honolulu. I have listed these as well as trails in the Windward Coast and North Shore areas. Unfortunately, many Oahu treks require special permission from the state, the armed services, or private owners. But you should find that the hikes suggested here, none of which require official sanction, will provide ample adventure.

To hike with a group or to obtain further information on hiking Oahu, contact the **Sierra Club** (212 Merchant Street, Room 201, Honolulu, HI 96813; 538-6616) or the **Hawaii Trail and Mountain Club** (P.O. Box 2238, Honolulu, HI 96804). Both agencies sponsor hikes regularly.

GREATER HONOLULU TRAILS If you're staying in Waikiki, the most easily accessible hike is the short jaunt up **Diamond Head** crater. There's a sweeping view of Honolulu from atop this famous landmark. The trail begins inside the crater, so take Diamond Head Road around to the inland side of Diamond Head, then follow the tunnel leading into the crater.

In the Koolau Mountains above Diamond Head there are two parallel trails that climb almost 2000 feet and afford excellent views of the Windward Coast. The head of **Wiliwilinui Trail** (3 miles long) can be reached by taking the Kalanianaole Highway (Routes H-1 and 72) east past the Kahala Mall Shopping Center. Then turn left on Laukahi Street and follow it a couple of miles to the top of the road. To get to **Lanipo Trail** (3 miles), located to the west of Wiliwilinui, take Waialae Avenue off Route H-1. Then turn up Wilhelmina Road and follow it to Maunalani Circle and the trailhead.

For spectacular views of the lush Palolo and Manoa Valleys, you can hike **Waahila Ridge Trail** (2 miles). To get there, take St. Louis Heights Drive (near the University of Hawaii campus) and then follow connecting roads up to Waahila Ridge State Recreation Area.

Another hike, along **Manoa Falls Trail** (0.8 mile), leads right through Manoa Valley. This is a pleasant jaunt that follows Waihi Stream through a densely vegetated area to a charming waterfall.

Manoa Cliffs Trail (3 miles), a pleasant family hike, follows a precipice along the west side of Manoa Valley. And **Puu Ohia Trail** (2 miles), which crosses Manoa Cliffs Trail, provides splendid views of the Manoa and Nuuanu valleys. Both trails begin from Tantalus Drive in the hills above Honolulu.

Makiki Valley Trail (1.1 miles) begins near Tantalus Drive. Composed of three interlinking trails, this loop passes stands of eucalyptus and bamboo trees and offers some sweeping views of Honolulu.

Another loop trail, **Judd Memorial** (1.3 miles), crosses Nuuanu Stream and traverses bamboo, eucalyptus, and Norfolk pine groves en route to the Jackass Ginger Pool. To get there, take the Pali Highway (Route 61) several miles north from Honolulu. Turn onto Nuuanu Pali Drive and follow it about a mile to Reservoir Number Two spillway.

Another hike in this general area, along **Waimano Trail** (7 miles), climbs 1600 feet to an astonishing vista point above Oahu's Windward Coast. There are swimming holes en route. To get there, take Kamehameha Highway (Route 90) west to Waimano Home Road (Route 730). Turn right and go two-and-a-half miles to a point along the road where you'll see a building on the right and an irrigation ditch on the left. The trail follows the ditch.

SOUTHEAST OAHU TRAILS   There are several excellent hikes along this shore. The first few are within 10 miles of Waikiki, near **Hanauma Bay**. From the beach at Hanauma you can hike two miles along the coast and cliffs to the Halona Blowhole. This trek passes the Toilet Bowl, a unique tidepool with a hole in the bottom that causes it to fill and then flush with the wave action. Waves sometimes wash the rocks along this path, so be prepared to get wet (and be careful!).

At the intersection where the short road leading down toward Hanauma Bay branches from Kalanianaole Highway (Route 72), there are two other trails. **Koko Head Trail**, a one-mile hike to the top of a volcanic cone, starts on the ocean side of the highway. This trek features some startling views of Hanauma Bay, Diamond Head, and the Koolau Range. Another one-mile hike, along **Koko Crater Trail**, leads from the highway up to a 1208-foot peak. The views from this crow's nest are equally spectacular.

WINDWARD COAST TRAILS   There are several other particularly pretty hikes much farther north, near the village of Hauula. **Sacred Falls Trail** (2.2 miles) gently ascends through a canyon and arrives at a waterfall and swimming hole. The trailhead for this popular trek is near Kamehameha Highway (Route 83) just south of Hauula.

Then, in Hauula, if you turn off Kamehameha Highway and head inland about a quarter-mile up Hauula Homestead Road, you'll come to Maakua Road. Walk up Maakua Road, which leads into the woods. About 300 yards after entering the woods, the road forks. Maakua Gulch Trail branches to the left. If you continue straight ahead you'll be on Hauula Trail, but if you veer left onto Maakua Gulch Trail, you'll encounter yet another trail branching off to the left in about 150 yards. This is Papapli Trail (also known as Maakua Trail).

Maakua Gulch Trail (3 miles), en route to a small waterfall, traverses a rugged canyon with extremely steep walls. Part of the trail lies along the stream bed, so be ready to get wet. **Hauula Trail** (2.5 miles) ascends along two ridges and provides fine vistas of the Koolau Range and the Windward

Coast. **Papali Trail** (2.5 miles) drops into Papali Gulch, then climbs high along a ridge from which you can view the surrounding countryside.

NORTH SHORE AND LEEWARD COAST TRAILS   In the mountains above Pearl Harbor, at Keaiwa Heiau State Park, you'll find the **Aiea Loop Trail** (4.8 miles). Set in a heavily forested area, this hike passes the wreckage of a World War II cargo plane. It provides an excellent chance to see some of the native trees—*lehua*, *ohia*, and *koa*—used by local woodworkers. (For directions to the state park, see the "Leeward Coast" section in this chapter.)

You can approach the trail to **Kaena Point** either from the North Shore or the Leeward Coast. It's a dry, rock-strewn path that leads to Oahu's northwest tip. There are tidepools and swimming spots en route, plus spectacular views of a rugged, uninhabited coastline. To get to the trailhead, just drive to the end of the paved portion of Route 930 on the North Shore or Route 93 on the Leeward Coast. Then follow the jeep trail out to Kaena Point. Either way, it's about a two-mile trek.

Transportation

BY AIR

There's one airport on Oahu and it's a behemoth. **Honolulu International Airport** is a Pacific crossroads, an essential link between North America and Asia. Most visitors arriving from the mainland land here first, and find it a convenient jumping-off point for venturing farther to the various neighbor islands. Aloha Airlines and Hawaiian Airlines provide regular jet service to the outer islands, while smaller outfits like Aloha Island Air and Air Molokai fly prop planes.

Honolulu International includes all the comforts of a major airport. Here you can check your bags or rent a locker; fuel up at a restaurant, coffee shop, or cocktail lounge; shop at any of several stores; or shower.

If you have spare time, stop by the **Pacific Aerospace Museum** (second floor; 839-0777; admission), a technology exhibition devoted to aviation and the islands. Here you can climb into a cockpit simulator and "fly" a plane, watch a 3-D movie, or view a model of the space shuttle.

To cover the eight or so miles into town, it's possible to hire a cab for approximately $13, plus a small charge for each bag. For $5, **Airport Motorcoach** (839-0911) will take you to your hotel or condominium. And city bus #19 or #20 travels through Downtown Honolulu and Waikiki. This is the cheapest transportation, but you're only allowed to carry on baggage that fits on your lap. So, unless you're traveling very light, you'll have to use another conveyance.

CAR RENTALS

Of all the islands, Oahu offers the most rental agencies. At the airport, **Avis Rent A Car** (834-5536), **Budget Rent A Car** (836-1700), **Dollar Rent A Car** (831-2330), and **Hertz Rent A Car** (831-3500) all have booths. Their convenient location helps to save time while minimizing the problem of picking up your car.

Several other outfits provide airport pick-up service. These include **Alamo Rent A Car** (833-4585), **Five-O Rent A Car** (836-1028), **Thrifty Rent A Car** (836-2388), **Tropical Rent A Car** (957-0800), and **World Rent A Car** (833-1866).

There are many other Honolulu-based companies offering very low rates but providing limited pick-up service at the airport. I've never found the inconvenience worth the savings. There you are—newly arrived from the mainland, uncertain about your environment, anxious to check in at the hotel— and you're immediately confronted with the Catch-22 of getting to your car. Do you rent a vehicle in which to pick up your rental car? Take a bus? Hitchhike? What do you do with your bags meanwhile?

If your budget is important, consider one of the following cheaper but less convenient outfits: **Honolulu Ford** (531-0491), **Sears Rent A Car** (599-2205), or **VIP Car Rental** (922-4605).

If you prefer to go in high style, rent a Rolls Royce from **Cloud Nine** (524-7999) or a vintage car at **Cruisin' Classics** (951-8331). **Aloha Funway Rentals** (1984 Kalakaua Avenue; 942-9696) rents Corvettes.

JEEP RENTALS

Dollar Rent A Car (831-2330) and **VIP Car Rental** (922-4605) provide jeeps.

MOTOR SCOOTER AND MOTORCYCLE RENTALS

Aloha Funway Rentals (1984 Kalakaua Avenue; 942-9696) rents scooters, motorcycles, and mopeds. In Haleiwa on the North Shore, try **Fantasy Cycles** (66-134 Kamehameha Highway; 637-3221).

PUBLIC TRANSPORTATION

Oahu has an excellent bus system that runs regularly to points all over the island and provides convenient service throughout Honolulu. Many of the beaches, hotels, restaurants, and points of interest mentioned in this chapter are just a bus ride away. It's even possible to pop your money in the fare box and ride around the entire island.

TheBus carries more than 250,000 people daily, loading them into any of 460 vehicles that rumble along city streets and country roads from 4:30 a.m. until midnight. There are also express buses traveling major highways.

If you stay in Waikiki you'll inevitably be sardined into a #19 or #20 bus for the ride through Honolulu's tourist mecca. Many bus drivers are Hawaiian; I saw some hysterical scenes on this line when tourists waited anxiously for their stop to be called, only to realize they couldn't understand the driver's pidgin. Hysterical, that is, after those early days when *I* was the visitor with the furrowed brow.

But you're surely more interested in meeting local people than tourists, and you can easily do it on any of the buses outside Waikiki. They're less crowded and a lot more fun for people-watching.

For information on bus routes call TheBus at 848-5555. And remember, the only carry-on luggage permitted is baggage small enough to fit on your lap.

In Waikiki you might want to check out the **pedicabs**. These three-wheeled rickshaws, now restricted to side streets, are expensive but entertaining conveyances. Several dollars will carry you from one place in Waikiki to another. Even if you decide not to ride around in this grand colonial style, you'll find the drivers are good sources of information. Many know the local scene intimately. If you're looking for a hot night spot or a good restaurant, check them out.

HITCHHIKING

Thumbing is not as popular on Oahu as one might think, so the competition for rides is not too great. The heavy traffic also increases your chances considerably. Officially, you're supposed to hitch from bus stops only. While I've seen people hitching in many different spots, I'd still recommend standing at a bus stop. Not only will you be within the law, but you'll also be able to catch a bus if you can't hitch a ride.

FLIGHTSEEING

The quickest way to see all Oahu has to offer is by taking to the air. In minutes you can experience the island's hidden waterfalls, secluded beaches, and volcanic landmarks. Tranquil gliders and hovering whirlybirds all fly low and slow to make sure you see what you missed on the trip over from the mainland. You can also take extended flights that include the outer islands.

Hawaii International Helicopters (100 Kaulele Place, Honolulu; 839-5509) tours feature Pearl Harbor, highlights of Honolulu, a nighttime city lights tour at sunset, and a circle trip covering Honolulu, Hanauma Bay, the Koolau Mountains, and the Windward Coast. There's also an hour-long loop tour of the island. **Papillon Hawaiian Helicopters** (836-1566) also offers a full menu of tours.

If you prefer fixed wing aircraft, consider **Scenic Air Tours Hawaii** (100 Iolana Place, Honolulu; 836-0044). Their Beechcrafts offer closeups of Punchbowl Crater, Diamond Head, Koko Head, and Hanauma Bay, as well as one or more of the neighbor islands.

To enjoy a one- or two-passenger glider trip, head out to **Glider Rides** (Dillingham Airfield, Mokuleia; 677-3404). On your 20-minute trip you're likely to see fields of sugar cane, marine mammals, surfers working the North Shore, and neighboring Lanai. You'll also enjoy peace and quiet while working your way down from 3000 feet.

Oahu Addresses and Phone Numbers

OAHU ISLAND

County Department of Parks and Recreation—Honolulu Municipal Building, 650 South King Street, Honolulu (523-4525)

Division of State Parks—1151 Punchbowl Street, Room 310, Honolulu (587-0300)

Hawaii Visitors Bureau—2270 Kalakaua Avenue, Room 801, Honolulu (923-1811)

Weather Report—(833-2849 for Honolulu; 836-0121 for entire island; 836-1952 for surfing weather)

HONOLULU

Ambulance—911

Books—Honolulu Book Shops, Ala Moana Center or 1001 Bishop Street (941-2274 or 537-6224)

Fire Department—911

Fishing Supplies—K. Kaya Fishing Supplies, 901 Kekaulike (538-1578)

Hardware—Kaimuki Ace Hardware, 3367 Waialae Avenue (732-2888)

Hospital—Queen's Medical Center, 1301 Punchbowl (538-9011)

Laundromat—Waikiki Ena Road Laundry, 478A Ena Road (942-3451)

Library—478 South King Street (586-3500)

Pharmacy—Long's Drugs, Ala Moana Center, 1450 Ala Moana Boulevard (941-4433)

Photo Supply—Francis Camera Shop, Ala Moana Center, 1450 Ala Moana Boulevard (946-2879)

Police Department—1455 South Beretania Street (943-3111; or 911 for emergencies)

Post Office—330 Saratoga Road (941-1062)

WINDWARD COAST

Ambulance—911

Fire Department—911

Laundromat—Kailua Laundromat, Aulike Street, Kailua (261-9201)

Police Department—1455 South Beretania Street (943-3111; or 911 for emergencies)

NORTH SHORE

Ambulance—911

Fire Department—911

Police Department—911

LEEWARD COAST

Ambulance—911

Fire Department—911

Laundromat—Waianae Speed Wash, 85-802 Farrington Highway (696-9115)

Police Department—911

CHAPTER FIVE

Hawaii

The Big Island, they call it, and even that is an understatement. Hawaii, all 4030 square miles, is almost twice as large as all the other Hawaiian islands combined. Its twin volcanic peaks, Mauna Kea and Mauna Loa, dwarf most mountains. Mauna Kea, rising 13,796 feet, is the largest island-based mountain in the world. Mauna Loa, the world's largest active volcano, which last erupted in 1950, looms 13,677 feet above sea level. This is actually 32,000 feet from the ocean floor, making it, by one system of reckoning, the tallest mountain on earth, grander even than Everest. And in bulk it is the world's largest. The entire Sierra Nevada chain could fit within this single peak.

Kilauea, a third volcano whose seething firepit has been erupting with startling frequency, is one of the world's most active craters. Since its most recent series of eruptions began in 1983, the volcano has swallowed almost 200 houses. In 1990 it completely destroyed the town of Kalapana, burying a once lively village beneath tons of black lava. There is little doubt that the Big Island is a place of geologic superlatives.

But size alone does not convey the Big Island's greatness. Its industry, too, is expansive. Despite the lava wasteland that covers large parts of its surface, and the volcanic gases that create a layer of "vog" during volcanic eruptions, the Big Island is the state's greatest producer of sugar, papayas, vegetables, anthuriums, macadamia nuts, and cattle. Its orchid industry, based in rain-drenched Hilo, is the world's largest. Over 22,000 varieties grow in the nurseries here.

Across the island in sun-soaked Kona, one of the nation's only coffee industries operates. Just off this spectacular western coast lie some of the finest deep-sea fishing grounds in the world. Between Hilo and Kona, and surrounding Waimea, sits the Parker Ranch. Sprawling across 225,000 acres, it is one of the world's largest independently owned cattle ranches.

Yet many of these measurements are taken against island standards. Compared to the mainland, the Big Island is a tiny speck in the sea. Across its broadest reach it measures a scant 93 miles long and 76 miles wide, smaller than Connecticut. The road around the island, totals only 300 miles, and can be driven in a day, though I'd recommend taking at least five. The island's 120,300 population comprises a mere ten percent of the state's citizens. Its lone city, Hilo, has a population of only 47,100.

But large or small, numbers cannot fully describe the Big Island, for there is a magic about the place that transcends statistics. Hawaii, also nicknamed the Orchid Island and Volcano Island, is the home of Pele, the goddess of volcanoes. Perhaps her fiery spirit is what infuses the Big Island with an unquantifiable quality. Or maybe the island's comparative youth (still growing in size from two active volcanoes, it is geologically the youngest spot on earth, one million years old) is what makes the elements seem nearer, more alluring, and strangely threatening here. Whatever it might be, the Big Island has always been where I feel closest to the Polynesian spirit. Of all the Hawaiian islands, this one I love the most.

It was here, possibly as early as 400 A.D., that Polynesian explorers first landed when they discovered the island chain. Until the advent of the white man, it was generally the most important island, supporting a large population and occupying a vital place in Hawaii's rich mythology. Little wonder then that Kamehameha the Great, the chief who would become Hawaii's first king, was born here in 1753. He established the archipelago's first capital in Kailua and ruled there until his death in 1819.

Within a year of the great leader's passing, two events occurred in Kailua that jolted the entire chain far more than any earthquake. First the king's heir, Liholiho, uprooted the centuries-old taboo system upon which ancient Polynesian religion rested. Then, in the spring of 1820, the first American missionaries dropped anchor off the coast of Kailua-Kona. It was also near here that Captain James Cook, history's greatest discoverer, was slain in 1779 by the same people who had earlier welcomed him as a god. Across the island another deity, Pele, was defied in 1824 when the high chieftess Kapiolani, a Christian, ate kapu fruit on the rim of Kilauea crater.

As stirring as the Big Island's story might be, much of its drama still awaits the visitor. For the land—the volcanoes, beaches, and valleys—is as vital and intriguing today as in the days of demigods and kings. This is a place for the adventurer to spend a lifetime.

On the east coast, buffeted by trade winds, lies Hilo, a lush tropical town that soaks up 140 inches of rain annually. Here anthuriums and orchids are cultivated in a number of spectacular nurseries. Just to the south—smoking, heaving, and sometimes erupting—sits Hawaii Volcanoes National Park.

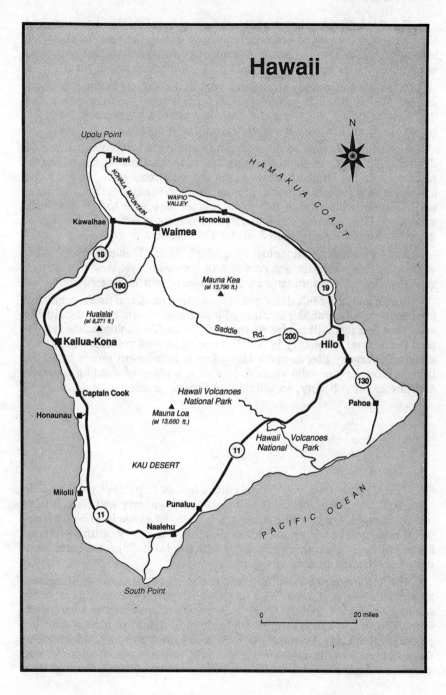

Hawaii

N

Upolu Point

Hawi

H A M A K U A   C O A S T

KOHALA MOUNTAIN

WAIPIO
VALLEY

Kawaihae

Honokaa

Waimea

19

190

Mauna Kea
(el 13,796 ft.)

19

Saddle   Rd.   200

Hilo

Hualalai
(el 8,271 ft.)

Kailua-Kona

130

Captain Cook

Hawaii Volcanoes
National Park

Pahoa

Honaunau

Mauna Loa
(el 13,680 ft.)

Hawaii   Volcanoes
National   Park

11

KAU DESERT

Milolii

Punaluu

PACIFIC   OCEAN

11

Naalehu

South Point

0   20 miles

The Puna District that straddles the coast between the volcanoes and Hilo has been the site of dramatic eruptions during the past decade. This lush rainforest is also the scene of a major political debate that has pitted environmentalists against developers of a geothermal power plant.

In the north, from the Hamakua Coast to the Kohala Peninsula, heavy erosion has cut through jutting cliffs to form spectacular canyons such as the Waipio Valley. All along the Hamakua plateau sugar plantations, fed by waters from Mauna Kea, stretch from the mountains to the surf.

In startling contrast to these verdant mountains is the desert-like Kau district at the southern tip of the island (and, for that matter, the southernmost point in the United States). Along the west coast stretches the Kona district, a vacationer's paradise. Suntan weather, sandy beaches, and coral reefs teeming with tropical fish make this an ideal area to just kick back and enjoy. The island's central tourist area is located here in Kailua-Kona, where Hawaiian royalty settled in the 19th century.

And for something unique to the Big Island, there's Waimea with its rolling grasslands, range animals, and *paniolos*, or Hawaiian-style cowboys. In fact, one of the biggest Hereford cattle herds is located here in the center of the island.

It's an island I don't think you should miss, an island that's beginning to change rapidly with the creation of a string of resorts along the Kohala coast, but one that still retains its original charm. To geologists the Big Island is a natural laboratory in which the mysteries of volcanic activity are a fact of everyday life; to many Hawaiians it is the most sacred of all the islands. To everyone who visits it, Hawaii is a place of startling contrasts and unspeakable beauty, an alluring and exotic tropical island.

Hilo

There's one thing you'll rarely miss in this tropical city—rain. Hilo gets about 140 inches a year. The Chamber of Commerce will claim it rains mostly at night, but don't be deceived. It's almost as likely to be dark and wet at midday. There is a good side to all this bothersome moisture—it transforms Hilo into an exotic city crowded with tropical foliage, the orchid capital of the United States.

Hilo is the closest you will approach in all Hawaii to a Somerset Maugham-style South Seas port town. With its turn-of-the-century stores, many badly needing a paint job, and old Chinese shops, it's a throwback to an era when tourists were few and Hawaii was a territory. Sections of town, especially around Waianuenue Avenue, have been refurbished and dabbed with 1990s flash, but much of the downtown is still a collection of ethnic eateries, swap shops, and Japanese groceries. The gutters are rusty, the rain awnings have sagged, and an enduring sense of character overhangs the place with the certainty and finality of the next downpour.

Hilo is a tropical wonderland, a rainforest with hotels, shops, and great places to visit. A visit to one of the city's many flower nurseries is an absolute must. These gardens grow orchids, anthuriums, and countless other flowers. Three that I highly recommend are **Orchids of Hawaii** (2801 Kilauea Avenue; 959-3581), **Nani Mau Gardens** (several miles south of Hilo near Route 11 at 421 Makalika; 959-3541; admission), and **Hilo Tropical Gardens** (1477 Kalanianaole Avenue; 935-4957).

Banyan Drive is another green thumb's delight. Sweeping past Hilo's plushest hotels, this waterfront road is shaded with rows of giant banyan trees. Next to this verdant arcade are the **Liliuokalani Gardens**, 30 acres exploding with color. These Japanese gardens, featuring both Hawaiian and Asian trees, are dotted with pagodas, arched bridges, and a ceremonial teahouse.

A short footbridge nearby crosses to **Coconut Island**, a palm-studded islet in Hilo Bay. This old Hawaiian sanctuary presents a dramatic view of Hilo Bay and, on a clear day, of Mauna Kea and Mauna Loa as well.

A stone's skip across from the island, at **Suisan Fish Market** (Banyan Drive and Lihiwai Street), fishing boats land their catches. Try to get there around 7:30 in the morning for a lively fish auction and a dose of local color.

It's not far to **Wailoa River State Park** (off Kamehameha Avenue), where grassy picnic areas surround beautiful **Waiakea Fishpond**. Across one of the pond's arching bridges, at Wailoa Visitor Center (933-4360), there are cultural exhibits and an information desk.

In downtown Hilo, the **Lyman Mission House** (276 Haili Street; 935-5021) is a fascinating example of a 19th-century missionary home. Built in 1839, the house is furnished with elegant period pieces that create a sense of this bygone era. A small admission fee buys a guided tour of the parsonage plus a look through the adjoining Hawaiian history museum, which focuses on Hawaiian culture and the islands' many ethnic groups. Upstairs from this ethnographic display you'll find an excellent exhibit of rocks and minerals.

The **East Hawaii Cultural Center Gallery** (141 Kalakaua Street; 961-5711) displays the work of local artists in a series of ever-changing exhibits. The building itself, an old police station that has achieved historic landmark status, is a work of art.

Fronting the library on nearby Waianuenue Avenue are the **Naha** and **Pinao Stones**. According to legend, whoever moved the massive Naha Stone would rule all the islands. Kamehameha overturned the boulder while still a youth, then grew to become Hawaii's first king.

Continue up Waianuenue Avenue to **Rainbow Falls**, a foaming cascade in Wailuku River State Park. Here, particularly in the morning, spray from the falls shimmers in spectral hues. It's another two miles to **Boiling Pots**, where a series of falls pours turbulently into circular lava pools. The rushing water, spilling down from Mauna Kea, bubbles up through the lava and boils over into the next pool.

Kaumana Drive, branching off Waianuenue Avenue, leads five miles out of town to **Kaumana Caves**. A stone stairway leads from the roadside down to two fern-choked lava tubes, formed during Mauna Loa's devastating 1881 eruption. Explore the lower tube, but avoid the other—it's dangerous.

Also be sure to visit the **Panaewa Rainforest Zoo** (one mile off the Mamalahoa Highway several miles south of town; 959-7224). Located in a lush region that receives over 125 inches of rain annually, this modest facility houses numerous rainforest animals as well as other species. There are water buffaloes and tigers, plus an array of exotic birds that include crowned cranes, macaws, parrots, Hawaiian stilts, and *nenes*.

HILO HOTELS

The fashionable hotel district in this rain-plagued city sits astride the bay along Banyan Drive. Most hotels offer moderately priced accommodations, while a few are designed to fit the contours of a more slender purse.

Near the far end of beautiful Banyan Drive lies the **Hilo Seaside Hotel** (126 Banyan Way; 935-0821). This charming place is actually on a side street fronting Reed's Bay, an arm of Hilo Bay. Owned by the Kimis, a Hawaiian family, it has the same friendly ambience that pervades their other hotels. There's a large lobby decorated with tile, *koa* wood and bamboo. A carp pond complete with footbridges dominates the grounds. The rooms are small and plainly decorated. Most are wallpapered in unattractive stripes and equipped with telephone, television, and a combination shower-tub (perfect for soaking away a rainy day). The lanais overlook lush gardens and the hotel swimming pool. All in all, for friendly ambience and a lovely setting, the Seaside is a prime choice. Moderate.

Hilo Bay Hotel (87 Banyan Drive; 935-0861) is another economical oceanfront establishment. The theme here is Polynesian, and proprietor "Uncle Billy" carries it off with flair: wicker furniture, thatch, and *tapa* in the lobby, a restaurant/cocktail lounge, a bayside swimming pool, and several carp ponds dotted about the tropical gardens. Standard rooms have wall-to-wall carpeting, televisions, telephones, and air conditioning, but are lacking in style and elegance. The walls are plaster, and the rooms are plainly furnished and located away from the water. They rent for a moderate price. Superior rooms (which overlook the gardens, are larger, more attractive, and come with kitchenettes) can be reserved for slightly more.

For luxurious living my favorite Hilo hostelry is the **Hawaii Naniloa Hotel** (93 Banyan Drive; 969-3333), a highrise affair located right on the water. Rooms are comfortably furnished and nicely adorned. Restaurants, bars, and a lounge are among the many amenities here, but the most alluring feature is the landscape—the tree-studded lawn is fringed with tidepools

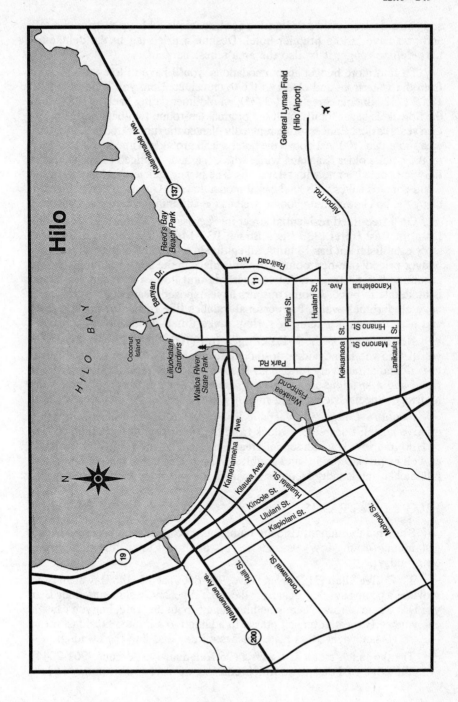

and volcanic rock. Add a swimming pool, spacious lobby, plus friendly staff and you have Hilo's premier hotel. Despite a price tag in the deluxe-to-ultra-deluxe range, it is also the area's best bargain.

To find more budget accommodations, you'll have to tote your bags up from the waterfront and closer to the town center. Here you'll find the **Hilo Hotel** (142 Kinoole Street; 961-3733), an oldtimer dating back to 1888 when the Spreckels sugar family built the original ten-room, two-bath hostelry. Fifteen years earlier, Princess Ruth reputedly planted the rubber tree that once towered more than 100 feet above the hotel's lush grounds. Time has left no trace on the hotel's older Kalakaua wing, where the budget-priced rooms are tastefully remodeled, some with televisions. The newer, quieter Niolopa Wing has wood-paneled suites with kitchens at moderate cost. Guests in both wings can enjoy the hotel swimming pool as well as the adjoining lounge and restaurant.

On a tree-lined residential street just across the Wailuku River sits the **Dolphin Bay Hotel** (333 Iliahi Street; 935-1466). This comfortable two-story establishment has 18 units, all equipped with kitchenettes. Studios are budget-priced; one-bedroom apartments place in the moderate range but can accommodate up to four. A two-bedroom unit houses as many as six and is moderate in price. Rooms upstairs have exposed-beam ceilings; all units have cinderblock walls, but personal touches like fresh flowers and fruit, and a garden with a running spring, make this a good choice.

Not far away at the **Wild Ginger Inn** (100 Puueo Street; 935-5556) you'll find rooms at budget-to-moderate prices. These are carpeted wall-to-wall and attractively furnished. There's a laundry room, rolling lawn out front, and a spacious lobby. Be prepared for some noise from the nearby highway. Special weekly and monthly rates.

Arnott's Lodge (98 Apapane Road; 969-7097) is a clean, bright attractive hostel. Located one block from the waterfront, it is on the outskirts of Hilo in a low-key residential area. There are dormitory rooms available as well as private singles and doubles. With prices in the budget range, and full kitchen and laundry facilities provided, it's one of the area's best bargains.

HILO RESTAURANTS

Scattered throughout Hilo are numerous cafés, lunch counters, and chain restaurants serving low-cost meals. This is a great town for ethnic eating on a budget.

J's Coffee Shop (71 Banyan Drive; 969-6660) at the Hilo Hawaiian Hotel provides a pennysaver's retreat from the more expensive restaurants along Banyan Drive's hotel row. There's nothing fancy about this café, but you can still enjoy a hearty meal at budget prices. In addition to a limited breakfast menu, they serve sandwiches and plate lunches all day and into the evening.

Try the lunch menu at **Gwen's** (96 Kalanianaole Avenue; 961-2044), near the edge of hotel row, which consists of sandwiches (many at low,

low cost) as well as Oriental and American platters. The menu's limited and the atmosphere nonexistent, but Gwen's place isn't bad for a quick meal. Breakfasts are served too; closed for dinner. Budget.

Ever try *adobo*? Or *laoya*? They're pork and pig's feet dishes served Filipino-style at Asian cafés in the rundown center of Hilo. One of these, **Sophie's Place** (207 Kilauea Avenue; 935-7300), serves lunch plates for little money. A great way to go ethnic. They also serve breakfast. Budget.

In the moderate price category, let's start with traditional and proceed to ethnic dining spots. **Ken's House of Pancakes** (1730 Kamehameha Avenue; 935-8711) has to top the list for all-American fare. If you've ever been to a Denny's or Howard Johnson's, you've been in Ken's. Endless rows of naugahyde booths, a long counter next to the kitchen, uniformed waitresses—the classic roadside America motif. The cuisine is on a par with the decorative taste: hamburgers and roast beef, mediocre in quality, moderate in cost. But when all else is closed, it's a good late-night option.

Another mediocre spot is **Hukilau Restaurant** (136 Banyan Way; 935-4222), adjacent to the popular Hilo Seaside Hotel. Decorated in tiled walls and *koa* paneling, the Hukilau features a fresh seafood menu complemented with meat 'n' potato favorites like pork chops, steak, and fried chicken. Dinners come with salad bar, soup, dessert, and beverage. For lunch, they offer sandwiches and other mid-day fare; also open at breakfast time. Moderate.

Uncle Billy's (87 Banyan Drive; 935-0861) at the nearby Hilo Bay Hotel sports a Hawaiian decor. In addition to its rattan furnishings, this cozy club hosts Polynesian dinner shows nightly. The menu is filled with surf-and-turf dishes priced comfortably. There's no lunch here, but they do offer breakfast daily. Budget to moderate.

Situated across the street from the golf course, **Strattons** (121 Banyan Drive; 961-6815) prepares breakfast, lunch, and dinner. The walls inside this restaurant-lounge are covered with unusual artworks and brass wall-hangings. Strattons' lunch and dinner are buffet affairs with beef, pork, chicken and fish dishes. You can also pay a visit to the salad bar. Prices range at the low end of the moderate category. For lunch you might also be interested in the hot and cold sandwiches and fried ice cream.

It's hard to say whether **Lehua's Bar & Grill** (90 Kamehameha Avenue; 935-8055) is retro or ultramodern: There are elements of both in the decor. Located in the historic heart of Hilo, the dining room is decorated with old photos—memorabilia from the Hawaii of yore, and modern art. One thing is certain, the menu is as up-to-date as you'll find anywhere: The fresh fish and steak dishes are charbroiled and the house specialties include stir-fried vegetables and spinach lasagna. Moderate.

In Hilo you'll find many more good Oriental restaurants than appealing American restaurants. For example, **Sachi's Gourmet** (250 Keawe Street; 935-6255), a small café downtown, serves Japanese meals. Sachi cooks several *donburi*, *udon*, and tempura dishes as well as several special seafood dishes. Open for breakfast, lunch, and dinner. Moderate.

For Chinese food, **Mun Cheong Lau Chop Suey Restaurant** (172 Kilauea Avenue; 935-3040) is the Orient's answer to the greasy spoon (greasy chopstick?) café. The place is as big as a barn and gaudily decorated with magenta walls and plastic lanterns. If you can get past the interior devastation, there's an ample menu listing numerous seafood, fowl, pork, and rice dishes at chop suey prices. And in case of late-evening munchie attacks, Mun Cheong stays open until 11 p.m. Moderate.

At **K. K. Tei Restaurant** (1550 Kamehameha Avenue; 961-3791) you can enjoy lunch or dinner while overlooking a lovely bonsai garden. The dining room offers a selection of traditional Japanese dishes. In addition to sukiyaki and tempura plates, the chefs prepare salmon, scallops, and shrimp. After dining, stroll past the pagodas and arched bridges that ornament K. K.'s Japanese Garden. Moderate.

Hilo boasts a very fine Japanese restaurant that combines excellent cooking with private dining. At **Restaurant Fuji** (142 Kinoole Street; 961-3733), in the Hilo Hotel, you can dine at the poolside lanai on delicious *teppanyaki* dishes or pass indoors to an attractive dining room. In addition to *wafu* steak, *dotenabe*, and tempura dishes, there are several *teishoku* (complete dinner) choices served with tofu, chicken salad, vegetables, and soup, plus an elaborate lunch menu. Moderate to deluxe.

One of the island's finest restaurants is found, surprisingly enough, in an old bank building in downtown Hilo. **Roussel's** (60 Keawe Street; 935-5111) is the creation of two brothers who replaced fluorescent lights with brass chandeliers and linoleum with hardwood floors, then converted the vault into a dining area. Painted in contemporary pastel hues, Roussel's specializes in French/Creole cuisine, offering up soft-shell crab, shrimp and oyster gumbo, blackened mahimahi, and trout amandine. Open for dinner only, it's priced in the moderate-to-deluxe range.

Hilo's foremost steak-and-seafood restaurant is **Harrington's** (115 Kalanianaole Street; 961-4966), a waterfront dining room that is particularly popular with local residents. Here you can dine in a congenial atmosphere to the strains of Hawaiian music in the background. Open for dinner only, Harrington's also has a lively bar scene and can be counted on for good food and a good time. Deluxe.

HILO MARKETS

The island's largest city, Hilo has several supermarkets. Foremost are **Sure Save** in the Kaikoo Mall on Kilauea Avenue and **Sack-N-Save** at 250 Kinoole Street in the Puainako Shopping Center.

Hilo hosts an excellent natural food outlet—**Abundant Life Natural Foods** (292 Kamehameha Avenue; 935-7411). It contains healthy supplies of vitamins, juices, and bath products, as well as fresh fruits and vegetables.

Suisan Company Limited (93 Lihiwai Street; 935-9349) has both fresh and frozen seafood.

Holsum/Oroweat Bakery Thrift Store (302 Kamehameha Avenue; 935-2164) offers day-old baked goods at unbeatable prices.

HILO SHOPPING

The most convenient way to shop in Hilo is at one of several shopping centers around the city. **Kaikoo Mall**, on Kilauea Avenue, is the main complex. Here you'll find jewelers, boutiques, curio and book stores, a photo shop, Penney's department store, and more. **Hilo Shopping Center**, also on Kilauea Avenue, contains numerous shops.

The latest addition to the Hilo shopping scene is **Prince Kuhio Plaza** (Route 11 just outside town), a full-facility complex featuring everything from small crafts shops to swank boutiques to a sprawling department store. The Big Island's largest mall, it's a gathering place for local shoppers and a convenient spot for visitors.

But bargains and locally crafted products are probably what you're after. So it's a good idea to window-shop through the centers, checking out products and prices, then do your buying at smaller shops. For woodwork, just head across the street from Kaikoo Mall to **Dan DeLuz Woods** (935-5587) at 760 Kilauea Avenue. The beautiful pieces are fashioned from banyan, sandalwood, *koa*, and *milo*, all priced reasonably. The DeLuzs, the craftspeople who own the shop, do all their carving in a back-room workshop. If you'd like a description of how the *tikis* and bowls are made, they're happy to provide an informal tour.

The Most Irresistible Shop in Hilo (110 Keawe; 935-9644) doesn't quite live up to its bold name but does create a strong attraction with jewelry, ceramics, books, toys, and piñatas.

For beach-reading materials, try **The Book Gallery** (Kaikoo Mall; 935-2447). This well-stocked shop has many popular titles. If maps, guidebooks, and volumes on Hawaiiana sound more inviting, **Basically Books** (46 Waianuenue Avenue; 961-0144) is an excellent choice.

Gamelan Gallery (277 Keawe Street; 969-7655) could well be a museum of Far Eastern arts and crafts. Here are Asian bronzes, Indonesian textiles, and New Guinea tribal masks. You'll also find jewelry and other fashionable items from all over East Asia.

Maile's Hawaii (216 Kamehameha Avenue; 935-8944), on the other hand, specializes in things Hawaiian. Whether it be books, clothing, jewelry, or knickknacks, you should find it here.

HILO NIGHTLIFE

The main scene centers around the big hotels along Banyan Drive. By far the best place is the Hawaii Naniloa Hotel (969-3333). This luxury hotel has a nicely appointed nightclub, **The Crown Room**. The lounge usually books local groups, but every once in a while it imports a mainland band for special events. There's a cover charge and two-drink minimum. Then there is the hotel's **Rainbow Lounge**, which has a karaoke bar.

Harrington's (135 Kalanianaole Avenue; 961-4966) hosts a jazz pianist during the week and a Hawaiian guitarist on weekends.

At **J.V.'s** (111 Banyan Drive; 961-5802) there's live entertainment every weekend.

The Menehune Lounge at the **Hilo Hawaiian Hotel** (71 Banyan Drive; 935-9361) has dancing nightly to a band playing contemporary music.

Lehua's Bar & Grill (90 Kamehameha Avenue; 935-8055) features dancing to a live band every Friday and Saturday. The sounds are blues and rock, usually from the '70s and '80s.

HILO BEACHES AND PARKS

Kalakaua Park—Located on the corner of busy Kinoole Street and Waianuenue Avenue, this pretty little park has a grand old banyan tree and a pleasant picnic area.

Reed's Bay Beach Park—Reed's Bay, a banyan-lined cove at the end of Banyan Drive, is a marvelous picnic spot. The bay is actually an arm of Hilo Bay, but unlike the larger body of water, Reed's Bay offers excellent swimming in smooth water (though an underwater spring keeps the water cold).

Onekahakaha, Kealoha, and **Leleiwi County Parks**—None of these three parks have sand beaches, but all possess lava pools or other shallow places for swimming. They also have grassy plots and picnic areas, plus restrooms and showers. Both tent and trailer camping are allowed at Onekahakaha and Kealoha (county permits are required).

If you fish along these shores, chances are good you'll net papio, threadfin, mountain bass, mullet, big-eyed scad, mackerel scad, milkfish, bonefish, or goatfish. Kealoha Park offers good snorkeling, surfing, spear-fishing, and throw-netting.

All three parks are located within five miles of Hilo, east along Kalanianaole Avenue.

Richardson's Ocean Park (★)—This black-sand beach, on Hilo Bay's south shore, is without doubt the finest beach in the area. From here you can see the entire sweep of Hilo Bay, with Mauna Kea hulking in the background. Palm and ironwood trees fringe the beach, while a lava outcropping protects swimmers.

Facilities: Restrooms, showers. **Richardson Ocean Park Center** (935-3830), an oceanographic museum, is located here. Restaurants and markets lie about two miles away in Hilo. *Swimming:* Excellent. Good body-surfing also. *Snorkeling:* Good in protected areas. *Surfing:* One of the best spots around Hilo. Winter break with right slides. Mornings and evenings are the prime times, but at all times beware of currents and riptides. Good bodyboarding also. *Fishing:* Common catches include papio, threadfin, mountain bass, mullet, big-eyed scad, mackerel scad, milkfish, bonefish, and goatfish.

Camping: Unofficial camping.

Getting there: Take Kalanianaole Street to within a quarter-mile of where the paved road ends; watch for the sign to Richardson Ocean Park. The beach is behind and to the right of the center.

Hamakua Coast

Route 19, the Mamalahoa Highway, leads north from Hilo along the rainy, windswept Hamakua Coast. Planted in sugar and teeming with exotic plant life, this elevated coastline is as lushly overgrown as Hilo.

A softly rolling plateau that edges from the slopes of Mauna Kea to the sea, the region is cut by sharp canyons and deep gulches. Waterfalls cascade down emerald walls and tumbling streams lead to lava-rock beaches. Beautiful is too tame a term for this enchanting countryside. There are stands of eucalyptus, shadowy forests, and misty fields of sugarcane. Plantation towns, filled with pastel-painted houses and adorned with flower gardens, lie along the route.

Several miles outside Hilo, follow the signs to the **Scenic Drive**. This old coast road winds past cane fields and shantytowns before rejoining the main highway. Alexander palms line the road. Watch for Onomea Bay: There you'll see a V-shaped rock formation where a sea arch collapsed in 1956.

You can also take in **Hawaii Tropical Botanical Garden** (964-5233; admission), an exotic nature preserve with streams, waterfalls, rugged coastline, and over 1800 plant species. This jungle garden, edged by the Pacific and inhabited by shore birds and giant sea turtles, is a place of uncommon beauty.

Back on the main road, you'll soon come to a turnoff heading inland to **Akaka Falls State Park**. Don't bypass it! A short nature trail leads past bamboo groves, ferns, *ti*, and orchids to Akaka Falls, which slide 442 feet down a sheer cliff face, and Kahuna Falls, 400 feet high. This 66-acre preserve is covered in a canopy of rainforest vegetation. There are birds of paradise, azaleas, and giant philodendrons whose leaves measure as much as two feet.

Countless gulches ribbon the landscape between Hilo and Honokaa. For a unique tour, take the road from Hakalau that winds down to **Hakalau Gulch** (★). Literally choked with vegetation, this gorge extends to a small beach. Towering above are an old sugar mill, a collapsing trestle, and the highway bridge.

Another side road several miles north corkscrews down to **Laupahoehoe Point**, a hauntingly beautiful peninsula from which 24 students and teachers were swept by the 1946 tidal wave. Here gently curving palm trees and spreading lawns contrast with the lash of the surf.

The plantation town of **Paauilo** offers a glimpse of vintage Hawaii: decaying storefronts, tinroof cottages, a sea-rusted sugar mill. Then it's on to Honokaa, the world center of macadamia nut growing. The **Hawaiian Holiday Macadamia Nut Factory** (775-7743) is open, but don't anticipate a wildly informative visit. This establishment concentrates more on selling macadamia products to tourists.

I'd bypass the place and head out Route 240 to **Waipio Valley**, the islands's largest valley. One mile wide and six miles long, this luxurious valley, sparsely populated today, once supported thousands of Hawaiians. Agriculturally bountiful, Waipio is also rich in history. Here in 1780 Kamehameha the Great acknowledged the war god who would propel him to victory. At that time the valley, which has been inhabited for over 1000 years, supported a population of about 4000 Hawaiians. It also looms large in island mythology. Wakea, the Zeus of Hawaii, loved the valley, as did two other members of the Polynesian pantheon, Kane and Kanaloa. The god Lono came here seeking a wife and Maui himself is said to have died in the Waipio Valley.

Taro patches and tumbledown cottages still dot the valley. From the lookout point at road's end, a jeep trail drops sharply into Waipio. Explorers can hike down, take an hour-and-a-half jeep tour with the **Waipio Valley Shuttle and Tours** (775-7121), or go on a **Waipio Valley Wagon Tour** (775-9518). Both tours visit the black-sand beach, then travel several miles up into the valley for eye-boggling views of 1200-foot Hiilawe Falls.

Eden for explorers, the valley floor is still planted with taro, guavas, bananas, and noni apples. Streams tumble through the territory and the rainforest is a riot of tropical colors. The homes of a few dozen dedicated residents dot the area and there are abandoned buildings, swimming holes, and cascades to be discovered. (If you don't have time to explore the valley, be sure to at least take in the vista from the **Waipio Valley Lookout** at the end of Route 240.)

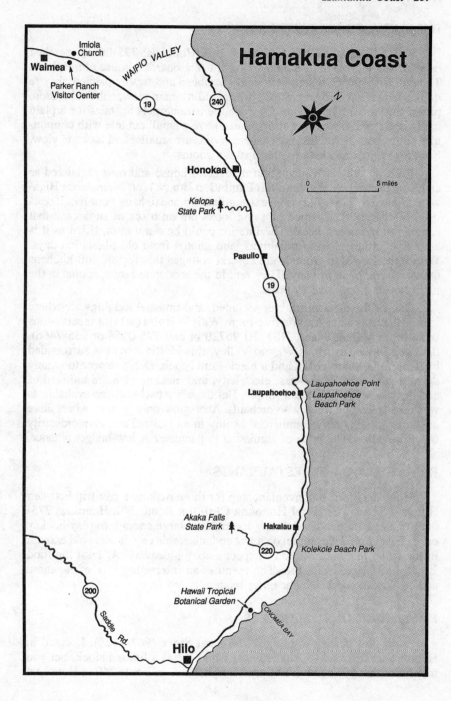

Hamakua Coast

Waimea

Imiola Church

Parker Ranch Visitor Center

WAIPIO VALLEY

19

240

N

0   5 miles

Honokaa

Kalopa State Park

Paauilo

19

Laupahoehoe Point

Laupahoehoe   Laupahoehoe Beach Park

Akaka Falls State Park   Hakalau

220   Kolekole Beach Park

200   Hawaii Tropical Botanical Garden

Saddle Rd.   ONOMEA BAY

Hilo

HAMAKUA COAST HOTELS

Hotel Honokaa Club (on Route 240, Honokaa; 775-0678), perched on a hillside above the Hamakua Coast, has a boardinghouse atmosphere. The rooms upstairs are kept thoroughly scrubbed and freshly painted; they're quite adequate. A budget price buys a splendid ocean view, color television, plus a tiny private bathroom. Or trade the trim carpets upstairs for a plain hardwood floor downstairs and you can have a small cubicle with community bathroom at even less cost. These rooms are smaller and lack the view, but they're just as clean as the upstairs rooms.

Built in 1921 as a plantation manager's house and now registered as an historic landmark, the **Paauhau Plantation Inn** (★) (off Mamalahoa Highway, Honokaa; 775-7222) is an extraordinary place to hang your hat. It rests on an elegantly landscaped plot and looks out on a sea of sugarcane that extends to the ocean itself. The interior could be a museum, filled as it is with fine antiques, *koa* furnishings, and photos from old plantation days. Within the five-acre grounds are several cottages that feature full kitchens and offer complete privacy. They rent in the moderate range; rooms in the main house are deluxe in price.

One of the most primitive, secluded, and unusual lodgings anywhere in the islands is Tom Araki's five-room **Waipio Hotel** (★) (for reservations write to 25 Malana Place, Hilo, HI 96720 or call 775-0368 or 935-7466). Set deep in the luxurious Waipio Valley, this idyllic retreat is surrounded by waterfalls, sharp cliffs, and a black-sand beach. Don't expect too many amenities here in Eden—gas, electricity, and meal service are unheard of and the rooms are small and simple. But there are two kitchens available as well as a landscape filled with orchards. Accessible only by four-wheel drive or shuttle, it's the only commercial facility in an isolated and extraordinarily beautiful valley. The price of admission to paradise? A low-budget pittance.

HAMAKUA COAST RESTAURANTS

Honokaa offers a convenient stop for those making a day-trip between Hilo and Kona. The **Hotel Honokaa Club** (on Route 240, Honokaa; 775-0678) has a banquet-sized dining room that's large enough to play hockey on. The last time I was there, on a wet and miserable day, it was cold enough inside to do just that. So don't expect a cozy hideaway. At least the food is hot, and priced well, too. The menu is an interesting mix of Japanese and American food. Dinner only; moderate.

HAMAKUA COAST MARKETS

Your best chance is **Ishigo's General Store** (963-6128). Located in Honomu on the road to Akaka Falls, Ishigo's has a limited stock, but you may find what you need. If not, try **M. Ujiki Inc.** on Route 240 in Honokaa.

HAMAKUA COAST SHOPPING

Several small shops between Hilo and Waimea are worth a visit. The **Akaka Falls Flea Market** (963-6171), on the road to Akaka Falls, is set in an old falsefront building. In addition to aloha wear it features shell jewelry.

Kamaaina Woods (775-7722), in Honokaa on Lehua Street (the road to the macadamia nut factory) has a splendid assortment of handmade bowls and decorations. With items fashioned from *milo*, mango, and *koa*, this shop is practically a museum. And if you are interested in learning more about these woods, you can view the factory through the window.

The Waipio Valley Artworks (775-0958), located on Route 240 near the Waipio Valley Lookout, is also cluttered with woodcarvings. Made from several different woods, some of these creations are extremely beautiful. This shop also features paintings, ceramics, quilts, and other items crafted by local artists.

HAMAKUA COAST BEACHES AND PARKS

Kolekole Beach Park—Located at the mouth of a wide gulch lush with tropical vegetation, this comfortable park has a large and pleasant grassy area. A stream and waterfall tumble through the park down to the rocky, surf-torn shore. The sandy beach and natural beauty of the place make it very popular among local residents.

Facilities: Picnic area, restrooms, electricity; there is no drinking water. Five miles to markets and restaurants in Honomu. *Swimming:* Okay in the stream, but the ocean here is forbiddingly rough. *Fishing:* Try for threadfin, menpachi, papio, ulua, and mountain bass.

Camping: Tent and trailer. County permit required.

Getting there: Located just off Mamalahoa Highway (Route 19) about 15 miles northwest of Hilo.

Laupahoehoe Beach Park—Set on a low-lying peninsula that was inundated by the 1946 tidal wave, this hauntingly beautiful park is still lashed by heavy surf. A precipitous pali and lava-strewn shoreline surround the area.

Facilities: Picnic area, restrooms, showers, and electricity. It's at least 15 miles to restaurants or markets in Honokaa, so bring a lunch. *Swimming, Snorkeling, Surfing:* Good at times, but usually very dangerous. *Fishing:* Common catches are mountain bass, ulua, papio, menpachi, and moi.

Camping: Tent and trailer camping permitted. County permit required.

Getting there: One mile off Route 19 down a well-marked twisting road, about 27 miles northwest of Hilo.

Kalopa State Park—A wooded retreat set in the mountains above the Hamakua Coast, this 615-acre park has both untouched expanses ripe for exploring and several beautifully landscaped acres. Ranging from 2000 to 2500 feet elevation, it's a great place for hiking or just for escaping.

Facilities: Picnic area, restrooms, showers, cabins. About five miles to markets and restaurants in Honokaa.

Camping: Tent camping allowed with a state permit. Cabins are also available; call 933-4200 for reservations.

Getting there: Take Route 19 southeast from Honokaa for about three miles. A well-marked paved road leads from the highway another two miles to the park.

Waimea

Just 15 miles from the tablelands of Honokaa and ten miles from the Kohala Coast, at an elevation of 2670 feet, sits Waimea. Covered with rolling grassland and bounded by towering mountains, Waimea (also called Kamuela) is cowboy country. Here *paniolos*, Hawaiian cowboys, ride the range on one of the world's largest independently owned cattle ranches. About 50,000 cattle roam Parker Ranch's sprawling 225,000-acre domain. Founded by John Palmer Parker, an adventurous sailor who jumped ship in 1809, the Parker preserve extends from sea level to over 9000 feet.

This cool rustic countryside, rare in a tropical retreat like Hawaii, is dotted with carpenter's Gothic houses and adorned with stables and picket fences. There are Victorian buildings and deep green trees, cattle grazing in the meadows, and horses edging along the fence line.

The museum at **Parker Ranch Visitor Center** (885-7655; admission) presents a history of the Parker family and includes a Duke Kahanamoku Room, depicting Hawaii's famous swimmer and surfer. The former will carry you back 100 years with its displays of Victorian-era furniture and clothing and the latter will place you in the early 20th century with an exhibit detailing "The Father of Modern Surfing."

And at the **Historic Parker Ranch Homes** (Mamalahoa Highway, one-half mile west of town) you can view the family's original 1840s-era ranch house and an adjoining century-old home (which doubles as a museum filled with extraordinary French Impressionist artwork). While the original home was built of *koa* and contains a collection of antique calabashes, the latter-day estate boasts lofty ceilings, glass chandeliers, and walls decorated with Renoirs, Chagalls, and Pissarros.

Another fine display is located at the **Kamuela Museum** (at the junction of Kawaihae Road and Kohala Mountain Road; 885-4724; admission). Founded by J. P. Parker's great-great-granddaughter, this private collection of everything from Royal Hawaiian artifacts to moon-flight relics is fascinating, if poorly organized.

For a splendid example of *koa* woodworking, visit **Imiola Congregational Church,** located along Mamalahoa Highway on the east side of town. Built in 1857, this clapboard church has an interior fashioned entirely from the native timber.

Backed by rolling ranchland (what else?) and surrounded by a stonewall enclosure is **Hale Kea** (Kawaihae Road one mile west of Waimea; 885-6095). This historic ranch estate has been transformed into a shopping mall/ museum with the accent on shopping mall. There are historic displays in the central building and the grounds offer an unusual collection of old wagons, carefully tended flower gardens, and a stable.

WAIMEA HOTELS

Set amid the Kohala Mountains in the cowboy town of Waimea are two hotels, both within walking distance of local markets and restaurants. **The Parker Ranch Lodge** (Kawaihae Road, Waimea; 885-4100), a modern multi-unit motel, is owned by Parker Ranch, which seems to control most everything in these parts. Rooms are large, carpeted, and equipped with telephones, shower-tub combinations, and color televisions; some have small kitchenettes. The ceilings are exposed beam; the furniture is knotty pine. Prices here run in the moderate range.

Kamuela Inn (Kawaihae Road, Waimea; 885-4243), a poor neighbor just down the street, has modest rooms. These are clean and bright with private baths. Many of the 31 units are equipped with a television and some have refrigerators. Guests are served a continental breakfast. Standard rooms and two-room units are moderately priced; suites in the new wing are deluxe-priced.

Combining style with personalized service, **Hawaii's Best Bed & Breakfasts** (P.O. Box 563, Kamuela 96743; 885-4550 or 800-262-9912) specializes in small, upscale bed-and-breakfast accommodations on all the islands. With more than 70 places to choose from, it places guests in a variety of privately owned facilities; most are deluxe in price. The unit I saw was a woodframe cottage that shared over an acre of land with the owner's house. Set in Waimea beside a stream and surrounded by trees and lofty green hills, it included a kitchen and sitting area.

WAIMEA RESTAURANTS

When in cowboy country do like the *paniolos* do. Up in the western-style town of Waimea the **Parker Ranch Broiler** (Parker Ranch Center; 885-7366) serves steak, steak, and steak. At lunch and dinner there's also chicken and seafood. The *koa*-paneled bar is right through them swingin' doors and the dining room's mighty purty. Moderate to deluxe.

Waimea is short on short-order restaurants. With all the fine-dining possibilities here there is not much in the way of inexpensive ethnic restaurants. You will find two in Waimea Center (Mamalahoa Highway): **Great Wall Chopsui** (885-7252) has steam-tray Chinese food and **Yong's Kalbi** (885-8440) serves Korean dishes. Both are budget-priced.

Providing excellent Italian dishes at budget prices is **Aloha Pasquale** (Kawaihae Road near the intersection with Mamalahoa Highway; 885-7277). This neighborhood café has pizza and spaghetti as well as meatball sandwiches and lasagna.

Hartwell's at Hale Kea (Kawaihae Road about one mile west of Waimea; 885-6095) mixes history with fine dining. Set in an 1897 plantation manager's house, this restaurant-cum-museum numbers five dining rooms, each furnished in period. In addition to the early decor you can enjoy a variety of dishes including duckling in lilikoi sauce, grilled lamb, Alaskan King crab and island fish. The appetizers are equally inviting—Chesapeake Bay crab cakes, grilled shiitake mushrooms, and brie baked in filo. Lunch and dinner. Deluxe.

One of my favorite Waimea dining spots is the **Edelweiss** restaurant (Kawaihae Road; 885-6800), a cozy club with a knockout interior design. The entire place was fashioned by a master carpenter who inlaid sugi pine, *koa*, and silver oak with the precision of a stonemason. Run by a German chef who gained his knowledge at prestigious addresses like Maui's plush Kapalua Bay Hotel, Edelweiss is a gourmet's delight. The dinner menu includes wienerschnitzel, roast duck, roast pork with sauerkraut, and a house specialty—sautéed veal, lamb, beef, and bacon with *pfifferling*. For lunch there is bratwurst and sauerkraut, turkey sandwiches, sauteed chicken breast, and club sandwiches. Priced moderate to deluxe.

Waimea's contribution to Hawaii regional cuisine is **Merriman's** (Opelo Plaza, Kawaihae Road; 885-6822), a very highly regarded restaurant that has received national attention. The interior follows a colorful neo-tropical theme and the menu is tailored to what is fresh and local. Since the locale is not simply Hawaii, but upcountry Hawaii, the cuisine combines the seashore and the cattle ranch. You might find fresh fish with spicy lilikoi sauce, wok-charred ahi, steak with kiawe-smoked tomato sauce, or veal sautéed with macadamia nuts. Ultra-deluxe.

WAIMEA MARKETS

Sure Save Super Market (885-7345), located in Waimea at the Parker Ranch Shopping Center, is the only large supermarket along this route. Open daily from 7 a.m. to 11 p.m.

Big Island Natural Foods (Parker Ranch Center, Waimea; 885-6323) has a large supply of vitamins, baked goods, spices, cosmetics, and so on.

If you're looking for meat products, definitely check out the **Kamuela Meat Market** (885-4601) in the Parker Ranch Center. The butchers sell delicious beef fresh from the ranch, and at good prices.

WAIMEA SHOPPING

Parker Ranch Center and **Waimea Center** are *the* shopping complexes in Waimea's cattle country. These modern centers feature sporting goods stores, boutiques, book shops, and more. If you're like me and enjoy browsing through stores in order to capture the flavor of a place, you'll find both malls in the center of Waimea.

Hale Kea (Kawaihae Road about one mile west of Waimea; 885-6095), a turn-of-the-century plantation manager's home, has been converted into an attractive museum/restaurant/shopping center. Restored to its original grandeur and adorned with antiques, the complex includes several original plantation buildings, each converted into arts and crafts shops.

Parker Square (Kawaihae Road, Waimea) specializes in "distinguished shops." Particularly recommended here is the **Gallery of Great Things** (885-7706), a store that fulfills the promise of its name.

WAIMEA NIGHTLIFE

Cattleman's Steak House (Waimea Center, Mamalahoa Highway; 885-4077) features dancing to live music Thursday through Saturday. The sounds range from Hawaiian to country-and-western. On Tuesday and Wednesday the program switches to karaoke.

Kohala Coast

Stretching from Anaehoomalu Beach to the northwestern tip of the Big Island are the districts of South and North Kohala. During the past two decades the southern section, which includes some of the island's prettiest beaches, has seen the building of one deluxe resort after another. Farther north, where Kohala Mountain forms a 5000-foot high spine, the territory remains much as it has for decades. As the Kaahumanu Highway (Route 19) gives way to the northerly Akoni Pule Highway (Route 270), the landscape eventually changes from dry and barren to tropical and luxurious.

Geologically, this was the section of the island that first rose from the sea. Later, as the volcanoes that formed Kohala Mountain became extinct, the region evolved into a center of historical importance. Kamehameha I was born and raised along this wind-blasted coastline and it was here that he initially consolidated his power base. The region is filled with ancient *heiaus* as well as more recent cemeteries that date to the era when sugar plantations dominated the local economy.

Exploring this region from Kailua-Kona you will find that Kaahumanu Highway cuts across a broad swath of lava-crusted country. There are views of Maui to the north, Mauna Kea to the east, and Hualalai to the south. Also along this desolate stretch of road is a type of graffiti unique to the Big Island. Setting white coral atop black lava, and vice versa, ingenious residents have spelled out their names and messages.

For evidence of Kohala's historic significance you need look no further than Puako, a small enclave about 30 miles north of Kailua-Kona. Take the side road leading into Puako and you will find some of the finest **petro-glyphs** in all the island. A well-marked trail near the road's end leads a half-mile inland past three sets of rock carvings. The first is just two hundred yards from the road; the second set, the best, is a few hundred yards farther; and the third lies near the trail's end.

From here, the highway moves north past the luxurious Mauna Kea Beach Hotel. Built by Laurence Rockefeller, it was the first of the five-star resorts to mushroom along the Kohala coastline.

The harbor of Kawaihae, one of the island's busiest ports, is the locale of two major *heiaus*, Mailekini and Puukohola, which have been dedicated as the **Puukohola National Historic Site**. Kamehameha built the impressive triple-tiered Puukohola in 1791 after a prophet related that doing so would ensure his victory over rival islands. At the temple dedication, the ambitious chief aided the prophecy by treacherously slaying his principal enemy. Measuring 224 feet by 100 feet, it was built of lava rocks and boulders that were fitted together using no mortar.

Just 12 miles to the north along Akoni Pule Highway (Route 270) is **Lapakahi State Historical Park** (889-5566), where a preserved village provides a unique glimpse into ancient Hawaiian ways. This is definitely worth a leisurely look-see. Dating back 600 years, this unique site includes fishing shrines, canoe sheds, house sites, and burial plots.

If time permits, take the turnoff to Upolu Airport (just west of Hawi) to reach **Mookini Heiau**, one of the island's most important temples. This holy place—dating to 480 A.D. and measuring 250 feet by 130 feet—is reached by taking a left at the airport, then following the dirt road for a mile-and-a-half. The **Birthplace of Kamehameha I**, marked with a plaque, lies one-third mile (and two gates) farther west along the same road. The boulders here are reputed to be the original birthstones.

The old plantation town of **Hawi**, with its trim houses and weather-blasted storefronts, harkens back to an earlier era. Like neighboring **Kapaau**, it is showing a few signs of refurbishment in the form of small galleries and local shops. Both are charming enclaves adorned with small churches and relics from the days when sugar was king.

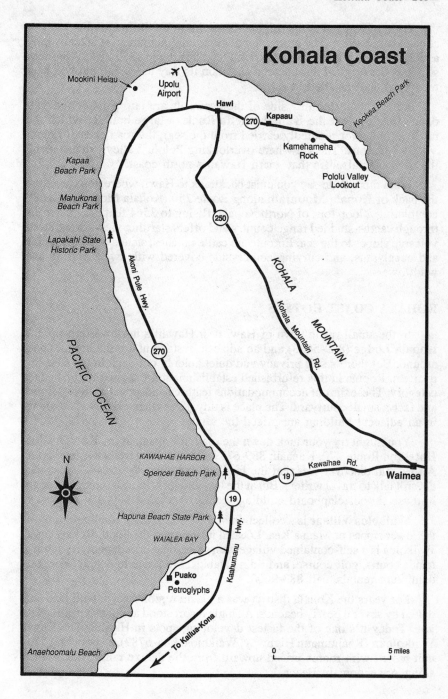

Kohala Coast

Keokea Beach Park

Mookini Heiau

Upolu Airport

Hawi

270 Kapaau

Kamehameha Rock

Pololu Valley Lookout

Kapaa Beach Park

Mahukona Beach Park

Lapakahi State Historic Park

250

KOHALA

MOUNTAIN

Kohala Mountain Rd.

Akoni Pule Hwy.

270

PACIFIC OCEAN

N

KAWAIHAE HARBOR

Spencer Beach Park

Kawaihae Rd.

19 Waimea

19

Hapuna Beach State Park

WAIALEA BAY

Kaahumanu Hwy.

Puako

Petroglyphs

To Kailua-Kona

Anaehoomalu Beach

0   5 miles

Pride of Kapaau is the original **Kamehameha Statue,** a nine-ton creation cast in bronze. The more famous Honolulu monument is actually only a replica of this gilt figure. Crafted in Florence around 1879 by an American sculptor, the original disappeared at sea on its way to Hawaii but was later recovered and installed here.

Along this lush, rainy side of the peninsula are taro patches and pandanus forests. Past the **Kamehameha Rock** (a large boulder which the mighty conqueror reputedly carried from the sea), the road ends at **Pololu Valley Lookout.** The view here overlooking Pololu Valley extends along the monumental cliffs that guard Hawaii's north coast.

From this cul-de-sac you must backtrack to Hawi, where you can climb the back of **Kohala Mountain** along Route 250 (Kohala Mountain Road), completing a loop tour of North Kohala. Rising to 3564 feet, the road rolls through cactus-studded range country and offers startling views down steep volcanic slopes to the sea. Enroute are cattle ranches, stands of Norfolk pine and eucalyptus, and curving countryside covered with sweet grasses and wildflowers.

KOHALA COAST HOTELS

In the small rustic town of Hawi near Hawaii's northwestern tip, the **Kohala Lodge** (889-5433) and an adjacent restaurant are the hottest spots around. But there's still privacy and quiet aplenty out back in the sleeping quarters. Rooms in this refurbished establishment are tagged in the budget category. These tinroof accommodations feature handsome hardwood floors and face a small courtyard. The place is tidy, if less than elegant. The rooms in an adjacent building are priced the same.

You might try your luck down the road in Kapaau at the **Kohala Club Hotel** (on Route 270, Kapaau; 889-6793). I hope you fare better than I did. All I could discover was that the landlady rents mostly to local folks and doesn't talk to travel writers. But at the low budget prices she charges, rooms in those tinroof clapboard buildings could be a good buy. Let me know.

Waikoloa Village is a collection of townhouse-style condominiums on the lower slopes of Mauna Kea. Located inland from the South Kohala coast, Waikoloa is a self-contained village with store, post office, pool, restaurant, tennis courts, golf course, and riding stables. Moderate to deluxe. For condominium rentals, call 883-9000.

For years the Kohala district was a placid region strewn with lava and dotted by several pearly beaches. A single resort stood along its virgin coastline. Today it's one of the fastest developing spots in Hawaii. The **Royal Waikoloan** (Kaahumanu Highway, Waikoloa; 885-6789), a sprawling 550-unit resort, with rooms priced upward from the deluxe range, now stands along Anaehoomalu Beach.

Several miles north, the **Mauna Lani Bay Hotel** (Kaahumanu Highway, Kawaihae; 885-6622), a 3200-acre resort, rests on another white-sand beach. Designed in the shape of an arrowhead and boasting 354 rooms, this luxurious facility offers two golf courses, ten tennis courts, and seven restaurants, several of which are award-winners. With brilliant green gardens set against black lava, the landscape combines curving lawns and palm-ringed fishponds. Each guest room is spaciously laid out and designed in a pastel motif. Ultra-deluxe.

The Kohala Coast's original resort, the **Mauna Kea Beach Hotel** (Kaahumanu Highway, Kawaihae; 882-7222), is a world-class complex that still ranks as one of the very finest hotels in the islands. Set on a crescent beach, boasting an 18-hole golf course and 500 manicured acres, the hotel is lavishly decorated and enjoys an impeccable reputation. Room rates for a modified American plan (breakfast and dinner included) begin high in the ultra-deluxe category.

KOHALA COAST RESTAURANTS

Outside the expensive resorts, you'll find very few restaurants along Hawaii's northwestern shore. Sailors say that any port is good in a storm, and on such a sparsely settled coast any restaurant is probably worth heading for.

If you cast anchor in Kawaihae, consider the budget-priced **Café Pesto** (Kawaihae Center; 882-1071). Pizza is the specialty at this simple café. But you'll also find linguini marinara, fettucine al pesto and even a Cajun shrimp dish.

The food is Mexican but the theme is surfing at **Tres Hombres Beach Grill** (882-1031), located in the same complex. There is a great display of surfing memorabilia and some of the bar counters are even fashioned from surfboards. The standard Mexican cuisine is moderately priced.

For very inexpensive food, try the **Blue Dolphin Restaurant** (across from Kawaihae Port; 882-7771). This take-out stand has a small dining pavilion in back. The plate lunches and sandwiches are budget-priced.

Up near Kohala's northern tip, in the timeworn town of Hawi, is **Honey's Country Kitchen** (889-0294). With a Western theme, this eatery serves up Hawaiian-style country cooking. The menu offers steak, pork, chicken, and teriyaki dishes. Budget to moderate.

For a taste of funky, traditional Hawaii there's **The Soda Fountain** (★) (just off Akoni Pule Highway about one mile east of Hawi; 889-0208). Set in a tinroof plantation building with bare walls and plastic tablecloths, it serves breakfast and lunch at super budget prices.

Generally, in outlying areas like the Kohala Peninsula, you'll find that although the restaurants are few and simple, they have a homey atmosphere about them that can never be captured in crowded urban areas. As I'm sure you're well aware, this fact sometimes makes dining in the outback almost as grand an adventure as hiking or camping.

With all the development that's been occurring along the Kohala Coast, it seems inevitable that gourmet restaurants would become an important part of the landscape. Thus far no independent dining rooms have opened; all are connected with one of the several resorts now dotting the shoreline.

For the ultimate luncheon buffet, try **The Terrace** (Kaahumanu Highway, Kawaihae; 882-7222) at the Mauna Kea Beach Hotel. This hotel, built on the Kohala coast by Laurence Rockefeller, is famous for its fabulous feasts. Every afternoon the staff spreads out assorted cold cuts and salads, plus steaming dishes such as hot sausages with sauerkraut and chicken paella, and a dessert table that resembles the window of a Parisian *patisserie*. The tab will be high, but this bounteous meal could be all you eat that day. In fact, you may want to skip breakfast if you plan on lunching here. Deluxe.

The Mauna Lani Bay Hotel (Kaahumanu Highway, Kawaihae; 885-6622) hosts some well-known, formal, ultra-deluxe-priced restaurants. The **Bay Terrace**, serving three meals, features an ever-changing dinner menu. The offerings may include fresh grilled salmon in an asparagus sauce or mahimahi with feta cheese. Beef dishes include prime rib with a spicy horseradish sauce and Black Angus steak. At lunch there are cold sandwiches as well as specialties like chicken fettucine, pizza, and sautéed prawns.

If you'd prefer fresh fish served with flair, try **Le Soleil** (885-6622). Specialties include baked Norwegian salmon with a horseradish crust. Meat eaters can try roasted rack of lamb with garlic flan or grilled veal chop stuffed with spinach and feta cheese.

Also located at the Mauna Lani Bay Hotel is the **Canoe House** (885-6622), one of the Big Island's most highly regarded dining rooms. Specializing in Pacific Rim cuisine and offering spectacular sunsets as an appetizer, it delivers fine food and a fine time. The menu, which changes frequently, is a creative mix of island and Asian dishes. Ultra-deluxe; dinner only.

At the Royal Waikoloan (Kaahumanu Highway, Waikoloa; 885-6789) there's a varied choice of restaurants. Depending on your purse, you can choose the moderate-priced **Garden Café**, a pleasant, open-air coffee shop; the wood-paneled **Tiara Room**, serving French-Polynesian cuisine and priced deluxe; or the similarly tabbed **Royal Terrace**.

KOHALA COAST MARKETS

On the western side of the island, there are several stores on the Kohala peninsula. **Kawaihae General Store** in Kawaihae has a small selection of groceries and dry goods. Between Kawaihae and Kailua there are no stores.

K. Takata Store (Route 27; Hawi; 889-5261) is an old market with an ample stock of groceries. It's the best place to shop north of Kailua.

A. Arakaki Store (889-5262), on Route 27 in Halaula, is conveniently located for campers and picnickers headed out to Pololu Valley.

KOHALA COAST SHOPPING

Way out on the Kohala peninsula, try not to miss **Vea Polynesian** (Akoni Pule Highway, Hawi; 889-5944). Owner Ika Vea, from Tonga, imports handiworks from his homeland as well as from Fiji, Samoa, and Tahiti. Ika also carves striking *tikis* and offers a variety of hula implements. The workmanship is of a very high quality, and the prices are often only 20 percent above wholesale.

A few miles farther along Akoni Pule Highway, in the falsefront town of Kapaau, you'll find **Ackerman Galleries** (889-5971). Divided into two different stores on opposite sides of the street, Ackerman's features fine art in one location and crafts items in the other.

Shopping in Kohala was once a matter of uncovering family-owned crafts shops in tiny towns. Now that it has become a major resort area, you can also browse at designer stores in several top-flight hotels. Simply drive along Akoni Pule Highway between Kailua and the Kohala Peninsula; you'll encounter, from south to north, the **Royal Waikoloan**, **Mauna Lani Bay Hotel**, and the **Mauna Kea Beach Hotel**. Each of these large resort complexes features an array of boutiques, knickknack shops, jewelers, sundries, and other outlets.

KOHALA COAST NIGHTLIFE

Night owls along the Kohala Coast roost at one of four resort hotels. The Mauna Kea Beach Hotel (Kaahumanu Highway, Kawaihae; 882-7222) has a Hawaiian band at **The Terrace** and features popular dance music in the **Batik Room**.

Nearby at the Mauna Lani Bay Hotel (Kaahumanu Highway, Kawaihae; 885-6622) there's a sleek rendezvous called **"the bar,"** which hosts a jazz band nightly. At other places in this spacious resort, you can also dance, listen to Hawaiian music, or imbibe in a lovely, open-air setting.

Up in Kawaihae, there is live music every Wednesday and Saturday at **Tres Hombres Beach Grill** (Kawaihae Center; 882-1031). On other nights you can enjoy the original collection of surfing memorabilia that decorates the place.

The night scene at the **Royal Waikoloan** (Kaahumanu Highway, Waikoloa; 885-6789) centers around several watering holes that offer a variety of diversions ranging from ocean views to live bands to Polynesian revues.

The **Lobby Lounge** at the Ritz-Carton Mauna Lani (1 North Kaniku Drive; 885-2000) hosts a trio and vocalist nightly. There's dancing to the sound of soft rock and jazz.

(Text continued on page 172.)

Skindiving the Gold Coast

Hawaii's Kona Coast offers some of the world's most spectacular skindiving and scuba diving. All along this western shoreline lie magnificent submerged caves, lava flows, cliffs, and coral reefs.

Protected from prevailing trade winds by Mauna Kea and Mauna Loa, Kona enjoys the gentlest conditions. Usually the weather is sunny, the water clear, and the surf mild. It's small wonder, then, that adventurers travel from all over the world to explore Kona's underwater world.

This brief description of the best skindiving spots, with a list of shops that provide equipment and tours, will lead you to the water's edge. For more detailed information, just drop by one of the area's dive shops.

KAILUA-KONA AREA SKINDIVING SPOTS

Kamakahonu Beach, the sand patch next to Kailua's King Kamehameha Kona Coast Hotel, is a crowded but conveniently located dive site. There are corals and many species of fish here, but watch out for heavy boat traffic along the nearby wharf. **Hale Halawai,** an oceanfront park in Kailua, has good snorkeling off its rocky beach. Nearby, off **Huggo's** restaurant, the underwater viewing is great, especially at night, when huge manta rays wing through here.

Old Airport Beach, just a stone's skip north of town, affords excellent diving all along its length. The entry is rocky, but once in, you'll find the waters spectacular. Many glass-bottom boats tour this area.

Honokohau Beach has some good spots south of the small-boat harbor. Stay away from the harbor itself, though; sharks are frequent.

Disappearing Sands Beach, several miles south of Kailua, offers some good spots around the rocks bordering the beach. But it's usually very crowded, so you might want to disappear yourself, to another beach. Try the diving just south of here at the four-mile marker.

Kahaluu Beach Park, a good place for beginners, abounds with tropical fish. There's also good diving off the **Kona Surf Hotel** at the south end of Alii Drive.

KOHALA COAST SKINDIVING SPOTS

Anaehoomalu Beach is good for beginners, but it lacks the scenic diversity of other areas. There's good diving at the end of the road leading

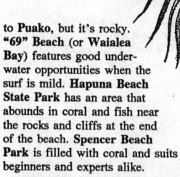

to **Puako**, but it's rocky. **"69" Beach (or Waialea Bay)** features good underwater opportunities when the surf is mild. **Hapuna Beach State Park** has an area that abounds in coral and fish near the rocks and cliffs at the end of the beach. **Spencer Beach Park** is filled with coral and suits beginners and experts alike.

Mahukona Beach Park is an old shipping area littered with underwater refuse which makes for great exploring. **Kapaa Beach Park** offers good diving, but it has a rocky entrance and tricky currents. **Keokea Beach Park,** an excellent spearfishing area, is often plagued by wind and high surf.

SOUTH KONA SKINDIVING SPOTS

Napoopoo Beach Park is an excellent diving spot—so good, in fact, that it draws diving tours and glass-bottom boats. The best diving is across Kealakekua Bay near the Captain Cook Monument.

Keei Beach features a lot of coral and, reportedly, a sea grotto. At **Puuhonua o Honaunau Park,** next to the City of Refuge, there's a rocky entry to some marvelous diving areas. **Hookena Beach Park** offers some good dive spots near the cliffs south of the beach. **Milolii** has some excellent diving areas as well as fascinating tidepools.

DIVING TOURS AND EQUIPMENT

The following shops rent and sell diving equipment or sponsor diving tours: **Jack's Diving Locker** (Coconut Grove Market Place, 75-5819 Alii Drive, Kailua; 329-7585) and **Fair Wind** (78-7128 Kaleopapa Road, Keauhou Bay; 322-2788).

KOHALA COAST BEACHES AND PARKS

Anaehoomalu Beach—An enchanting area, this is one of the island's most beautiful beaches. There are palm trees, a luxurious lagoon, and a long crescent of white sand. Turn from the sea and take in the gorgeous mountain scenery. Or explore the nearby petroglyph field and archaeological ruins. Very popular; often crowded; fronted by a major resort complex.

Facilities: Picnic tables, restrooms, showers. Restaurants available in the adjacent Royal Waikoloan. *Swimming:* Excellent along this partially protected shore. *Snorkeling:* See the "Skindiving the Gold Coast" section in this chapter. *Fishing:* Mullet, threadfin, big-eyed scad, bonefish, and papio are among the usual catches here.

Camping: None.

Getting there: Located a half-mile off Kaahumanu Highway, about 25 miles north of Kailua near the 76-mile marker.

"69" Beach or **Waialea Bay** (★)—No, it's not what you might think. This lovely beach is named for a nearby highway marker rather than for licentious beach parties. The white-sand shoreline extends several hundred yards along a rocky cove. Despite houses nearby, the spot is fairly secluded; fallen *kiawe* trees along the beachfront provide tiny hideaways.

Facilities: None. Three miles to market and restaurants in Kawaihae. *Swimming:* Very good, but exercise caution. *Snorkeling:* See the "Skindiving the Gold Coast" section in this chapter. *Surfing:* Good breaks near the southwest end of the bay and off the northwest point. Long paddle out.

Camping: Not permitted.

Getting there: The name "69" derives from a highway mileage marker near the entrance to Hapuna Beach Park, three miles south of Kawaihae. From Kaahumanu Highway, turn into the park entrance. Then take the paved road that runs southwest from the park (between the beach and the A-frames). Go about six-tenths of a mile on this road and then turn right on a dirt road (the road at the very bottom of the hill). When the road forks, after about one-tenth mile, go left. Follow this new road another one-tenth mile around to the beach.

Hapuna Beach State Park—Here's one of the state's prettiest parks. A well-tended lawn—studded with *hala*, coconut, and *kiawe* trees—rolls down to a wide corridor of white sand that extends for one-half mile, with points of lava at either end. Maui's Haleakala crater looms across the water. This is a popular and generally very crowded place. Unfortunately, a major resort hotel is currently under construction at one end of the beach.

Facilities: Numerous picnic areas; restrooms, showers, electricity; information, 882-7995. Three miles to market and restaurants in Kawaihae. *Swimming:* Excellent at north end of beach. *Snorkeling:* See the "Skindiving the Gold Coast" section in this chapter. *Fishing:* You can hope to hook papio, red bigeye, mullet, threadfin, and menpachi.

the Gold Coast" section in this chapter. *Fishing:* You can hope to hook papio, red bigeye, mullet, threadfin, and menpachi.

Camping: Screened A-frame shelters, located on a rise above the beach, can be rented. These cottages are equipped with table, sleeping platforms, and electricity; they sleep up to four people. Bring your own bedding. Toilet and kitchen facilities are shared among all six A-frames. For reservations, contact Kapuna Beach Services (882-1095). No tent or trailer camping is allowed here.

Getting there: Located on Kaahumanu Highway, three miles south of Kawaihae.

Spencer Beach Park—Lacking the uncommon beauty of Anaehoomalu or Hapuna, this spacious park is still lovely. There's a wide swath of white sand, backed by a lawn and edged with *kiawe* and coconut trees. Very popular camping grounds.

Facilities: Picnic area, restrooms, showers, large pavilion, tennis courts, electricity. A market and restaurants are less than a mile away in Kawaihae. *Swimming:* Excellent. *Snorkeling:* See the "Skindiving the Gold Coast" section in this chapter. *Fishing:* Common catches are papio, red bigeye, mullet, threadfin, and menpachi.

Camping: Both tent and trailer camping are okay, but a county permit is required. The county has limited the number of campers here. Reservations are required.

Getting there: The park is located off Akoni Pule Highway one mile south of Kawaihae.

Mahukona Beach Park—This now-abandoned harbor village and boat landing lies along a rocky windswept shore. The lawn is shaded with *kiawe* trees; there's no sandy beach here at all. Nicer areas lie to the south, but if you seek a site far from the frenzied crowd, this is a good retreat.

Facilities: Picnic area, restrooms, electricity, no drinking water. About 13 miles from restaurants and markets in Kawaihae. *Swimming:* Poor access from rocks. *Snorkeling:* See the "Skindiving the Gold Coast" section in this chapter. *Fishing:* Frequent catches include threadfin, mullet, menpachi, papio, and red bigeye.

Camping: Tent and trailer. County permit required.

Getting there: Located off Akoni Pule Highway about 13 miles north of Kawaihae.

Kapaa Beach Park—Besides a spectacular view of Maui, this rocky, wind-plagued park has little to offer. It does have a miniature cove bounded by *kiawe* trees, but lacks any sand, which is sometimes nice to have on a beach.

Facilities: Picnic area, restrooms. No drinking water. About 14 miles to markets and restaurants in Kawaihae. *Swimming:* Poor access over rocks.

Snorkeling: See the "Skindiving the Gold Coast" section in this chapter. *Fishing:* At last, a sport benefiting from all those rocks! Stand out there and try for threadfin, mullet, red bigeye, papio, and menpachi.

Camping: Tents and trailers are allowed, but the terrain is very rocky for tent camping. County permit required.

Getting there: The park is off Akoni Pule Highway about 14 miles north of Kawaihae.

Keokea Beach Park—Seclusion is the password to this beautiful little park with its cliff-rimmed cove and tiered lawn fringed by *hala* and palm trees. Set way out on the Kohala peninsula, this retreat receives very heavy rainfall.

Facilities: Picnic area, restrooms, showers. Four miles to restaurants and markets in Hawi. *Swimming:* Only with extreme caution. *Snorkeling:* See the "Skindiving the Gold Coast" section in this chapter. *Fishing:* Mullet, papio, red bigeye, threadfin, and menpachi are the main catches here.

Camping: Tent and trailer. County permit required.

Getting there: Take Akoni Pule Highway about six miles past Hawi. Turn at the sign and follow the winding road one mile.

Kailua-Kona Area

At the center of the tourist scene on the Kona Coast is the contemporary town of Kailua. Here, extending for five miles along Alii Drive from the King Kamemeha Hotel to Keauhou Bay, is a string of hotels, restaurants, condominiums, and shopping malls. Like a little Waikiki, Kailua-Kona is the commercial focus for this entire side of the island.

Despite the tinsel and tourist trappings, this old fishing village and former haunt of Hawaiian royalty still retains some of its charm. If you tour **Kailua wharf** (Alii Drive) around 4 p.m., the fishing boats may be hauling freshly caught marlin onto the docks. Some of the finest marlin grounds in the world lie off this shoreline and the region is renowned for other deep-sea fish. The wharf itself is a departure point not only for fishing charters but for snorkeling tours and glass-bottom boat cruises as well. It's also a favorite place for viewing Kona's fabled sunsets.

On the grounds of the nearby King Kamehameha Hotel (75-5660 Palani Road; 329-2911) rests **Ahuena Heiau**, an important historical site that has been partially reconstructed and combined, in truly tacky fashion, with a hotel luau facility. This compound represents the royal grounds used by Kamehameha I for several years during the early 19th century.

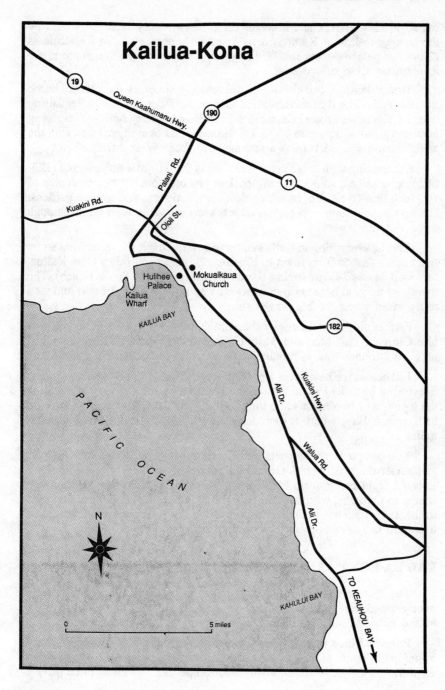

ing royal Hawaiian relics. It seems that this two-story estate was built by the brother-in-law of Kamehameha I and later used by King Kalakaua as a summer palace during the 1880s. Among the fine furnishings are many handcrafted from native *koa*.

Mokuaikaua Church, directly across the street, is the oldest church in the islands. The first missionaries anchored offshore in 1820 after sailing over 18,000 miles around Cape Horn from Boston. They built the imposing lava-and-coral structure in 1836. By the way, that churchyard tree with the weird salami-shaped fruit is a sausage tree from West Africa.

Contrasting with these venerable sites is the **Atlantis Submarine** (329-6626; admission), an 80-ton craft parked just offshore. Diving to depths of 150 feet, this 46-passenger sub explores tropical reefs and sponge gardens. During the hour-long voyage, passengers view the underwater world through large viewing ports.

Almost everything in Kailua sits astride Alii Drive, the waterfront street that extends south from town to Keauhou Bay. Several miles from Kailua, this road passes **Disappearing Sands Beach** (or Magic Sands Beach). The lovely white sand here is often washed away by heavy winter surf and then redeposited when the big waves subside.

Farther along, on the rocky shore of Kahaluu Bay, is **St. Peter's Catholic Church**. This blue-and-white clapboard chapel, precariously perched on a lava foundation, is reputedly the world's second-smallest church.

Just across the bay, at the Keauhou Beach Hotel (322-3441), are several interesting historical sites. Ask in the hotel lobby for a free map detailing the location of two *heiaus* and the **King's Pool**. Then you can continue on to Keauhou Bay, where a monument marks the **Birthplace of Kamehameha III**.

You can pay your respects to the crew of the space shuttle *Challenger* at the **Astronaut Ellison S. Onizuka Space Center** (329-3441, admission). Located eight miles north of Kailua at Keahole Airport, this pavilion is a tribute to Onizuka, who lived in Hawaii, and the other astronauts who died in the 1986 tragedy. Videos and interactive displays trace the astronauts' lives and the development of the space program.

KAILUA-KONA AREA HOTELS

The Kona Coast is as expensive as it is beautiful. Hawaiian royalty once resided here, and their former playground is still the haunt of well-heeled tourists. As a result, bargains are as rare as rainy days.

Patey's Place in Paradise (75-195 Ana Olaola Street; 326-7018), a hostel in the center of Kailua, is small, clean, and conveniently priced. There are dormitory-style accommodations for 20 people as well as three private rooms that sleep two. Kitchen facilities, a television room, and free airport pickup are provided. Budget.

Kona Seaside Hotel (75-5646 Palani Road; 329-2455) is a sprawling 228-room complex set in the heart of Kailua. Located across the street from the ocean, this multi-faceted facility features the Tower Wing with moderate-priced rooms and the Garden Wing where the deluxe-priced facilities come with mini-kitchenettes. Rooms in the Pool Wing, also moderately tabbed, are smaller and less fashionable but are conveniently placed around one of the hotel's two swimming pools. While the more expensive rooms add lanais and wall-to-wall carpeting, all the accommodations are tastefully done. A lounge and restaurant are adjacent.

Kona Bay Hotel (75-5739 Alii Drive; 329-1393) is part of the old Kona Inn, the rest of which fell to Kailua developers, who have perversely transformed it into yet another shopping mall. What remains is a four-story semicircular structure with a pool, bar, restaurant, and lounge in the center. The rooms are large, tastefully furnished, and quiet. Some have lava walls that provide a pleasant backdrop plus excellent soundproofing. The staff is friendly, and the atmosphere is very appealing. I once spent a relaxing month here and highly recommend the place. Moderate.

Kona Islander Inn (75-5776 Kuakini Highway; 329-3181) occupies several three-story buildings spread across a lush swath of land. Set between Alii Drive and Route 11 on Kailua's outskirts, this chain hotel has a large lobby and an oval pool flanked by MacArthur palms. All rooms have small lanais, cable televisions, refrigerators, carpets, and air conditioning. Tastefully appointed, but lacking a good ocean view. Moderate.

Kona Tiki Hotel (75-5968 Alii Drive; 329-1425), a mile down the road, is a quaint hotel neatly situated on the ocean. The rooms are bright and clean. Despite the contrasting decorative themes and the noise from Alii Drive, I recommend this 15-unit establishment for its oceanview lanais, oceanfront pool, barbecue, garden, and complimentary continental breakfast. Rooms equipped with mini-kitchenettes (sink, refrigerator, and two-burner stove crowded into one unit) rent for moderate prices.

Also tabbed in the moderate range, but a better bargain still, are the rooms at **Kona White Sands Apartment Hotel** (77-6467 Alii Drive; 329-3210). Located just across the street from Disappearing Sands Beach (the nicest beach along Alii Drive), this ten-unit hotel offers both studios and one-bedroom apartments. Each comes with kitchenette; deluxe rooms have ceiling fans. The cinderblock and plasterboard walls are pretty plain, but who needs fancy interior decoration with that knockout ocean view? Rooms are cross-ventilated, and the cooling breeze will probably bring along noise from cars and sun revelers. That's the extra price for living this close to the Kona Coast. Many people are willing to pay it, so you'll have to reserve a room far in advance. (Contact Hawaii Resorts Management, 75-5776 Kuakini Highway, Suite 105-C, Kailua-Kona, HI 96740; 800-553-5035 from the mainland).

Anchoring one end of Kailua Bay is the town's most historic hotel. The **King Kamehameha Kona Beach Hotel** (75-5660 Palani Road; 329-2911), priced higher than its young neighbors, is nonetheless deserving of note. The lobby alone is worth the price of admission: It's a wood-paneled affair along which you can trace the history of ancient Hawaii. For its guests, the "King Kam" has a pool, tennis courts, and jacuzzi, plus a host of other amenities ranging from an activities desk to room service. The rooms themselves are quite spacious, fashionably decorated, and equipped with positively everything. You'll find plush carpeting, color televisions, air conditioning, refrigerators, and lanais with spectacular views of the ocean or mountains. Deluxe to ultra-deluxe.

Situated on a lava-rock beach just outside Kailua is the **Kailua Plantation House** (75-5948 Alii Drive; 329-3727). This contemporary two-story, plantation-style bed and breakfast has five rooms, all with private baths and lanais. There's a jacuzzi and tiny pool along the oceanfront and a comfortable sitting room for guests. The entire place, painted white with oak trim, is light, bright, and airy. Island art adorns the walls and a sense of easy elegance pervades the place. Deluxe.

Keauhou Beach Hotel (78-6740 Alii Drive; 332-3441) is a true sleeper. A large, blocky, six-story hotel, it hardly seems on the outside to possess the Hawaiian spirit. But the grounds include an ancient *heiau* and other archaeological sites and the waterfront location boasts magnificent tidepools that extend for acres. The complex includes an oceanfront swimming pool, restaurant, a cozy waterfront bar, and tennis courts. With prices that start in the moderate-to-deluxe range, the hotel also offers room service.

Architecturally, one of the region's most intriguing spots is the **Kona Surf Resort** (78-128 Ehukai Street; 322-3411), a 537-room hotel. Situated on 14 acres along a peninsula that juts into Keauhou Bay, the facility fans out into four wings. At the center of the configuration is a lobby area complete with restaurants, lounges, and shops. It lacks a sand beach, but there is a freshwater as well as a saltwater pool and the snorkeling in the bay is good; adjacent to tennis and golf. While most rooms are in the ultra-deluxe range, there are standard rooms at deluxe prices.

Of course, when money is no object the place to stay is **Kona Village Resort** (★) (P.O. Box 1299, Kaupulehu-Kona, HI 96745; 325-5555), a very plush, very private colony located several miles north of Kailua. Favored by movie stars and other celebrities seeking escape from autograph hounds and aggressive agents, this regal retreat is set along a white-sand cove in an ancient Hawaiian fishing village. The individual guest cottages are thatched-roof structures (*hales*), variously designed to represent the traditional houses of Hawaiian, Tahitian, Fijian, Samoan, and other Polynesian groups. There are no televisions, radios, clocks, or air conditioning; but you will find serenity, solitude, and a well-heeled version of hidden Hawaii, not to mention tennis courts, sailboats, outrigger canoes, and glass-bottom excursion boats. Prices are in the ultra-deluxe class and are based on the American plan.

KAILUA-KONA AREA CONDOMINIUMS

Kona Alii (75-5782 Alii Drive; 329-2000). One-bedroom, two-bath apartments run from $80 double (and from $60 during the off-season, April 1 to December 15). This seven-story building is just across the street from the ocean.

The Sea Village (75-6002 Alii Drive, about one mile south of Kailua; 329-1000). One-bedroom garden view units start at $90 single or double; two bedrooms, two baths, $114 for one to four people; prices increase from mid-December to mid-April. Jacuzzi, swimming pool, and tennis courts. Oceanfront, but no beach.

Kona Riviera Villa (75-6124 Alii Drive; 329-1996) is a relatively small condominium on a lava-rock beach outside Kailua. It's attractively landscaped, has a pool, and rents studio units for $70 ($60 from April 15 to December 14).

Kona Bali Kai (76-6246 Alii Drive; 329-9381). Studio apartments are $90 single or double ($110 during peak season), one-bedroom apartments with mountain views go for $110 ($130 peak) for one to four people. One and two bedrooms with ocean views start at $145 ($160 peak). Jacuzzi and pool. One mile from Disappearing Sands Beach.

Kona Magic Sands (77-6452 Alii Drive; 329-6488). Studio apartment, $65 ($70 peak) single or double. Located on the ocean, next to Disappearing Sands Beach. Three-night minimum.

Aston Kona By The Sea (75-6106 Alii Drive; 327-2300) is a large, trimly landscaped complex on a lava-rock beach. The suites are one- and two-bedroom; all have two baths and a lanai; there's a pool and jacuzzi. Rates start at $180 ($160 from April 1 to December 21).

KAILUA-KONA AREA RESTAURANTS

For anyone on a tight budget, Kailua would seem an unlikely place to find a decent meal. Most restaurants along the Gold Coast cater to gilded tourists and wealthy residents. If you work at it, though, you'll locate a few low-cost eating places.

Kona Coast Shopping Center houses several short-order joints. **Betty's Chinese Kitchen** (329-3770) serves tasty, nutritious, budget-priced meals at its cafeteria-style emporium. **Kim's Place** (329-4677) has an assortment of low-priced Japanese and Korean dishes. Open for lunch and dinner, they prepare *yakitori*, teriyaki, *tonkatsu,* and tempura. On the Korean side of the menu there's *bolgogi* and *kalbi*. If you'd prefer something simpler, Kim's also has hamburger steaks and mahimahi sandwiches. Budget.

If these places don't intrigue you, head downhill to the North Kona Shopping Center. **Kuakini Café** (329-1166) is not as bad as all that. Matter of fact, some people find the plate lunches and hamburgers down-right *ono*. Budget.

For budget-priced dining in opulent surroundings, you should stop by the **Kona Veranda Coffee Shop** (329-2911) in the Hotel King Kamehameha. Open for breakfast as well as lunch, this pleasant café serves standard American fare as well as more imaginative island dishes. Of course the opulence comes not so much from the coffee shop as the hotel facilities. The "King Kam" is a famous hotel, featuring a lobby that contains a collection of ancient Hawaiian artifacts worthy of any museum. The hotel's beach and shopping mall also provide post-prandial opportunities.

Sibu Café (Banyan Court, Alii Drive; 329-1112) prepares a host of Indonesian dishes daily for lunch and dinner. Among the tangy favorites at this outdoor café are beef *saté*, tofu and vegetable stir-fry, and Balinese chicken (which is marinated, cooked over an open flame, then served with peanut sauce). Budget.

Tolkien fans should stop by **Tom Bombadil's** (75-5864 Walua Road; 329-1292) quaint little place near Alii Drive. The murals decorating this small café represent scenes from the *Lord of the Rings* trilogy. In addition to pizza, Tom serves sandwiches straight from Goldberry's pantry. But take heed: In these parts a roast beef sandwich translates as "The Pride of Gondor," turkey is a "Withywindle," and for ham and cheese read "Rivendell." Tom also serves fish and chicken dishes as well as salads. If you ever get past the menu, you'll find the food quite delicious. Budget to moderate.

The **Oceanview Inn** (on Alii Drive; 329-9998), a large, informal dining room opposite Kailua Bay, has a voluminous lunch and dinner menu. Chinese, Hawaiian, fresh fish, and meat dishes, served all day, comprise only part of the selection. This is a perfect opportunity to try local fish, caught several miles offshore in some of the world's finest fishing grounds. There's also a complete breakfast menu. Budget.

The best buy in the moderate-price category is right next door at **Stan's Restaurant** (75-5687 Alii Drive; 329-4500), where you can order from a unique menu that lists dinners by price. Here you'll find numerous steak, seafood, and chicken concoctions. This open-air establishment overlooking Kailua Bay offers significantly more atmosphere than the Oceanview. There are rattan furnishings, a cocktail lounge, and a windswept waiting area. Lunch isn't served, but breakfast features coconut, macadamia nut, or banana hotcakes.

Kona Amigos (75-5669 Alii Drive; 326-2840), on the same waterfront drive, specializes in south-of-the-border cuisine. Here you'll dine out on a lanai overlooking Kailua Bay or in one of several rooms attractively paneled in *lauhala* and bamboo. Open for lunch and dinner, this Mexican restaurant offers crab enchiladas, fajitas, steak sandwiches, and fresh fish dishes. Moderate.

Another popular oceanfront dining room is **Marty's Steak and Seafood** (Alii Drive; 329-1571). It's an open-air affair, with torches lighting the perimeter. The entire restaurant is situated on a balustraded balcony overlooking the water, making it an enchanting place to dine (or simply enjoy a beer). Of course, that view is costly: The dinner menu rises from the moderate to the deluxe category; lunch is similarly priced. But I've always found Marty's dishes worth the asking price. So if you're in the mood for steak, chops, crab, lobster, or scampi, stop by.

Guiseppe's Italian Café (75-5699 Alii Drive; 329-7888), a hole-in-the-wall bistro punched into a corner of the Kailua Bay Inn Shopping Plaza, has moderately priced Italian food. The menu is pretty standard as is the red-checkered oilcloth interior.

Aesthetically speaking, **Kona Ranch House** (75-5653 Ololi Street; 329-7061) swings both ways. One section of the trimly appointed restaurant features informal dining in an understated and comfortable environment. In the adjoining Plantation Lanai facility you can treat yourself to a candle-light-and-linen-tablecloth experience. The menu is the same for both sections of this switch-hitting establishment. Drop in for lunch or dinner and you'll find an inventory of entrées ranging from ribs to chicken and from New York steak to fresh fish. There are also inexpensive sandwiches and appetizer dishes. At breakfast Kona Ranch House offers an array of egg dishes. So take your pick of locales, easy or elegant, and enjoy good food at moderate prices.

For a touch of class at a reasonable cost, consider **Eclipse Restaurant** (75-5711 Kuakini Highway; 329-4686). Open for lunch and dinner, this sleek dining room offers New York steak, prawns, a vegetarian dish, and the catch of the day at moderate prices. The place is finished in fine woods and decorated with original artworks, etched glass, and potted palms. You can gaze into the aquarium, lounge at the brass-rail bar, or stay after hours when it changes face to become a danceclub. Appealing ambience, moderately good food, outstanding service.

The commemorative sign at the **Kona Inn** (75-5744 Alii Drive; 329-4455) tells the tale of the old inn—how it was built back in the steamship era when Kona was gaining fame as a marlin fishing ground. The bad news is that the original hotel was razed and replaced with a mall—of which this contemporary namesake is a part. The good news is that the restaurant is quite attractive—an open-air, oceanfront affair with two separate dining facilities. The Kona Inn Café Grill serves grilled appetizers and sandwiches. The dining room serves several fresh fish dishes daily as well as prime rib and Hawaiian-style chicken; dinner only. Moderate to deluxe.

Jameson's By the Sea (77-6452 Alii Drive near Disappearing Sands Beach; 329-3195) is a lovely waterfront restaurant with an emphasis on fresh local seafood dishes. Tucked unpretentiously into the corner of a large condominium, Jameson's conveys a modest sense of elegance: bentwood furniture, potted palms, a seascape from the lanai or through plate-glass windows, and good service. Choose from an enticing menu of fresh local catches, steaks, veal, chicken dishes, and other gourmet delights. Lunch and dinner weekdays, dinner only on weekends. Deluxe.

For continental cuisine in a fashionable setting, consider **La Bourgogne French Restaurant** (Kuakini Plaza on Kuakini Highway, four miles south of Kailua; 329-6711). Open for dinner only, this French country dining room features New York steak with peppercorn sauce, roast saddle of lamb, veal sweetbreads with Madeira sauce, coquilles St. Jacques, and fresh fish selections. For appetizers there are escargots, truffled mousse, and steak tartar. Round off the meal with cherries jubilee or chocolate mousse and you have a French feast right here in tropical Hawaii. Deluxe.

KAILUA-KONA AREA MARKETS

The best place to shop anywhere along the Kona Coast is in the town of Kailua. This commercial center features several supermarkets as well as a number of specialty shops. One of the first choices among supermarkets is **Food 4 Less** (75-5595 Palani Road; 326-2729) in the center of Kailua. It has everything you could possibly need.

If you'd prefer another supermarket with a similar selection, try **K.T.A. Super Store** (329-1677) in the Kona Coast Shopping Center. It's open every day from 6 a.m. to midnight, and is another of the Kailua-Kona area's most convenient and accessible shopping facilities.

Kona Healthways (329-2296), in the Kona Coast Shopping Center, has an ample stock of vitamins, bathing supplies, grains, fruits, and vegetables. By the simple fact that it is the only store of its kind in the area, it wins my recommendation.

KAILUA-KONA AREA SHOPPING

You might remember that song about how "L.A. is a great big freeway." Well, the Hawaiian version could easily be "Kailua is a great big mall." I've never seen so many shopping arcades squeezed into so small a space. Here are goldsmiths, boutiques, jewelers galore, travel agencies, sundries, knickknack shops, sandal-makers, T-shirt shops, and much, much more, all crowded onto Alii Drive.

Personally, I think most of the items sold along this strip are plastic or overpriced, and in some cases, both. You may find something worth buying, but you'll probably discover it's best to browse here and buy outside town. One place I do recommend is **Middle Earth Bookshoppe** (Kona Plaza Shopping Arcade, 75-5719 Alii Drive; 329-2123). Here you'll find a good selection of Hawaiian books, as well as paperbacks and current bestsellers.

The **Kona Inn Shopping Village**, which parallels the waterfront along Alii Drive, features dozens of shops. Because of its convenient location and variety of stores, it is the center of the visitor shopping scene.

Kona Marketplace (Alii Drive) across the street is another prime tourist destination.

Each year, however, this consumer scene shifts farther south. Shopping malls grow by accretion in Kailua. One of the newest and more tastefully designed is **Waterfront Row** (75-5770 Alii Drive), a raw-wood-and-plank-floor complex with perhaps a dozen stores and restaurants.

B. T. Pottery (75-5707-B Alii Drive; 326-4989) is a husband-and-wife craft shop that features pottery inlaid with black sand as well as an array of handmade jewelry.

The **Hulihee Palace Gift Shop** (Alii Drive; 329-1877), a small store located behind the palace, specializes in Hawaiian handicrafts and literature on the islands.

In addition to these centers along Alii Drive, there are two large shopping malls a couple blocks up from the water. **Kona Coast Shopping Center** and **Lanihau Center** sit on either side of Palani Road near the Kaahumanu Highway intersection. The latter contains one of the town's few bookstores, a **Waldenbooks** (329-0015).

The **King Kamehameha Kona Beach Hotel** (75-5660 Palani Road; 329-2911) has a cluster of shops. My favorite is **Meleo Polynesian Handcraft** (326-2205), which handles *tapa* cloth, lauhala weavings, sandalwood pieces, *hula* instruments, and Hawaiian jewelry.

KAILUA-KONA AREA NIGHTLIFE

What action there is here is near the shorefront on Alii Drive. **Huggo's** (Alii Drive and Kakakai Road; 329-1493) features live Hawaiian music every evening, while live rock bands play nightly at **Jolly Roger** (75-5776 Alii Drive; 329-1344). Both places have stunning ocean views and are usually packed to the gills.

The **Billfish Bar,** located poolside at the King Kamehameha Kona Beach Hotel (75-5660 Palani Road; 329-2911), has live Hawaiian music nightly.

Fisherman's Landing (75-5744 Alii Drive; 326-2555) in the Kona Inn Shopping Village is a restaurant/lounge with a Hawaiian soloist and knock-out sunset views nightly.

For an evening of slow rhythms and dancing cheek-to-cheek, there's the **Windjammer Lounge** (329-3111) at the Kona Hilton. When I went by recently, the band was playing Hawaiian sounds.

There's dancing to live music nightly after 10 p.m. at the **Eclipse Restaurant** (75-5711 Kuakini Highway; 329-4686). Cover on weekends.

Another good bet is the **Kona Surf Resort** (78-128 Ehukai Street, Keauhou; 322-3411), which sports two lounges and a karaoke disco Friday and Saturday night.

KAILUA-KONA AREA BEACHES AND PARKS

Hale Halawai—This small oceanfront park, fringed with coconut trees, has an activities pavilion but no beach. Its central location in Kailua does make the park a perfect place to watch the sunset, though.

Getting there: Situated near the intersection of Alii Drive and Hualalai Road.

Old Airport State Recreation Area (★)—This white-sand beach parallels Kailua's former landing strip, extending for a half-mile along a lava-crusted shore. Very popular with Kailuans, this is a conveniently located spot for catching some rays.

Facilities: Picnic area, restrooms, showers. You can walk to the Kailua markets and restaurants less than a half-mile away. *Swimming:* Shallow, with rocky bottom. There are a few sand channels for entering the water; and there is a sandy inlet good for children just north of the lighthouse. *Snorkeling:* See the "Skindiving the Gold Coast" section in this chapter. *Fishing:* The principal catches are threadfin, big-eyed scad, bonefish, papio, and especially mullet.

Getting there: Located just a few hundred yards north of the King Kamehameha Kona Beach Hotel in Kailua.

Honokohau Beach (★)—This is Kailua's nude beach. Folks come for miles to soak up the sun on this long narrow strand. Bordered by a lagoon, backdropped by distant mountains, protected by a shallow reef, and highly recommended for the adventurous.

Facilities: Zilch. It's three miles to the many markets and restaurants in Kailua. *Swimming:* Well protected, but very shallow. *Snorkeling:* See the "Skindiving the Gold Coast" section in this chapter. *Fishing:* Mullet, threadfin, big-eyed scad, bonefish, and papio are commonly caught. Good luck. *Surfing:* Good.

Camping: A prime area for unofficial camping.

Getting there: Take Kaahumanu Highway a couple miles north from Kailua. Turn onto the road to Honokohau Small Boat Harbor. From the north side of the harbor, walk about 600 yards farther north to the beach.

Disappearing Sands Beach—A small strand studded with volcanic rocks, this spot is also called **Magic Sands**. It seems that the white sand periodically washes away, exposing a lava shoreline. When still carpeted with sand, this is a very popular and crowded place.

Facilities: Restrooms and showers, with markets and restaurants nearby. *Swimming:* Good. Also a favorite area for bodysurfing. *Snorkeling:* See the "Skindiving the Gold Coast" section in this chapter. *Surfing:* Principally bodysurfing here. The best surfing spot in Kona is just north of here at "Banyans," with breaks year-round over a shallow reef. Right and left slides. *Fishing:* Major catches include mullet, threadfin, big-eyed scad, bonefish, and papio.

Getting there: Located on Alii Drive four miles south of Kailua.

Kahaluu Beach Park—Set along the south shore of Kahaluu Bay, this county park is fringed with palm trees. The salt-and-pepper beach is small and often crowded.

Facilities: Picnic areas, showers, and restrooms. A small market and restaurant are next door at the Keauhou Beach Hotel. *Swimming:* Excellent; the cove is partially protected by outlying rocks. *Snorkeling:* See the "Skindiving the Gold Coast" section in this chapter. *Surfing:* Good near the reef during periods of high surf. *Fishing:* For mullet, threadfin, big-eyed scad, bonefish, and papio. The bay is also a good spot for throw netting and surround netting.

Getting there: Located on Alii Drive five miles south of Kailua.

Kona/Kau District

One element that comes as a visual shock to many first-time visitors to the Kona Coast is the endless stretch of black lava that blankets this dry terrain. Backdropped by 8271-foot Hualalai and standing in the windshadow of both Mauna Loa and Mauna Kea, Kailua and the entire Kona region project the bald unreality of a moonscape.

But the ragged shoreline has been trimmed with stands of palm trees and sections along the roadways are splashed with bougainvillea. Even in this land of lava you don't need to venture far to discover soft foliage and tropical colors. Along the lower slopes of Hualalei just above Kailua lies **Kona's coffee country**. This 20-mile long belt, located between the 1000- and 2000-foot elevation and reaching south to Honaunau, is an unending succession of plantations glistening with the shiny green leaves and red berries of coffee orchards. If you prefer your vegetation decaffeinated, there are mango trees, banana fronds, macadamia nut orchards, and sunbursts of wildflowers. To make sure you remember that even amid all the black lava you *are* still in the tropics, old coffee shacks and tinroof general stores dot the countryside.

So rather than heading directly south from Kailua, make sure you take in the full sweep of Kona's coffee country. Just take Palani Road (Route

190) uphill from Kailua, then turn right onto Route 180. This winding road cuts through old Kona in the heart of the growing region—watch for orchards of the small trees. Before the coast road was built, this was the main route. Today it's somewhat off the beaten track, passing through funky old country towns like Holualoa before joining the Mamalahoa Highway (Route 11) in Honalo.

Once on this latter highway, you'll encounter the old Greenwell Store (Mamalahoa Highway, Kealakekua; 323-3222), a stone building that dates to 1867, and a perfect place to combine shopping with museum browsing. The **Kona Historical Society Museum** has taken over this former general store. Today it's filled with artifacts from Kona's early days plus contemporary postcards, calendars, and other items. Of particular interest are the marvelous collections of photographs and antique bottles.

This main route continues south along the western slopes of **Hualalai**. Near the town of Captain Cook, Napoopoo Road leads down to Kealakekua Bay. First it passes the **Royal Kona Coffee Mill** (328-2511). I don't know about you, but I'm a confirmed "caffiend," happily addicted to java for years. So it was mighty interesting to watch how the potent stuff goes from berry to bean to bag, with a few stops between. If you haven't tried Kona coffee, one of the few brews grown in the United States, this is the time.

At the **Fuku-Bonsai Center** (78-6767 Mamalahoa Highway; 322-9222; admission) on the southern outskirts of Holualoa, you can take a self-guided tour through a series of bonsai gardens. Among the most fascinating miniatures are the banyans. There is also a fine gift shop on the premises.

Kealakekua Bay is a marine reserve with technicolor coral reefs and an array of tropical fish species. Here you can also check out the reconstructed temple, **Hikiau Heiau**, where Captain James Cook once performed a Christian burial service for one of his crewmen. Cook himself had little time left to live. Shortly after the ceremony, he was killed and possibly eaten by natives who had originally welcomed him as a god. A white obelisk, the **Captain Cook Monument**, rises across the bay where the famous mariner fell in 1779. The cliffs looming behind this marker are honeycombed with **Hawaiian burial caves**.

Puuhonua o Honaunau National Historical Park (328-2288) sits four miles south of Kealakekua Bay on Route 160. This ancient holy ground, also known as the City of Refuge, was one of the few places to which *kapu* breakers and refugees could flee for sanctuary. Once inside the Great Wall, a lava barricade ten feet high and 17 feet wide, they were safe from pursuers. Free booklets are available for self-guided tours to the palace, *heiaus*, and menacing wooden idols that made this beachfront refuge one of Hawaii's most sacred spots. The heiaus, dating back to the 16th and 17th centuries, are among the finest examples of ancient architecture on the Big Island. Also explore the house models, built to traditional specifications, the royal fishpond, and the displays of ancient arts and crafts.

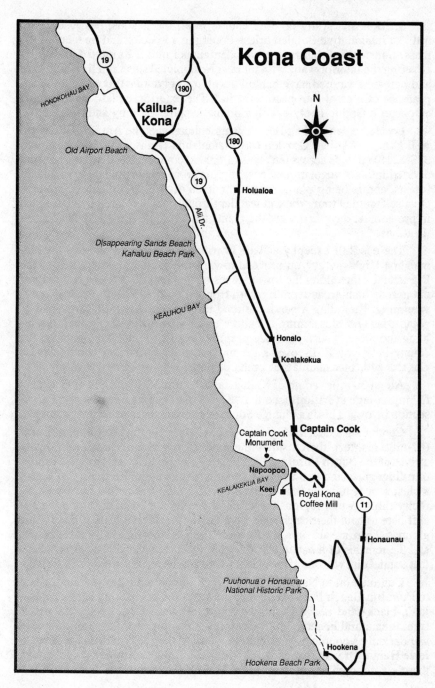

Kona Coast

N

HONOKOHAU BAY

Kailua-Kona

Old Airport Beach

Disappearing Sands Beach
Kahaluu Beach Park

KEAUHOU BAY

Holualoa

Alii Dr.

Honalo

Kealakekua

Captain Cook
Monument

Captain Cook

Napoopoo

KEALAKEKUA BAY

Keei

Royal Kona
Coffee Mill

Honaunau

Puuhonua o Honaunau
National Historic Park

Hookena

Hookena Beach Park

St. Benedict's, my favorite church in all the islands, lies just up the hill. An imaginative Belgian priest, hoping to add color and imagery to the mass, transformed this rickety wooden chapel into a **Painted Church** by covering the interior walls with murals. He depicted several religious scenes and painted a vaulted nave behind the altar to give this tiny church the appearance of a great European cathedral. The exterior, equally charming, is carpenter's Gothic in style with a dramatic spire. Stop by and take a look.

Located on an ancient Hawaiian agricultural site, the **Amy B. H. Greenwell Ethnobotanical Garden** (off Mamalahoa Highway in Captain Cook; 323-3318) spreads across ten acres of upland countryside. The land is being divided into six vegetation zones, varying from seaside plants to mountain forests, and is being planted with hundreds of wild and domestic species. On a self-guided tour, you can wander through fields cleared by Hawaiians in pre-contact days and view the plants that were vital to early island civilizations.

There is little except you, dark lava, and the black macadam of the Mamalahoa Highway as you proceed toward the southern extremities of the Big Island. Here along the lower slopes of Mauna Loa, lifeless lava fingers cut across lush areas teeming with tropical colors. The contrast is overwhelming: Rounding a bend, the road travels from an overgrown land of poinsettias and blossoming trees to a bleak area torn by upheaval, resembling the moon's surface. Once past the lava flows that have ravaged the countryside, you'll discover a terrain that, though dry and windblown, is planted with macadamia nut orchards and fields of cattle-range grasses.

About 30 miles south of Kailua, take the turnoff to the quaint Hawaiian fishing village at **Milolii** (see the "Kona/Kau District Beaches and Parks" section below). This is a vintage South Seas scene that should not be missed.

Continuing south, the highway passes **James Stewart's Hoomau Ranch** (87-mile marker), then a sprawling **macadamia nut orchard,** and finally arrives at the **South Point** turnoff. South Point Road leads through 11 miles of rolling grassland to the nation's southernmost point. En route you'll pass a cluster of windmills that draw energy from the trades that blow with ferocity through this region. Fishermen have built **platforms** along the sea cliff here to haul their catches up from the boats that troll these prime fishing grounds. There are also **ancient Hawaiian canoe moorings** in the rocks below, and the remains of a *heiau* near the light tower. Some archaeologists believe that South Point was one of the places where Polynesian discoverers first settled.

Continue on to **Naalehu,** the nation's southernmost town, and then on to **Punaluu Beach Park.** With its palm trees and enchanting lagoon, Punaluu's black-sand beach is simply gorgeous. The tourist complex detracts from the natural beauty, but to escape the madding mobs the explorer need wander only a couple of hundred yards east to the rocky remains of **Kaneeleele Heiau.** Or venture about one-third mile south to **Ninole Cove.** Though there's a condominium complex nearby, this spot is a bit more secluded.

Many of the stones along Ninole's pebbly beach are filled with holes containing "baby" stones that are said to multiply.

From Punaluu to Volcanoes National Park, the highway passes through largely uninhabited grassland and sugarcane areas. **Pahala**, the only town along this stretch, is a plantation colony. For an interesting side trip, go through Pahala to **Wood Valley Temple** (★) (P.O. Box 250, Pahala, HI 96777; 928-8539), where a Tibetan Buddhist monk and his followers have taken over an old Japanese temple. Situated on 25 acres, the temple was dedicated in 1980 by the Dalai Lama. A tranquil but dynamic place, it is painted in floral colors and adorned with a gilded statue of the Buddha. Since the small staff here has many responsibilities, call ahead before arriving at the temple. To get there, go right onto Pikake Street at the first stop sign in Pahala. When it forks after a little more than four miles, go left and proceed two-tenths of a mile to the temple. The road continues up into luxuriant **Wood Valley** (★), the scene of a devastating 1868 earthquake and mudslide.

KONA/KAU DISTRICT HOTELS

For a funky country place high in the mountains overlooking the Kona Coast, try the **Kona Hotel** (Route 180, Holualoa; 324-1155). Catering primarily to workers, this 11-unit hotel remains a real sleeper. It might be difficult to book a room during the week, but on weekends, the lunchpail crowd heads home and you can rent a small place at an unbelievable low-budget rate. No reservations, thank you. Shared bathroom facilities. It's five miles to the beaches and action around Kailua, but if you're after an inexpensive retreat, this is the place.

Down the road in Honalo, **Teshima's Inn** (Mamalahoa Highway; 322-9140) has small, cozy rooms at similar rates. These are set in an L-shaped structure fronting a Japanese garden. The rooms have linoleum floors and wood-paneled walls decorated with Japanese art. Here you're 1300 feet above sea level and seven miles from Kailua. This charming inn is run by Mrs. Teshima, a delightful Japanese woman who has operated the establishment for years.

One of the more unique places to stay on the Big Island is **The Dragonfly Ranch** (Route 160, Honaunau; 328-9570). Spread across two acres, several hideaways and a main house comprise this "tropical fantasy lodging." The grounds are as thick and luxurious as a well-tended jungle and the atmosphere is decidedly New Age. The "honeymoon suite" has an outdoor waterbed complete with canopy and mosquito netting and the "redwood cottage" conveys a woodsy, informal feeling. Each of the four units, which rent in the moderate- and deluxe-price categories, have partial kitchen facilities. Don't expect telephones and air-conditioning, but do prepare yourself for an experience.

At **H. Manago Hotel** (323-2642), on Mamalahoa Highway in the town of Captain Cook, you'll have a varied choice of accommodations. Rooms with communal bath in the creaky old section are budget-priced. The battered furniture, torn linoleum floors, and annoying street noise make for rather funky living here. Rooms in the new section rise in price as you ascend the stairs. First-floor accommodations are the least expensive and rooms on the ethereal third floor are the most expensive, but all reside in the budget range. The only advantage for the extra cost is a better view. All these rooms are small and tastelessly furnished—somehow orange carpets don't make it with naugahyde chairs. But you'll find visual relief in the marvelous views of mountain and sea from the tiny lanais. There's also a restaurant and television room in the old section.

Shirakawa Motel (Mamalahoa Highway, Waiohinu; 929-7462), the country's southernmost hotel, sits on stunningly beautiful grounds. There's a fruit farm out back and poinsettias lining the driveway. When I last stopped by, a rainbow arched across the landscape and birds loudly rioted in the nearby hills. Located 1000 feet above sea level, this corrugated-roof, 13-room hostelry offers quaint rooms with faded furniture and functional kitchenettes at budget prices. Without cooking facilities, the bill is even less. Write P.O. Box 467, Naalehu, HI 96772 for reservations.

Wood Valley Temple (★) (928-8539), a Buddhist retreat four miles outside Pahala, has dormitory-style and private rooms at budget prices. Set on 25 landscaped acres, it provides a serene resting place. There are Buddhist services performed in Tibetan every morning and evening and a congenial staff. The guest rooms are pretty basic but have been pleasantly decorated and are quite comfortable. Baths are shared and guests have access to the ample kitchen facilities. Call for reservations; two-night minimum.

KONA/KAU DISTRICT RESTAURANTS

From Kailua south, the Mamalahoa Highway heads up *mauka* into the mountains above the Kona Coast. There are numerous restaurants in the little towns that dot the first 15 miles. All sit right on the highway.

Teshima's (322-9140), a pleasant restaurant in Honalo, is a good place to enjoy a Japanese meal or a drink in the lounge. Modestly decorated with lanterns and Oriental paintings, this busy café has a lunch menu priced in the moderate range. Dinner features several Japanese delicacies. Breakfast is also served.

There's a different mood entirely at the **Aloha Theatre Café** (322-3383) in Kainaliu. Here in the lobby of the town's capacious movie house, a young crew serves delicious breakfasts as well as sandwiches and Mexican dishes during lunch and dinner. So if for some bizarre reason you've always longed to dine in the lobby of a movie theatre . . . if not, you can eat out on the oceanview lanai. Moderate.

H. Manago Hotel (323-2642) in the town of Captain Cook, has a full-size dining room. Primarily intended for hotel guests, the menu is limited and the hours restricted to "meal times" (7 to 9 a.m., 11 a.m. to 2 p.m., and 5 to 7 p.m. Tuesday through Thursday). Lunch and dinner platters, consisting of a few daily specials, are moderately priced; sandwiches are also available.

In Kealakekua Ranch Center, a shopping center on Mamalahoa Highway in Captain Cook, there are two budget-priced eateries. **Real Mexican Food** (323-3036) is a take-out stand and **Hong Kong Chop Suey** (323-3373) is one of those Chinese restaurants that have (literally) about 100 items on the menu.

In the Kau district along Mamalahoa Highway, the **Ohana Drive-Inn** (78-mile marker; 929-7679) has breakfast items, sandwiches, and hot platters. Fancy it's not, just a counter for ordering and a few tables. Budget.

For something more comfortable, try the **South Point Restaurant & Bar** (76-mile marker on Mamalahoa Highway; 929-9343). At this small dining room, the menu includes steak, prawns, and teriyaki chicken. In an area lacking in full-service dining facilities, this moderate-to-deluxe-priced restaurant is a welcome oasis.

Down in Naalehu, the nation's southernmost town, you'll find the **Naalehu Coffee Shop** (929-7238). Some people like the place. I was completely put off by all the tourist trappings: books, slides, knickknacks—even the wall decorations are for sale. But the banana bread is good and the menu is varied. There are full-course breakfasts; at lunchtime they serve sandwiches with salad; the dinner menu has beef, seafood, and chicken dishes.

KONA/KAU DISTRICT MARKETS

Strung along Mamalahoa Highway south of Kailua is a series of small towns that contain tiny markets. The only real supermarket en route is **Sure Save** (323-2695) at the Kealakekua Ranch Center in Captain Cook.

The Aloha Village Store (on Mamalahoa Highway, Kainaliu; 322-9941) has an ample stock of vitamins, juices, fruits, and other health food items.

Down the road in Kealia, **Ohana O Ka Aina Cooperative** (322-2425) has a similar inventory, plus an herb shop and juice bar.

Sea Fresh Hawaii (Mamalahoa Highway, Captain Cook; 323-3040), about ten miles south of Kailua, has fresh seafood.

Ocean View General Store (929-9966), in the Kau district around the 78-mile marker on Mamalahoa Highway, has an ample inventory of groceries.

Down at the southern end of the island the **Food Fair Super Market** (929-7527) on Mamalahoa Highway in Naalehu is the prime place to stock up.

KONA/KAU DISTRICT SHOPPING

After escaping the tourist traps in Kailua, you can start seriously shopping in South Kona. Since numerous shops dot the Mamalahoa Highway as it travels south, I'll list the most interesting ones in the order they appear.

For hats and baskets woven from pandanus and bamboo and sold at phenomenally low prices, turn off the main road onto Route 18 and check out **Kimura Lauhala Shop** (324-0053) in Holualoa.

Holualoa is also a center for art galleries. Within the ambit of this one-street town you'll find the **Kona Arts Center** (Route 18), housed in an old church, plus several privately owned galleries nearby.

Among the most noteworthy is **Studio 7 Gallery** (Route 18; 324-1335), a beautifully designed multi-room showplace that displays pottery, paintings, and prints.

Banana Patch (Route 18, Holualoa; 322-3676) has an imaginative collection of African handicrafts as well as jewelry and collectibles.

Blue Ginger Gallery (Mamalahoa Highway, Kainaliu; 322-3898) displays an impressive array of crafts items produced by local artisans. There are ceramics, custom glass pieces, woodwork, volcanic glass jewelry, and hand-painted silk scarves.

Two other places I recommend are **Paradise Found** (322-2111) in Kainaliu for contemporary and Hawaiian-style clothes, and **Country Store Antiques** (323-3005) in Captain Cook for things old and aging.

Kakanahou Hawaiian Foundation (Mamalahoa Highway, Kealakekua; 322-3901), an apprentice school teaching Hawaiians native arts, sells hand-wrought *hula* drums and other instruments, as well as masks and other handicrafts.

My favorite shop is **Kealakekua's Grass Shack** (Mamalahoa Highway, Kealakekua; 323-2877). This place is crowded with Hawaiiana, not just from native Polynesians, but from the island's late arrivals as well—Americans, Chinese, Japanese, Portuguese. As owner John Jens explains, "We go all the way from *poi* to tofu." There are *milo* and *koa* wood pieces, black coral jewelry, handwoven baskets, and much more. Most interesting of all, to me at least, are the antique tools and handicrafts that Jens has gathered. This transplanted Dutchman is something of an authority on Hawaiian history and culture, combining a scholar's knowledge with a native's love for the islands. Ask him for a tour of his mini-museum and garden. It'll be an education in things Hawaiian.

Cottage Gallery (Mamalahoa Highway, Honaunau; 328-9392) is an artists' cooperative displaying the work—paintings, ceramics, jewelry, clothing, sculpture—of many local artists.

KONA/KAU DISTRICT NIGHTLIFE

The **Aloha Theater** (Mamalahoa Highway, Kainaliu; 322-9924), home to the Aloha Performing Arts Center, features an ongoing series of theatrical performances. In addition to plays, it also periodically schedules concerts.

KONA/KAU DISTRICT BEACHES AND PARKS

Napoopoo Beach Park—Many small boats moor at this black-rock beach on Kealakekua Bay. Set amidst cliffs that rim the harbor, it's a charming spot. Unfortunately, it draws caravans of tour buses on their way to the nearby Hikiau Heiau and Captain Cook Monument. Kealakekua Bay, one mile wide and filled with marine life, is an underwater preserve that attracts snorkelers and glass-bottom boats.

Facilities: Picnic area, restrooms. Try the soda stand just up from the beach. Two miles to the markets and restaurants in the town of Captain Cook. *Swimming:* Very good. *Snorkeling:* See the "Skindiving the Gold Coast" section in this chapter. *Surfing:* In the bay there are good-sized summer breaks. Just north, at "Ins and Outs," the surf breaks year-round. *Fishing:* A good locale for mullet, moi, bonefish, papio, and big-eyed scad.

Getting there: In the town of Captain Cook, take Napoopoo Road, which leads two miles down to Kealakekua Bay.

Keei Beach (★)—This salt-and-pepper beach extends for a quarter-mile along a lava-studded shoreline. Situated next to the creaky village of Keei, this otherwise mediocre beach offers marvelous views of Kealakekua Bay. It is far enough from the tourist area, however, that you'll probably encounter only local people along this hidden beach. What a pity—no white shoes and polyester here!

Facilities: None. Both markets and restaurants will be found several miles away in the town of Captain Cook. *Swimming:* The very shallow water makes swimming safe, but limited. Try the north end. *Snorkeling:* See the "Skindiving the Gold Coast" section in this chapter. *Fishing:* Try here for mullet, threadfin, bonefish, papio, and big-eyed scad.

Camping: You could pitch a tent, but only with difficulty along this narrow strand.

Getting there: Take the Mamalahoa Highway to Captain Cook, then follow Napoopoo Road down to Kealakekua Bay. At the bottom of the hill, go left toward the Puuhonua O Honaunau National Historical Park. Take this road a half-mile, then turn right onto a lava-bed road. Now follow this road another half-mile to the beach.

Puuhonua o Honaunau Park—This park, part of the Puuhonua o Honaunau National Historical Park (City of Refuge), is an excellent picnic spot when you're sightseeing. Besides the picnic tables and other facilities, enjoy the sandy sunbathing area. There's no beach, but the tidepools along the lava shoreline are fascinating.

Getting there: Located off Route 160 just south of the National Historical Park displays.

Hookena Beach Park—Popular with adventurous travelers, this is a wide, black-sand beach, bordered by sheer rock walls. Coconut trees abound along this lovely strand, and there's a great view of the South Kona coast.

Facilities: Picnic area, restrooms. Unpotable water. A small market is four miles away in Kealia. *Swimming:* Very good; bodysurfing also. *Snorkeling:* See the "Skindiving the Gold Coast" section in this chapter. *Fishing:* Mullet, threadfin, bonefish, papio, and big-eyed scad are among the most common catches.

Getting there: Take the Mamalahoa Highway south from Kailua for about 21 miles to Hookena. Turn onto the paved road at the marker and follow it two miles to the park.

Milolii Beach Park (★)—Even if you don't feel like a character from Somerset Maugham, you may think you're amid the setting for one of his tropical stories. This still-thriving fishing village is vintage South Seas, from tumbledown shacks to fishing nets drying in the sun. There are patches of beach near the village, but the most splendid resources are the tidepools, some of the most beautiful I've ever seen.

Facilities: Restrooms, picnic area, swings, and basketball court, but no running water. There's a small market up the street in town. *Swimming:* This area is fringed with reefs that create safe but shallow areas. Exercise extreme caution if you go beyond the reefs. *Snorkeling:* See the "Skindiving the Gold Coast" section in this chapter. *Fishing:* A prime area for mullet, bonefish, papio, threadfin, and big-eyed scad.

Camping: Permitted only in the seaside parking lot. Get there early and you can park a tent beneath the ironwood trees with the sea washing in just below. County permit required.

Getting there: Take the Mamalahoa Highway south from Kailua for about 33 miles. Turn off onto a well-marked macadam road leading five miles down to the village.

Manuka State Park—This lovely botanic park, almost 2000 feet above sea level, has a beautiful ocean view. The rolling terrain is planted with both native and imported trees and carpeted with grass.

Facilities: Picnic area, restrooms.

Camping: No tent and trailers allowed, but you can park your sleeping bag in the pavilion. A state permit is required.

Getting there: Located on the Mamalahoa Highway about 41 miles south of Kailua.

Whittington Beach Park—This pretty little park features a small patch of lawn dotted with coconut, *hala*, and ironwood trees. It's set on a lava-rimmed shoreline near the cement skeleton of a former sugar wharf. There are some marvelous tidepools here.

Facilities: Picnic area, restrooms, showers, and electricity. It's three miles to the markets and restaurants in Naalehu. *Swimming:* Access to the water over the sharp lava rocks is pretty rough on the feet. *Snorkeling:* Very good. *Surfing:* Summer break; left slide. *Fishing:* Mullet, menpachi, red bigeye, ulua, and papio are the most frequent species caught.

Camping: Tent and trailer camping allowed; county permit required.

Getting there: Across from the abandoned sugar mill on Mamalahoa Highway, three miles north of Naalehu.

Punaluu Beach Park—A black-sand beach fringed with palms and bordered by a breathtaking lagoon, this area, unfortunately, is regularly assaulted by tour buses. Still, it's a place of awesome beauty, one I would not recommend bypassing. For more privacy, you can always check out **Ninole Cove**, a short walk from Punaluu. This attractive area has a tiny beach, grassy area, and lagoon. It's a good swimming spot for children.

Facilities: Picnic area, restrooms, showers, and electricity. There's a restaurant nearby, with a museum and tourist complex on the premises. *Swimming:* With caution. Try the northeastern end of the beach. *Snorkeling:* Mediocre. *Surfing:* Short ride over a shallow reef; right slide. *Fishing:* Principal catches are red bigeye, menpachi, ulua, and papio.

Camping: Tents and trailers are allowed; county permit required.

Getting there: Located about a mile off Mamalahoa Highway, eight miles north of Naalehu.

Hawaii Volcanoes National Park

Covering 344 square miles and extending from 13,677-foot Mauna Loa to 4090-foot Kilauea to the Puna shoreline, this incredible park is deservedly the most popular feature on the Big Island. Its two live volcanoes, among the most active in the world, make the region as elemental and unpredictable as the next eruption. During the last two centuries these firepits have covered almost 200,000 acres with black lava, destroying almost everything in their path.

Unlike Washington's Mt. St. Helens and Mt. Pinatubo in the Philippines, eruptions here are not explosive. So even Kilauea, which has destroyed several hundred homes and devoured an entire town during the last decade, has gained a reputation as a "drive-in volcano" where you can stand shoulder to shoulder with geologists and journalists watching Madame Pele vent her wrath.

Also contained within this singular park are rainforests, black-sand beaches, rare species of flora and fauna, and jungles of ferns. If you approach the park from the southwest, traveling up the Mamalahoa Highway (Route 11), the points of interest begin within a mile of the park boundary. Here at the trailhead for **Footprints Trail**, you can follow a two-mile-long path that leads to the area where Halemaumau's hellish eruption overwhelmed a Hawaiian army in 1790. The troops, off to battle Kamehameha for control of the island, left the impressions of their dying steps in molten lava. Many tracks have eroded, but two centuries later some still remain imprinted on the ground.

Continuing along the highway, turn up Mauna Loa Strip Road to the **Tree Molds.** Lava flowing through an *ohia* forest created these amazing fossils. The molten rock ignited the trees and then cooled, leaving deep pits in the shape of the incinerated tree trunks. It's a little farther to **Kipuka Puaulu** or **Bird Park,** a nature trail leading through a densely forested bird sanctuary. *Kipuka* means an "island" surrounded by lava and this one is filled with *koa, kolea,* and *ohia* trees. If the weather's clear, you can continue along this narrow, winding road by foot for about ten miles to a **lookout** perched 6662 feet high on the side of Mauna Loa.

Back on the main road, continue east a few miles to **Kilauea Visitor Center** (967-7311), which contains a museum, a film on recent eruptions, souvenir shop, and information desk. Across the road at **Volcano House,** there's a hotel and restaurant. An earlier Volcano House, built in 1877, currently houses the **Volcano Art Center,** right next to the visitor complex.

From here you can pick up Crater Rim Drive, one of the islands' most spectacular scenic routes. This 11-mile loop passes lava flows and steam vents in its circuit around **Kilauea Crater.** It also takes in everything from a rainforest to a desert and provides views of several craters.

Proceeding clockwise around the crater, the road leads near **Thurston Lava Tube,** a 450-foot tunnel set amid "the fern jungle," a dense tangle of luxurious vegetation. The tube itself, created when outer layers of lava cooled while the inner flow drained out, reaches heights of 10 to 20 feet. You can hike through the tunnel and along nearby **Devastation Trail,** a half-mile boardwalk that cuts through a skeletal forest of *ohia* trees devastated in a 1959 eruption.

Another short path leads to **Halemaumau Crater.** This firepit, which erupted most recently in 1982, is the home of Pele, the goddess of volcanoes. Even today steam and sulfurous gas blast from this hellhole, filling the air with a pungent odor and adding a sickly yellow-green luster to the cliffs. Halemaumau is actually a crater within a crater, its entire bulk contained in Kilauea's gaping maw.

Around the southern and western edges of the crater, the road passes part of the **Kau Desert,** a landscape so barren that astronauts bound for the moon were brought here to train for their lunar landing. At the **Jaggar Museum,** adjacent to the park observatory, you can catch an eagle-eye glimpse into Halemaumau Crater and take in a series of state-of-the-art displays on volcanology and Hawaiian volcano myths. Then the road continues on to a succession of steam vents from which hot mists rise continually.

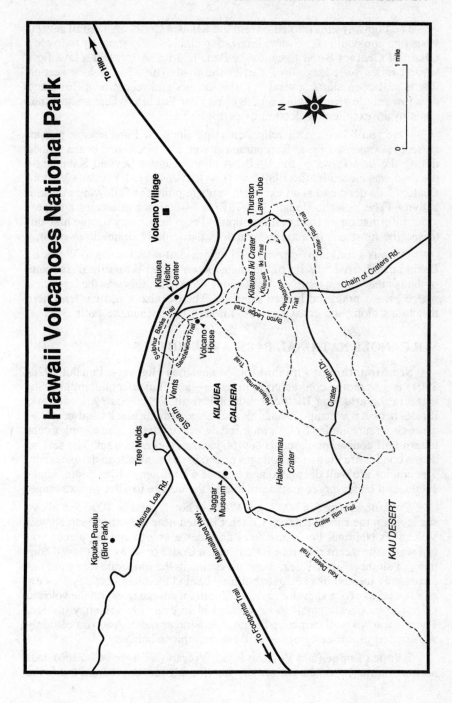

Hawaii Volcanoes National Park

The highway zips into Hilo from the Kilauea Crater area. Until several years ago you could take a more interesting and leisurely route by following **Chain of Craters Road** down to the Puna district. At present a lava flow several miles wide has closed part of the road. The 27-mile-long section that is still open skirts several volcanic craters and recent lava flows and dips toward the sea, arriving on the coast near **Puuloa,** where a short trail leads to an excellent collection of petroglyphs.

Here you'll hug the shoreline, coursing along the Puna seaside past an ancient Hawaiian village at **Kamoamoa** as well as a black-sand beach formed during the lava flows of the 1980s. A short distance beyond Kamoamoa the road was closed by the 1989 lava flow that destroyed Wahaula Visitors Center. This dead end is an excellent vantage point for following volcanic activity. (The Volcano Update, 967-7977, a 24-hour recorded message, provides information on the latest eruptions.) From here many people hike out to see the most recent activity, which is particularly dramatic at night.

There is a trail at road's end leading one-and-a-half miles to Wahaula. Behind the charred remains of the visitor's center lies **Wahaula Heiau,** one of the islands' oldest temples. Built about 1250 A.D., this was the last *heiau* where priests practiced human sacrifice. There's also a **nature trail** here that loops along the coast and cuts through an earthquake fault.

VOLCANOES NATIONAL PARK AREA HOTELS

Sea Mountain at Punaluu (off Mamalahoa Highway, Punaluu; 928-8301) is a welcome contradiction in terms—a secluded condominium. Situated in the arid Kau District south of Hawaii Volcanoes National Park, it rests between volcanic headlands and a spectacular black-sand beach. A green oasis surrounded by lava rock and desert vegetation, the complex contains a golf course, pool, tennis courts, jacuzzi, and restaurant. The several dozen condos are multi-unit cottages priced in the moderate to deluxe range. The condos are well decorated and include a bedroom, sitting room, kitchenette, and lanai; larger units available in the deluxe to ultra-deluxe range.

Volcano House (967-7321), a 42-room hotel, perches 4000 feet above sea level on the rim of Kilauea Crater. Situated near the entrance to Hawaii Volcanoes National Park, this hotel provides a unique resting place. You can watch the steam rise from Halemaumau Crater or study the rugged contours of slumbering Kilauea. Standard rooms in the moderate range are unfortunately located in a separate building behind the main hotel. For a view of Kilauea, ask for a superior or deluxe room (at deluxe rates) on the volcano side. The rooms are small and decorated in an ever tidy and cozy fashion. There's wall-to-wall carpeting but no television or radio. And you certainly won't need an air conditioner at these breathless heights.

Kilauea Lodge (Old Volcano Road, Volcano Village; 967-7366) does not rest on the lip of the crater, but that doesn't prevent it from being the finest place in the area to stay. Set on tropically wooded grounds, this 12-unit hideaway nevertheless conveys a mountain atmosphere. Some guest rooms have fireplaces, quilts, and oak furnishings. This coziness carries over into an inviting common room shared by guests and furnished with rocking chairs and a tile fireplace. The lodge, built in 1938 as a boys' camp, rests at the 3700-foot elevation and combines the best features of a Hawaiian plantation house and an alpine ski lodge. It also provides a memorable contrast to the ocean-oriented places that you'll probably be staying in during the rest of your visit. Deluxe.

There are also a number of small, privately run bed-and-breakfast inns around the volcano area. For information, contact **Volcano Accommodations** (967-8662), a central agency that can help book reservations.

VOLCANOES NATIONAL PARK AREA RESTAURANTS

Along the lengthy stretch from Naalehu to Hawaii Volcanoes National Park, one of the few dining spots you'll encounter is the **Seamountain Golf Course & Lounge** (928-6222) in Punaluu. Situated a short distance from the black-sand beach, this restaurant serves a lunch consisting of hot sandwiches plus a few platters. The deluxe-priced dinner entrées include mahi florentine, scampi, steak, and crab legs. Topping the cuisine are the views, which range across the links out to the distant volcanic slopes.

If you'd like to dine amid comfortable accommodations overlooking a splendid lagoon, head to the nearby **Punaluu Black Sands Restaurant** (928-8528). Situated at Punaluu black-sand beach, it combines good food with spectacular views. Open for lunch only, this eatery offers a moderately priced buffet featuring sautéed mahimahi, chicken, a salad bar, rice, potatoes, hot vegetables, and dessert. Sandwiches are also available.

Speaking of vistas, **Volcano House Restaurant** (967-7321)—perched on the rim of Kilauea Crater—affords extraordinary views. Located at the 4000-foot elevation in Hawaii Volcanoes National Park, this spacious dining room looks out on sheer lava walls and angry steam vents. If you can tear yourself away from the stunning scenery, there's an ample dinner menu highlighted by mahimahi, prime rib, chicken, or a variety of seafood dishes. Dinners are priced in the deluxe range. Lunch is buffet-style and there's also a complete breakfast menu.

For quick, inexpensive meals you can't top the **Volcano Store Diner** (Old Volcano Road, Volcano Village; 967-7707). Adjacent to the only grocery hereabouts, this take-out-stand-with-tables has sandwiches and plate lunches at budget prices.

And for those languorous evenings when time is irrelevant and budgets forgotten, there is **Kilauea Lodge** (Old Volcano Road, Volcano Village; 967-7366). Here you can sit beside a grand fireplace in an atmosphere that mixes tropical artwork with alpine sensibility. The exposed-beam ceiling and elegant hardwood tables comfortably contrast with a menu that features "prawns Mauna Loa," shrimp tempura, catch of the day, and chicken Milanese. Dinner only; deluxe.

VOLCANOES NATIONAL PARK AREA MARKET

The Volcano Store (Old Volcano Road, Volcano Village; 967-7210), located just outside the National Park, has a limited stock of groceries.

VOLCANOES NATIONAL PARK BEACHES AND PARKS

Kipuka Nene—Easily accessible by paved road, this windswept campsite nevertheless offers considerable privacy. Tourists use the road less than most other thoroughfares in Hawaii Volcanoes National Park, and the park remains relatively secluded. It's surrounded by a forest of dead trees and backdropped by Mauna Loa.

Facilities: Picnic area, water tank, and pit toilets. About ten miles back are a restaurant and information booth in the park center.

Camping: Tent and trailer camping. No permit is required, but there is a seven-day limit.

Getting there: Once in Hawaii Volcanoes National Park, take Chain of Craters Road south from Crater Rim Road. Turn right onto Hilina Pali Road and follow it for five miles until Kipuka Nene appears on the left.

Namakani Paio—Situated in a lovely eucalyptus grove at the southern end of Volcanoes National Park, this campground offers both outdoor and cabin camping.

Facilities: Picnic area, restrooms. You're several miles from the restaurant and information booth in the park center. Showers are not available for campers.

Camping: Tent and trailer camping. No permit required, but, as always, campers should note that there is a seven-day limit. Cabins are rented from the Volcano House (967-7321). Each cabin has one double and two single beds, plus an outdoor grill. No firewood or cooking utensils are provided. The units rent for $32 a day for two people, $7 for each additional person up to four. Sheets, blankets, and towels are provided, but it's recommended that you bring a sleeping bag.

Getting there: Namakani Paio is located on Mamalahoa Highway about two miles west of park headquarters and 31 miles southwest of Hilo.

Kamoamoa Campground—Located near an ancient Hawaiian village in the Puna section of Hawaii Volcanoes National Park, this campground sits astride a rugged, wave-whipped coastline. There are ruins to explore and an ample seaside lawn for picnicking. Since recent lava flows have swept this area, it is also a unique spot to check out the action.

Facilities: Picnic area, outhouses; no running water. *Swimming, Snorkeling, Surfing:* None. The coast is far too rugged. *Fishing:* Only Hawaiians living in the area are permitted to fish these waters.

Camping: An excellent campground with about a half-dozen private campsites, each equipped with a picnic table and grill. No permit is required.

Getting there: Located on Chain of Craters Road about 30 miles south of Hilo in Hawaii Volcanoes National Park.

Saddle Road

This alternate route across the island climbs from Hilo to an elevation of over 6500 feet (bring a sweater!). While the eastern section is heavily wooded with *ohia* and fern forests, most of the later roadway passes through the lava wasteland that divides **Mauna Kea** and **Mauna Loa**. You cross lava flows from 1855 and 1935 while gaining elevation that will provide you with the finest view of these mountains anywhere on the island.

Near the 27-mile marker, the road to Mauna Kea leads 13 miles up to the 13,796-foot summit. The first six miles are passable by passenger car and take in a lookout and the **Onizuka Center for International Astronomy** (961-2180). Beyond this point you will need a four-wheel drive vehicle. Be sure to call ahead since the visitor station at the center sponsors tours of the summit and star-gazing opportunities. At the summit you'll find the Mauna Kea Observatory complex, one of the finest observatories in the world. You'll also be treated to some of the most otherworldly views in the world. For a four-wheel-drive tour of the summit, you can also contact **Waipio Valley Shuttle and Tours** (775-7121).

Mauna Kea State Park, with cabins and recreation area, lies about midway along the Saddle Road. Take the dirt road that goes behind the park for several hundred yards to a **bird sanctuary.** Among the species you'll see is the *nene*, an extremely rare goose native to Hawaii.

Saddle Road continues past a United States military base, then descends through stands of eucalyptus into Waimea cattle country. Here you can pick up the Mamalahoa Highway (Route 190) southwest to Kailua. Passing through sparsely populated range country over 2000 feet in elevation, this road has sensational views of the Kona Coast and Maui. Near the rustic village of **Puuanahulu** stands **Puuwaawaa**, the island's largest cinder cone.

It's only 87 miles from Hilo to Kailua by way of this interior shortcut. Before setting out, pack warm clothing and check your gas gauge—there are no service stations or stores en route. And consult your car rental agency: some do not permit driving on Saddle Road.

SADDLE ROAD AREA PARKS

Mauna Kea State Park—Situated on the tableland between Mauna Kea and Mauna Loa, this is an excellent base camp for climbing either mountain. The cabins here are also convenient for skiers headed up to Mauna Kea. With its stunning mountain views, sparse vegetation, and chilly weather, this rarefied playground hardly seems like Hawaii. For remoteness and seclusion, you can't choose a better spot. To be sure you fully enjoy it, dress warmly.

Facilities: Picnic area, restrooms, cabins. You'll need to go back 35 miles to the restaurants and markets of Hilo if you need supplies, so plan ahead.

Camping: No tents or trailers allowed. The cabins can be rented from the Division of State Parks, 75 Aupuni Street, Hilo, Hawaii, HI 96721 (933-4200). The individual cabins, each accommodating up to six people, have two bedrooms, bath, kitchenette, and an electric heater. Cabins have loads of cooking utensils and sufficient bedding. Rates are on a sliding scale from $10 single, $14 double, to $30 for six. There are also four-plex cabinettes that rent for $8 single, $12 double, on up to $28 for eight people (kids under 12 are half-price). These aren't nearly as nice as the individual cabins. They are one-bedroom units crowded with eight bunks; cooking is done in a community dining and recreation area next door.

Getting there: On the Saddle Road about 35 miles west of Hilo.

Puna District

That bulging triangle in the southeast corner of the Big Island is the Puna District, a kind of living geology lab where lush rainforest is cut by frequent lava flows. Here at the state's easternmost point, black-sand beaches, formed when hot lava meets the ocean and explodes into crystals, combine with anthurium farms and papaya orchards to create a region both luxurious and unpredictable. There are lava tubes, arches, and caves galore, all formed by the lava that flows inexorably down from the rift zones of Kilauea.

Now that Chain of Craters Road is covered in a layer of black lava, the only way to visit the area is by following Route 130, which will carry you through the tumbledown plantation town of **Keaau** and near the artistic little community of **Pahoa**, or along Route 137, an enchanting country road that hugs the coast.

During the Spring of 1990, **lava flows** poured through Kalapana, severing Routes 130 and 137 and covering many houses. Kalapana, once home to more than 400 people, was largely destroyed. Today, a few isolated houses form oases in a desert of black lava. Just above the town, where both highways come to an abrupt halt, you can see how the lava crossed the road and gain an excellent view of any current activity. In fact, for the past several years this has been the best vantage point on the island to watch for volcanic action.

What you will not see here is the original black-sand beach at Kaimu, which was covered by lava. But another **black-sand beach**, formed by the 1990 flow, has taken its place! The ancient canoe ramp is also buried beneath black rock and the Star of the Sea Painted Church—a tiny 1920s-era chapel painted in imaginative fashion to make it resemble a grand cathedral—has been moved to a temporary location near the end of Route 130.

Since the latest series of eruptions began in January 1983, the area has been in constant turmoil. During one phase, an average 650,000 tons of lava a day was spewing from the vent. In all it has covered 30 square miles of

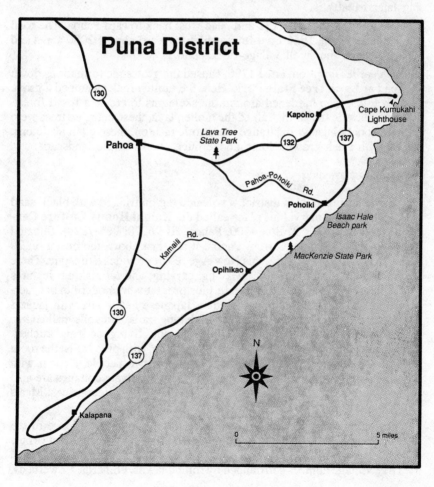

the Big Island, created new land masses along the ocean, destroyed about 200 houses, and fashioned several new black-sand beaches.

After exploring the area of recent volcanic action, you can backtrack along the coast via Route 137, which proceeds northeast through jungly undergrowth and past dazzling seascapes to the tiny villages of **Opihikao** and **Pohoiki**.

At the intersection of Route 137 and Route 132, take a right onto the dirt road and follow it seaward toward the site of a truly eerie occurrence. When the 1960 lava flow swept down to destroy this entire region, it spared the **Cape Kumukahi Lighthouse** on the state's easternmost point. Today you can see where the wall of lava parted, flowed around the beacon, then closed again as it continued to the sea. In the process, it added about 500 yards of land to the point—an awesome demonstration of how young this Big Island really is.

Now return to Route 132 and head west back toward Pahoa. The road passes more of the **1960 lava flow**, which covered almost 2000 acres and totally leveled the small village of Kapoho.

An earlier eruption, circa 1790, caused the grotesque formations down the road at **Lava Tree State Park**. Here the molten rock swamped a grove of *ohia* trees, then hardened around the skeletons to create a fossil forest. When fissures in the earth drained the molten lava, these petrified trees were left as a lonely legacy. In strange and exotic fashion, these giant skeletons, mixed with fresh growth, loom above huge cracks in the landscape.

PUNA DISTRICT HOTELS

In the beautiful Puna district, a volcanic region fringed with black-sand beaches, there's a marvelous place called the **Kalani Honua Culture Center and Retreat** (RR 2, Box 4500, Pahoa, HI 96778; 965-7828). Situated on Route 137 20 minutes from Pahoa, it sits just above the ocean on 20 acres. In addition to lodging, this New Age resort provides a lifestyle. There are occasional classes in *hula*, weaving, carving, and *lei* making; lectures on the history and culture of Hawaii; plus programs in modern dance, aerobics, and yoga. The facilities include a Japanese health spa with jacuzzi and sauna, a swimming pool, tennis court, hiking trails, and volleyball courts. Guests stay in multi-unit lodges, sharing a spacious living room and kitchen. Sleeping accommodations are basic but appealing, with pine walls; the room decorations are crafted at the center. For one or two people, a room with shared or private bath runs in the moderate range; private cottages are also for rent at moderate cost. Campsites are available at budget prices. Meals are $24 a day per person, or you can cook for yourself.

An enterprising family has converted the manager's residence of the old Puna Sugar Plantation into the **Banyan House Bed and Breakfast** (Route 130 about one mile southeast of Keaau; 966-8598). Set on ten tropical acres, the 1898 vintage home is surrounded by rolling lawns, orchards, flowerbeds, and jungle. Each of the four guest rooms (one with private bath) are decorated in a different theme, from plantation wicker to antique, and are comfortably tabbed in the moderate range. The public rooms are very spacious and there are ocean views from several parts of the house. It provides a unique opportunity to experience turn-of-the-century Hawaii.

PUNA DISTRICT RESTAURANTS

In the rustic town of Pahoa, there's **Luquin's Mexican Restaurant** (965-9990), a friendly Mexican eatery. Serving a variety of dishes from south of the border, it offers lunch and dinner daily at budget prices.

Paradise West (965-9733), a local café also located on the main drag in Pahoa, serves three hearty meals a day at moderate prices. Breakfast includes whole-grain pancakes and eggs with the catch of the day; lunch consists of hamburgers, sandwiches, and soup. The dinner menu changes nightly: You might be treated to fresh ahi, rib-eye steak, roast chicken, or even tofu enchiladas. "Everything here is homemade." How can you go wrong?

PUNA DISTRICT MARKETS

In Pahoa, people often set up stands along the roadside. These freelance operations are great places to purchase fresh fish and home-grown fruits and vegetables. There are a few small markets, including the **Wiki Wiki Mart** (Keaau; 966-8588) and **Da Store** (Route 130, Pahoa; 965-9411). For health foods, consider **Pahoa Natural Groceries** (Route 130, Pahoa; 965-8322).

PUNA DISTRICT SHOPPING

Out in the volcano region, on the road down to the Puna district, you'll pass through the tiny town of **Pahoa**. Either side of Route 130, the main drag, is lined with falsefront buildings. Each one seems to contain yet another ingenious craft shop run by a local resident.

PUNA DISTRICT BEACHES AND PARKS

Isaac Hale Beach Park—This small park on the Puna coast is pretty but run-down. There's a patch of black sand here and some hot springs nearby. A boat landing ramp makes this a popular park with local people.

Facilities: Picnic area, restrooms. Several miles away from groceries in Pahoa. *Swimming:* Okay when the sea remains calm. *Surfing:* Summer and winter breaks in the center of the bay. *Fishing:* The most common catches here are papio, moi, mountain bass, menpachi, red bigeye, ulua, and goatfish.

Camping: Tent and trailer camping. County permit required. I much prefer nearby MacKenzie State Park for overnighting.

Getting there: Located on Route 137 about two miles northeast of MacKenzie State Park.

MacKenzie State Park—This beautiful 13-acre park lies in an ironwood grove along a rocky coastline. King's Highway, an ancient Hawaiian trail, bisects the area.

Facilities: Picnic area and restrooms. It's several miles away from groceries in Pahoa. *Swimming, Snorkeling, Surfing:* None; a sea cliff borders the park. *Fishing:* Good shore fishing from rock ledges.

Camping: Tent camping; a state permit is required.

Getting there: On Route 137 near the village of Opihikao.

Kaimu Black Sand Beach—This narrow swath of black sand was covered with lava during the 1990 lava flows. The palm trees that ran to the water's edge, adding to the spectacular scenery along the crescent-shaped beach, were also destroyed. Within a short time, however, a new black-sand beach had been formed. At last report, the new beach was even larger than the original one. When the new beach officially opens to the public, the following information may once again characterize the area:

Swimming and Snorkeling: Extremely dangerous. *Surfing:* Summer and winter breaks, right and left sides. *Fishing:* For goatfish, ulua, red bigeye, menpachi, mountain bass, threadfin, and papio.

Getting there: Located on Route 137 about 30 miles south of Hilo.

The Sporting Life

CAMPING

There are few activities on the Big Island more pleasurable than camping. Beautiful state and county parks dot the island, while enticing hiking trails lead to remote mountain and coastal areas.

No matter what you plan to do on the island, keep in mind that the Kona side is generally dry, while the Hilo side receives considerable rain. Also remember that the mountains can be quite cold and usually call for extra clothing and gear.

Camping at **county parks** requires a permit. These cost $1 per person per day (50¢ for children age 13 through 17). Pick up permits from the County Department of Parks and Recreation, 25 Aupuni Street, Hilo, Hawaii, HI 96720 (961-8311) or at the Kona Recreation Office, P.O. Box 314, Captain Cook, Hawaii, HI 96740 (323-3046). County permits are issued for both tent and trailer camping, and can be obtained for up to two weeks at each park (one week during the summer).

Free **state parks** permits can be obtained through the State Department of Land and Natural Resources, Division of State Parks, 75 Aupuni Street, Hilo, Hawaii, HI 96721 (933-4200). Maximum stay at each park is five days. For information on cabin rentals and camping in Volcanoes National Park, see the individual listings in the "Beaches and Parks" sections in this chapter.

Hilo Hawaii Sales and Surplus (284 Keawe Street, Hilo; 935-6398) and **Honsport** (111 East Puainako, Hilo; 959-5816) sell camping equipment. **Pacific United Rent-All** (1080 Kilauea Avenue, Hilo; 935-2974) rents tents, backpacks, sleeping bags, stoves, coolers, and other camping equipment.

SKINDIVING

The Big Island's coastal waters offer some of the most enticing dive sites in Hawaii. Good visibility, lava and coral formations and, of course, an intriguing variety of marine life assure plenty of fun. Whether you choose a beach or boat dive, you'll find the waters relatively uncrowded. Snorkelers will be attracted to beautiful Kealakekua Bay where Captain Cook met his maker.

Nautilus Dive Center (382 Kamemameha Avenue, Hilo; 935-6939) operates one- and two-tank shore dives off the Hilo coast. You'll see a variety of marine life, including sea turtles, as well as coral formations and caves.

Sandwich Isle Divers (Kona Marketplace, Kailua; 329-9188) arranges dive trips to Turtle Pinnacles, Pine Trees, Golden Arches, Kaiwi Point, and Kaloko Arches along the Kona Coast. **King Kamehameha Divers** (King Kamehameha Hotel, Kailua; 329-5662) offers daytime and night dives off the Kona Coast. There's expert instruction for beginners and experienced divers will enjoy exploring caves and archaeological sites.

Sea Paradise Scuba (71-7128 Kaleopapa Street, Kailua; 322-2500) leads trips to lava tubes, caverns, caves, and other fascinating formations at 25 locations south of Kailua. **Big Island Dives** (Gentry's Kona Marina, Honokohau Harbor, Kailua; 329-6068) offers daytime and night dives along the Kona Coast.

Kohala Divers (Kawaihae Shopping Center, Kawaihae; 882-7774) is a full-service diving center providing scuba and snorkeling lessons as well as gear rental. (Also see the "Skindiving the Gold Coast" section in this chapter.)

SURFING AND WINDSURFING

For surfing U.S.A., consider the dynamic Kona Coast as well as Hilo Bay. Winter is peak season for surfing popular spots such as Lyman's, Banyan's, and Hunnels south of Kailua. Also popular is Pohiki in the Puna area near the Kilauea volcano. Windsurfing is good year-round. Try Anaehoomalu Beach on the Kona Coast or the South Point area.

Orchid Land Surfboards (832 Kilauea Avenue, Hilo; 935-1533) rents and sells surfboards. **Ocean Sports Hawaii** (Royal Waikoloan, Waikoloa;

885-5555) rents sailboards and offers lessons. At the Kona Inn Shopping Village, **Hobie Sports Kona** (75-5744 Alii Drive; 329-1001) also rents surfboards and recommends the best locations.

FISHING

The waters off the Kona Coast are among the Pacific's finest fishing grounds, particularly for marlin. Many charter boats operate out of Kailua; check the phone book for names or simply walk along the pier and inquire.

Kona Charter Skippers' Association (75-5663 Palani Road, Kailua; 329-3600) represents one of the larger outfits. They sponsor daily charters for marlin, yellowfin tuna, skipjack, and mahimahi. Using boats 26 to 50 feet in length, they charge $90 per person for a half day or $130 for a full day.

Head up to the tuna tower to survey the fishing scene aboard **Pamela** (Honokohau Harbor; 329-1525), a 38-foot vessel that focuses on marlin, short-nosed bullfish, yellowfin, and wahoo.

Omega Sportfishing (Honokohau Harbor, Kailua; 325-7859) operates full- and half-day charters. Another company offering similar service is **Kona Marlin Center** (Honokohau Harbor, Kailua; 329-7529).

SAILING AND PARASAILING

One of the authentic pleasures of a Big Island visit is a sail along the Kona or Kohala coast. Choose from a pleasure sail or take an adventure trip that includes a snorkeling excursion.

Among the popular operators is **Kamanu Charters** (Honokohau Harbor, Kailua; 329-2021), which offers half-day trips featuring snorkeling at Kaiwi Point. **Hawaii Bluewater Sailing** (Kawaihae Harbor; 326-1986) operates half-day, full-day, and overnight trips. The short four-hour sail includes snorkeling. **The Maile** (Kawaihae Harbor; 326-5174) is a 50-foot gulfstar sailboat available for a variety of trips around the Big Island. **Aloha Kai Sailing** (Honokohau Harbor, Kailua; 882-7575) charters boats for personalized trips ideal for watching marine life and visiting hidden coves.

Another sport that's gaining increased notoriety is parasailing, in which you're strapped to a parachute that is towed aloft by a motorboat. For information, contact **Kona Water Sports, Inc.** (Kailua; 329-1593).

KAYAKING

Kona Kai-Yak (74-5563 Kaiwi Street, Kailua; 326-2922) offers beginner lessons as well as half- and full-day excursions. Kayak trips depart from boat ramps and secluded beaches up and down the Kona Coast. You can explore secluded spots like Kukio Bay and Kua Bay. Kayak rentals are also available here.

WHALE WATCHING AND SEA TOURS

Between November and May, when about 400 humpback whales inhabit Hawaiian waters, a popular spectator sport is spotting whales in the channels around the islands.

During the winter months, University of Hawaii marine mammal research experts guide two-and-a-half-hour tours for **Hawaiian Cruises** (Kailua pier; 329-6411). **Captain Zodiac** (Honokohau Harbor; 329-3199) also leads four-hour daily trips along the Kona Coast. You may see whales, dolphins, sea turtles, and other marine life as you journey along the coast and head into sea caves. There's a stop at Kealakekua Bay for snorkeling.

Captain Dan McSweeney's Whale Watching Adventures (Honokohau Harbor, Kailua; 322-0028) operates three-and-a-half-hour cruises. If you don't see whales, the company will give you another trip at no charge. **Hawaiian Cruises** (74-5606-A Pawai Place, Kailua; 329-6411) offers two-and-a-half-hour trips led by University of Hawaii naturalists.

SKIING

See the "Ski Hawaii" section in this chapter.

GOLF

Some of the best golfing in the United States is found on the Big Island. From the stunning links on the Kohala Coast to community courses in the Hilo area, this island has everything you need for a golf-oriented vacation. Sunny conditions on the Kona side mean you generally don't need to worry about taking a rain check. Throw in views of the lava landscape, verdant shorelines, and swaying banyan trees, and you've created a duffer's view of paradise.

Naniloa Country Club (120 Banyan Drive, Hilo; 935-3000) is a nine-hole, par-35 course overlooking Hilo Bay. This narrow course may look easy but don't be deceived: Water hazards and trees along the fairways create plenty of challenges.

Hilo Municipal Golf Course (340 Haihai Street, Hilo; 959-7711) is one of the best bargains on the islands. This verdant 18-hole course has great views of the water and the mountains. Be sure to reserve tee times on the weekends. You can sharpen your skills on the driving range and practice greens.

Hamakua Country Club (Honokaa; 775-7244) is another inexpensive choice. Located on the north shore about 40 miles from Hilo, this nine-hole course bans power carts. While it lacks the amenities of the resort links, Hamakua has a nice neighborhood feel.

Creating a great golf course is easy if you just dip into Laurence Rockefeller's deep pockets, hire Robert Trent Jones Sr, and buy some lava-strewn oceanfront terrain. What you'll end up with is the 18-hole **Mauna Kea Beach Golf Course** (Kawaihae; 882-7222). Quite a challenge, the original links have been complemented by the new 18-hole **Hapuna Golf Course** (882-1035) created by Arnold Palmer.

Waikoloa Village Golf Course (Waikoloa; 883-9621) is a 72-hole layout that also includes a driving range and practice greens. This windy course designed by Robert Trent Jones Jr. has great views of Mauna Kea and Mauna Loa. Nearby **Waikoloa Beach Resort Golf Course** (Waikoloa; 885-6789) and the adjacent **Waikoloa Kings' Golf Club** (Waikoloa; 885-4647) are also popular. Convenient to the Hyatt Regency Waikoloa and the Royal Waikoloan, each course has unique features. The beach course heads through petroglyph fields while the Kings Golf Club also has beautiful lava hazards.

Mauna Lani Golf Course (Kalahuipuaa; 885-6655) has two 18-hole links built across rugged lava beds. If you miss the fairway, don't expect to find your ball out there in the volcanic landscape. There's also a driving range and practice greens.

At the **Kona Country Club** (78-7000 Alii Drive, Kailua; 808-322-2595), a pair of 18-hole golf courses are ideal for those who want to bunker down. Bring along your camera to capture memorable views of the ocean course. Or head uphill to fully enjoy the challenging Mauka course. If you're looking for overwater holes and hidden hazards, you've come to the right place.

Volcano Golf and Country Club (Volcanoes National Park; 967-7331) is the only course we know located in the vicinity of an erupting volcano. The high elevation (4200 feet) will give your ball an extra lift on this 18-hole course. **Sea Mountain Golf Course** (Punaluu; 928-6222) is a popular 18-hole course located south of Kilauea volcano. It's beautifully landscaped with banyan trees.

TENNIS

Public tennis courts are convenient to all of the Big Island's popular resort destinations. In Hilo, you can play at the courts at Kalanikoa and Piilani streets or Kilauea and Ponahawai streets.

In Waimea, try Waimea Park on Lindsey Road off Route 19. In the Kailua area head for Kailua Park (Old Airport Road), Hiashi Hara Park (Mamalahoa Highway, Keauhou), or the courts at the intersection of Palani and Hualalai roads.

Call the **County Department of Parks and Recreation** (961-8311) for information on public courts; contact the **Hawaii Visitors Bureau** (961-5797 or 329-7787) for information concerning private courts.

BICYCLING

Hawaii offers very good roads and many unpopulated stretches that make it ideal for cyclers. Much of the island is mountainous with some fairly

Ski Hawaii

During your island tour you'll inevitably pull up behind some joker with a bumper sticker reading "Think Snow." Around you trade winds may be bending the palm trees, sunbronzed crowds will be heading to the beach, and the thermometer will be approaching 80°. Snow will be the furthest thing from your mind.

When I first came to Hawaii, I thought the only white powder on the islands was the illegal stuff that drifts along mirrors and is plowed with a razor. But up on the 13,796-foot slopes of Mauna Kea, you're liable to see a bikini-clad skier schussing across a mantle of newly fallen snow! Any time from December until March, there may be enough dry snow to create ski runs several miles long and fill bowls a half-mile wide and almost a mile long. The slopes range from beginner to expert: some have a vertical drop of over 5000 feet.

Situated above the clouds about 80 percent of the time, this snow lover's oasis is baked by a tropical sun many times more powerful than at the beach. So it's easy to tan and easier yet to burn. Combined with the thin air and winds up to 100 miles per hour, Hawaii's ski slopes are not for the faint-hearted or fair-skinned.

But if you're seeking an incredible adventure and want a view of the Hawaiian islands from a 13,000-foot crow's nest, the heights of Mauna Kea await.

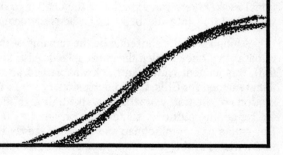

steep grades in the interior. Saddle Road, the roads to Waimea, and the road from Hilo up to Volcanoes National Park will all make a heavy breather of you, but the coast roads are generally flat or gently rolling. Most roads have shoulders and light traffic.

Keep in mind that the northeast side of the island receives heavy rainfall, while the Kona side is almost always sunny. But wet side or dry, the scenery is spectacular throughout. South of Hilo, **Teo's Safaris** (Keaau; 982-5221) leads off-road tours in the Olaa rainforest and along the coast.

BIKE RENTALS In Kailua, try **Dave's Bike and Triathlon Shop** (King Kamehameha Square; 329-4522). They rent 10-speed, 12-speed, and mountain bikes and do repairs. Rentals are also available at **Hawaiian Pedals** (Kona Inn Shopping Village, Kailua; 329-2294). In addition, Teo's Safaris (mentioned above) rents bikes.

BIKE REPAIRS These shops will do repair work and will cheerfully sell you bike accessories: **The Bike Shop** (258 Kamehameha Avenue, Hilo; 935-7588), **Mid-Pacific Wheels** (1133-C Manono Street, Hilo; 935-6211), and **B & L Bike & Sports** (74-5576-B Pawai Place, Kailua; 329-3309).

STARGAZING TOURS

Paradise Safaris' Sunset Stargazing Trips (Kailua; 322-2366) picks you up at your hotel and takes you to the Mauna Loa summit for stargazing. Astronomer Pat Wright sets up a telescope and conducts a brief lesson.

HIKING

Of all the islands in the chain, Hawaii has the finest hiking trails. The reason? Quite simply, it's the Big Island's size. Larger than all the other islands combined and boasting the highest peaks, Hawaii offers the greatest diversity to explorers.

Mauna Loa and Mauna Kea, each rising over 13,000 feet, provide rugged mountain climbing. To the north, the Kohala Mountains feature trails through dense tropical terrain and along awesome cliffs. In Volcanoes National Park, hikers can experience the challenge of walking through a lava wasteland and into the belly of an active volcano.

Along Hawaii's shoreline lie the remains of the Makahiki trail, a series of paths that once circled the entire island. Also known as the William Ellis trail, this ancient Hawaiian track was named after the Makahiki gods and then renamed for Ellis, the bold missionary who explored it in 1823. Today, sections of the trail can still be walked, though much of it is destroyed. Of the remaining portions, some cross private land and others are unmarked. But with a topographic map and a pair of sturdy boots you can still follow in the tracks of the gods, and, for that matter, in the tracks of William Ellis.

Hawaii's official hiking trails run through four areas: Volcanoes National Park, Kau Desert, Mauna Kea, and the Kohala Mountains. These are popular and well-defined trails, many of which are described below.

VOLCANOES NATIONAL PARK TRAILS The most interesting and easily accessible trails lead through the **Kilauea Crater** area. The crater, two-and-one-half miles long and 4000 feet above sea level, can be explored either by hiking along one extended trail or over several shorter connecting trails.

Crater Rim Trail (11.6 miles long) begins near park headquarters and encircles Kilauea Crater. An excellent introduction to the volcanoes, this lengthy loop trail passes steam vents, the Kau Desert, the fractured Southwest Rift area, and a fascinating fern forest. The views from atop the crater are spectacular.

Sulphur Banks Trail (0.3 mile) begins at park headquarters and parallels Crater Rim Road past steam vents and sulphur deposits.

Halemaumau Trail (3.1 miles) starts near Volcano House, then descends into Kilauea Crater. The trail crosses the crater floor and affords astonishing views down into steaming Halemaumau crater, then climbs back up to join Crater Rim Trail. This has got to be one of the park's finest hikes.

Kilauea Iki Trail (4 miles) loops from the Thurston Lava Tube parking lot down into Kilauea Iki crater and returns via Crater Rim Trail. Crossing the crater floor, the trail passes over a lava crust beneath which lies a brewing pool of molten rock. Step lightly.

Sandalwood Trail (1.5 miles) loops from near the Volcano House past sandalwood and *ohia* trees and then along the side of Kilauea Crater.

Byron Ledge Trail (2.5 miles) branches off Halemaumau Trail, crosses the Kilauea caldera floor, and then climbs along Byron Ledge before rejoining Halemaumau. This makes an excellent connecting trail.

The **Wahaula Trail**, created after the 1989 destruction of the Wahaula Visitor Center, goes for 1.5 miles from the end of Chain of Craters Road to the ruins of the center. There is also a *heiau* here, the oldest in Hawaii, which was largely unaffected by the flow.

Volcanoes National Park's premier hike is along **Mauna Loa Trail**. This tough 19.5-mile trek, requiring at least four days, leads to the top of the world's largest shield volcano. Cold-weather equipment and a sturdy constitution are absolute necessities for this challenging adventure.

Climbers usually hike seven miles the first day from the trailhead at the end of Mauna Loa Strip Road up to Red Hill. At this 10,035-foot way station, there is a rudimentary cabin with no provisions. A hearty eleven-mile trek the second day leads to another cabin inside Mokuaweoweo caldera, then to Mauna Loa's summit. The return trip takes one or two days, depending on how fast you want to come down.

Beware of altitude sickness and hypothermia, and be sure to register for a permit at park headquarters before and after hiking. Purification tablets for the water and white gas for the stoves are also essential. Don't treat this as a casual jaunt; it's a real trek. Good planning will ensure your safety and enjoyment.

A dirt road, usually passable by passenger car, climbs from Saddle Road to an area near Mauna Loa summit. This alternative hiking route lacks the adventure but reduces the difficulty of a Mauna Loa ascent.

KAU AREA TRAILS   From Volcanoes National Park's southern section several trails lead into the hot, arid Kau Desert. All are long, dusty trails offering solitude to the adventurous hiker.

Halape Trail (7.2 miles) begins at Kipuka Nene campground on Hilina Pali Road and rapidly drops 3000 feet to a sand beach at Halape. There is also a shelter at Halape.

Kau Desert Trail (18.9 miles) branches off Crater Rim Trail and drops 2000 feet en route to the lookout at the end of Hilina Pali Road. The shelter along the way, at Kipuka Pepeiau, provides a welcome resting place on this lengthy trek.

Mauna Iki Trail (8.8 miles) leads from Mamalahoa Highway to Hilina Pali Road. The trail passes near Footprints Trail, where a sudden volcanic eruption in 1790 engulfed a Hawaiian army at war with Kamehameha.

MAUNA KEA TRAIL   This hike is not nearly as rigorous as the trek up Mauna Loa, but the scenery is just as stunning. A road leads off Saddle Road for nine miles to the trailhead at Kilohana. From this 9620-foot elevation, it is six miles to the 13,796-foot summit. Begin early and plan to make the hike in one day since no camping is permitted along the way.

In addition to vistas as breathtaking as the altitude, Mauna Kea features the state's highest lake, Lake Waiau, at 13,020 feet. From atop the state's highest peak, you'll have a spectacular view of Maui's Haleakala crater.

KOHALA MOUNTAIN TRAILS   Stretching along Kohala peninsula's northeast coast is a series of sheer cliffs and wide valleys rivaling Kauai's Na Pali Coast in beauty. At either end of this rainswept *pali* are lush, still valleys that can only be reached by hiking trails.

Pololu Valley Trail (0.5 mile) descends from the Pololu Valley lookout at the end of Akoni Pule Highway to the valley floor 300 feet below. From here, a series of trails leading through the Kohala Mountains begins. Unfortunately, these trails are controlled by the Kohala Corporation and are closed to hikers.

Waipio Valley Trail begins from Waipio Valley lookout at the end of Route 24. Waipio is comparable to Kauai's Kalalau Valley: a broad, lush, awesomely beautiful valley ribboned with waterfalls and rich in history. From the trailhead, a jeep trail drops steeply for one mile to the valley floor. Here the trail joins one road leading up into the valley and another heading to the beach. The high road goes toward 1200-foot Hiilawe Falls and to a now-abandoned Peace Corps training camp.

Waipio Valley is ripe for exploring, but if you want to leave civilization completely behind, continue instead along the **Waimanu Valley Trail**. This seven-mile track begins at the base of the cliff that marks Waipio's northwest border. It climbs sharply up the 1200-foot rock face in a series of switchbacks, then continues up and down across numerous gulches, and finally descends into Waimanu Valley. This exotic place, half the size of Waipio Valley, is equally as lush. Here, in addition to wild pigs, mountain apple trees, and ancient ruins, you'll find naturally running water (requiring purification) and great spots for beachfront picnics. You may never want to leave.

Transportation

BY AIR

Four airports serve the Big Island—Hilo International Airport (General Lyman Field) near Hilo, Kailua-Kona's Keahole Airport, Upolu Airport on the Kohala peninsula, and Kamuela Airport near Waimea.

The main landing facility is **Keahole Airport**. Many mainland visitors fly here rather than to Honolulu to avoid Oahu's crowds. United Airlines, which provides the most frequent service to Hawaii, is the only carrier flying from the mainland to Kailua-Kona. United provides several flights daily to this airport.

This windswept facility has snack bars, cocktail lounges, and souvenir shops, but no lockers or bus service. A nine-mile cab ride into town costs about $16.

Passengers flying between the islands use Aloha Airlines, Hawaiian Airlines, and Aloha Island Air. The first two provide frequent jet service from Oahu and the other islands, while the other flies prop planes. Personally I prefer Aloha Airlines because of their punctuality and excellent service record.

Hilo International Airport (General Lyman Field), once the island's main jetport, is now more like a small city airport. It is served by the same inter-island carriers as Keahole Airport. Here you'll find a cafeteria-style restaurant, cocktail lounge, gift shop, newsstand, and lockers, but no bus service. Covering the two miles into town means renting a car, hailing a cab, hitching, or hoofing.

Upolu Airport is a desolate landing strip on the Kohala peninsula along the island's northwest coast. There are no facilities whatever and only prop planes land here.

Kamuela Airport, two miles outside the cowboy town of Waimea, is served by Aloha Island Air. There are waiting rooms, but no shops of any kind here. Both airline and car rental offices are often closed unless a flight is scheduled, so it's best to make all reservations in advance.

CAR RENTALS

Big Island rental agencies generally charge slightly more than is charged on the other islands because of the longer distances traveled. Also, they often charge a fee ($30 or so) for cars rented in Hilo or Kona and dropped off in the other locale. It's wise to remember that you will be driving farther on Hawaii, sometimes through quite rural areas; it may sound obvious, but remember to watch your gas gauge.

When choosing a rental agency, check whether they permit driving on the Saddle Road across the island and on South Point Road, both good paved roads with few potholes and many points of interest. I think it's quite unfair, even irrational, that some rental companies revoke insurance coverage if you drive these thoroughfares. But my protests will be of little benefit in case of an accident. So check first or be prepared to take your chances!

That said, my favorite car rental operations are the smaller companies. Like the nationally known firms, they generally have booths either in Hilo or Kona, or both. (The first phone number listed here is for Hilo, the second for Kona.) Generally, the lesser-known outfits tend to be easier on the purse than nationally acclaimed companies. I have always found Hawaii's small, independent car rental agencies provide comparable service, and therefore I generally recommend them. So with your budget in mind, consider the following companies: **Sunshine Rent A Car** (935-1108; 329-2926) or **Robert's Hawaii Rent A Car** (935-2858; 329-1688).

Several other companies have franchises at the Hilo and Kailua-Kona airports. Among these are **Thrifty Rent A Car** (935-1936; 329-1730), **National Inter-Rent** (935-0891; 329-1674), **Dollar Rent A Car** (961-6059; 329-2744), **Avis** (935-1290; 329-1191), **Hertz Rent A Car** (935-2896; 329-3566), and **Budget Rent A Car** (935-6878; 329-8511).

Many outfits located outside the Hilo International Airport and Keahole Airport feature competitive rates and free service to and from the airport. These include **Tropical Rent A Car** (935-3385; 329-2437), which is located at the Hilo International Airport and near Keahole.

(See Chapter Two for a complete explanation of car rentals in the islands.)

JEEP RENTALS

Budget Rent A Car (935-6878; 329-8511) rents four-wheel drives.

MOTOR SCOOTER RENTALS

Mopeds are available for rent from **Rent Scootah** (74-5563 Kaiwi Street, #4; 329-3250) and **Scoots R Us** (75-5819 Alii Drive; 329-3250) in Kailua.

PUBLIC TRANSPORTATION

The **Hele-On Bus** provides cross-island service Monday through Saturday between Hilo and Kailua-Kona. There are also limited intra-city buses serving Hilo. Other buses drive to the Kona and Kau coasts. The Hele-On runs Monday through Saturday; fares range from 75¢ for short rides to $6 for the Hilo–Kailua cross-island run.

The Hilo bus terminal is on Kamehameha Avenue at Mamo Street. You'll see few bus stops indicated on the island. The official stops are generally unmarked, and you can hail a bus anywhere along its route. Just wave your hand. When it's time to get off, the driver will stop anywhere you wish. For information and schedules, call **County Hawaiian Transit** at 935-8241 or 961-8343.

HITCHHIKING

Thumbing is very popular in Hawaii. Like any place, your luck will vary here, depending on your location, looks, the time, the tides, whatever. Generally, populated areas and tourist attractions are good spots for a ride. If you venture from these beaten paths, remember that the Big Island has long stretches with nothing but macadam and lava.

Check the Hele-On bus schedule before setting out just in case you get stranded. If your luck fails, you can hail a bus from anywhere along the roadside.

FLIGHTSEEING

Thanks to the Kilauea eruption, the Big Island offers a wide variety of aerial sightseeing opportunities. In addition to the lava flows, you'll see remote coastlines, the slopes of Mauna Kea, and coffee plantations. Bring your camera because the lava flow is one of Hawaii's greatest sightseeing opportunities.

Hilo Bay Air (Hilo Airport; 969-1545) operates three daily flights over Kilauea's Puu Oo vent and the black-sand beaches. Riders also view current lava activity and waterfalls. Rides last from 40 minutes to one hour.

Volcano Helitours (Mile Marker 30, Mamalahoa Highway, Volcano; 967-7578) offers a narrated 45-minute tour of all active eruptions.

At **Mauna Kea Helicopters** (Mamalahoa Highway at the Kamuela Airport, Waimea; 885-6400) you have a choice of three flights lasting up to two hours. Passengers view the valleys and waterfalls on the island's northern end, as well as volcanic activity at Kilauea.

Big Island Air (Keahole Airport; 329-4868) takes passengers on a circle island tour featuring Kilauea and the north end valleys and waterfalls. Flights last about 1 hour and 45 minutes.

Papillon Helicopters (Waikoloa Heliport and Keahole Airport; 329-0551) offers flights from both sides of the island featuring Kilauea, the Kohala Coast, Waipio Valley, waterfalls, and the rainforest. Trips last 35 minutes to two hours. Similar tours are offered by **Kenai Helicopters** (Waikoloa Beach Drive, Waikoloa; 329-7424).

Hawaii Addresses and Phone Numbers

HAWAII ISLAND

County Department of Parks and Recreation—25 Aupuni Street, Hilo (961-8311)

Hawaii Visitors Bureau—180 Kinoole, Hilo (961-5797); and Kona Plaza Shopping Arcade, Alii Drive, Kailua (329-7787)

State Department of Land and Natural Resources—75 Aupuni Street, Hilo (933-4200)

Volcanoes National Park Headquarters—(967-7311)

Weather Report—(935-8555 for Hilo; 961-5582 for entire island)

HILO

Ambulance—(961-6022)

Barber Shop—Faye's Barber Shop, 710 Kilauea Avenue (935-4990)

Books—Book Gallery 2, Kaikoo Mall (935-2447)

Fire Department—(961-6022)

Fishing Supplies—S. Tokunaga Store, 26 Hoku Street (935-6965)

Hardware—Garden Exchange, 300 Keawe Street (961-2875)

Hospital—Hilo Hospital, 1190 Waianuenue Avenue (969-4111)

Library—300 Waianuenue Avenue (933-4650)

Liquor—Kadota Liquor, 194 Hualalai Street (935-1802)

Pharmacy—Long's Drugs, 555 Kilauea Avenue (935-3357)

Photo Supply—Hawaii Photo Supply, 250 Keawe Street (935-6995)

Police Department—349 Kapiolani Street (935-3311)

Post Office—Hilo International Airport (935-2821) and 154 Waianuenue Avenue (935-6685)

KAILUA-KONA

Ambulance—(961-6022)

Barber Shop—Delilah's Barber, King Kamehameha Kona Coast Hotel (329-2577)

Books—Middle Earth Bookshoppe, 75-5719 Alii Drive (329-2123)

Fire Department—(961-6022)

Fishing Supplies—Yama's Specialty Shop, 75-5943 Alii Drive (329-1712)

Hardware—Trojan Lumber Company, 74-5488 Kaiwi Street (329-3536)

Hospital—Kona Hospital, Kealakekua town (322-9311)

Laundromat—Hele Mai Laundromat, North Kona Shopping Center (329-3494)

Library—Hualalai Road (329-2196)

Pharmacy—Pay 'n' Save Drug Store, Kona Coast Shopping Center, Palani Road (329-3577)

Photo Supply—Kona Photo Center, North Kona Shopping Center (329-3676)

Police Department—(329-3838)

Post Office—Palani Road (329-1927)

CHAPTER SIX

Maui

Residents of Maui, Hawaii's second-largest island, proudly describe their Valley Isle by explaining that "Maui *no ka oi*." Maui is the greatest. During the last decade, few of the island's visitors have disputed the claim. They return each year in increasing numbers, lured by the enchantment of a place possessing 33 miles of public beaches, one of the world's largest dormant volcanoes, beautiful people, a breeding ground for rare humpback whales, and a climate that varies from subtropic to subarctic.

Named after one of the most important demigods in the Polynesian pantheon, Maui has retained its mythic aura. The island is famous as a chic retreat and jet-set landing ground. To many people, Maui *is* Hawaii.

But to others, who have watched the rapid changes during the past two decades, Maui is no longer the greatest. They point to the 2.3 million tourists (second only to Oahu) who visited during a recent year, to the condominiums and resort hotels mushrooming along the prettiest beaches, and to the increasing traffic over once rural roads. And they have a new slogan. "Maui is *pau*." Maui is finished. Overtouristed. Overpopulated. Overdeveloped.

Today, among the island's 91,300 population, it seems like every other person is in the real estate business. On a land mass measuring 729 square miles, just half the size of Long Island, their goods are in short supply. During the 1970s and 1980s, land prices shot up faster than practically anywhere else in the country.

Yet over 75 percent of the island remains unpopulated. Despite pressures from land speculation and a mondo-condo mentality, Maui still offers exotic, untouched expanses for the explorer. Most development is concentrated along the south and west coasts in Kihei, Wailea, and Kaanapali. The rest of the island, though more crowded than neighboring islands, is an adventurer's oasis.

The second-youngest island in the chain, Maui was created about fifteen million years ago by two volcanoes. Haleakala, the larger, rises over 10,000 feet, and offers excellent hiking and camping within its gaping crater. The earlier of the two firepits created the West Maui Mountains, 5788 feet at their highest. Because of their relative age, and the fact they receive 400 inches of rainfall a year, they are more heavily eroded than the smooth surfaces of Haleakala. Between the two heights lies Central Maui, an isthmus formed when the volcanoes flowed together.

The twin cities of Kahului and Wailuku, Maui's commercial and civic centers, respectively, sit in this saddle. Most of the isthmus is planted in sugar, which became king in Maui after the decline of whaling in the 1860s. A road through the cane fields leads south to Kihei's sunsplashed resorts and beaches.

Another road loops around the West Maui Mountains. It passes prime whale-watching areas along the south coast and bisects Lahaina, an old whaling town that is now the jet-set capital of the island. Next to this timeworn harbor stretches the town of Kaanapali with its limitless beaches and endless condominiums. Past these plastic palisades, near the island's northwest tip, lie hidden beaches, overhanging cliffs, and spectacular vistas.

The road girdling Haleakala's lower slopes passes equally beautiful areas. Along the rainswept northeast coast are sheer rock faces ribboned with waterfalls and gorges choked with tropic vegetation. The lush, somnolent town of Hana gives way along the southeast shore to a dry, unpopulated expanse ripe for exploration.

On the middle slopes of Haleakala, in Maui's Upcountry region, small farms dot the landscape. Here, in addition to guavas, avocados, and lichee nuts, grow the sweet Kula onions for which the Valley Isle is famous.

Back in the days of California's gold rush, Maui found its own underground nuggets in potatoes: Countless bushels were grown in this area and shipped to a hungry San Francisco market. Today the crop is used to prepare Maui potato chips. With the possible exception of marijuana, these delicious snacks are the island's most renowned agricultural product.

Because of its strategic location between Oahu and Hawaii, Maui has played a vital role in Hawaiian history. Kahekili, Maui's last king, gained control of all the islands except Hawaii before being overwhelmed by Kamehameha in 1790. Lahaina, long a vacation spot for island rulers, became a political center under Hawaii's first three kings and an important commercial center soon after Captain Cook sighted the island in 1778. It served as a supply depot for ships, then as a port for sandalwood exports. By the 1840s, Lahaina was the world capital of whaling. Now, together with the other equally beautiful sections of the Valley Isle, it is a mecca for vacationers.

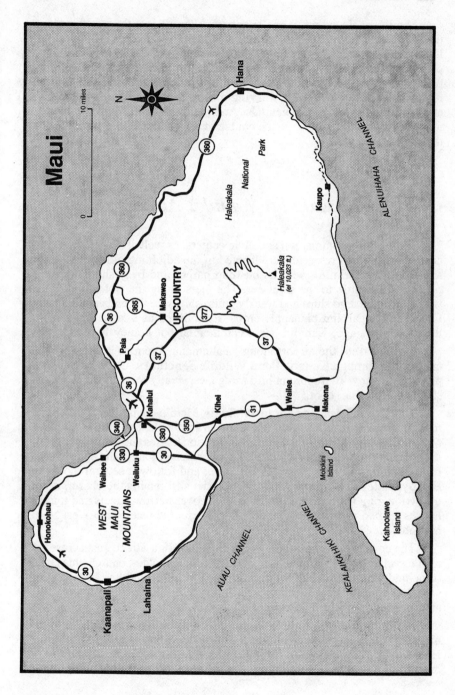

Maui

Maui's magic has cast a spell upon travelers all over the world, making the island a vacation paradise. Like most modern paradises, it is being steadily gilded in plastic and concrete. Yet much of the old charm remains. Some people even claim that the sun shines longer on the Valley Isle than any place on earth. They point to the legend of the demigod Maui who created his own daylight savings by weaving a rope from his sister's pubic hair and lassoing the sun by its genitals. And many hope he has one last trick to perform, one that will slow the course of development just as he slowed the track of the sun.

Kahului-Wailuku Area

The island's commercial and civic centers, as well as the greatest concentration of Maui residents, are located in the adjoining cities of Kahului and Wailuku. **Kahului,** with its bustling harbor and busy shopping complexes, offers little to the sightseer. The piers along the waterfront, lined with container-cargo ships and weekly cruise ships, are the embarkation point for Maui's sugar and pineapple crops. Established as a sugar town more than a century ago, Kahului has a commercial but homey feel about it.

Coming from the airport along Kaahumanu Avenue (Route 32), you can wander through **Kanaha Pond Wildlife Sanctuary.** Once a royal fishpond, this is now an important bird refuge, especially for the rare Hawaiian stilt and Hawaiian coot.

The highway leads uphill to **Wailuku,** Maui's county seat. Older and more interesting than Kahului, Wailuku sits astride the foothills of the West Maui Mountains. A mix of woodframe plantation houses and suburban homes, it even boasts a multi-story civic building. For a short tour of the aging woodfront quarter, take a right on Market Street and follow it several blocks to **Happy Valley.** This former red-light district still retains the charm, if not the action, of a bygone era. Here you'll discover narrow streets and tinroof houses framed by the sharply rising, deeply creased face of the West Maui Mountains.

The county government buildings sit along High Street. Just across the road rests picturesque **Kaahumanu Church.** Maui's oldest church, this grand stone-and-plaster structure was constructed in 1876, and has been kept in excellent condition for its many visitors. With a lofty white spire, it is the area's most dramatic manmade landmark.

Nearby you'll find **Hale Hoikeike** (2375-A Main Street; 244-3326; admission), the Maui Historical Society museum. Housed in the Old Bailey House (completed in 1850), the home of a former missionary, the displays include 19th-century Hawaiian artifacts, remnants from the early sugarcane

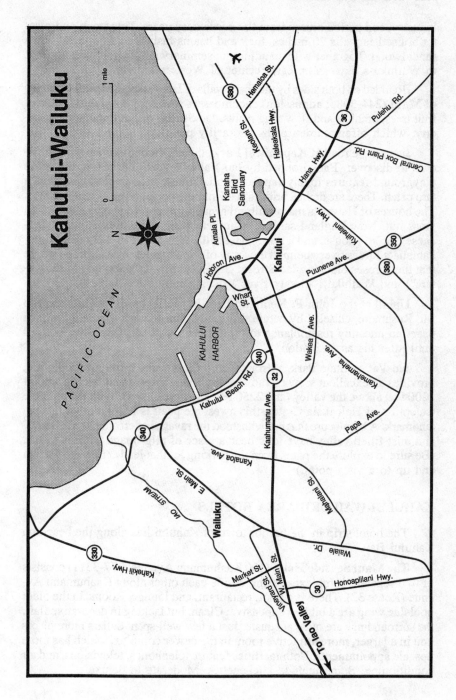

industry, and period pieces from the missionary years. This stone-and-plaster house has walls 20 inches thick and beams fashioned from hand-hewn sandalwood. Together with an adjoining seminary building, it harkens back to Wailuku's days as an early center of Western culture.

Bounded on both sides by the sharp walls of Iao Valley, **Tropical Gardens of Maui** (244-3085; admission) encompasses four densely planted acres of fruit trees, orchids, and flowering plants. Iao Stream rushes through the property, which offers garden paths and a lily pond.

Just up the road at **Kepaniwai Park,** there's an outdoor cultural showcase to discover. Backdropped by Iao Valley's adze-like peaks, this adult playground features lovely Japanese and Chinese monuments as well as a taro patch. There are arched bridges, a swimming pool, and an Oriental garden. The houses of Hawaii's many cultural groups are represented by a Hawaiian grass hut, New England saltbox (complete with white picket fence), Japanese bamboo house, and a Portuguese villa. It was here in 1790 that Kamehameha's forces overwhelmed the army of a Maui chief in a battle so terrible that the corpses blocking Iao Stream gave Kepaniwai ("damming of the waters") and Wailuku ("bloody river") their names.

Uphill at the **John F. Kennedy Profile** you'll see Hawaii's answer to Mt. Rushmore, chiseled by nature. Ironically, this geologic formation, which bears an uncanny resemblance to the former president, was never noticed until after his assassination.

Iao Valley State Park, surrounded by those same moss-mantled cliffs, provides an excellent view of **Iao Needle,** a single spire that rises to a point 1200 feet above the valley (and 2250 feet above sea level). With the possible exception of Haleakala Crater, this awesome peak is Maui's most famous landmark. A basalt core that has withstood the ravages of erosion, the "Needle" and mist-filled valley have long been a place of pilgrimage for Hawaiians. (Be sure to explore the paths from the parking lot that lead across Iao Stream and up to a vista point.)

KAHULUI-WAILUKU AREA HOTELS

The hotel strip in the harbor town of Kahului lies along the beach on Kahului Bay.

The **Maui Seaside Hotel** (100 Kaahumanu Avenue; 877-3311) consists of two separate complexes sitting beside each other along Kaahumanu Avenue (Route 32). There is a pool, restaurant, and lounge. Rooms in the older poolside wing are a bit less expensive: Clean, but lacking in decorative flair, the surroundings are quite adequate. Just a few well-spent dollars more places you in a larger, more attractive room in the newer complex, which has more upscale appointments. Both facilities feature telephones, televisions, and air conditioning. Some include kitchenettes. Moderate to deluxe.

The nearby **Maui Palms Hotel** (170 Kaahumanu Avenue; 877-0071) has comfortable and spacious rooms at moderate prices with wall-to-wall carpeting, telephone, and color television, but lacks decoration. This beachfront facility has a pool tucked between the lobby and the rooms. There's also an Asian-American restaurant on the premises that provides a convenient dining facility for folks staying anywhere along Kahului's hotel row. The grounds are studded with palms; considering the price, the ambience is quite appealing.

Even by Maui's mellow standards, life at the **Banana Bungalow** (310 North Market Street, Wailuku; 244-5090) is *low* key. When I stopped by there was no one around. The rooms—plain, clean units with shared baths—are among the cheapest on the island. There are shared facilities with three or four to a room as well as private singles and doubles. A cross between a hotel and a hostel, you'll find Banana Bungalow has an ambience unlike any place else on the Valley Isle. Television lounge; laundry facilities; continental breakfast. Budget.

Northshore Inn (2080 Vineyard Street, Wailuku; 242-8999) is another clean, trim hostel-cum-hotel with shared rooms and private singles or doubles at budget rates. The lobby/television room is decorated with surfboards, flags, and modern art, and the place has an easy, windswept air about it. There are laundry and kitchen facilities; baths are shared. Every room has a refrigerator and overhead fan.

KAHULUI-WAILUKU AREA RESTAURANTS

The best place in Kahului for a quick, inexpensive meal is at one of several shopping arcades along Kaahumanu Avenue (Route 32). For common fare, head over to the Maui Mall. Here you can drop in at **Restaurant Matsu** (871-0822), a short-order eatery that features such Japanese selections as tempura, yakitori, sushi, and *saimin*. Next door at **Siu's Chinese Kitchen** (871-0828), they serve *dim sum* and other Chinese specialties. To round off the calorie count, you can try a cup of *guri guri* sherbet at **Tasaka Guri Guri Shop** (871-4513). All are budget-priced.

For Asian food, I recommend **Ma-Chan's Of Maui** (199 Dairy Road, Kahului; 877-7818). It features a cafeteria as well as a full-fledged restaurant. Budget.

If you're staying at one of Kahului's bayfront hotels, you might try **Vi's Restaurant** (Kaahumanu Avenue; 877-6494) in the Maui Seaside Hotel. This open-air Polynesian-style establishment has seafood and other assorted dinners. The ambience here is quite pleasant, and the staff congenial, but in the past the service has sometimes been slow. Vi doesn't serve lunch, but at breakfast time (7 a.m. to 9:30 a.m.) she sometimes features a menu that includes banana and coconut hot cakes as well as an assortment of mainland-style dishes. Moderate.

The **East-West Dining Room** (877-0071) lies along Kaahumanu Avenue in the Maui Palms Hotel. This spacious open-air restaurant looks past the hotel lawn out over Kahului Bay. True to its name, the East-West serves a Japanese buffet at dinner, and at lunch features American cuisine. Both the lunch and evening buffets are priced comfortably. The latter includes shrimp tempura, scallops, mixed vegetables, yakitori chicken, teriyaki steak, many different types of Japanese salad, and a host of other dishes. Moderate.

It's locals only (and that is *never* a bad sign!) at **Mickey's** (Kaahumanu and Lono avenues, Kahului; 871-7555). This steak-and-seafood house, trimmed in hardwood and etched glass, is quiet and intimate. Lunch or dinner here means fresh fish prepared in any of eight different ways or accompanied by a steak. Though deluxe in price, Mickey's has a moderate-priced early-bird menu from 5:00 to 6:30 p.m.

At **The Chart House** (500 North Puunene Avenue, Kahului; 877-2476) you can lean back in a captain's chair and gaze past the woodwork and candle-light out over Kahului Bay. There's a lavish salad-bar-in-the-round centered in the main dining room, an open grill just to the side, and a cozy bar off in the wings. The menu offers a surf-and-turf selection with many dishes. Deluxe.

Up the road apiece in Wailuku there are numerous ethnic restaurants guaranteed to please both the palate and the purse. The first, **Sam Sato's** (318 North Market Street; 244-7124), features Japanese and American cuisine. Open for breakfast and lunch, it specializes in *manju* (a bean cake pastry), dry *mein* (a noodle dish), and the ubiquitous *saimin*. The nearby **Fujiya** (133 Market Street; 244-0206) stirs up some similar money-belt-tightening Asian meals. Either place is well worth a visit.

Siam Thai Cuisine (123 North Market Street, Wailuku; 244-3817) is always a good choice for Southeast Asian fare. Attractively decorated with posters and artworks from Thailand, it features a complete menu that includes *dozens* of delicious dishes at budget prices. A local favorite.

Local, budget-priced, and attractively decorated—what more can you ask? Well, **Chums** (1900 Main Street, Wailuku; 244-1000) will go one more and add tasty food. Settle into a hardwood booth and order from an island-style menu that includes *saimin*, won ton soup, curry stew, teriyaki pork, and mahimahi. Or play it safe with a sandwich or salad.

Saeng's Thai Cuisine (2119 Vineyard Street, Wailuku; 244-1567) sits in a beautifully designed building embellished with fine woodwork and adorned with Asian accouterments. The menu, which lists *six pages* of dishes from Thailand, is like an encyclopedia of fine dining. Meals, served in the dining room or out on a windswept veranda, begin with sateh and spring rolls, venture on to dishes like the "evil prince" and "tofu delight," and end over tea and tapioca pudding.

Wailuku is becoming more hip by the month, and the center of "hipdom" is a tiny espresso house with a hand-painted floor and a pizza/quesadilla/

salad menu. At **Café Kup a Kuppa** (79 Church Street; 244-0500) you can order scrambled eggs or bagel with lox and cream cheese for breakfast; lunch includes chicken, turkey, vegetable, or tuna sandwiches, and daily specials like quiche; no dinner; budget.

Like its Waikiki counterpart, **Hamburger Mary's** (2010 Main Street, Wailuku; 244-7776) is a center for gays. Imaginatively decorated with surfboards and antique posters, it attracts a mixed clientele with an appealing menu of hamburgers (who would have guessed?), sandwiches, salads, and steaks. There's also a hearty breakfast menu. Moderate.

Wailuku's low-rent district lies along Lower Main Street, where a string of ethnic restaurants caters almost exclusively to local residents. These are informal, family-owned, formica-and-naugahyde-chair cafés that serve good food at budget prices. For Japanese food, there's **Tokyo Tei** (1063 Lower Main Street; 242-9630). Southeast Asia is represented by **Vietnam Cuisine** (1246 Lower Main Street; 244-7845). And if you're craving Chinese food, try **Moon Hoe Seafood Restaurant** (752 Lower Main Street; 242-7778).

KAHULUI-WAILUKU AREA MARKETS

Kahului features two sprawling supermarkets: **Foodland** (877-2808) in Kaahumanu Center and **Star Super Market** (877-3341) in the Maui Mall, both located on Kaahumanu Avenue.

Down to Earth Natural Foods (1910 Vineyard Street; 242-6821) in Wailuku has a complete line of health food items and fresh produce. Add to that a healthy stock of herbs and you have what amounts to a natural food supermarket. This gets my dollar for being the best place on Maui to shop for natural foods.

There are also stores in two of the shopping centers lining Kaahumanu Avenue: **Ah Fook's Super Market** (877-3308) in Kahului Shopping Center and **Maui Natural Foods** (877-3018) in the Maui Mall.

Wakamatsu Fish Market (145 Market Street; 244-4111) in Wailuku has fresh fish daily.

Love's Bakery Thrift Shop (344 Ano Street; 877-3160) in Kahului and **Holsum/Oroweat Thrift Shop** (1380 Lower Main Street; 242-9155) in Wailuku sell day-old baked goods at old-fashioned prices.

For Japanese gourmet foods, try **Shirokiya** (877-5551) in the Kaahumanu Center.

KAHULUI-WAILUKU AREA SHOPPING

For everyday shopping needs, you should find the Kahului malls very convenient. Three sprawling centers are strung along Kaahumanu Avenue (Route 32).

Kaahumanu Center is the best and most modern, with **Liberty House** (877-3361) and **Sears** (877-2221) department stores, a photo studio, **Waldenbooks** (871-6112), boutiques, shoe stores, candy stores, a sundries shop, and a jeweler.

Nearby **Maui Mall** has a similar inventory of shops. **Sir Wilfred's Tobacconist** (877-3711) stocks a connoisseur's selection of tobaccos and coffees, and even has a coffee bar.

You might also try **Kahului Shopping Center**, though I prefer the other, more convenient malls.

The Coral Factory (877-7631), out near Kahului Airport, features a wide variety of black and pink coral jewelry at low prices. The folks here will show you how they create all their own products.

Up in Wailuku, a tumbledown town with a friendly face, you'll find the little shops and solicitous merchants that we have come to associate with small-town America. Along North Market Street you'll discover several imaginative shops operated by low-key entrepreneurs. There's **Traders of the Lost Ark** (62 North Market Street; 242-7753), with ancestral carvings and art from Africa, Asia, and the Pacific; **Hula Moons** (130 North Market Street; 244-1693) with a marvelous collection of Hawaiiana antiques; **Memory Lane** (158 North Market Street; 244-4196), featuring antiques and unusual collectibles; and **Wailuku Gallery** (28 North Market Street; 244-4544), which specializes in works by Maui artists.

There are rasta posters and T-shirts, plus a colorful inventory of island wear, at **Maui Reggae** (10 North Market Street, Wailuku; 242-8858).

A Touch of Glass (1977 Main Street, Wailuku; 244-1977) has an array of original and amazingly beautiful stained-glass pieces. This studio/gallery even offers courses in the art.

KAHULUI-WAILUKU AREA NIGHTLIFE

If Kahului can be said to have an entertainment strip, Kaahumanu Avenue (Route 32) is the place. You can enjoy a Sakura band and dancing at the **Maui Palms Hotel** (877-0071) on the weekends. The nearby **Red Dragon Room** fires up on weekends at the Maui Beach Hotel (877-0051). Every Friday and Saturday night, the Dragon rolls back the banquet tables and wheels in the Red Dragon Disco. There's a cover and two-drink minimum.

Up in Wailuku, **Aki's** (309 North Market; 244-8122) entertains a local crowd almost every night around its bar. Located in Wailuku's Happy Valley section, it's a good place to meet people, or just to sit back and enjoy a tall, cool drink.

Another neighborhood hangout just up the street and around the corner is the **Vineyard Tavern** (2171 Vineyard; 244-9597). With a falsefront exterior and swinging doors, this establishment is reminiscent of a Wild West saloon. But the jukebox music is contemporary and the ambience is definitely Mauian.

The gay nightspot on Maui is **Hamburger Mary's** (2010 Main Street, Wailuku; 244-7776), an attractive watering hole with overhead fans and a collection of antique wallhangings worthy of a museum. There's deejay music and dancing nightly. Attracting both gay men and women, Hamburger Mary's also draws a straight crowd, especially on Thursday night when the cruise ship is in port.

KAHULUI-WAILUKU AREA BEACHES AND PARKS

Hoaloha Park—This is Kahului's only beach, but unfortunately the nearby harbor facilities detract from the natural beauty of its white sands. There's heavy boat traffic on one side and several hotels on the other, so I don't recommend the place. It is a good spot, however, to beachcomb (particularly for Maui diamonds).

Facilities: Picnic tables available. *Swimming:* Poor. *Snorkeling:* Poor. *Surfing:* Good breaks (two to six feet) off the jetty mouth near the north shore of Kahului Harbor. Left slide. *Fishing:* Goatfish, papio, and triggerfish can be hooked from the pier; ulua and papio are often caught along the shore.

Getting there: Next to the Kahului hotels on Kaahumanu Avenue (Route 32).

Kepaniwai County Park—Here in this beautiful park, surrounded by sheer cliffs, you'll discover paths over arched bridges and through gardens, plus pagodas, a thatch-roofed hut, a taro patch, and banana, papaya, and coconut trees. An ideal and romantic spot for picnicking.

Facilities: Picnic pavilions, restrooms, and a swimming pool.

Getting there: Located in Wailuku on the road to Iao Valley.

Waihee Beach Park—Located outside Wailuku on the rural road that circles the West Maui Mountains, this pretty park is used almost exclusively by local residents. Bordered by a golf course and shaded with ironwood trees and *naupaka* bushes, it features a sandy beach and one of Maui's longest and widest reefs. There's a grassy area perfect for picnicking; also good for beachcombing and *limu* gathering.

Facilities: Picnic areas, restrooms, showers; restaurants and groceries are four miles away in Wailuku. *Swimming:* Good. *Snorkeling:* Good. *Fishing:* Good.

Getting there: From Route 340 in Waiehu turn right on Halewaiu Road. Take beach access road from Waiehu Golf Course.

Central Maui and the Road to Lahaina

Three highways cross the isthmus separating West Maui from the slopes of Haleakala. From Kahului, Mokulele Highway (Route 350) tracks south to Kihei through this rich agricultural area. The Kuihelani Highway (Route 380), running diagonally across sugar cane plantations, joins the Honoapiilani Highway (Route 30) in its course from Wailuku along the West Maui Mountains. The low-lying area that supports this network of roadways wasformed by lava flows from Haleakala and the West Maui Mountains.

The **Alexander & Baldwin Sugar Museum** (Puunene Avenue and Hansen Road, Puunene; 871-8058; admission), situated on the grounds of a working plantation, provides a brief introduction to Hawaii's main crop. Tracing the history of sugar cultivation in the islands, its displays portray everything from early life in the cane fields to contemporary methods for producing refined sugar.

Along Honoapiilani Highway (Route 30), the road to Lahaina, lies **Maui Tropical Plantation** (244-7643; admission for the tram), a 120-acre enclave complete with orchards and groves displaying dozens of island fruit plants. Here you'll see avocados, papayas, bananas, pineapples, mangoes, and macadamia nuts growing in lush profusion. There's a tropical nursery, museum, aquaculture display, and a tram that will carry you through this ersatz plantation.

Then, as you pass the small boat harbor at **Maalaea Bay**, the highway hugs the southwest coast. There are excellent lookouts along this elevated roadway, especially near the lighthouse at **McGregor Point**. During whale season (see the "Whale-Watching" section in this chapter) you might spy a leviathan from this landlocked crow's nest. Just offshore there are prime whale breeding areas.

Down the road from McGregor Point, you'll see three islands anchored offshore. As you look seaward, the portside islet is **Molokini**, the crescent-shaped remains of a volcanic crater. **Kahoolawe,** a barren, desiccated island used for naval target practice, sits in the center. Hawaiian activists are demanding an end to the bombing of this sacred isle and have staged dramatic demonstrations by occupying its forbidden shores. The humpbacked island to starboard is **Lanai**. As you continue toward Kaanapali, **Molokai** sails into view.

The road drops back to sea level as it approaches the timeworn village of **Olowalu**. Here, in 1790, more than 100 Hawaiians were slaughtered by the crew of an American ship to avenge the death of one single sailor. Known as the "Olowalu Massacre," this incident contributed significantly to the ill will that developed between the islanders and the interlopers during the next century.

Lahaina

Maui's top tourist destination is a waterfront enclave that stretches for over two miles along a natural harbor, but measures only a couple of blocks deep. Simultaneously chic and funky, Lahaina has gained an international reputation for its art galleries, falsefront stores, and waterfront restaurants.

It also happens to be one of Hawaii's most historic towns. A royal seat since the 16th century, Lahaina was long a playground for the *alii*. The royal surfing grounds lay just south of today's town center, and in 1802, Kamehameha I established his headquarters here, taking up residence in the Brick Palace, the first Western-style building in Hawaii.

It was in Lahaina that the first high school and first printing press west of the Rockies were established in 1831. From Lahaina, Kamehameha III promulgated Hawaii's first constitution in 1840, and established a legislative body that met in town until the capital was eventually moved to Honolulu.

During the 1820s, this quaint port also became a vital watering place for whaling ships and evolved into the whaling capital of the world. At its peak in the mid-1840s, the whaling trade brought over 400 ships a year into the harbor.

To the raffish sailors who favored it for its superb anchorage, grog shops, and uninhibited women, Lahaina was heaven itself. To the stiff-collared missionaries who arrived in 1823, the town was a hellhole—a place of sin, abomination, and vile degradation. Some of Lahaina's most colorful history was written when the Congregationalists prevented naked women from swimming out to meet the whalers. Their belligerent brethren anchored in the harbor replied by cannonballing mission homes and rioting along the waterfront.

The town declined with the loss of the whaling trade in the 1860s, and was transformed into a quiet sugar plantation town, serving the Pioneer Sugar Mill that opened during the same decade. Not until developers began building resorts in nearby Kaanapali a century later did it fully revive. During the 1960s, Lahaina was designated a national historic landmark and restoration of many important sites was begun. By the 1970s, the place was a gathering spot not only for the jet set but the ultra hip as well. Clubs like the Blue Max made Lahaina a hot nightspot where famous musicians came to vacation and jam.

Today the town retains much of its old charm in the ramshackle storefronts that line the water along Front Street. Most points of interest lie within a half-mile of the old sea wall that protects this narrow thoroughfare from the ocean, so the best way to explore the town is on foot.

Start at **Lahaina Harbor** (Wharf Street) and take a stroll along the docks. In addition to tour boats, pleasure craft from around the world put in here or cast anchor in the Lahaina Roads just offshore. During the heyday of the whaling industry in the 1840s, the Auau Channel between Lahaina and Lanai was a forest of masts. **Carthaginian II** (661-8527; admission), the steel-hulled schooner at dock's end, preserves those days in a shipboard museum. Actually a turn-of-the-century schooner that was converted into a replica of an old square-rigged sailing ship, this floating display case features videotapes on whales and intriguing artifacts from days of yore.

Across Wharf Street sits the **Pioneer Inn** (661-3636), a rambling hostelry built in 1901. With its second-story veranda and Old Whaler's Grog Shop, this woodframe hotel is a great place to bend an elbow and breathe in the salt air.

Just north of here a Hawaii Visitors Bureau sign points out the chair-shaped **Hauola Stone**, a source of healing power for ancient Hawaiians, who sat in the natural formation and let the waves wash over them.

There is nothing left of the **Brick Palace** (just inshore from the Hauola Stone), the two-story structure commissioned in 1798 by Kamehameha I. Built by an English convict, the palace was used by the king in 1802 and 1803. Today the original foundation has been outlined with brick paving.

To the south, a 120-year-old **banyan tree** (Front and Hotel streets), among the oldest and largest in the islands, extends its rooting branches across almost an entire acre. Planted in 1873 to mark the advent of Protestant missionaries in Maui 50 years earlier, this shady canopy is a resting place for tourists and mynah birds alike.

The sprawling giant presses right to the **Old Courthouse** door. Built in 1859 from the remains of the palace of King Kamehameha III, the building was fashioned from coral blocks. The **Old Jail** in the basement now incongruously houses an art gallery (661-0111).

Those stone ruins on either side of the courthouse are restorations of the **Old Fort**, built during the 1830s to protect Lahaina from the sins and cannonballs of lawless sailors. The original structure was torn down two decades later to build a jail, but during its heyday the fortress guarded the waterfront with 47 cannons.

Across Front Street you'll find the **Baldwin Home** (661-3262; admission), Maui's oldest building. Constructed of coral and stone in the early 1830s, the place sheltered the family of Reverend Dwight Baldwin, a medical missionary. Today the house contains period pieces and family heirlooms, including some of the good doctor's rather fiendish-looking medical implements. Beneath the hand-hewn *ohia* ceiling beams rest the Baldwin's Steinway piano; the dining room includes the family's china, a fragile cargo that made the voyage around Cape Horn; and in the master bedroom stands a four-poster bed fashioned from native *koa*. The **Master's Reading Room** next door, an 1833 storehouse and library, is home to the local historical society and not open to the public.

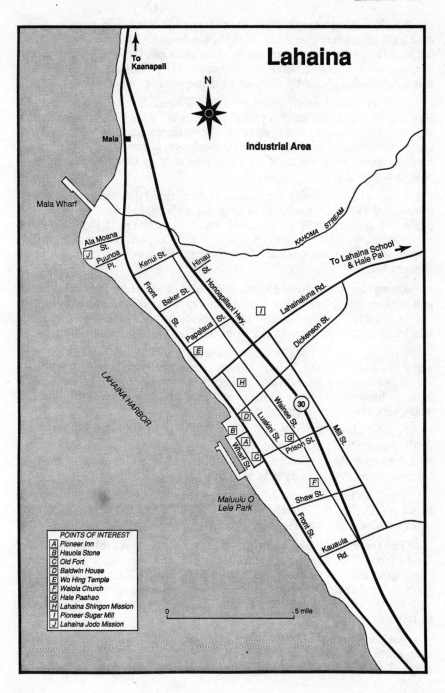

Lahaina

To Kaanapali

N

Industrial Area

Mala

Mala Wharf

Ala Moana St.
Puunoa Pl.
J

Kenui St.

Hinau St.

KAHOMA STREAM

To Lahaina School & Hale Pai

Front St.

Baker St.

Honoapiilani Hwy.

Lahainaluna Rd.

I

Dickenson St.

Papalaua St.

E

LAHAINA HARBOR

H

Wainee St.

30

D

Luakini St.

B

A

G

Prison St.

Mill St.

Wharf St.

C

F

Maluulu O Lele Park

Shaw St.

Front St.

Kauaula Rd.

POINTS OF INTEREST
A Pioneer Inn
B Hauola Stone
C Old Fort
D Baldwin House
E Wo Hing Temple
F Waiola Church
G Hale Paahao
H Lahaina Shingon Mission
I Pioneer Sugar Mill
J Lahaina Jodo Mission

0   .5 mile

The **Wo Hing Temple** (858 Front Street; 661-3262; admission), a Chinese gathering place that dates to 1912, has been lovingly restored. While the temple has been converted into a small museum, the old cookhouse adjacent is used to show films of the islands made by Thomas Edison in 1898 and 1906 during the early days of motion pictures.

Several other historic spots lie along Wainee Street, which parallels Front Street. **Waiola Cemetery**, with its overgrown lawn and eroded tombstones, contains graves dating to 1823. Queen Keopuolani, wife of Kamehameha I and the mother of Hawaii's next two kings, is buried here. Surrounded by blossoming plumeria trees are the graves of early missionaries and Hawaiian commoners.

Maui's first Christian services were performed that same year on the grounds of **Waiola Church** next door. Today's chapel, built in 1953, occupies the spot where Wainee Church was constructed in 1832. The earlier structure, Hawaii's first stone church, seated 3000 parishioners and played a vital role in the conversion of the local population to Christianity and western ways.

Down the street rise the menacing walls of old **Hale Paahao** (Prison and Wainee streets), a prison built by convicts in 1854 and used to house rowdy sailors as well as more hardened types. The coral blocks used to build this local hoosegow were taken from the Old Fort on Front Street.

Just north of the jail along Wainee Street sits the **Episcopal Cemetery** and **Hale Aloha**. Walter Murray Gibson, a controversial figure in 19th-century Hawaii politics who eventually became an adviser to King David Kalakaua, is buried here. Hale Aloha, completed in 1858 and restored several years ago, served as a church meetinghouse.

Nearby **Maria Lanakila Church** (Wainee and Dickenson streets), built in 1928 to replace a 19th-century chapel, is a lovely white-washed building with interior pillars. Adjacent is the **Seamen's Cemetery**, a poorly maintained ground where early sailors were laid to rest.

The **Lahaina Shingon Mission** (Luakini Street between Lahainaluna Road and Dickenson Street), a simple plantation-era structure with an ornately gilded altar, represents a gathering place for Buddhists.

The proverbial kids-from-eight-to-eighty set will love the **Sugar Cane Train** (661-0089; admission), a reconstructed 1890-era steam train. Operating around the West Maui resort area, the Lahaina-Kaanapali & Pacific Railroad engine and open passenger cars chug along a six-mile route midway between the mountains and ocean. The main station is off Hinau Street in Lahaina.

And don't miss **Lahaina Jodo Mission**, a Buddhist enclave one-half mile north of Lahaina on Ala Moana Street. There's a temple and three-tiered pagoda here, as well as the largest ceremonial bell in Hawaii. The giant bronze Buddha, with the West Maui Mountains in the background, is a sight to behold.

For a splendid view of Lahaina, head uphill along Lahainaluna Road to **Lahainaluna School**. Established by missionaries in 1831, it is one of the country's oldest high schools. Today this historic facility serves as a public high school for the Lahaina area. **Hale Pai,** a printing house dating to 1836, is located nearby. Here early textbooks and Hawaii's first newspaper were printed. Having played a key role in the development of Hawaiian as a written language, Hale Pai is now a fascinating museum devoted to printing.

On the way uphill you will pass **Pioneer Sugar Mill**, a sugar company tracing back to 1860.

LAHAINA HOTELS

To fully capture the spirit of Lahaina, there's only one place to stay— the **Pioneer Inn** (658 Wharf Street; 661-3636). Located smack on Lahaina's waterfront, this rickety wooden hostelry is the center of the area's action. On one side, sloops, ketches, and glass-bottom boats are berthed; on the other side lies bustling Front Street with its falsefront shops. The Inn is noisy, vibrant, and crowded with tenants and tourists. On the ground floor, you can hunker down over a glass of grog at the seaman's saloon, or stroll past the restaurants and shops lining the Inn's lushly planted courtyard.

Upstairs are the rooms. In the older section, over the bar, dark, noisy rooms with communal bathrooms price in the budget range. With private bath they're a little higher, though still in the budget category. You probably won't be able to sleep until the bar closes around 1 a.m., but you can sit on the lanai watching the moon reflect off the water. Or you can book a room in the newer, brighter, and quieter section overlooking the courtyard; moderate price. Like the older digs, these are small and plainly decorated, with telephones and overhead fans. But they trade stall showers for shower-tub combinations, swap a shared lanai for a private one, provide air conditioning, and add a touch of sanity to the surroundings. If you seek adventure, try the old rooms; if you value your sleep, go for the new.

While the building is actually quite modern, the **Plantation Inn** (174 Lahainaluna Road, Lahaina; 667-9225) possesses the look and ambience of a turn-of-the-century hostelry. Modeled after the plantation architecture of an earlier era, it features 18 rooms decorated in period. Each is adorned with poster beds, stained-glass windows, and tile bathrooms. Combining the atmosphere of the past with the amenities of the present, guest rooms also feature televisions, refrigerators and airconditioning, as well as VCRs on request. There's a pool, gazebo, and activities area on the premises. The deluxe price tag includes a continental breakfast at the inn's restaurant.

The Oscar for most original inn goes to the **Lahaina Hotel** (127 Lahainaluna Street; 661-0577). Constructed earlier this century, this 13-room beauty was fully restored and appointed in Gay Nineties finery. Each room is wall to ceiling with gorgeous antiques—leaded glass lamps, mirrored armoires, original oil paintings, cast iron beds, and brass locks. Attention to detail is a way of life: The place simply exudes the aura of another era. If you don't stay here, stop by and visit. Deluxe.

The **Maui Islander Hotel** (660 Wainee Street; 667-9766) is a warren of woodframe buildings spread across lushly landscaped grounds. The ambience is an odd combination of tropical retreat and motel atmosphere. With 372 rooms, it's too large to be cozy. But with trimly decorated rooms and small studios (including kitchens) renting in the moderate-to-deluxe range, it's a good value. Swimming pool; laundry; tennis court; picnic area.

LAHAINA CONDOMINIUMS

Perhaps the nicest place to stay on this side of the island is **Puamana** (★) (Pualima Place; 667-2551), a 28-acre retreat located about a mile southeast of Lahaina. This townhouse complex, a 1920s-era sugar plantation, rests along a rock-strewn beach. The oceanfront clubhouse, open to guests, was once the plantation manager's house, and the landscaped grounds are still given over to mango, plumeria, and torch ginger trees. Guests stay in low-slung plantation-style buildings that sport shake-shingle roofs and house from two to six units. Prices begin in the deluxe range for one-bedroom facilities that contain kitchens and sleep up to four people. To round out the amenities there are three pools and a tennis court. Three-night minimum.

Lahaina Shores Hotel (475 Front Street, Lahaina; 661-4835). Though it's more expensive than many others, this sprawling condominium has the advantage of a beachfront location in Lahaina. Studio apartments begin at $95, while one-bedroom units start at $120.

LAHAINA RESTAURANTS

One of my favorite light-food stops is a devil-may-care place called the **Sunrise Café** (located around back at 693 Front Street; 661-3326). Set in a tiny clapboard house with a fresh, airy look, it serves salads, sandwiches, and espresso, but no hot entrées. Budget.

You'll also fare well at one of Lahaina's many shopping complexes, especially Lahaina Square on Wainee Street. Here **Amilio's Delicatessen** (661-8551) has sandwiches for vegetarians and carnivores alike. Amilio's manages to serve practically everything that you'd expect from a self-respecting deli, and the folks here do it with a special flair. Budget.

Across the street in the Lahaina Shopping Center, **Thai Chef Restaurant** (667-2814) has an inviting assortment of South East Asian dishes at lunch and dinner. Moderate.

Lani's Pancake Cottage (The Wharf Mall, 658 Front Street; 661-0955) has more to offer than the name implies. In addition to breakfast fare, they feature a dozen different sandwiches plus fried chicken and fish and chips. Dark and cozy, Lani's is budget-priced.

Also try **Local Food** (888 Wainee Street; 667-2882), a take-out stand that sells—what else—local food (in the form of plate lunches). Budget.

In keeping with the rickety old hostelry upstairs, Pioneer Inn (658 Wharf Street; 661-3636) has a patchwork of restaurants on its ground floor. **Snug Harbor,** the main dining room, is a cozy anchorage dotted with nautical fixtures. Outside, on the **South Seas Patio,** you can dine beneath umbrellas and palm trees. And across the lobby, on the **Harpooner's Lanai,** there's a view overlooking the Lahaina waterfront. The galley in Snug Harbor fixes steak and seafood dinners plus a vegetarian special—eggplant and zucchini. Lunch, served in the ever-friendly and commodious Harpooner's Lanai, features a soup-and-sandwich menu, with seafood chowder and Portuguese bean soup topping the bill. You can cast anchor at breakfast, too. Moderate.

I can't say much for the nomenclature, but the prices are worth note at **Cheeseburgers in Paradise** (811 Front Street; 661-4855). This is a rare catch indeed—an inexpensive restaurant smack on the Lahaina waterfront. Granted, you won't find much on the menu other than standard breakfasts, hamburgers, salads, and sandwiches. But if some couples can live on love, why can't the rest of us live on ocean views? Budget to moderate.

For a taste of the Orient, I'd head to the Lahaina Shopping Center (Wainee Street between Papalua Street and Lahainaluna Road) and the **Golden Palace Chinese Restaurant** (661-3126). Boldly decorated with Chinese reliefs, this dimly lighted establishment has an extensive Cantonese menu. There are beef, fowl, pork, and seafood dishes, as well as chop suey. In the afternoon, the Palace combines sweet-and-sour ribs, roast pork, chop suey, shrimp, and rice. Moderate.

Nearby, in the same complex, is **Musashi Japanese Cuisine** (Lahaina Shopping Center; 667-6207). Highly regarded by area residents, it has a sushi bar and table seating. Prices are moderate and the menu includes a full selection of standard Japanese dishes.

Dine on the upper level at the **Tree House Restaurant** (Lahaina Market Place, Front Street and Lahainaluna Road; 661-3235) and you'll catch a breeze through the branches. This Swiss Family Robinson-style dining place specializes in shrimp and chicken dishes with a few fresh fish entrées added for good measure. Moderate prices make it a good value.

Offering a partial view of the water at moderate prices is **Moondoggies** (666 Front Street; 661-3966). This balcony restaurant is on the wrong side of Front Street but does provide an easy, you-can-sit-at-the-bar-or-take-a-table atmosphere. Wherever you rest your *okole*, you can dine on pasta, pizza, pupus, sandwiches, soups, or salad.

Light, bright, and airy, **Compadres** (661-7189) in the Lahaina Cannery Mall (Front and Kapunakea streets) is a great place to sip a margarita or enjoy a Mexican meal. The tropical ambience is as appealing as the steaming dishes served here. Moderate.

The preferred style of dining in Lahaina is steak and seafood at one of the waterfront restaurants along Front Street. And the common denominator is the ever popular, usually crowded **Kimo's** (845 Front Street; 661-4811), where you can enjoy all the tropical amenities at a moderate price.

Personally, I prefer the **Lahaina Broiler** (885 Front Street; 661-3111), a more stylish address where you can experience the same open-air atmosphere. Offering several fresh fish dishes, as well as an assortment of beef and chicken entrées, it prices in the moderate-to-deluxe category.

Slightly (I said *slightly*) off the tourist track but still offering a classic Lahaina-dinner-on-the-water-with-sunset-view experience is the **Old Lahaina Café and Luau** (505 Front Street; 661-3303). Overhead fans, oceanfront location, nautical feel—it's all here. The menu matches the occasion with fresh island fish, jumbo prawns (prepared five different ways), and a special luau plate. Also open for breakfast and lunch; moderate to deluxe.

At **Longhi's** (888 Front Street; 667-2288), a European-style café that specializes in Italian dishes, informality is the password. The menu changes daily and is never written down; the waiter simply tells you the day's offerings. Usually there'll be several pasta dishes, sautéed vegetables, salads, a shellfish creation, steak, a wine-soaked chicken or veal dish, and perhaps eggplant parmigiana. Longhi's prepares most of its own bread and pasta, buys Maui-grown produce, and imports many cheeses from New York. The dinners, priced ultra-deluxe, reflect this diligence. Breakfasts and lunches are cooked with the same care. Definitely recommended, especially for vegetarians, who can choose from many of the dishes offered.

Hawaiian regional cuisine is the order of the day at **Avalon Restaurant & Bar** (844 Front Street; 667-5559), an open-air establishment in Mariner's Alley. Decorated in lauhala and bamboo, adorned with the work of local artists, it is owned by Mark and Judy Ellman. Mark is the master chef—preparing wok-fried opakapaka in black bean sauce, Chinese duck with plum sauce, and other flaming delectables—while Judy greets the folks out front. Try it for lunch or dinner; deluxe.

David Paul's Lahaina Grill (127 Lahainaluna Road; 667-5117), headlining New American cuisine (with a Southwestern accent), is an intimate dining room with a personalized touch. According to owner/chef David Paul, the menu represents "a gathering of technique, flavors, and skills from around the world, utilizing local ingredients to translate each dish into an exceptional dining experience." Order the tequila shrimp and fire cracker rice, soft-shell crabs, kona coffee-roasted rack of lamb, or macadamia-smoked tenderloin and decide for yourself whether he carries it off. Ultra-deluxe in price.

The defining experience in Lahaina dining is **Gerard's Restaurant** (174 Lahainaluna Road; 661-8939). Here you'll encounter a French restaurant in a colonial setting with tropical surroundings. Housed in the Plantation Inn, a bed and breakfast reminiscent of early New Orleans, Gerard's provides a chandelier-and-pattern-wallpaper dining room as well as a veranda complete with overhead fans and whitewashed balustrade. The chef prepares fresh fish, rack of lamb, calf veal liver, braised Makawao rabbit, and sweetbreads. Of course, that is after having started off with ahi steak tartar or crab bisque. Ultra-deluxe.

Near the top of the cognoscenti's list of gourmet establishments is an unlikely looking French restaurant in Olowalu called **Chez Paul** (Honoapiilani Highway; 661-3843). The place is located several miles outside Lahaina in a dilapidated building that also houses Olowalu's funky general store. But for years this little hideaway has had a reputation far transcending its surroundings. You'll probably drive right past the place at first, but when you do find it, you'll discover a menu featuring such delicacies as *tournedos*, duck *à l'orange*, veal prepared with apples, scampi, and several other entrées. While the tab runs in the ethereal ultra-deluxe range, the rave reviews this prim dining room receives make it worth every franc.

LAHAINA MARKETS

Lahaina features two supermarkets: **Foodland** (661-0975) in Lahaina Square Shopping Center on Honoapiilani Highway and **Nagasako Supermarket** (661-0989) in the nearby Lahaina Shopping Center. Foodland is open daily from 6 a.m. to midnight. You can shop at Nagasako from 7 a.m. until 9 p.m. every day except Sunday (until 7 p.m.).

For health-food items, stop by **Westside Natural Food** (136 Dickenson Street; 667-2855).

South of Lahaina, along Honoapiilani Highway in Olowalu, the **Olowalu General Store** (661-3774) has a limited supply of grocery items.

LAHAINA SHOPPING

Lahaina's a great place to combine shopping with sightseeing. Most shops are right on Front Street in the historic wooden buildings facing the water. For a walking tour of the stores and waterfront, start from the Pioneer

Inn at the south end of the strip and walk north on the *makai* or ocean side. Then come back along the *mauka* or mountain side of the street.

One of the first shops you will encounter on this consumer's tour of Lahaina will be **Sgt. Leisure Resort Patrol** (701 Front Street; 667-0661), which has an array of imaginative T-shirts.

The Gecko Store (703 Front Street; 661-1078), the only shop I've seen with a sand floor, also stocks inexpensive beachwear. The **Endangered Species Store** (707 Front Street; 661-0208), which features a multitude of conservation-minded items such as oils and lotions from the rainforest, is a worthy stop. You will also find *koa* products, chimes, statues, and a vast array of T-shirts and stuffed animals.

Past the sea wall, in an overgrown cottage set back from the street, lie several shops including **Pacific Vision** (819 Front Street; 661-0188), with its hand-etched glass and crystal pieces. And just down the street at **South Seas Trading Post** (851 Front Street; 661-3168), you can barter greenbacks for Nepali wedding necklaces, Chinese porcelain opium pillows, or New Guinea masks.

There are just a few more street numbers before this shopper's promenade ends. Then if you cross the road and walk back in the opposite direction, with the sea to your right, you'll pass **The Gallery** (716 Front Street; 661-0696), which has jade and pearl pieces among its inventory of exotic jewelry. You'll also find antiques and artworks at this unusual shop.

Nearby at **The Wharf** (658 Front Street) mall, there's a maze of stores. One notable shop is **Casablanca** (661-8692), featuring floral patterns in its line of women's fashions.

Then it's upstairs to **The Whaler's Book Shoppe** (667-9544). This nifty outlet features an unbeatable combination—good books and fine coffee. One of the best bookstores around, it doubles as a coffeehouse where you can sit back, read, and sip a cup of Kona brew.

Village Gallery has three locations (120 Dickenson Street, 661-4402; Lahaina Cannery, Front and Kapunakea streets, 661-3280; and Embassy Suites Hotel, 104 Kaanapali Shores Place, 667-5115), all featuring paintings by modern Hawaiian artists. Amid the tourist schlock there is some brilliant artwork.

The **Lahaina Cannery Mall** (Front and Kapunakea streets; 661-5304), a massive complex designed in the style of an old canning factory, is the area's most ambitious project. Dozens of shops are housed in this multi-tiered facility. **Lahaina Printsellers** (667-7843), one of my favorite Maui shops, has an astounding collection of ancient maps and engravings from Polynesia and other parts of the world. **Alexia Natural Fashions** (661-4110) offers stylish women's clothing from the island of Cyprus and other romantic locales.

Another major shopping complex, **Lahaina Center**, opened a few years ago along Front Street (corner of Papalaua Street). Covering 150,000 square feet, with space for scores of shops, it could become one of the island's top shopping destinations. But to date, many spaces remain unfilled and the mall has a long way to go before it competes with the Lahaina Cannery.

Dickenson Square (Dickenson and Wainee streets) represents another theme mall, fashioned after an early 20th-century plantation manor.

505 Front Street, located at 505 Front Street, is an attractive wood-frame mall built to resemble a New England fishing village. Situated south of central Lahaina, it has a few shops, including galleries, boutiques, and jewelry stores.

LAHAINA NIGHTLIFE

Front Street's the strip in Lahaina—a dilapidated row of buildings from which stream some of the freshest sounds around.

The place of places along this surging waterfront is **Longhi's** (888 Front Street; 667-2288). The upper story of this well-known restaurant is painted brilliant white and decorated in a startling black-and-white motif; the dance-floor is native *koa* wood. The result is a club that draws a jet-set crowd. You'll hear a local jazz or rock group working out on stage every Friday and Saturday from 10:30 p.m. to 1:30 a.m. Cover.

Over at the **Old Whaler's Grog Shop** (661-3636), the standard fare is country-western or blues and jazz. Tucked into a corner of the Pioneer Inn, this spot features a nautical motif complete with harpoons, figureheads, and paintings of naked ladies. Usually packed to the bulkheads with a lively crew, it's a great place to hunker down over a glass of rum.

Moose McGillycuddy's (667-7758), a hot club fronting Front Street, has a large dancefloor and video-disco format. The house is congenial and the drinks imaginatively mixed; for contemporary melodies with dinner, arrive before 10 p.m.

Lahaina's favorite pastime is watching the sunset over the ocean while sipping a tall, cool one at a waterfront watering place. Prime places for this very rewarding activity are **Kimo's** (845 Front Street; 661-4811) and the **Lahaina Broiler** (885 Front Street; 661-3111). After the sun finishes performing, the Lahaina Broiler features do-it-yourself karaoke entertainment.

If it's Friday, you can also browse the art galleries of Lahaina, which sponsor a special **Art Night** every week.

Blackie's Bar (667-7979), located on Honoapiilani Highway between Lahaina and Kaanapali, serves up live jazz four nights a week.

LAHAINA BEACHES AND PARKS

Papalaua State Wayside Park—*Kiawe* trees and scrub vegetation spread right to the shoreline along Papalaua Beach Park. There are sandy patches between the trees large enough to spread a towel, but I prefer sunbathing at beaches closer to Lahaina. Bounded on one side by Honoapiilani Highway, this narrow beach extends for a mile to join a nicer, lawn-fringed park, and then stretches on toward Olowalu for several more miles. If you want to be alone, just head down the shore.

Facilities: There's an outhouse and picnic area at the state wayside and picnic facilities at the grassy park. You'll find a small market several miles away in Olowalu. *Swimming:* Good. *Snorkeling:* Okay out past the surf break. *Surfing:* Excellent at "Thousand Peaks" breaks; also very good several miles east in Maalaea Bay.

Getting there: The park is located on Honoapiilani Highway about ten miles south of Lahaina.

Olowalu Beaches—Both to the north and south of Olowalu General Store lie narrow corridors of white sand. This is an excellent area to hunt Maui diamonds.

Facilities: None. Market nearby. *Swimming:* Very good. *Snorkeling:* South of the general store, where road and water meet, you'll find an excellent coral reef. *Surfing:* Good breaks about a half-mile north of the general store. Right and left slide. *Fishing:* Often ulua are caught from Olowalu landing.

Getting there: Go south from Lahaina on Honoapiilani Highway for about six miles.

Launiupoko State Wayside Park—There's a seaside lawn shaded by palm trees, but no beach here. A rock sea wall slopes gently for entering swimmers, but offers little to sunbathers. Launiupoko is located near the West Maui Mountains, with great views of Kahoolawe and Lanai.

Facilities: Picnic area, restrooms, showers. Restaurants and markets are three miles away in Lahaina. *Swimming:* Mediocre. *Snorkeling:* Mediocre. *Fishing:* Good surf-casting from here south for three miles.

Getting there: The park is located three miles south of Lahaina on Honoapiilani Highway.

Puamana State Wayside Park—A grass-covered strip and narrow beach wedged between Honoapiilani Highway and the ocean, Puamana Park is dotted with ironwood trees. The excellent views make this a choice spot for a picnic. It's located on Honoapiilani Highway, about two miles south of Lahaina.

Maluulu o Lele Park—This park has one thing going for it—a convenient location in Lahaina. Otherwise, it's heavily littered, shadowed by a theme mall, and sometimes crowded. If you do stop by, try to forget all that and concentrate on the sandy beach, lawn, and truly startling view of Lanai directly across the Auau Channel.

Facilities: Restrooms and tennis courts are across the street near the playing field. *Swimming:* Okay. *Snorkeling:* Good past the reef. *Surfing:* Summer breaks near the sea wall in Lahaina Harbor. *Fishing:* Threadfin and ulua are common catches here.

Getting there: Easy to find, this park is right on Front Street next to 505 Front Street mall in Lahaina.

Lahaina Beach—This curving stretch of white sand is the best beach in Lahaina. It lacks privacy but certainly not beauty. From here, you can look back to Lahaina town and the West Maui Mountains, or out over the ocean to Kahoolawe, Lanai, and Molokai. Or just close your eyes and soak up the sun.

Facilities: Restrooms, showers. Restaurants and markets nearby in Lahaina. *Swimming:* Good, well-protected, shallow. *Snorkeling:* Fair. *Surfing:* Summer breaks nearby at Mala Wharf. Left slide. *Fishing:* Threadfin and ulua are often caught.

Getting there: Take Front Street north from Lahaina for about a half-mile. Turn left on Puunoa Place and follow it to the beach.

Wahikuli State Wayside Park—This narrow stretch of beach and lawn, just off the road between Lahaina and Kaanapali, faces Lanai and Molokai. There are facilities aplenty, which might be why this pretty park is so popular and crowded.

Facilities: Picnic areas, restrooms; tennis courts across the street. Markets and restaurants nearby in Lahaina. *Swimming:* Very good. *Snorkeling:* Fair. There's a better spot just north of here near the Lahaina Canoe Club. *Surfing:* Poor. *Fishing:* The most common catches here are ulua and threadfin.

Getting there: Located on Honoapiilani Highway between Lahaina and Kaanapali.

Hanakaoo Beach Park—Conveniently located beside Kaanapali Beach Resort, this long, narrow facility features a white-sand beach and grassy picnic ground. The road is nearby, but the views of Lanai are outstanding.

Facilities: Picnic areas, restrooms, showers. Restaurants and groceries nearby. *Swimming:* Good. *Snorkeling:* Fair. *Surfing:* Poor. *Fishing:* Common catches include ulua and threadfin.

Getting there: Located on Honoapiilani Highway between Lahaina and Kaanapali.

(Text continued on page 248.)

Shell Hunting

With over 1500 varieties of shells washing up on its beaches, Hawaii has some of the world's finest shelling. The miles of sandy beach along Maui's south shore are a prime area for handpicking free souvenirs. Along the shores are countless shell specimens with names like horned helmet, Hebrew cone, Hawaiian olive, and Episcopal miter. Or you might find glass balls from Japan and sunbleached driftwood.

Beachcombing is the easiest method of shell gathering. Take along a small container and stroll through the backwash of the waves, watching for ripples from shells lying under the sand. You can also dive in shallow water where the ocean's surge will uncover shells.

It's tempting to walk along the top of coral reefs seeking shells and other marine souvenirs, but these living formations maintain a delicate ecological balance. Reefs in Hawaii and all over the planet are dying because of such plunder. In order to

protect this underwater world, try to collect only shells and souvenirs that are adrift on the beach and no longer necessary to the marine ecology.

The best shelling spots along Maui's south shore are Makena, Kihei beaches, Maalaea Bay, Olowalu, the sandy stretch from Kaanapali to Napili Bay, D. T. Fleming Park, and Honolua Bay. On the north coast, the stretch from Waiehu to Waihee (west of Kahului) and the beaches around Hana are the choicest hunting grounds.

After heavy rainfall, watch near stream mouths for Hawaiian olivines and in stream beds for Maui diamonds. Olivines are small, semiprecious stones of an olive hue. Maui diamonds are quartz stones and make beautiful jewelry. The best places to find Maui diamonds are near the Kahului Bay hotel strip and in Olowalu Stream.

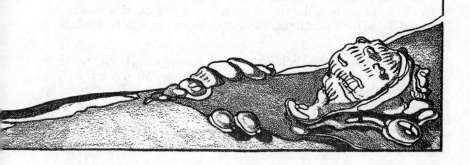

Kaanapali-Kapalua Area

Even in the case of Maui's notorious land developers, there is method to the madness. The stretch of coastline extending for six miles along Maui's western shore, crowded to the extreme with hotels and condominiums, is anchored by two *planned* resorts. Like handsome bookends supporting an uneven array of dog-eared paperbacks, Kaanapali and Kapalua add class to the arrangement.

Supporting the south end, **Kaanapali** is a 500-acre enclave that extends along three miles of sandy beach and includes six hotels, a half-dozen condominiums, two golf courses, and an attractive shopping mall. Back in the 19th century it was a dry and barren segment of the sugar plantation that operated from Lahaina. Raw sugar was hauled by train from the mill out to Black Rock, a dramatic outcropping along Kaanapali Beach, where the produce was loaded onto waiting ships.

In 1962, Kaanapali's first resort opened near Black Rock and development soon spread in both directions. Important to developers, who built the Sheraton Maui hotel around it, **Black Rock** (Puu Kekaa) is a volcanic cinder cone from which ancient Hawaiians believed that the dead departed the earth in their journey to the spirit world. According to legend, the great 18th-century Maui chief Kahekili proved his bravery by leaping from the rock to the ocean below.

Kaanapali's modern-day contribution to Pacific culture is the **Whalers Village Museum** (Whalers Village, 2435 Kaanapali Parkway; 661-5992), a three-room display that spills over into outdoor sections of the Whalers Village shopping mall. The "golden era of whaling" is portrayed in scrimshaw exhibits, a scale model whaling ship, harpoons, and other artifacts from the days when Lahaina was one of the world's great whaling ports.

An earlier chief, Piilani, built a road through the area in the 16th century and gave his name to modern-day Route 30, the Honoapiilani Highway. Translated as "the bays of Piilani," the road passes several inlets north of Kaanapali that have been developed in haphazard fashion. Honokowai, Kahana, and Napili form a continuous wall of condominiums that sprawls north to Kapalua Bay.

Kapalua, the bookend holding the north side in place, is a former pineapple plantation that was converted into a luxurious 750-acre resort. Here two major hotels, three golf courses, and several villa-style communities blanket the hillside from the white sands of Kapalua Bay to the deep-green foothills of the West Maui Mountains. Like the entire strip along Maui's western flank, Kapalua enjoys otherworldly sunsets and dramatic views of Lanai and Molokai.

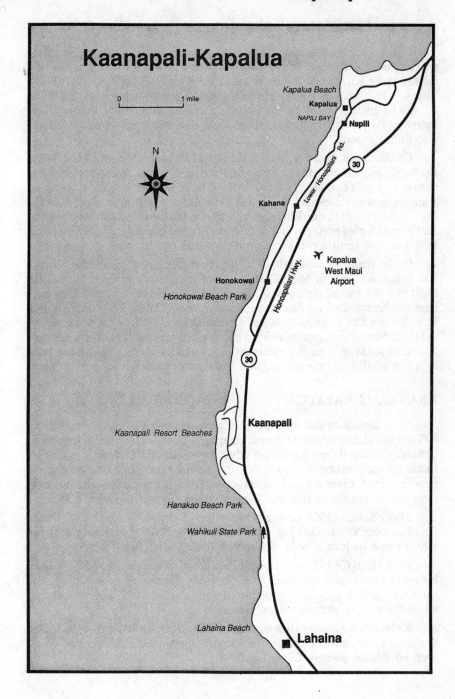

Kaanapali-Kapalua

0   1 mile

N

Kapalua Beach

Kapalua

NAPILI BAY   **Napili**

Ⓝ 30

Kahana

Honoapiilani Rd.

Lower Honoapiilani Rd.

Honoapiilani Hwy.

✈ Kapalua
West Maui
Airport

Honokowai

Honokowai Beach Park

Ⓝ 30

Kaanapali

Kaanapali Resort Beaches

Hanakao Beach Park

Wahikuli State Park

Lahaina Beach

■ **Lahaina**

KAANAPALI-KAPALUA AREA HOTELS

In the Kaanapali area the modestly priced hotel is not an endangered species, it's totally extinct! The closest you will come to a money-saving facility is the **Kaanapali Beach Hotel** (2525 Kaanapali Parkway; 661-0011). This 431-room hostelry sits right on the beach, sports many restaurants and a large lobby, and rents rooms in the deluxe-to-ultra-deluxe range. Guest rooms enjoy private lanais and guests lounge around a grassy courtyard and a swimming pool.

Or check out, and check in to, the **Royal Lahaina Resort** (2780 Kekaa Drive, Kaanapali; 661-3611). Spreading across 27 acres, it encompasses 542 rooms, two golf courses, 11 tennis courts, three swimming pools, three restaurants, and a white-sand beach that extends for a half-mile. Rooms in the highrise hotel start in the deluxe price category, but the nicest accommodations are the multi-plex cottages that dot the landscaped grounds. These also begin in the deluxe territory; the ones with kitchen facilities are ultra-deluxe.

In the realm of luxury hotels, the **Hyatt Regency Maui** (200 Nohea Kai Drive, Kaanapali; 661-1234) is one of the better addresses in Hawaii. Built in 1980, its atrium lobby, Asian artwork, and freeform swimming pool have set the standard for deluxe resorts ever since. Unlike more recent hotels, in which the size of guest rooms is sacrificed for the sake of lavish grounds, the Hyatt Regency maintains an ideal balance between public and private areas. If you're seeking beautiful surroundings, friendly service, and beachfront location at ultra-deluxe prices, this 815-room extravaganza is the ticket.

KAANAPALI-KAPALUA AREA CONDOMINIUMS

Most condos in this area are on the beach or just across the road from it. They are ideally situated for swimming or sunbathing; the major drawback, ironically, is that there are so many other condos around. Generally, I have selected the most economical facilities, but I think you'll find they meet basic requirements for comfort and convenience. For a better idea of what to anticipate, check out the section on "Condominium Living" in Chapter Two.

Maui Sands (3600 Lower Honoapiilani Road, Kaanapali; 669-1902). One-bedroom apartments begin at $75 single or double; two bedrooms run $90 for one to four people. Seven-night minimum. Beachfront.

Paki Maui (3615 Lower Honoapiilani Road, Kaanapali; 669-8235). One-bedroom apartments run from $139 to $159, depending on the view, and sleep one to four people; two-bedroom units start at $199, accommodating up to six people. Jacuzzi. Beachfront.

Kaleialoha (Lower Honoapiilani Road, Honokowai; 669-8197). Studio apartments, $75 double; one-bedroom apartments, $85 double; $7.50 each additional person. Oceanfront.

Aston Kaanapali Shores (3445 Lower Honoapiilani Road; 667-2211). Studios from $159 double ($129 from April 1 to December 21); one-bedroom units for $189 and $159, respectively. Large and expensive, but it's right on Kaanapali Beach and has two pools, jacuzzis, tennis courts, restaurant, and shops.

Aston Maui Park (3626 Lower Honoapiilani Road; 669-6622). Studios from $89 ($79 from April 1 to December 21). Across street from beach.

Honokowai Palms (3666 Lower Honoapiilani Road, Honokowai; 669-6130). One-bedroom apartments (up to four people) with lanai and ocean view run $65 double. Two-bedroom units without lanai are $75 for one to six people. Located right across the street from the ocean.

Hale Maui (Lower Honoapiilani Road; 669-6312) has one-bedroom condos for $65 double. Not on the waterfront; no pool.

Hale Ono Loa (3823 Lower Honoapiilani Road; 669-9680) has one-bedroom units at $85 for up to four people and two-bedroom units for $150. Oceanfront but no beach.

Polynesian Shores (3975 Lower Honoapiilani Road, Honokowai; 669-6065). One-bedroom apartments, $95 double; two-bedroom apartments, $125 double; three-bedroom apartments, $145 double. All units have ocean view.

Mahina Surf (4057 Lower Honoapiilani Road; 669-4534). One-bedroom units start at $100 double ($85 from April 15 to December 14); two-bedroom accommodations are $115 and $100, respectively. Oceanfront on a lava-rock beach.

Kahana Reef (4471 Lower Honoapiilani Road, Kahana; 669-6491). Studio apartments, $85 single or double; one-bedroom apartments are $90 single or double; $15 more from December 19 to Easter. All units are oceanfront and have daily maid service.

The Napili Bay (33 Hui Drive, Napili; 669-6044). Studio apartments are $100 double for garden and partial ocean views and $125 for oceanfront. Rates drop to the $75-$85 range in the off-season.

Napili Point Resort (5295 Lower Honoapiilani Road; 669-9222). One-bedroom condos are $164 for up to four people ($134 from April 20 to December 21). Oceanfront on rocky beach.

The Coconut Inn (181 Hui Road, Napili; 669-5712) has studios for $85 and one-bedroom units for $95 ($75 and $85, respectively, from April 1 to December 24). It's small (40 units) and cozy. Woodframe buildings encircle a courtyard with pool and pond. Several blocks from beach.

KAANAPALI-KAPALUA AREA RESTAURANTS

Luigi's Pasta & Pizzeria (661-3160) is located near the entrance to Kaanapali Beach Resort. A patio restaurant overlooking a golf course, it's a pretty place to dine on pizza, pasta, and other Italian favorites. Open for lunch and dinner, they expand the menu every evening to include veal marsala, chicken parmesan, and shrimp scampi. Moderate.

The **Kaanapali Beach Hotel Koffee Shop** (Kaanapali Beach Hotel; 661-0011) serves cafeteria-style meals at prices that are surprisingly out of place for this expensive hotel. But don't expect too much for so little. The menu is limited to a few egg dishes at breakfast, sandwiches and plate lunches, and dinners. Budget to moderate.

Chico's Cantina (Whalers Village; 667-2777) is one of those tacky theme restaurants that prove either entertaining or annoying, depending on your disposition and mood. Surfboards tacked to the wall, a car in the middle of the restaurant—that sort of thing. If you manage to get as far as the food, you'll find fajitas, chimichangas, burritos, and other moderate-priced Mexican dishes.

You can dine by the water at **Leilani's On The Beach** (Whalers Village; 661-4495). The sunsets are otherworldly at this breezy veranda-style dining room. Trimmed in dark woods and lava rock, it's dominated by an outrigger canoe that hangs suspended from the ceiling. On the menu you'll find Malaysian shrimp, spinach and cheese ravioli, Cajun-style fresh fish, ginger chicken, and teriyaki steak. Touristy but appealing; deluxe.

Some Place Different features early-bird specials at moderate prices from 5:30 to 6:30 p.m. Located poolside at the Sheraton Maui (Kaanapali Parkway; 661-0031), this terrace restaurant looks out on the ocean and the island of Lanai. Serving three meals daily, it offers a surf-and-turf menu at deluxe prices.

Chopsticks (661-3611), a dinner-only dining room at the Royal Lahaina Resort (2780 Kekaa Drive, Kaanapali), covers the entire Pacific Rim. The menu divides into China, Thailand, Japan, and Polynesia, with a half-dozen entrées from each locale. Wicker chairs, shell lamps, decorative fans, and dragons' heads continue the theme. Add to these features a price structure in the moderate range and you have one of Kaanapali's best values.

Dollie's Pub and Café (4310 Lower Honoapiilani Road, Kahana; 669-0266) has lasagna, fettucine alfredo, chicken marinara, pizza, and sandwiches at budget prices. This is a sports-on-the-television bar with a small kitchen and dining room adjacent; noisy but cheap.

There's not much of an ocean view at **Kahana Keyes Restaurant** (4327 Lower Honoapiilani Road, Kahana; 669-8071), but you will find a moderately priced menu and wood-trimmed dining room. The bill of fare is pretty standard—steak and seafood; and the decor is comforting if uninspired. Check out the early-bird specials from 5:00 to 7:00 p.m.

One of Maui's prettiest restaurants, **Sound of the Falls** is the plush Westin Maui Hotel's (Kaanapali Parkway, Kaanapali; 667-2525) signature dining room. Specializing in sunsets and French-with-a-touch-of-Asia cuisine, it sits beside tumbling waterfalls and gazes out on Lanai. Broad pillars support this high-ceilinged pavilion and a colony of resident flamingoes adds to the elegance. Open for dinner and Sunday brunch, this is the place for whole-boned baby hen, kiawe-grilled scallops, seared beef chops, and opakapaka in Chardonnay cream. Ultra-deluxe.

There's little doubt that Hawaii's finest sunsets occur off the southwest coast of Maui. One of the best spots to catch the spectacle is **The Bay Club** (1 Bay Drive, Kapalua; 669-5656) at the Kapalua Bay Hotel, an oceanfront dining room that looks out on Molokai and Lanai. More than just a feast for the eyes, this open-air restaurant offers a gourmet menu at lunch and dinner. You can watch the sky melt from deep blue to flaming red while dining on bouillabaisse, scallops with capers, Pacific lobster tail, veal scallopine, or filet mignon. A rough life indeed. Ultra-deluxe.

For something less expensive, consider **The Market Café** (669-4888). It's located in the Kapalua Shops adjacent to the Kapalua Bay Hotel (1 Bay Drive, Kapalua) and shares its space with a gourmet market. Comfortably equipped with wooden booths and bentwood chairs, the dining area presents fresh fish, steak teriyaki, chicken tettrazini, and several other Italian specialties at moderate prices. They also serve very inexpensive breakfast and lunches.

KAANAPALI-KAPALUA AREA MARKETS

Out in the Kaanapali area, the best place to shop is **The Food Pantry** (669-6208), a small supermarket on Lower Honoapiilani Road in Honokowai.

Toward Kapalua, try the **Napili Market** (669-1600), a well-stocked supermarket in Napili Plaza on Honoapiilani Highway.

KAANAPALI-KAPALUA AREA SHOPPING

Worthy of mention is **Whalers Village** in the Kaanapali Beach Resort on Route 30. This sprawling complex combines a shopping mall with an outdoor museum. Numbered among the stores you'll find gift emporia featuring coral and shells, a shirt store with wild island designs, other stores offering fine men's and women's fashions, and a **Waldenbooks** (661-8638) bookstore.

Several shops in this split-level complex should not be missed. **Nohea Gallery** (661-1012) has a tasteful collection of artwork by island artists, and **The Secret Jungle** (661-8651) next door specializes in the cloisonné jewelry and silk-screened fabrics of Laurel Burch. Around the corner at **Lahaina Printsellers Ltd.** (667-7617), they purvey "fine antique maps and prints," while at **Blue Ginger Designs** (667-5433) they feature original styles in women's and children's clothing.

And then, to help make shopping the grand adventure it should be, there are the displays. Within this mazework mall you'll discover blunderbusses, intricate scrimshaw pieces, the skeletal remains of leviathans, and whaling boats with iron harpoons splayed from the bow. Practically everything, in fact, that a whaler (or a cruising shopper) could desire.

For serious shoppers, ready to spend money or be damned, there is nothing to compare with the neighboring hotels. Set like gems within this tourist cluster are several world-class hotels, each hosting numerous elegant shops.

Foremost is the **Hyatt Regency Maui,** along whose wood-paneled lobby are stores that might well be deemed mini-museums. One shop contains exquisite pieces of hand-chiseled crystal. Another, called **Elephant Walk** (667-2848), displays *koa* wood furniture, baskets, and Niihau shell jewelry. There are art galleries, fabric shops, candy stores, a luggage shop, and more—set in an open-air lobby that is filled with rare statuary and exotic birds.

The shopping annex at the Kapalua Bay Hotel (1 Bay Drive, Kapalua) is another upscale address. Among the temptations is **Mandalay** (669-6170), specializing in silks and cottons from Asia. There are blouses and jackets for women as well as a small collection of artfully crafted jewelry. Also stop by **South Seas of Kapalua** (669-1249), which has native masks from New Guinea and other artwork from Oceania.

KAANAPALI-KAPALUA AREA NIGHTLIFE

At the Maui Marriott (667-1200), the **Makai Bar** cooks every night with a duo or trio performing Hawaiian and Pop numbers. If you'd rather get up there and perform yourself, you can join the hostess in a karaoke-style sing-along at the **Lobby Bar** on Thursday, Friday, or Saturday.

One of Maui's premier night spots, tucked into the basement of one of the island's finest hotels, is a disco called **Spats II** (Hyatt Regency Maui, Kaanapali Beach Resort; 661-1234). Named after a hot Waikiki club, this opulent lounge doubles as an elegant Italian restaurant. That's why you see marble tabletops, antique armchairs, and brass chandeliers surrounding the wood-inlay dancefloor. The music is strictly soundtrack, though it draws the crowds. No cover or minimum, but there is a strict dress code that bars sandals while requiring slacks and collar shirts. (While you're nightowling here, take a stroll through the Hyatt Regency's atrium-style lobby. The hotel is lavishly decorated with rare artworks and inhabited by exotic birds.)

Possibly the prettiest place in these parts to enjoy a late night drink 'neath the tropic moon is **El Crab Catcher** (661-4423). Located in the Whalers Village mall, this club features contemporary Hawaiian music on Friday and Saturday nights. The place is located right on the water, so you can listen to a slow set, then stroll the beach.

The Sheraton Maui (Kaanapali Parkway; 661-0031) is a prime nightspot both early and later in the evening. Just before sunset you can watch the torchlighting and cliff-diving ceremony from the **Sundowner Bar**. Then adjourn to **On The Rocks,** where there's live dance music Sunday through Wednesday and a karaoke program the rest of the week.

There's Hawaiian-style entertainment nightly at the **Royal Ocean Lounge,** a beachfront watering hole on the grounds of the Royal Lahaina Resort (2780 Kekaa Drive, Kaanapali; 661-3611). Arrive early and you can watch the sunset between Lanai and Molokai.

The **Villa Lounge** and the **Colonnade Lounge** at the Westin Maui (2365 Kaanapali Parkway, Kaanapali; 667-2525) have live music on alternating nights. The sounds range from jazz to blues to country rock.

For soft entertainment in a relaxed setting, try the **Bay Club** (669-8008) at the Kapalua Bay Hotel. This open-air piano bar is set in a lovely restaurant overlooking the water. The melodies are as serene and relaxing as the views of neighboring Molokai.

KAANAPALI-KAPALUA AREA BEACHES AND PARKS

Kaanapali Resort Beaches—The sprawling complex of Kaanapali hotels sits astride a beautiful white-sand beach that extends for three miles. Looking out on Lanai and Molokai, this is a classic palm-fringed strand. The entire area is heavily developed, and crowded by flaccid tourists glistening in coconut oil. But it *is* an extraordinarily fine beach.

Facilities: Restaurants and groceries are nearby. *Swimming:* Very good. *Skindiving:* Excellent around Black Rock at the Sheraton Maui.

Getting there: Take the public right-of-way to the beach from any of the Kaanapali resort hotels.

Honokowai Beach Park—Compared to the beaches fronting Kaanapali's nearby resorts, this is a bit disappointing. The large lawn is pleasant enough, but the beach itself is small, with a reef that projects right to the shoreline. The view of Molokai is awesome, though.

Facilities: Picnic tables, restrooms, showers. Directly across the street is a supermarket. *Swimming:* Good. *Snorkeling:* Good. *Surfing:* Not usually good. *Fishing:* Threadfin and ulua are among the most frequent catches.

Getting there: On Lower Honoapiilani Road (which is the oceanfront section of Route 30) north of Kaanapali in Honokowai.

Napili Bay—You'll find wall-to-wall condominiums along this small cove. There's a crowded but beautiful white-sand beach studded with palm trees and looking out on Molokai.

Facilities: Restaurants and groceries nearby. *Swimming:* Good. *Snorkeling:* Good. *Surfing:* Good for beginners.

Getting there: It's located several miles north of Kaanapali, with rights-of-way to the beach from Lower Honoapiilani Road via Napili Place or Hui Drive.

Kapalua Beach—This is the next cove over from Napili Bay. It's equally beautiful, but not as heavily developed. The crescent of white sand that lines Kapalua Bay is bounded on either end by rocky points and backdropped by a line of coconut trees and the Kapalua Bay Hotel.

Facilities: Restaurants and groceries are nearby. *Swimming:* Very good. *Snorkeling:* Fair.

Getting there: There's a right-of-way to the beach from Lower Honoapiilani Road near the Napili Kai Beach Club.

D. T. Fleming Park—One of Maui's nicest beach parks, D. T. Fleming has a spacious white-sand beach plus a rolling lawn shaded with palm and ironwood trees. Unfortunately, a major resort resides just uphill from the beach. Sometimes windy, the park is plagued by rough and dangerous surf in winter. There's a nice view of Molokai's rugged East End.

Facilities: Restrooms, picnic area, showers. It's a mile to the market in Napili. *Swimming:* Good swimming and bodysurfing. *Snorkeling:* Fair. *Surfing:* Good breaks nearby at "Little Makaha," named after the famous Oahu beach. *Fishing:* Prime catches here are ulua and papio.

Getting there: Located just off Honoapiilani Highway, about seven miles north of Kaanapali.

Northwest Maui

To escape from the mondo condo jungle of the Kaanapali-Kapalua area and travel north on the Honoapiilani Highway is to journey from the ridiculous to the sublime. As you curve along the edge of the West Maui Mountains, en route around the side of the island to Kahului and Wailuku, you'll pass several hidden beaches that lie along an exotic and undeveloped shore.

Near the rocky beach and lush valley at **Honokohau Bay**, the Honoapiilani Highway (Route 30) becomes the Kahekili Highway (Route 340). This macadam track snakes high above the ocean, hugging the coastline. From the highway rises a series of multihued **sandstone cliffs** that seems alien to this volcanic region.

After several miles, the road turns to dirt and soon deteriorates into a bone-jangling series of ruts punctuated with potholes. The scenery is some of the most magnificent on Maui. About a mile down the dirt road sits the rustic village of **Kahakuloa** (★). Nestled in an overgrown valley beside a deep blue bay, the community is protected by a solitary headland rising directly from the sea. Woodframe houses and churches, which appear ready to fall to the next gusting wind, are spotted throughout this enchanting area. Kahakuloa is cattle country, and you'll find that the villagers live and farm much as their forefathers did.

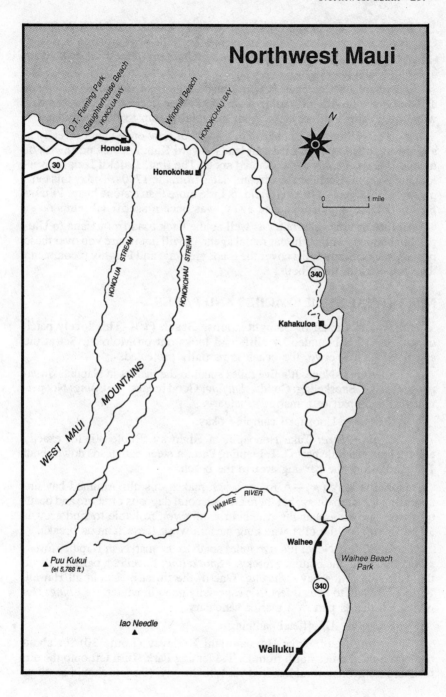

The road ascends again and improves somewhat outside Kahakuloa. Opening below you, one valley after another falls seaward in a series of spine-backed ridges. Above the road, the mountain range rises toward its 5788-foot summit at Puu Kukui.

There are lush gulches farther along as the road returns to pavement and descends into the plantation town of **Waihee**. Here cane fields, dotted with small farm houses, slope from the roadside up to the foothills.

You're still on the Kahekili Highway, but now once again it really is a highway, a well-paved road that leads toward Kahului. Just northwest of town a side road leads to two sacred spots. The first, **Halekii Heiau**, overlooking Kahului Bay and Iao Stream, dates from the 1700s. Today this temple, once as large as a football field, is little more than a stone heap. **Pihana Kalani Heiau**, a short distance away, was once a sacrificial temple.

Before driving this route, as well as the back road from Hana to Ulupalakua, remember that the car rental agencies will not insure you over these rugged tracks. Many folks cover the roads anyway, and I highly recommend that you explore them both.

NORTHWEST MAUI BEACHES AND PARKS

Mokuleia Beach or **Slaughterhouse Beach** (★)—This lovely patch of white sand is bounded by cliffs and looks out on Molokai. Set at the end of a shallow cove, the beach is partially protected.

Facilities: None. It's five miles south to the market in Napili. *Swimming:* Good. Snorkeling: Good. *Surfing:* Good breaks. *Fishing:* Not permitted; this is part of a marine sanctuary.

Camping: Unofficial camping okay.

Getting there: Take Honoapiilani Highway (Route 30) for exactly eight-tenths of a mile past D. T. Fleming Park. A steep path leads down about 100 yards from the parking area to the beach.

Honolua Bay (★)—A rocky beach makes this cliff-rimmed bay unappealing for sunbathers, but there are rich coral deposits offshore and beautiful trees growing near the water. In winter you're liable to find crowds along the top of the cliff watching surfers work these famous breaks.

Facilities: None. It's five miles south to the market in Napili. *Swimming:* Good, but the bottom is rocky. *Snorkeling:* Excellent, particularly on the west side of the bay. *Surfing:* One of the finest breaks in all Hawaii. Perfect tubes up to fifteen feet. It's especially good in winter. *Fishing:* Not permitted; this is part of a marine sanctuary.

Camping: Unofficial camping.

Getting there: Take Honoapiilani Highway (Route 30) for about one-and-a-third miles north from D. T. Fleming Park. Turn left onto the dirt road and follow it several hundred yards to the bay. (Surfers should continue another eight-tenths of a mile on the highway, then turn left onto the dirt road bordering the nearby pineapple field. A path from this road leads down a cliff to a small beach and the best breaks.)

Punalau Beach or Windmill Beach (★)—A white-sand beach studded with rocks, Windmill Beach is surrounded by cliffs and intriguing rock formations. Very secluded.

Facilities: None. Seven miles to the market in Napili. *Swimming:* Okay when calm. *Snorkeling:* Excellent when calm. A fascinating reef extends along the coast all through this area. *Surfing:* Fine peak in winter. Left and right slide. *Fishing:* Leatherback, papio, milkfish, moano, and big-eyed scad are the primary catches.

Camping: Permit required from Maui Pineapple Co., Honolua Division, 4900 Honoapiilani Highway, Lahaina (669-6201) and must be obtained in person. No charge; three-day limit.

Getting there: Go just three-and-a-half miles north from D. T. Fleming Park on Honoapiilani Highway (Route 30), then turn left onto the dirt road. Follow it a short distance to the beach.

Honokohau Bay—This rocky beach is surrounded by cliffs. To the interior, a lush valley rises steadily into the folds of the West Maui Mountains.

Facilities: None. It's nine miles to markets in Napili. *Swimming:* Good when calm. *Snorkeling:* Good when calm. *Surfing:* Rugged two- to twelve-foot breaks. *Fishing:* Milkfish, papio, leatherback, moano, and big-eyed scad are the principal species caught in these waters.

Camping: Too rocky.

Getting there: Follow Honoapiilani Highway (Route 30) about six miles north of D. T. Fleming Park.

Kihei-Wailea Area

Stretching from Maalaea Bay to Makena is a nearly continuous succession of beautiful beaches that make Kihei and Wailea favored resort destinations. Second only to the Lahaina-Kaanapali area in popularity, this seaside enclave rests in the rainshadow of Haleakala, which looms in the background. Maui's southeastern shore receives only ten inches of rain a year, making it the driest, sunniest spot on the island. It also experiences heavy winds, particularly in the afternoon, which sweep across the island's isthmus.

Since the 1970s, this long, lean stretch of coast has become a developer's playground. Kihei in particular, lacking a master plan, has grown by accretion from a small local community into a haphazard collection of condominiums and mini-malls. It's an unattractive, six-mile strip lined by a golden beach.

Situated strategically along this beachfront are cement **pillboxes**, reminders of World War II's threatened Japanese invasion. Placed along Kihei Road just north of town, they are not far from **Kealia Pond Bird Sanctuary**, a 300-acre reserve frequented by migratory waterfowl as well as Hawaiian stilts and Hawaiian coots.

To the south lies Wailea, an urbane answer to the random growth patterns of its scruffy neighbor. Wailea is a planned resort, all 1450 manicured acres of it. Here kiawe scrubland has been transformed into a flowering oasis that is home to five top-class hotels and six condominiums, as well as the required retinue of golf courses, tennis courts, and overpriced shops. Like Kihei, it is blessed with beautiful beaches.

You'll have to go well past Wailea, to where the coast road becomes a dirt track, to escape the tourist complexes. I highly recommend visiting **Makena Beach**, located along Makena Alanui Road about four miles beyond Wailea. Although development has struck here, too, Makena is still one of Maui's finest strands. A hippie hangout in the 1960s and early 1970s, it still retains a freewheeling atmosphere, especially at nearby "Little Makena," Maui's most famous nude beach.

Past here the road gets rough as it presses south to **Ahihi-Kinau Reserve**. Encompassing over 2000 acres of land and ocean bottom, this preserve harbors an amazing array of marine life and contains the remains of an early Hawaiian fishing village. Almost 100 larval fish species and about two dozen species of stony coral have been found in this ecologically rich reserve.

The road continues on, bisecting the **1790 lava flow**, which resulted from Haleakala's last eruption. The flow created Cape Kinau, a thumb-shaped peninsula dividing Ahihi Bay and **La Perouse Bay**. When I drove this route recently in a compact rental car, I reached La Perouse Bay before being forced by poor road conditions to turn back. The bay is named for the ill-starred French navigator, Jean de Francois La Perouse, who anchored here in 1786, the first westerner to visit Maui. After a brief sojourn in this enchanting spot, he sailed off and was later lost at sea.

KIHEI-WAILEA AREA HOTELS

Like Kaanapali, this oceanfront strip features condominiums, but there are a couple of moderately priced hotels. The **Nona Lani Cottages** (455 South Kihei Road, Kihei; 879-2497) tops the list, with eight quaint wooden cottages situated across busy Kihei Road from a white-sand beach. Each is a one-bedroom unit with lanai, all-electric kitchen, and a living room capable of housing two extra sleepers. There's wall-to-wall carpeting and a shower-tub combination, plus television, but no phone or air conditioner. Like most cottages in Hawaii, these are extremely popular, so you'll need to reserve them far

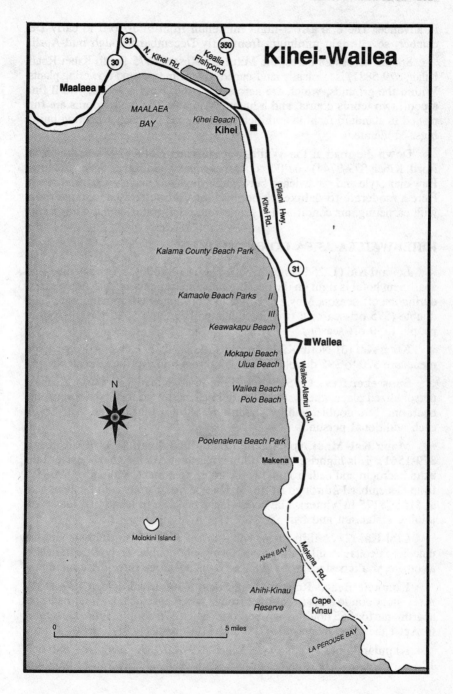

Kihei-Wailea

Maalaea

MAALAEA BAY

Kealia Fishpond

N. Kihei Rd.

Kihei Beach

Kihei

Piilani Hwy.

Kihei Rd.

Kalama County Beach Park

Kamaole Beach Parks

I
II
III

Keawakapu Beach

■**Wailea**

Mokapu Beach
Ulua Beach

Wailea-Alanui Rd.

Wailea Beach
Polo Beach

N

Poolenalena Beach Park

Makena ■

Molokini Island

Makena Rd.

AHIHI BAY

Ahihi-Kinau

Reserve

Cape Kinau

LA PEROUSE BAY

0   5 miles

in advance. There is a four-night minimum from mid-April to early December; seven-night minimum from early December through mid-April.

Spread across 28 acres, the **Maui Lu Resort** (575 South Kihei Road, Kihei; 879-5881) is tropically landscaped with palm trees and flowering plants. Within the grounds, which are across the street from a beach, you'll find a pool, two tennis courts, and a huge restaurant. The guest rooms are furnished in standard fashion and located in a series of interconnecting buildings. Moderate.

Down the road at the **Wailea Oceanfront Hotel** (2980 South Kihei Road, Kihei; 879-7744) you'll find a series of six buildings designed in mock-Hawaiian style and sandwiched between the highway and a white-sand beach. Here a moderate-to-deluxe tab books a tiny, attractively decorated room with carpeting, air conditioning, television, refrigerator, and a clock radio.

KIHEI-WAILEA AREA CONDOMINIUMS

Leilani Kai (1226 Uluniu Street, Kihei; 879-2606). This cozy nine-unit apartment hotel is right on the beach. Studio apartments are $75 double ($60 during the off-season, May 1 to November 30); one-bedroom units are $100 double ($75 off-season); two bedrooms will run you $125 for one to four people ($90 off-season).

Kihei Kai (61 North Kihei Road, Kihei; 879-2357). One-bedroom apartments are $70 to $95 double ($55 to $80 from mid-April to December 14).

Sunseeker Resort (551 South Kihei Road, Kihei; 879-1261). A small, personalized place where studios with kitchenettes go for $50 double, one-bedrooms $60 double, and two-bedrooms $80 for four people. Add $6 for each additional person.

Mana Kai–Maui Apartment Hotel (2960 South Kihei Road, Kihei; 879-1561). This highrise condominium has "hotel units" that consist of the extra bedroom and bath from a two-bedroom apartment, renting for $90 ($95 from December 17 through April 15). One-bedroom units with kitchens start at $155 ($175 in winter). The condo has a beachfront location, plus an adjoining restaurant and bar.

Lihi Kai (2121 Iliili Road, Kihei; 879-2335). This establishment has nine beach cottages, all renting for $59 single or double. To be sure of getting a cottage, you'd best make reservations far in advance. Three-night minimum.

Kamaole Beach Royale (2385 South Kihei Road, Kihei; 879-3131). A six-story condo across the street from a beach park, this has one-bedroom apartments for $65 double; two-bedroom units, $75 double. From December to April the rates increase to $90 and $100, respectively.

Kapulanikai (73 Kapu Place, Kihei; 879-1607). A cozy place with only 12 apartments, all of which overlook the ocean. The two-story buildings are constructed of wood and capped with tile roofs. One-bedroom apartments rent for $80 single or double ($65 from April to mid-December).

KIHEI-WAILEA AREA RESTAURANTS

Now that condominiums have mushroomed from its white sands, Kihei is no longer a poor person's paradise. Yet there are still several short-order griddles like **Suda's Snack Shop** (61 South Kihei Road, Kihei; 879-2668) around. Budget.

You'll find another take-out window at **Azeka's Market Snack Shop** (879-0611) in nearby Azeka Place Shopping Center. For atmosphere there's a parking lot, but for food there's a fair choice, with hamburgers and plate lunches priced low. Budget.

Surfside Spirits and Deli (1993 South Kihei Road, Kihei; 879-1385) has a take-out delicatessen serving sandwiches, salads, and slaw. Prices are in the budget range.

At **Canton Chef** (2463 South Kihei Road, Kihei; 879-1988), on the other hand, the cuisine ranges from roast duck to beef with oyster sauce. This traditional Chinese restaurant offers almost 100 different choices including a selection of spicy Szechuan dishes.

For a relaxed meal, I like **Luigi's Pasta & Pizzeria** (Azeka Place Shopping Center, 1280 South Kihei Road, Kihei; 879-4446). Built on three levels and decorated in a nautical motif, it has a comfortable laid-back atmosphere. Dinner consists of Italian dishes like chicken parmesan and fettuccine alfredo as well as shrimp and steak platters. At lunch they serve up soup, salad, and sandwiches, plus several entrées. A gathering place for local residents, Luigi's is easygoing and friendly.

Margarita's Beach Cantina (101 North Kihei Road, Kihei; 879-5311) is one of those big brassy Mexican restaurants that are ever more frequent along the beaches. The kind that have live sports on big-screen television and a buzzing night scene. The menu covers lunch and dinner, includes everything it should, and is moderately priced.

For inexpensive Korean food, there's **The Kal Bi House** (1212 South Kihei Road, Kihei; 874-8454). Squeezed into a corner of Kihei Center and furnished with molded-plastic seats, it's not much on atmosphere. But it's hard to beat their budget-priced barbecued ribs and other favorites.

If you prefer something from Southeast Asia, **Royal Thai Cuisine** (Azeka Place Shopping Center, 1280 South Kihei Road, Kihei; 874-0813) sits across the street in yet another shopping mall. Here the chairs are wood, the menu includes *dozens* of dishes, and prices are moderate.

Did you say Greek? No problem. Just a few malls away (this one is called Kai Nani Village) is the **Greek Bistro** (2511 South Kihei Road,

Kihei; 879-9330) with a full selection of Mediterranean dishes. These come to you at a moderate price tag.

Or forget this ethnic theme and head next door to the **Kihei Prime Rib and Seafood House** (2511 South Kihei Road, Kihei; 879-1954). A reliable if undistinguished dining room, it offers a good salad bar and numerous beef and fresh fish dishes. There are views across the road overlooking the ocean. Deluxe; there's a moderate-priced early-bird special from 5:00 to 6:00 p.m.

The **Longhouse Restaurant** at the Maui Lu Resort (575 South Kihei Road, Kihei; 879-5881) is a cavernous hall with bandstand and sunken dining room. You'll sometimes be serenaded at dinner by one of the resident musicians. The menu is a surf-and-turf affair priced in the moderate-to-deluxe range. They also serve breakfast and lunch, but you won't be serenaded over your eggs benedict.

Island Fish House (1945 South Kihei Road, Kihei; 879-7771) has the most complete seafood menu around. Not only is the selection broad (usually including about five fresh Hawaiian fish dishes), but the style of preparation varies as well. Opakapaka, yellowfin tuna, ono, mahimahi, and paka dishes come poached, sautéed, deep-fried, charbroiled, baked, and teriyaki style. There are also a number of imported shellfish dishes, plus an extensive wine list. The casual decor at this cozy haunt is simple, but the dishes are elaborately prepared. Dinner only. Deluxe.

All those *Travel/Holiday Magazine* awards at the entrance to **Raffles** (3550 Wailea-Alanui Drive, Wailea; 879-4900) signify that this is Stouffer Wailea Resort's signature restaurant and one of the most highly respected dining rooms on the island. With its bamboo drapes and brass chandeliers, the place is a study in British colonial elegance. The cuisine, however, is island classic: rack of lamb with mango chutney, ahi in wasabi ginger cream, ono with papaya, and breast of chicken with Maui onion. The tab naturally is ultra-deluxe. Dinner and Sunday brunch only.

Seasons, the signature restaurant at the Four Seasons Resort Wailea (3900 Wailea-Alanui Drive, Wailea; 874-8000) gained a vaunted reputation soon after it opened a few years ago. Marble trim, chairs upholstered in leather, and knockout ocean views create the suitable ambience. But it is the Hawaii regional cuisine for which the dining room is particularly known. Specializing in fresh fish and locally grown produce, it is one of Maui's top restaurants. Ultra-deluxe.

KIHEI-WAILEA AREA MARKETS

Foodland (879-9350), a large supermarket in Kihei Town Center on South Kihei Road, and **Star Market** (1310 South Kihei Road; 879-5871) have the largest grocery selections in the area (open 24 hours daily). **Azeka's Market** (879-0611) up the road is often price-competitive, though.

If you're camping at Makena, you'll find **Wailea Pantry** (879-3044) in Wailea fairly convenient, but I'm afraid you'll pay for the convenience. This small store, situated in the posh Wailea Shopping Village, is painfully overpriced.

Paradise Fruit Maui (Rainbow Mall, 2439 South Kihei Road, Kihei; 879-1723) has delicious fresh fruit and health foods at low overhead prices.

KIHEI-WAILEA SHOPPING

Shopping in Kihei is centered in the malls and doesn't hold a lot of promise. You'll find swimwear shops and an assortment of other outlets, but nothing with style and panache. Foremost among the malls is **Kihei Center**, which stretches along the 1200 South block of Kihei Road.

Across the street in **Azeka Place Shopping Center** (1280 South Kihei Road, Kihei) you'll find more of the same.

Kukui Mall just down the road has that most wonderful of inventions— a bookstore: a **Waldenbooks** (874-3688) bookstore to be exact.

If you don't find what you're searching for at any of these addresses, there are countless other strip malls along Kihei Road.

Or, if you prefer more sophisticated shops, continue on to Wailea. The elite counterpart to middle-class Kihei, this resort complex features 27 different stores in **Wailea Shopping Village**.

You'll also find signature shops at the large resorts that now dominate the scene in Wailea: Foremost among them are the **Grand Hyatt Wailea** (3850 Wailea-Alanui Drive, Wailea; 875-1234) and **Four Seasons Resort Wailea** (3900 Wailea Alanui, Wailea; 874-8000).

KIHEI-WAILEA AREA NIGHTLIFE

Every Wednesday night, **Luigi's Pasta & Pizzeria** (Azeka Place Shopping Center, 1280 South Kihei Road, Kihei; 879-4446) remakes the third tier of its multideck restaurant into a disco. Despite the deejay spinning platters, the place still looks like a converted restaurant, but it's the hottest spot in Kihei's lukewarm night scene.

The Maui Lu Resort's **Longhouse** (879-5881) features a Polynesian revue Wednesday and Friday.

Down in Wailea, the **Inu Inu Lounge** at the Hotel Inter-Continental (3700 Wailea-Alanui Drive; 879-1922) mixes smoky dance music with a little jazz and rock 'n' roll on Thursday, Friday, and Saturday nights.

Leave it to the Grand Hyatt Wailea (that's Grand Hyatt with the accent on Grand) to have Maui's most elaborate high-tech nightclub. **Tsunami** (3850 Wailea-Alanui Drive, Wailea; 875-1234) cost $4 million to build, features 20 video monitors, and has a 14-foot-wide karaoke screen. Cover.

For a quiet drink to the tinkle of a piano, try **Raffles** (3550 Wailea-Alanui Drive, Wailea; 879-4900), the spiffy restaurant at the Stouffer Wailea Beach Resort.

There is a Hawaiian soloist performing nightly at the **Molokini Lounge** (874-1111) over in Makena at the Maui Prince Hotel.

KIHEI-WAILEA AREA BEACHES AND PARKS

Kihei Beach—This narrow, palm-fringed beach stretches from Maalaea Bay to Kihei. It can be seen from several points along Kihei Road and is everywhere accessible from the highway. There are buildings and numerous condominiums along this strip, but few large crowds on the beach. Beach joggers take note: You can run for miles along this unbroken strand, but watch for heavy winds in the afternoon.

Facilities: There are picnic tables and restrooms at **Kihei Memorial Park** (located midway along the beach). Markets and restaurants are nearby. *Swimming:* Well-protected by shoals, but very shallow. *Snorkeling:* Fair (better at Kamaole beaches). *Surfing:* Poor. *Fishing:* Bonefish, papio, mullet, goatfish, ulua, moano, and mountain bass.

Getting there: Kihei Beach runs along Kihei Road between Maalaea and Kihei.

Kalama County Beach Park—This long, broad park has an ample lawn but very little beach. Rather than lapping along the sand, waves wash up against a stone sea wall. Backdropped by Haleakala, the park has stunning views of West Maui, Lanai, and Kahoolawe. Here's an excellent place for a picnic, but before you pack your lunch, remember that Kalama, like all Kihei's beaches, is swept by afternoon winds.

Facilities: Picnic areas, restrooms, showers, tennis courts. Restaurants and markets nearby. *Swimming:* Shoals provide ample protection, but they also create shallows throughout this area; good for children. *Snorkeling:* Fair. *Surfing:* Summer breaks over a coral reef. Left and right slide. *Fishing:* Poor.

Getting there: It's located on South Kihei Road across from Kihei Town Center.

Kamaole Beach Parks I, II, and III—Strung like beads along the Kihei shore are these three beautiful parks, their white sands fringed with grass and studded with trees. With Haleakala in the background, they all offer magnificent views of the West Maui Mountains, Lanai, and Kahoolawe. All are windswept in the afternoon, though.

Facilities: Each is equipped with picnic areas, restrooms, and showers. Kamaole III also has a playground. Restaurants and markets are nearby. *Swimming:* Very good on all three beaches. *Snorkeling:* Best near the rocks fringing Kamaole III. *Fishing:* Common catches include bonefish, papio, mullet, goatfish, ulua, moano, and mountain bass.

Getting there: On South Kihei Road near Kihei Town Center.

Keawakapu Beach—Ho hum, another of Kihei's beautiful white-sand beaches. Like other nearby beach parks, Keawakapu has marvelous views of the West Maui Mountains and Lanai, but is plagued by afternoon winds. The half-mile-long beach is bordered on both ends by lava points.

Facilities: Showers. Short distance to the markets and restaurants of Kihei and Wailea. *Swimming:* Good, but not as well-protected as Kamaole beaches. *Snorkeling:* Good around rocks. *Fishing:* Excellent. Numerous species can be caught here.

Getting there: On South Kihei Road between Kihei and Wailea.

Mokapu and **Ulua beaches**—Two crescent-shaped beaches fringed with palms and looking out toward Lanai and Kahoolawe, these have much of their natural beauty spoiled by the nearby hotel and condominium developments. Both beaches feature landscaped miniparks and are popular with bodysurfers.

Facilities: Restrooms and showers. *Swimming:* Good. *Snorkeling:* Good here.

Getting there: Follow the signs near Stouffer's Wailea Beach Hotel in Wailea.

Wailea Beach—Another beach in the ultra-modern Wailea development, this lovely white-sand strip, once fringed with *kiawe* trees, is now dominated by two very large, very upscale resorts. Popular with bodysurfers.

Facilities: Restrooms and showers. *Swimming:* Good. *Snorkeling:* Also good.

Getting there: Located adjacent to the Four Seasons Wailea Resort just a half-mile south of Wailea Shopping Village.

Polo Beach—Though not quite so attractive as Wailea Beach, Polo still has a lot to offer. There's a bountiful stretch of white sand, plus great views of Kahoolawe and Molokini. The beach has a landscaped minipark and is popular with bodysurfers.

Facilities: There are restrooms and showers. *Swimming:* Good here. *Snorkeling:* Excellent.

Getting there: About one mile south of Wailea Shopping Village.

Poolenalena (or **Paipu**) **Beach Park**—This lovely white-sand beach has been transformed into an attractive little facility frequented by people from throughout the area. Next to Makena, it is the prettiest beach in the Kihei-Wailea region.

Facilities: None. Two miles from the market in Wailea. *Swimming:* Good. *Snorkeling:* Fair. *Fishing:* Very good; many species are caught here.

Camping: Unofficial tenting is very common under the *kiawe* trees that front the beach.

Getting there: It's located on Makena-Alanui Road about 1.7 miles south of Wailea Shopping Village.

Black Sands Beach or Oneuli Beach (★)—This is a long, narrow, salt-and-pepper beach located just north of Red Hill, a shoreline cinder cone. Fringed with *kiawe* trees, this stretch of beach is less attractive but more secluded than Makena.

Facilities: Nonexistent; four miles to the market in Wailea. *Swimming:* Good. *Snorkeling:* Fair. *Fishing:* Very good; many species caught.

Camping: Unofficial camping okay.

Getting there: Follow Makena-Alanui Road south from Wailea Shopping Village for three-and-three-quarters miles. Turn right on the dirt road at the north end of Red Hill, then bear right to the beach.

Makena Beach or Oneloa Beach (★)—Much more than a beach, Makena is an institution. For over a decade, it's been a countercultural gathering place. There are even stories about rock stars jamming here during Makena's heyday in the early 1970s. While once a hideaway for hippies, the beach today is increasingly popular with straight tourists and is slated for mondo-condo development. Hurry—so far this long, wide corridor of white sand curving south from Red Hill is still the most beautiful beach on Maui.

Little Beach (Puu Olai Beach), a pretty white-sand beach next to Makena Beach, is a nude beach. It's just across Red Hill from the main beach. But if you go nude here or at Makena, watch out for police; they regularly bust nudists.

Facilities: None. About four miles to the market in Wailea. *Swimming:* Good. Good bodysurfing at Little Makena. *Snorkeling:* Good near the rocks at the north end of the beach. *Fishing:* Very good; many species caught here.

Camping: Unofficial camping is very popular here, but beware of ripoffs.

Getting there: Follow Makena-Alanui Road for about four-and-one-half miles south from Wailea Shopping Village. Watch for Red Hill, the large cinder cone on your right. Just past Red Hill, turn right onto any of several dirt roads and continue to the beach.

Hana Highway

The Hana Highway (Route 360), a bumpy, tortuous road between Kahului and Hana, is one of the most beautiful drives in all Hawaii. It may in fact be one of the prettiest drives in the world. The road courses through a rainforest, a luxurious jungle crowded with ferns and African tulip trees, and leads to black-sand beaches and rain-drenched hamlets. The vegetation is so thick it seems to be spilling out from the mountainside in a cascade of greenery. You'll be traveling the windward side of Haleakala, hugging its lower slopes en route to a small Hawaiian town that receives 70 inches of rain a year.

There are over 600 twists and turns and 56 one-lane bridges along this adequately maintained paved road. It will take at least three hours to drive the 51 miles to Hana. To make the entire circuit around the south coast, plan either to sleep in Hana or to leave very early and drive all day. If you can, take your time—there's a lot to see.

About seven miles east of Kahului, you'll pass the quaint, weather-beaten town of **Paia**. This old sugar plantation town, now a burgeoning artist colony, has been painted in nursery colors. Along either of Paia's two streets, falsefront buildings have been freshly refurbished.

Hookipa Beach Park, one of the world's premier windsurfing spots, lies about three miles east of town. Brilliantly colored sails race along the horizon as windsurfers perform acrobatic stunts, cartwheeling across the waves.

Within the next ten miles the roadway is transformed, as your slow, winding adventure begins. You'll drive past sugarcane fields, across verdant gorges, through valleys dotted with tumbledown cottages, and along fern-cloaked hillsides.

Route 36 becomes Route 360, beginning a new series of mileage markers that are helpful in locating sites along the way. Near the two-mile marker, a short trail leads to an idyllic swimming hole at **Twin Falls** (the path begins from the west side of the Hoolawa Stream bridge on the right side of the road).

Nearby Huelo, a tiny "rooster town" (so named because nothing ever seems to be stirring except the roosters), is known for the **Kaulanapueo Church**. A coral chapel built in 1853, this New England-style sanctuary strikes a dramatic pose with the sea as a backdrop.

Farther along, on **Waikamoi Ridge**, you'll see picnic areas and a nature trail. Here you can visit a bamboo forest, learn about native vegetation, and explore the countryside.

Another picnic area, at **Puohokamoa Falls** (11-mile marker), nestles beside a waterfall and large pool. If you packed a lunch, this is a perfect place to enjoy it. Trails above and below the main pool lead to other waterfalls.

A few zigzags farther, at **Kaumahina State Wayside** (12-mile marker), a tree-studded park overlooks Honomanu Gulch and Keanae Peninsula. From here the road descends the gulch, where a side road leads left to **Honomanu Bay** (14-mile marker) and its black-sand beach.

Above Keanae Peninsula, you'll pass **Keanae Arboretum** (16-mile marker). You can stroll freely through these splendid tropical gardens, which feature many native Hawaiian plants including several dozen varieties of taro. Another section of the gardens is devoted to exotic tropical plants and there is a mile-long trail that leads into a natural rainforest.

Just past here, turn left onto the road to the **Keanae Peninsula** (★) (17-mile marker). This rocky, windswept point offers stunning views of Haleakala. You'll pass rustic houses, a patchwork of garden plots, and a coral-and-stone church built around 1860. A picture of serenity and rural perfection, Keanae is inhabited by native Hawaiians who still grow taro and pound poi. Their home is a lush rainforest—a quiltwork of taro plots, banana trees, palms—that runs to the rim of a ragged coastline.

Another side road descends to **Wailua** (18-mile marker), a Hawaiian agricultural and fishing village. Here is another luxurious checkerboard where taro gardens alternate with banana patches and the landscape is adorned with clapboard houses and a classic 1860 church.

Back on the main road, there's yet another picnic area and waterfall at **Puaa Kaa State Park** (22-mile marker). The cascade tumbles into a natural pool in a setting framed by eucalyptus and banana trees.

Past here, another side road bumps three miles through picturesque **Nahiku** (★) (25-mile marker) to a bluff overlooking the sea. The view spreads across three bays all the way back to Wailua. Directly below, the ocean pounds against rock outcroppings, spraying salt mist across a stunning vista. Set in one of the wettest spots along the entire coast, Nahiku village is inundated by rainforest and graced by yet another 19th-century church.

Kahanu Gardens (31-mile marker; 248-8912; admission), a 120-acre tropical reserve, features a pandanus forest, stands of coconut and breadfruit trees, and a vast assortment of indigenous and exotic plants. Part of the National Tropical Botanical Garden, it lies a mile-and-a-half down Ulaino Road. Call beforehand to check road conditions and confirm that the gardens are open.

Several miles before Hana, be sure to stop at **Waianapanapa State Park**. Here you'll find a black-sand beach here and two lava tubes, Waianapanapa and Waiomao caves. Strong swimmers and scuba divers can dive into a pool and swim underwater to reach Waianapanapa Cave, a legendary meeting place for lovers. Hawaiian mythology tells of a Hawaiian princess who hid from her cruel husband here, only to be discovered by him and slain. Now every spring the waters hereabouts are said to run red with her blood. Offshore you will also see several sea arches and nearby a blowhole that spouts periodically.

To reach the secluded hamlet of **Hana,** you can take the old Hawaiian shoreline trail (see the "Hiking" section at the end of this chapter) or continue on along the highway. This Eden-like town, carpeted with pandanus, taro, and banana trees, sits above an inviting bay. Known as "heavenly Hana," it's a ranch town inhabited primarily by part-Hawaiians. Because of its remote location it has changed little over the years. The rain that continually buffets Hana makes it a prime agricultural area and adds to the luxuriant, unsettling beauty of the place.

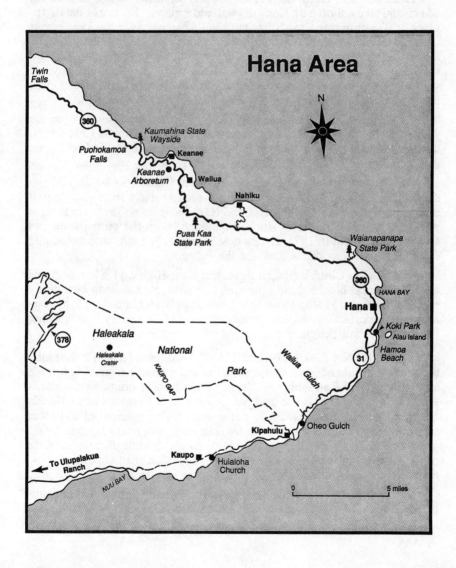

Because of its strategic location directly across from the Big Island, Hana was an early battleground in the wars between the chiefs of Maui and the Big Island, who conquered, lost, and regained the region in a succession of bloody struggles. During the 19th century it became a sugar plantation, employing different ethnic groups who were brought in to work the fields. Then, in 1946, Paul Fagan, a San Francisco industrialist, bought 14,000 acres and created the Hana Ranch, turning the area into grazing land for Hereford cattle and opening the exclusive Hotel Hana Maui.

Head down to **Hana Bay**. Here you can stroll the beach, explore the wharf, and take a short path along the water to a plaque that marks the **Birthplace of Kaahumanu**, King Kamehameha I's favorite wife and a key player in the 1819 overthrow of the ancestral Hawaiian religious system. To reach this sacred spot, pick up the trail leading from the boat landing on the right side of the bay. It leads along the base of **Kauiki Hill**, a cinder cone covered with ironwood trees that was the scene of fierce battles between Kahekili, the renowned Maui chief, and the Big Island chief Kalaniopuu.

Near the Hotel Hana Maui (where you can request a key to open the gate), you can drive or hike up a short road to **Mount Lyons** (that camel-humped hill with the cross on top). From this aerie, a memorial to Paul Fagan, there's a fine view of Hana Bay and the surrounding coastline.

Also be sure to take in the **Hana Cultural Center** (248-8622; admission). This enticing little gallery displays such artifacts from Hana's past as primitive stone tools, rare shells, and Hawaiian games. There are antique photographs and elaborately stitched quilts. Also on the grounds, the old **Court House**, built in 1871, is a modest but appealing structure containing three small benches and a desk for the judge.

Wananalua Church (Hauoli Street and Hana Highway), a lovely chapel built from coral blocks during the mid-19th century, has been beautifully refurbished. Located atop an ancient *heiau*, stately and imposing in appearance, it is a perfect expression of the days when Christianity was crushing the old Hawaiian beliefs.

FROM HANA TO ULUPALAKUA   The backroad from Hana around the southwest side of Maui is one of the island's great adventures. It leads along the side of Haleakala past dense rainforest and tumbling waterfalls to an arid expanse covered by lava flows, and then opens onto Maui's vaunted Upcountry region. Since a five-mile stretch is unpaved and other sections are punctuated with potholes, car rental companies generally do not permit driving on parts of this route; so check with them in advance or be prepared to take your chances. Also check on road conditions: The road is sometimes closed during periods of heavy rain.

Past Hana, the road, now designated the Piilani Highway and renumbered as Route 31 (with mileage markers that descend in sequence), worsens as it winds toward an overgrown ravine where **Wailua Falls** (45-mile marker) and another waterfall pour down sharp cliff faces.

At **Oheo Gulch** (42-mile marker), better known as **Seven Sacred Pools**, a series of waterfalls tumbles into two dozen (not seven!) pools before reaching the sea. The pools are rock-bound, some are bordered by cliffs, and several provide excellent swimming holes. This is an eerie and beautiful place from which you can see up and down the rugged coastline.

Another special spot, **Charles Lindbergh's grave** (★) (41-mile marker), rests on a promontory overlooking the ocean. The great aviator spent his last days here and lies buried beside Palapala Hoomau Church. The white-washed chapel and surrounding shade trees create a place of serenity and remarkable beauty. (To find the grave, continue 1.2 miles past Oheo Gulch. Watch for the church through the trees on the left. Turn left onto an unpaved road and drive several hundred yards, paralleling a stone fence. Turn left into the churchyard.)

Not far from here, in **Kipahulu**, the paved road gives way to dirt. It's five miles to the nearest pavement, so your car should have good shock absorbers. The road rises along seaside cliffs, some of which are so steep they jut out to overhang the road. This is wild, uninhabited country, ripe for exploration.

Huialoha Church, built in 1859, rests below the road on a wind-wracked peninsula. The last time I visited this aging worship hall, horses were graz-ing in the churchyard. Nearby you'll encounter the tinroof town of **Kaupo**, with its funky general store. Directly above the town is **Kaupo Gap**, through which billowing clouds pour into Haleakala Crater.

The road bumps inland, then returns seaward to **Nuu Bay's** rocky beach. From here the rustic route climbs into a desolate area scarred by lava and inhabited with scrub vegetation. The sea views are magnificent as the road bisects the **1790 lava flow**. This was the last volcanic eruption on Maui; it left its mark in a torn and terrible landscape that slopes for miles to the sea.

It's several miles farther to **Ulupalakua Ranch**, a lush counterpoint to the lava wasteland behind. With its grassy acres and curving rangeland, it provides a perfect introduction to Maui's Upcountry region.

HANA HIGHWAY HOTELS

Along the Hana Highway out in Paia, about seven miles from Kahului, sits **Nalu Kai Lodge** (579-8009). Tucked behind the Kihata Restaurant near the town hub, this eight-unit resting place is a real sleeper. The last time I was by, only three rooms were available; the others were accommodating permanent residents. If you snag one of the vacant rooms, you'll check into a small, plain cubicle with no carpeting and little decoration. Sound un-appealing? Well, even bare walls sometimes look good at low-budget prices.

A very convenient budget accommodation on the Hana Highway is the **Maui YMCA** (242-9007) in Keanae. For $8 a night, both men and women are welcome to roll out their sleeping bags on bunks in the dormitory. Set in a spacious wooden house overlooking the sea, this crash pad comes complete with a kitchen, hot showers, and a gymnasium. Sorry, maximum stay is five nights.

Aloha Cottages (248-8420), perched on a hillside above Hana Bay, has two-bedroom units at moderate prices. Situated amid papaya and banana trees, these cozy cottages feature hardwood floors and walls fashioned from redwood. The decor is simple, the kitchens are all-electric, and many of the furnishings are rattan. Representing one of Hana's best bargains, the cottages have been recommended many times over the years by readers and friends. There are only five units at this small complex, so advance reservations are a good idea.

You can also consider heading down toward the water to the **Hana Kai Maui Resort** (248-8426). Located smack on a rocky beach, these two twin-story buildings sit amid lush surroundings. The ornamental pool is a freshwater affair fed by toe-dipping spring water. The location and exotic grounds rate a big plus. The bill? A studio apartment or a one-bedroom condominium will price in the deluxe category.

Speaking of scenery, **Heavenly Hana Inn** (248-8442) is blessed indeed. Located about two miles outside Hana, this hostelry is entered through a Japanese gate. On either side, stone lions guard a luxuriant garden. The interior mirrors this elegance. There's an Oriental touch to each two-bedroom apartment—Japanese screens, bamboo towel racks, Asian art objects. The walls are wood-paneled, the lanai's screened, the kitchenette is equipped with the usual accouterments. They also have two cottages available, one near the beach at Hana Bay. Moderate to deluxe.

The finest resting place of all is the **Hotel Hana Maui** (248-8211), a luxurious retreat on a hillside above the bay. From ocean views to tropical landscape to rolling lawn, this friendly inn is a unique, world-class resort. Spread across the grounds are plush rooms, suites, and cottages, all elegantly designed, with prices in the ultra-deluxe range for two people on the American plan. The staff has been here for generations, lending a sense of home to an enchanting locale. Highly recommended.

And don't forget the cabins at **Waianapanapa State Park** (see the "Hana Highway Beaches and Parks" section below).

HANA HIGHWAY RESTAURANTS

Paia, an artsy little town just a few miles out on the Hana Highway, has several restaurants to choose from. If you don't choose any of them, however, be forewarned—there are no pit stops between here and Hana.

Wunderbar (89 Hana Highway, Paia; 579-8808) is an uneasy cross between a European dining room and an American bar and grill. You can order a beer at the bar or select from a German menu that includes wienerschnitzel, beef stroganoff, and Bavarian hunter steak. They also have full, American-style breakfast and lunch menus. Moderate to deluxe.

The Vegan Restaurant (115 Baldwin Avenue, Paia; 579-9144) is the prime address hereabouts for vegetarian food. Place your order at the counter—there are salads, sandwiches, and a few hot entrées. Budget.

Just down the street you'll find **Kihata Restaurant** (115 Hana Highway, Paia; 579-9035). This old-style restaurant, with bamboo partitions and a screen door that slams, is another favorite watering place for Paia residents. There's a glistening formica counter up front, and a cluster of tables in back. Dining in this local hangout is definitely casual. And the menu is ethnic: In addition to sushi bar specialties, it includes Japanese noodle dishes, *tonkatsu* (deep-fried pork), teriyaki, and tempura. But the meals are comfortably priced and the local color is free.

Or, for masterfully prepared food without the sophisticated trappings, try **Mama's Fish House** (on Hana Highway; 579-8488) outside Paia. Unlike most well-heeled restaurants, this oceanfront nook is simply decorated: shell *leis*, an old Hawaiian photo here, a painting there, plus potted plants. Elegant simplicity. During lunch, there's a varied menu that includes California cuisine-style dishes and ever-changing specialties. Other than a few steak dishes, the dinner menu is entirely seafood. The evening entrées include abalone, bouillabaisse, scampi, and fresh Hawaiian lobster. Another of Mama's treats is fresh fish: There are always at least four varieties, prepared ten different ways. Deluxe.

If you plan to stay in Hana for any length of time, pack some groceries in with the raingear. You'll find only three restaurants along the entire eastern stretch of the island. Luckily, they cover the gamut from budget to ultra-deluxe. **Tutu's At Hana Bay** (248-8224), located within whistling distance of the water, whips up sandwiches, hamburgers, and teriyaki chicken for breakfast and lunch. Budget.

Hana Ranch Restaurant (248-8255) is a small, spiffy establishment decorated with blond woods and offering great ocean views. There's a full bar here plus a flagstone lanai for outdoor dining. Open daily for lunch, they serve dinner every Friday and Saturday. Lunch is buffet style; in the evening they offer fresh fish, chops, steak, and baby back ribs; deluxe. There's also a budget-priced **take-out stand** serving breakfast and lunch, with picnic tables overlooking the ocean.

Hana's premier restaurant is the dining room of the **Hotel Hana Maui** (248-8211). This extraordinary resort, perched on a hillside overlooking the ocean, serves gourmet meals to its guests and the public alike. At lunch there's an á la carte menu that includes tiger shrimp, New York steak, and mahimahi. The evening meal is a fixed-price affair with stir-fry shrimp, veal chops, and three special entrées every night. Ultra-deluxe.

HANA HIGHWAY MARKETS

You'd better stock up before coming if you plan to spend very long in this remote region. There are few restaurants and even fewer stores. **Hana Ranch Store** (248-8261) and **Hasegawa General Store** (248-8231), both in Hana, have limited stocks of grocery items.

Over on the Hana Highway in Paia, **Nagata Store** (579-9252) has a small supply of groceries. If you can't find what you need here, check the **Paia General Store** (579-9514) or **H & P Market & Seafood** (579-9640) down the street.

Mana Foods (49 Baldwin Avenue, Paia; 579-8078) has a complete stock of health foods and organic produce.

Clear across the island, along the back road from Hana, there's a sleeper called **Kaupo General Store** (248-8059). You'll find it tucked away in the southeast corner of the island. Whether it'll be open when you get there, or have what you want, isn't something I'd bet on, though.

HANA HIGHWAY SHOPPING

Paia, a rustic falsefront town seven miles outside Kahului, is my favorite place to shop on Maui. Many fine artisans live in the Upcountry area and come down to sell their wares at the small shops lining the Hana Highway. The town itself is a work of art, with old wooden buildings that provide a welcome respite from the crowded shores of Kaanapali and Kihei. I'll mention just the shops I like most. Browse through town to see for yourself. If you discover places I missed, please let me know.

On display at the **Maui Crafts Guild** (43 Hana Highway; 579-9697) are prints by local artists. There are also numerous gift items, including a line of ceramics that ranges from functional to fanciful. You'll also discover craftspeople here working with wood, baskets, and textiles.

Paia Trading Company (106 Hana Highway; 579-9472) has a few interesting antiques and a lot of junk. Among the more noteworthy items: turquoise and silver jewelry, wooden washboards, apothecary jars, and antique glassware.

Eddie Flotte Watercolors (83 Hana Highway, Paia; 579-9641) features original artworks by an original character. Flotte's paintings capture the down-home lifestyles of Upcountry residents.

Summerhouse Boutique (83 Hana Highway; 579-9201) might be called a chic sundries shop. They sell everything from sunglasses, jewelry, postcards, and porcelain dolls to swimwear and natural fiber garments.

Around the corner on Baldwin Avenue lies another shop worth browsing. **The Clothes Addict** (12 Baldwin Avenue; 579-9266) features a fine selection of women's fashions, including designer clothing, manufactured designs, and locally made styles. They also have '30s and '40s *aloha* shirts for men, as well as informal beachwear.

In Hana there are several elegant shops at the Hotel Hana Maui. One of my favorites is **Hana Coast Gallery** (248-8636), which features fine paintings by Maui artists, as well as pieces by novelist Henry Miller.

HANA HIGHWAY NIGHTLIFE

Wunderbar (89 Hana Highway, Paia; 579-8808) usually has deejay music or live bands on Thursday, Friday, and Saturday nights.

Out in Hana you can enjoy a drink in the lounge at the **Hotel Hana Maui** (248-8211) and plan to turn in early.

HANA HIGHWAY BEACHES AND PARKS

H. A. Baldwin Park—This spacious county park, located several miles east of Kahului on the Hana Highway, is bordered by a playing field on one side and a crescent-shaped beach on the other. Palm and ironwood trees dot the half-mile-long beach. There's good shell collecting and a great view of West Maui. This otherwise lovely park has at times been the scene of robberies and violence; if you camp here (which I do not recommend), exercise caution.

Facilities: Picnic area complete with large pavilion, showers, restrooms, and playground. Markets and restaurants are a short distance away in Paia. *Swimming:* Good, but beware of currents. *Snorkeling:* Not recommended. *Surfing:* Winter breaks. Right slide. Good bodysurfing. *Fishing:* Good for threadfin, mountain bass, goatfish, and ulua.

Camping: Tent camping. County permit required.

Getting there: Turn left off Route 360, about seven miles east of Kahului.

Hookipa Beach Park—For surfers, this is one of the best spots on Maui, but for windsurfers, Hookipa is one of the prime places *in the world*. On any day you're liable to see a hundred sails with boards attached skimming the whitecaps. The beach itself is little more than a narrow rectangle of sand paralleled by a rocky shelf. Offshore, however, top-ranked wind-surfers may be performing airborne stunts.

Facilities: Picnic areas, restrooms, showers; restaurants and groceries are three miles away in Paia. *Swimming:* Good only when surf is low.

Getting there: Located on the Hana Highway about three miles east of Paia.

Honomanu Bay (★)—This tranquil black-sand-and-rock beach, sur-rounded by pandanus-covered hills and bisected by a stream, is a very beau-tiful and secluded spot. There are no facilities, and the water is often too rough for swimming, but it's a favorite with surfers.

Getting there: Located off the Hana Highway (Route 360) about 30 miles east of Kahului. Turn off onto the dirt road east of Kaumahina State Wayside; follow it to the beach.

Waianapanapa State Park—Set in a heavenly seaside locale, this is one of Hawaii's prettiest parks. The entire area is lush with tropical foliage, especially palmy pandanus trees. There's a black-sand beach, sea arches, a blowhole, and two legendary caves. But pack your parkas; wind and rain are frequent. The cabins and campsites make this a very popular spot.

Facilities: Picnic area, restrooms, showers, cabins. About four miles to markets and restaurants in Hana. *Swimming:* Good when the water's calm. *Snorkeling:* Good when the water's calm. *Fishing:* Good.

Camping: State permit required. Campsites are on a grass-covered bluff overlooking the sea. The cabins are rented through the Division of State Parks (see "The Sporting Life" section in this chapter). These are plain but attractive accommodations renting on a sliding scale (starting at $10 single and $14 double up to $30 for six people). Each one contains a small bedroom with two bunk beds, plus a living room that can double as an extra bedroom. All cabins are equipped with bedding and complete kitchen facilities, and some have ocean views.

Getting there: Just off the Hana Highway (Route 360) about four miles north of the town of Hana.

Hana Beach Park—Tucked into a well-protected corner of Hana Bay, this park features a large pavilion and a curving stretch of sandy beach.

Facilities: Picnic area, restrooms, showers. Snack bar across the street. *Swimming:* Good. *Snorkeling:* Good near the lighthouse. *Surfing:* Sum-mer and winter breaks on the north side of the bay. Left slide. *Fishing:* There are bonefish, ulua, and papio, plus runs of moilii in June and July.

Getting there: Located on Hana Bay.

Red Sand Beach (★)—Known to the Hawaiians as Kaihalulu ("roar-ing sea") Beach, this is one of the most exotic and truly secluded beaches in all Hawaii. It is protected by lofty cliffs and can be reached only over a precarious trail. A volcanic cinder beach, the sand is reddish in hue and coarse underfoot. Most dramatic of all is the lava barrier that crosses the mouth of this natural amphitheater, protecting the beach and creating an inshore pool.

Facilities: None. *Swimming:* Good. *Snorkeling:* Good. *Fishing:* Good.

Getting there: The beach is located on the far side of Kauiki Hill in Hana. Follow Uakea Road to its southern terminus. There is a grassy plot on the left between Hana School and the parking lot for the Hotel Hana Maui's "sea ranch cottages." Here you will find a trail leading into the undergrowth. It traverses an overgrown Japanese cemetery and curves around Kauiki Hill, then descends precipitously to the beach. Be careful!

Hamoa Beach—A stretch of salt-and-pepper sand with rock outcroppings at each end, this strand is at the head of Mokae Cove. It's a pretty place, but the Hotel Hana Maui uses the beach as a semi-private preserve. There are separate restrooms for guests and non-guests and a dining pavilion available only to guests, so a sense of segregation pervades the beach. Less problematic is **Koki Beach Park**, a sandy plot paralleled by a grassy park. Backdropped by lofty red cinder cliffs, Koki can be very windy and is plagued by currents. With a small island and sea arch offshore, it can also be very pretty.

Facilities: Restrooms and picnic areas; restaurants and groceries are a few miles away in Hana. *Swimming:* Good, but exercise caution. *Surfing:* Good surfing at Hamoa and good bodysurfing at both beaches.

Getting there: Follow the Hana Highway south from Hana for a little over a mile. Turn left on Haneoo Road and follow it a half-mile to Koki or a mile to Hamoa.

Oheo Gulch or **Seven Sacred Pools**—The stream that tumbles down Haleakala through the National Park's Kipahulu section forms several large pools and numerous small ones. The main pools, known to many as the Seven Sacred Pools, descend from above the Hana Highway to the sea. This is a truly enchanting area—swept by frequent wind and rain, and shadowed by Haleakala. It overlooks Maui's rugged eastern shore. You can swim in the pools' chilly waters and camp nearby on a bluff above the sea.

Facilities: There are picnic tables and outhouses.

Camping: Three-day limit for campers; no permit required. Bring your own drinking water.

Getting there: The pools are located on the Hana Highway about ten miles south of Hana.

Upcountry

Maui's Upcountry is a verdant mountainous belt that encircles Haleakala along its middle slopes. Situated between coastline and crater rim, it's a region of ample rainfall and sparse population that is ideal for camping, hiking, or just wandering.

Here the flat fields of sugarcane and pineapples that blanket central Maui give way to open ranchland where curving hills are filled with grazing horses. Farmers plant tomatoes, cabbages, carrots, and the region's famous Maui onions. Proteas, those delicate flowers native to Australia and South Africa, grow in colorful profusion. Hibiscus, jacandras, and other wildflowers sweep along the hillsides like a rain storm. And on the region's two ranches—20,000-acre Haleakala Ranch and 30,000-acre Ulupalakua Ranch—Angus and Hereford cattle complete a picture far removed from Hawaii's tropical beaches.

Home to *paniolos*, Hawaii's version of the American cowboy, the Upcountry region lies along the highways that lead to the crest of Haleakala crater. Route 37, Haleakala Highway, becomes the Kula Highway as it ascends to the Kula uplands where the **Church of the Holy Ghost** (12-mile marker), a unique octagonal chapel, was built in 1897.

This roadway angles southwest through Ulupalakua Ranch to the ruins of the **Makee Sugar Mill**, a once flourishing enterprise built in 1878. A currently flourishing business, **Tedeschi Winery** (878-6058), sits just across the road. Producing a pineapple wine called Maui Blanc, the winery rests in an old jailhouse built of lava and coral in 1857. Here at Hawaii's only winery you can stop for a taster's tour.

You can also turn up Route 377 to **Kula Botanical Gardens** (878-1715; admission). An excellent place for picnicking, the landscaped slopes contain an aviary, pond, "Taboo Garden" with poisonous plants, and 40 varieties of protea, the flowering shrub that grows so beautifully in this region. Several farms, including **Sunrise Protea Farm** (Haleakala Crater Road; 878-2119), devoted primarily to proteas, are located nearby.

Another intriguing place is the tiny town of **Makawao**, where battered buildings and falsefront stores create an Old West atmosphere. This is the capital of Maui's cowboy country, similar to Waimea on the Big Island, with a rodeo every Fourth of July.

From Makawao the possibilities for exploring the Upcountry area are many. There are two **loop tours** (★) I particularly recommend. The first climbs from town along Olinda Road (Route 390) past **Pookela Church**, a coral sanctuary built in the 1850s. It continues through a frequently rain-drenched region to the **Tree Growth Research Area**, jointly sponsored by state and federal forestry services. You can circle back down toward Makawao on Piiholo Road past **Olinda Vista Nursery** (878-3251) and the **University**

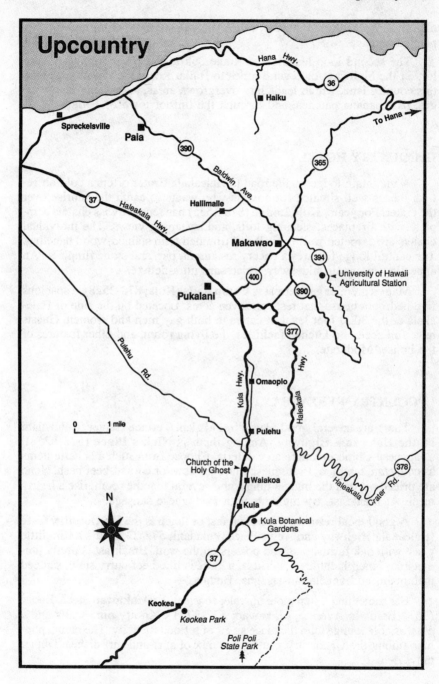

of Hawaii Agricultural Station, where you will see more of the area's richly planted acreage.

The second loop leads down Route 365 to the Hana Highway. Turn left on the highway for several miles to Haiku Road, then head left along this country lane, which leads into overgrown areas, across one-lane bridges, past banana patches, and through the tinroof town of **Haiku.**

UPCOUNTRY HOTELS

A mountain lodge on the road to Haleakala Crater offers a cold-air retreat that is well-situated for anyone who wants to catch the sunrise over the crater. For years, **Kula Lodge** (878-1535) has rented Swiss chalets complete with fireplaces, sleeping lofts, and sweeping views. The individual chalets are carpeted wall-to-wall and trimmed with stained-wood paneling. The central lodge features a cheery restaurant, bar, and stone fireplace. An appealing mountain hideaway; prices are ultra-deluxe.

Maui's premier gay retreat is **Camp Kula** (Kula; 878-2528), a spacious five-bedroom house that rests on seven acres. Located on the side of Haleakala at the 3000-foot level, it caters to both gay men and women. Guests have full access to kitchen facilities, the living room, and other features of the house. Moderate.

UPCOUNTRY RESTAURANTS

There are several good places in Pukalani Terrace Center in Pukalani on the Haleakala Highway. Among them is **Nick's Place** (572-8258), a Japanese-Chinese-American cafeteria. Choose from such à la carte items as *chow fun*, tempura, Portuguese sausage, stew, or corned-beef hash. None are priced beyond the budget range, and several together comprise a hearty meal. At breakfast, try the eggs with Portuguese sausage.

A good local restaurant for breakfast or lunch is the **Up Country Café** (Haleakala Highway and Aewa Place, Pukalani; 572-2395) It's a trim little place with oak furnishings and posters on the wall. Breakfast is pretty predictable; lunch includes a half-dozen entrées like beef curry stew, sautéed mahimahi, and vegetarian lasagna. Budget.

For something a step more upscale, consider the **Makawao Steak House** (3612 Baldwin Avenue, Makawao; 572-8711). Knotty pine walls and a comfortable lounge lend the place an air of refined rusticity. The menu, popular among the Upcountry gentry, is a mix of surf-and-turf dishes. Dinner only; deluxe.

In Makawao, you can go Mediterranean at **Casanova Italian Restaurant & Deli** (1188 Makawao Avenue; 572-0220), a stylish bistro that serves Italian-style seafood and pasta dishes at deluxe and moderate prices, respectively. For something faster, cheaper, and more casual, you can try the adjacent deli.

Or head across the street to **Polli's Mexican Restaurant** (1202 Makawao Avenue, Makawao; 572-7808). This sombreros-on-the-wall-and-oilcloth-on-the-tables eatery offers a full selection of Mexican dishes at moderate prices. A local gathering place popular with residents throughout Maui's Upcountry region, Polli's has become an institution over the years. It will inevitably be crowded with natives and tourists alike, all dining on tacos, burritos, tamales, and tostadas.

Upcountry's contribution to the culinary revolution that has been sweeping Hawaii the past few years is **Haliimaile General Store** (900 Haliimaile Road, Haliimaile; 572-2666). A former plantation store that has been converted into a chic gathering place, it puts a creative spin on American cuisine and serves roast duckling, fresh island fish, and beef from the Big Island at deluxe prices.

UPCOUNTRY MARKETS

Along the Haleakala Highway (Route 37) there's a **Foodland** (572-0674) in the Pukalani Terrace Center, open 24 hours.

You can also count on **Down To Earth Natural Foods** (1161 Makawao Avenue, Makawao; 572-1488) for a selection of health foods and New Age supplies.

UPCOUNTRY SHOPPING

Baldwin Avenue in Makawao has developed over the years into a prime arts-and-crafts center. Housed in the falsefront stores that line the street you'll find galleries galore and a few boutiques besides.

The Courtyard (3620 Baldwin Avenue), an attractive woodframe mall, contains **Hot Island Glass** (572-4527), with a museum-quality collection of handblown glass pieces. Also here is **Viewpoints Gallery** (572-0781), which puts many of the higher-priced Lahaina galleries to shame.

The kids will love **Maui Child Toys & Books** (3643 Baldwin Avenue, Makawao; 572-2765), and women will find fashions by Upcountry designers at **Goodie's** (3633 Baldwin Avenue, Makawao; 572-0288). **Gecko Trading Company** (3621 Baldwin Avenue; 572-0249) is a small shop that also features contemporary fashions at reasonable prices. Both are enchanting spots in a town well worth exploring.

On the outskirts of Makawao, the 1917 Mediterranean-style Baldwin mansion is home to the **Hui Noeau Visual Arts Center** (2841 Baldwin Avenue; 572-6560). Here you can purchase works by Maui artists or take the plunge yourself at one of the regular workshops on painting, printmaking, pottery, and sculpture.

UPCOUNTRY NIGHTLIFE

There are live bands on the weekends and disco music several weeknights at **Casanova Italian Restaurant** (1188 Makawao Avenue, Makawao; 572-0220). One of Upcountry's few nightspots, it features dancing and good times. Cover.

UPCOUNTRY PARKS

Poli Poli State Park—Located at the 6200-foot elevation on the slopes of Haleakala, this densely forested park is an ideal mountain retreat. Monterey and sugi pine, eucalyptus and Monterey cypress grow in stately profusion; not far from the campground there's a grove of redwoods. From Poli Poli's ethereal heights you can look out over Central and West Maui, as well as the islands of Lanai, Molokai, and Kahoolawe. Miles of trails, some leading up to Haleakala Crater, crisscross the park.

Facilities: Picnic area, restrooms, running water, cabin.

Camping: State permit required. The cabin houses up to ten people and rents on a sliding scale from $10 single and $14 double up to $50 for ten people. The spacious cabin (three bedrooms) is sparsely furnished and lacks electricity. It does have a wood heating stove, gas cooking stove, gas lanterns, kitchen utensils, and bedding. It can be rented from the Division of State Parks (see "The Sporting Life" section at the end of this chapter for the address).

Getting there: From Kahului, take Haleakala Highway (Route 37) through Pukalani and past Waiakoa to Route 377. Turn left on 377 and follow it a short distance to the road marked for Poli Poli. This ten-mile road to the park is paved about halfway up. The second half of the track is extremely rough and often muddy. It is advisable to take a four-wheel-drive vehicle, especially if more than two people are in the car.

Keokea Park—A pleasant picnic spot on Route 37 in Keokea. There's a rolling lawn with picnic tables and restrooms.

Haleakala National Park

It seems only fitting that the approach to Haleakala Crater is along one of the world's fastest-climbing roads. From Kahului to the crater rim—a distance of 40 miles along Routes 37, 377, and 378—the macadam road rises from sea level to over 10,000 feet, and the silence is broken only by the sound of ears popping from the ascent.

At the crater lip, 10,023-feet in elevation, you look out over an awesome expanse—seven miles long, over two miles wide, 21 miles around. This dormant volcano, which last erupted in 1790, is the central feature of a 27,284-acre national park that extends all the way through the Kipahulu Valley to the sea. The crater floor, 3000 feet below the rim, is a multihued wasteland filled with cinder cones, lava flows, and mini-craters. It's a legendary place, with a mythic tradition that's as vital as its geologic history. It was from Haleakala ("House of the Sun") that the demigod Maui lassoed the sun and slowed its track across the sky to give his mother more daylight to dry her *tapa* cloth.

In the afternoon, the volcano's colors are most vivid, but during the morning the crater is more likely to be free of clouds. Before going up Haleakala, call 572-7749 or 871-5054 for a weather report. Then you can decide what time of day will be best for your explorations. Many people arrive at dawn to see the sun rise over the edge of the crater, one of the greatest experiences in all Hawaii. Remember that it takes an hour-and-a half to two hours to reach the summit from Kahului, longer from the Kaanapali-Kapalua area. Be sure to bring warm clothes since the temperature drop from sea level to 10,000 feet can be 30° or more.

On the way up you'll pass **Hosmer Grove**, a picnic area and campground surrounded by eucalyptus, spruce, juniper, and cedar trees.

National Park Headquarters, located at 7030-feet elevation, contains an information desk and maps, and makes a good starting point. Be sure to see the *nene*, a rare species of Hawaiian goose, located in a pen adjacent to the center.

The first crater view comes at **Leleiwi Overlook**, an 8800-foot perch from which you'll be able to see all the way from Hana across the island to Kihei. Here at sunset, under correct meteorological conditions, you can see your shadow projected on the clouds and haloed by a rainbow. To experience this "Specter of the Brocken," stand atop the crater rim looking toward the cloud-filled crater with the setting sun at your back.

Up the hill, a side road leads to **Kalahaku Overlook**, a 9325-foot aerie that offers a unique view of several cinder cones within the crater. Just below the parking lot are numerous **silverswords**. Related to sunflowers, these spike-leaved plants grow only on Maui and the Big Island. They re-

(Text continued on page 288.)

In the Belly of the Volcano

While the views along the crater rim are awesome, the best way to see Haleakala is from the inside looking out. With 32 miles of hiking trails, two campsites, and three cabins, the crater provides a tremendous opportunity for explorers. Within the belly of this monstrous volcano, you'll see such geologic features as cinder cones, lava tubes, and spatter vents. The Hawaiians marked their passing with stone altars, shelters, and adze quarries. You may also spy the rare *nene* (a Hawaiian relative of the Canada goose), as well as chukar partridges, pheasants, mynahs, and white-tailed tropicbirds.

The crater floor is a unique environment, one of constant change and unpredictable weather. Rainfall varies from 12 inches annually in the southwestern corner to 200 inches at Paliku. Temperatures, usually hovering between 55° and 75° during daylight, may fall below freezing at night. Campers should come prepared with warm clothing and sleeping gear, a tent, poncho, lantern, and stove (no open fires are permitted). Don't forget the sunburn lotion, as the elevation on the crater bottom averages 6700 feet and the ultraviolet radiation is intense.

Within the crater you can explore three main trails. **Sliding Sands Trail**, a steep cinder and ash path, begins near the Haleakala Visitor Center. It descends from the crater rim along the south wall to Kapalaoa cabin, then on to Paliku cabin. In the course of this ten-mile trek, the trail drops over 3000 feet. From Paliku, the **Kaupo Trail** leaves the crater through Kaupo Gap and descends to the tiny town of Kaupo, eight miles away on Maui's southeast coast. **Halemauu Trail** (10 miles) begins from the road three-and-a-half miles beyond National Park Headquarters and descends 1400 feet to the crater floor. It passes Holua cabin and eventually joins Sliding Sands Trail near the Paliku cabin.

There are campgrounds at **Holua** and **Paliku** that require a permit from National Park Headquarters. Permits are given out on a first-come, first-served basis (not available in advance), so plan accordingly. The campgrounds have pit toilets and running water. Camping is limited to two days at one site and three days total at both. There is also a 12-person cabin at each campsite and at **Kapalaoa**. Equipped with wood stoves, pit toilets, cooking utensils, and mattresses, these primitive facilities are extremely popular. So popular, in fact, that guests are chosen by lottery three months in advance. For more information, write Haleakala National Park, P.O. Box 369, Makawao, Maui, HI 96768, or call 572-9306.

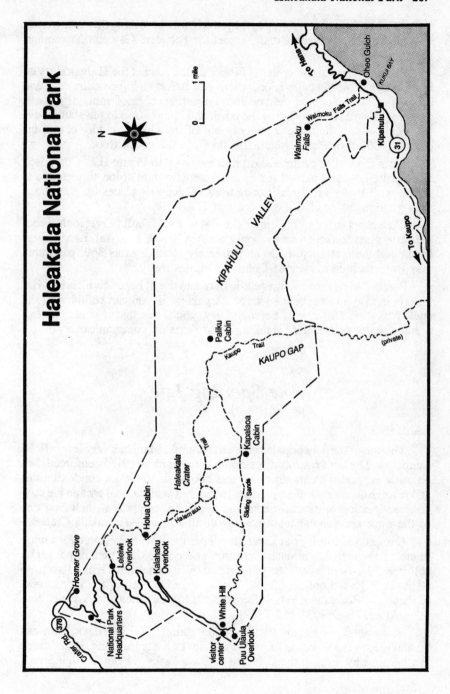

main low bristling plants for up to 20 years before blooming into a flowering stalk. Each plant blossoms once, sometime between May and November, and then dies.

The best view of the crater is farther up the road at the **Haleakala Visitor Center**, 9745-feet elevation, where you'll find an information desk and a series of exhibits about the volcano. From this coign of vantage you can gaze out toward Koolau Gap to the north and Kaupo Gap to the south. Several peaks along the crater rim loom out of the clouds; cinder cones, including 1000-foot Puu o Maui, rise up from the crater floor.

From the visitor center a short trail heads up to **White Hill**. Composed of andesite lava and named for its characteristic light color, this mound is dotted with stone windbreaks once used as sleeping places by Hawaiians who periodically visited the summit of Haleakala.

It's a short drive to the crater summit at **Puu Ulaula Overlook**. From the plate-glass lookout you can view the Big Island, Molokai, Lanai, West Maui, and the crater itself. On an extremely clear day this 360° panorama may even include a view of Oahu, 130 miles away.

Perched high above atmospheric haze and the lights of civilization, Haleakala is also an excellent spot for stargazing. If you can continue to the end of Skyline Drive, past **Science City**, you'll see that it is also an important center for satellite tracking and television communications.

The Sporting Life

CAMPING

Though extremely popular with adventurers, Maui has very few official campsites. The laws restricting camping here are more strictly enforced than on other islands. The emphasis on this boom island favors condominiums and resort hotels rather than outdoor living, but you can still escape the concrete congestion at several parks and unofficial campsites (including one of the most spectacular tenting areas in all Hawaii—Haleakala Crater).

Camping at **county parks** requires a permit. These are issued for a maximum of three nights at each campsite, and cost $3 per person per night, children 50¢. Permits can be obtained at War Memorial Gym adjacent to Baldwin High School, Route 32, Wailuku, or by writing the Department of Parks and Recreation, Permit Department, 1580 Kaahumanu Avenue, Wailuku, Maui, HI 96793 (243-7389).

State park permits are free and allow camping for five days. They can be obtained at the Division of State Parks in the State Building, High Street, Wailuku, or by writing the Division of State Parks, 54 South High Street,

Wailuku, Maui, HI 96793 (243-5354). You can also rent cabins at Waianapanapa and Poli Poli state parks through this office.

If you plan on camping in Haleakala Crater, you must obtain a permit on the day you are camping. You can do so at Haleakala National Park headquarters, located on the way to the crater. These permits are allocated on a first-come, first-served basis.

Remember, rainfall is heavy along the northeast shore around Hana, but infrequent on the south coast. Also, Haleakala crater gets quite cold; you'll need heavy clothing and sleeping gear.

For camping equipment, check **Maui Expeditions** (87 South Puunene Avenue, Kahului; 871-8787), which sells and rents supplies. **Maui Sporting Goods** (92 North Main Street, Wailuku; 224-0011) has a large selection of gear for sale while **Gaspro Inc.** (365 Hanakai Street, Kahului; 877-0056) sells a limited amount of camping equipment.

SKINDIVING

Maui offers a wide variety of snorkeling and diving opportunities ranging from Black Rock off Kaanapali to Honolua Bay. While most of the dive operators are located near the island's south coast resorts, there are also good diving and snorkeling opportunities on the north shore at Paia's Baldwin Beach Park, as well as Hana's Waianapanapa State Park. From Maui it's also easy to reach neighboring destinations such as the Molokini Crater Marine Preserve and reefs off Lanai.

Extended Horizons (Mala Wharf, Lahaina; 667-0611) offers trips to Lanai for divers of varying abilities, as well as a variety of snorkeling trips. **Destination Pacific** (1223 Front Street, Lahaina; 667-4348) offers marine biologist-led dives to gems like the cathedrals of Lanai. Introductory courses, including free pool clinics, make it easy to learn how to explore the deep. **Ocean Riders Adventure Rafting** (Mala Wharf, Lahaina; 661-3586) specializes in all-day snorkeling trips to Lanai and, if weather permits, Molokai. **Lahaina Divers Inc.** (710 Front Street, Lahaina; 661-4505) is another popular dive operator.

Underwater Habitat (36 Keala Place, Kihei; 879-3483) runs scuba and snorkeling trips off Wailea Point, Holoa Point, and Molokini Crater. Certification classes and night dives are available. **Molokini Divers** (Kihei Boat Harbor, Kihei; 879-0055) features scuba and snorkeling trips to this popular islet. Visibility of 150 feet makes this marine preserve a great place to splash down. Another popular tour operator that also rents equipment is **Maui Dive Shop** (Azeka Place Shopping Center, South Kihei Road, Kihei, 879-3388; and Kihei Town Center, South Kihei Road, Kihei, 879-1919).

Popular with underwater photographers, **Mike Severns Diving** (Kihei Boat Ramp, Kihei; 879-6596) runs trips for certified divers to Molokini,

Makena, and Kahoolawe. His dives focus on the southwest rift of Haleakala, a fascinating place to study marine life. Led by informative biologists, these trips are an excellent way to see Hawaii's hidden marine life.

SURFING AND WINDSURFING

If you must go down to the sea again, why not do it on a board. You'll find the best waves and winds on Maui's north and northwest shores. Popular spots include Hookipa Beach near Paia and Kanaha Beach Park in the Kahului area, as well as Napili Bay on the south coast. You can also take beginner lessons in the Lahaina area.

A good place to start is **Maui Surfing School** (adjacent to Lahaina Harbor; 875-0625). Instructor Andrea Thomas offers small classes and free board rental, and guarantees you'll be able to surf after one lesson.

Thanks to a convenient radio communication system, **Maui Windsurfing Company** (520 Keolani Place, Kahului; 877-4816) instructors remain in constant contact with their students. Lessons are at Kanaha Beach Park, which has a protected area ideal for beginners. Safe, onshore winds blow you back toward the beach. Rentals are also available.

Kaanapali Windsurfing School (Whalers Village, Kaanapali; 667-1964) offers surfing and windsurfing lessons on the adjacent beach. Ninety-minute windsurfing lessons come with a guarantee of success. Four-person surfing classes are also offered, weather permitting. Rentals are available.

At **Maui Sailing Center** (101 North Kihei Road, Kihei; 879-5935) you can learn to windsurf off Maalaea Bay's Sugar Beach. Begin your lesson on a simulator and then master this fine art in the water accompanied by your instructor. Surfboard rentals are available, as well.

You can also rent or buy equipment at **Lightning Bolt** (55 Kaahumanu Avenue, Kahului; 877-3484).

FISHING

The deep blue sea around Maui can be nirvana for sportfishing. Choose between party boats, diesel cruisers, and yachts custom-designed for trolling. All provide equipment and bait. Just bring your own food and drinks and you're in business. If it's not too rough, your skipper may head for the productive game fishing waters between Maui and the Big Island. If conditions are choppy, you're more likely to fish the leeward side of the island or off neighboring Lanai.

Ideal for groups up to four, **Robalo One** (Lahaina Harbor; 661-0480) is a stable 23-foot vessel that hits speeds up to 40 miles per hour in pursuit of game fish. You'll catch snapper, wrasse, barracuda, or jack crevalle on half-day trips.

Lucky Strike Charters (Lahaina; 661-4606) uses live opelu bait to help you catch larger barracuda, shark, ulua, amberjack, ono, and mahimahi swimming 150 feet below the surface. Combination trolling and bottom fishing is available.

Islander II (Lahaina Harbor; 667-6625) and **Hinatea** (Lahaina Harbor; 667-7548) are matching sportfishing boats offering identical trips into coastal waters. On half- and full-day trips you'll fish for marlin, tuna, mahimahi, wahoo, and shark.

In the Kihei area, contact **Carol Ann Charters** (Maalea Harbor; 877-2181) for half- and full-day fishing trips great for catching marlin, tuna, mahimahi, and ono. Choose between light or heavy tackle with **Rascal Charters** (Maalaea Harbor; 874-8633) when you fish for ahi, ono, and marlin. Half- and full-day trips aboard a 31-foot vessel include game and bottom fishing.

SAILING

Eager to protect the whales who winter in these waters, local officials have forced power craft to keep their distance from these cetaceans. But these restrictions do not apply to the many sailing vessels that offer whale-watching opportunities off the Maui coast. You can also enjoy dive trips or pure performance rides on these beautiful vessels.

Sentinel Yacht Charters (Lahaina Harbor; 661-8110) specializes in six-person whale-watching trips aboard a 41-foot sloop, as well as snorkeling excursions. Special trips include Molokai and Lanai. **Scotch Mist Sailing Charters** (Lahaina Harbor; 661-0386) offers half-day snorkeling trips to Lanai, as well as trips to the coral gardens of west Maui. Whale-watching, champagne sunset sails, and moonlight sails are also available. **First Class** (Lahaina Harbor; 667-7733) runs both snorkeling and performance sailing trips.

PARASAILING

Lahaina and Kaanapali Beach are ideal places to become airborne. Wonderful views of Maui's west side and neighboring Molokai add to the fun. The typical trip includes 30 to 45 minutes shuttling out and back to the launch point and eight to ten minutes in the air. **Parasail Kaanapali** (Mala Wharf, Lahaina; 669-6555) riders rise as high as 750 to 850 feet. **West Maui Parasail** (Lahaina Harbor; 661-4060) offers similar trips. **UFO Parasailing** (Whalers Village, Kaanapali; 661-7836) lets you ascend up to 600 feet and, if you wish, fly with a companion.

KAYAKING

A sport that's growing in popularity, kayaking is an ideal way to explore the shore. A good place to learn this adventure sport is **Ocean Kayaking**

(158 Nanakila Place, Kihei; 874-6330). Guided tours include the Makena-La Perouse area on Maui's south shore, a north shore tour exploring the Honolua Bay/Honokohau area, and a sunset excursion along Papawai Point. Along the way you might spot dolphins, flying fish, or whales. In the Kihei area, **Maui Kayaks** (50-J Waiohuli Street, Kihei; 874-3536) offers half- and full-day tours that include snorkeling and whale-watching. Kayaks are also available from **Kaanapali Windsurfing School** (Whalers Village, Kaanapali; 667-1964).

RAFTING

Rafting trips are an ideal way to enjoy the Maui coast. Easily combined with dive and whale-watching trips, these sturdy craft are a great way to reach hidden coves and beaches.

Sea Sails Ocean Rafting (727 Wainee Street, Lahaina; 667-7798) features rafting trips that circumnavigate Lanai. Snorkeling and diving are also offered. **Hawaiian Rafting Adventures** (1223 Front Street, Lahaina; 661-7333) operates half- and full-day trips to Lanai. Whale-watching trips are great fun in the winter months. **Ocean Riders Adventure Rafting** (Mala Wharf, Lahaina; 661-3586) will take you out to Lanai and, weather permitting, Molokai, for a glorious day of snorkeling. All trips are aboard rigid-hull inflatable boats. **Blue Water Rafting** (Kihei Boat Ramp, Kihei; 879-7238) offers both rafting and snorkeling trips to Molokini.

WATERSKIING

If you've always wanted to learn how to waterski, consider **Kaanapali Water Skiing** (164 Wahikuli Road, Lahaina; 661-3324). Equipment rentals are available.

HORSEBACK RIDING

Maui's beautiful volcanic landscape, beaches, and sculptured valleys are ideal for equestrians. A variety of beautiful rides are available across the island. From the shoreline of Hana to the slopes of Haleakala, you can count on seeing wildlife, lava fields, and great sunsets.

Makena Stables (Old Makena Road, Makena; 879-0244) leads trail rides across the scenic 30,000-acre Ulupalakua Ranch on the south slope of Haleakala. As you cross this rugged ranchland you may spot axis deer, Hawaiian owls, and pheasants. Mountain trails cross a 200-year-old lava flow.

At **Thompson Ranch and Riding Stables** (Thompson Road, Kula; 878-1910) visitors ride through pastureland on short day and sunset rides that offer views of the other islands. The full-day Haleakala ride enters the crater at 10,000 feet.

Whale-Watching

Every year the humpback whales return to the Lahaina Roads after summering in the Bering Sea. Measuring 45 feet and weighing over 40 tons, these rare giants make the migration south in order to breed in Maui's warm waters.

Any time from November until May you can see them swimming in the tropic seas between Maui, Molokai, Lanai, and Kahoolawe. The best months for whale-watching are January to April; the most favorable times are from 8 until 11 a.m. and 1:30 to 5 p.m. Rough, windy days are best for watching them at their acrobatics—breaching, tail-slapping, etc.

About 400 to 500 of the world's 7000 humpbacks make the annual migration to Lahaina. Today they are an endangered species, protected by federal law from whalers. Several local organizations study these leviathans and serve as excellent information sources. The **Pacific Whale Foundation** can be contacted at 879-8861 (or call their whale hotline at 800-942-5311); **Maui Whale Watchers** and the local chapter of the **American Cetacean Society** have no central numbers but post public notices of their meetings. The Pacific Whale Foundation issues daily reports over local radio stations.

A prime area for whale-watching lies along Honoapiilani Highway between Maalaea Bay and Lahaina, particularly at McGregor Point. **Island Marine Activities** (661-8397) and the Pacific Whale Foundation offer whale-spotting cruises.

So while you're visiting Maui always keep an eye peeled seaward for vaporous spume and a rolling hump. The place you're standing might suddenly become an ideal crow's nest.

Hit the trail on Maui's north shore with **Adventures on Horseback** (Makawao; 242-7445) and you'll ride along 300-foot cliffs, see beautiful rainforests, and take a break to swim in waterfall-fed pools.

Oheo Stables (Hana Highway, one mile south of Oheo Gulch; 667-2222) offers two-and-a-half hour excursions within Haleakala National Park. Trips ascend through a tropical rainforest and include views of waterfalls and the Kipahulu Valley. Highlights include the view from Pipiwai lookout above Oheo Gulch.

For tours of Haleakala National Park, contact **Pony Express Tours** (667-2202), which leads half- and full-day horseback trips through the crater. **Charlie's Trail Rides and Pack Trips** (248-8209) leads overnight horseback trips from Kaupo through the crater.

GOLF

With more than a dozen public and private courses, Maui features excellent golfing opportunities. Choices range from championship links to inexpensive community courses. A number of resorts offer a choice of courses ideal for golfers looking for change of pace.

Waiehu Memorial Golf Course (Waiehu Beach Road, Waiehu; 243-7400) is the island's lone public course. In addition to an 18-hole course, there's a driving range and practice green.

Sandalwood (2500 Honoapiilani Highway, Waikapu; 242-7090) is one of Maui's newest courses. Somewhat hilly, this par 72-course was designed by Nelson Wright. Four holes have lakes or ponds. There's a full-service restaurant and pro shop on the premises, as well as a practice range and four putting greens.

Designed by Robert Trent Jones Sr., the **Royal Kaanapali Golf Courses** (Kaanapali Beach Resort, Kaanapali; 661-3691) are among the island's finest. The championship par-71 North Course has a slight incline. The easier South Course is intersected by Maui's popular sugarcane train.

With three courses, the **Kapalua Golf Club** (300 Kapalua Drive, Kapalua; 669-8044) is one of the best places to golf on Maui. For a real challenge, try the par-73 Plantation Course, built in the heart of pineapple country. The oceanfront Bay Course was created by Arnold Palmer himself. The Village Course ascends into the foothills.

The **Wailea Golf Club** (879-2966), in the heart of the Wailea Resort complex, features two championship courses.

Next to the Maui Prince Resort, **Makena Golf Course** (5415 Makena-Alanui Road, Wailea; 879-3344) is a fool's paradise with 64 traps waiting to trip you up. Rolling terrain and beautiful views of the neighbor islands make these links a treat.

TENNIS

Public tennis courts are easily found throughout the island. Almost all are lighted and convenient to major resort destinations. In Wailuku, try **Wailuku War Memorial** (1580 Kaahumanu Avenue), or the public courts at Wells and Market streets or on Onehee Street.

In the Lahaina area, you'll enjoy the courts at the **Lahaina Civic Center** (1840 Honoapiilani Highway) or at **Malu-ulu-olele Park** (Front and Shaw streets).

Kihei public courts are found at **Kalanu Park** (Kihei Road) and **Maui Sunset Condominiums** (Waipulani Road).

For general information, call the County Department of Parks and Recreation at 243-7389 or the Hawaii Visitor's Bureau at 871-8691.

BICYCLING

If you've ever wanted to zip down a mountainside or go off-road in volcanic highlands, you've come to the right place. While Maui is best known for its downhill cycling trips, there are also many other challenging adventures. For example, you can enjoy the remote route from Hana to Ulupalakua or head from Kapalua to Wailuku via Kahakuloa.

Chris' Bike Adventures (Kula; 877-8000) runs such intriguing trips as the Haleakala Wine Trek, a tour of the mountain's remote backside, and a trip along the island's hidden northwest coast, complete with off-road biking. Half- and full-day trips include lunch.

At **Maui Downhill** (199 Dairy Road, Kahului; 871-2155) you'll enjoy sunrise trips, morning runs, and day tours on Haleakala. The sunrise run is a beautiful 38-mile trip from the crater to sea-level. Other, less strenuous trails also offer great views of the mountain, ranchlands, and verdant forests. Similar trips are offered by **Cruiser Bob's Haleakala Downhill** (99 Hana Highway, Paia; 667-7717). Equipment includes full-face helmets, windbreaker pants, and custom megabrakes.

Fun Rentals (193 Lahaianaluna Road, Lahaina; 661-3053) rents mountain bikes and ten-speed cruisers. The **Bike Shop** has a store in Kahului (111 Hana Highway; 877-5848) that sells bikes and accessories, and does repair work.

HIKING

Many people complain that Maui is overdeveloped. The wall-to-wall condominiums lining the Kaanapali and Kihei beachfront can be pretty depressing to the outdoors lover. But happily there is a way to escape. Hike right out of it.

The Valley Isle has many fine trails that lead through Hana's rainforest, Haleakala's magnificent crater, up to West Maui's peaks, and across the south shore's arid lava flows. Any of them will carry you far from the madding crowd. It's quite simple on Maui to trade the tourist enclaves for virgin mountains, untrammeled beaches, and eerie volcanic terrain.

If you're unfamiliar with the island, or uncomfortable about exploring solo, you might consider an organized tour. The National Park Service (Haleakala National Park, Box 369, Makawao, Maui, HI 96768; 572-9306) provides information to hikers interested in exploring Haleakala or other sections of the island. If you'd rather head off alone, check the trail descriptions below for a basic guide to most of Maui's major trails.

KAHULUI-WAILUKU AREA TRAILS   The main trails in this Central Maui region lie in Iao Valley, Kahului, and along Kakekili Highway (Route 340).

Two trails begin near the parking lot at Iao Valley State Park. **Tableland Trail** (2 miles long) climbs about 500 feet from the park lookout shelter to the tableland above Iao Valley. A detour along a short loop trail provides spectacular views of Iao Valley and Wailuku.

Iao Stream Trail (1 mile) leads from the park parking lot for half a mile along the stream. The second half of the trek involves wading through the stream or hopping across the shoreline rocks. But your efforts will be rewarded with some excellent swimming holes en route. You might want to plan your time so you can relax and swim.

Not far from the Kahului Airport on Route 380, bird watchers will be delighted to find a trail meandering through the **Kanaha Pond Wildlife Sanctuary**. This jaunt follows two loop roads, each one mile long, and passes the natural habitat of the rare Hawaiian stilt and the Hawaiian coot. Permits are necessary from the State Division of Forestry (243-5352).

Northwest of Kahului, along the Kahekili Highway, are two trails well worth exploring, the Waihee Ridge and Kahakuloa Valley trails.

Waihee Ridge Trail (2.5 miles) begins just below Maluhia Boy Scout Camp outside the town of Waihee. The trail passes through a guava thicket and scrub forest and climbs 1500 feet en route to a peak overlooking West and Central Maui.

Kahakuloa Valley Trail (2 miles) requires driving over the rugged, dirt-road section of Kahekili Highway to the picturesque town of Kahakuloa. This is one of the most beautiful, untouched spots on Maui. The trail begins across the road from a schoolhouse and passes burial caves, stands of guava and passion fruit, and old agricultural terraces.

KIHEI-WAILEA AREA TRAILS   **King's Highway Coastal Trail** (5.5 miles) follows an ancient Hawaiian route over the 1790 lava flow. The trail begins near La Perouse Bay at the end of the rugged road that connects La Perouse Bay with Makena Beach and Wailea. It heads inland through groves of *kiawe* trees, then skirts the coast and finally leads to Kanaloa Point. From this point the trail continues across private land.

HANA AREA TRAILS **Hana-Waianapanapa Coastal Trail** (3 miles), part of the ancient King's Highway, skirts the coastline between Waianapanapa State Park and Hana Bay. The trail passes a *heiau*, sea arch, blowhole, and numerous caves while winding through lush stands of *hala* trees.

Waimoku Falls Trail (Seven Pools Walk) (2 miles) leads from the bridge at Oheo Gulch up to Waimoku Falls. On the way, it goes by four pools and traverses a bamboo forest. Mosquito repellant advised.

UPCOUNTRY TRAILS The main trails in Maui's beautiful Upcountry lie on Haleakala's southern slopes. They branch out from Poli Poli State Park through the Kula and Kahikinui Forest Reserves.

Redwood Trail (1.7 miles) descends from Poli Poli's 6200-foot elevation through impressive stands of redwoods to the ranger's cabin at 5300 feet. There is a dilapidated public shelter in the old CCC camp at trail's end. A four-wheel drive is required to reach the trailhead.

Plum Trail (2.3 miles) begins at the CCC camp and climbs gently south to Haleakala Ridge Trail. The route passes plum trees as well as stands of ash, redwood, and sugi pine. There are shelters at both ends of the trail.

Tie Trail (0.5 mile) descends 500 feet through cedar, ash, and sugi pine groves to link Redwood and Plum Trails. There is a shelter at the Redwood junction.

Poli Poli Trail (0.6 mile) cuts through cypress, cedars, and pines en route from Poli Poli Campground to Haleakala Ridge Trail.

Boundary Trail (4.4 miles) begins at the cattle guard marking the Kula Forest Reserve boundary along the road to Poli Poli. It crosses numerous gulches planted in cedar, eucalyptus, and pine. The trail terminates at the ranger's cabin.

Waiohuli Trail (1.4 miles) descends 800 feet from Poli Poli Road to join Boundary Trail. Along the way it passes young pine and grasslands, then drops down through groves of cedar, redwood, and ash. There is a shelter at the Boundary Trail junction.

Skyline Trail (6.5 miles) begins at 9750 feet, near the top of Haleakala's southwest rift, and descends more than 3000 feet to the top of Haleakala Ridge Trail. The trail passes a rugged, treeless area resembling the moon's surface. Then it drops below timberline at 8600 feet and eventually into dense scrub. The unobstructed views of Maui and the neighboring islands are awesome. Bring your own water.

Haleakala Ridge Trail (1.6 miles) starts from Skyline Trail's terminus at 6550 feet and descends along Haleakala's southwest rift to 5600 feet. There are spectacular views in all directions and a shelter at trail's end.

(For **Haleakala Crater** trails, see the "In the Belly of the Volcano" section in this chapter.)

Transportation

BY AIR

Three airports serve Maui—Kahului Airport, Kapalua-West Maui Airport, and Hana Airport.

The **Kahului Airport** is the main landing facility and should be your destination if you're staying in the Central Maui region or on the southeast coast in the Kihei-Wailea area. United Airlines is the only carrier with non-stop service from the mainland. American Airlines and Delta Air Lines stop in Honolulu en route. Currently Aloha Airlines, Hawaiian Airlines, Aloha Island Air, and Air Molokai fly here from other islands in the chain. The first two companies fly jets, while Aloha Island Air uses both jets and propeller-driven planes. Air Molokai uses propeller-driven planes only; the prop planes often feature the lowest fares.

If you decide to land in Kahului, you'll arrive at a bustling airport that has been expanded. I never realized how popular Maui was until I first pushed through the mobs of new arrivals here. In addition to the masses, you'll find a coffee shop and lounge, snack bar, newsstand, gift shop, *lei* stand, and information booth (872-3893), but no lockers. **Trans-Hawaiian** (877-7308) provides shuttle service both to and from the airport.

Kapalua-West Maui Airport serves the Lahaina-Kaanapali area. Hawaiian Airlines and Aloha Island Air fly into the facility, which features a snack bar and sundries shop.

Hana Airport, really only a short landing strip and a one-room terminal, sits near the ocean in Maui's lush northeastern corner. Only Aloha Island Air lands in this isolated community. And don't expect very much ground transportation waiting for you. There is no bus service, though there is a car rental agency.

BY BOAT

If you'd prefer to arrive by boat, **Sea Link of Hawaii** (661-8397) provides round-trip service from Molokai aboard the 118-foot *Maui Princess*.

CAR RENTALS

If, like most visitors to Maui, you arrive at the airport in Kahului, you certainly won't want for car rental agencies. There are quite a few with booths right at the airport. A number of others are located around town.

Naturally, the most convenient means of renting a car is through one of the outfits at the airport. The problem with these companies, however, is that you pay for the convenience. The airport agencies are as follows:

Andres Rent A Car (877-5378), Sunshine Rent A Car (871-6222), Dollar Rent A Car (877-2731), Avis Rent A Car (871-7575), Budget Rent A Car (871-8811), and Hertz Rent A Car (877-5167).

Then there are the agencies located away from the airport. Some of them will provide airport pick-up service when your plane arrives. I recommend that you check in advance and reserve a car from an outfit that extends this service. The others might be a little cheaper, but I've never considered the inconvenience worth the savings. Without a ride you'll be confronted with the Catch-22 situation of getting to your car. Do you rent a car in which to pick up your rental car? Take a bus? Or are you supposed to hitchhike?

Enough said. The rental agencies outside the airport include several companies that rent older model cars at very competitive rates. These are Word of Mouth Rent A Used Car (877-2436), Tropical Rent A Car (877-0002), VIP Car Rentals (877-2054), Sunshine Rent A Car (871-6222), National Inter-Rent (877-5347), and Thrifty Rent A Car (871-7596).

If you find yourself in the Lahaina-Kaanapali area wanting to rent a car, try Dollar Rent A Car (667-2651), Budget Rent A Car (661-8721), Avis Rent A Car (661-4588), Hertz Rent A Car (661-3195), Thrifty Rent A Car (667-9541), Rainbow Rent A Car (661-8734), National Inter-Rent (667-9737), or Tropical Rent A Car (661-0061). Among these agencies, Dollar, Budget, and Hertz are located at the Kapalua West Maui Airport.

Dollar Rent A Car (248-8237) is the sole company in Hana.

Kihei is served by Avis Rent A Car (879-1905) and Kihei Rent A Car (879-7257).

As elsewhere in the islands, there are a few points to remember when renting a car on Maui. First, the car rental agencies will charge several dollars a day extra for complete insurance coverage. Also, many of them will forbid you from driving the road around the West Maui Mountains and the road from Hana around the southeast side of the island.

(See Chapter Two for a complete explanation of car rentals in Hawaii.)

JEEP RENTALS

There are several companies on the island of Maui that rent four-wheel-drive vehicles. Among the outfits offering jeeps are Adventures Rent A Jeep (456 Dairy Road, Kahului; 877-6626) and Sunshine Rent A Car (933 Koeheke Road, Kahului; 871-6222).

But for the most part, Maui roads, including cane roads, are accessible by car, so you probably won't need a jeep. If you hit the rainy season, though, and want to explore the back roads, it can't hurt.

MOTOR SCOOTER AND MOTORCYCLE RENTALS

A & B Moped Rental (Honokowai General Store, Honokowai; 669-0027) rents mopeds by the hour or day. These vehicles provide an exhilarating and economical way to explore the area. Though they are not intended for long trips or busy roadways, they're ideal for short jaunts to the beach.

PUBLIC TRANSPORTATION

There is almost no general transportation on Maui and the little that is provided lies concentrated in one small sector of the island. The **Lahaina Express** (661-8748) travels between Lahaina and Kaanapali. Picking up the baton in Kaanapali, the **Kaanapali Trolley** (667-7411) runs through this popular resort area; a sister trolley services the Kapalua West Maui Airport.

Outside the immediate Lahaina-Kaanapali area you'll have to rely on **Trans-Hawaiian** (877-7308). This well-known carrier operates shuttle services regularly from Kahului to Lahaina-Kaanapali for $13.

HITCHHIKING

Officially, hitching is illegal on Maui, and the police have been known to arrest people. The local technique is not to extend your thumb. Just stand by the side of the road and face oncoming traffic as you would if you were hitching, but keep your hand down. Local people and some of the tourists will know you're hitching, and the police will leave you alone. If you do use your thumb, you'll be marking yourself as an outsider to the locals, and the police may feel the need to remind you of the law.

As everywhere else, luck hitching here varies. But the heavy traffic in most areas enhances your chances considerably.

FLIGHTSEEING

Much of Maui's best scenery is accessed via serpentine roads or steep mountain drives. While the views are stunning, the best way to get a bird's-eye view is from the air. Helicopters, fixed wing aircraft, and gliders all make it easy to see the volcanic uplands, waterfall splashed cliffs, and dreamy back country beaches.

Cardinal Helicopters (Kahului Airport; 877-2400) operates 45-minute to two-hour tours focusing on such destinations as Haleakala crater, Hana's rainforests, and waterfalls. Your trip includes a video recording of the entire journey. **Papillon Helicopters** (Kahului Heliport; 877-0022) offers a 30-minute tour of the West Maui Mountains featuring Waihee Valley and the Honokohau Valley, as well as the Kapalua and Kaanapali areas.

There's also a west Maui/Molokai flight highlighting the tallest waterfall in the state, Molokai's Kahiwa. **Hawaii Helicopters** (Kahului Heliport; 877-3900) offers tours ranging from 30 minutes to five hours. The longer tours stop in Hana for 45 minutes to three hours, offering a chance to explore this verdant area's beaches and waterfalls via van.

At **American Pacific Air** (Kahului Airport; 871-8115) you can choose between a 45-minute tour of West Maui or a one-hour-and-40-minute circle tour of the entire island aboard four- and six-seater Cessnas.

For aerobatic flights and scenic tours in an open cockpit aircraft, try **Biplane Barnstormers** (878-2860). Trips range from 20 minutes to an hour and 40 minutes and reach a wide variety of destinations around the island. A special 30-minute aerobatic flight, guaranteed to knock your socks off, includes barrel rolls, loops, and four-leaf clovers.

Maui Addresses and Phone Numbers

MAUI ISLAND

County Department of Parks and Recreation—Wailuku (243-7230; permits, 243-7389)

Division of State Parks—Wailuku (243-5354)

Haleakala National Park Headquarters—(572-7749 and 572-9306)

State Department of Land and Natural Resources—(243-5352)

Weather Report—(877-5111 for entire island; 871-5054 for recreational areas; 572-7749 for Haleakala National Park)

KAHULUI-WAILUKU

Ambulance—911

Barber Shop—Kahului Barber Shop, Kahului Shopping Center, Kaahumanu Avenue (871-4221)

Books—Waldenbooks, Maui Mall Shopping Center, Kaahumanu Avenue (877-0181)

Fire Department—911

Fishing Supplies—New Maui Fishing Supply, 54 Market Street, Wailuku (244-3449)

Hardware—Monarch Home Centers, Maui Mall, Kaahumanu Avenue (871-7373)

Hospital—Maui Memorial Hospital, 221 Mahalani Street, Wailuku (244-9056)

Laundromat—W & F Washerette, 125 South Wakea Avenue (877-0353)

Library—251 High Street, Wailuku (244-3945)

Liquor—Party Pantry, 261 Dairy Road, Kahului (871-7690)

Pharmacy—Long's Drugs, Maui Mall, Kaahumanu Avenue (877-0041)
Photo Supply—Maui Photo Center, Maui Mall, Kaahumanu Avenue (871-4311)
Police Department—911
Post Office—250 Imikala, Wailuku (244-4815)

LAHAINA

Ambulance—911
Barber Shop—For Shear, 724 Luakini Street (667-2866)
Books—Whaler's Book Shoppe, The Wharf Mall, Front Street (667-9544)
Fire Department—911
Fishing Supplies—Lahaina Fishing Supply, Lahaina Shopping Center, Wainee Street (661-8348)
Hardware—Monarch Home Centers, 1087 Limahana (661-4025)
Library—Wharf Street (661-0566)
Liquor—Lahaina Mini-Mart, 193 Lahainaluna Road (667-2100)
Pharmacy—Lahaina Pharmacy, Lahaina Shopping Center, Wainee Street (661-3119)
Photo Supply—Lahaina Camera Center, Lahaina Shopping Center, Wainee Street (661-3306)
Police Department—911
Post Office—1760 Honoapiilani Highway (667-6611)

KIHEI-WAILEA

Ambulance—911
Fire Department—911
Police Department—911

HANA

Ambulance—911
Fire Department—911
Police Department—911

CHAPTER SEVEN

Lanai

Eight miles from Maui, across the historic whaling anchorage at Lahaina Roads, lies the pear-shaped island of Lanai. The word *lanai*, usually
meaning "porch," is more appropriately translated as "swelling" on this humpbacked isle. In profile the island, formed by an extinct volcano, resembles
the humpback whales that frequent its waters. It rises in a curved ridge from
the south, then gradually tapers to the north. The east side is cut by deep
gulches, while the west is bounded by spectacular sea cliffs rising 1500 to 2000
feet. Lanaihale, the island's tallest peak, stands 3370 feet above sea level.

First discovered by Captain Cook's men in 1779, Lanai was long avoided
by mariners, who feared its reef-shrouded shores and saw little future in
the dry, barren landscape. You can still see testaments to their fear in the
rotting hulks that lie off Shipwreck Beach.

Ancient Hawaiians believed Lanai was inhabited only by evil spirits
until Kaululaau, son of the great Maui chief Kakaalaneo, killed the spirits.
Kaululaau, a Hawaiian-style juvenile delinquent who chopped down fruit
trees with the gay abandon of young George Washington, had been exiled
for such destructive behavior to Lanai by his father. After the wild youth
redeemed himself by making the island safe from malevolent spirits, Lanai
was settled by Hawaiians and controlled by powerful Maui chiefs.

Most archaeologists doubt that the native population, which lived from
taro cultivation and fishing along the eastern shore, ever exceeded 2500.
Even periods of peak population were punctuated by long intervals when
the island was all but deserted. Lying in Maui's wind shadow, Lanai's rainfall ranges from 40 inches along its northeast face to a meager 12 inches
annually in the barren southwest corner. Covered in scrub vegetation along

much of its surface, the island still supports several rare endemic bird species as well as axis deer, mouflon sheep, and pronghorn antelope.

Like Molokai, its neighbor to the north, Lanai for centuries was a satellite of Maui. (Even today it is part of Maui County.) Then in 1778 it was overwhelmed by the forces of Kalaniopuu, the king of the Big Island. Later in the century, an even more powerful monarch, Kamehameha the Great, set up a summer residence along the south coast in Kaunolu.

During the 19th century, Lanai was a ranchers' island with large sections of flat range land given over to grazing. Missionaries became active saving souls and securing property in 1835 and by the 1860s one of their number had gained control of Lanai's better acreage. This was Walter Murray Gibson, a Mormon maverick whose life story reads like a sleazy novel. Despite being excommunicated by the Mormon church, Gibson went on to become a formidable figure in Hawaiian politics.

Gibson was not the only man with a dream for Lanai. George Munro, a New Zealand naturalist, came to the island in 1911 as manager of a plantation complex that originally tried to grow sugar on the island and then turned to cattle raising. While his herds grazed the island's tablelands, Munro worked in the rugged highlands. He extended the native forest, planting countless trees to capture moisture and protect eroded hillsides. He restored areas ravaged by feral goats and imported the stately Norfolk pines that still lend a mountain ambience to Lanai City. And, most important, Munro introduced an ecological awareness that hopefully will continue to pervade this enchanting island.

The land that Gibson and Munro oversaw changed hands several times until James Dole bought the entire island in 1922 for a mere $1.1 million. Dole, descended from missionaries, was possessed of a more earthly vision than his forebears. Pineapples. He converted the island to pineapple cultivation, built Lanai City, and changed the face of Lanai forever.

Filipinos, now about 50 percent of the island's population, were imported to work the fields. Until a few years ago they were bent to their labors all over Lanai, wearing goggles and gloves to protect against the sharp spines that bristle from the low-lying plants. Pineapples are cultivated through plastic sheets to conserve precious water and harvesting is done by hand. Up until the early 1990s, you could see hundreds of acres covered in plastic. Downtown Lanai would roll up the streets at 9 p.m., but the lights would burn bright in the pineapple fields as crews worked through the night loading the hefty fruits onto conveyor belts.

That was yesterday, back when Lanai retained something of an ambiguous reputation. Most tourists, hearing that Lanai was nothing but pineapples and possessed only 20 miles of paved roads and a single 10-room hotel, left the place to the antelopes and wild goats.

Now, however, the sleeping midget is beginning to awaken. You still rent your car in an old gas station with scuffed floors and deer trophies on

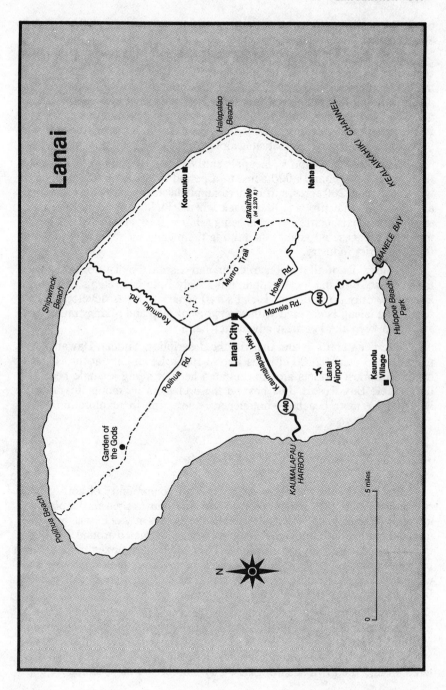

Lanai

Halepalao Beach

KEALAIKAHIKI CHANNEL

Keomuku

Naha

Lanaihale
(el 3,370 ft.)

MANELE BAY

Shipwreck Beach

Munro Trail

Hoike Rd.

Keomuku Rd.

Manele Rd.

440

Hulopoe Beach Park

Polihua Rd.

Lanai City

Kaumalapau Hwy.

Lanai Airport

Kaunolu Village

Garden of the Gods

440

KAUMALAPAU HARBOR

Polihua Beach

5 miles

N

0

the wall. And there are still only three paved roads on the island. But nothing else here will ever be the same.

Stores are being renovated, old plantation homes are receiving fresh coats of paint, and new housing developments are going up. Castle & Cooke, the conglomerate that owns the island, has poured $350 million into the place, building two resorts and transforming little Lanai into luxurious Lanai. The Manele Bay Hotel, a 250-room oceanfront extravaganza, opened in 1991 just one year after the christening of the Lodge at Koele, a rustic but refined 102-room resort situated along Lanai's forested mountain slopes.

Meanwhile the island's pineapple cultivation is declining precipitously from a peak of about 18,000 acres to a period in the near future when it will total a mere 200 acres, sufficient to supply island needs and give visitors a glimpse at what life was like "back when." Fields are being converted to alfalfa and oats; cattle raising is being reintroduced; and the island's Filipino and Japanese population is quitting the plantation and going to work for the tourist industry.

In the midst of all the construction, and despite the disturbing changes in the lifestyle of the local people, this lovely little isle retains its charm. Even now only a fraction of Lanai's 140 square miles is developed. The rest of the island is covered with a network of jeep and hiking trails guaranteed to keep the heartiest adventurer happy.

Here is an entire island that fits the description "hidden Hawaii." Almost all of Lanai's 2100 citizens live in rustic Lanai City at the island's center and most tourists are concentrated here or along a single beach at the Manele Bay Resort. Just beyond these clusters lie mountains, ranchlands, and remote beaches—untouched realms ripe for exploration.

Lanai City

Situated at 1645 feet, **Lanai City** is a trim community of corrugated-roof houses and small garden plots. Tourist brochures present the place as a quaint New England village, but until the Lodge at Koele was built the town was rather drab. Most of the houses were constructed around the 1920s in traditional company-town fashion. They are square boxes topped with tin roofs and tend to look alike. Norfolk pines break the monotony, and now that Lanai is much more self-conscious, many homes are freshly painted in a rainbow assortment of hues.

It is still a company town, but today the company is harvesting tourists instead of planting pineapples. Several housing developments and condominium complexes have been built on the outskirts to house hotel employees and the airport is about to undergo major expansion. With everything centered around the town square, Lanai City embraces almost the entire population of the island. Situated at the center of the island at an elevation midway between the beach and the mountain peaks, it is cool and breezy with a temperate climate.

Nevertheless, the really interesting places on Lanai lie outside town, and most require driving or hiking over jeep trails. It's advisable to get specific directions wherever you go, since the maze of pineapple roads can confuse even the most intrepid pathfinder. Where possible, I've included directions; otherwise, check with the jeep rental shops in Lanai City or at the hotels.

To be extra safe, ask about road conditions, too. The slightest rain can turn a dusty jeep road into a slick surface, and a downpour can transmogrify it into an impassable quagmire. I once dumped a jeep into a three-foot ditch when the trail to Polihua Beach collapsed. It had been raining steadily for three days and the soft shoulder couldn't support the weight of a vehicle. I was 11 miles from Lanai City with the wheels hopelessly embedded and an hour left until dark. The way back led past pretty menacing country, heavily eroded and difficult to track through. Rain clouds brought the night on in a rush. I gathered up my poncho and canteen, convinced myself that the worst to come would be a cold and wet night outdoors, and began trekking back to civilization. Fortunately, after five miserable hours I made it. But the entire incident could have been avoided if I had first checked road conditions and had allowed at least several hours of daylight for my return.

This shouldn't discourage you, though. With the proper precautions, exploring Lanai can be a unique experience, challenging but safe. To make things easy, I'll start with a journey to the island's northeastern shore, part of which is over a paved road. Then I'll continue clockwise around the island.

LANAI CITY HOTELS

Prior to the 1990s the only inn on the entire island was the **Hotel Lanai** (★) (565-7211), a modest mountain retreat. Set 1600 feet above sea level and surrounded by Norfolk pines, it offers clean, medium-sized rooms equipped with private baths. The lodge was built in the '20s, as was most of Lanai City, but was refurbished several years ago when it passed to new management. It features a restaurant and lounge, and is a local gathering place. A lot of folks hang out in the lobby here, making for a warm, friendly atmosphere, and the staff is congenial. Small standard rooms, medium-sized accommodations, and rooms with lanais are priced in the deluxe range.

There are only ten units in this U-shaped hostelry, so reservations can be troublesome if even a dozen or so budget-minded tourists or locals descend on the island. To reserve in advance, write to Hotel Lanai, P.O. Box A-119, Lanai City, HI 96763 or call 800-624-8849 toll-free from the mainland. It's advisable to arrange transportation with the hotel at the time of making reservations.

The **Lodge at Koele** (Lanai City; 565-7300), a fashionable 102-room hideaway, is a study in style and decorum. The most noteworthy feature is the lobby, a vaulted-ceiling affair faced on either end with a stone fireplace that rises to the roofline. Etched-glass skylights extend the length of the room, illuminating the "great hall." The Victorian guest rooms are done with four-poster beds, lacquer boxes, statuettes, and decorative plates. To make sure you remember that even here amid the Norfolk pines you are still in Hawaii, an overhead fan beats the air in languid motions.

Backdropped by mountains and surrounded by miles of pineapple fields, the emphasis at the Lodge is on staying put. There are cloisters lined with wicker chairs, a croquet court, a swimming pool that looks out on field and forest, and a congenial staff to take care of every request. Ultra-deluxe.

If you prefer to rent a house, contact **Lanai Realty** (P.O. Box 67, Lanai City, HI 96763; 565-6597). They have three-bedroom homes renting in the deluxe range and a four-bedroom house that is priced ultra-deluxe.

LANAI CITY RESTAURANTS

The **Hotel Lanai** (565-7211) in Lanai City offers wholesome meals at modest prices. Lunch and dinner menus feature an assortment of steak, seafood, and other platters, plus sandwiches. Lunches and dinners are both tabbed in the moderate range. The full-course breakfasts in this cozy dining facility vary in cost, depending on how full your course is. Decorated with island photographs along the knotty pine walls, this is a cozy place to share a meal. You can strike up a conversation with a local resident, sit back and enjoy the mountain air, or bask in the glow of the restaurant's two fireplaces. Watch the hours, though, or you'll get shut out. Breakfast is served only from 7:30 to 10 a.m., lunch from 11:30 a.m. to 1:30 p.m., and dinner from 5:30 to 9 p.m.

If the hotel restaurant is closed, Lanai City has both a budget- and a moderate-priced alternative. The first is **S. T. Property** (565-6537), a luncheonette that sits in one corner of a store lined with flashing video machines, and serves breakfast and lunch.

Your second alternative, the **Blue Ginger Café** (★) (409 7th Street; 565-6363), rests in an old plantation house and serves three solid meals a day. Simple drawings of tropical fish adorn the place and the red paint on the cement floor has worn away almost completely. But the white walls shine and the dinners are served piping hot. Breakfasts and plate lunches are pretty standard, but the evening meal is sophisticated enough to include T-bone steak, shrimp Cantonese, and lemon chicken. Moderate.

On Lanai, isolation is the engine of ingenuity. Confronted with all that land and so few people, **The Lodge at Koele** (565-7300) transformed sections of the island into an organic garden, hog farm, and cattle ranch. After adding a master chef, they had the ingredients for a gourmet restaurant that would be the pride not only of tiny Lanai but any island. The meals in this personalized dining room are as enticing as the hotel's sumptuous surroundings. Breakfast, lunch, and dinner are all culinary extravaganzas. The day begins with sweet rice waffles and lilikoi-coconut chutney, breakfast bread pudding, or bacon and eggs fresh from the farm. By evening the chef progresses to steamed seafood gyoza, loin of rabbit, marinated axis deer, and veal chop with pumpkin. Ultra-deluxe.

LANAI CITY MARKETS

For standard food needs, try **Richard's Shopping Center** (565-6047) on 8th Street in Lanai City. This "shopping center" is really only a small grocery store with a dry goods department. Richard's is open daily except Sunday from 8:30 a.m. to noon and from 1:30 to 5:30 p.m.

If, by some strange circumstance, you can't find what you're seeking here, head down the street to **Pine Isle Market** (565-6488).

LANAI CITY SHOPPING

Granted, it doesn't have much competition (in fact it doesn't have *any* competition), but **Island Collections** (373 7th Street; 565-6405) in Lanai City would be remarkable regardless of where it was located. Many of the paintings and sculptures were done by artists on the island and depict the plantation culture that was once Lanai's lifeblood but is now fast becoming its legacy.

Otherwise, you will have to seek out the gift shop at **The Lodge at Koele** (565-7300).

LANAI CITY NIGHTLIFE

Visitors find this a great spot to get the sleep they missed in Lahaina or Honolulu. If rest isn't a problem, Lanai may be a good place to catch up on your reading or letter writing. One thing is certain—once the sun goes down, there'll be little to distract you. You can have a drink while listening to local gossip at the **Hotel Lanai** (565-7211) or while mixing with the gentry at **The Lodge At Koele** (565-7300), where the lounge possesses a kind of gentlemen's library atmosphere with an etched-glass-and-hardwood interior. But on an average evening, even these night owl's nests will be closed by 10 o'clock. In addition to its plush lounge, The Lodge at Koele features hula dancers or other live entertainment in the lobby (The Grand Hall) nightly.

Northeast—Shipwreck Beach and Naha

From Lanai City, Route 430 (Keomuku Road) winds north through hot, arid country. The scrub growth and red soil in this barren area resemble a bleak southwestern landscape, but the sweeping views of Maui and Molokai could be found only in Hawaii.

By the way, those stones piled atop one another along the road are neither an expression of ancient Hawaiian culture nor proof of the latest UFO landing. They were placed there by imaginative hikers. Each one is an *ahu*, representative of a Hawaiian tradition in which columns of three or so stones are built to help ensure good luck.

Near the end of the macadam road you can turn left onto a dirt road. This track leads past colonies of intermittently inhabited squatters' shacks, many built from the hulks of vessels grounded on nearby **Shipwreck Beach**. The coral reef paralleling the beach has been a nemesis to sailors since whaling days. The rusting remains of a barge and a 1950s-era oil tanker still bear witness to the navigational hazards along this coast. Needless to say, this is one of the best areas in Hawaii for beachcombing. Look in particular for the Japanese glass fishing floats that are carried here on currents all the way from Asia.

At the end of the dirt road, a path marked with white paint leads to clusters of ancient **petroglyphs** depicting simple island scenes. Those interested in extensively exploring the coast can hike all the way from Shipwreck eight miles west to Polihua Beach along jeep trails and shoreline.

Back on the main road (continuing straight ahead as if you had never made that left turn that led to Shipwreck Beach) you will discover that the macadam gives way to a dirt road that leads along the northeast shore for 12 teeth-clicking miles. It was along this now-deserted coast that the ancient Hawaiian population lived. Numbering perhaps 2000 in pre-Western times, they fished the coast and cultivated taro.

The ghost town of **Keomuku**, marked by a ramshackle church that is slated for refurbishment, lies six miles down the road. It's another mile and a half to **Kahea Heiau**, a holy place that many claim is the reason Keomuku was deserted. It seems that stones from this temple were used to build the nearby Maunalei Sugar Company plantation despite warnings against disturbing the sacred rocks. So when the plantation failed in 1901 after its sweet water mysteriously turned brackish, the Hawaiians had a heavenly explanation. It was shortly after this incident that most of the rest of Lanai's populace moved up to Lanai City, leaving only spirits along the coast.

Club Lanai (871-1144), the waterfront complex that caters to day visitors from Maui, is located along the beach nearby. One way to spend just a day on Lanai is to catch a round-trip catamaran ride from Lahaina with this outfit. You'll land at a seven-acre visitor park along a sandy beach on the island's eastern shore. This private facility provides a dining area and bar as well as an array of equipment for beach and water sports. Guests snorkel on a coral reef, learn Hawaiian arts and crafts, and stroll along the strand. They do not, however, get an opportunity to tour around the island. Meals are provided. All you do is show up at Pier 4 in Lahaina Harbor at 7:15 a.m. to board a catamaran that returns you to Lahaina around 3 p.m.

Several miles farther, past numerous salt-and-pepper-colored beaches, the road ends at the old Hawaiian village of **Naha**. Today nothing remains of this once prosperous colony.

NORTHEAST—SHIPWRECK AND NAHA BEACHES AND PARKS

Shipwreck Beach—This strand is actually a string of small sandy patches that stretches for eight miles along the north coast, all the way to Polihua Beach. The glass fishing balls, driftwood, and occasional nautilus shells on the beach make this a beachcomber's paradise. The remains of misguided ships that gave the beach its name also add to the allure. Sometimes windy.

Facilities: None. Ten miles to Lanai City restaurants and markets. *Swimming:* Shallow, with a sandy bottom. Protecting reef 200 yards offshore. *Snorkeling:* Very good along the reef; though the water is murky during part of the year. There's also diving for lobsters. *Fishing:* Here you'll find good fishing for threadfin, bonefish, and ulua in the area between the squatters' houses and the petroglyphs.

Getting there: Head north from Lanai City on Route 430 (Keomuku Road). See the "Northeast—Shipwreck Beach and Naha" section above for more details.

Halepalaoa Beach and **Naha Beach**—A string of salt-and-pepper-colored sand beaches lies along the 12-mile dirt road to Naha. While most are unattractive and crowded with shoals, they do offer great views of Molokai, Maui, and Kahoolawe. The Naha road winds in and out along the seafront, with numerous access roads leading to the shore. The prettiest strand is Halepalaoa Beach, a mile-long white-sand corridor partially bordered by sand dunes. Club Lanai, a day-trip center for visitors from Maui, is located here.

Facilities: Several beaches, including Naha, have small picnic areas and makeshift facilities on grassy plots. *Swimming:* Most beaches are well-protected by shoals, but the waters are shallow. *Snorkeling:* Good. *Fishing:* The reefs are too far away to make this a prime angling area.

Getting there: Take Route 430 north from Lanai City and continue on after it turns southward and becomes a dirt road. The dirt road extends for about 12 miles, ending at Naha; Halepalaoa Beach is about seven miles out along the dirt road.

The Munro Trail

Named for New Zealand naturalist George Munro, this seven-mile jeep trail climbs through rainforest and stands of conifers en route to **Lanaihale** (★), the highest point on Lanai. From this 3370-foot perch you can see every major Hawaiian island except Kauai.

On the way to Lanaihale, about two miles up the trail, you'll pass **Hookio Gulch**. The ridge beyond is carved with a defense work of protective notches made by warriors who tried futilely to defend Lanai against invaders from Hawaii in 1778.

A footpath leads to an overlook above 2000-foot deep **Hauola Gulch**, Lanai's deepest canyon. Here you may see axis deer clinging to the sharp rockfaces, seeming to defy gravity as they pick their way along the heights.

This knife-edge ridge, little more than 100 feet wide in places, is studded with ironwood and eucalyptus trees, as well as the stately Norfolk pines that New Zealand naturalist George Munro personally planted along the heights. From this aerie the slopes fall away to reveal the twin humps of Maui. The Big Island rests far below you, anchored in open ocean. The sea itself is a flat, shimmering expanse.

From Lanaihale you can either turn around or continue and descend through open fields to Hoike Road, which will connect with Route 440. The Munro Trail begins in Koele off Route 430 (Keomuku Road) about a mile north of Lanai City. Be sure to check road conditions and try to go early in the morning before clouds gather along the ridgetop. While it's rough going at times, the trail affords such magnificent views from its windswept heights that it simply must not be ignored by the adventurous sightseer.

Southeast—Manele Bay

Heading south from Lanai City on Route 440 (Manele Road), you'll be traveling through the Palawai Basin, the crater of the extinct volcano that formed the island. This was also the heart of Lanai's once extensive pineapple plantation.

The explorer can detour off the main highway to the **Luahiwa petroglyphs** (★). Finding them requires obtaining explicit directions, then driving through a field, and finally climbing a short distance up a steep bluff. But the Luahiwa petroglyphs—portraying human figures, deer, paddles, and turtles—are among the finest rock carvings in Hawaii and are definitely worth the search. As you approach each cluster of boulders, you'll see pictographic stories begin to unfold. One in particular depicts a large outrigger canoe, sails unfurled, being loaded Noah-style with livestock. Preparing, perhaps, for the ancient migration north to the Hawaiian Islands? To locate the petroglyphs, head south from Lanai City on Route 440. Turn left at the first dirt road. Follow the lower road as it curves along the bottom of the hillside. After passing below a watertank and pipeline, the road forks and you follow the left fork. The road goes into a horseshoe curve; when you come out of the curve there will be black boulders on the hillside above you to the left. Spread across a few acres, they contain the petroglyphs.

The main road leads through agricultural fields and winds down to the twin inlets at **Manele Bay** and **Hulopoe Bay**, which together comprise a marine life conservation area. Just offshore from the cinder cone that separates these two harbors is a sea stack, **Puu Pehe**, known not only for its beauty but its legends as well. Puu Pehe was a lovely Maui girl kidnapped by a Lanai warrior who kept her hidden in a sea cave. One day when he went off in search of water, a huge sea wave swept the girl to her death. Stricken with grief and remorse, the young warrior buried her on top of the rock island and then jumped to his death from its heights.

The small-boat harbor at Manele, rimmed by lava cliffs along the far shore, contains ruins of ancient Hawaiian houses. You'll also see an old wooden chute protruding from the rocks, a loading platform used years ago to lead cattle onto ships. Today this rock-rimmed anchorage is a mooring place for fishing boats and yachts. Hulopoe offers the island's finest beach, a crescent of white sand with gentle waves, crystalline waters, and a fine park facility. You'll find the stone ruins of an ancient Hawaiian home and canoe house at the north end of the beach. Just above the beach, on the grounds in front of the plush Manele Bay Hotel, stands the remains of an *ahu* or traditional Hawaiian shrine.

SOUTHEAST—MANELE BAY HOTELS

While The Lodge at Koele is situated at 1600-feet elevation in Lanai City, eight miles from the ocean, Lanai's other fashionable new resort, the **Manele Bay Hotel** (565-7600) is a traditional beachfront resort. Set on a bluff overlooking the best beach on the island, it is a 250-room extravaganza designed along both Asian and Mediterranean lines and surrounded by artistically planted gardens. Elegance here is in no way subdued: It speaks from the stone floors and white columns, the dark-paneled library, and the recessed ceilings. The two-tiered lobby combines art deco windows with traditional Hawaiian murals; the lower level is a terrace with glass doors that open onto ocean views.

Guest rooms look out either on the beach or the grounds, which are sculpted into five different theme gardens—Japanese, Bromeliad, Hawaiian, Chinese, and Cosmopolitan. Each room is spacious, done in pastel hues and decorated with Asian armoires and color sketches of Hawaiian flora. The four-poster beds are accented with quilts and upholstered throw pillows. Add a four-leaf clover-shaped pool, six tennis courts, spa, and workout room and you will realize that sleepy little Lanai is never going to be the same again. Ultra-deluxe.

SOUTHEAST—MANELE BAY RESTAURANTS

Outside Lanai City the dining choices, a grand total of two, are concentrated at the Manele Bay Hotel. Here, ladies and gentlemen, lunch is served at the **Pool Grille** (565-7700) beneath a bougainvillea-covered trellis. Set poolside just above the beach, this patio dining facility features several island salads, including a seasonal fruit offering. There is also a standard assortment of sandwiches, as well as grilled mahimahi on nori bread and other specialties. Lunch only; moderate.

This spacious resort offers more formal dining in the **Hulopoe Court Restaurant** (565-7700), a high-ceiling dining room with glass doors that open onto a veranda overlooking the ocean. Island murals adorn the walls and pineapple motif chandeliers dominate the room. The decor blends Asian and Polynesian styles and the menu picks up the theme with island, Asian, and Western dishes. Breakfast and dinner only; deluxe.

SOUTHEAST—MANELE BAY NIGHTLIFE

Down along Hulopoe Beach at the Manele Bay Hotel, the **Hale Ahe Ahe Lounge** (565-2000) combines several different settings, each equally inviting. The lounge itself has dark textured walls, hardwood bar, and a clubby ambience. It features piano or contemporary Hawaiian music nightly. Out on the terrace you can settle into a comfortable armchair or lean against the rail and enjoy the ocean view. The adjacent Holokai Room is a gameroom complete with backgammon board and an air of relaxed elegance.

SOUTHEAST—MANELE BAY BEACHES AND PARKS

Hulopoe Beach Park—Lanai's finest beach also possesses the island's only fully developed park. Set in a half-moon inlet and fringed with kiawe trees, this white-sand beach is an excellent spot for all sorts of recreation. It is also the site of the 250-room Manele Bay Hotel, which rests on a bluff about 50 yards above the waterfront. Part of a marine life conservation area, Hulopoe has a lava terrace with outstanding tidepools along its eastern point. There is also a wading area for children at this end of the park. If you continue a short distance along this eastern shoreline you'll also encounter **Puu Pehe Cove**, a small beach with abundant marine life that is excellent for swimming and snorkeling. Little wonder that Hulopoe is the island's favorite picnic spot.

Facilities: Picnic area, restrooms, showers. Eight miles from the markets and restaurants of Lanai City. *Swimming:* Excellent. The beach is partially protected. *Snorkeling:* Excellent. *Surfing:* Good for both surfboards and bodysurfing. *Fishing:* A prime area for threadfin, ulua, and bonefish, this is also the most accessible surf-casting beach on the island.

Camping: This is it! There are three campsites at the far end of the beach. Permits are issued by the Lanai Company (565-7233), P.O. Box L, Lanai City, Lanai, HI 96763. Expect to pay a $5 registration fee plus a charge of $5 per camper per day.

Getting there: Take Route 440 (Manele Road) south from Lanai City for eight miles.

Manele Bay—Primarily a small-boat harbor, this cliff-fringed inlet is populated by sailboats from across the Pacific. You can carouse with the crews, walk along the jetty, or scramble up the rocks for a knockout view of Maui's Haleakala crater.

Facilities: There's a park for picnicking, and just around the corner at Hulopoe Beach are facilities for camping, swimming, and other sports. *Swimming:* Very good since the harbor is well protected, but you need to be wary of boat traffic. *Snorkeling:* Good. *Fishing:* Good. Since this is part of the marine life preserve there are restrictions.

Getting there: Take Route 440 south from Lanai City.

Southwest—Kaumalapau Harbor and Kaunolu

A southwesterly course along Route 440 (Kaumalapau Highway) will carry you steadily downhill for about six miles to **Kaumalapau Harbor**. This busy little harbor was built by pineapple interests and used primarily to ship the fruit on barges to Honolulu. During the heyday of Lanai's pineapple industry, more than a million pineapples a day were loaded onto waiting ships. On either side of Kaumalapau, you can see the *pali*, which rises straight up as high as 1000 feet, protecting Lanai's southwestern flank. These lofty sea cliffs are an ideal vantage point for watching the sunset.

The most interesting point along this route involves a detour near the airport and a journey down a *very* rugged jeep trail to **Kaunolu Village** (★). A summer retreat of Kamehameha the Great and now a national historic landmark, this ancient fishing community still contains the ruins of more than 80 houses as well as stone shelters, petroglyphs, and graves. Pick your way through it carefully, lest you step on a ghost. Kamehameha's house, once perched on the eastern ridge, looked across to **Halulu Heiau** on the west side of Kaunolu Bay. Commanding a dominant view of the entire region, these rocky remains are bounded on three sides by cliffs that vault 1000 feet from the ocean.

From nearby **Kahekili's Leap,** warriors proved their courage by plunging more than 60 feet into the water below. If they cleared a 15-foot outcropping and survived the free fall into 12 feet of water, they were deemed noble soldiers worthy of their great king.

Just offshore from this daredevil launching pad lies **Shark Island,** a rock formation that bears an uncanny resemblance to a shark fin. Could it be that warriors skilled enough to survive Kahekili's Leap had then to confront the malevolent spirit of a shark?

Northwest—Polihua Beach

From Lanai City, a graded pineapple road that disintegrates into an ungraded dirt track leads about seven miles to the **Garden of the Gods** (★). This heavily eroded area resembles the Dakota Badlands and features multi-hued boulders that change color dramatically during sunrise and sunset. A fantasy land of stone, the Garden of the Gods is planted with ancient lava flows tortured by the elements into as many suggestive shapes as the imagination can conjure. The colors here vibrate with psychedelic intensity and the rocks loom up around you as though they were the gods themselves—hard, cold, dark beings possessed of untold power and otherworldly beauty.

Past this surreal but sacred spot, Polihua Trail, a rugged jeep road, descends several miles to the ocean. **Polihua Beach,** stretching more than a mile and a half, is the longest and widest white-sand beach on the island. Once a prime nesting beach for green sea turtles, it is an excellent spot to watch whales as they pass close by the shoreline.

NORTHWEST—POLIHUA BEACH BEACHES & PARKS

Polihua Beach (★)—A wide white-sand beach situated along Lanai's northwest shore, this isolated strand, with a stunning view of Molokai, rivals Kauai's trackless beaches. Often very windy.

Facilities: None. *Swimming:* Exercise caution; strong winds and currents prevail throughout this region. *Snorkeling:* The water here is sometimes muddy; when it's clear, you can dive for lobsters. *Fishing:* According to local fishermen, this is the best spot on the island. Common catches include papio, ulua, bonefish, threadfin, and red snapper.

Getting there: It's located about 11 miles from Lanai City through pineapple fields and the Garden of the Gods. The last half of the drive is over a rugged jeep trail. For specific directions and road conditions, check with the jeep rental garages.

The Sporting Life

CAMPING

With so much virgin territory, Lanai should be ideal for camping. But here, as on the other islands, landowners restrict outdoors lovers. The villain is the outfit that manages the island. It permits island residents to camp where they like, but herds visitors into one area on the south coast. This campsite, at Hulopoe Beach, has facilities for three tents. Once filled to capacity, no other camping is permitted on the entire island! So make reservations early.

GOLF

The premier course on the island is one designed by Greg Norman and Ted Robinson, **The Experience at Koele** (565-7300). The nine-hole **Cavendish Golf Course**, also in Lanai City, is open to the public as well. Plans are afoot to open another course near the Manele Bay Hotel.

TENNIS

Call the County Department of Parks and Recreation (565-6979) for information on the public courts in Lanai City. Courts are also available at **The Lodge at Koele** (565-7300) in Lanai City and the **Manele Bay Hotel** (565-7700) near Hulopoe Beach.

HORSEBACK RIDING

The Lodge at Koele (565-7300) offers horseback riding and equestrian tours. They also feature wagon rides.

BICYCLING

Given the lack of paved roads, bicycle use is somewhat restricted on Lanai. There are a few nice rides from Lanai City, but all are steep in places and pass over pockmarked sections of road. One goes south eight miles to Manele Bay and the beach at Hulopoe, another diverts west to busy little Kaumalapau Harbor, and the last heads north 14 miles to Shipwreck Beach.

Lanai City Service Inc. (565-7227) is a good place to obtain information concerning Lanai roads.

HIKING

Hikers on Lanai are granted much greater freedom than campers. Jeep trails and access roads are open to the public; the only restriction is that hikers cannot camp along the trails. Since all Lanai's trails lead either to beaches or points of interest, they are described in the regional sightseeing and "Beaches and Parks" sections above.

Transportation

BY AIR

Planes to Lanai land at **Lanai Airport** (565-6757) amid an endless maze of tilled fields four miles from downtown Lanai City. This tiny landing strip, slated for major expansion, currently has no shops, lockers, car rentals, or public transportation. A few rooms house airline offices. Aloha Airlines and Hawaiian Airlines offer jet service to the island. Aloha Island Air and Air Molokai fly propeller-driven planes and feature competitive rates.

If you're staying at any of the island hotels, they will provide transportation into town, as will any of the island's car rental agencies if you're renting a vehicle from them.

BY BOAT

A ferry service called **Expeditions** (P.O. Box 1763, Lahaina, HI 96767; 661-3756) operates out of Maui and links Lahaina with Manele Bay on Lanai. There are four boats per day in each direction. The 45-minute crossing provides a unique way to arrive on the island.

CAR AND JEEP RENTALS

Lanai City Service Inc. (565-7227) and **Oshiro's Service Station** (565-6952) rent cars. (Lanai City Service is affiliated with Dollar Rent A Car.) Both outlets have automatic compacts with free mileage. But renting a car on Lanai is like carrying water wings to the desert: there's simply nowhere to go. Rental cars are restricted to pavement, while most of Lanai's roads are jeep trails: four-wheel drive is the only way to fly.

The first time I visited the island of Lanai, I rented a vintage 1942 jeep. The vehicle had bad brakes, no emergency brake, malfunctioning windshield wipers, and no seat belts. It was, however, equipped with an efficient shock absorber—me. Today, both Lanai companies described above rent new and reliable jeeps.

TOURS

At **Oshiro's Service Station** (565-6952) they offer guided tours, custom-designed to your personal interests. Generally ranging from two to four hours, these tours can cover places of major interest or obscure corners of the island.

There are also boat tours of Lanai offered by several Maui-based outfits. Some of these include **Trilogy** (661-4743) and **Ocean Activities Center** (879-4485).

HITCHHIKING

Officially, it's illegal, but actually it's common. The folks in these parts are pretty friendly, so rides are easy to get. The trick lies in finding someone who's going as far as you are—like all the way out to Shipwreck Beach or out to the Garden of the Gods.

Lanai Addresses and Phone Numbers

LANAI ISLAND

Camping Permits—Lanai Company, Lanai City (565-7233)
Weather—(565-6033)

LANAI CITY

Ambulance—(911)
Fire Department—(911)
Hospital—Lanai Community Hospital, 628 7th Street (565-6411)
Laundromat—On 7th Street next to Emura Jewelry
Library—Fraser Avenue (565-6996)
Police Department—312 8th Street (911)
Post Office—731 Lanai Avenue (565-6517)

CHAPTER EIGHT

Molokai

Between the bustling islands of Oahu and Maui lies an isle which in shape resembles Manhattan, but which in spirit and rhythm is far more than an ocean away from the smog-shrouded shores of the Big Apple. Molokai, Hawaii's fifth-largest island, is thirty-eight miles long and ten miles wide. The slender isle was created by three volcanoes that mark its present geographic regions: one at West End where the arid Mauna Loa tableland rises to 1381 feet, another at East End where a rugged mountain range along the north coast is topped by 4970-foot Mount Kamakou, and the third, a geologic afterthought, which created the low, flat Kalaupapa Peninsula.

Considering that the island measures a modest 260 square miles, its geographic diversity is amazing. Arriving at Hoolehua Airport near the island's center, travelers feel as though they have touched down somewhere in the American Midwest. Red dust, dry heat, and curving prairie surround the small landing strip and extend to the west end of Molokai. This natural pastureland gives way in the southcentral region to low-lying, relatively swampy ground and brown-sand beaches with murky water.

The prettiest strands lie along the western shore, where Papohaku Beach forms one of the largest white-sand beaches in the state, and at the east end around Halawa Valley, a region of heavy rainfall and lush tropic vegetation. To the north is the vaunted *pali*, which rises in a vertical wall 2000 feet from the surf, creating the tallest sea cliffs in the world. Here, too, is an awesome succession of sharp, narrow valleys cloaked in green moss.

Kaunakakai, a sleepy port town on the south shore, is the island's hub. From here a road runs to the eastern and western coasts. Kalaupapa and the northern *pali* are accessible overland only by mule and hiking trails.

Even in a region of islands, Molokai has always been something of a backwater. To the early Hawaiians it appeared desiccated and inhospitable and they named it *molo*, "barren," *kai*, "sea." The rich Halawa Valley was settled in the 7th century and the island developed a haunting reputation for sorcery and mystical occurrences.

In ancient times it was also called *pule-oo* or "powerful prayer" and was revered for the potency of its priests. According to legend, Molokai was the child of the god Wakea and his mistress Hina, whose cave still lies along the southeastern edge of the island.

When Captain James Cook "discovered" the island in November 1778, he found it bleak and inhospitable. Not until 1786 did a Western navigator, Captain George Dixon, bother to land. When Kamehameha the Great took it in 1795, he was actually en route to the much grander prize of Oahu. His war canoes are said to have loomed along four miles of shoreline when he attacked the island at Pakuhiwa Battleground and slaughtered the island's outnumbered defenders.

The next wave of invaders arrived in 1832 when Protestant missionaries introduced the Polynesians to the marvels of Christianity. Around 1850 a German immigrant named Rudolph Meyer arrived in Molokai, married a Hawaiian chieftess, and began a reign as manager of the Molokai Ranch that lasted for almost a half-century.

Leprosy struck the Hawaiian Islands during the 19th century, and wind-plagued Kalaupapa Peninsula became the living hell to which the disease's victims were exiled. Beginning in 1866, lepers were torn from their families and literally cast to their fates along this stark shore. Here Father Damien de Veuster, a Belgian priest, the Martyr of Molokai, came to live, work, and eventually die among the afflicted.

For years Molokai was labeled "The Lonely Isle" or "The Forgotten Isle." By 1910 a population that once totaled 10,000 had decreased to one-tenth the size. Then in 1921, Polynesians began settling homesteads under the Hawaiian Homes Act, which granted a 40-acre homestead to anyone with over 50 percent Hawaiian ancestry. Molokai eventually became "The Friendly Isle," with the largest proportion of native Hawaiians anywhere in the world (except for the island of Niihau, which is closed to outsiders). With them they brought a legacy from old Hawaii, the spirit of *aloha*, which still lives on this marvelous island. Young Hawaiians, sometimes hostile on the more crowded islands, are often outgoing and generous here. And of all the islands, Molokai offers you the best opportunity to "go native" by staying with a Hawaiian family.

During the 1920s, while Hawaiians were being granted the hardscrabble land that had not already been bought up on the island, Libby (which later sold out to Dole) and Del Monte began producing pineapples across the richer stretches of the island. The company towns of Maunaloa and Kua-

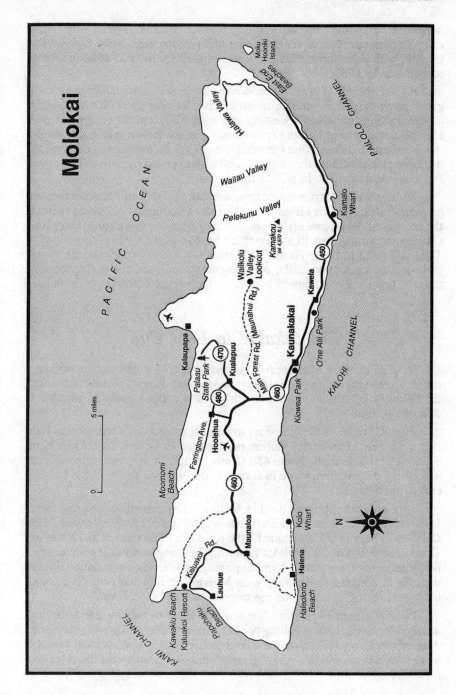

Molokai

PACIFIC OCEAN

Moku Hooniki Island

East End Beaches

PAILOLO CHANNEL

Halawa Valley

Wailau Valley

Pelekunu Valley

Kamalo Wharf

Kamakou
(w/ 4,970 ft.)

450

Wailkolu Valley Lookout

Kawela

Kaunakakai

Main Forest Rd. (Maunahui Rd.)

One Alii Park

Kalaupapa

470

Kualapuu

Palaau State Park

460

460

Kiowea Park

KALOHI CHANNEL

480

Hoolehua

Farrington Ave.

5 miles

0

Moomomi Beach

460

Maunaloa

Kolo Wharf

Kaluakoi Rd.

Halena

Papohaku Beach

Lauhue

Haleolono Beach

Kawakiu Beach

Kaluakoi Resort

KAIWI CHANNEL

N

lapuu sprang up and Molokai's rolling prairies became covered with fields of spike-topped fruits. Over the years competition from Asia became increasingly intense, forcing Dole to shut its operation in 1975 and Del Monte to pull out in 1982.

As elsewhere in Hawaii, the economic powers realized that if they couldn't grow crops they had better cultivate tourists. During the 1970s thousands of acres along the island's western end were allocated for resort and residential development and the sprawling Kaluakoi Resort was built. While this hotel and condominium complex has only been marginally successful, a master plan for future development, bitterly opposed by native Hawaiians and environmentalists, is still in the works.

Today the island's population numbers about 6700. It still does not possess a single traffic light or elevator and the weak economy has saved it from the ravages of development that plagued the rest of Hawaii during the 1980s. Change is coming, but like everything on Molokai, it is arriving slowly. Time still remains to see Hawaii as it once was and to experience the trackless beaches, vaulting seacliffs, sweeping ranchlands, and forested mountains that led ancient Hawaiians to believe in the mystical powers of Molokai.

Kaunakakai to East End

You don't need a scorecard, or even a map for that matter, to keep track of the sightseeing possibilities on Molokai. Across its brief expanse, the Friendly Isle offers several rewards to the curious, none of which are difficult to find.

First of course is the falsefront town of Kaunakakai, a commercial hub that more resembles a way station on the road to Dodge City. From here a simple two-lane road, Route 450 (Kamehameha V Highway), threads its way along the southern shore in search of the Halawa Valley at the far east end of the island.

It is only too appropriate that **Kaunakakai** gained its greatest fame from someone who never existed. Known for a song written about "The Cock-eyed Mayor of Kaunakakai," the town has in fact never had a mayor. This somnolent village, with its falsefront buildings and tiny civic center, is administered from Maui. Poor but proud, it possesses a population of less than 2000, and has a main drag (Ala Malama Street) that extends a grand total of three blocks but still represents the hub of Molokai.

Nearby is the **wharf**, extending seaward almost a half-mile and offering a mooring place for a few fishing boats, charter outfits, and private sailboats. A good place to gaze out on the island of Lanai, it is also an ideal vantage from which to take in the velvet green slopes that rise toward the ridgeline of Molokai.

Close to the pier landing rest the rocky remains of **Kamehameha V's Summer Home,** where Hawaii's king luxuriated during the late-19th century.

From Kaunakakai to Halawa Valley, a narrow macadam road leads past almost 30 miles of seascapes and historic sites. Route 450 runs straight along the south shore for about 20 miles, presenting views across the Kalohi and Pailolo channels to Lanai and Maui. Then the road snakes upward and curves inland before descending again into Halawa Valley.

Due to the calm, shallow waters along the southeastern shoreline, this area once supported one of the greatest concentrations of fishponds in Hawaii. Numbering as many as five dozen during the pre-Western period, these ancient aquaculture structures were built of lava and coral by commoners to raise fish for Hawaiian royalty. Small fish were trapped within these stone pens, fattened, and eventually harvested. You will see the rebuilt remains of several as you drive along the coast, including **Kalokoeli Fishpond,** two miles east of Kaunakakai, **Keawanui Fishpond,** about 12 miles east of town, and **Ualapue Fishpond,** a mile farther east.

About five miles from town lies Kawela, once an ancient city of refuge, now known as the place where two battles were fought at **Pakuhiwa Battleground.** In his drive to become Hawaii's first monarch, Kamehameha the Great launched a canoe flotilla that reportedly extended four miles along this shore.

This is also the site of **Kakahaia National Wildlife Refuge,** a 42-acre habitat that is a nesting area for a dozen species of coastal and sea birds. Centered around Kakahaia Beach Park, the preserve includes a 15-acre freshwater pond that rests immediately inland from the coast.

Just past the ten-mile marker (indicating that you are ten miles east of Kaunakakai), a dirt road leads to **Kamalo Wharf,** an old pineapple shipping point. This natural harbor, once a major commercial center (by Molokai standards!), is now a gathering place for occasional fishermen and boats.

It's a half-mile farther to **St. Joseph Catholic Church,** a tiny chapel built by Father Damien in 1876. A statue of the bespectacled priest, clad in a cape and leaning on a cane, graces the property. A small cemetery completes this placid tableau.

A monument (past the 11-mile marker) designates the **Smith and Bronte Landing,** an inhospitable spot where two aviators crash-landed after completing the first civilian transpacific flight in 1927. The 25-hour flight from California, scheduled to land in Honolulu, ended abruptly when the plane ran out of gas. (An opening in the trees past the 12-mile marker reveals the aforementioned Keawanui Fishpond, one of Molokai's largest.)

Set back from the road in a clearing framed by mountains is **Our Lady of the Sorrows Catholic Church** (14 miles east of Kaunakakai). Originally built by Father Damien in 1874 and reconstructed almost a century later, it's a pretty chapel surrounded by coconut trees and flanked by a small cemetery.

One of the largest temples in the islands, **Iliiliopae Heiau** (★) (15 miles east of Kaunakakai; for permission and directions, call 558-8380), rests hidden in the underbrush on private land just inland from the highway. Measuring about 100 yards in length and 40 yards in width, it was once a center of sorcery and human sacrifice that today consists of a stone platform and adjoining terraces. This is also the trailhead for the Wailau Valley Trail. According to legend, the *heiau*'s stones were all transported from this distant valley and assembled in a single night.

The best way to visit this ancient site is on the **Molokai Wagon Ride** (located near Mapulehu Mango Grove, 15 miles east of Kaunakakai; 558-8380). This horse-drawn tour, conducted by several delightful local fellows, also visits the nearby **Mapulehu Mango Grove**, a stand of 2000 fruit trees that were planted during the 1930s and now represent one of the largest such groves in the world. The wagon ride winds up at a picturesque beach where guests enjoy a Molokai-style party complete with coconut husking and Hawaiian net throwing.

At the **Mapulehu Glass House** (15 miles east of Kaunakakai; 558-8160) you can tour a tropical flower garden. Spanning ten acres and centered around a decades-old greenhouse, it's a paradise of flowering ginger and other exotic plants.

The ruins of the island's first **sugar mill** stand near Route 450's 20-mile marker. All that remains of this early factory, which burned down about a century ago, is a solitary stack.

Just beyond the marker is Kumimi Beach, which presents your first view of **Moku Hooniki Island** as well as otherworldly vistas of Maui.

The road now begins a sinuous course along a string of pearl-white beaches, then climbs above a rocky coastline. As you curve upward into Molokai's tropical heights, the roadside flora becomes increasingly colorful and dense. First you encounter the open pastures and rolling ranchland of 14,000-acre **Puu O Hoku Ranch**, then dive into the tropical foliage of Molokai's windblown northeast coast.

As the road winds high above **Halawa Valley** (★) it offers several vista points from which to view this V-shaped canyon bounded by green walls. Directly below, tropical greenery gives way to white surf and then aquamarine ocean. A river bisects this luxuriant region. At the far end, surrounded by sheer walls, two waterfalls—Hipuapua and Moaula—spill down the mountainside. Obviously East End has withheld its most spectacular scenery until the last.

Archaeologists believe that Molokai's first settlement was established here, possibly as early as the 7th century. The ancient Hawaiians terraced the surrounding slopes, planting taro and living off the largesse of the sea. Then in 1946 (and again in 1957) a tidal wave swept through the valley, leveling buildings and leaving salt deposits that destroyed the agricultural industry. Today you can drive down into the valley, where you'll find a park, a lovely curve of sandy beach, fresh-water Halawa Stream, an old church, and several other structures. A hiking trail leads to 250-foot Moaula Falls and 500-foot Hipuapua Falls, which lie to the interior of this awesomely beautiful vale.

KAUNAKAKAI TO EAST END HOTELS

The choicest spot on the island to combine local color with a relaxing atmosphere is the cozy **Pau Hana Inn** (★) (553-5342), Molokai's oldest hotel. The beachfront is lackluster, but there's a lovely view across the Kalohi Channel to Lanai. You'll find a quiet, lazy ambience here with cottages and buildings spotted about the lawns. Relax and enjoy the lush vegetation, small swimming pool, and the restaurant and bar down near the waterfront.

Standard rooms are budget-to-moderate-priced. They're small but have been refurbished with new furniture, carpeting, and ceiling fans. Deluxe units are larger and newer. Add a fan, lanai, tub, and extra double bed and you'll pay something in the deluxe price range. These rooms are a good choice if you're traveling with friends—they can be rented with tiny kitchenettes. (To make reservations from the mainland, you can call 800-423-6656.)

There's Polynesian architecture but less island spirit at **Hotel Molokai** (553-5347). Set on a small unappealing beach two miles east of Kaunakakai, this hotel charges a moderate price for a very tiny room with twin beds. I found spotty mirrors, bumpy rugs, shared lanai, and a tacky interior of shingled (yes, shingled) walls. All that's okay in a low-rent hostelry, but why pay more for less? Actually, you're probably paying for what's outside: a shrub-rimmed lawn with coconut trees, and along the shore a pool, restaurant-lounge, and thatch pavilions.

Amid all this splendor you'll find a cluster of brown-shingle buildings with elegantly curved Polynesian roofs and plate-glass windows reflecting the view. These are the deluxe rooms (priced in the moderate to deluxe range); they have wood paneling, high-beamed ceilings, and a much more appealing atmosphere.

If you're traveling with several folks or want kitchen facilities, there are also condominiums: **Molokai Shores** (553-5954) and **Wavecrest Resort** (558-8103). Both offer oceanfront accommodations with full kitchen, lanai, and color television. Each is a series of low-slung buildings that forms a U-shaped configuration around a landscaped lawn extending to the beach. Within the grounds are palm trees, a swimming pool, and barbecue areas. Of the two, Wavecrest, 13 miles east of Kaunakakai, is the best bargain even though there is a three-night minimum. In addition to a few extra features including a putting green, tennis courts, and a dishwasher, the rates are slightly lower (in the moderate range) than Molokai Shores, just one mile east of Kaunakakai.

KAUNAKAKAI TO EAST END RESTAURANTS

A gourmet will starve on Molokai, but someone looking for a square meal at fair prices should depart well-fed. The budget restaurants are clustered along Ala Malama Street in Kaunakakai.

Kanemitsu's Bakery (★) (553-5855) serves tasty meals at appetizing prices. A local institution, it's a simple café with molded seats, formica tables, and an interesting folk art mural presenting a map of Molokai. The dinner special varies but the price is budget whether you are dining on pork chops, beef teriyaki, breaded mahimahi, or fried chicken. Kanemitsu's is also a favorite with the breakfast crowd, which is drawn in by the bakery as well as a menu of omelettes, hot cakes, and egg dishes served with Portuguese sausage or that island favorite, Spam.

If you're into Filipino food, try **Oviedo's Lunch Counter** (553-5014), a nearby café. This mom 'n' pop restaurant serves up spicy steaming dishes at low, low prices. You'll find plank board walls surrounding a few plastic chairs and yellow formica tables. The steam-tray cuisine includes chicken papaya, pig's feet, turkey tail adobo, and mongo beans. Budget.

Outpost Natural Foods (553-3377) has a take-out counter at the back of its tiny health food store. Here you can fuel up with delicious sandwiches, salads, and smoothies that are both nutritious and inexpensive. There are also burritos and daily specials. Open for lunch only; budget.

The **Pau Hana Inn** (553-5342) charges more, but you can dine in a spacious dining room overlooking a century-old banyan tree that faces the ocean. The lunch and dinner menus offer standard fare and come with a salad bar; prices are moderate; breakfast also served.

This is Molokai's classic Hawaiian retreat. The lingua franca at this local hangout is pidgin English and the password is *laid-back*. While enjoying a meal here you'll find all the accoutrements to furnish a tropical dream, from overhead fans to Hawaiian altos plucking slack-key guitars. Charm is the Pau Hana's middle name, which is why it's such a popular spot among savvy travelers.

The Hotel Molokai (553-5347), two miles east of Kaunakakai, hosts hungry travelers in its attractive **Holoholo Dining Room**. In an open-air setting just a stone's skip from shore you can order from a surf-and-turf menu featuring such delectables as prime rib with coconut sauce, mahimahi, and Hawaiian-style stew. Prices are on the deluxe side.

KAUNAKAKAI TO EAST END MARKETS

The nearest Molokai approaches to a supermarket is **Misaki's** (553-5505), a medium-sized grocery store on Kaunakakai's main drag, Ala Malama Street. The prices are higher and the selection smaller here than at the chain markets, so it's wise to bring a few provisions from the larger islands. Open 8:30 a.m. to 8:30 p.m., Sunday 9 a.m. to noon.

Outpost Natural Foods (553-3377), down the street and around the corner from Misaki's, offers a friendly atmosphere as well as juices, herbs, dried fruit, fresh fruit, and other health food items.

Try **Kanemitsu's Bakery** (553-5855) for delicious Molokai honey, bread, and pastries.

On the East End, **Wavecrest Resort**, 12 miles out, has a "general store" with a very limited supply of groceries (primarily canned goods) and a hearty stock of liquor. About 15 miles from Kaunakakai, a small outlet called the **Neighborhood Store 'n' Snack Bar** sells fresh fruit and groceries.

KAUNAKAKAI TO EAST END SHOPPING

You needn't worry about falling into the shop-till-you-drop syndrome on Molokai. Long before you have even begun to think about being tired you will have visited every store on the island. Shopping is still an adventure here, since the few stores operating are all owned by local people and provide a window into life on Molokai.

Ala Malama Street, Kaunakakai's main street, offers a modest row of shops. **Molokai Island Creations** (553-5926) specializes in clothing, jewelry, glassware, and gift items made by Molokai artists.

Imports Gift Shop (553-5734) features casual wear, cultured and mabe pearls, and Hawaiian heirloom jewelry.

They collect antique bottles as well as contemporary shell necklaces and assorted knickknacks at **Collectibles 'n' Such,** and for beachwear you can try **Molokai Surf** (553-5093).

Molokai Fish & Dive (553-5926), "home of the 'original' Molokai T-shirt designs," features its signature clothing as well as beach items and sporting equipment.

KAUNAKAKAI TO EAST END NIGHTLIFE

Confirmed partygoers will find Molokai a pretty dead scene. Probably the best place around is the venerable **Pau Hana Inn** (553-5342) in Kaunakakai. It's certainly popular among the local folks. The Pau Hana Inn blazes with local color weeknights and cranks up the band on weekends when they charge a cover. The ocean view stars nightly.

Hotel Molokai's **Holoholo Dining Room** (553-5347), two miles east of Kaunakakai, is an easy place to kick back, relax, and enjoy dinner music on Thursday, Friday, and Saturday.

KAUNAKAKAI TO EAST END BEACHES AND PARKS

O'ne Alii Park—This spacious park features a large grass-covered field and coconut grove plus a narrow beach with an excellent view of Lanai.

Facilities: Picnic area, restrooms, showers, electricity at the pavilion. Markets and restaurants are four miles away in Kaunakakai. *Swimming:* A reef far offshore makes this area very shallow and affords ample protection. Excellent for children. *Snorkeling:* Mediocre. *Surfing:* All the action is far out on the reef and that's rarely any good. *Fishing:* Surf-casting isn't bad here but it's even better farther to the east. Most common catches are manini, red and white goatfish, parrotfish, papio, ulua, milkfish, and mullet.

Camping: Tent camping only. Very popular and therefore sometimes crowded and noisy. County permit required.

Getting there: Located four miles east of Kaunakakai on Route 450.

Kakahaia Beach Park—This is a long, narrow park wedged tightly between the road and the ocean. A national wildlife refuge, Kakahaia is an important nesting area for native and migratory birds. Picnicking, swimming, snorkeling, surfing, and fishing are much the same as at O'ne Alii Park. Day use only. Head east on Route 450 from Kaunakakai for six miles.

Pukoo Beach—This crescent-shaped strand is mirrored by another curving beach just to the west. Very popular with fishermen, it has a shallow, rocky bottom. Maui lies directly across the channel and there are also marvelous views of Lanai.

Facilities: None. *Swimming:* Mediocre. *Fishing:* Good.

Getting there: Neighborhood Store 'n' Snack Bar, located on Route 450 near the 15-mile marker, is your landmark. Just past here, traveling east, turn into the second driveway on the right. This access road leads a short distance to the beach.

Kumimi Beach, Pohakuloa Point, and **Other East End Beaches**— Beginning near the 18-mile marker on Route 450, and extending for about four miles, lies this string of small sandy beaches. These are among the island's loveliest, featuring white sands and spectacular views of the islands of Maui and Lanai.

Facilities: There is a small market near the 15-mile marker. *Swimming:* Very good, but beware of heavy currents and high surf. *Snorkeling:* Very good. There's a lot of coral in this area. The diving for lobsters is pretty good. *Surfing:* Numerous breaks throughout this area. **Pohakuloa Point** (or **Rock Point**), located eight-tenths of a mile past the 20-mile marker, is one of Molokai's top surfing spots. *Fishing:* Particularly good. Barracuda are sometimes caught in the deeper regions. Also bonefish, mountain bass, threadfin, manini, red and white goatfish, ulua, papio, parrotfish, milkfish, and mullet.

Getting there: These pocket beaches are located along Route 450 between the 18- and 22-mile markers.

Halawa Beach Park—Set in lush Halawa Valley, one of Molokai's most splendid areas, the park is tucked neatly between mountains and sea on a grassy plot dotted with coconut palms and ironwood trees. Cliffs, waterfalls, two pocket beaches—altogether a heavenly spot, though sometimes rainy and almost always windy.

Facilities: The park is a bit weatherbeaten and overgrown. Picnic area; restrooms; running water that must be boiled or treated chemically. *Swimming:* Very good. Partially protected by the bay, but exercise caution anyway. *Snorkeling:* Good, though water is sometimes murky. *Surfing:* One of the very best spots on the island. *Fishing:* Reefs studding this area make it a prime locale for many of the species caught along East End Beaches.

Camping: Not permitted in the park, but people camp on the other side of Halawa Stream on property owned by Puu O Hoku Ranch.

Getting there: Located at the far end of Route 450, about 30 miles east of Kaunakakai.

Kaunakakai to West End

Generally, if you are not pointed east on Molokai, you are headed westerly. The thoroughfare that carries you across the prairie-like plains of west Molokai is Route 460, the Maunaloa Highway, another two-lane track. Along the way you can venture off in search of the plantation town of Kualapuu and the vista point overlooking Kalaupapa, but eventually you will arrive at road's end out in the woodframe town of Maunaloa. From this red-dust municipality it's a short jaunt to Papohaku Beach, Molokai's western shore.

Just a mile west of the cock-eyed town of Kaunakakai on Route 460 is the **Kapuaiwa Grove**, planted in the 1860s by Kamehameha V. This magnificent stand of coconut palms, once 1000 in number, served as a resting place for Hawaii's king. Royal palms are among the tallest of the species and the grove creates the sensation of being in a tropical dream sequence, with hundreds of palm trees flashing green and yellow fronds and extending to the lip of the ocean. Some appear to stand in columns, but others have bent so far to the wind they have fallen out of formation.

Strung like rosary beads opposite the grove are seven tiny churches. This **Church Row** includes Protestant, Mormon, Jehovah's Witness, and several other denominations. Like sentinels protecting the island from the devil, they too are gathered in rows. The most intriguing are the oldest, tiny woodframe structures with modest steeples. These one-room chapels lack worldly frills like stained glass and are furnished with creaky wooden pews that seat a few dozen parishioners. Stop by and inquire about services; visitors are always welcome.

A side trip along Route 470 leads past the tinroof town of **Kualapuu**. Filled with modest plantation houses, it harkens back to an earlier era when Molokai cultivated pineapples rather than tourists. Today its claim to fame is a 1.4 million gallon reservoir that is reportedly the largest rubber-lined water tank in the world.

Fittingly, Kualapuu is home to the **R. W. Meyer Sugar Mill** (Route 470; 567-6436; admission), an 1878 steam-generated operation that has been restored in sparkling fashion. The mule-driven cane crusher, copper clarifiers, and dependable old steam engine are ready and waiting for Molokai to return to its old ways. There are also well-presented displays and heirlooms of the German immigrant family that owned the mill.

Route 470 passes the stable for the Molokai Mule Ride and soon ends at the **Kalaupapa Lookout**. Here cliffs as green as Ireland fall away in dizzying fashion to reveal a softly sloping tableland 1600 feet below, the Kalaupapa Peninsula. Fringed by white-sand beaches, this geologic afterthought extends over two miles out from the foot of the *pali*. A lighthouse and landing strip occupy the point of the peninsula. Nearer the cliffs, a cluster of houses comprises the famous leper colony; while neighboring Kauhako Crater, a nicely rounded circle far below you, represents a vestige of the volcano that created this appendage. Ringed by rock and water, protected by the tallest sea cliffs in the world, Kalaupapa Peninsula is a magnificent sight indeed.

A short hike from the lookout, **Phallic Rock** protrudes obscenely from the ground amid an ironwood stand as thick as pubic hair. This geologic formation, so realistic it almost seems sculpted, was said to represent the Hawaiian fertility god, who was turned to stone when his wife caught him admiring a beautiful young girl. Legend says that a woman offering gifts and spending the night here will return home pregnant.

Route 460 continues over dry rolling plains toward Molokai's West End. This arid plateau, windswept and covered by deep red, iron-rich soil, was once planted in pineapple. Today Molokai Ranch, which still owns much of the region, has turned to hay cultivation to feed cattle.

If nothing else, the West End is rich in myth and history. As Hawaiian storytellers recount, the region around Maunaloa, the volcano that formed this side of the island, was once a cultural focus of the Polynesians. It was here that the hula originated; from the slopes of Maunaloa the goddess Laka spread knowledge of the sensuous dance to all the other islands.

Easier to substantiate historically is the fact that the Kaluakoi area was a rich adze quarry, one of the most important in all Hawaii. The rock, vital to a Stone Age society, was fashioned into tools that were in turn used to create weapons, canoes, bowls, and other necessities.

Like the pineapple industry itself, Route 460 ends in **Maunaloa**. With the departure of Dole's operations in 1975, this company town assumed the dusty, falsefront visage of the Wild West after the mines petered out and

Molokai's Outback

For a splendid tour of Molokai's mountainous interior, take a drive or hike on the Main Forest Road. This bumpy dirt road is studded with "4-Wheel Drive Only" signs along its ten-mile length, but it's passable by car in dry weather.

Deer, quail, pheasant, doves, and chukkar partridge populate the route. Numerous secondary roads and trails lead to the very edge of the mammoth Molokai Forest Reserve, through which the main road passes. These side roads offer excellent possibilities for adventurous hikers.

After nine miles, the main road passes **Lua Moku Iliahi**, known to the English-speaking world as the **Sandalwood Measuring Pit**. This depression, dug into the earth to match the hull size of an old sailing vessel, was used by 19th-century Hawaiians to gauge the amount of sandalwood needed to fill a ship. It's another mile to **Waikolu Picnic Grove**, a heavily wooded retreat ideal for lunching or camping. Here you'll find picnic facilities and an outhouse. (State permit required to camp.) Across the road, **Waikolu Valley Lookout** perches above Waikolu Valley, which descends precipitously 3000 feet to the sea.

Here you can also explore **Kamakou Preserve,** a 2774-acre sanctuary managed by The Nature Conservancy. Home to more than 200 plants that live only in Hawaii, the preserve is a lush rainforest from which Molokai draws most of its water supply. There are also a number of rare forest birds, including the Molokai thrush and Molokai creeper. For information on visiting the reserve, call 553-5236.

To reach the Main Forest Road, take Route 460 west from Kaunakakai. There is a white bridge a little more than three-and-a-half miles from town, just before the four-mile marker. Take a right on the dirt road right before the bridge and you're on the Main Forest Road.

the saloons shut down. In true revival spirit, however, local craftspeople and artists have converted a few buildings into shops and galleries. Besides these more recent additions to the rustic landscape, the old post office remains and there is a classic general store. Framed by Norfolk pines and filled with 1920s-era tinroof plantation houses, Maunaloa itself is a classic.

Perhaps the island's most unexpected and exotic feature is the nearby **Molokai Ranch Wildlife Park** (P.O. Box 8, Maunaloa, HI 96770; 552-2767; admission). Part of Molokai Ranch's sprawling 52,000-acre spread, this game preserve is roamed by more than 1000 animals. Barbary sheep, eland, sable, antelope, ibex, zebra, crown crane, axis deer, giraffe, greater kudu, and oryx are among the species that have transformed Molokai's West End into a kind of "Little Africa." The park also features a "giraffe picnic" where you can feed and pet the curious critters. Van tours and camera safaris of this unusual refuge are scheduled daily.

Any tour of West End should of course finish at *the west end*. **Papohaku Beach**, a sparkling three-mile long swath of white sand, would be a fitting finale to any tour. Reached by taking Kaluakoi Road from Route 460 and driving through the rolling hills of sprawling Kaluakoi Resort, Papohaku is one of the largest beaches in the state. During World War II troops practiced shore landings along this coast. But today you will have the beach and surrounding sand dunes almost entirely to yourself.

KAUNAKAKAI TO WEST END HOTELS

Far from the madding crowd on the west end of Molokai, you'll find a 6700-acre master-planned complex, the Kaluakoi Resort. Divided into the 178-room **Kaluakoi Hotel** (552-2555), the cottage-like condos of **Kaluakoi Villas** (552-2721), and two other condominium complexes, it is set near a luxurious three-mile-long beach. This is Molokai's premier resting spot, offering both seclusion and comfort.

Here you'll find the essence of plush living: wasp-waisted pool, tennis courts, golf course, a view of Oahu across the channel, and an oceanfront lounge and restaurant. The hotel rooms are located in eight-plex *hales* and have all the necessities: lanai, color television, tile bathroom, overhead fan, rattan furniture. For an ultra-deluxe price tag, you can buy a piece of that ocean view in a studio unit with a kitchenette. The villas are more spacious, also include a kitchenette, and are priced deluxe.

Ke Nani Kai (552-2761), a 120-unit condominium located within Kaluakoi Resort, has one-bedroom units at deluxe rates. From December through March there's a five-night minimum. The complex includes a pool, tennis courts, and an outdoor party area with barbecues.

Paniolo Hale (552-2731), also part of the resort complex, has 77 units starting in the deluxe price range. These also include all the amenities and offer access to a swimming pool and paddle tennis.

KAUNAKAKAI TO WEST END RESTAURANTS

Everyone has heard of fast food but what about slow food? **Kualapuu Cook House** (★) (Route 480, Kualapuu; 567-6185) bills itself as the international headquarters for a "slow food chain." Set in an old plantation house, it serves *saimin*, chili, and hamburgers. If you want to get serious about it, there is chicken stir-fry, teriyaki plate, and mahimahi dinners. The pies are homemade and the place is bright with local color. Budget.

Out in Maunaloa, there's a gathering spot called **Jojo's Café** (552-2803). Priced along the border between budget and moderate, its menu includes a variety of ethnic and all-American dishes. Like many of the mom 'n' pop businesses on Molokai, it is located in a tinroof plantation house. You can expect a counter, homespun decor, and an easy friendly atmosphere.

The aforementioned Kaluakoi Hotel (552-2555), on the island's far west end, has a pennysaver **snack bar** with sandwiches. That's just light artillery to back up the hotel's big gun, the **Ohia Lodge**, Molokai's finest restaurant. This multilevel, handsomely appointed establishment (high-beamed ceiling, rattan furnishings) looks out on the distant lights of Oahu. The dinner buffet changes daily, but usually features entrées such as mahimahi, pork loin, and teriyaki chicken. You can also order from an extensive surf-and-turf menu. Seeking a place to splurge? Well, this is it. Breakfast and dinner; deluxe.

KAUNAKAKAI TO WEST END MARKETS

Out West End way, **Maunaloa General Store** (552-5852), in Maunaloa a few miles away from Kaluakoi Resort, has a limited stock of grocery items.

KAUNAKAKAI TO WEST END SHOPPING

Over on Molokai's West End in the red-dust town of Maunaloa you'll stumble upon two great shops that share the same building and the same telephone, 552-2364. **Big Wind Kite Factory** (★) has an astonishing assortment of high flyers. There are diamond kites, dancer kites, windsocks, and rainbow tail kites. You can even pick up flags and banners here. At **The Plantation Gallery** there are aloha shirts, batik sarongs, tribal art, shell necklaces, deer horn scrimshaw, and other original pieces by over 30 Molokai craftspeople.

There are also a few shops at **Kaluakoi Hotel** (552-2555) down the road in the Kaluakoi Resort complex.

KAUNAKAKAI TO WEST END NIGHTLIFE

To step out in style, head west to Kaluakoi Hotel's **Ohia Lounge** (552-2555). The rattan furnishings, carpets, overhead fans, and marvelous view of Honolulu, not to mention the band on the weekends, make it *the* place.

KAUNAKAKAI TO WEST END BEACHES AND PARKS

Kiowea Park—Watch for falling coconuts in the beautiful Kapuaiwa Grove, which is the centerpiece of this beach park. Towering palm trees extend almost to the water, leaving little space for a beach. (This park is generally restricted to homesteaders, but if you stop for a picnic you may be allowed by the locals to stay.) A nice place to visit, but I wouldn't want to fall asleep in the shade of a coconut tree.

Facilities: Picnic area; restrooms. One mile to Kaunakakai's restaurants and markets. *Swimming:* Beach well-protected by a distant reef, but the bottom is shallow and rocky. *Snorkeling:* Mediocre. *Surfing:* Forget it. *Fishing:* Common catches include mullet, manini, parrotfish, milkfish, and papio, plus red, white, and striped goatfish.

Camping: Camping is usually restricted to homesteaders. If the park is vacant however, the Hawaiian Homelands Department in Hoolehua (567-6104) will issue permits for $5; hours are Monday through Friday from 7:45 a.m. to 4:30 p.m.

Getting there: The park is located one mile west of Kaunakakai on Route 460.

Palaau State Park—Set in a densely forested area, this 34-acre park is ideal for a mountain sojourn. Several short trails lead to petroglyphs, a startling phallic rock, and the awesome Kalaupapa Lookout. The trail down to Kalaupapa Peninsula is also nearby.

Facilities: Picnic area; restrooms. Twelve miles to markets and restaurants in Kaunakakai.

Camping: State permit required. Tent camping only.

Getting there: Take Route 460 six miles west from Kaunakakai, then follow Route 470 about six more miles.

Moomomi Beach (★)—A small, remote beach studded with rocks and frequented only by local people—what more could you ask? While Moomomi is a small pocket beach, many people use the name to refer to a three-mile length of coastline that extends west from the pocket beach and includes two other strands, Kawaaloa Beach and Keonelele Beach. This latter beach forms the coastal border of the **Moomomi Dunes**, a unique series of massive sand dunes that extend as far as four miles inland, covering Molokai's northwestern corner. Also known as the Desert Strip, this unique ecosystem is overseen by the Nature Conservancy (553-5236), which can provide information and tours. The preserve protects five endangered plant species and is a habitat for the endangered Hawaiian green sea turtle.

Facilities: None *Swimming:* Good, but use caution; partially protected. Rocky bottom. *Snorkeling:* Very good along reefs and rocks. *Surf-*

ing: Fair breaks at the mouth of the inlet. *Fishing:* Good surf-casting from the rocky headland to the west.

Camping: Camping on a grassy plot elevated from the beach is allowed on weekends. Obtain permit and keys at Molokai Ranch.

Getting there: Take Route 460 west from Kaunakakai to Hoolehua. Go right on Route 481 (Puupeelua Avenue), then left on Farrington Avenue. Farrington starts as a paved road, then turns to dirt. After two-and-two-tenths miles of dirt track, the road forks. Take the right fork and follow it a half-mile to the beach. A four-wheel drive vehicle may be required.

Halena and Other South Coast Beaches (★)—Don't tell anyone, but there's a dirt road running several miles along a string of trackless beaches on the south shore. The first one, **Halena**, is a very funky ghost camp complete with a dozen weatherbeaten shacks and a few primitive facilities. To the west lies **Haleolono Beach**, with its pleasant bay and lagoon. To the east is **Kolo Wharf** (an abandoned pier collapsing into the sea), plus numerous fishponds, coconut groves, and small sand beaches. This is an excellent area to explore, camp, hike, fish, and commune with hidden Hawaii.

Facilities: The shacks, picnic facilities, and running water are open to visitors at Halena. After that you're on your own. Better boil or chemically treat the water. *Swimming:* The water is muddy, but otherwise swimming is good. *Snorkeling:* Muddy water. *Fishing:* You might reel in mountain bass, threadfin, inenui, or even red goatfish. This is also a prime area for limpets.

Camping: Molokai Ranch permits camping along all the beaches in this region. Obtain permits and keys in advance (see information in the "Camping" section at the end of the chapter).

Getting there: Take Route 460 to Maunaloa. As you first enter town (before the road curves into the main section), you'll see houses on the left and a dirt road extending perpendicularly to the right. Usually the roads in this region are locked, making access impossible to everyone but hikers. If you're determined to explore the area anyway, then follow this road two-and-eight-tenths miles to the Molokai Ranch gate and continue along the rugged road that extends beyond the gate. Take this road one-and-eight-tenths miles to where it forks.

Now, to get to Halena, take a right at the fork, then a quick left (there are signs posted), then drive a short way, just a few hundred yards, to the end. The shore is nearby; simply walk west along the beach several hundred yards to the shacks.

To get to Haleolono Beach, walk about a mile west along the beach from Halena.

To get to Kolo Wharf and the other beaches, go straight where the road forks. Kolo is two miles east over an equally rugged road. Sand beaches, coconut groves, and fishponds extend for another six miles past Kolo. Then the road turns inland, improving considerably, and continues for seven miles more until it meets the main road two miles west of Kaunakakai.

For information about road access contact Molokai Ranch (552-2767).

Kawakui Beach (★)—This idyllic spot is my favorite Molokai campground. Here a small inlet, tucked away in Molokai's northwest corner, is edged by a beautiful beach with a sandy bottom. Nearby is a shady grove of kiawe trees, fringed by the rocky coastline. On a clear night you can see the lights of Oahu across Kaiwi Channel.

Facilities: Forget it. Try Kaunakakai, 19 miles behind you. *Swimming:* Very good. The inlet offers some protection, but exercise caution. *Snorkeling:* Good near the rocks when the surf is low. *Surfing:* Good, but variable. Shore wind plagues this area. *Fishing:* Mountain bass, threadfin, inenui, and red goatfish are commonly caught here.

Camping: That shady grove is a perfect site to pitch a tent. Camping permitted by Molokai Ranch (552-2767) on Friday, Saturday, Sunday, and holidays only. Permit required in advance, no fee.

Getting there: Take Route 460 west from Kaunakakai for about 12 miles. Then take a right onto the dirt road that leads downhill. Follow this bumpy dirt road about seven miles to the beach. The road forks a few hundred yards before the ocean. Take the right fork to Kawakui; the left fork leads to a series of white-sand beaches offering excellent possibilities for exploring and swimming. (A key to open the gates en route must be obtained from Molokai Ranch at their office in Kaunakakai; 552-2767.)

Papohaku Beach—This splendid beach extends for three miles along Molokai's west coast; it's an excellent place to explore, collect *puka* shells, or just lie back and enjoy the view of Oahu. Backed by kiawe trees and low sand dunes, Papohaku is the largest beach on the island, averaging 100 yards in width.

Facilities: Picnic areas, restrooms, showers; the Kaluakoi Hotel, with snack bar and restaurant, is about a half-mile away. *Swimming:* Excellent, but use caution. *Snorkeling:* Mediocre; there's not much rock or coral here. *Surfing:* Good breaks when the wind isn't blowing from the shore. Use caution, especially in the winter months. Also popular with bodysurfers. *Fishing:* Mountain bass, threadfin, inenui, and red goatfish are the most common catches.

Camping: Tent only. County permit required.

Getting there: To get to the beach, take Route 460 for about 14 miles from Kaunakakai. Turn right onto the road to the Kaluakoi Resort. Continue past the hotel (don't turn onto the hotel road) and down the hill. Follow this macadam track, Kaluakoi Road, as it parallels the beach. Side roads from Kaluakoi Road and Pohakuloa Road (an adjoining thoroughfare) lead to Papohaku and other beaches.

Kalaupapa

The ultimate Molokai experience is the pilgrimage to the Kalaupapa leper colony along the rugged north shore of the island. Isolated on a 12-square-mile lava tongue that protrudes from the north shore, this sacred and historic site can be reached only by foot, mule, or plane.

Here about 130 victims of Hansen's Disease live in solitude. Doctors have controlled the affliction since 1946 with sulfone drugs, and all the patients are free to leave. But many are 60 to 85 years old, and have lived on this windswept peninsula most of their lives.

Their story goes back to 1866 when the Hawaiian government began exiling lepers to this lonely spot on Molokai's rain-plagued north coast. In those days Kalaupapa was a Hawaiian fishing village, and lepers were segregated in the **old settlement** at Kalawao on the windy eastern side of the peninsula. The place was treeless and barren—a wasteland haunted by slow death. Lepers were shipped along the coast and pushed overboard. Abandoned with insufficient provisions and no shelter, they struggled against both the elements and disease.

To this lawless realm came Joseph Damien de Veuster, Father Damien. The Catholic priest, arriving in 1873, brought a spirit and energy that gave the colony new life. He built a church, attended to the afflicted, and died of leprosy 16 years later. Perhaps it is the spirit of this "Martyr of Molokai" that even today marks the indescribable quality of Kalaupapa. There is something unique and inspiring about the place, something you'll have to discover yourself.

To visit Kalaupapa you can fly, hike, or ride muleback; there are no roads leading to this remote destination. Once there you must take a guided tour; no independent exploring is permitted. And no children under 16 are allowed. Flights and hiking tours are organized by **Damien Tours** (567-6171) and **Molokai Mule Ride** (567-6088). For flight information, check **Aloha Island Air** (567-6115).

As far as I'm concerned, the mule ride is the only way to go. The Molokai Mule Ride conducts tours daily, weather permitting. You saddle up near the Kalaupapa Lookout and descend a 1664-foot precipice. Kalaupapa unfolds below as you switchback through lush vegetation on a three-mile-long trail. The ride? Exhilarating, frightening, but safe. And the views are otherworldly.

On the tour you will learn that Kalaupapa has been designated a national historical park. Among the points of interest within this refuge are numerous windblasted structures, a volcanic crater, and several monuments. You'll also visit Philomena Church, built by Father Damien in the 1870s, and Kalawao Park, an exotically beautiful spot on the lush eastern side of the peninsula.

Definitely visit Kalaupapa. Fly in and you'll undergo an unforgettable experience; hike or ride a mule and it will become a pilgrimage.

The Sporting Life

CAMPING

With so little development and such an expanse of untouched land, Molokai would seem a haven for campers. Unfortunately, large segments of the island are owned by Molokai Ranch and other private interests; with the exception of a few beaches on Molokai Ranch property, these tracts are closed off behind locked gates.

There *are* a few parks for camping. A county permit is required for O'ne Alii Park. Permits cost $3 per person a day and are obtained at the County Parks and Recreation (553-5141) office in Kaunakakai. Office hours are 8 a.m. to 12 noon, Monday through Friday, so get your permit in advance.

Permits for Kiowea Park, when available, are issued by the Hawaiian Homelands Department (567-6104) in Hoolehua. The fee is $5 per night at Kiowea for a group of any size.

Camping at Palaau State Park is free but requires a permit from the Department of Agriculture (567-6150), situated next to the Hoolehua Post Office in Hoolehua.

A $10 per person per day fee (plus a $10 key deposit at Halena and South Coast beaches) is required for campgrounds on Molokai Ranch property. For information contact Molokai Ranch, P.O. Box 8, Maunaloa, HI 96770 (552-2767), Monday through Friday, 7:45 a.m. to 4:30 p.m.

Molokai Fish and Dive Corporation (553-5926) in Kaunakakai sells camping gear.

SKINDIVING, FISHING, AND SAILING

Molokai Fish and Dive Corporation (553-5926) sells a small variety of diving equipment.

For deep-sea fishing contact **Alyce C Commercial and Sport Fishing** (558-8377) in Kaunakakai.

If you'd rather go sailing, step aboard *Satan's Doll*, a 42-foot sloop operated by **Molokai Charters** (553-5852), located on the wharf in Kaunakakai. They sponsor sunset cruises, whale-watching tours, and excursions to Lanai.

TENNIS

There are courts open to the public at the **Kaunakakai Community Center** in Kaunakakai.

GOLF

Ironwood Hills Golf Course (Kalae; 567-6000) and **Kaluakoi Golf Course** (Kaluakoi Resort; 552-2739) are all that Molokai has to offer to the golfing set.

HORSEBACK RIDING

Molokai Wagon Ride (558-8380) sponsors wagon and saddle tours to scenic and historic sites at Mapulehu in eastern Molokai; this outfit also rents horses.

BICYCLING

Traffic is light and slow-moving, making Molokai an ideal place for two-wheeling adventurers. The roads are generally good, with some potholes out East End near Halawa Valley. The terrain is mostly flat or gently rolling, with a few steep ascents. Winds are strong and sometimes make for tough going. Sorry, no bicycle shops of any kind here.

HIKING

Molokai features some splendid country and numerous areas that seem prime for hiking, but few trails have been built or maintained and most private land is off-limits to visitors. Some excellent hiking possibilities, but no official trails, are offered along the beaches described above. Palaau State Park also has several short jaunts to points of interest.

The only lengthy treks lead to the island's rugged north coast. Four valleys—Halawa, Wailau, Pelekunu, and Waikolu—cut through the sheer cliffs guarding this windswept shore.

The **Pelekunu Trail** begins several hundred yards beyond the Waikolu Valley Lookout (see the section on "Molokai's Outback"). I had trouble gathering information on this trail; some sources insisted it didn't even exist. I did learn that it is unmaintained and *extremely* difficult. The trail leads to a lookout point and then drops into the valley.

The **Wailau Trail** is another very difficult trail; it takes six to eight hours and passes through some muddy rainforest regions. The trailhead is off Route 450 about 15 miles east of Kaunakakai. To reach it, you must obtain permission from Pearl Petro (P.O. Box 25, Kaunakakai, HI 96748; 558-8113) to cross private land. The trail extends across nearly the entire island from south to north.

The **Kalaupapa Trail**, used for the island's famous mule ride, is the easiest and best-maintained trail descending the north *pali*. A trail description is given in the "Kalaupapa" section in this chapter. To hike here you must obtain permission and pay $22 for a mandatory tour of the leper colony. Call Damien Tours (567-6171) or Molokai Mule Ride (567-6088) for permission and information.

The only valley accessible by car is Halawa. The **Halawa Valley Trail,** one of Molokai's prettiest hikes, extends for two miles from the mouth of the valley to the base of Moaula Falls. This 250-foot cascade tumbles down a sheer cliff to a cold mountain pool perfect for swimming. Hipuapua Falls, a sister cascade just a third of a mile north, shoots 500 feet down the *pali.* This can be reached by taking a trail near Moaula Falls, then climbing along the rocks.

The trail to Moaula Falls is well-marked and relatively easy to hike. It takes about 90 minutes each way and climbs 250 feet. The path passes several homes as well as the remains of houses wiped out when the 1946 tidal wave swept the valley. Numerous fruit trees line the way and wildlife abounds. If you decide to swim in the pool, you might heed the warning of ancient Hawaiians. They would tie a stone to a *ti* leaf and set it adrift here. If the leaf floated, they plunged in; if it sank, they recognized that the legendary lizard *moo* would drown anyone disturbing his lair.

To get to the trail, take Route 450 to Halawa Valley. The trail is marked near the end of the road a short distance from the beach.

Transportation

BY AIR

When your plane touches down at **Molokai Airport,** you'll realize what a one-canoe island you're visiting. There's a snack bar and adjoining lounge, which seem to open and close all day, plus a few car rental and airline offices. It's seven miles to the main town of Kaunakakai. There is no public transportation available. However, shuttle service can be arranged through some of the hotels or reserved in advance with **Roberts Hawaii** (552-2751).

The airport is served by several airlines: Hawaiian Airlines carries passengers in turbo prop planes. Aloha Island Air and Air Molokai fly small prop planes and are the most exciting way to reach Molokai. To fly direct from Honolulu to Kalaupapa, try Aloha Island Air, which can always be relied upon for friendly service.

BY BOAT

If you'd prefer to arrive by boat, **Sea Link of Hawaii** (553-5736) provides round-trip service from Maui aboard the 118-foot *Maui Princess.* The 75-minute cruise provides a unique opportunity to travel between the islands by sea.

CAR RENTALS

Molokai being a small island, there's not much in the way of car rentals. At last count, only four firms were supplying visitors with infernal combustion machines. But considering that Molokai is off the flight path of tourists, there should be enough cars for visiting adventurers.

The existing companies, in no particular order, are as follows: **Dollar Rent A Car** (567-6156), **Budget Rent A Car** (567-6877), **Tropical Rent A Car** (567-6118), and **Avis Rent A Car** (567-6814). Any of them should prove quite adequate.

JEEP RENTALS

Avis Rent A Car (567-6814) and **Budget Rent A Car** (567-6877) rent jeeps, but require that you drive them only on paved roads!

HITCHHIKING

Thumbing is officially illegal. Actually the law is not enforced and police are rarely even seen on the roads. The traffic is light, but rides are frequent (and there's never very far to go). So happy trucking.

TOURS

Several Maui-based companies, including **Papillon Helicopters** (669-4884), provide flight-seeing tours of Molokai. Because of the otherworldly beauty of Molokai's northern sea cliffs, these helicopter excursions are memorable (and expensive!) experiences.

Molokai Addresses and Phone Numbers

MOLOKAI ISLAND

County Parks and Recreation—Kaunakakai (553-5141)
Department of Agriculture, Hoolehua (567-6150)
Hawaiian Homelands Department—Hoolehua (567-6104)
Weather—(552-2477)

KAUNAKAKAI

Ambulance—911
Fire Department—911
Library—Ala Malama Street (553-5483)

Liquor—Molokai Wines and Spirits, Ala Malama Street (553-5009)
Pharmacy and Photo Supply—Molokai Drugs, Ala Malama Street (553-5790)
Police Department—(553-5355, or 911 for emergencies)
Post Office—Ala Malama Street (553-5845)

CHAPTER NINE

Kauai

Note: As this book went to press, the entire island of Kauai was being rebuilt in the wake of Hurricane Iniki. Since the chapter was researched just prior to the storm, it describes Kauai as it was before the natural disaster occurred.

The force-four hurricane, which struck the island in September 1992 with 135-mile-per-hour winds and 160-mile-per-hour gusts, left 8000 people homeless and caused over one billion dollars damage. Crops were flattened, utility poles toppled, and houses demolished. Every hotel on the island sustained damage.

Plans for 1993 are to completely rebuild the island. Construction crews are repairing hotels and restaurants. Fields are being replanted and landscaping is continuing apace.

Since the entire island was raked by the storm and almost every facility on Kauai was affected, you should double-check the information contained in this chapter by calling ahead to make sure that a particular facility has reopened and is able to provide the same services as before the storm.

The Kauai hotline (800-262-1400) provides 24-hour updates.

Seventy miles northwest of Oahu, across a storm-wracked channel that long protected against invaders, lies Kauai. If ever an island deserved to be called a jewel of the sea, this "Garden Isle" is the one. Across Kauai's brief 33-mile expanse lies a spectacular and wildly varied landscape.

Along the north shore is the Hanalei Valley, a lush patchwork of tropical agriculture, and the rugged Na Pali Coast with cliffs rising 2700 feet above the boiling surf. Spanning 14 miles of pristine coastline, the narrow valleys and sheer walls of Na Pali are so impenetrable that a road entirely encircling the island has never been built. Here, among razor-edged spires and flower-choked gorges, the producers of the movie South Pacific found their Bali Hai. To the east flows the fabled Wailua River, a sacred area to Hawaiians that today supports a sizable population in the blue-collar towns of Wailua and Kapaa.

Along the south coast stretch the matchless beaches of Poipu, with white sands and an emerald sea that seem drawn from a South Seas vision. It was here in November 1982 that Hurricane Iwa, packing 110-mile-an-hour winds and carrying devastating tidal waves, overwhelmed the island. Ironically, it was also this area that sustained some of the most severe damage when Hurricane Iniki struck in September 1992.

The tourist enclave of Poipu gives way to rustic Hanapepe, an agricultural town asleep since the turn of the century, and Waimea, where in 1778 Captain James Cook became the first Westerner to tread Hawaiian soil. In Kauai's arid southwestern corner, where palm trees surrender to cactus plants, snow-white beaches sweep for miles along Barking Sands and Polihale.

In the island's center, Mount Waialeale rises 5148 feet (Mount Kawaikini at 5243 feet is the island's tallest peak) to trap a continuous stream of dark-bellied clouds that spill more than 450 inches of rain annually, making this gloomy peak the wettest spot on earth and creating the headwaters for the richest river system in all Hawaii—the Hanapepe, Hanalei, Wailua, and Waimea rivers. Also draining Waialeale is the Alakai Swamp, a wilderness bog that covers 30 square miles of the island's interior. Yet to the west, just a thunderstorm away, lies a barren landscape seemingly borrowed from Arizona and featuring the 2857-foot-deep Waimea Canyon, the Grand Canyon of the Pacific.

From Lihue, Kauai's largest and most important city, Route 50 (Kaumualii Highway) travels to the south while Route 56 (Kuhio Highway) heads along the north shore. Another highway climbs past Waimea Canyon into the mountainous interior.

Papayas, taro, and bananas grow in lush profusion along these roads, and marijuana is grown deep in the hills and narrow valleys, but sugar is still Kauai's major crop. Tourism has overtaken agriculture in the Kauai economy and is becoming increasingly vital to the island's 51,000 population. The tourist industry has multiplied in the past two decades, and the ominous construction of condos in Poipu and Princeville threatens to turn Kauai into the Maui of the 1990s.

Particularly disconcerting is the decline of the sugar industry, which is intensifying demands to replace agricultural income with tourist dollars. But the Garden Isle still offers hidden beaches and remote valleys to any traveler possessing a native's sensibility. And even though sugar is in re-

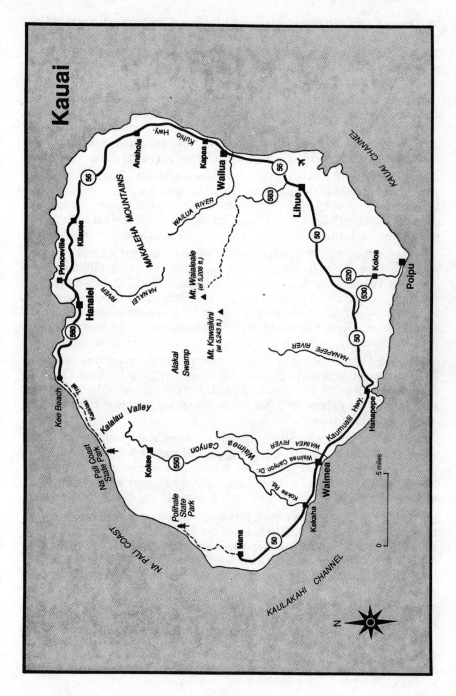

Kauai

treat, cane fields still dominate the island. Here more than anywhere in Hawaii, visitors have a window on 19th-century island life, when sugar was king. For miles in every direction, deep-green sugar stalks cover the landscape, edging from the lip of the ocean to the foot of the mountains.

Island sugar mills are redolent with the cloyingly sweet smell of their produce, and mammoth cane trucks, sugar stalks protruding like bristles from a wild boar, charge down dusty roads. Depending on the phase of the growing cycle, visitors pass fields crowded with mature cane, tall as Midwest corn, or deep-red earth planted with rows of seedlings. In the evening, when harvested cane is set afire, black smoke billows from deep within the fields.

Historically, Kauai is Hawaii's premier island—the first to be created geologically and the first "discovered" by white men. It was here that Madame Pele, goddess of volcanoes, initially tried to make her home. Perhaps because of the island's moist, tropical climate, she failed to find a place dry enough to start her fire and left in frustration for the islands to the southeast.

Formed by a single volcano that became extinct about six million years ago, Kauai is believed by some anthropologists to be the original island populated by Polynesians. After Captain Cook arrived in 1778, explorers continued to visit the island periodically. Ten years later, settlers began to arrive, and in 1820 the first missionaries landed in the company of Prince George, son of Kauai's King Kaumualii. By 1835, the Koloa sugar plantation was founded, becoming the first successful sugar mill in Hawaii.

Kauai was the site not only of the original but the anomalous, as well. In 1817, George Scheffer, a Prussian adventurer representing Czar Nicholas of Russia, built a fort in Waimea. He soon lost the support of both the Czar and Kauai's King Kaumualii, but left as his legacy the stone ruins of Russia's imperialist effort.

Kauai was the only island not conquered by Kamehameha the Great when he established the Hawaiian kingdom. Thwarted twice in his attempts to land an attack force—once in 1796 when high seas prevented an invasion from Oahu and again in 1802 when his battle-ready army was suddenly ravaged by disease—he finally won over Kaumualii by diplomacy in 1810.

But Kauai's most fascinating history is told by mythmakers recounting tales of the *Menehunes*, the Hobbits of the Pacific. These miniature forest people labored like giants to create awesome structures. Mysterious ruins such as the Menehune Fishpond outside Lihue reputedly date back before the Polynesians and are attributed by the mythically inclined to an earlier, unknown race. Supernaturally strong and very industrious, the *Menehunes* worked only at night, completing each project by dawn or else leaving it forever unfinished. Several times they made so much noise in their strenuous laboring that they frightened birds as far away as Oahu.

They were a merry, gentle people with ugly red faces and big eyes set beneath long eyebrows. Two to three feet tall, each practiced a trade in which he was a master. They inhabited caves, hollow logs, and banana-leaf huts, and eventually grew to a population of 500,000 adults.

Some say the *Menehunes* came from the lost continent of Mu, which stretched across Polynesia to Fiji before it was swallowed by floods. Where they finally traveled to is less certain. After the Polynesians settled Kauai, the *Menehune* king, concerned that his people were intermarrying with an alien race, ordered the *Menehunes* to leave the island. But many, unwilling to depart so luxurious a home, hid in the forests. There, near hiking trails and remote campsites, you may see them even today.

Lihue Area

Unappealing in appearance, Lihue sits at the crossroads between the tropical regions of the north and the sunsplashed beaches to the south. So a visit to Lihue is inevitable. Commercial and civic center of the island, the town is an odd amalgam of contemporary Hawaii and traditional plantation life. The sugar mill at the edge of town, with its aging conveyor belts and twin smoke stacks, is still a vital element in the landscape. A portion of the 6000 population continues to live in woodframe plantation houses, and cane fields surround the town. But the airport here is an international landing strip that has grown considerably during the past two decades and Lihue possesses Kauai's main port, Nawiliwili Harbor. Lihue also boasts the island's largest concentration of restaurants and shopping centers.

Among the attractions you will find is the **Kauai Museum** (4428 Rice Street; 245-6931; admission), a two-building complex rich in Hawaiiana. This is a prime spot to learn about the history, culture, and natural history of the island. The main building focuses on Hawaiian heritage with its displays of quilts, feather *leis*, and ancient calabashes. In the adjacent exhibition, Kauai's natural history unfolds and 19th-century plantation life is revealed in a collection of old photographs.

Providing an even wider window on Kauai's sugarcane heritage, **Grove Farm Homestead** (Lihue; 245-3202; admission) is a beautifully preserved 80-acre spread. Founded in 1864 by the son of missionaries, the plantation is like an outdoor museum with the main house, farm office, workers' homes, and a private cottage still intact. Surrounding these tinroof buildings are banana patches, grape arbors, gardens, and pastures. Two-hour guided tours of this fascinating facility are available by reservation. Call in advance or write to Box 1631, Lihue, HI 96766 and they will provide directions.

Another interesting side trip from Lihue is down Rice Street to busy **Nawiliwili Harbor**. This deep-water port, with its cruise ships and cargo vessels, is a major transit point for island sugar. Nearby **Kalapaki Beach** is one of Kauai's most popular strands, both because of its proximity to Lihue and its pretty white sands.

If you've ever sensed that life in the United States is approaching ancient Rome in decadence, there's no better place to prove the point than the **Westin Kauai** (Nawiliwili Harbor; 245-5050). A cross between Nero's city and a modern-day Fellini film, this sprawling resort comes complete with fountains, pillars, reflecting pools, manmade lagoons, and monumental statuary. You can tour the place in a 19th-century British-style carriage drawn by Clydesdales or climb aboard an Italian-style mahogany launch and explore the resort's inland waterways. The latter trip will carry you past Monkey Island, inhabited by Colobus monkeys, and Kangaroo Island, home to wallabies and the endangered Red Kangaroo. Zebras share another island with pheasants from China and ostriches. On the other islets in the lagoons, there are gazelles and flamingoes, llamas and cranes. Then if you venture into the hotel, you'll see the strange species that inhabits this bizarre place.

From Nawiliwili Harbor, you can continue on to the **Menehune** (or **Alakoko) Fishpond**. This 900-foot-long pond, spread across a valley floor and backdropped by the Hoary Head Mountain Range, dates back well before the Polynesians. Or so the mythmakers would like you to believe. Legend has it that a line of leprechaun-like *Menehunes* 25 miles long passed rocks from hand to hand and built the pond in a single night. Their only request of the prince and princess for whom they built the structure was that these two mortals not watch them while they worked. When the *Menehunes* discovered that curiosity had overcome the two, who were watching the midget workers by the light of the moon, the *Menehunes* turned them into the pillars of stone you see on the mountainside above the fishpond. To get there, take Rice Street to Nawiliwili, then right on Route 58, a quick left on Niumalu Road, and finally right on Hulemalu Road.

Also visible from the vista overlooking the fishpond, and accessible to kayakers, is the adjoining **Huleia National Wildlife Refuge (★)**, a 238-acre preserve that rises from the river basin up the wooded slopes of Huleia Valley. This estuary is home to 31 bird species including four different endangered species of waterbirds—the Hawaiian stilt, Hawaiian duck, Hawaiian gallinule, and Hawaiian coot.

A short distance from Lihue, Kuhio Highway (Route 56), the main road to Kauai's north shore, descends into the rustic village of **Kapaia**. Sagging wood structures and a gulch choked with banana plants mark this valley. On the right, **Lihue Hongwanji Temple**, one of the island's oldest, smiles from beneath a modern-day facelift.

To the left, off Kuhio Highway, Maalo Road threads through three miles of sugarcane to **Wailua Falls**. These twin cascades tumble 80 feet into a heavenly pool fringed with *hala* trees. A steep, difficult trail leads down to the luxurious pool at the base of the falls; or if you're not that ambitious, a more easily accessible pool lies just a couple hundred yards past the falls.

Follow Kuhio Highway and you'll arrive in **Hanamaulu,** an old plantation town where falsefront stores and tinroof houses line the roadway.

Or you can head a mile-and-a-half southwest from Lihue on Kaumualii Highway (Route 50) to **Kilohana** (245-5608) for a view of the luxurious side of island life. This 16,000-square-foot Tudor mansion was once home to one of the island's most prominent families. Today, the 1935 house serves as a center for arts-and-crafts shops and museum displays, and the 35 surrounding acres are devoted to a re-creation of traditional plantation life. Wander down the "coral path" and you'll pass a tropical garden and a succession

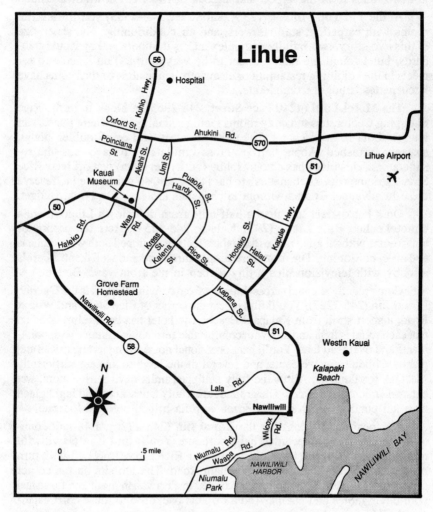

of corrugated-roof houses. Papaya, banana, and avocado trees line the route and roosters crow in the distance. Directly behind the plantation grounds, fields of sugarcane roll to the foothills of the mountains. Carriages pulled by Clydesdales tour the grounds and wagon tours lead out into the cane fields.

LIHUE AREA HOTELS

If you are in search of budget-priced lodging facilities, there are few places in all Hawaii as inviting as Lihue. Three low-cost establishments are located just two miles from the airport and a block or two from downtown Lihue.

At the **Tip Top Motel** (3173 Akahi Street; 245-2333) you'll find trim rooms with carpeting, stall showers, and air conditioning. The sheer size of this two-story, two-building complex makes it impersonal by Kauai standards, but I found the management to be very warm. You'll have to eat meals in the adjoining restaurant or elsewhere, since none of the rooms have kitchenettes. Budget to moderate.

The **Motel Lani** (4240 Rice Street; 245-2965), a block from the Rice Shopping Center, has ten cozy rooms facing a small patio where guests can lounge about in lawn chairs. The units are clean and comfortable, though sparsely furnished. About half are cross-ventilated; all have fans and refrigerators. This place has a noisy lobby (with television) just off busy Rice Street. Rooms with kitchenettes are hard to obtain, so you'll need to reserve these in advance. Rooms without kitchenettes are easier to book. Budget.

On a back street less than a half-mile from downtown Lihue, there's a motel called **Hale Lihue** (2931 Kalena; 245-3151). Here the proprietor rents rooms without kitchenettes and others that are equipped both with kitchens and air conditioning. The rooms are simply furnished and well-kept. There's a lobby with television plus a tiny garden in the front yard. Budget.

Conveniently situated across the street from Nawiliwili Park is the **Garden Island Inn** (245-7227). You'll find it near the corner of Rice Street and Wilcox Road, a short stroll from Kalapaki Beach. The hotel has been refurbished so that each room is light and airy with comfortable furnishings, attractive appointments and overhead fans. You'll hear occasional noise from passing trucks and planes. Children are welcome, and several of the large rooms are sufficiently spacious for families. All of the fully equipped units have refrigerators, wet bars, and microwave ovens. The grounds are trimly landscaped and highlighted by a koi pond in which several dozen carp flash their colors. Moderate.

For local charm, consider the **Kauai Inn** (245-2720), a 48-unit country-style inn set in a secluded neighborhood. You'll find it in Nawiliwili, near Niumalu Park and the harbor. Just take Rice Street to Nawiliwili, turn right on Route 58, then left on Niumalu Road. The inn sits on the corner of Hulemalu Street. The rooms are decorated in a Hawaiian motif and furnished with rattan tables and chairs. Add a tropical backdrop to these corrugated-roof buildings and you have a touch of the islands at a moderate price.

Banyan Harbor Resort (3411 Wilcox Road; 245-7333), a collection of woodframe buildings across a busy street from Nawiliwili Harbor, has two-bedroom condominiums for rent at deluxe prices. Most of the 148 units here are leased by the month, but a handful rent by the night.

LIHUE AREA RESTAURANTS

Lihue is rich in low-cost local restaurants. For the money, the best breakfast spot on the island is **Ma's Family** (★) (4277 Halenani Street; 245-3142). This nondescript café makes up in clientele what it lacks in physical beauty. Early in the morning the place is crowded with Hawaiians on their way to the cane fields. In the world of breakfasts, this is the bargain basement. Or if you want to go Hawaiian at lunch, order a lau lau, poi, and salmon dish. Closed for dinner. Budget.

What Ma's is to breakfast, **Hamura Saimin** (2956 Kress Street; 245-3271) is to lunch and dinner. It's just around the corner, so you're liable to see the same faces lining Hamura's curving counter. When I ate there the place was packed, but I was the only turista around. I had the "saimin special," a combination of noodles, won tons, eggs, meat, onion, vegetables, and fish cake in a delicious broth. Budget.

Yokozuna Ramen (246-1008), on the Lihue Shopping Center's lower level (Rice Street and Kuhio Highway), serves delicious lunches and dinners. Ramen, miso soup, and various Japanese dishes are among the offerings. Budget.

For good food at moderate prices, Lihue is also a prime spot. This is the Kauai county seat, and the center of most island business, so it contains numerous restaurants that cater largely to local folks. To the discerning diner, of course, that means you can enjoy outstanding cuisine and avoid tourist prices. Even if you're not staying around town, try to stop by for at least one meal during your Kauai sojourn.

At **Eggbert's Restaurant** (4483 Rice Street; 245-6325) you'll find more than just a clever name. Here you can create your own omelette, choosing any of 50 variations ranging from a Portuguese sausage concoction to the "vegetarian's delight," a combination of garden delicacies including just about everything a green thumb can grow. Moderate.

Rather go Japanese? Try **Restaurant Kiibo** (2991 Umi Street, Lihue; 245-2650). The place used to be just a noodle house, but a remodeling job has changed the interior into a contemporary-style restaurant. The cuisine has also evolved. Today, you'll find the lunch and dinner menu filled with yakitori, tempura, and tofu dishes as well as sushi and sashimi. Moderate.

The **Barbeque Inn** (2982 Kress Street; 245-2921) offers Asian dishes as well as all-American meals. Breakfasts at this comfortable establishment are pretty standard; the lunch menu includes salads, soups, sandwiches, burgers, and a daily special that often features teriyaki and curry dishes; at dinner, there's steak, lobster, shrimp tempura, and scampi. Moderate to deluxe.

A favorite among tourists is the **Tip Top Café and Bakery** (3173 Akahi Street; 245-2333). Visitors can take their pick of table, booth, or counter in this large and impersonal eatery. Breakfasts are inexpensive (and the macadamia nut pancakes are delicious). Lunch entrées are not very imaginative and have received negative reviews from readers. The dinner menu is limited, but priced comfortably. The well-known bakery serves delicious cakes and pies, plus macadamia nut cookies, the house specialty. My advice? Hit the bakery, skip the restaurant.

If you're in Nawiliwili, check out **Kalapaki Beach Burgers** (3474 Rice Street; 246-6330) near the Westin Kauai entrance. They serve a variety of ethnic foods plus mainland standards. Budget.

You can't beat the location at nearby **Kalapaki Beach Deli** (Anchor Cove Shopping Center, 3412 Rice Street; 245-1778). This glorified take-out stand, with a small patio dining area, sits several coconut trees up from the beach. There are pancakes and quiche for breakfast and deli sandwiches the rest of the day. Budget to moderate.

The Pacific Ocean Plaza across the street promises several good restaurants, including the popular **Kauai Chop Suey** (245-8790) with its ample, moderately priced Chinese menu. **Café Portofino** (245-2121), located in the same complex, is a bright and attractive Italian restaurant with a partial ocean view. Comfortably furnished and nicely decorated, it features several pasta dishes as well as house specialties like stuffed calamari, scampi, eggplant parmigiana, and sautéed rabbit. There's also a spiffy espresso bar at this moderate-priced dining room.

Also down Rice Street on the shore of Nawiliwili Harbor sits the **Club Jetty** (245-4970). This cozy restaurant sports a view of both the busy port and the Hoary Head Mountains. There's live music later in the evening, and a Cantonese menu with á la carte plates as well as multi-course meals. They also serve steak and seafood dishes. I found the cooking adequate and the staff very friendly. Moderate.

J. J.'s Broiler Room (3614 Rice Street; 246-4422) is widely known for its "Slavonic steak," a tenderloin that's broiled, then sliced thin and basted with a wine, butter, and garlic sauce. This family-style eatery offers standard steak dishes, seafood platters, and a salad bar, and enjoys a waterfront location overlooking Kalapaki Beach. With its windswept terrace and open-air dining room, it has a sunny Southern California ambience. Deluxe.

When it comes to special occasions and fine dining, the address in these parts is the **Westin Kauai** (Nawiliwili Harbor; 245-5050) and the adjacent Kauai Lagoons. This lavishly baroque complex offers numerous restaurants, three of which I recommend.

For traditional Japanese dining, there is **Tempura Garden,** a classic restaurant set within a flowering landscape. The menu includes several complete dinners: the nabemono dinner, for instance, consists of meats and vegetables prepared in a Japanese pot and served with bean paste soup, fresh fruit, and pickled vegetables. The presentations of sushi, tempura, and other kyoto-style dishes are elegant and delicious. Ultra-deluxe.

Sharky's Fish Market is more relaxed, an open-air bistro on a hillside above the Pacific. A great place to down a margarita, order from the oyster bar, or get serious and select one of the half-dozen or so fresh fish dishes. There is also fresh pasta, lobster, and "landlubber" dishes like steak and teriyaki chicken. Deluxe.

You'll have to take a hotel boat to reach the **Inn on the Cliffs.** I don't know that this exactly qualifies it as part of "hidden Hawaii," but it certainly makes it a popular spot. Bounded on one side by a lagoon and on the other by open ocean, it serves up otherworldly views and gourmet cuisine. As at Sharky's, expect fresh seafood, pasta, and a few meat entrées like lamb chops, steak, and chicken breast in tarragon sauce. Deluxe to ultra-deluxe.

If it's atmosphere and a taste of the Orient you're after, reserve a tea room at the **Hanamaulu Café** (245-2511) on Kuhio Highway in Hanamaulu. My favorite is the garden room overlooking a rock-bound pond filled with carp. Lunch and dinner are the same here, with an excellent selection of Japanese and Chinese dishes. There's also a sushi bar. Children's portions are available. Moderate.

Take a plantation manor, add a flowering garden, and you have the setting for **Gaylord's** (at Kilohana on Kaumualii Highway, one-and-one-half miles southwest of Lihue; 245-9593). Elevating patio dining to a high art, this alfresco restaurant looks out on the spacious lawns and spreading trees of Kilohana plantation. The menu features fresh island fish, Alaskan king crab, shrimp, duck with juniper berry sauce, and barbecued baby back ribs. A rare combination of Old World elegance and tropical ambience; lunch, dinner, and Sunday brunch; ultra-deluxe.

LIHUE AREA MARKETS

Lihue has by far the greatest number of grocery, health food, and fresh fish stores on the island. This commercial center is an ideal place to stock up for a camping trip, hike, or lengthy sojourn in an efficiency apartment.

The **Big Save Market** (Lihue Shopping Center, 4444 Rice Street; 245-6571) is one of Lihue's main grocery stores. It's open 7 a.m. to 11 p.m. every day.

Hale O Health (Rice Shopping Center, 4300 block of Rice Street; 245-9053) has an excellent line of vitamins, juices, and bath supplies, plus natural foods and sandwiches.

If you hanker for fresh fish, be sure to check out **Fish Co. Seafoods** (4361 Rice Street).

Don't miss the **Sunshine Market (★)** every Friday afternoon in the parking lot of the town stadium (Hoolako Street) or the convention center (4191 Hardy Street). Local folks turn out to sell homegrown produce, "talk story," and generally have a good time. It's a great place to buy island fruits and vegetables at bargain prices, and an even better spot to meet Kauai's farmers.

Love's Thrift Store (4100 Rice Street; 245-6113) sells day-old bakery products including delicious breads for about 50 percent off.

North of Lihue, the **Kauai Variety Store** (246-0449) on Kuhio Highway in Hanamaulu has a small grocery stock.

LIHUE AREA SHOPPING

For everyday needs and common items, try the local shopping centers. The **Lihue Shopping Center** (Rice Street and Kuhio Highway) contains a clothes shop and small department store. **Rice Shopping Center** (4300 block of Rice Street) has a few stores, including a boutique.

Who would have guessed that Nawiliwili, formerly a rough-hewn harbor district, would become a major shopping area. It began with the **Westin Kauai** (245-5050), a sprawling resort with enough exclusive stores to keep even a gold credit card past the credit limit. This extraordinary resort also features a network of lagoons along which are several more shopping complexes. Happy fishing!

Then **Anchor Cove**, a beachside mall, went up along Rice Street at the entrance to the Westin Kauai. Later, **Pacific Ocean Plaza** (3501 Rice Street), a glass-and-stucco shopping center, joined the contingent. So don't worry: If you can't find it here, by the time you are done looking, they will have opened another mall somewhere nearby.

At the **Kapaia Stitchery** (245-2281), on Kuhio Highway just north of town in the hamlet of Kapaia, half the items are designed and stitched by local women. There's an array of T-shirts, *aloha* shirts, Hawaiian quilting kits, and dresses, plus stunning patchwork quilts. This is an excellent place to buy Hawaiian fabrics. In addition to the handmade quality, the prices here are often lower than in larger stores.

Kukui Grove Center (Kaumualii Highway, one-half mile southwest of Lihue) is the island's largest shopping mall, an ultra-modern complex. Here are department stores, bookshops, specialty stores, and many other establishments. Though lacking the intimacy of Kauai's independent handicraft outlets, the center provides such a concentration of goods that it's hard to bypass.

Kilohana (Kaumualii Highway, one-and-one-half miles southwest of Lihue) is one of Hawaii's most beautiful complexes. Set in a grand plantation house, it rests amid acres of manicured grounds. Many rooms in this museum-cum-mall are furnished in period to recapture 1930s-era plantation life. The galleries, boutiques, and crafts shops are equally enchanting. Don't miss **Stone's Gallery** (245-6684) with its outstanding selection of artwork from Oceania.

If you can't find what you're after in Lihue, you've always got the rest of the island. Failing that, you'll just have to wait for that plane flight back to the Big Papaya, Honolulu.

LIHUE AREA NIGHTLIFE

You'll find a lot of local color at the **Lihue Café** (2978 Umi Street; 245-6471). The drinks are cheap, the tourists are few.

The **Club Jetty** (245-4970), down on the harbor at Nawiliwili, features live entertainment every night from 10 p.m. to 4 a.m. This rocking seaside spot is recommended for anyone in search of a good time. Cover.

Legends Night Club (3501 Rice Street, Nawiliwili; 246-0491) in the nearby Pacific Ocean Plaza mall features Hawaiian and reggae sounds, and boasts the area's largest dancefloor. The motif is tropical and the club is equally hot. Cover for the occasional live band.

The **Westin Kauai** (245-5050) on Kalapaki Beach in Nawiliwili offers low-key evening entertainment. At **The Colonnade,** you'll find a bar overlooking the pool area that features live contemporary Hawaiian music. For something more formal, you can head out to the **Inn on the Cliffs,** which features piano or jazz duos in a luxurious lounge dramatically poised above the Pacific.

LIHUE AREA BEACHES AND PARKS

Kalapaki Beach—This wide strand stretches for a quarter-mile in front of the plush Westin Kauai hotel. Popular with surfers since ancient Hawaiian times, it is situated right on Nawiliwili Bay, an appealing but busy harbor. It is also one of the best swimming beaches on the island since the harbor protects it from heavy shorebreak. Out past the harbor, the Hoary Head mountains rise in the background.

Facilities: Nawiliwili Park, next to the beach, has a picnic area and restrooms. Snack bars and restaurants are nearby. Be sure to check out the **Pine Tree Inn** (★), a small pavilion painted with local color. *Swimming:* Excellent. *Snorkeling:* Fair. *Surfing:* Beginner's surfing is best in the right center of Nawiliwili Bay. Right slide. More experienced surfers will find good breaks next to the rock wall near the lighthouse. Left slide. There's also good surfing on the right side of the bay. Nicknamed "Hang Ten," these breaks are a good place for nose-riding. Left slide. *Fishing:* Both off the pier and near the lighthouse are good spots for mullet, big-eyed scad, papio, bonefish, and threadfin; sometimes ulua, oama, and red bigeye can be caught here, too.

Getting there: Take Rice Street from Lihue to Nawiliwili Park. Enter Kalapaki Beach from the park.

Niumalu Beach Park—This tree-lined park is tucked into a corner of Nawiliwili Harbor near a sugar-loading facility and a small-boat harbor. With neighbors like this and no swimming facilities, the park's key feature is its proximity to Lihue. It is popular nonetheless with campers and picnickers and the adjacent Huleia River attracts kayakers, fishermen, and crabbers.

Facilities: Picnic area, restrooms, showers, playground. Restaurants are nearby.

Camping: County permit required. Tent and trailer camping.

Getting there: Take Rice Street to Nawiliwili, turn right on Route 58, then left on Niumalu Road.

Ninini Beach (★)—Hidden along a rocky coastline between Nawiliwili Bay and the lighthouse on Ninini Point are two small sand beaches. Lying at the base of a sea cliff, these pocket beaches are separated by a lava rock formation and are usually protected from currents and winds. The smaller beach is a quarter-mile from Ninini Point and the larger is known as **Running Waters Beach,** named for the numerous springs that bubble out of the lava and percolate up into the sand. Both are excellent for sunbathing. Since they're pretty close to civilization, I don't recommend camping at either beach.

Facilities: None. *Swimming:* Excellent. *Snorkeling:* Very good. *Surfing:* Bodysurfers frequent Running Waters Beach.

Getting there: Take the road leading through the Westin Kauai Hotel property in Nawiliwili. Follow this road to the golf course clubhouse. Park and walk across the golf course in a direction several degrees to the right of the lighthouse. The smaller beach can be reached by walking from Running Water Beach toward the lighthouse for about three-tenths of a mile.

Hanamaulu Beach Park—Here's an idyllic park nestled in Hanamaulu Bay and crowded with ironwood and coconut trees. The beach is a narrow corridor of sand at the head of Hanamaulu Bay, well protected from the open ocean. I found this a great place for picnicking and shell collecting.

Facilities: Picnic area, restrooms, showers, playground. One mile from restaurants and the small market in Hanamaulu. *Swimming:* Well-protected bay affords excellent opportunities, but the water is usually murky so there is not much snorkeling. *Fishing:* Common catches include bonefish, mullet, and big-eyed scad.

Camping: Needles from the ironwood trees make a natural bed at this lovely site. Tent and trailer camping; county permit required.

Getting there: Take Kuhio Highway to Hanamaulu, then turn down the road leading to the bay.

Hidden Beaches and Cane Roads

Strung like jewels along Kauai's shore lies a series of hidden beaches that are known only to local people. Among these are some of the loveliest beaches on the entire island, removed from tourist areas, uninhabited, some lacking so much as a footprint. For the wanderer, they are an uncharted domain, and to the camper they can be a secret retreat.

Over a dozen of these hideaways are described in the accompanying sections on Kauai's beaches. Some are located right alongside public thoroughfares; others require long hikes down little-used footpaths. Most can be reached only by private cane roads. These graded dirt roads are owned by sugar plantations and marked with menacing "No Trespassing" signs. Officially, the public is not permitted, and few tourists ever travel along them. But local people use cane roads all the time.

They do so with the greatest courtesy and discretion, realizing that they are treading on private property. They watch cautiously for approaching cane trucks, and yield to plantation traffic. Most important, they respect the awesome beauty of these areas by leaving the beaches as they found them. As one Hawaiian explained to me, the golden rule for visitors is this: "If you want to go native, act like one!"

I certainly recommend that you go native, and I can't think of a better place to do so than one of Kauai's secluded beaches.

Poipu Area

All during the 1980s and now in the 1990s, the Poipu Beach region has represented the fastest-growing tourist destination on Kauai. With the continual construction of new condominiums and the opening of the Hyatt Regency Kauai in 1991, it's one of the hottest spots in the entire state. What you will find in this warm, dry, sunny southeastern corner is a prime example of everyone's favorite combination—the old and the new.

The traditional comes in the form of Koloa town, site of Hawaii's first successful sugar mill, a 19th-century plantation town that has been refurbished in tropical colors. For the modern, you need look only a couple miles down the road to Poipu, a series of scalloped beaches that has become action central for real estate developers.

Anchoring these enclaves to the east is Puuhi Mount, scene of the last volcanic eruption on Kauai. To the north rises the Hoary Head Range, a wall of wooded mountains that divides the district from the Huleia Valley and Lihue. Everywhere else (everywhere, that is, that isn't being developed) you'll find sugar, acres of sugar, miles of sugar: cane fields that are losing to the encroachment of contractors but that appear nevertheless to be sweeping down from the mountains, poised to overwhelm everything in their path.

Before King Sugar retakes his territory, you'll want to drive out from Lihue along Kaumualii Highway (Route 50) to explore the south coast. Along the way, if you possess a Rorschach-test imagination, you'll see **Queen Victoria's Profile** etched in the Hoary Head Range. (Need a helping eye? Watch for the Hawaii Visitors Bureau sign on the side of the highway.)

When you turn south toward Poipu on Maluhia Road (Route 52), you won't need a road sign to find **Eucalyptus Avenue**, an arcade of towering trees that forms a shadowy tunnel en route to the timeworn town of **Koloa**. The remains of the original sugar plantation stand in an unassuming pile on the right side of the road as you enter town; a plaque near this old chimney commemorates the birth of Hawaii's sugar industry, a business that dominated life in the islands throughout most of the 19th century. A sugar mill continues to operate just outside town and Koloa still consists primarily of company-town houses and humble churches surrounded by fields of sugarcane. But the main street was gentrified during the 1980s as tropical-colored paints were added to the old woodframe and falsefront town center. The tiny **Koloa History Center**, located in the freshly refurbished Old Koloa Town Mall (Koloa Road), provides a brief introduction to the history of the area in the form of artifacts from the old plantation days.

If a one-word association test were applied to **Poipu**, the word would be "beach." There really is no town here, just a skein of hotels, condominiums, and stores built along a series of white-sand beaches. Nevertheless, this is Kauai's premier playground, a sun-soaked realm that promises good weather and good times. Scene of devastating damage during the 1982 Hurricane Iwa, Poipu recovered so rapidly it barely missed a beat in the parade of development.

While civilization has encroached to the very side of sea, nature continues to display its wonders along the colorful reefs and pearly sands. Most remarkable of all is **Spouting Horn** (end of Lawai Road), an underwater lava tube with an opening along the shore. Surf crashing through the tube dramatically transforms this blowhole into a miniature Old Faithful. Try to time your visit with the high tide when the spumes from Spouting Horn reach their greatest heights. The mournful sounds issuing from the blowhole are said to be the plaintive cries of a legendary lizard or *moo*. It seems that he was returning from another island where he had been told of the death of his two sisters. Blinded by tears he missed his landing and was swept into the blowhole. (You should also look around at this intriguing coastline, which is covered by coral outcroppings and tidepools and is the location of several archaeological sites.)

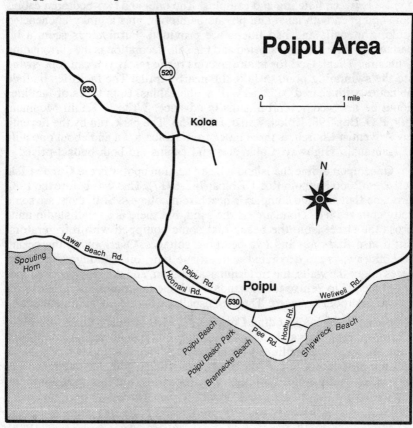

Civilization meets nature (and they live happily ever after) at the **National Tropical Botanical Garden** (★) (332-7361; admission), a spectacular 186-acre tropical plant research facility off Route 53 about three miles from Koloa. The three-hour guided tours of this remarkable place take in some of the 7000 (7000!) plant species that reside in the gardens. They also include a visit to the Allerton Garden, a 100-acre paradise that was first planted by Hawaii's Queen Emma in the 1870s. With the Lawai River coursing through the property, flowering gardens are intermingled with pools, fountains, and waterfalls. Advance reservations recommended.

POIPU AREA HOTELS

One place for people wanting to rough it or to establish a base camp is **Kahili Mountain Park** (742-9921). Facing the Hoary Head Range and backdropped by Kahili Mountain, this 197-acre domain offers an easy compromise between hoteling and camping. The one- and two-bedroom cabins come equipped with lanai and private bathroom, plus a funky kitchenette. Cooking utensils and bed linens are provided. Furnishings seem a bit spartan: the floors are uncarpeted and the sole decoration is the surrounding mountains. Thank God for nature. At this rustic resort you can rope-swing into the swimming pond or hike the nearby trails. The facilities include cabinettes with shared baths as well as the cabins. Both types of facilities should be reserved several months in advance. Write to Kahili Mountain Park, P.O. Box 298, Koloa, Kauai, HI 96756. The park, run by the Seventh Day Adventist Church, is three miles from Koloa town and about one mile off Kaumualii Highway. Cabinettes and cabins are both budget-priced.

Once upon a time the island's best vacation spot was the **Garden Isle Cottages** (2666 Puuholo Road, Koloa; 742-6717). That was before the 1982 hurricane flattened the complex's beachfront cottages. Still, there are some pretty cottages left. None are on the sand, but there are small studio units across the street from the beach that come equipped with refrigerators. You'll also find one- and two-bedroom cottages. Overlooking the ocean, these hideaways are decorated with artistic flair: oil paintings and woven pieces adorn the walls, the furnishings are rattan, and the kitchens are modern. Moderate to deluxe for the studios and one-bedrooms, ultra-deluxe for the two-bedroom cottages. There is usually a two-night minimum stay.

Similarly, **Koloa Landing Cottages** (2704-B Hoonani Road; 742-1470) in Poipu offers guests a choice between two studio units and three cottages. These are attractive facilities with kitchens. All studios and two of the cottages are moderately priced; the third cottage rents in the deluxe range and holds up to four people. With their garden setting and family atmosphere, they evoke a comfortable sense of familiarity. Three-night minimum.

Poipu Bed & Breakfast Inn (2720 Hoonani Road; 742-1146) is a lovely woodframe house with four guest rooms renting in the deluxe range. White wicker furniture and merry-go-round horses (there's one in the living room and in three of the bedrooms) dominate the decor. You can also expect wall-to-wall carpeting and overhead fans. There are small porches in front and back plus a yard complete with garden and mango tree.

Another bed and breakfast run by the same people is the **Ocean Front Inn** (2650 Hoonani Road; 742-1146). This five-bedroom house sits across the street from the ocean. It's trimly decorated, has a large front porch and backyard patio, and prices in the deluxe range. Each room comes equipped with a microwave and refrigerator.

For a place right on the water, there's **Gloria's Spouting Horn Bed & Breakfast** (4464 Lawai Beach Road; 742-6995), a 1940s-era plantation house with five guest rooms decorated in American oak and English walnut antiques. Open and airy, Gloria's has an oceanfront living room and a lanai that sits just above the waves. Here's a place where you can play a Baldwin piano, lie in a hammock, or go surfing outside your front door. And the prices start in the moderate range!

Pricey as Poipu can be, even a deluxe-priced hotel seems like a relief. Especially when it's right on the sand like the **Poipu Beach Hotel** (2251 Poipu Road; 742-1681). This low-slung establishment, shaped in a "U" with a swimming pool at the center, is designed in the plantation style popular on Kauai. Guest rooms are comfortable if uninspired in decor. Face it, you're paying for the location, and at this price you're getting a lot of location for the dollar.

One hotel that sets the definition for style in Poipu is the **Stouffer Waiohai Beach Resort** (2249 Poipu Road; 742-9511). In this case, style means a windswept lobby trimmed with marble, a cluster of signature shops, and three swimming pools that flank a white-sand beach. Rooms are furnished in rattan and the grounds appear to be cared for by a bevy of hair stylists. Add a health spa and award-winning restaurant to round out the description; ultra-deluxe.

Another fashionable address, **Kiahuna Plantation** (2253 Poipu Road, Poipu; 742-6411), is a 35-acre beachfront spread. Landscaped with lily ponds, lagoon, and a spectacular cactus garden, the complex offers condominiums at ultra-deluxe prices. The units are housed in attractive plantation-style structures, which are dotted about the resort's rolling lawns.

POIPU AREA CONDOMINIUMS

At **Sunset Kahili Condominium** (1763 Pee Road; 742-1691) one-bedroom apartments are $88 double, two bedrooms will run $113 for one to four people. Some units have ocean views. Three-night minimum.

One of the most unique condominiums around is **Poipu Crater Resort** (★) (Hoohu Road; 742-7260). It's also one of the best deals. This entire 30-unit facility rests in the bowl of an extinct volcano. The accommodations are contained in attractive woodframe houses; all are two-bedroom condos and rent for about $90. Pool, tennis courts, jacuzzi, barbecue; 600 yards from the beach.

Poipu Kai Resort (1941 Poipu Road; 742-6464) consists of a succession of separate buildings spread around a spacious lawn. There are five pools and nine tennis courts on the property plus a restaurant, jacuzzi, and barbecues. It's located across the street from Brennecke Beach. One-bedroom condominiums start at $165 ($150 from April 1 to December 21).

Poipu Shores (1775 Pee Road; 742-7700) is a small (39 unit) complex right on the ocean with a swimming pool so close to the water the waves seem poised to break across it. One-bedroom units start at $150 ($135 off-season); three-night minimum.

Poipu Kapili (2221 Kapili Road; 742-6449), neatly situated a short stroll from Poipu Beach, has one-bedroom oceanview condos from $175 (with a free rental car). It's a 60-unit complex with pool and tennis courts.

Out on the road to Spouting Horn, **Lawai Beach Resort** (5017 Lawai Road; 742-9581), a large complex across the street from the ocean, has one-bedroom units starting at $140 ($125 during off-season). There are two pools plus tennis courts and spas.

At nearby **Kuhio Shores** (5050 Lawai Road; 742-6120) one-bedroom apartments are $95 for one to four people; two bedrooms, two baths, cost $125 for one to six people. On the shore, but lacking a beach. There's a four-night minimum.

The best way to shop for value and location among Poipu condominiums is to contact one of the local rental agencies: **Poipu Beach Resort Association** (2360 Kiahuna Plantation Drive; 742-7444), **Grantham Resorts** (2721 Poipu Road; 742-7220), or **R & R Realty & Rentals** (1661 Pee Road; 742-7555). Talk to them at length. Ask them about the best deals they have to offer during the season you're going. If interested, you can also ask about packages that include rental cars.

POIPU AREA RESTAURANTS

"Snack bar" comes closer to describing the low-priced dining facilities here than "restaurant." This lovely beach area hosts no full-sized budget restaurants. In Koloa town, two miles from Poipu, there's the **Kauai Kitchens** snack bar (742-1712) next to the Big Save Market on Koloa Road. No dinner. Budget.

Also in Koloa, you might consider **Koloa Broiler** (5412 Koloa Road; 742-9122). Nothing fancy; it's a bright, airy café with a broil-your-own kitchen and adjoining bar. There's steak, beef kabob, mahimahi, chicken, fresh island fish, and hamburger to choose from. Of course, the quality of the food depends on your own culinary abilities; this could prove to be

Kauai's best (or worst) restaurant. The one thing you can bank on is that this family-style establishment will transform dining from a spectator sport to a way of meeting fellow chefs. Moderate.

If you're hankering for Mexican food, there's **Pancho & Lefty's** (Old Koloa Town Mall, Koloa Road, Koloa; 742-7377). A tad overpriced, it's a pine-paneled dining room with sombreros, ristras, and woven baskets decorating the walls. There's a popular bar and a menu that includes fajitas, tacos, enchiladas, burritos, and other south-of-the-border standbys. Moderate.

The Japanese are represented in tiny Koloa town by **Taisho Restaurant** (5470 Koloa Road; 742-1838), a simple and appealing dining spot. There are two small dining areas, decorated in traditional Asian fashion, and a full Japanese menu. Cozy and moderately priced.

Budget-priced cafés in Poipu are rare as unicorns. The best place to look for a quick, inexpensive meal is in the Poipu Shopping Village on Poipu Road. Here you'll find take-out stands dispensing hot dogs, sub sandwiches, and other nutritious items. A particularly good deal is **Pizza Bella** (742-9571), where they serve not only pizzas but lasagna, pasta marinara, soups, and salads too. You can dine inside or on a small patio within the mall.

Keoki's Paradise (Poipu Shopping Village; 742-7534) is a beautiful patio-style restaurant centered around a tropical garden and pond. Open for dinner only, they feature a steak-and-seafood menu at moderate cost. The setting alone makes it worth a visit.

Overlooking Poipu Beach is **Brennecke's Beach Broiler** (Hoone Road; 742-7588). Downstairs at this two-level dining spot you'll find a budget-priced snack bar and deli serving sandwiches. The upper deck is occupied by an open-air restaurant that serves appetizers from noon to 4 p.m. daily, then stokes the kiawe broiler for a dinner that includes several fresh fish dishes, steak, chicken, and seafood kabob. There's also pasta at this deluxe-priced nook.

Pink is the color of the day, everyday, at **Flamingo Cantina** (2301 Nalo Road, Poipu; 742-9505). The bar, walls, even the porch rail are pink. Which doesn't really tell you that this is a Mexican restaurant, and a very popular one at that. During lunch they prepare a taco bar. In the evening they pass out the menus, complete with flautas, arroz con pollo, chile rellenos, and a Mexican pizza. Moderate.

With windsurf sails on the ceiling, T-shirts on the walls, and a neon fish logo, the **Poipu Beach Café** (Poipu Beach Hotel, 2251 Poipu Road; 742-1681) is nothing if not hip. A popular nightclub later in the evening, it features a dinner menu that includes pizza, linguine, beef ribs, ginger-grilled mahimahi, and tempura-fried shrimp. Dinner only; moderate.

My first choice in the ethereal realm of ultra-deluxe-priced restaurants is the **Plantation Gardens Restaurant** (2253 Poipu Road; 742-1695) at Kiahuna Plantation. Despite rather modest furnishings, the open-air design here creates a sense of elegance. The view extends along a carefully tended cactus garden, which encircles this old sugar planter's manor house. Only dinner is served; the evening menu features seafood and also offers steak, chicken, and prime rib dishes. If you'd like to dine well in a tropical garden setting, this old plantation is the perfect spot.

Stouffer Waiohai Beach Resort's signature restaurant, **Tamarind** (2249 Poipu Road, Poipu; 742-9511), is another of the island's top gourmet dining rooms. The sleek decor in this continental-and-Asian restaurant is highlighted by Japanese paper lanterns ribbed with teak. Surrounded by brass pillars and Thai silks, you'll enjoy *ono* in black bean-ginger sauce, duckling with a Maui onion-pineapple relish, or Western-style dishes like veal medallions and rack of lamb. Ultra-deluxe.

The signature restaurant at the Hyatt Regency Kauai is **Dondero's** (1571 Poipu Road; 742-1234), a fashionable Italian dining place. Here you can begin with carpaccio or seafood ravioli, progress to minestrone or an appetizer pizza, then get serious with a list of entrées that includes cioppino, veal scallopine, shrimp wrapped in pancetta, sautéed scallops, and lamb chops. Festive and original, it's a solid choice for a special meal. Dinner only; deluxe to ultra-deluxe.

POIPU AREA MARKETS

There's a **Big Save Market** (742-1614) on Koloa Road in Koloa. The store includes a dry goods section and is definitely the place to shop on the way to Poipu Beach.

If you're already soaking up the sun at Poipu, you have two grocery options. **Brennecke's Mini-Deli** (742-1582) is conveniently situated on Hoone Road across the street from Poipu Beach Park. This mom 'n' pop business has liquor, cold drinks, and a limited selection of groceries. To increase your choices and decrease your food bill, head up Poipu Road to **Kukuiula Store** (742-1601) at the intersection of Poipu and Lawai roads. This market offers prices nearly competitive with Big Save.

POIPU AREA SHOPPING

On the way to Poipu, the former plantation town of Koloa supports a cluster of shops as well as a miniature mall. Several trendy clothing stores line Koloa Road. The mall, called **Old Koloa Town** (even though it was totally overhauled in the 1980s), houses a string of small jewelry stores, a T-shirt shop, and a photo studio.

Bougainvilla (5492 Koloa Road, Koloa; 742-9232) has hand-painted clothing and collectible jewelry.

Poipu Shopping Village on Poipu Road is a sprawling complex dotted with upscale shops. There are dozens of stores to choose from, including several galleries and boutiques, as well as a sundries shop.

After browsing here, if you care to go from the middle class to the très cher, you might consider the shops at the **Stouffer Waiohai Beach Resort** (2249 Poipu Road; 742-9511). Located on Poipu Beach, this resort complex offers a wide selection of stores from which to choose.

Speaking of upscale, you can always venture down to the **Hyatt Regency Kauai** (1571 Poipu Road; 742-1234). It's a spectacular property, well worth touring, and also offers a half-dozen sleek shops.

My favorite shopping spot around Poipu has always been at the **Spouting Horn** (end of Lawai Road). Here, next to the parking lot that serves visitors to the blowhole, local merchants set up tables to sell their wares. You're liable to find coral and puka shell necklaces, trident shell trumpets, rare Niihau shell necklaces, and some marvelous mother-of-pearl pieces. You are free to barter, of course, though the prices are pretty good to begin with. If you're interested in jewelry, and want to meet local artisans, this is an intriguing spot.

POIPU AREA NIGHTLIFE

The **Poipu Beach Café** (2251 Poipu Road; 742-9511) at the Poipu Beach Hotel features live music nightly, a large dancefloor with two stages, and lots of pink and green neon.

The **Drum Lounge** at the nearby Sheraton Kauai Beach Resort (742-1661) beats out dance rhythms every night of the week. I admit I had mixed feelings about the music, but the view from this seaside watering hole is simply spectacular.

Stouffer's Waiohai Beach Resort (2249 Poipu Road; 742-9511), also located on Poipu Beach, hosts several plush nightspots. The **Tamarind Lounge** offers piano or guitar music; seaside at the **Terrace Bar** you can watch the moon over the water or buy a drink to go and take a stroll along the beach.

To catch a more local crowd, head down to **Brennecke's Beach Broiler** (Hoone Road; 742-7588). There's no music, but the crowds are young and the views otherworldly.

The Hyatt Regency Kauai (1571 Poipu Road; 742-1234), a lavish resort on Shipwreck Beach, hosts several top nightspots. My favorite is **Stevenson's Library**, a stately wood-paneled lounge that evokes a sense of colonial-era Polynesia. For a drink in the open air by the beach, try the **Tidepools Lounge**. To dance to live and deejay music, check out **Kuhio's**. The bands turn up every Thursday through Saturday and the deejay plays Top-40 tunes during the breaks. (On Wednesday, it's deejay only, and during the rest of the week Kuhio's is closed.)

POIPU AREA BEACHES AND PARKS

Poipu Beach and **Waiohai Beach**—Extending from the Sheraton to the Waiohai hotel are two adjacent white-sand beaches lined with hotels and crowded with visitors. Popular with sunbathers, swimmers, and water sport aficionados, both are protected by a series of offshore reefs.

Facilities: There is full range of facilities in the hotels that line both strands. *Swimming:* Excellent. *Surfing:* At Poipu Beach there is good surfing for beginners near the beach, for intermediate surfers about 100 yards offshore, and for expert surfers about a half-mile out at "First Break." This beach is also popular with windsurfers. Waiohai Beach has an offshore break near the reef known as "Waiohai." *Fishing:* The beach area is usually crowded but there is fishing from the nearby rocks.

Getting there: Located along Poipu Road near the Waiohai hotel.

Poipu Beach Park—This has got to be one of the loveliest little parks around. There's a well-kept lawn for picnickers and finicky sunbathers, a crescent-shaped beach with protecting reef, and the sunny skies of Poipu.

Facilities: Picnic area, restrooms, showers, playground, lifeguards. Market and restaurants across the street. *Swimming:* Excellent. *Snorkeling:* The entire area has some of the best diving on the island. *Surfing:* An offshore sandbar makes for good bodysurfing. *Fishing:* Bonefish, rockfish, and papio are common. There's good spearfishing on the nearby reefs.

Getting there: Located on Hoone Road in Poipu.

Brennecke Beach—This tiny pocket beach looms large in the imagination of bodysurfers everywhere. A sandbar near the shore and Brennecke's now-famous shorebreak make it one of the hottest bodysurfing spots in Hawaii. As a result, the water is often crowded.

Facilities: There are restaurants and stores nearby; restrooms, showers, and other facilities are available a short distance away at Poipu Beach Park. *Swimming:* Good only when surf is flat. *Surfing:* Boards are not permitted. The best bodysurfing is usually in the summer. *Fishing:* Good from nearby rocks.

Getting there: Located on Hoone Road in Poipu.

Shipwreck Beach—Back in the 1980s (remember way back then?), this was one of the greatest of Kauai's hidden beaches. Then condominiums began crawling along the coast and eventually the Hyatt Regency Kauai was built right on the beach. Today, it's a sandy but rock-studded beach, quite beautiful but bordered by a major resort.

Facilities: There is a full host of (expensive) facilities at the hotel. Otherwise, it's a mile to markets and restaurants around Poipu Beach. *Swimming:* Good when surf is low. *Surfing:* This is an outstanding bodysurfing and windsurfing area. The best spot is at the east end of the beach. *Fishing:* Good from nearby Makawehi Point.

Getting there: From the Poipu Beach area, follow Poipu Road east and simply look for the Hyatt Regency Kauai, which borders the beach.

Mahaulepu Beach (★)—If you've come to Hawaii seeking that South Seas dream, head out to these lovely strands. Mahaulepu is a dreamy corridor of white sand winding for two miles along a reef-protected shoreline and including several strands and pocket beaches. In addition to being incredibly beautiful and ripe with potential for outdoor sports, Mahaulepu is important scientifically. Remains of extinct birds have been found here; flocks of seabirds inhabit the area; and petroglyphs have been discovered along the shoreline. If that's not enough, the beach boasts 100-foot-high sand dunes and a mushroom-shaped sea stack.

Facilities: None. *Swimming:* Good along the well-protected sections of beach. *Snorkeling:* Good. *Surfing:* Good. *Fishing:* Good from the rocky areas along this stretch.

Camping: Local residents say that the best camping is in the ironwood grove along the beach.

Getting there: From the Poipu Beach area, follow Poipu Road east past the Hyatt Regency Kauai at Shipwreck Beach. Beyond Shipwreck, the pavement ends and the thoroughfare becomes a cane road. Continue on the main cane road (which is like a dirt road continuation of Poipu Road). Follow this road for about two miles (even when it curves toward the mountains and away from the ocean). Numerous minor cane roads will intersect from the right and left: ignore them. Finally, you will come to a crossroads with a major cane road (along which a line of telephone poles runs). Turn right and follow this road for about a mile (you'll pass a quarry off in the distance to the right), then watch on the right for roads leading to the beach.

Waimea Area

The Western world's relationship with Hawaii, a tumultuous affair dating back more than two centuries, began in southwest Kauai when Captain James Cook set anchor at Waimea Bay. Cook landed on the leeward side of the island, a hot, dry expanse rimmed by white-sand beaches and dominated to the interior by Waimea Canyon, "the Grand Canyon of the Pacific."

Like the district surrounding Poipu, this is sugarcane country. Several small harbors dot the coast and the population is concentrated in company towns consisting of old plantation cottages and falsefront stores.

One of the first plantation towns you'll encounter driving west on Kaumualii Highway (Route 50) is Kalaheo. Here, a left on Papalina Road will lead a mile up to **Kukuiolono Park**, a lightly visited Japanese garden complete with stone bridge, ornamental pool, and florid landscaping. Take a stroll through this peaceful retreat and you'll also enjoy a stunning view that sweeps across a patchwork of cane fields to the sea.

Back on the main road, nearby **Olu Pua Gardens and Plantation** (332-8182; admission) features an international assortment of plant life cultivated in patterns that represent different themes. There's a hibiscus garden, a palm garden, a section devoted to edible plants, and a tropically luxurious "jungle garden." After paying a hefty admission fee, you are led through this former plantation estate by a tour guide.

En route from one tinroof town to the next, you'll pass the **Hanapepe Valley Lookout**, which offers a view of native plant life dramatically set in a gorge ringed by eroded cliffs.

Be sure to take the nearby fork into **Hanapepe** (★), a vintage village complete with wooden sidewalks and weather-beaten storefronts. During the 1924 sugar strike, 16 workers were killed here by police. Even today, the independent spirit of those martyrs pervades this proud little town. For a sense of Hanapepe during the plantation days, drive out Awawa Road. Precipitous red lava cliffs rim the roadside, while rickety cottages and intricately tilled fields carpet the valley below.

Fort Elizabeth State Historic Park, just outside Waimea near the mouth of the Waimea River, is now just a rubble heap. Historically, it represents a fruitless attempt by a maverick adventurer working for a Russian trading company to gain a foothold in the islands in 1817. Designed in the shape of a six-pointed star, the original fort bristled with guns and had walls 30 feet thick.

An earlier event, Captain James Cook's 1778 "discovery" of Hawaii, is commemorated with a lava monolith near his landing place in Waimea. Watch for roadside markers to **Cook's Monument** (on the road to Lucy Wright Park).

Cook was not the only outsider to assume a role in Waimea's history. It seems that those industrious leprechauns who built the fishpond outside Lihue were also at work here constructing the **Menehune Ditch** (★) (outside town on Menehune Road). This waterway, built with hand-hewn stones in a fashion unfamiliar to the Polynesians, has long puzzled archaeologists.

As interesting as this lengthy aqueduct is a nearby **swinging footbridge** that crosses the Waimea River. Swaying with every step you take across it, the wood-and-wire span is a rather unsettling way to get from one side of the river to the other.

You'll pass the town of Kekeha, home of a sugar mill and a colony of plantation houses, before arriving at the next stop on Kaumualii Highway's scenic itinerary—**Barking Sands Airfield**. Actually, it's not the airfield but the sands that belong on your itinerary. These lofty sand dunes, among the largest on the island, make a woofing sound when ground underfoot. This, according to scientists, is due to tiny cavities in each grain

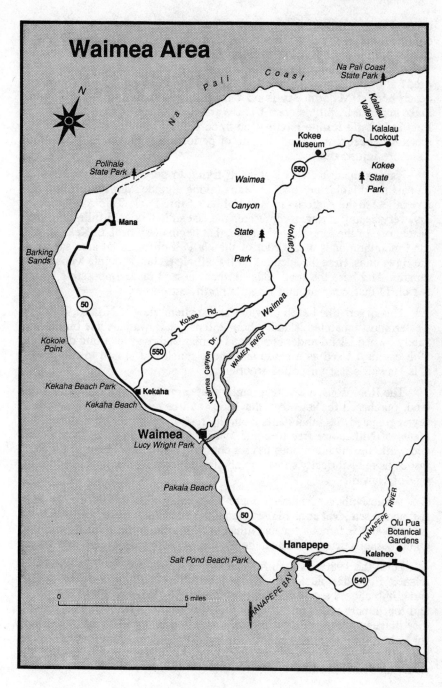

Waimea Area

of sand that cause them to resonate when rubbed together. (Similar sands are found in Egypt's Sinai Desert, the Gobi Desert of Mongolia, and in Saudia Arabia.) If you have trouble making the sound, remember what one local wag told me: The hills actually got their name from tourists becoming "dog-tired" after futilely trying to elicit a growl from the mute sand. (Since the beach here at Major's Bay is on a military reservation, call 335-4346 to make sure the facility is open.) There are also guided tours of the adjacent **Pacific Missile Range Facility**, an important launch area for military and meteorological rockets and the site of periodic war games; call 335-4242 for more information.

Having made a fool of yourself trying to get sand to bark, continue on past the dilapidated town of Mana (along a graded dirt road for the last five miles) to the endless sands of **Polihale State Park**. This very hot, very dry, very beautiful retreat represents the last stretch of a 15-mile-long sand beach, one of the longest in the state, that begins way back in Kekaha. The sand marathon ends at the foot of the Na Pali cliffs, in an area sacred to the Hawaiians. Here the ancients built **Polihale Heiau**, a temple whose ruins remain. And here the road ends, further passage made impossible by the sea cliffs that wrap around Kauai's northwest corner.

This desert-like beach provides an excellent view of **Niihau**, Hawaii's westernmost inhabited island. About 230 native Hawaiians live on this privately owned island under conditions similar to those prevailing during the 19th century. Used as a cattle and sheep ranch and closed to the public, it is Hawaii's last unspoiled frontier.

The Robinsons, a Scottish family that came to Hawaii from New Zealand, purchased the island in the 1860s and have protected (some critics say segregated) its inhabitants from the rest of the world ever since. Residents of Niihau are free to come and go from the island as they please, and while the situation does have a company-town aura about it, the Robinsons have historically shown an abiding concern for the people and ecology of Hawaii.

While Niihau measures a mere 73 square miles and rises only 1281 feet above sea level at its highest point, the island lays claim to rich fishing grounds and is famous for its Niihau shell necklaces, fashioned from rare and tiny shells that wash up on the windward shore only a few times a year.

Until the 1980s, Niihau fully deserved its nickname, "The Forbidden Island." But today outsiders with a sense of adventure (and some extra cash) can climb aboard a **Niihau Helicopter** (★) (Kaumakani; 335-3500) flight and tour a part of the island. You'll fly over most of the island, avoiding the village where the population is concentrated, and land on a remote beach for a short hike along the shore. You won't meet any Niihau residents, but you will have an experience that could prove to be your ultimate encounter with "hidden Hawaii."

Another candidate in the contest for ultimate adventure—one that is free, doesn't require a helicopter, and always lies open to exploration—is **Waimea Canyon**. Touring the "Grand Canyon of the Pacific" involves a side trip from either Waimea or Kekaha. Waimea Canyon Road leads from the former and Kokee Road climbs from the latter; they join about halfway up the mountain. For an overview of the entire region, go up along Waimea Canyon Road, since it hugs the canyon rim and provides the best views, then follow Kokee Road down.

As the paved road snakes along the side of this 2857-foot-deep canyon, a staggering panorama opens. The red and orange hues of a barren southwestern landscape are splashed with tropic greens and yellows. Far below, the Waimea River, which carved this ten-mile-long chasm, cuts a sinuous course. Several vista points provide crow's-nest views of the territory, including one (Poohinahina Overlook at 3500-feet elevation) that provides views of the canyon to the east and Niihau in the west.

The road continues deep into Kauai's cool interior before arriving at **Kokee State Park** (335-5871). Here you'll find a restaurant, cabins, and the **Kokee Museum**, a small display space devoted to the flora, fauna, and natural history of the area. This intriguing exhibit also features collections of shells and Hawaiian artifacts.

It's a short drive onward and upward to the **Kalalau Lookout**. Here, Kauai's other face is reflected in knife-edged cliffs and overgrown gorges that drop to the sea 4000 feet below. Another nearby overlook gazes out across the Alakai Swamp to Mt. Waialeale. (Because of cloud cover in the valley, it's best to arrive at the overlook before 10 a.m. or after 4 p.m.) One more spectacular scene along the way, one more reason to bring you back to this magnificent island.

WAIMEA AREA HOTELS

Accommodations on Kauai's southwest side include beachside cottages in Waimea and ethereal facilities in Kokee State Park.

Waimea Plantation Cottages (★) (Kaumualii Highway, Waimea; 338-1625) is one of the most alluring and secluded facilities on the entire island. Here in a spectacular coconut grove, fronting a salt-and-pepper beach, is a cluster of rustic 1920s-era plantation cottages. Each has been carefully restored and many are furnished with period pieces. One, two, and multi-bedroom houses, with full kitchens, rent for deluxe prices; maid service is every fourth day. Like the rest of the complex, the swimming pool follows the style of an earlier era (most visitors swim here since the offshore waters are usually murky). The place is a little gem out on Kauai's remote westside. I highly recommend it.

Nestled in secluded woods between Waimea Canyon and the Kalalau Valley Lookout are the **Kokee Lodge Cabins** (335-6061). Each of the 12 mountain cabins, varying in size from one large room to two-bedroom complexes, comes with complete kitchen, wood-burning stove, and rustic furnishings. These knotty-pine cabins, 3600 feet above sea level, are a mountaineer's dream. With forest and hiking trails all around, Kokee is ideal for the adventurer. It gets chilly here, so bring a jacket or sweater. And try to make reservations for the cabins in advance; this place is popular! If you can't make future plans, you'll have to call and hope for a cancellation or last-minute reservation. Rates are the same for each cabin; some cabins sleep as many as seven people. Budget.

Catering to gay men and women, **Black Bamboo** (Kalaheo; 332-7518) is a plantation-style house with views of the ocean in the distance. There are three units at this casual retreat, one of which is a studio with kitchenette; all are moderately priced. The rooms are attractively decorated and equipped with overhead fans. Guests share a lounge area and a trimly landscaped yard with a pool and jacuzzi. Continental breakfast.

WAIMEA AREA RESTAURANTS

Traveling west toward Waimea Canyon and Barking Sands, you'll find the watering places decrease as rapidly as the rainfall. Most restaurants en route are cafés and take-out stands. If you're on a budget, you're in luck; if you're looking for an exclusive, elegant establishment, you'll find slim pickings out Waimea way.

At the **Kalaheo Steak House** (4444 Papalina Road, Kalaheo; 332-9780) you'll step into a comfortable wood-paneled dining room. Pull up a chair, rest your elbows on the table (it's permitted), and choose among sirloin, filet mignon, scampi, Cornish hens, and several other appealing entrées. It's dinner only at this moderate-priced restaurant.

Camp House Grill (Kaumualii Highway, Kalaheo; 332-9755) is a trim little café with an island-style lunch and dinner menu. Favored by nearby residents, they serve huli huli chicken and pork ribs. Budget to moderate.

On Kaumualii Highway in Hanapepe is **Susie's All Kind Burgers** (335-3999), a postage-stamp-sized eatery with breakfasts and lunch platters. This place is a real sleeper. When I went in it was elbow to elbow with local people and tourists. At lunch you can order a teriyaki chicken plate, fish filet, or deli sandwich, as well as hamburgers. Budget.

The best restaurant along this highway is Hanapepe's **Green Garden Restaurant** (335-5422). Dining is indoors, but the tropical plants convey a genuine garden feeling. At breakfast you can enjoy eggs and hot cakes along with a steaming cup of coffee. The lunch menu features a broad selection of meat, seafood, and Asian platters, all priced comfortably. And for dinner, the deliciously varied menu ranges from pork chow mein to rock lobster tail. I particularly enjoyed the seafood special, a platter of mahimahi, shrimp, oysters, and scallops. Children's portions are available. Moderate.

If you'd prefer to go ethnic, there's **Sinaloa Mexican Restaurant** (1-3959 Kaumualii Highway, Hanapepe; 335-0006), a brightly colored café sporting overhead fans, tile counter, and a kind of pastel rainbow atmosphere. The prices stand in budget territory and the menu covers the spectrum of south-of-the-border dishes.

In Waimea, there's **Yumi's** (338-1731), a short-order restaurant with a rotating menu. They serve breakfast and lunch. Budget.

Decorated with everything from buddhas and New Guinea masks to tapestries and cruise ship menus, the **International Museum Café** (9875 Waimea Road, Waimea; 338-0403) is a scene. It serves fresh fish and vegetable dishes at moderate prices and draws a local crowd.

The decor at **Wrangler's Restaurant** (Kaumualii Highway, Waimea; 338-1218), as you might have guessed, is Western. The old wagon wheels, dusty saddles, kerosene lanterns, and trophy horns evoke Hawaii's *paniolo* country. But the prize antiques here are the jukeboxes, which once played 78s and featured tunes by Nat King Cole and Jimmy Dorsey. The food? At lunch they serve Mexican-style meals, local platters, and hamburgers. For dinner there are also pork chops, steaks, seafood, and regional specials. Moderate.

The only real sit-down establishment past Waimea is **Toi's Thai Kitchen** (337-9922) on Kekaha Road in Kekaha. The lunch and dinner menu consists primarily of Thai food, but hamburgers, fried chicken, and mahimahi are also served. Dining is on a patio and the menu includes satays, curries, and several ginger-sauce dishes. Moderate.

When you're up in the heights above Waimea Canyon, hungry as a bear after hibernation, you'll be mighty glad to discover **Kokee Lodge** (335-6061) in remote Kokee State Park. From the dining room of this homey hideaway, you can gaze out at the surrounding forest; or step over to the lounge with its stone fireplace and *koa* bar. The breakfast menu consists of a variety of egg dishes, pancakes, and fresh fruit. The house specialty is the home-smoked meats sliced in sandwiches at lunch. Every Friday and Saturday they also serve dinner—a full-course affair with smoked beef and turkey dishes, Korean-style ribs, grilled fish, and stuffed Cornish game hen. There are also salads and special desserts, and for noncarnivores a vegetarian fettuccine dish. In addition to the bounteous fare, you'll find moderate prices and a friendly staff.

WAIMEA AREA MARKETS

There are two **Big Save Markets** along Kaumualii Highway (Route 50). Traveling west from Lihue, the first is in the Eleele Shopping Center (338-1621) and the second is in the center of Waimea (335-3127). Also along the highway is the **Menehune Food Mart** convenience store (332-8027) in Kalaheo. For groceries past Waimea, try the **Menehune Food Mart** (337-1335) on Kekaha Road in Kekaha.

WAIMEA AREA SHOPPING

Hanapepe, a turn-of-the-century town with a falsefront main street, is steadily developing into an art center.

The James Hoyle Gallery (3900 Hanapepe Road, Hanapepe; 335-3582) displays the scintillating works of the famous Hawaii artist.

Nearby **Andy Lopez Gallery** (3878 Hanapepe Road, Hanapepe; 335-3853) features originals and limited-edition prints by the owner. Many of his island images are drawn directly from town scenes of Hanapepe.

Across the street at the **Dawn M. Traina Gallery** (3871 Hanapepe Road, Hanapepe; 335-3993) are a series of portraits by another local artist.

This is also the home of **Kauai Fine Arts** (★) (3848 Hanapepe Road, Hanapepe; 335-3778), a singular gallery with an outstanding collection of antique maps and prints. With a varnished pine interior that creates a captain's cabin atmosphere, this is one of my favorite Kauai shops.

Hanapepe Bookstore (3830 Hanapepe Road, Hanapepe; 335-5011) doesn't actually stock very many books, but it does have an espresso bar! After downing a cup, you can wander across the street and indulge in a delicious Hawaiian pastime at **Longies Crackseed Center** (335-3440), where the candy jars are filled with dried fruit.

It's a small store with a big name, **Kashuba Fine Art & Gifts International** (9883 Waimea Road, Waimea; 338-1750). But crowded into these confines is a choice selection of contemporary and Hawaiian pieces.

Collectibles & Fine Junque (9821 Kaumualii Highway, Waimea; 338-9855) has an amazing collection of glassware, *aloha* shirts, dolls, and old bottles. It's a good place to pick up antiques or knickknacks.

WAIMEA AREA BEACHES AND PARKS

Salt Pond Beach Park—A pretty, crescent-shaped beach with a protecting reef and numerous coconut trees, this park is very popular with local folks and may be crowded and noisy on weekends. It's a good place to collect shells, though. The road leading to the park passes salt ponds that date back hundreds of years and are still used today to evaporate sea water and produce salt.

Facilities: Picnic area, restrooms, showers. Markets and restaurants are a mile away in Hanapepe. *Swimming:* Good, well-protected. *Snorkeling:* Fair diving near rocks and along the offshore reef. *Surfing:* There's a shore break by the mouth of the Hanapepe River nearby in Port Allen. Sandy and shallow with small waves, this area is safe for beginners. Left and right slides. Along the outer harbor edge near Port Allen Airport runway there are summer breaks, for good surfers only, which involve climbing down a rocky shoreline. At Salt Pond there are occasional summer breaks requiring a long paddle out. Left and right slides. This is also a very popular windsurfing area. *Fishing:* Rockfish and mullet are the most common catches here.

Camping: County permit required. Tent camping only.

Getting there: Take Kaumualii Highway to Hanapepe. Turn onto Route 543 and follow it to the end.

Pakala Beach (★)—This long narrow ribbon of sand is bounded by trees and set in perfectly lush surroundings. Surfers will probably be the only other people around. They may come out of the water long enough to watch the spectacular sunsets with you and to tell you of the fabled summer waves that reach heights of 10 to 12 feet. If this book were rating beaches by the star system, Pakala Beach would deserve a constellation.

Facilities: None. Markets and restaurants are two miles away in Waimea. *Swimming:* Good when surf is low. *Snorkeling:* Good along the reef when surf is down. *Surfing:* You're at one of Hawaii's top summer surfing spots. The incredibly long walls that form along a wide shallow reef allow you to hang ten seemingly forever. Hence the nickname for these breaks— "Infinity." Long paddle out. *Fishing:* Good from the rock outcropping off to the left.

Camping: Camping is not recommended here; the area behind the beach is strictly private.

Getting there: Listen carefully—along Kaumualii Highway near the 21-mile marker (two miles east of Waimea) you'll see a concrete bridge crossing Aakukui stream with the name "Aakukui" chiseled in the cement. Go through the gate just below the bridge and follow the well-worn path to the beach.

Lucy Wright Park—This five-acre park at the Waimea River mouth is popular with locals and therefore sometimes a little crowded. Despite a sandy beach, the park is not as appealing as others nearby: the water is often murky from cane field spillage. If you're in need of a campground you might stop here, otherwise I don't recommend the park.

Facilities: Picnic area, restrooms, showers, playground. Markets and snack bars nearby in Waimea. *Swimming:* Fair, unless the water is muddy. *Surfing:* Varies from small breaks for beginners to extremely long walls that build four different breaks. Surfing is best near the river mouth. Left slide. *Fishing:* In Waimea Bay, for parrotfish, red goatfish, squirrelfish, papio, bonefish, big-eyed scad, and threadfin. You can also fish from the pier a few hundred feet west of the park.

Camping: County permit required. Tent camping only.

Getting there: Located in Waimea.

Kekaha Beach—This narrow beach parallels Kaumualii Highway for several miles along the eastern edge of Kekaha. Although close to the highway, the lovely white strand offers some marvelous picnic spots, but the rough surf and powerful currents make swimming dangerous. There are numerous surfing spots along this strip; the foremost, called "Davidson's," lies off Oomano Point.

Kekaha Beach Park—Set on a beautiful ribbon of sand, this 20-acre park is a great place to kick back, picnic, and catch the sun setting over Niihau.

Facilities: Picnic facilities and restrooms; restaurants and markets are nearby in Kekaha. *Swimming:* Good when surf is down; otherwise it can be dangerous. *Surfing:* Immediately west of the park are several breaks, including "Inters" (near Kaumualii Highway and Akialoa Street) and "First Ditch" and "Second Ditch," located in front of two drainage ditches. *Fishing:* For threadfin.

Getting there: Located on Kaumualii Highway in Kekaha.

Kokole Point (★)—Out by an old landing strip/drag strip, a local dump, and a rifle range, there is a wide sandy beach that stretches forever and offers unofficial camping and outrageous sunsets. Fishermen, joggers, and beachcombers love the place, but those who hold it nearest their hearts are surfers.

Facilities: None. *Swimming:* Currents and high surf usually make it unadvisable. *Surfing:* The breaks here go by such names as "Rifle Range," "Targets," and "Whispering Sands." *Fishing:* Good.

Camping: Local people pitch their tents here regularly.

Getting there: Just take the road that leads off Kaumualii Highway one mile west of Kekaha (there's a sign directing traffic to the dump). Follow any of the dirt roads in as far as possible. These will lead either to the dump or to a nearby landing strip. Walk the last three-tenths of a mile to the beach.

Barking Sands—The military installation at Major's Bay is bounded by very wide beaches that extend for miles. You'll see the Barking Sands dunes and magnificent sunsets and get some of the best views of Niihau anywhere on Kauai. Hot, dry weather: a great place to get thoroughly baked, but beware of sunburns. The Pacific Missile Range Facility is located here, and the area is sometimes used for war games.

Facilities: Markets and restaurants are several miles away in Kekaha. *Swimming:* Good, but exercise caution. Snorkeling is good along the coral reefs. *Surfing:* Major's Bay is an excellent surfing spot with both summer and winter breaks. Other breaks include "Rockets" near the rocket launch pad, "Kinkini" at the south end of the airfield runway, and "Family Housing" just offshore from the base housing facility. Windsurfers also frequent Major's Bay and "Kinkini." *Fishing:* The most common catches are bonefish, threadfin, and ulua. A particularly good fishing spot is around Nohili Point.

Camping: Check with the security guards (335-4346) at the front entrance. Camping only on weekends and holidays.

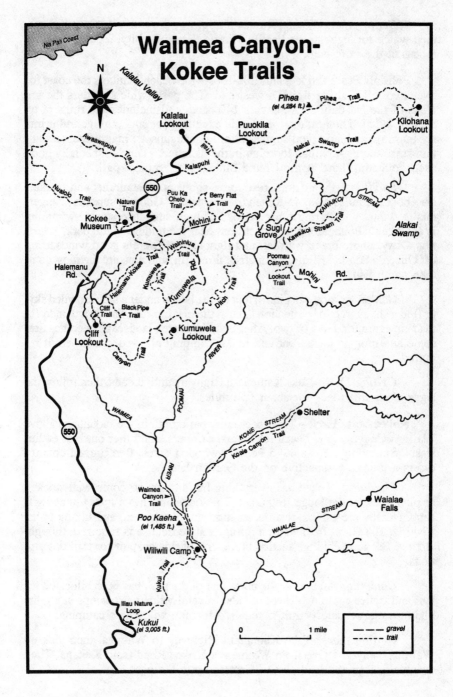

Waimea Canyon-Kokee Trails

Getting there: Take Kaumualii Highway several miles past Kekaha, then watch for signs to the Pacific Missile Range Facility. You can request a pass at the front gate.

Polihale State Park—This 300-foot-wide beach blankets the coast for over two miles along Kauai's west end. The park, which borders the sea cliffs of the Na Pali Coast, covers 140 acres and includes the ruins of an ancient *heiau*. The hot, dry weather is excellent for sunbathing, and prime for burning, so load up on suntan lotion. Great sunsets; magnificent mountain surroundings; Niihau looming in the distance. There's especially good shell collecting here at the United State's westernmost park.

Facilities: Picnic area, restrooms, showers. Restaurants and markets are about ten miles away in Kekaha. *Swimming:* Good in summer; dangerous in winter and during other periods of high surf. The safest swimming is at Queen's Pond, along the beachfront near the middle of the park. *Surfing:* Okay. Shore break with left and right slides. There's good windsurfing off Queen's Pond. *Fishing:* Bonefish, threadfin, and ulua are the most common game fish.

Camping: You can pitch a tent on the beach under a star-crowded sky, or find a shady tree for protection against the blazing sun. This is a wonderful place to camp for a day or two. After that, the barren landscape becomes tiresome and monotonous. Tent and trailer camping allowed. State permit required.

Getting there: Take Kaumualii Highway until it ends, then follow the signs along dirt roads for about five miles.

Kokee State Park—This spectacular park, high in the mountains above Waimea Canyon, is a mecca for hikers, campers, and other outdoor enthusiasts. Sprawling across 4345 heavily wooded acres, this rugged country offers a unique perspective on the Garden Isle.

Facilities: Kokee has everything but a store, so come well-stocked or plan to eat at the lodge restaurant. The lodge also has a museum and gift shop. Nearby are cabins, restrooms, showers, picnic area, and hiking trails. *Fishing:* Excellent freshwater angling; a state license is required, though. *Hiking:* See the "Hiking" section at the end of this chapter for trail descriptions.

Camping: An area at the north end of the park has been allocated for tent and trailer camping. There are also several wilderness camps along the hiking trails. A state permit is required for non-wilderness camping.

Getting there: Take Kaumualii Highway to Waimea, then pick up Waimea Canyon Drive from Waimea or Kokee Road from Kekaha. They eventually join and lead about 20 miles up to the park.

Wailua-Kapaa Area

If Lihue is the commercial center of Kauai, Wailua is the cultural heart of the island. Here along the Wailua River, the only navigable river in Hawaii, the *alii* built *heiaus* and perpetuated their princely lines.

What attracted them to Kauai's east coast was the weather along this windward shore, cooler in the summer than the baking sands of Poipu but not so moist as the tropical rainforests to the north. There are broad surfing beaches here as well as cascades and grottoes up along the Wailua River. Hawaiian royalty added fishponds and coconut groves to these natural features and forbade commoners from entering their domain.

The oral tradition they handed down tells of a Tahitian holy man named Puna, one of the first Polynesians to arrive in Hawaii, who chose this sacred spot to live. Other legends recount the lost tribe of Mu, a pre-Polynesian people, dwarfish and cruel, who inhabited caves far up the Wailua River.

Developed as a resort destination before Poipu and Princeville, this area has nevertheless avoided the overdevelopment that plagues other parts of the island. Wailua and Kapaa, while hosting the famous Coco Palms Hotel and a string of oceanfront condominiums, remain working-class towns, maintaining a contemporary version of the cultural pride of the ancient *alii*.

Lydgate State Park (Kuhio Highway, Wailua), perfectly situated at the confluence of the Wailua River and the ocean, bears the rocky remains of the **Hauola Place of Refuge**. Here *kapu* breakers under sentence of death could flee; once inside its perimeter, their crimes were absolved. A stone retaining wall also marks the ancient **Hikina Heiau**.

On the other side of the highway you can step from the sacred to the profane. Billing itself as "Kauai's best-kept secret," **Smith's Tropical Paradise** (174 Wailua Road, Wailua; 822-4654; admission) is actually the island's biggest tourist trap. Covering 30 riverside acres is a series of gardens and mock Pacific villages in the form of a tropical theme park. There are hibiscus, bamboo, and Japanese gardens as well as re-creations of life in Polynesia, the Philippines, and elsewhere. In the evening they stage a luau and show.

Fittingly, the adjacent marina is the departure point for boat trips up the Wailua River to **Fern Grotto** (822-4111). The scenery along the way is magnificent as you pass along a tropical riverfront that is luxuriously overgrown. The grotto itself is a 40-foot cavern draped with feathery ferns, a place so beautiful and romantic that many people choose to be married here. But the boat ride is one of the most cloyingly commercial experiences in Hawaii, a 20-minute voyage during which you are crowded together with legions of tourists and led in chants by a narrator with an amplifier.

Across the river, Route 580 provides an idyllic escape. Before experiencing Wailua's natural and cultural wonders, take in the gorgeous **Coco Palms Resort** (Kuhio Highway and Route 580, Wailua; 822-4921), which will provide an idea of Hollywood's version of idyllic. The beautiful grounds of this plush resort include one of Hawaii's largest coconut groves, a princely stand of palms that actually were planted by a 19th-century German intent on starting a copra plantation. You're welcome to tour the grounds, but beware of falling coconuts!

At sundown every night, the ancient royal lagoon behind the hotel is the site of a famous torchlighting ceremony to which everyone, guest or not, is invited. Parts of *South Pacific*, Elvis Presley's *Blue Hawaii*, and Rita Hayworth's *Sadie Thompson* were filmed here and the hotel grounds still contain some of the props from classic movies.

Past Coco Palms, the road courses through Kauai's most historic region, the domain of ancient Hawaiian royalty. Watch for Hawaii Visitors Bureau signs pointing out the **Holo-Holo-Ku Heiau**, one of the oldest temples on the island, a place where human sacrifices were performed. A short distance uphill, you'll find a small but interesting Japanese cemetery. Ironically, this is also the site of **Pohaku-Ho-O-Hanau**, a sacred spot where royal women came to give birth.

As you continue up Route 580, the lush Wailua Valley opens to view. On the left along the hilltop rest the rocky remains of **Poliahu Heiau**. A short path leads down to the **Bell Stone**, which resounded when struck with a rock, loudly signaling the birth of royal infants. All these places, vital to Hawaiian myth, were located along the old King's Highway, a sacred thoroughfare used only by island rulers.

For some vivid **mountain scenery** (★), continue on Route 580 past **Opaekaa Falls**. The road passes through **Wailua Homesteads**, a ranch and farm region filled with fruit orchards and macadamia nut trees. It ends at **Keahua Forestry Arboretum**, where hiking trails wind through groves of painted gum trees. The adjoining state forest climbs all the way to Waialeale, providing unique views of the world's wettest place.

From Route 580 you can also pick up Route 581 as it rolls through field and forest before spilling into Kapaa. En route you'll encounter **Kamokila Hawaiian Village** (★) (822-1192; admission), a reconstructed Polynesian village featuring demonstrations of native crafts and guided boat tours. Authentically constructed and manned by informative guides, it is well worth visiting. There are *imu* pits, a warrior's house, chief's sleeping quarters, even a place where medicinal herbs were made. You'll also learn the principles of taro raising, mat weaving, and poi manufacturing.

As the road dips down into **Kapaa**, you'll be passing from one Hawaiian era to another. This 19th-century town, with its falsefront stores and second-story balconies, is home to everyday folks. This is where the local

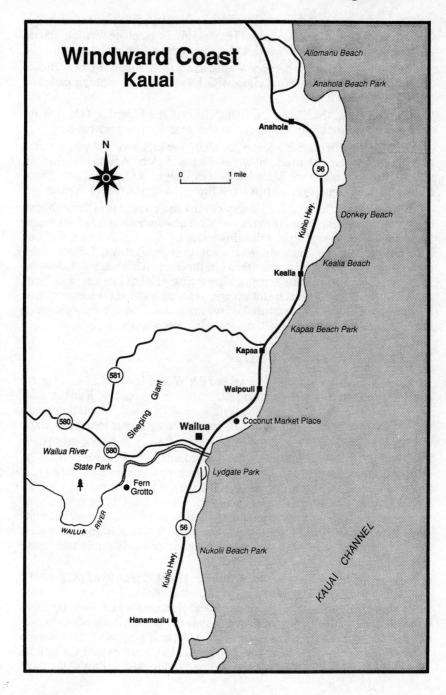

Windward Coast
Kauai

N

0   1 mile

Aliomanu Beach

Anahola Beach Park

Anahola

56

Kuhio Hwy.

Donkey Beach

Kealia Beach

Kealia

Kapaa Beach Park

Kapaa

Waipouli

Wailua   ● Coconut Market Place

Sleeping Giant

581

580

580

Wailua River
State Park

Fern Grotto

Lydgate Park

WAILUA   RIVER

56

Kuhio Hwy.

Nukolii Beach Park

KAUAI CHANNEL

Hanamaulu

plumber, carpenter, and fisherman live. The population is Japanese, Hawaiian, Caucasian, Filipino, and Chinese. They reside in small plantation houses and attend the local churches that dot the surrounding countryside.

In its northerly course between Wailua and Kapaa, Kuhio Highway (Route 50) passes the **Coconut Plantation** with its sprawling shopping mall and grove of royal palm trees.

From Kapaa, there's an excellent view of the **Sleeping Giant,** a recumbent figure naturally hewn out of the nearby mountain range.

Follow the direction his feet point along the highway and you'll arrive at a curving ribbon of sand known as Kealia Beach. Across the road, in various states of disrepair, are a local school, store, and post office. These clapboard buildings represent in its entirety the tiny town of **Kealia**.

From Kealia, the Kuhio Highway climbs and turns inland through sugarcane fields and continues through the town of **Anahola,** a small Hawaiian homestead settlement. Beyond this tiny town, a "Hole in the Mountain" was once chiseled by the elements. According to legend, it was formed when an angry giant hurled his spear through the rock. This natural formation in the **Anahola Mountains,** a major sightseeing point of interest, was clearly visible from the highway. But several years ago, the same elements that created the feature destroyed it. Today, the mountains are a single uninterrupted wall of angling rock and clinging vegetation.

WAILUA-KAPAA AREA HOTELS

Tucked between a coconut grove and the Wailua River, the **Fern Grotto Inn** (4561 Kuamoo Road, Wailua; 822-2560) enjoys one of Kauai's most idyllic locations. Amid this garden setting stands a classic plantation house and several smaller structures. Rooms rent in the moderate to deluxe range.

Kauai's venerable hotel, the **Coco Palms Resort** (4-241 Kuhio Highway, Wailua; 822-4921) is one of the most romantic in all the islands. With 45 acres of coconut groves, lagoons, and thatch-roofed bungalows, the place retains an air of old Hawaii. Granted, it has evolved into a sprawling facility with 390 rooms, nine tennis courts, and two restaurants. But the Coco Palms still sports the lava-rock spas, giant clamshell wash basins, and torchlit pathways that harken back to the days when Hawaii was a little-known destination. Located across the street from a beach; prices begin in the deluxe range and rise rapidly to ultra-deluxe.

To get any closer to the water than the **Hotel Coral Reef** (822-4481), you'd have to pitch a tent in the sand. Located on Kuhio Highway in Kapaa, it's within strolling distance of markets and restaurants and is an excellent choice for the wanderer without wheels. A floral garden leads out to a comfortable strip of sand next to Kapaa Beach Park. If you check into the old section, the rooms are a little less expensive, but don't expect the Hilton. Newly refurbished rooms are carpeted and come with a fan; some have ocean views. The new section, priced in the moderate range, is quite modern. Here you can enjoy a touch of wood paneling, soft beds, refrigerator, and a delightful seascape just beyond those sliding glass doors. No kitchenettes, but continental breakfast is included. Budget.

The **Kauai Sands Hotel** (822-4951) costs a little more, but it's still a bargain. This beachfront accommodation (at 420 Papaloa Road near the Coconut Plantation in Wailua) is part of the only hotel chain in the world owned by a Hawaiian family, the Kimis. You'll find a relaxed and spacious lobby, restaurant, two pools, a well-tended lawn, carpeting, lanai, imaginative decor, and a touch of Hawaiiana. Moderate.

The nearby **Kauai Beach Boy** (822-3441), a link in the Colony Resorts hotel chain, is another extremely appealing place. Located behind the Coconut Market Place, it's popular with swimmers and shoppers alike. There's a pool, bar, and shuffleboard courts amid the hotel's central grounds, plus a windswept lobby with adjoining shops and restaurant. For pleasant surroundings near the center of the action, it's definitely among the area's top choices. The rooms are air conditioned and include televisions, refrigerators, and lanais. The decor is quite tasteful, and the rates, considering what the hotel provides, are reasonable. Deluxe.

Keapana Center (★) (5620 Keapana Road; 822-7968), set in the mountains outside Kapaa, is a lush three-acre complex offering a restful environment and otherworldly views. With five guest rooms, this hilltop bed and breakfast provides a unique escape that somehow seems perfectly suited to the slow rhythms of Kauai. From here, you can hike the surrounding mountains, drive to a nearby beach, or relax on the windswept lanai with its hammock and inviting armchairs. A rare retreat. Moderate.

WAILUA-KAPAA AREA CONDOMINIUMS

Wailua Bay View (320 Papaloa Road, Kapaa; 822-3651). One-bedroom apartments, $100 for up to four people; three-night minimum stay. Ocean view.

Kapaa Sands (380 Papaloa Road, Kapaa; 822-4901). Studio apartments, $75 single or double, $85 for an ocean view. Two-bedroom apartments, $99 (one to four people); $109 for an ocean view.

Mokihana of Kauai (796 Kuhio Highway, Kapaa; 822-3971). Studio apartments run $55 single or double. These units are supplied with a hotplate and small refrigerator. Oceanfront; three-night minimum.

Kauai Kailani (856 Kuhio Highway, Kapaa; 822-3391). Two-bedroom apartments, $65 single or double; $70 for three; $75 for four; $80 for five people. A lot of square footage for the money. There's one catch—reservations are difficult to obtain and should be made a year in advance. Three-night minimum.

WAILUA-KAPAA AREA RESTAURANTS

For oceanfront dining, it's hard to match the **Seashell Restaurant** (Kuhio Highway, Wailua; 822-3632). This restaurant-in-the-round is an open-air affair resting directly above Wailua Beach. The menu is dinner only and features fresh island fish, New Zealand lobster, cioppino, steak, and prawns with pasta. Deluxe.

There are short-order stands galore at the Coconut Market Place (Kuhio Highway, Wailua). **Paradise Chicken-N-Ribs** (822-2505) delivers what its name promises. **Taco Dude** (822-1919) sells tacos and burritos. **Don's Deli and Picnic Basket** (822-7025) is the perfect stop for beachgoers. **Sunshine Grill** (822-9981) features good old American food like hot dogs and hamburgers. The **Fish Hut** (822-1712) lives up to its name. Any time from early morning until eight or nine at night, several of these stands will be open. An interesting way to dine here is by going from one to the next, nibbling small portions along the way. Budget.

Hidden (but certainly not hiding) in the wings at Coconut Market Place is **Buzz's Steak & Lobster** (822-7491). Dim lighting, potted palms, tropical paintings, overhead fans—all these spell Polynesia. There is a surf-and-broiler menu for lunch and dinner. I also recommend the salad bar. Prices begin in the moderate range and rise steadily.

Kalua pig, lomi salmon, and poi highlight the menu at the **Aloha Diner** (Waipouli Complex, 971 F Kuhio Highway, Waipouli; 822-3851). There are only a few tables in this tiny place, but they prepare heaping dishes of Hawaiian food at budget prices.

The **Waipouli Delicatessen and Restaurant** (Kuhio Highway, Waipouli; 822-9311) is a small Japanese-style luncheonette owned by a delightful Asian woman. Budget.

It's beef, beef, and beef at **The Bull Shed** (796 Kuhio Highway, Kapaa; 822-3791). We're talking about prime rib, beef kebab, top sirloin, garlic tenderloin, and teriyaki steak. All this in a captain's-chair-and-fish-trophy restaurant that's so close to the surf your feet feel wet. Speaking of surf, they also serve lobster, broiled shrimp, Alaskan King crab, and fresh fish. Dinner only; moderate to deluxe.

For a light, healthful meal, you can cross the street to **Papaya's Natural Foods & Café** (Kauai Village Shopping Center, 4-831 Kuhio Highway, Kapaa; 823-0191). This take-out-counter-with-tables has pasta, pizza, sandwiches, vegetable stir fry, grilled fish, and vegetables. For breakfast, you can order buckwheat pancakes or tropical millet. Budget.

One of Kauai's hottest restaurants, **A Pacific Café** (★) (Kauai Village Shopping Center, 4-138 Kuhio Highway, Kapaa; 822-0013) serves beautifully presented Pacific Rim cuisine. The accent is on freshness, with an open-kitchen design and a menu that changes daily. The restaurant ranks high among local critics, who rave about the opakapaka with orange saffron sauce, swordfish with ratatouille, curry lobster, grilled ahi with eggplant, and wok-seared sirloin. The decor is a simple mix of Asian and Hawaiian with paintings by local artists adorning the walls. Dinner only; deluxe.

Up Kapaa way on Kuhio Highway in the center of town, there's a restaurant known to Mexican food aficionados for miles around. **El Café** (822-3362) draws a hungry crowd of young locals for dinner. The owners raise a lot of their own beef and vegetables, and they serve monstrous portions. If you're not hungry, order à la carte. If you are, choose from a solid menu ranging from enchiladas to burritos to chile rellenos. Children's portions are available and all meals can be converted to cater to vegetarians. Definitely worth checking out. Moderate.

One of the loveliest dining spots hereabouts is **Kapaa Fish & Chowder House** (4-1639 Kuhio Highway, Kapaa; 822-7488). These creative restaurateurs have converted a warehouse into a collection of cozy rooms. Each is trimly decorated, comfortably furnished, and adorned with nautical items and an assortment of potted plants; the back room is a garden patio. Open for lunch and dinner, they serve stir-fry fish dishes, shellfish, tiger prawns, calamari, prime rib, New York steak, and chicken. Moderate to deluxe.

Numbah one among local dives is **Fast Freddy's Diner** (4-1302 Kuhio Highway, Kapaa; 822-0488), a hole in the wall that attracts a whole lot of people. Most breakfasts are under $3 here; lunch, which consists of sandwiches, is not much more; at dinnertime there are teriyaki chicken, mahimahi, and steak platters, also at budget prices. Local color to da max.

The best hamburgers on the island are reputedly found at **Duane's Ono Burger** (822-9181) on Kuhio Highway in Anahola. If you do a taste test, let me know the results. Moderate.

WAILUA-KAPAA AREA MARKETS

Foodland (Waipouli Town Center, Waipouli; 822-7271) and **Safeway** (Kauai Village Shopping Center, Kapaa; 822-2464) are the major grocery stores in this area.

There's a **Big Save Market** (822-4971) on Kuhio Highway at the Kapaa Shopping Center.

Café Espresso, located at the Coconut Market Place (Kuhio Highway, Wailua; 822-9421), has a good selection of coffees and teas as well as locally preserved jams. There's also an espresso bar and an assortment of baked goods here.

Ambrose's Kapuna Natural Foods (822-7112), conveniently located on Kuhio Highway in Waipouli, is a recommended shopping place for health food aficionados. At this store you should be able to locate herbs and spices, fresh fruits and vegetables, as well as other natural food items.

Pono Fish Market (4-939 Kuhio Highway, Kapaa; 822-0955) has a variety of fresh, smoked, and dried fish.

To the north is the **Whaler's General Store** (822-5818) along Kuhio Highway in Anahola. This well-stocked market is the largest store between Kapaa and Princeville.

WAILUA-KAPAA AREA SHOPPING

One of the top shopping spots on Kauai is the **Coconut Market Place** (Kuhio Highway, Wailua). This theme mall consists of wooden stores designed to resemble little plantation houses. For decor you'll find the pipes, valves, gears, and waterwheels characteristic of every tropical plantation. This is a good place for clothing, flowers, curios, jewelry, toys, Asian imports, T-shirts, luggage, sweets, plus leather goods, betters, and bests. If you don't want to buy, you can always browse or have a snack at the many short-order stands here. In any case, it's worth a walk through.

Two galleries within the Market Place are worthy of note. **Kahn Galleries** (822-4277) and **Island Images** (822-3636) feature premier Hawaiian artwork by artists such as George Sumner, Jan Parker, Pegge Hopper, Roy Tabora, and Randy Puckett. Original paintings, lithographs, and sculptures are available through Kahn Galleries and fine art prints and lithographs can be purchased at Island Images.

There's also a **Waldenbooks** (822-9362) conveniently situated in Coconut Market Place that sells an array of local books and national bestsellers.

The nearby **Coco Palms Hotel** has several shops selling beautiful handicrafts. Prices are rather steep, but the quality here is superb. There are *tapa* pieces, glassware, delicate woodcarvings, intricate fishbone statuary, and an assortment of fine jewelry. And that's just on the ground floor of this two-tiered emporium. Topside, you'll find a couple of clothing shops with designs for every lifestyle from island to mainland.

Kauai Village Shopping Center (Kuhio Highway), a multi-store complex in the center of Kapaa, is another of Kauai's shopping destinations. Anchored by a grocery store, it features a string of small shops. Of particular interest is the **Kauai Village Museum and Gift Shop** (822-9272), which is actually more like a museum than a shop. The collection here includes many fine Polynesian artifacts.

It's not really **The Only Show in Town** (1495 Kuhio Highway, Kapaa; 822-1442), but this eclectic antique, clothing, and art shop is the only place around where you'll find old *aloha* shirts, fur pieces, early-20th-century cigarette packs, statuettes, Polynesian spearheads, and collectible bottles, all under a single roof.

Also stop by **Nightengayles** (1312 Kuhio Highway, Kapaa; 822-3729) up the street. Here you'll find specialty clothing, glass vases, and handwrought jewelry.

WAILUA-KAPAA AREA NIGHTLIFE

Gilligans (4331 Kauai Beach Drive; 245-1955), at the Kauai Hilton, is a chic video disco with big crowds, big screen, and a pink marble bar.

Also check out the **Jolly Roger** (822-3451); located in the Coconut Market Place, it's a karaoke bar with a lively crowd.

The **Lagoon Terrace** at Coco Palms Hotel (Kuhio Highway, Wailua; 822-4921) has a torchlighting ceremony at 7:30 p.m. and dance music from 10 p.m. to 1 a.m. every evening. The music is low-key, the setting is dreamlike. There's also a Polynesian show at 9 p.m. just across the corridor in the **Lagoon Dining Room**. Cover.

For an early-evening drink overlooking the water, the most enchanting spot is at the **Seashell Restaurant** (Kuhio Highway, Wailua; 822-3632), situated on Wailua Beach. Sit at a table outside under the palms, order a tall, cool one, and watch the surf walk along the sand.

WAILUA-KAPAA AREA BEACHES AND PARKS

Nukolii Beach Park (★)—Located adjacent to the Kauai Hilton Hotel, this is a long narrow strand with a shallow bottom. From the park, the beach extends for several miles all the way to Lydgate State Park in Wailua. One of the island's prettiest beaches, it provides an opportunity to use the park facilities or to escape to more secluded sections (which parallel Wailua Golf Course). A dirt road parallels the beach north of the park for about a half-mile, but if you seek seclusion, just start hiking farther north along the shore. You'll find places galore for swimming, camping, fishing, surfing, and so on.

Facilities: A small market and restaurants are nearby in Hanamaulu. *Swimming:* Good; well-protected and shallow. *Snorkeling:* Good diving among reefs. *Surfing:* Good breaks on shallow reef at "Graveyards." *Fishing:* Best near reefs.

Camping: There are numerous spots for unofficial camping along the beachfront.

Getting there: The beach park is at the end of Kauai Hilton Road. To reach the more secluded sections, go north from Lihue on Kuhio Highway and take a right onto the road that runs along the southern end of the Wailua

Golf Course. This paved road rapidly becomes a dirt strip studded with pot-holes. Driving slowly, proceed a quarter-mile, then take the first left turn. It's another quarter-mile to the beach; when the road forks, take either branch.

Lydgate Park—The awesome ironwood grove and long stretches of rugged coastline make this one of Kauai's loveliest parks. Located near the Wailua River, it is also one of the most popular. Two large lava pools, one perfect for children and the other protecting swimmers and snorkelers, make it a great place to spend the day.

Facilities: Picnic area, showers, and restrooms. Wailua's restaurants, markets, and sightseeing attractions are all close. Nearby Wailua River State Park features sacred historic sites and breathtaking views of river and mountains. *Swimming:* Very good. *Surfing:* Long paddle out to breaks off mouth of Wailua River. Right slide. Also popular with windsurfers. *Fishing:* Ulua is the most common catch.

Getting there: From Kuhio Highway, turn toward the beach at Leho Drive, the road just south of the Wailua River.

Kapaa Beach Park—While it sports an attractive little beach, this 15-acre facility doesn't measure up to its neighbors. Located a block from the highway as the road passes through central Kapaa, the park is flanked by ramshackle houses and a local playing field.

Facilities: Picnic area, restrooms. *Swimming:* Fair. *Fishing:* Fair. There is good squidding and torchfishing.

Getting there: Located a block from Kuhio Highway, Kapaa.

Kealia Beach—This strand is one of those neighbors that makes Kapaa Beach the pimply kid next door: It's a wide, magnificent beach curving for about a half-mile along Kuhio Highway.

Facilities: None. The one-store town of Kealia is just across the road. *Swimming:* Good, but requires caution. *Surfing:* Good surfing and bodysurfing at the north end of the beach. *Fishing:* For papio, threadfin, and ulua.

Camping: Unofficial camping at the north end of the beach.

Getting there: Located on Kuhio Highway, Kealia.

Donkey Beach (★)—This broad, curving beach is flanked by a grassy meadow and towering ironwoods. Favored as a hideaway and nude beach by local folks, it's a gem that should not be overlooked. Also note that the two-mile stretch from here north to Anahola is lined by low sea cliffs that open onto at least four pocket beaches. This entire area is popular with beachcombers, who sometimes find hand-blown Japanese glass fishing balls. (Several other hidden beaches are strung anonymously along cane roads paralleling the coast from Kealia to Anahola. You should watch for them as you travel through this area.)

Facilities: None. *Swimming:* Good, but remember that currents here can be treacherous and the nearest lifeguard is a world away. *Surfing:* Right off Donkey Beach there is good surfing and bodysurfing. Just north of the beach is "14 Crack," a popular left slide break. *Fishing:* Popular for both pole fishing and throw-netting.

Camping: Unofficial camping is common.

Getting there: Follow Kuhio Highway north from Kealia. At the 11-mile marker the road begins to climb slowly, then descend. At the end of the descent, just before the 12-mile marker, there is a cane road on the right. Take this road; bear right and watch for Donkey's Beach on the left within a half-mile. (Since the road is presently chained, you'll have to hike in from Kuhio Highway.)

Anahola Beach Park—A slender ribbon of sand curves along wind-swept Anahola Bay. At the south end, guarded by ironwood trees, lies this pretty little park. Very popular with neighborhood residents, this is a prime beachcombing spot where you may find Japanese glass fishing balls.

Facilities: Picnic area, restrooms, showers. Less than a mile to the market and snack bar in Anahola. *Swimming:* There is a protecting reef here; but as elsewhere, use caution because of the strong currents. *Snorkeling:* Good behind the reef. *Surfing:* Long paddle out to summer and winter breaks along the reef. Left and right slides. There is a break called "Unreals" offshore from the old landing. Also a popular bodysurfing beach. *Fishing:* Good torch-fishing for lobsters. Fish commonly caught include papio, rudderfish, ulua, threadfin, bonefish, and big-eyed scad.

Getting there: Turn onto Anahola Road from Kuhio Highway in Anahola; follow it three-quarters of a mile, then turn onto a dirt road that forks left to the beach.

Aliomanu Beach—On the far side of Anahola Bay, separated from the park by a lagoon, sits another sandy beach. Shady ironwood trees, several roadside houses, and a picnic table dot this area, which is a favorite among locals. What makes Aliomanu particularly popular is the offshore reef, one of Kauai's longest and widest fringing reefs. This is an excellent area for gathering edible seaweed.

Facilities: It is a mile to the market and snack bar in Anahola. *Swimming:* Fairly safe in the lagoon but use caution seaside. *Fishing:* Local residents spear octopus and go torchfishing here.

Camping: There is unofficial camping along the beach.

Getting there: To get there, turn off Kuhio Highway onto Aliomanu Road just past Anahola.

North Shore

It is no accident that when it came to choose a location for Bali Hai, the producers of *South Pacific* ended their search on the North Shore of Kauai. The most beautiful place in Hawaii, indeed one of the prettiest places on earth, this 30-mile stretch of lace-white surf and emerald-green mountains became Hollywood's version of paradise.

While the scenery is so spectacular as to seem mythic, there is nothing insubstantial about the North Shore. The tiny villages that dot the waterfront are populated by people with a strong sense of defending their environment. With development concentrated in the resort complex of Princeville, Hanalei remains a tiny town of taro fields and one-lane bridges. The village of Kilauea is still a sanctuary for a vast population of waterfowl and attempts to widen the North Shore's lone road have been fought with religious intensity.

Backdropping this thin line of civilization is the **Na Pali Coast.** Here, sharp sea cliffs vault thousands of feet from the ocean, silver waterfalls streaming along their fluted surfaces. There are pocket beaches ringed by menacing rock formations and long, wide strands as inviting as a warm tub.

The North Shore is wet and tropical, drawing enough precipitation to dampen the enthusiasm of many tourists. It is suited for travelers who don't mind a little rain on their parade if it carries with it rainbows and seabirds and a touch of magic in the air.

Your civic introduction to this realm comes in **Kilauea,** a former sugar town with a cluster of stores and a couple noteworthy churches. The cottages that once housed plantation workers are freshly painted and decorated with flowering gardens and the place possesses an air of humble well-being.

But as everywhere along the North Shore, mankind is a bit player in the natural drama being presented here. To take in that scene, you need venture no farther than **Kilauea National Wildlife Refuge (★)** (end of Kilauea Road; 828-1520). Here on Kilauea Point, a lofty peninsula that falls away into precipitous rockfaces, you'll have the same bird's-eye view of the Na Pali Coast as the boobies, tropicbirds, albatrosses, and frigate birds that nest in the cliffs. As you stand along this lonely point, gazing into the trees and along the cliffs, birds—graceful, sleek, exotic birds—swarm like bees. A vital rookery, the preserve is also home to Hawaiian monk seals and green turtles, as well as occasional whales and dolphins.

Counterpoint to this natural pageant is the **Kilauea Lighthouse,** a 52-foot-high beacon built in 1913 that bears the world's largest clamshell lens. Capable of casting its light almost 100 miles, it is the first sign of land seen by mariners venturing east from Asia. This old lighthouse, now replaced by a more modern beacon, sits on the northernmost point of Kauai. The nearby visitor center houses a small wildlife exhibit with examples of the

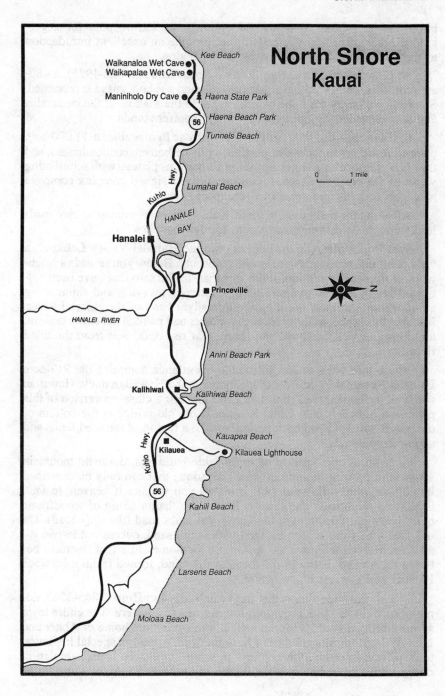

Waikanaloa Wet Cave ●
Waikapalae Wet Cave ●
Maniniholo Dry Cave ●

Kee Beach

North Shore
Kauai

Haena State Park

56

Haena Beach Park

Tunnels Beach

Kuhio Hwy.

Lumahai Beach

0   1 mile

HANALEI
BAY

Hanalei ■

HANALEI RIVER

■ Princeville

Anini Beach Park

Kalihiwai ■   Kalihiwai Beach

Kuhio Hwy.

Kauapea Beach

Kilauea ■   ● Kilauea Lighthouse

56

Kahili Beach

Larsens Beach

Moloaa Beach

N

birds inhabiting the surrounding cliffs. It is also the starting point for ranger-guided hikes of nearby Crater Hill that provide an excellent introduction to the bird life and natural history of the region.

At **Guava Kai Plantation** (Kuawa Road, Kilauea; 828-1925), a 480-acre complex, you can wander past orchards and see how guava is processed. Set along a country road, the plantation sits in the shadow of the mountains and is surrounded by open meadows and conifer stands.

Civilization stakes its claim once again at **Princeville**, a 11,000-acre planned resort community that combines private homes, condominiums, and the elegant Princeville Hotel. Set along a luxurious plateau with scintillating views of the Na Pali Coast, it is a tastefully designed complex complete with golf courses and acres of open space.

All along the main thoroughfare, Kuhio Highway, numerous side roads lead through fields and meadows to **hidden beaches**.

Past Princeville, the road opens onto the **Hanalei Valley Lookout**, a vista point that transcends prose with its beauty. Below you spreads a patchwork of tropical vegetation, fields of broad-leafed taro that have been cultivated for over 1200 years. This green carpet, swaying and shimmering along the valley floor, is cut by the thin silver band of the Hanalei River. Framing this scene, as though a higher power had painted the entire tableau, are deep-green cliffs, fluted and sharp, that rise 3500 feet from the tilled fields.

These taro patches and surrounding wetlands comprise the 917-acre **Hanalei National Wildlife Refuge**, home to the Hawaiian duck, Hawaiian stilt, and the endangered Hawaiian gallinule. For a close-up version of this panorama, turn left onto Ohiki Road near the old bridge at the bottom of the hill. It will lead you back several eras to a region of terraced fields and simple homesteads.

In town, a combination of ramshackle buildings, dramatic mountain views, and curving beaches creates a mystique that can only be described in a single word—**Hanalei** (★). It makes you wonder if heaven, in fact, is built of clapboard. The town is little more than a string of woodframe bungalows and falsefront stores lining the main road (the *only* road). On one side a half-moon bay, rimmed with white sand, curves out in two directions. Behind the town the *pali*, those awesome cliffs that fluctuate between dream and reality in the focus of the mind, form a frontier between Hanalei and the rest of the world.

It's almost superfluous that the **Waioli Mission House** (245-3202; admission), built in 1836, provides glimpses of a bygone era: The entire town seems a reflection of its former self. But this one-time home of Abner and Lucy Wilcox, missionaries from New England, extends a special invitation to step back into the 19th century. A small but stately house, shiplap in design with a second-story patio, it sits amid palm and *hala* trees on a broad lawn. The rooms look undisturbed since the days when the Wilcoxes prayed and proselytized. The china rests in the cupboard and an old rocker sits in one room while the canopied bed and cradle still occupy a bedroom. The walls are decorated with paintings of the Wilcox family and knickknacks from their era are scattered about the entire house.

The road winds on from Hanalei past single-lane bridges and overgrown villages. The air seems moister and the real world more distant as you pass **Lumahai Beach** (Kuhio Highway about five miles west of Hanalei), a sandy scimitar where Mitzi Gaynor vowed to "wash that man right out of my hair" in the 1957 movie *South Pacific*.

Several caves along this route were created eons ago when this entire area was underwater. The first is **Maniniholo Dry Cave**, which geologists claim is a lava tube but which legend insists was created by *Menehunes*. The **Waikapalae** and **Waikanaloa Wet Caves** nearby are said to be the work of Pele, the Hawaiian fire goddess, who sought fire in the earth but discovered only water.

The legendary gives way to the cinematic once more at **Kee Beach**, a lovely strand with protecting reef that was used to film some of the torrid love scenes in *The Thorn Birds*. This is the end of the road, beyond which the fabled Kalalau Trail winds along the Na Pali Coast.

NORTH SHORE HOTELS AND CONDOMINIUMS

The North Shore is short on bargains, but at **Hanalei Bay Inn** (Kuhio Highway, Hanalei; 826-9333) there are studio units with kitchenettes available at moderate prices. They are attractive, well-maintained rooms with woven lauhala facing on some walls, carpeting, and decorative prints. Hawaiian-owned and carefully tended, this intimate inn sits amid a garden 100 yards from the beach.

At the YMCA's **Camp Naue** (P.O. Box 1786, Lihue, Kauai, HI 96766; 246-9090), located beachfront in Haena, there are dormitory accommodations at budget prices. Bring your own bedding and kitchen utensils. There is also an adjacent area for camping.

The only other reasonably priced resting places around Hanalei are the condos. In the Princeville resort complex, a few miles east of Hanalei, are several: **The Cliffs at Princeville** (826-6219) has condominiums from $110; **Pali Ke Kua** (826-9066) offers one- and two-bedroom apartments for $105 and up; **Kaeo Kai** (826-6549) has studios from $130. These are modern, fully equipped units with all the amenities. There is a swimming pool on each property.

Hanalei Colony Resort (Kuhio Highway, Hanalei; 826-6235) is the only oceanfront condominium complex and the most highly recommended. Two-bedroom apartments, $95 single or double; $115 ocean view; $150 oceanfront.

For information on other condominiums and to learn where the best deals are available during any particular time, check with **Hanalei Aloha Rental Management** (P.O. Box 1109, Hanalei, HI 96714; 826-7288).

Hanalei Bay Resort (5380 Honoiki Road, Princeville; 826-6522), spectacularly perched on a hillside overlooking the coastline, provides full vacation facilities at rates that start in the deluxe range. Outstanding for the price, the 22-acre property, which descends to a beach, contains a restaurant, lounge, tennis courts, and a spacious swimming pool. The guest rooms are located in multi-plex cabanas dotted around the grounds; some, priced ultra-deluxe, include kitchens.

The North Shore's premier resting place is a clifftop roost called the **Princeville Hotel** (Princeville; 826-9644). Situated on a point and sporting one of the best views this side of paradise, it's a 252-room complex decorated in European style. The hotel rises above a white-sand beach and features several restaurants and shops as well as a pool and jacuzzi. Trimmed in gold plating and marble, this is a concierge-and-doorman resort long on service and short on Hawaiian spirit. Ultra-deluxe.

NORTH SHORE RESTAURANTS

In the resort complex of Princeville, **Café Zelo's** (Princeville Marketplace; 826-9700) starts with espresso and cappuccino, moves on to sizzling fajitas and meatball sandwiches, then finishes the bill of fare with chocolate suicide cake. This nifty café also offers soups, salads, pasta, and hamburgers. Moderate.

Another popular Princeville dining room, the **Beamreach Restaurant** (Pali Ke Kua, 5300 Ka Haku Road; 826-9131) is a steak-and-seafood emporium with a nautical theme. Expect a beam ceiling, dark-wood paneling, and poster-size photographs of sailboat races. Fare from the galley is all-American with a sprinkling of salt water—shrimp scampi, scallops bourguignon, plus steak and lobster combinations. Predictable but dependable; deluxe in price.

Any restaurant critic in the world would immediately award five stars to the view at **Bali Hai Restaurant** (Hanalei Bay Resort, 5380 Honoiki Road, Princeville; 826-6522). Perched on a deck high above Hanalei Bay, it overlooks a broad sweep of mountains and sea. The menu at this deluxe-priced establishment features classic island fare, ranging from mahimahi to teriyaki chicken to filet mignon. Reservations required.

A pleasant veranda-style dining room adorned with fresh flowers, **Casa di Amici** (2484 Keneke; 828-1388) in nearby Kilauea has established a solid reputation for excellent pasta dishes. The idea here is to combine a pasta (linguine, farfalle, fettucine) with your favorite sauce—pesto, bolognese, abruzzi, and so on. If you're not up to the challenge, they also have saltimbocca, tournedos rossini, chicken marsala, scampi, and a host of other gourmet Italian dishes. Deluxe.

If you'd simply like a pizza, at a reasonable budget-to-moderate price, the little town of Kilauea also supports **Pau Hana Pizza** (828-2020), a combination kitchen and bakery that cooks up some delicious pies.

As beautiful and popular as Hanalei happens to be, the area possesses only a few low-priced facilities. If you've ever tried to find a place to stay here, you know how tight things can be. And the budget restaurant situation is not a whole lot better.

There are several luncheonettes, including the **Hanalei Snack Shop** (Hanalei; 826-6783), which has sandwiches and platters.

There are baby back ribs and mesquite-grilled chicken at **U.S. Barbecue** (next to Ching Young Village; 826-6994). This budget-priced take-out stand also has submarine sandwiches, hot dogs, and meatball sandwiches.

The **Black Pot Luau Hut Restaurant** (Aku Road; 826-9871) is a low-key café offering plate lunches of corned beef or chicken hekka, an assortment of sandwiches, and local treats like lau lau, kalua pig, poki, and stir-fry. If you're feeling bold, order the multicourse luau plate. Budget.

The **Hanalei Shell House** (826-7977) in Hanalei is devoted to a small restaurant serving breakfasts complete with omelettes, hash browns, and macadamia nut pancakes. For lunch they serve up seafood taquitos, vegetarian omelettes, and quesadillas. There are also hamburgers, sandwiches, and salads. The dinner menu changes frequently, but might feature steak au poivre, seafood tortellini, and fresh fish prepared in any of a half-dozen ways. Very highly recommended. Moderate.

Foong Wong (Ching Young Village; 826-6996), a second-story Chinese restaurant, offers a complete menu that ranges from local favorites like cake noodle and pork hash to more traditional Szechuan and Cantonese dishes. Chinese prints and detailed lighting fixtures add to the ambiance of this simple restaurant. Moderate.

Hanalei dining facilities jump from one extreme to the other with few moderate-priced restaurants between. Among the expensive establishments, however, there are several that warrant a stretch in the old budget.

At **Charo's** (adjacent to Hanalei Colony Resort on Kuhio Highway, five miles west of Hanalei; 826-6422) you'll discover the best of two worlds—oceanfront dining and good food. Owned by the renowned entertainer, Charo, this breezy establishment sits in a secluded corner of Kauai. With tile floor, colorful furnishings, and bamboo decor, it's a great spot for drinking and dining. The dinner menu features Mexican entrées as well as a few fresh fish, steak, chicken, and shrimp dishes. At lunch there are sandwiches and fish platters. Deluxe.

The **Tahiti Nui Restaurant** (in the center of Hanalei; 826-6277) has a luau every Wednesday and Friday night at 6:30. If you miss it, catch a taste of local cooking by trying their calamari, prawn, steak, or island fish dishes. And check out the bamboo-fringed lanai, or the lounge decorated with Pacific Island carvings and overhung with a thatch canopy. Best of all, strike up a conversation with Louise, the robust Tahitian who owns the place. Deluxe.

From the large aquarium in the foyer to the porthole windows to the Japanese fishing balls, the **Hanalei Dolphin Restaurant** (826-6113) presents an interesting aquatic decor. Built smack on the bank of the Hanalei River, this eatery offers a turf-and-surf menu that includes fresh fish, shrimp dishes, buffalo steak, and New York steak. Open nightly from 6 until 10; no reservations are taken. Deluxe.

NORTH SHORE MARKETS

The best place on the North Shore is **Foodland** (826-9880) in the Princeville shopping complex just off Kuhio Highway. It's very well stocked and open from 7 a.m. to 11 p.m.

Hanalei supports one large grocery store on Kuhio Highway, **Big Save** (826-6652) in the Ching Young Village complex.

About four miles west of Hanalei, **Wainiha General Store** (826-6251) has a small assortment of food items. It's your last chance for provisions before reaching the end of the road at Haena.

Hanalei Health & Natural Foods (Ching Young Village Shopping Center, Kuhio Highway, Hanalei) has an assortment of health-related items.

Banana Joe's Tropical Fruit Farm (5-2719 Kuhio Highway, Kilauea) has ripe, delicious fruits as well as smoothies, fruit salads, and dehydrated fruit. They can also arrange farm tours.

NORTH SHORE SHOPPING

Kong Lung Co. (828-1822) in Kilauea has a marvelous assortment of Pacific and Asian treasures as well as a selection of Hawaiian books. Don't miss this one.

Just behind this shop is **Crater Hill Gallery** (828-1828) with a tasteful selection of furniture and fine art pieces.

Princeville is the closest you will come to a shopping center on the North Shore. Here **Princeville Center**, located just off Kuhio Highway, features a cluster of shops that represents the prime spot in the area for window browsers.

In Hanalei, **Ching Young Village** is a small shopping mall that contains a variety store, clothing shops, and several other outlets.

Across the street you'll find the **Hanalei Center,** which houses several shops in the Old Hanalei School Building.

Ola's (next to Hanalei Dolphin Restaurant; 826-6937) showcases the work of over 100 craftspeople from Hawaii and the mainland. Some of the artistry in this tiny shop is outstanding.

On the Road To Hanalei (next to Ching Young Village; 826-7360) has *tapa* cloth, woodcarvings, jewelry, quilts, and other locally fashioned craft items.

If you're interested in homemade goods, you'll find a few more stores in Hanalei and other small towns along the North Shore.

NORTH SHORE NIGHTLIFE

In all the world there are few entertainment spots with as grand a view as the Princeville Hotel's **Living Room Lounge** (Princeville; 826-9644). Overlooking Hanalei Bay and the Na Pali Coast, it also features a trio playing contemporary music nightly.

At nearby Hanalei Bay Resort's **Happy Talk Lounge** (5380 Honoiki Road, Princeville; 826-6522), you can enjoy the views of Hanalei Bay and relax with either Hawaiian music or jazz.

For a tropical drink amid a tropical setting, place your orders at **Tahiti Nui Restaurant** (826-6277) or the **Dolphin Restaurant** (826-6113), both in Hanalei.

The **Hanalei Gourmet** (Hanalei Center across the street from Ching Young Village; 826-2524) has a guitarist/vocalist every night.

NORTH SHORE BEACHES AND PARKS

Moloaa Beach (★)—Nestled in Moloaa Bay, a small inlet surrounded by rolling hills, Moloaa Beach is relatively secluded, though there are a few homes nearby. A meandering stream divides the beach into two strands. You'll see horses grazing on the nearby bluff, and a coral reef shadowing the shore. There is good beachcombing at the west end of the strand.

Facilities: None. *Swimming:* With caution. *Snorkeling:* Good. *Fishing:* Good. *Skindiving:* For lobster.

Getting there: Take Koolau Road where it branches off Kuhio Highway near the 16-mile marker. Go one-and-three-tenths miles, then turn onto Moloaa Road. Follow this to the end. All roads are paved.

Larsens Beach (★)—This narrow, sandy beach extends seemingly forever through a very secluded area. Rolling hills, covered with small trees and scrub, rim the strand. A protecting reef provides excellent swimming and snorkeling. Glass fishing balls and other collectibles wash ashore regularly, making this a prime beachcombing spot. It is also very popular for seaweed gathering and throw-netting.

Facilities: None. *Fishing:* Good.

Camping: This is a splendid place to set up an unofficial camp.

Getting there: It's hard to get to, but more than worth it when you arrive. Take Koolau Road as it branches off Kuhio Highway near the 16-mile marker. Go two-and-one-half miles to a cane road on the right, which switches back in the opposite direction. Get on this road, then take an immediate left onto another dirt road (lined on either side with barbed wire). Don't let the fences scare you—this is a public right of way. Follow it a mile to the end. Hike through the gate and down the road. This leads a half-mile down to the beach, which is on your left. (There is also an access road from Koolau Road that is one-and-one-fifth miles from the intersection of Koolau Road and Kuhio Highway.)

Kahili Beach (★)—Tucked away in Kilauea Bay, this beach is bordered by tree-covered hills and a rock quarry. It's a lovely, semi-secluded spot with a lagoon that represents one of Hawaii's most pristine estuaries. Kahili is also a prime beachcombing spot. For a spectacular view of windswept cliffs, follow the short quarry road that climbs steeply from the parking area.

Facilities: None. *Swimming:* Good when sea is calm. *Surfing:* The favorite break is "Rock Quarry," located offshore from the stream. *Fishing:* Good. The reef at the east end of the beach is also a favored net-throwing spot.

Camping: Unofficial camping.

Getting there: Take Kilauea Road from its beginning for seven-tenths mile toward the lighthouse in Kilauea. You'll pass through town; on the outskirts of town, before the road veers up toward the lighthouse, turn right onto the narrow dirt road. This road leads one-and-one-half miles to the beach.

Kauapea Beach or Secret Beach (★)—Inaccessibility means seclusion along this hidden strand. Ideal for birdwatching, swimming, and unofficial camping, this half-mile-long beach lies just below Kilauea Lighthouse. Very wide and extremely beautiful, it is popular with nudists and adventurers alike.

Facilities: None.

Camping: An excellent spot for unofficial camping.

Getting there: The beach can be seen from Kilauea Lighthouse, but getting there is another matter. From Kuhio Highway just west of Kilauea turn onto Kalihiwai Road (be sure to get on the eastern section of Kalihiwai Road, near Banana Joe's Tropical Fruit Farm). The road immediately curves left; go right onto the first dirt road; proceed three-tenths mile to a parking lot; from here follow the fenceline down into a ravine to the beach.

Kalihiwai Beach (★)—Bounded by sheer rock wall on one side and a rolling green hill on the other, this semi-secluded beach is crowded with ironwood trees. Behind the ironwoods, the Kalihiwai River has created a large, shallow lagoon across which stretches the skeleton of a bridge, a last grim relic of the devastating 1946 tidal wave.

Facilities: Picnic table. Market and restaurants are about a mile away in Kilauea. *Swimming:* With caution. *Surfing:* "Kalihiwai" is one of the top surfing breaks on the North Shore. Also popular for bodysurfing. *Fishing:* Bonefish and threadfin are the most common catches. This is also a popular spot for surround-netting of akule.

Camping: Unofficial camping under the ironwoods.

Getting there: Take heed—there are two Kalihiwai Roads branching off Kuhio Highway between Kilauea and Kalihiwai. (The washed-out bridge once connected them.) Take the one closest to Lihue. This bumpy macadam road leads a short distance directly to the beach.

Anini Beach Park—Here a grass-covered park fronts a narrow ribbon of sand, while a protecting reef parallels the beach 200 yards offshore. I thought this an ideal place for kids: The ocean is glass smooth and the beach-combing is excellent. As a result, it's very popular and sometimes crowded.

Facilities: Picnic area, restrooms, shower. A market and restaurants are about two miles away in Kilauea; the Princeville shopping complex is eight miles distant. *Swimming:* Excellent and very safe. *Snorkeling:* Excellent. *Surfing:* Winter breaks on very shallow reef. Left and right slides. Also a very popular windsurfing site. *Fishing:* Bonefish, papio, and ulua are regularly caught here. This is also an excellent place for torchfishing, throw-netting, spearing octopus, and harvesting seaweed.

Camping: Pleasant, but lacks privacy. County permit required. Tent camping only.

Getting there: Between Kilauea and Hanalei, turn off Kuhio Highway onto the second Kalihiwai Road (the one farthest from Lihue, on the Hanalei side of the Kalihiwai River). Then take Anini Road to the beach.

Other Anini Beaches—Anini Road snakes along the shoreline for several miles on either side of Anini Beach Park. Numerous dirt roads lead a short distance off Anini Road to secluded beaches. These offer the same natural features as the park, plus privacy.

Princeville Beaches—There are three beaches directly below the plateau on which the Princeville resort complex rests. The most popular is *Puu Poa Beach*, a long and wide strand located next to the Princeville Hotel and reached through the hotel. It offers good swimming and easy access to the hotel's (expensive) facilities but is often crowded. The other two are pocket beaches. *Sealodge Beach*, reached via a right of way near unit two of the Sealodge condominium, is a white-sand beach backdropped by cliffs.

Offshore is a surfing break called "Little Grass Shacks." *Pali Ke Kua Beach* consists of two mirror-image beaches, one below Pali Ke Kua condominium and the other below Puu Poa. They are both good spots for swimming and snorkeling and feature a surfing break called "Hideaways."

Hanalei Bay Beaches—A sandy, horseshoe-shaped strip of sand curves the full length of Hanalei Bay. Along this two-mile strand there are four beach parks. *Black Pot Beach Park*, a local gathering place, lies at the eastern end of the bay and is bounded on one side by the Hanalei River and on the other by a 300-foot-long pier (Hanalei Landing). With showers and lifeguard facilities available, it is very popular with watersport enthusiasts of all stripes—swimmers, surfers, bodysurfers, windsurfers, kayakers, and anglers. It is located at the eastern end of Weke Road. *Hanalei Pavilion Beach Park*, located along Weke Road between Pilikoa and Aku roads, is a favorite picnic spot. *Waioli Beach Park*, a small facility set in an ironwood grove, is situated near the center of the half-moon-shaped bay. It can be reached from the end of either Hee or Amaama roads. *Waikoko Beach* is a slender strand paralleled by a shallow reef. Popular with families who come here to swim and snorkel, it lies along Kuhio Highway on the western side of the bay.

Facilities: All have picnic areas, restrooms, and marvelous ocean and mountain views. *Swimming:* The safest swimming is in the summer when the surf is relatively low. *Surfing:* There are three major breaks here. "Impossible" breaks require a long paddle out from the pier; right slide. "Pine Tree" breaks, off Waioli Beach Park, are in the center of the bay. "Waikoko" breaks are on the shallow reef along the western side of the bay. All are winter breaks. Surfing in Hanalei is serious business, so be careful. Early morning and late afternoon are the best surfing times. The bay is also a popular body-surfing area. *Fishing:* Fishing for squirrelfish, rockfish, red bigeye, oama, big-eyed scad, ulua, and papio. Crabbing off Hanalei Landing pier.

Camping: Tent camping permitted on weekends and holidays. A county permit is required.

Getting there: Located in Hanalei just off Kuhio Highway.

Lumahai Beach—Many people know this strand as the Nurse's Beach in the movie *South Pacific*. Snuggled in a cove and surrounded by lush green hills, Lumahai extends for three-fourths of a mile. With white sand against black lava, it's a particularly pretty spot.

Facilities: None. *Swimming:* Exercise extreme caution and swim only when the sea is very calm. *Fishing:* Good for papio and ulua.

Getting there: Watch for a vista point near the five-mile marker on Kuhio Highway. From here, a crooked footpath leads to the beach.

Tunnels Beach and **Other Haena Beaches**—There are beach access roads all along Kuhio Highway near Haena. Taking any of these dirt roads will shortly lead you to secluded strands. Most popular of all is "Tunnels," a sandy beach with a great offshore reef. One of Kauai's best spots for water sports, this is where many of the boats headed along the Na Pali Coast are launched. According to divers, the name "Tunnels" derives from the underwater arches and tunnels in the reef; but surfers claim it's from the perfect tunnel-shaped waves. Windsurfers consider this one of the best sites on Kauai. You'll also find swimmers, sunbathers, and beachcombers here.

Facilities: None. *Swimming:* Good. *Snorkeling:* Excellent. *Fishing:* Kepuhi Point is one of the best fishing spots on the North Shore; Tunnels attracts fishermen with nets and poles.

Getting there: These beaches are located along Kuhio Highway near Wainiha Bay and Kepuhi Point. Tunnels is two-fifths mile east of Maniniholo Dry Cave.

Haena Beach Park—This grassy park, bounded by the sea on one side and a sheer lava cliff on the other, is right across the street from Maniniholo Dry Cave. It's very popular with young folks and provides good opportunities for beachcombing.

Facilities: Picnic area, restrooms, shower. Markets and restaurants are a few miles away in Hanalei. *Swimming:* There are very strong ocean currents here, which make swimming impossible. *Surfing:* "Cannon's" breaks on a shallow reef in front of Maniniholo Dry Cave. For experts only. Right slide. *Fishing:* Excellent surfcasting and torchfishing for red bigeye, squirrelfish, papio, and ulua. Cardinal fish are sometimes caught on the reef at low tide during the full moon.

Camping: It's an attractive campground, sometimes crowded, open to both tents and trailers, and requiring a county permit. There is also camping nearby at the YMCA's Camp Naue (246-9090).

Getting there: On Kuhio Highway five miles west of Hanalei.

Haena State Park and **Kee Beach**—At the end of Kuhio Highway, where the Kalalau trail begins, 230-acre Haena State Park encompasses a long stretch of white sand, with Kee Beach at its western end. This reef-shrouded beach is one of the most popular on the North Shore. When the surf is gentle, swimming is superb. At such times, this is one of the best snorkeling beaches on Kauai, with its coral reef brilliantly colored and crowded with tropical fish. The Haena shoreline is also one of the island's best shelling beaches.

Facilities: Restrooms and showers. *Surfing:* Good at "Cannons" and "Bobo's" breaks. Also a prime windsurfing area. *Fishing:* Good along the reef.

Camping: A camping facility is planned here.

Getting there: Located at the end of Kuhio Highway

The Sporting Life

CAMPING

To visit Kauai without enjoying at least one camping trip is to miss a splendid opportunity. This lovely isle is dotted with county and state parks that feature ideal locations and complete facilities. There are also many hidden beaches where unofficial camping is common.

Camping at **county parks** requires a permit. These are issued for seven days. You are allowed to camp seven consecutive days at one county park and a total of 60 days at all county parks. Permits cost $3 per person per night; children under 18 are free. Permits can be obtained weekdays at the Department of Parks and Recreation (4193 Hardy Street, Lihue; 245-1881). At all other times, permits are issued by the Kauai Police Department (3060 Umi Street, Lihue; 245-9711).

State park permits are free. They allow camping five consecutive days at each park, and should be requested at least seven days in advance in winter, one month in advance during the summer. These permits are issued by the Department of Land and Natural Resources (3060 Eiwa Street, Lihue, HI 96766; 241-3444).

The State Division of Forestry (241-3433) also maintains camping areas in the **forest reserves**. These are free; permits are available at the State Division of Forestry, 3060 Eiwa Street, Room 306, Lihue, HI 96766. Camping is limited at each site. Check with the forest division for information.

Camping elsewhere on the island is officially prohibited but actually quite common. Local folks use discretion in selecting hidden beaches, marked in this book by a (★), for camping, and so can you. By the way, an extra effort should be made to keep these areas clean. One of the best suggestions I've ever heard is to leave your campsite cleaner than when you arrived.

Rainfall is much heavier along the North Shore than along the south coast, but be prepared for showers anywhere. The Kokee area gets chilly, so pack accordingly. And remember, boil or chemically treat all water from Kauai's streams. Water from some of these streams can cause dysentery, and none of the waterways are certified safe by the Health Department.

To rent or buy camping supplies and equipment, check with **Jungle Bob's** (Ching Young Village, Kuhio Highway, Hanalei; 826-6664). They have tents, packs, stoves, and other equipment available.

SKINDIVING

The Garden Isle offers snorkeling and scuba opportunities at such spots as Haena Beach, Moloaa, and Koloa Landing. Even if you have your own equipment, it's a good idea to stop by one of the local dive shops to pick up a map, as well as advice on local conditions. To familiarize yourself with the region's treasures you may want to begin with a group tour. **Snorkel Bob's Kauai** (4480 Ahukini Road, Lihue; 245-9433) rents snorkeling equipment returnable at branches on all the other islands. Scuba and snorkeling lessons are available at the **Sheraton Kauai Beach Resort** (2440 Hoonani Road, Poipu; 742-1661). **Kauai Seasports** (2827 Poipu Road, Poipu; 742-9303) rents snorkeling and scuba equipment and offers lessons, tours, and day and night dives. **Aloha Destinations** (Koloa and Poipu roads, Koloa; 742-7548) rents snorkeling gear and arranges dive trips around the island. **Fathom Five Divers** (Poipu Road, Poipu; 742-6991) and **Aquatics Kauai** (733 Kuhio Highway, Kapaa; 822-9213) rent both diving and snorkeling equipment. To rent snorkeling equipment also try **Sand People** (Hanalei; 826-6981). Another good possibility for rentals is **Hanalei Surf Company** (5-5161 Kuhio Highway, Hanalei; 826-9000).

SURFING AND WINDSURFING

Summer breaks in the south and winter breaks in the north constitute the surfing scene here. Gentler conditions are typically found at the Poipu beaches. If you're qualified, you might want to take on challenging North Shore beaches like Hanalei. Keep in mind that conditions can be extremely dangerous during the winter months. Don't try this area unless you're an expert. Both **Progressive Expressions** (5428 Koloa Road, Koloa; 742-6041) and **Waiohai Beach Services** (Waiohai Beach Resort, Poipu; 742-7051) rent surfboards. Surfing champing Margo Oberg offers surfing lessons at **Kiahuna Plantation Resort** on Poipu Beach (Poipu; 742-6411). Windsurfing rentals, surfboards, boogie boards, lessons, or sales are also available at **Hanalei Surf Company** (5-5161 Kuhio Highway, Hanalei; 826-9000).

FISHING

Both saltwater and freshwater fishing opportunities make Kauai popular with anglers. Intriguing possibilities include overnight adventures off the Niihau coast, fishing for giant tuna and marlin. Keep a sharp eye out on your trip and you may spot spinner dolphins or breaching whales along the way.

Sea Lure Fishing Charters (Nawiliwili Harbor, Lihue; 808-822-5963) provides everything you need to fish for marlin, ahi, ono, and aku on Kauai's south and east coasts. **Sport Fishing Kauai** (Kukuiula Harbor; 742-7013) cruises up to ten miles offshore in search of a similar catch. Head inland to fish for large and small bass on Kauai's reservoirs with **Cast and Catch** (Koloa; 332-9707). For deep-sea fishing, consult **Alana Lynn Too** (Kapaa; 245-7446). **Fishing For Fun** (Nawiliwili Harbor; 822-3899) takes groups of four on cruises to the leeward side of Niihau for nocturnal bait fishing. After spending the night aboard the 32-foot-long *Dankat*, you'll head to Lehua Island and across the Kaulakahi Channel to the Barking Sands area for the ultimate 24-hour fishing experience. Passengers are encouraged to bring snorkeling equipment.

BOAT TOURS

The trade winds ensure excellent sailing in Kauai waters. From a catamaran trip along the southern shore to a thrilling trip along the rugged Na Pali Coast, these waters are ideal for cruising. Many of the cruises stop at isolated beaches and also offer excellent snorkeling opportunities. **True Blue Charters** (Westin Kauai Hotel, Kalapaki Beach, Lihue; 246-6333) rents sailboats and runs skippered cruises off the island's east coast.

For south coast sailing tours on the 46-foot-long *Akialoa* catamaran, weigh anchor with **Captain Andy's Sailing Adventures** (Kukuiula Harbor; 822-7833). Along the way, you may spot humpback whales or giant green sea turtles. Sunset and moonlight sails are among the intriguing possibilities. Craft include Hobie Cats and Nomads. **Paradise River Rentals** (3155 Kuhio Highway, Kapaa; 335-5081 or 742-1080) rents Boston Whalers, Zodiacs, and Porta-Boats ideal for exploring rivers and wildlife refuges. **Blue Water Sailing** (Hanalei Bay from May to September; Port Allen Boat Harbor, October to April, 822-0525) runs half- and all-day trips to popular destinations like the Na Pali Coast. Sunset sails are also available.

Captain Zodiac (Hanalei; 826-9371) offers rafting expeditions along the Na Pali Coast. Two- to five-hour trips include visits to sea caves, beautiful reefs, and an ancient fishing village. Backpacker drop-offs, sunrise and sunset cruises, and whale watching along the south shore in the winter months are also featured. **Na Pali Adventures** (Hanalei; 826-6804) also serves the Na Pali Coast with motor-powered catamarans. Snorkeling equipment is provided on these narrated tours of historic Kauai. Zodiac and catamaran tours of the Na Pali Coast are also offered by **Hanalei Sea Tours** (Hanalei; 826-7254).

AERIAL TOURS

Whether you choose a whirlybird's-eye view from a helicopter or prefer the serenity of a glider, aerial sightseeing is one of Kauai's great thrills. From simple flyovers to thrilling acrobatic flights, you'll gain a unique perspective on the island's canyons and rainforests, hidden beaches, and tropical retreats.

Island Helicopters (Lihue Airport, 245-8588), **Bruce Needham Helicopters** (Port Allen, 335-3115), and **Papillon Helicopters** (Lihue, 245-6664; and Princeville, 826-6591) all feature unique glimpses of scenic treasures like Waialeale, the Na Pali Coast, and Waimea Canyon. **Tradewinds Glider Rides** (Lihue; 335-5086) takes the adventurous on a 40-minute "Top Gun" tour, a 20-minute scenic tour of Hanapepe Valley and the ancient salt ponds, and an acrobatic "Thrillseeker" that loops the loop. If you're really into acrobatics, consider **Classic Biplanes** (Lihue Airport; 245-2563). In addition to exciting wingovers, you can also enjoy a biplane tour of the island. **Niihau Helicopters** (Kaumakani; 335-3500), on the other hand, specializes in trips to the Forbidden Isle.

KAYAKING

Kayaking is one of Kauai's fastest growing water sports. And why not. Choose from verdant river valleys or, if you like, go down to the sea again. **Kauai By Kayak** (Lihue; 245-9662) paddles up the Huleia River to a picturesque wildlife refuge. **Outfitters Kauai** (Poipu Road, Poipu Beach; 742-9667) goes around Spouting Horn in Poipu where you'll paddle past a lava tube. **Kayak Kauai Outfitters** (Kapaa, 822-9179; Hanalei, 826-9844) rents kayaks and runs introductory reef paddle and snorkel trips. They also sponsor river tours of Fern Grotto, as well as day and overnight tours of the Na Pali Coast. More experienced kayakers can explore sea caves along the Na Pali Coast. This trip includes a lunch break at the ruins of an ancient Hawaiian fishing village. **Luana of Hawaii** (Chin Young Village Shopping Center, Hanalei; 826-9195) kayaks up the Hanalei River in glass bottom craft. Extra added attractions on these guided trips include waterfalls and mountain scenery.

WATERSKIING

If you've ever wondered what it feels like to waterski through paradise, why not head for the Wailua River. This serene tributary is the perfect place to glide through verdant canyons graced by waterfalls. You can practice your slalom technique, try out a pair of trick skis, or enjoy yourself on the hydroslide.

Kauai Water Ski and Sports (4-356 Kuhio Highway, Kapaa; 822-3574) offers a wide variety of trips ranging from beginner lessons to advanced waterskiing. Hot doggers will want to try out the competition slalom course.

HORSEBACK RIDING

From scenic coastal trail rides to journeys up the Hanalei Valley, Kauai is an equestrian's delight. Colorful Waimea Canyon offers another intriguing possibility.

In the Poipu area, try **CJM Country Stables** (742-6096). Possibilities include rides along the south shore and a three-hour breakfast trip to the romantic Haupu Valley. Another highlight is the three-hour trip past the isolated coves of Mahaulepu Beach. You may be tempted to return later on foot to explore these hidden spots.

Garden Isle Ranch (Kaumualii Highway, Waimea; 338-0052) offers rides in the Waimea Canyon region. A best bet here is the sunset ride. In the Hanalei area, call **Pooku Stables** (Kuhio Highway, Princeville; 826-6777) for picnic rides to waterfalls and stunning viewpoints overlooking Hanalei Valley.

GOLF

Some of the best golfing in Hawaii is found on the Garden Isle. In addition to outstanding resort courses at Princeville, the Westin Kauai, and the Hyatt Regency Kauai, you can enjoy several excellent public courses. Beautifully situated with dramatic ocean and mountain backdrops, all of these links will make your game a pleasure.

Kiele Course, created by Jack Nicklaus, and **The Kauai Lagoons Course** (Westin Kauai, Nawiliwili; 246-5078) are two of the island's best-known golfing spots. Next door to the Hyatt Regency Kauai is the demanding 18-hole **Poipu Bay Resort Golf Course** (Poipu; 742-8711). On the south side of the island, **Kukuiolono Golf Course** (Kalaheo; 332-9151) is also popular. If your idea of a public golf course is long lines and boring terrain, head for the **Wailua Golf Course** (Wailua; 245-2163). The golfing public is well served here and the low green fees make this beauty a best buy. With 27 holes, the **Princeville Makai Golf Course** (Princeville; 826-3580), designed by Robert Trent Jones, is complemented by the demanding 18-hole **Prince** course next door. Special discounts apply for twilight golf and there's also a driving range to help sharpen your skills.

TENNIS

With a wide variety of public and resort courses available, it's a good idea to include a racket in your carry-on luggage. The **County Department of Parks and Recreation** (245-8821) is your best source of information on public courts.

You'll find free public courts in Lihue (Hardy Street), Koloa (Maluhia Road), Hanapepe (Puoolo Road), Waimea (Kaumuali Road), and Kekaha (Elepaio Road). In Wailua you'll find courts at Wailua Homestead (Kamalu Road) and Wailua Houselots (corner of Lanikila and Nonou streets).

BICYCLING

There are no bikeways on Kauai and most roads have very narrow shoulders, but the Garden Isle is still the most popular island for bicycling. Roads are good, and except for the steep 20-mile climb along Waimea Canyon, the terrain is either flat or gently rolling. The spectacular scenery and network of public parks make this a cyclist's dream.

RENTALS In Poipu, head for **Outfitters Kauai** (2827-A Poipu Road; 742-9667). **Aquatics Kauai** (733 Kuhio Highway, Kapaa; 822-9213) rents 15-speed mountain bikes as well as touring bikes. In Hanalei, try **Pedal 'n Paddle** (Ching Young Village; 826-9069).

REPAIRS **Bicycles Kauai** (1379 Kuhio Highway, Kapaa; 822-3315) can supply you with needed parts and take care of any emergency repairs.

GUIDED TOURS   **Kauai Downhill** (Lihue; 245-1774) features 12-mile rides coasting down the Waimea Canyon Road. **Kayak Kauai Outfitters** (Hanalei; 826-9844) offers morning and afternoon trips through jungle scenery on the Hanalei River to the Hanalei Wildlife Refuge. After seeing fascinating waterfowl, you'll return to Hanalei Bay for snorkeling.

HIKING

Trekking is among the finest, and certainly least expensive, ways of touring the Garden Isle. Kauai's trails are concentrated in the Na Pali Coast and Waimea Canyon-Kokee regions, with a few others near the Wailua River. Most are well maintained and carefully charted. For further information, contact the State Department of Land and Natural Resources (241-3444).

WAILUA RIVER TRAILS   While none of these hikes actually follow the Wailua, all begin near Route 580, which parallels the river.

Nonou Mountain Trail—**East Side** (1.8 miles long) begins off Haleilio Road in the Wailua Houselots and climbs 1250 feet to the Sleeping Giant's head at Mount Nonou summit.

Nonou Mountain Trail—West Side (1.5 miles) begins off Route 581 and ascends 1000 feet to join the East Side trail.

Keahua Arboretum Trail (0.5 mile) begins two miles past the University of Hawaii Wailua Experiment Station on Route 580. This nature trail is lined with native and foreign plants identified in a field guide available from the State Division of Forestry (241-3433).

Kuilau Ridge Trail (2.1 miles) begins on Route 580 near the Keahua Arboretum. This scenic hike goes past several vista points and picnic areas.

WAIMEA CANYON-KOKEE TRAILS   Kokee State Park has about 45 miles of hiking trails that offer treks through rugged, beautiful country. Along the mountain paths listed here, you'll discover some of the finest hiking in all Hawaii.

Alakai Swamp Trail (3.5 miles) passes through bogs and scrub rainforests to the Kilohana Lookout above Hanalei Bay. This very muddy trail begins off Mohihi (Camp 10) Road.

Awaawapuhi Trail (3.3 miles) starts on Route 55 midway between Kokee Museum and Kalalau Lookout. It leads through a forest to a vista at 2500-feet elevation that overlooks sheer cliffs and the ocean. The trail then connects with Nualolo Trail for an eight-and-a-half-mile loop.

Berry Flat Trail (1 mile) and Puu Ka Ohelo Trail (0.3 mile) combine off Mohihi (Camp 10) Road to form a loop that passes an interesting assortment of trees, including California redwood, ohia, sugi pine, and koa.

٭   **Black Pipe Trail** (0.4 mile) links Canyon Trail with Halemanu Road. It follows a cliff past stands of the rare iliau plant, a relative of Maui's famous silversword.

Hiking Kalalau

Kauai's premier hike, one of the finest treks in all the islands, follows an 11-mile trail along the rugged Na Pali Coast. This ancient Hawaiian trail to Kalalau Valley descends into dense rainforests and climbs along windswept cliffs. Streams and mountain pools along the path provide refreshing swimming holes. Wild orchids, guavas, *kukui* nuts, mangoes, and mountain apples grow in abundance.

The trail begins near Kee Beach at the end of Kuhio Highway. After a strenuous two-mile course the trail drops into Hanakapiai Valley. From here, two side trails—the **Hanakapiai Valley Loop Trail** (1.3 miles) and its extension, the **Hanakapiai Falls Trail**—climb through the valley and up to Hanakapiai Falls, respectively. Fringed by cliffs and possessing a marvelous sand beach, Hanakapiai makes an excellent rest point or final destination.

If you bypass the side trails and continue along the Kalalau Trail, you'll find that as it climbs out of Hanakapiai Valley, it becomes slightly rougher. Sharp grass presses close to the path as it leads through thick foliage, then along precipitous cliff faces. Four miles from Hanakapiai Valley, the trail arrives at Hanakoa Valley. There are several shacks and campsites here as well as a steep one-third-mile trail that goes up to Hanakoa Falls.

The final trek to Kalalau, the most difficult section of the trail, passes scenery so spectacular as to seem unreal. Knife-point peaks, illuminated by shafts of sunlight, rise thousands of feet. Frigate birds hang poised against the trade winds. Wisps of cloud fringe the cliffs. The silence is ominous, almost tangible. A foot from the trail, the ledge falls away into another sheer wall, which plummets a thousand feet and more to the surf below.

The narrow, serpentine trail then winds down to Kalalau Valley. A well-fed stream rumbles through this two-mile-wide vale. If you must use the water here, be sure to boil or otherwise purify it. Farther along, a white-sand beach sweeps past a series of caves to the far end of the valley. You may want to stop awhile and explore the caves, but if you swim here or at Hanakapiai, exercise extreme caution. The undertow and riptides are wicked.

Kalalau has many fine campsites near the beach, but firewood is scarce and cutting trees is *kapu*, so you'd best bring a campstove. Camping at Hanakapiai, Hanakoa, or Kalalau will necessitate a state permit. Anyone hiking beyond Hanakapiai also needs a permit. These are available from the State Parks office (241-3444) at 3060 Eiwa Street in Lihue.

Canyon Trail (1.4 miles) forks off Cliff Trail and follows Waimea Canyon's northern rim to a vista sweeping down the canyon to the sea.

Cliff Trail (0.1 mile) begins at the end of the right fork of Halemanu Road and offers an easy hike to a viewpoint above Waimea Canyon.

Ditch Trail (3.5 miles) runs from Kumuwela Road at one end to Mohihi Road at the other. It's a rugged trail with spectacular views of forest areas and the Poomau River.

Halemanu-Kokee Trail (1.2 miles) sets out from the old ranger station. Bird watchers should especially enjoy this easy jaunt.

Iliau Nature Loop (0.3 mile) starts along Route 55 on a short course past 20 local plant species, including the iliau, endemic only to the Garden Isle. This trail offers good views of both Waimea Canyon and Waialae Falls.

Kalapuhi Trail (1.7 miles) begins at Route 55 en route to a plum grove. The plums are in season every other year. In a good year, you can enjoy both plums and a fine hike; other years, you'll have to settle for the latter.

Kawaikoi Stream Trail (1.8 miles), a loop trail, starts on Mohihi (Camp 10) Road across from Sugi Grove and follows near the stream through a manmade forest.

Koaie Canyon Trail (3 miles) branches off the Waimea Canyon trail near Poo Kaeha. It crosses the Waimea River and passes ancient terraces and rock walls en route to Lonomea camp, a wilderness campsite. Here you'll find a shelter and a stream chock-full of swimming holes.

Kukui Trail (2.5 miles) leads from Route 55 near Puu Kukui and descends 2000 feet to the Waimea River. You'll encounter switchbacks along the west side of Waimea Canyon; the trail ends at Wiliwili Camp, a wilderness campsite. You must register at the trailhead.

Kumuwela Trail (0.8 mile) begins off Mohihi (Camp 10) Road and passes through a fern-choked gulch.

Nature Trail (0.1 mile) begins behind the Kokee Museum and passes through a *koa* forest.

Nualolo Trail (3.8 miles) starts near Park headquarters. Along the way you'll be able to see Nualolo Valley on the Na Pali Coast.

Pihea Trail (3.8 miles) offers excellent views of Kalalau Valley and the Alakai Swamp. Pihea also features a variety of birds and plant life. This trail begins at Puu O Kila Lookout.

Poomau Canyon Lookout Trail (0.3 mile) heads through a stand of Japanese sugi trees and a native rainforest. It begins from Mohihi (Camp 10) Road and ends at a vista overlooking Poomau and Waimea Canyons.

Waimea Canyon Trail (8 miles) can be reached from the Kukui Trail. It follows the Waimea River through the center of the canyon.

Waininiua Trail (0.4 mile) leads from the unpaved Kumuwela Road through a forest where ginger grows.

Transportation

BY AIR

Visiting Kauai means flying to the jetport near Lihue or the landing strip near Princeville. Unless you're staying on the north shore, it is more convenient to fly to the more centrally located Lihue Airport. United Airlines, Aloha Airlines, and Hawaiian Airlines operate here; Aloha Island Air flies in and out of Princeville.

The **Lihue Airport** has a restaurant, cocktail lounge, lockers, newsstand, and flower shop. What you won't find are buses, far more useful to most travelers than cocktails and flowers. Transportation (it's two miles into town) requires reserving a seat on a shuttle, renting a car, hailing a cab, hitching, or hoofing. Cabs generally charge about $4 to Lihue. At **Princeville**, it's either walk or rent a vehicle from **Avis Rent A Car** (826-9773) or **Hertz Rent A Car** (826-7455), which are the only rental agencies in these parts.

CAR RENTALS

Across the street from the terminal at Lihue Airport you'll find a series of booths containing car rental firms. These include **Dollar Rent A Car** (245-3651), **National Car Rental** (245-5636), **Thrifty Rent A Car** (245-7388), **Alamo Rent A Car** (246-0645), **Sunshine Rent A Car** (245-9541), **Avis Rent A Car** (245-3512), **Budget Rent A Car** (245-9031), and, of course, America's most popular (and most expensive) agency, **Hertz Rent A Car** (245-3356). There are also rental companies located in resort areas like Poipu and Wailua.

Tropical Rent A Car (245-6988) is a budget-priced agency located outside the airport. Another off-site possibility is **Westside U-Drive** (332-8644) in Poipu.

JEEP RENTALS

Budget Rent A Car (Lihue Airport; 245-9031) has four-wheel-drive vehicles. However, most Kauai roads, including cane roads, are accessible by car so you probably won't need a jeep.

MOTOR SCOOTER RENTALS

Slow but sporting, mopeds are as much a form of entertainment as transportation. I don't recommend them for getting around the island, but if you'd like to buzz around the neighborhood, contact **Pedal 'n Paddle** (Ching Young Village, Hanalei; 826-9069).

PUBLIC TRANSPORTATION

Kauai Bus (246-4622) is an hourly shuttle that travels between Lihue and Kapaa from 9:30 a.m. to 2:30 p.m. It stops at about a dozen places, including the major shopping centers and the Lihue Airport.

HITCHHIKING AND WALKING

Hitching is permitted on Kauai provided you stay off the paved portion of the road. Like everywhere else, luck hitchhiking varies here. In the summer, there will be many extended thumbs along the road, particularly in the Hanalei area. The folks who pick up strangers are usually fellow tourists or local *haoles*.

Walking on the highways is permitted against the flow of traffic and well off the roadways, but I encountered no problem walking with traffic while thumbing.

TOURS AND DROPOFFS

Na Pali Cruise Line (335-5078) offers day and dinner cruises onboard the 130-foot *Na Pali Queen*.

Kauai Mountain Tours (245-7224) has four-wheel-drive tours into the mountains of Kokee State Park around Waimea Canyon.

Kauai Addresses and Phone Numbers

KAUAI ISLAND

County Department of Parks and Recreation—(245-1881)
Department of Land and Natural Resources—3060 Eiwa Street, Lihue (241-3444)
Hawaii Visitors Bureau—3016 Umi Street, Lihue (245-3971)
Weather—(245-6001)

LIHUE

Ambulance—911
Barber Shop—Ikeda Barber Shop, 4446 Hardy Street (245-4983)
Books—Waldenbooks, Kukui Grove Center, Kaumualii Highway (245-7162)
Fire Department—911
Fishing Supplies—Lihue Fishing Supply, 2985 Kalena (245-4930)
Hardware—Ace Hardware, 4018 Rice Street (245-4091)

Hospital—Wilcox Memorial, 3420 Kuhio Highway (245-1100)
Library—4344 Hardy Street (245-3617)
Liquor—City Liquor, 4347-B Rice Street (245-3733)
Pharmacy—Long's Drug Store, Kukui Grove Center, Kaumualii Highway (245-7771)
Photo Supply—Don's Camera Center, 4286 Rice Street (245-6581)
Police Department—3060 Umi Street (245-9711 or 911 for emergencies)
Post Office—4441 Rice Street (245-4994)

POIPU AREA

Ambulance—911
Fire Department—911
Laundromat—Beside Big Save Market, Koloa Road, Koloa
Police Department—911

WAIMEA AREA

Ambulance—911
Fire Department—911
Laundromat—Menehune Center Laundromat, 9887 Waimea Road, Waimea
Police Department—338-1831 or 911 for emergencies

WAILUA AREA

Ambulance—911
Fire Department—911
Laundromat—In Kapaa Shopping Center, Kapaa (822-3113)
Police Department—911

HANALEI AREA

Ambulance—911
Fire Department—911
Police Department—826-6214 or 911 for emergencies

Recommended Reading

The Beaches of Oahu, by John R.K. Clark. Univeristy of Hawaii Press, 1977. This book, and companion volumes that cover the other islands, provides excellent background information on all the beaches.

Hawaii, by James Michener. Bantam Books, 1978. This lengthy historic novel skillfully blends fact and fiction, dramatically tracing the entire course of Hawaiian history.

Hawaii Pono, by Lawrence H. Fuchs. Harcourt Brace Jovanovich, 1961. A brilliant sociological study of 20th-century Hawaii which vividly portrays the islands' ethnic groups.

Hawaii: The Sugar-Coated Fortress, by Francine Du Plessix Gray. Random House, 1972. A hard-hitting analysis of modern-day Hawaii which details the tragic effect Western civilization has had on the Hawaiian people.

Hawaiian Antiquities, by David Malo. Bishop Museum Press, 1971. Written by a Hawaiian scholar in the nineteenth century, this study contains a wealth of information on pre-European Hawaiian culture.

Hawaiian Hiking Trails, by Craig Chisholm. Fernglen Press, 1986. The best single-volume hiking guide available, this handbook provides excellent descriptions of Hawaii's most popular treks.

The Legends and Myths of Hawaii, by David Kalakaua. Charles E. Tuttle Company, 1972. Written by Hawaii's last king, this fascinating collection includes fables of the great chiefs and priests who once ruled the islands.

Oahu Handook, by J.D. Bisignani. Moon Publications, 1990. An excellent resource for anyone seeking detailed information about Oahu, this book is part of a series that covers all the islands.

Polynesian Researches: Hawaii, by William Ellis. Charles E. Tuttle Company, 1969. This missionary's journal originally appeared in the 1820s. Despite some tedious sermonizing, it poignantly portrays Hawaii at a historic crossroads and graphically describes volcanoes and other natural phenomena on the big island.

Shoal of Time, by Gavan Daws. University Press of Hawaii, 1974. The finest history written on Hawaii, this volume is not only informative but entertaining as well.

Shore Fishing in Hawaii, by Edward Y. Hosaka. Petroglyph Press, n.d. This how-to guide is filled with handy tips on surf-casting, fabricating your own equipment, and identifying Hawaii's fish species.

Index

Abbreviations used in index for island names are (H) Hawaii; (K) Kauai; (L) Lanai; (M) Maui; (Mo) Molokai; and (Oa) Oahu.

Adventure travel, 34–35
Aerial tours: (K) 411
Ahihi-Kinau Reserve (M), 260
Ahuena Heiau (H), 174
Air travel, 25–27; (H) 215–16; (K) 417; (L) 320; (M) 299; (Mo) 345; (Oa) 137–38
Airports. *See* Air travel; *see also names of specific airports*
Akaka Falls State Park (H), 155
Ala Moana Regional Park (Oa), 87
Alakokos Fishpond (K), 354
Alexander & Baldwin Sugar Museum (M), 232
Aliomanu Beach (K), 395
Aloha Tower (Oa), 79
Amy B. H. Greenwell Ethnobotanical Garden (H), 188
Anaehoomalu Beach (H), 170–71, 172
Anahola (K): markets, 392; restaurants, 391; sightseeing, 388
Anahola Beach Park (K), 395
Anahola Mountains (K), 388
Anini Beach Park (K), 406
Anini beaches (K), 406
Arizona Memorial (Oa), 91–92
Astronaut Ellison S. Onizuka Space Center (H), 176
Atlantis Submarine (H), 176
Atlantis Submarine (Oa), 59

Babysitters, 41
Baldwin Home (M), 234
Banyan Drive (Hilo) (H), 147
Banyan tree (M), 234
Banzai Pipeline (Oa), 115, 116, 121
Barking Sands (K), 382, 384
Barking Sands Airfield (K), 374, 376
Beaches, hidden (K), 363

Bed and breakfast referral services: (H) 161, 199; (Oa) 66
Bed and breakfasts. *See* Hotels *in area and city entries*
Bell Stone (K), 386
Bellows Beach Park (Oa), 103–104
Bicycling: (H) 210, 212; (K) 413–14; (L) 319; (M) 295; (Mo) 344; (Oa) 134–35
Big Island. *See* Hawaii (island)
Bird Park (H), 196
Bird sanctuary (H), 201
Birthplace of Kaahumanu (M), 272
Birthplace of Kamehameha I (H), 164
Birthplace of Kamehameha III (H), 176
Bishop Museum (Oa), 90–91
Black Pot Beach Park (K), 407
Black Rock (M), 248
Black Sands Beach (M), 268
Boat tours: (K) 411
Boats (inter-island), 27; (L) 320; (M) 299; (Mo) 345
Boiling Pots (H), 147–48
Brennecke Beach (K), 372
Brick Palace (M), 234
Brigham Young University (Oa), 106
Burial caves (H), 186
Byodo-In Temple (Oa), 105

Cabins. *See* Hotels *in area and city entries*
Calendar of events, 30–32
Camping, 44; (H) 206–207; (K) 409; (L) 319; (M) 288–89; (Mo) 343; (Oa) 130
Cane roads (K), 363
Canoe moorings (H), 188
Cape Kumukahi Lighthouse (H), 204
Captain Cook (town) (H): hotels, 189–90; markets, 191; restaurants, 190–191; shopping, 192; sightseeing, 186, 188

Captain Cook Monument: (H) 186; (K) 374

Car rentals, 36, 40; (H) 216; (K) 417; (L) 320; (M) 299-300; (Mo) 346; (Oa) 138. *See also* Jeep rentals

Carthaginian II (M), 234

Central Maui (M), 232

Central Oahu (Oa): sightseeing, 123-24

Chain of Craters Road (H), 198

Children, traveling with, 40

Chinaman's Hat (Oa), 106

Chinatown (Oa), 79-80

Chinatown walking tours (Oa), 80

Church of the Holy Ghost (M), 280

Church Row (Mo), 333

City of Refuge (H), 186

Club Lanai (L), 312-13

Coco Palms Resort (K), 386

Coconut Island (H), 147

Coconut Plantation (K), 388

Condominiums, 36-37. *See also* Condominiums *in area and city entries*

Contemporary Arts Center (Oa), 90

Cook's Monument: (H) 186; (K) 374

Coral Queen (Oa), 105

Coral reefs, 48, 246-47

Cost of living, 20

Cottages. *See* Hotels *in area and city entries*

Court House (M), 272

Crabbing, 46

Crouching Lion (Oa), 106

Cruises, 27, 79

Cuisine, 20

Cultural Plaza (Oa), 80

Culture, 2

Currency, 40

Customs requirements, 39-40

D. T. Fleming Park (M), 256

Diamond Head (Oa), 61

Diamond Head Beach Park (Oa), 93, 97

Diamond Head Lighthouse (Oa), 93

Disabled travelers, 38

Disappearing Sands Beach (H), 170, 176, 184-85

Dole Cannery Square (Oa), 81

Dole Pineapple Pavilion (Oa), 123

Donkey Beach (K), 394-95

Downtown Honolulu (Oa), 75-87; addresses and phone numbers, 140-41; beaches and parks, 87; hotels, 81; map, 77; markets, 84-85; nightlife, 86-87; restaurants, 84; shopping, 85-86; sightseeing, 75-81

Drugs, 19, 51

East End area. *See* Kaunakakai to East End area (Mo)

East End Beaches (Mo), 332

East Hawaii Cultural Center Gallery (H), 147

East-West Center (Oa), 92

Economy, 19-20

Ehukai Beach Park (Oa), 116, 121

Endangered species, 44

Episcopal Cemetery (M), 236

Events calendar, 30-32

Ewa (Oa): sightseeing, 126

Falls of Clyde (Oa), 78

Fern Grotto (K), 385

Ferry service, 27; (L) 320; (M) 299; (Mo) 345

Fish and fishing, 45-47, 50; (H) 208; (K) 410; (M) 290-91; (Mo) 343; (Oa) 132

Fishponds (Mo), 327

Flightseeing: (H) 217-18; (M) 301-302; (Oa) 139-40

Foreign travelers, 39-40

Fort De Russy Army Museum (Oa), 59

Fort De Russy Beach (Oa), 59

Fort Elizabeth State Historic Park (K), 374

Fort Street Mall (Oa), 79

Foster Botanical Garden (Oa), 80

Fruit, 50-51, 52-53

Fuku-Bonsai Center (H), 186

Garden of the Gods (L), 318

Gathering, 45-47, 50

Gay- and lesbian-friendly establishments: (K) hotels, 378; (M) hotels, 282; restaurants, 229, 231; (Oa) hotels, 65; nightlife, 75; restaurants, 64-65; shopping, 73

Geology, 1

Glider rides (Oa), 118

Goat Island (Oa), 114
Golf: (H) 209-10; (K) 413; (L) 319; (M) 294; (Mo) 344; (Oa) 133-34
Greater Honolulu (Oa), 88-97; addresses and phone numbers, 140-41; beaches and parks, 96-97; hotels, 93-94; map, 89; markets, 95; nightlife, 96; restaurants, 94-95; shopping, 96; sightseeing, 88-93; trails, 135-36
Grove Farm Homestead (K), 353
Guava Kai Plantation (K), 398

H.A. Baldwin Park (M), 277
Haena Beach Park (K), 408
Haena beaches (K), 407-408
Haena State Park (K), 408
Haiku (M): sightseeing, 282
Haiku Gardens (Oa), 105
Hakalau Gulch (H), 156
Halaula (H): markets, 169
Halawa Beach Park (Mo), 333
Halawa Valley (Mo), 328-29
Hale Aloha (M), 236
Hale Halawai (H), 170, 184
Hale Hoikeike (M), 224, 226
Hale Kea (H), 161
Hale Paahoa (M), 236
Hale Pai (M), 237
Haleakala National Park (M), 285-88; map, 287; visitor center, 288
Haleiwa (Oa): markets, 120; nightlife, 121; restaurants, 119-20; shopping, 120-21; sightseeing, 115-16
Haleiwa Beach Park (Oa), 122
Halemaumau Crater (H), 196
Halena Beach (Mo), 339
Haleolono Beach (Mo), 339
Halepalaoa Beach (L), 313
Haliimaile (M): restaurants, 283
Halona Blowhole (Oa), 98, 100
Halona Cove Beach (Oa), 102
Halulu Heiau (L), 317
Hamakua Coast (H), 155-60; beaches and parks, 159-60; hotels, 158; map, 157; markets, 158; restaurants, 158; shopping, 159; sightseeing, 155-57
Hamoa Beach (M), 279
Hana (M): addresses and phone numbers, 303; hotels, 274; markets, 276; nightlife, 277; restaurants, 275-76; shopping, 277; sightseeing, 271-72
Hana Airport (M), 299
Hana Bay (M), 272
Hana Beach Park, 278
Hana Cultural Center (M), 272
Hana Highway area (M), 269-79; beaches and parks, 277-79; hotels, 273-74; map, 271; markets, 276; nightlife, 277; restaurants, 274-76; shopping, 276-77; sightseeing, 269-73; trails, 298
Hanakaoo Beach Park (M), 245
Hanakapiai Valley (K), 415
Hanalei (K): addresses and phone numbers, 419; condominiums, 399; hotels, 399; markets, 402; nightlife, 404; restaurants, 401; shopping, 402, 404; sightseeing, 398
Hanalei Bay beaches (K), 407
Hanalei National Wildlife Refuge (K), 398
Hanalei Pavilion Beach Park (K), 407
Hanalei Valley Lookout (K), 398
Hanalo (H): hotels, 189; restaurants, 190
Hanamaulu (K): markets, 360; restaurants, 359
Hanamaulu Beach Park (K), 362
Hanapepe (K): restaurants, 378-79; shopping, 380; sightseeing, 374
Hanapepe Valley Lookout (K), 374
Hanauma Bay (Oa), 98
Hanauma Bay Beach Park (Oa), 102
Happy Valley (M), 224
Hapuna Beach State Park (H), 171, 172-73
Hauola Gulch (L), 314
Hauola Place of Refuge (K), 385
Hauola Stone (M), 234
Hauula (Oa): markets, 110; sightseeing, 106
Hauula Beach Park (Oa), 112
Hauula Congregational Christian Church (Oa), 106
Hauula Door of Faith Church (Oa), 106
Hawaii (island), 143-219; addresses and phone numbers, 218-19; Hamakua Coast, 155-60; Hilo, 146-55, 218; history, 143-44, 146; Kailua-Kona area, 174-85, 219; Kohala Coast, 163-74, 214-15; Kona/Kau District, 185-95, 214; maps, 145, 149, 157,

165, 175, 187, 197, 203; Puna District, 202-206; Saddle Road, 201-202; sports, 206-15; transportation, 215-18; Volcanoes National Park, 195-201, 213-14; Waimea, 160-63
Hawaii Children's Museum (Oa), 81
Hawaii Maritime Center (Oa), 78
Hawaii State Library Service, 38
Hawaii Tropical Botanical Garden (H), 155
Hawaii Visitors Bureau, 38
Hawaii Volcanoes National Park. *See* Volcanoes National Park (H)
Hawaiian Electric Beach Park (Oa), 128
Hawaiian Holiday Macadamia Nut Factory (H), 156
Hawaiian Islands: calendar of events, 30-32; cost of living, 20; cuisine, 20; culture, 2-4; economy, 19-20; geography, 18; geology, 1; Hawaii, 143-219; history, 1-17; Kauai, 349-419; Lanai, 305-21; Maui, 221-303; Molokai, 323-47; Oahu, 55-141; people, 18-19; time zone, 18; transportation, 25-27; visitor information, 38; weather, 29, 146, 259, 286, 305, 350
Hawaiian language, 21-23
Hawaiian Plantation Village (Oa), 124
Hawi (H): hotels, 166; markets, 168; restaurants, 167; shopping, 169; sightseeing, 164
Heeia State Park (Oa), 105
Hikiau Heiau (H), 186
Hikina Heiau (K), 385
Hiking, 44; (H) 212-15; (K) 414-16; (L) 319; (M) 295-96, 298; (Mo) 344-45; (Oa) 135-37
Hilo (H), 146-55; addresses and phone numbers, 218; beaches and parks, 154-55; hotels, 148-50; map, 149; markets, 152-53; nightlife, 154; restaurants, 150-52; shopping, 153; sightseeing, 146-48; weather, 146
Hilo International Airport (H), 215
Hilo Tropical Gardens (H), 147
Historic Parker Ranch Homes (H), 160
Hitchhiking: (H) 217; (K) 418; (L) 321; (M) 301; (Mo) 346; (Oa) 139
Hoaloha Park (M), 231
Holo-Holo-Ku Heiau (K), 386

Holua (M): parks, 286
Holualoa (H): hotels, 189; shopping, 192; sightseeing, 186
Honaunau (H): hotels, 189; shopping, 192
Honokaa (H): hotels, 158; markets, 158; restaurants, 158; shopping, 159
Honokohau Bay (M), 256, 259
Honokohau Beach (H), 170, 184
Honokowai Beach Park (M), 255
Honolowai (M): condominiums, 250-51
Honolua Bay (M), 258-59
Honolulu. *See* Downtown Honolulu; Greater Honolulu; Waikiki
Honolulu Academy of Arts (Oa), 81
Honolulu Hale (Oa), 76
Honolulu International Airport (Oa), 137
Honolulu Memorial Park (Oa), 88
Honolulu Myohoji Temple (Oa), 88
Honolulu Zoo (Oa), 61
Honomanu Bay (M), 270, 278
Honomu (H): markets, 158
Hookena Beach Park (H), 171, 194
Hookio Gulch (L), 314
Hookipa Beach Park (M), 269, 277-78
Hoomaluhia Park (Oa), 104-105
Horseback riding: (K) 412; (L) 319; (M) 292, 294; (Mo) 344; (Oa) 133·
Hosmer Grove (M), 285
Hospitals, 41
Hostels: (H) 150; (Oa) 63, 93
Hotels, 37. *See also* Hotels *in area and city entries*
Hualalai (H), 186
Huelo (M): sightseeing, 269
Huialoha Church (M), 273
Hukilau Beach (Oa), 114
Huleia National Wildlife Refuge (K), 354
Hulihee Palace (H), 174, 176
Hulopoe Bay (L), 315
Hulopoe Beach Park (L), 316-17
Hurricane Iniki, 28, 349

Iao Needle (M), 226
Iao Valley State Park (M), 226
Iliiliopae Heiau (Mo), 328
Ilikai Hotel (Oa), 59
Imiola Congregational Church (H), 161

Inter-island carriers (air and sea), 26–27; (L) 320; (M) 249; (Mo) 345
International driver's license, 40
Iolani Barracks and Bandstand (Oa), 76
Iolani Palace (Oa), 76
Isaac Hale Beach Park (H), 205–206
Izumo Taishakyo Mission (Oa), 80

Jaggar Museum (H), 196
James Stewart's Hoomau Ranch (H), 188
Jeep rentals: (H) 216; (K) 417; (L) 320; (M) 300; (Mo) 346; (Oa) 138
Jellyfish, 49
John F. Kennedy Profile (M), 226

Kaaawa (Oa): hotels, 108; markets, 110; restaurants, 110
Kaahumanu Birthplace (M), 272
Kaahumanu Church (M), 224
Kaalawai Beach (Oa), 97
Kaanapali Resort Beaches (M), 255
Kaanapali-Kapalua area (M), 248–56; beaches and parks, 255–56; condominiums, 250–51; hotels, 250; map, 249; markets, 253; nightlife, 254–55; restaurants, 251–53; shopping, 253–54; sightseeing, 248–49
Kaena Point (Oa), 118, 127
Kahakuloa (M): sightseeing, 256
Kahala (Oa), 92–93
Kahala Beach (Oa), 97
Kahana (M): condominiums, 251
Kahana Bay (Oa), 106
Kahana Valley State Park (Oa), 112
Kahanamoku Beach (Oa), 59
Kahanu Gardens (M), 270
Kahe Point Beach Park (Oa), 128
Kahea Heiau (L), 312
Kahekili's Leap (L), 318
Kahili Beach (K), 405
Kahoolawe (island), 18, 232
Kahuku (Oa): restaurants, 109; sightseeing, 108
Kahuku Golf Course Park (Oa), 115
Kahuku Sugar Mill (Oa), 108
Kahului Airport (M), 299
Kahului-Wailuku area (M), 224–31; addresses and phone numbers, 302–303; beaches and parks, 231; hotels, 226–27; map, 225; markets, 229; nightlife, 230–31; restaurants, 227–29; shopping, 224–30; sightseeing, 224–26; trails, 296
Kaiaka Recreation Area (Oa), 122
Kaihalulu Beach (Red Sand Beach) (M), 278–79
Kailua (Oa): hotels, 108; markets, 110–11; nightlife, 111; restaurants, 109; shopping, 111; sightseeing, 104–105
Kailua-Kona area (H), 174–85; addresses and phone numbers, 219; beaches and parks, 170, 184–85; condominiums, 179; hotels, 176–79; map, 175; markets, 182; nightlife, 183–84; restaurants, 179–82; shopping, 182–83; sightseeing, 174–76
Kailua wharf (H), 174
Kaimu Black Sand Beach (H), 206
Kainaliu (H): markets, 191; nightlife, 192; restaurants, 190; shopping, 192
Kakahaia Beach Park (Mo), 332
Kakahaia National Wildlife Refuge (Mo), 327
Kakela Beach (Oa), 112
Kalahaku Overlook (M), 285
Kalaheo (K): hotels, 378; markets, 379; restaurants, 378; sightseeing, 373–74
Kalahuu Beach Park (H), 170, 185
Kalakaua Park (H), 154
Kalalau Lookout (K), 377
Kalalau Valley (K), 415
Kalama County Beach Park (M), 266
Kalapaki Beach (K), 353–54, 361–62
Kalapuna (H): sightseeing, 202
Kalaupapa (Mo), 342
Kalaupapa Lookout (Mo), 334
Kalawao (Mo): sightseeing, 342
Kalawao Park (Mo), 342
Kalihiwai Beach (K), 406
Kalokoeli Fishpond (Mo), 327
Kalopa State Park (H), 159–60
Kamakahonu Beach (H), 170
Kamakou Preserve (Mo), 335
Kamalo Wharf (Mo), 327
Kamaole Beach Parks I, II, and III (M), 266–67
Kamehameha I Birthplace (H), 164
Kamehameha III Birthplace (H), 176

Kamehameha V's Summer Home
(Mo), 327
Kamehameha Rock (H), 166
Kamehameha Statue (H), 166
Kamehameha Statue (Oa), 78
Kamoamoa (H): sightseeing, 198
Kamoamoa Campground (H), 200
Kamokila Hawaiian Village (K), 386
Kamuela. *See* Waimea
Kamuela Airport (H), 216
Kamuela Museum (H), 160
Kanaha Pond Wildlife Sanctuary (M), 224
Kaneaki Heiau (Oa), 126
Kaneana Cave (Oa), 126
Kaneeleele Heiau (H), 188
Kaneohe (Oa): hotels, 108; markets,
110; restaurants, 109-10; shopping,
11; sightseeing, 104
Kaneohe Bay (Oa), 105
Kapaa. *See* Wailua-Kapaa area
Kapaa Beach Park (H), 171, 173-74
Kapaa Beach Park (K), 394
Kapaau (H): hotels, 166; shopping,
169; sightseeing, 164, 166
Kapaia (K): shopping, 360; sightseeing,
354
Kapalaoa (M): parks, 286
Kapalua. *See* Kaanapali-Kapalua area (M)
Kapalua Beach (M), 256
Kapalua-West Maui Airport (M), 299
Kapiolani Park (Oa), 60, 62
Kapiolani Rose Garden (Oa), 60
Kapuaiwa Grove (Mo), 333
Kau District. *See* Kona/Kau District
Kau Desert (H), 196
Kauai (island), 349-419; addresses and
phone numbers, 418-19; history, 349-
50, 352-53; Lihue area, 353-62, 418;
maps, 351, 355, 365, 375, 383, 387,
397; North Shore, 396-408; Poipu
area, 364-73, 419; sports, 409-16;
transportation, 417-18; Wailua-
Kapaa area, 385-95, 414, 419; Wai-
mea area, 373-84, 414, 416, 419;
weather, 350
Kauai Museum (K), 353
Kauapea Beach (K), 405
Kauiki Hill (M), 272
Kaulanapueo Church (M), 269
Kaumahina State Wayside (M), 270

Kaumalapau Harbor (L), 317
Kaumana Caves (H), 148
Kaunakakai to East End area (Mo),
326-333; addresses and phone numbers, 346-47; beaches and parks, 332-
33; hotels, 329; markets, 330-31;
nightlife, 331; restaurants, 330; shopping, 331; sightseeing, 326-29
Kaunakakai to West End area (Mo),
333-40; beaches and parks, 338-40;
hotels, 336; markets, 337; nightlife,
337; restaurants, 337; shopping, 337;
sightseeing, 333-36
Kaunolu Village (L): sightseeing, 317
Kaupo (M): markets, 226; sightseeing,
273
Kaupo Gap (M), 273
Kawaihae (H): hotels, 167; markets,
168; nightlife, 169, restaurants, 167-
68; sightseeing, 164
Kawaihao Church (Oa), 76
Kawakui Beach (Mo), 340
Kayaking: (H) 208; (K) 412; (M) 291-
92; (Oa) 132-33
Keaau (H): hotels, 204-205; sight
seeing, 202
Keahole Airport (H), 215
Keahua Forestry Arboretum (K), 386
Keaiwa Heiau State Recreation Area
(Oa), 96-97
Kealakekua (H): shopping, 192; sight-
seeing, 186
Kealakekua Bay (H), 186
Kealia (H): markets, 191
Kealia (K): sightseeing, 388
Kealia Beach (K), 394
Kealia Pond Bird Sanctuary (M), 260
Kealoha County Park (H), 154
Keanae (M): hotels, 274
Keanae Arboretum (M), 270
Keanae Peninsula (M), 270
Keauhou (H): nightlife, 184
Keauu Beach Park (Oa), 129
Keawakapu Beach (M), 267
Keawanui Fishpond (Mo), 327
Kee Beach (K), 399, 408
Keei Beach (H), 193
Kekaha (K): markets, 379; restaurants,
379; sightseeing, 374
Kekaha Beach (K), 381-82

Kekaha Beach Park (K), 382
Keokea Beach Park (H), 171, 174
Keokea Park (M), 284
Keomuku (L): sightseeing, 312
Kepaniwai County Park (M), 231
Kepaniwai Park (M), 226
Kewalo Boat Basin (Oa), 78
Kihei Beach (M), 266
Kihei Memorial Park (M), 266
Kihei-Wailea area (M), 259-68; addresses and phone numbers, 303; beaches and parks, 266-68; condominiums, 262-63; hotels, 260, 262; map, 261; markets, 264-65; nightlife, 265-66; restaurants, 263-64; shopping, 265; sightseeing, 259-60, 261; trails, 296
Kilauea (H), 195, 197, 198
Kilauea (K): markets, 402; restaurants, 400-401; shopping, 402; sightseeing, 396, 398
Kilauea Crater (H), 196
Kilauea Lighthouse (K), 396, 398
Kilauea National Wildlife Refuge (K), 396
Kilauea Visitor Center (H), 196
Kilohana (K), 355-56, 359, 360-61
King's Pool (H), 176
Kiowea Park (Mo), 338
Kipahulu (M): sightseeing, 273
Kipuka Nene (H), 200
Kipuka Puaulu (H), 196
Kodak Hula Show (Oa), 61
Kohala Coast (H), 163-74; beaches and parks, 170-71, 172-74; hotels, 166-67; map, 165; markets, 168-69; nightlife, 169; restaurants, 167-68; shopping, 169; sightseeing, 163-66; trails, 214-15
Kohala Mountain (H), 166
Kokee State Park (K): beaches and parks, 384; hotels, 377-78; restaurants, 379; sightseeing, 377; trails, 414, 416
Koki Beach Park (M), 279
Koko Crater (Oa), 98
Koko Crater Botanic Gardens (Oa), 100
Koko Head (Oa), 98
Kokole Point (K), 382
Kolekole Beach Park (H), 159

Kolekole Pass (Oa), 123
Kolo Wharf (Mo), 339-40
Koloa (K): hotels, 366; markets, 370; restaurants, 368-69; shopping, 370; sightseeing, 364
Koloa History Center (K), 364
Kona Coast. *See* Kailua-Kona area (H)
Kona Historical Society Museum (H), 186
Kona/Kau District (H), 185-95; beaches and parks, 171, 193-95; hotels, 189-90; map, 187; markets, 191; nightlife, 192; restaurants, 190-91; shopping, 191-92; sightseeing, 185-89; trails, 214
Kona's coffee country (H), 185-86
Koolau Range (Oa), 101
Kualapuu (Mo): restaurants, 337; sightseeing, 334
Kualoa Beach Park (Oa), 111
Kuhio Beach Park (Oa), 60
Kuilei Cliffs Beach Park (Oa), 97
Kukaniloho (Oa), 123
Kukuiolono Park (K), 373-74
Kula (M): hotels, 282
Kula Botanical Gardens (M), 280
Kumimi Beach (Mo), 332

La Perouse Bay (M), 260
Lahaina (M), 233-45; addresses and phone numbers, 303; beaches and parks, 244-45; condominiums, 238; hotels, 237-38; map, 235; markets, 241; nightlife, 243; restaurants, 238-41; shopping, 241-43; sightseeing, 233-37
Lahaina Beach (M), 245
Lahaina Harbor (M), 233-34
Lahaina Jodo Mission (M), 236-37
Lahaina Shingon Mission (M), 236
Lahainaluna School (M), 237
Laie (Oa): hotels, 109; sightseeing, 106, 108
Laie Point (Oa), 108
Lanai (island), 305-21; addresses and phone numbers, 321; history, 305-306, 308; Lanai City, 308-11, 321; map, 307; Munro Trail, 314; northeast area, 312-13; southeast area, 314-17; southwest area, 317-18;

sports, 319; transportation, 320-21; weather, 305

Lanai Airport (L), 320

Lanai City (L), 308-11; addresses and phone numbers, 321; hotels, 309-10; markets, 311; nightlife, 311; restaurants, 310-11; shopping, 311; sightseeing, 308-309

Lanaihale (L), 314

Language, 21-23

Lapakahi State Historical Park (H), 164

Larsens Beach (K), 404-405

Launiupoko State Wayside Park (M), 244

Laupahoehoe Beach Park (H), 159

Laupahoehoe Point (H), 156

Lava flows: (H) 202-204; (M) 260, 273

Lava Tree State Park (H), 204

Leeward Coast (Oa), 124-29; addresses and phone numbers, 137; beaches and parks, 128-29; hotels, 126-27; map, 125; markets, 127; nightlife, 128; restaurants, 127; sightseeing, 124-26; trails, 137

Leleiwi County Park (H), 154

Leleiwi Overlook (M), 285

Leper colony (Mo), 342

Lesbian- and gay-friendly establishments: (K) hotels, 378; (M) hotels, 282; restaurants, 229, 231; (Oa) hotels, 65; nightlife, 75; restaurants, 64-65; shopping, 73

Lihue Airport (K), 417

Lihue area (K), 353-62; beaches and parks, 361-62; hotels, 356-57; map, 355, markets, 359-60; nightlife, 361; restaurants, 357-59; shopping, 360-61; sightseeing, 353-56

Lihue Hongwanji Temple (K), 354

Liliuokalani Gardens (H), 147

Lindbergh's grave (M), 273

Little Beach (M), 268

Little Grass Shack (Oa), 92

Lua Moku Iliahi (Mo), 335

Luahiwa petroglyphs (L), 314-15

Lualualei Beach Park (Oa), 128

Lucy Wright Park (K), 381

Lumahai Beach (K), 399, 407

Lydgate Park (K), 394

Lyman Mission House (H), 147

Lyon Arboretum (Oa), 92

Maalaea Bay (M), 232

MacKenzie State Park (H), 206

Magic Sands Beach (Disappearing Sands Beach) (H), 170, 176, 184-85

Mahaulepu Beach (K), 373

Mahukona Beach Park (H), 171, 173

Mail, 38

Maili Beach Park (Oa), 128

Makaha (Oa): hotels, 126-27; nightlife, 128; restaurants, 127; sightseeing, 126

Makaha Beach (Oa), 126

Makaha Beach Park (Oa), 129

Makapuu Beach (Oa), 100

Makapuu Beach Park (Oa), 103

Makapuu Point (Oa), 100

Makawao (M): markets, 283; nightlife, 284; restaurants, 282-83; shopping, 283-84; sightseeing, 280

Makee Sugar Mill (M), 280

Makena Beach (M), 260, 268

Malaekahana State Recreation Area (Oa), 114-15

Maluulu o Lele Park (M), 244-45

Manele Bay (L): beaches and parks, 317; hotels, 315-16; nightlife, 316; restaurants, 316; sightseeing, 315

Maniniholo Dry Cave (K), 399

Manoa Valley (Oa), 92

Manuka State Park (H), 194

Mapulehu Glass House (Mo), 328

Mapulehu Mango Grove (Mo), 328

Maria Lanakila Church (M), 236

Marijuana, 19, 51

Master's Reading Room (M), 234

Maui (island), 221-303; addresses and phone numbers, 302-303; central Maui, 232; Haleakala National Park, 285-88; Hana Highway, 269-79, 298; history, 221-22, 224; Kaanapali-Kapalua area, 248-56; Kahului-Wailuku area, 224-31, 296, 302-303; Kihei-Wailea area, 259-68, 296, 303; Lahaina, 233-45, 303; maps, 223, 225, 235, 249, 257, 261, 271, 281, 287; northwest Maui, 256-59; sports, 288-98; transportation, 299-302; Upcountry, 280-84, 298; weather, 286

Maui Tropical Plantation (M), 232

Mauna Kea (H), 201, 211

Mauna Kea State Park (H), 201, 202; trails, 214
Mauna Loa (H), 195, 196, 201
Maunakea Marketplace (Oa), 80
Maunaloa (Mo): markets, 337; restaurants, 337; shopping, 337; sightseeing, 334, 336
McGregor Point (M), 232
Measurements, 40
Menehune Ditch (K), 374
Menehune Fishpond (K), 354
Menehunes, 352–53, 354
Merchant Street (Oa), 79
Milolii (H): sightseeing, 188
Milolii Beach Park (H), 171, 194
Mission Houses Museum (Oa), 75–76
Mission Memorial Building (Oa), 76
Mokapu Beach (M), 267
Moku Hooniki Island, 328
Mokuaikaua Church (H), 176
Mokuleia Beach (M), 258
Mokuleia Beach (Oa), 122
Mokuleia Beach Park (Oa), 122
Moloaa Beach (K), 404
Molokai (island), 323–47; addresses and phone numbers, 346–47, history, 323–24, 326; Kalaupapa, 342; Kaunakakai to East End, 326–33; Kaunakakai to West End, 333–40; map, 325; outback, 335; sports, 343–45; transportation, 345–46
Molokai Airport (Mo), 345
Molokai Ranch Wildlife Park (Mo), 336
Molokai Wagon Ride (Mo), 328
Molokini (island), 232
Mookini Heiau (H), 164
Moomomi Beach (Mo), 338–39
Moomomi Dunes (Mo), 338–39
Mopeds. *See* Motor scooter and motorcycle rentals
Mormon Temple (Oa), 106
Mosquitoes, 44
Motor scooter and motorcycle rentals: (H) 217; (K) 417; (M) 301; (Oa) 138
Mount Lyons (M), 272
Munro Trail (L), 314

Na Pali Coast (K), 396, 415
Naalehu (H): markets, 191; restaurants, 191; sightseeing, 188

Naha (village) (L): sightseeing, 313
Naha Beach (L), 313
Naha Stone (H), 147
Nahiku (M): sightseeing, 270
Namakani Paio (H), 200
Nanakuli Beach Park (Oa), 128
Nani Mau Gardens (H), 147
Napili (M): condominiums, 251
Napili Bay (M), 255
Napoopoo Beach Park (H), 171, 193
National Memorial Cemetery (Oa), 90
National Tropical Botanical Garden (K), 366
Nawiliwili (K): hotels, 356–57; nightlife, 361; restaurants, 358–59; shopping, 360; sightseeing, 353–54
Niihau (island), 18, 376
Niihau Helicopter (K), 376
Ninini Beach (K), 362
Ninole Cove (H), 188–89, 195
Niumalu Beach Park (K), 362
North Shore (K), 396–408; beaches and parks, 404–408; condominiums, 399–400; hotels, 399–400; map, 397; markets, 402; nightlife, 404; restaurants, 400–402; shopping, 402, 404; sightseeing, 396–99
North Shore (Oa): 115–22; addresses and phone numbers, 137; beaches and parks, 121–22; hotels, 118; map, 117; markets, 120; nightlife, 121; restaurants, 119–20; shopping, 120–21; sightseeing, 115–18; trails, 137
Northeast Lanai (L), 312–13; beaches and parks, 313; sightseeing, 312–13
Northwest Lanai (L), 318; beaches and parks, 318
Northwest Maui (M), 256–59; beaches and parks, 258–59; map, 257; sightseeing, 256–58
Nukolii Beach Park (K), 393–94
Nuu Bay (M): sightseeing, 273
Nuuanu Avenue (Honolulu) (Oa), 88
Nuuanu Pali Drive (Oa), 91
Nuuanu Pali Lookout (Oa), 91

Oahu (island), 55–141; addresses and phone numbers, 140–141; central Oahu, 123–24; history, 56, 58; Honolulu, 75–97, 135–36, 140–41; Lee-

ward Coast, 124–29, 137, 141; maps, 57, 61, 77, 89, 99, 107, 117, 125; North Shore, 115–22, 137, 141; southeast Oahu, 98–104, 136; sports, 130–37; transportation, 137–40; Waikiki, 58–75; Windward Coast, 104–12, 114–15, 136–37, 141
Ocean safety, 48
Oheo Gulch (M), 273, 279
Old Airport Beach (H), 170
Old Airport State Recreation Area (H), 170, 184
Old Courthouse (M), 234
Old Fort (M), 234
Old Jail (M), 234
Old Sugar Mill (Oa), 106
Older travelers, 39
Olinda Vista Nursery (M), 280, 282
Olomana Peak (Oa), 101
Olowalu (M): markets, 241; restaurants, 241; sightseeing, 232
Olowalu Beaches (M), 244
Olu Pua Gardens and Plantation (K), 374
O'ne Alii Park (Mo), 332
Onekahakaha County Park (H), 154
Oneloa Beach (M), 268
Oneuli Beach (M), 268
Onizuka Center for International Astronomy (H), 201
Opaekaa Falls (K), 386
Opihikao (H): sightseeing, 204
Orchids of Hawaii (H), 147
Our Lady of the Sorrows Catholic Church (Mo), 327
Outrigger canoes (Oa), 60

Paaulio (H): sightseeing, 156
Pacific Missile Range Facility (K), 376
Pacific Whaling Museum (Oa), 100
Packing, 33, 36; for children, 41
Pahala (H): hotels, 190; sightseeing, 189
Pahoa (H): hotels, 204; markets, 205; restaurants, 205; shopping, 205; sightseeing, 202
Paia (M): hotels, 273; markets, 276; nightlife, 277; restaurants, 274–75; shopping, 276; sightseeing, 269
Painted Church (H), 188
Paipu Beach Park (M), 267–68

Pakala Beach (K), 381
Pakuhiwa Battleground (Mo), 327
Palaau State Park (Mo), 338
Paliku (M): parks, 286
Panaewa Rainforest Zoo (H), 148
Papalaua State Wayside Park (M), 244
Papohaku Beach (Mo), 336, 340
Paradise Park (Oa), 92
Parasailing: (H) 208; (M) 291
Parker Ranch Visitor Center (H), 160
Passports, 39
Pearl Harbor (Oa), 91–92
Petroglyphs: (H) 164; (L) 312, 314–15
Phallic Rock (Mo), 334
Philomena Church (Mo), 342
Pidgin language, 21–23
Pihana Halekii Heiau (M), 258
Pillboxes (M), 260
Pinao Stone (H), 147
Pineapple Variety Garden (Oa), 123
Pioneer Inn (M), 234
Pioneer Sugar Mill (M), 237
Pohaku-Ho-O-Hanau (K), 386
Pohakuloa Point (Mo), 332
Pohoiki (H): sightseeing, 204
Poipu area (K), 364–73; addresses and phone numbers, 419; beaches and parks, 372–73; condominiums, 367–68; hotels, 366–67; map, 364; markets, 370; nightlife, 371; shopping, 370–71; sightseeing, 364–66
Poipu Beach (K), 372
Poipu Beach Park (K), 372
Poison ivy, 44
Poli Poli State Park (M), 284
Poliahu Heiau (K), 386
Polihale Heiau (K), 376
Polihale State Park (K), 376, 384
Polihua Beach (L), 318
Polo Beach (M), 267
Pololu Valley Lookout (H), 166
Polynesian Cultural Center (Oa), 106, 108
Pookela Church (M), 280
Poolenalena Beach Park (M), 267–68
Portuguese man-of-wars, 49
Pounders Beach (Oa), 114
Princeville (K): condominiums, 399; hotels, 400; markets, 402; nightlife, 404; restaurants, 400; shopping, 402; sightseeing, 398

Princeville beaches (K), 406–407
Princeville Landing Strip (K), 417
Puaa Kaa State Park (M), 270
Puako (H): sightseeing, 164
Puamana State Wayside Park (M), 244
Public transportation: (H) 217; (K) 418;
   (M) 301; (Oa) 138–39
Pukalani (M): markets, 282; restaurants,
   282
Pukoo Beach (Mo), 332
Puna District (H), 202–206; beaches and
   parks, 205–206; hotels, 204–205; map,
   203; markets, 205; restaurants, 205;
   shopping, 205; sightseeing, 204–205
Punalau Beach (M), 259
Punaluu (H): hotels, 198; restaurants, 199
Punaluu (Oa): hotels, 108–109; nightlife,
   111; restaurants, 110; shopping, 111;
   sightseeing, 106
Punaluu Beach Park (H), 188, 195
Punaluu Beach Park (Oa), 112
Punchbowl (Oa), 88, 90
Puohokamoa Falls (M), 269
Pupukea Beach Park (Oa), 121
Puu O Makuha Heiau (Oa), 116
Puu O Hoku Ranch (Mo), 328
Puu Olai Beach (M), 268
Puu Pehe (L), 315
Puu Pehe Cove (L), 316–17
Puu Ualakaa Park (Oa), 90
Puu Ulaula Overlook (M), 288
Puuanahulu (H): sightseeing, 201
Puuhonua O Honaunau National Histor-
   ical Park (H), 186
Puuhonua O Honaunau Park (H), 171, 193
Puukohola National Historic Site (H), 164
Puuloa (H): sightseeing, 198
Puunene (M): sightseeing, 232
Puuwaawaa (H), 201

Queen Emma's Summer Palace (Oa), 91
Queen Victoria's Profile (K), 364
Queen's Surf (Oa), 60

R. W. Meyer Sugar Mill (Mo), 334
Rabbit Island (Oa), 100
Rafting: (M) 292
Rainbow Falls (H), 147

Rainfall, 29; (H) 146; (K) 350; (L) 305;
   (M) 259, 286
Red Sand Beach (M), 278–79
Reed's Bay Beach Park (H), 154
Rental agencies: (K) 368, 400; (Oa) 67
Restaurants, 37. *See also* Restaurants *in
   area and city entries*
Richardson Ocean Park Center (H), 155
Richardson's Ocean Park (H), 154–55
Rip currents, 48
Rock Point (Mo), 332
Royal Hawaiian (Oa), 59
Royal Kona Coffee Mills (H), 186
Royal Mausoleum (Oa), 88
Royal-Moana Beach (Oa), 59
Running Waters Beach (K), 362

Saddle Road area (H), 201–202; parks,
   202; sightseeing, 201–202
Sailing: (H) 208; (M) 291; (Mo) 343;
   (Oa) 132
Salt Pond Beach Park (K), 380–81
Sand Island State Park (Oa), 87
Sandalwood Measuring Pit (Mo), 335
Sandy Beach (Oa), 100, 102–103
Sans Souci Beach (Oa), 61
Science City (M), 288
Sea Life Park (Oa), 100
Sea tours: (H) 209
Sea urchins, 49
Seamen's Cemetery (M), 236
Seasons, 28–29. *See also* Weather
Seaweed gathering, 50
Secret Beach (K), 405
Senator Fong's Plantation and Gardens
   (Oa), 105
Seven Sacred Pools (M), 273, 279
Shark Island (L), 318
Sharks, 49
Shave ice, 113
Shell hunting: (M) 246–47
Shellfish gathering, 47, 50
Sheraton Moana Surfrider Hotel (Oa), 59
Sheraton Waikiki (Oa), 59
Shipwreck Beach (K), 372–73
Shipwreck Beach (L), 312, 313
Silverswords (M), 285, 288, 297
"69" Beach (H), 171, 172
Skiing: (H) 211

Skindiving: (H) 170-71, 207; (K) 409-10; (M) 289-90; (Mo) 343; (Oa) 130-31
Slaughterhouse Beach (M), 258
Sleeping Giant (K), 388
Smith and Bronte Landing (Mo), 327
Smith's Tropical Paradise (K), 385
Snakes, 44
Snow cones, 113
Soto Mission of Hawaii (Oa), 88
South Coast beaches (Mo), 339-40
South Point (H), 188
Southeast Lanai (L), 314-17; beaches and parks, 316-17; hotels, 315-16; nightlife, 316; restaurants, 316; sightseeing, 314-15
Southeast Oahu (Oa), 98-104; beaches and parks, 102-104; map, 99; markets, 102; restaurants, 101; sightseeing, 98-101; trails, 136
Southwest Lanai (L), 317-18
Spearfishing, 45
Spencer Beach Park (H), 171, 173
Sprouting Horn (K), 365
Squidding, 46-47
St. Joseph Catholic Church (Mo), 327
St. Peter's Catholic Church (H), 176
Star of the Sea Painted Church (H), 203
Stargazing tours: (H) 212
State Capitol Building (Oa), 78
Sugar Cane Train (M), 236
Sugar mill (Mo), 328
Suisan Fish Market (H), 147
Sunrise Protea Farm (M), 280
Sunset Beach (Oa), 115-16, 121
Surfing: (H) 207-208; (K) 410; (M) 290; (Oa) 131
Swanzy Beach Park (Oa), 112

Tantalus (Oa), 90
Tedeschi Winery (M), 280
Temperature. *See* Weather
Tennis: (H) 210; (K) 413; (L) 319; (M) 295; (Mo) 343; (Oa) 134
Tenrikyo Mission (Oa), 88
Thurston Lava Tube (H), 196
Time zone, 18
Toilet Bowl (Oa), 98
Torchfishing, 45
Tourist seasons, 28-29

Tours: (K) 418; (L) 320; (Mo) 346
Tree Growth Research Area (M), 280
Tree molds (H), 196
Tropical fruit, 50-51, 52-53
Tropical Gardens of Maui (M), 226
Tunnels Beach (K), 407-408
Twin Falls (M), 269

Ualapue Fishpond (Mo), 327
Ulua Beach (M), 267
Ulupalakua Ranch (M), 273
Ulupo Heiau (Oa), 104
University of Hawaii (Oa), 92
University of Hawaii Agricultural Station (M), 280, 282
Upcountry (M), 280-84; hotels, 282; map, 281; markets, 283; nightlife, 284; parks, 284; restaurants, 282-83; shopping, 283-84; sightseeing, 280-82; trails, 298
Upolu Airport (H), 216
USS Arizona (Oa), 91-92
USS Bowfin/Pacific Submarine Museum (Oa), 92

Visas, 39
Visitor information, 38
Volcano Art Center (H), 196
Volcano House (H), 196, 198, 199
Volcano Update (H), 198
Volcano Village (H): hotels, 198-99; markets, 200; restaurants, 199-200
Volcanoes National Park (H), 195-201; beaches and parks, 200-201; hotels, 198-99; map, 197; markets, 200; restaurants, 199-200; sightseeing, 195-98; trails, 213-14; visitor center, 196

Wahaula Heiau (H), 198
Wahiawa (Oa): sightseeing, 123
Wahiawa Botanical Gardens (Oa), 123
Wahikuli State Wayside Park (M), 245
Waiahole (Oa): markets, 111
Waiahole Valley (Oa), 106
Waiakea Fishpond (H), 147
Waialae Beach Park (Oa), 97
Waialea Bay (H), 171, 172

Waianae (Oa): markets, 127; restaurants, 127; sightseeing, 126
Waianapanapa State Park (M), 270, 278
Waihee (M): sightseeing, 258
Waihee Beach Park (M), 231
Waikamoi Ridge (M), 269
Waikanaloa Wet Cave (K), 399
Waikane (Oa): markets, 111
Waikane Valley (Oa), 106
Waikapalae Wet Cave (K), 399
Waikiki (Oa), 58-75; condominiums, 67; hotels, 62-67; map, 61; markets, 71; nightlife, 73-75; restaurants, 68-71; shopping, 71-73; sightseeing, 58-62
Waikiki Aquarium (Oa), 60
Waikoko Beach (K), 407
Waikoloa (H): hotels, 166; nightlife, 169; restaurants, 168
Waikolu Picnic Grove (Mo), 335
Waikolu Valley Lookout (Mo), 335
Wailea. *See* Kihei-Wailea area (M)
Wailea Beach (M), 267
Wailoa River State Park (H), 147
Wailua (M): sightseeing, 270
Wailua Falls (K), 354
Wailua Falls (M), 273
Wailua Homesteads (K), 386
Wailua-Kapaa area (K), 385-95; addresses and phone numbers, 419; beaches and parks, 393-95; condominiums, 389; hotels, 388-89; map, 387; markets, 391-92; nightlife, 393; restaurants, 390-91; shopping, 392-93; sightseeing, 385-88; trails, 414
Wailuku. *See* Kahului-Wailuku area
Waimanalo (Oa): markets, 102; restaurants, 101; sightseeing, 101
Waimanalo Bay State Recreation Area (Oa), 103
Waimanalo Beach Park (Oa), 103
Waimea (H), 160-63; hotels, 161; markets, 162-63; nightlife, 163; restaurants, 161-62; shopping, 163; sightseeing, 160-61
Waimea area (K), 373-84; addresses and phone numbers, 419; beaches and parks, 380-82; hotels, 377-78; map, 375; markets, 379; restaurants, 378-79; shopping, 380; sightseeing, 373-77
Waimea Bay (Oa), 116

Waimea Bay Beach Park (Oa), 121-22
Waimea Canyon (K): map, 383; sightseeing, 377; trails, 414, 416
Waimea Falls Park (Oa), 116
Waiohai Beach (K), 372
Waiohinu (H): hotels, 190
Waiola Cemetery (M), 236
Waiola Church (M), 236
Waioli Beach Park (K), 407
Waioli Mission House (K), 398-99
Waipahu (Oa): sightseeing, 124
Waipio Valley (H): hotels, 158; shopping, 159; sightseeing, 156
Waipio Valley Lookout (H), 156
Waipouli (K): markets, 391-92; restaurants, 390
Wamamalu Beach Park (Oa), 103
Wananalua Church (M), 272
Waoli Tea Room (Oa), 92
Water safety, 48
Waterskiing: (K) 412; (M) 292
Weather, 29; (H) 146; (K) 350; (L) 305; (M) 259, 286
Weights, 40
West End area. *See* Kaunakakai to West End area (Mo)
Westin Kauai (K), 354
Whale-watching: (H) 209; (M) 232, 293
Whalers Village Museum (M), 248
White Hill (M), 288
Whittington Beach Park (H), 194-95
Windmill Beach (M), 259
Windsurfing: (H) 207-208; (K) 410; (M) 290; (Oa) 131
Windward Coast (Oa), 104-12, 114-15; addresses and phone numbers, 136-37; beaches and parks, 111-12, 114-15; hotels, 108-109; map, 107; markets, 110-11; nightlife, 111; restaurants, 109-10; shopping, 111; sightseeing, 104-108; trails, 141
Wineries: (M) 280
Wo Hing Temple (M), 235
Women travelers, 39
Wood Valley (H), 189
Wood Valley Temple (H), 189

Yokohama Bay (Oa), 127
Yokohama Bay State Park (Oa), 129

Also Available From Ulysses Press

HIDDEN BOSTON AND CAPE COD
This compact guide ventures to historic Boston and the windswept Massachusetts coastline. 228 pages. $7.95

HIDDEN COAST OF CALIFORNIA
Explores the fabled California coast from Mexico to Oregon, describing over 1000 miles of spectacular beaches. 468 pages. $13.95

HIDDEN FLORIDA
From Miami to the Panhandle, from the Keys to Cape Canaveral, this award-winning guide combs the state. 528 pages. $14.95

HIDDEN FLORIDA KEYS AND EVERGLADES
Covers an area unlike any other in the world—the tropical Florida Keys and mysterious Everglades. 156 pages. $7.95

HIDDEN MEXICO
Covers the entire 6000-mile Mexican coastline in the most comprehensive fashion ever. 444 pages. $13.95

HIDDEN NEW ENGLAND
A perfect companion for exploring from Massachusetts colonial villages to the fog-shrouded coast of Maine. 564 pages. $14.95

HIDDEN PACIFIC NORTHWEST
Covers Oregon, Washington, and British Columbia. Seattle sightseeing, Oregon beaches, Cascades campgrounds, and more! 528 pages. $14.95

HIDDEN SAN FRANCISCO AND NORTHERN CALIFORNIA
A major resource for travelers exploring the San Francisco Bay area and beyond. 444 pages. $14.95

HIDDEN SOUTHERN CALIFORNIA
The most complete guidebook to Los Angeles and Southern California in print. 516 pages. $14.95

HIDDEN SOUTHWEST
Explores Arizona, New Mexico, Utah, and Colorado, describing Native American sites, campgrounds, and desert adventures. 504 pages. $14.95

CALIFORNIA: The Ultimate Guidebook
Definitive. From the Pacific to the desert to the Sierra Nevada, it captures the best of the Golden State. 504 pages. $13.95

DISNEY WORLD AND BEYOND: The Ultimate Family Guidebook
Unique and comprehensive, this guide to Orlando's theme parks and outlying areas is a must for family travelers. 300 pages. $9.95

DISNEY WORLD AND BEYOND: Family Fun Cards
This guidebook you can shuffle covers Orlando's theme parks with a deck of 90 cards, each describing a different ride or exhibit. $7.95

DISNEYLAND AND BEYOND: The Ultimate Family Guidebook
The only guidebook to cover all Southern California theme parks. Includes three chapters of daytrip possibilities for families. 240 pages. $9.95

FLORIDA'S GOLD COAST: The Ultimate Guidebook
Captures the tenor and tempo of Florida's most popular stretch of shoreline—Palm Beach, Fort Lauderdale, and Miami. 192 pages. $8.95

THE MAYA ROUTE: The Ultimate Guidebook
Travel the route of the ancient Mayans. Yucatán Peninsula, Belize, Guatemala, and Honduras are explored. 300 pages. $12.95

THE NEW KEY TO COSTA RICA
Hailed by *The New York Times* as the "best guidebook" to the area. A classic adventurer's handbook covering the entire country. 312 pages. $13.95

FOR A FREE CATALOG OR TO ORDER DIRECT   For each book send an additional $2 postage and handling (California residents include 8% sales tax) to Ulysses Press, 3286 Adeline Street, Suite 1, Berkeley, CA 94703. Or call **800-377-2542** or 510-601-8301 and charge your order.

About the Author

Ray Riegert is the author of seven travel books, including *Hidden San Francisco and Northern California*. His most popular work, *Hidden Hawaii*, has won the coveted Lowell Thomas Travel Journalism Award for Best Guidebook. In addition to his role as publisher of Ulysses Press, he has written for the *Chicago Tribune*, *Saturday Evening Post*, *San Francisco Examiner & Chronicle*, and *Travel & Leisure*. A member of the Society of American Travel Writers, Ray lives in the San Francisco Bay Area with his wife, travel publisher Leslie Henriques, and their son Keith and daughter Alice.